BUSINESS POLICY AND STRATEGIC MANAGEMENT

PLANNING, STRATEGY, AND ACTION

GEORGE SAWYER
City College of New York

Harcourt Brace Jovanovich, Publishers
San Diego   New York   Chicago   Austin   Washington, D.C.
London   Sydney   Tokyo   Toronto

TO MARGO

Copyright © 1990 by Harcourt Brace Jovanovich, Inc.

All rights reserved. No part of this publication may be reproduced or transmitted in any form or by any means, electronic or mechanical, including photocopy, recording or any information storage and retrieval system, without permission in writing from the publisher.

Requests for permission to make copies of any part of the work should be mailed to: Copyrights and Permissions Department, Harcourt Brace Jovanovich, Publishers, Orlando, Florida 32887.

This work is an adaptation of DESIGNING STRATEGY by George Sawyer, copyright © 1986 John Wiley & Sons, Inc. Adapted courtesy of John Wiley & Sons, Inc.

ISBN: 0-15-505680-8

Library of Congress Catalog Card Number: 89-84237

Printed in the United States of America

PREFACE

A manager should know how to design strategies, know how to sustain or create the organization necessary to execute them, and know something about strategic management. *Business Policy and Strategic Management* tries to explain what policies are, how they are related to strategies, and how a manager builds a strategic dimension into his or her actions. And because this book is also about putting together a strategy, translating that strategy into policy, and carrying that policy into action, it has the subtitle: *Planning, Strategy, and Action.*

A strategy outlines to the members of an organization how to perform some specific task—bringing a new product or service to market, increasing customer satisfaction, or getting an old product accepted for new uses. There are various sorts of strategy because of the many different things organizations need to do. The book defines primary strategies at three levels: (1) for a product or service, (2) for a business, or (3) for an enterprise as a whole. The book also describes contributing strategies—those that guide other departments and units as they help to make the primary strategies happen. Because these strategies differ in their ease of execution, some can be put into action successfully by almost anyone, while others should be attempted only by the very best organizations.

By separating a strategy problem into its components—elements of product strategy, degrees of product differentiation, sources of product profit, and enterprise strategy—this book encourages the consideration of these variables into a framework that aids in understanding the fundamentals of the strategy design process. This framework encourages a more orderly approach that is easier to learn and use and that is therefore likely to yield better strategies. And while no one will become expert in designing strategy solely from one book or one course, the well-organized foundation presented here can make the learning far more rapid and effective.

Some strategies are easy for an organization to execute and others more difficult. To be successful, the strategy selected must be one the organization can execute. If not, extra preparation time and resources are needed for upgrading the organization's capabilities—or only a less demanding strategy can succeed. This book discusses the strategic management requirements for high performance, and how to create a high performance organization when the strategy requires it.

Strategic management has become the major conceptual theme of the policy and strategy field because today's managers need to be able to do more than define strategic choices; they must be able to put these choices into action successfully through a strategic management process that also ensures that these strategies continue to be appropriate and effective as environment, market, and organization change. This dynamic aspect of strategic management needs emphasis because it is such an important component of the international effort to gain industrial leadership. *Business Policy and Strategic Management* builds in this emphasis.

This book is in five parts. Parts I and II lay out the basic policy and strategy definitions; the product, market, and business foundations of strategy; and the enterprise or governing strategy framework that controls lower-level actions. Part III deals with an organization's means of controlling and maintaining a continuing profitable fit into its environment. This includes such topics as strategic control, management of social impact and opportunity, and the organization's management of the strategy for the people, the operation, and self-renewal. Part IV outlines the product or business strategy design process and discusses the way in which the design must be reconciled with the governing enterprise strategies and the necessary fit into the strategic planning and strategic management pattern used in a particular firm. Part V takes the strategy design framework that has been related largely to medium and large business organizations up to that point and demonstrates its extension to public agencies and not-for-profit corporations, to small businesses, and to businesses in other countries and cultures. Along the way, this section deals briefly with the nature of top management and top managers and with some of the political and ethical problems of strategic management.

Business Policy and Strategic management is organized into twenty-one chapters, each of which concludes with two cases and questions that provide a review of the material in that chapter. The cases illustrate the issues the chapter has presented and provide an opportunity for reinforcement through discussion. When important new concepts are introduced in the text, they are followed by specific examples demonstrating their application. Where groups of new concepts are introduced (e.g., the elements of product strategy), they are followed both by a set of examples of the application of these concepts and an exercise for students to test their mastery. Additional cases at the back of the book can provide the basis for further discussion of specific issues or of a financial analysis of their consequences. The book is indexed for easy cross-reference and significant definitions are summarized in the Glossary. Some of the material presented here is derived from earlier good work in the field and has been so credited in the footnotes. Some of the material is adapted from previous books written by the author.*

---

*George C. Sawyer, *Corporate Planning as a Creative Process: Action Laid Out in Advance* (Oxford, Ohio: Planning Executives Institute, 1983); also *Business and Its Environment: Managing Social Impact* (Englewood Cliffs, New Jersey: Prentice-Hall, 1985); also *Designing Strategy: A How-To Book for Managers* (New York: Wiley, 1986).

This book is designed for upper-level undergraduate use in a capstone or integrating policy course, but it can easily be extended to the graduate level by requiring greater comparison with current issues in business and non-business organizations and a more fundamental examination of the cases. The intent is to aid the undergraduate or graduate instructor in moving a strategic management/business policy course beyond exposing students to examples of past strategic decisions, and beyond teaching key decision elements such as value added or market positioning. This is not to be done by displacing these valuable techniques and concepts, but by offering an overall strategy design framework into which the student can integrate functional knowledge gained in earlier courses with these and other strategic management concepts.

This book's purpose is to provide a clear, comprehensive first summary of an important and demanding subject. Major separate study areas open out beyond it—in such areas as strategic marketing, value-driven planning, leadership strategy, organizing strategy, and strategic operations management—but these areas will be better addressed from a sound foundation in business policy and strategic management.

Integration of strategy and policy issues into a workable strategic management framework requires a new pattern of emphasis, on levels of strategy, on translation of strategy into strategic management action, and on the linkage of planning and strategy to action. The objective of this book is to help its readers learn and apply that pattern.

The author is grateful for the advice provided by these reviewers: Howard Babson, Columbus State Community College; Lew Brown and Holly Buttner, University of North Carolina, Greensboro; and Dean Schroeder, University of Massachusetts.

LIST OF FIGURES

1-1	The Mission, or Social Role. Where to Hunt for Profits?	4
1-2	Fundamentals	12
1-3	Mission, Goals, and Strategy as Part of Strategy Design	12
2-1	Actions Lead to Policies	26
2-2	Moving from Mission to Action	30
2-3	The Types and Levels of Strategy	32
2-4	Linking Strategy to Action	34
2-5	Action as the Objective	35
3-1	Elements of Product and Business Strategy	46
3-2	Examples of Product and Service Strategy	50
3-3	Examples of Product Line and Service Line Strategies	51
3-4	Differentiating the Product or Service	53
3-5	A Short-life-cycle Product	56
3-6	A Long-life-cycle Product	57
3-7	Sources of Business Profit	59
3-8	Example of Sources of Business Profit	60
3-9	Product or Service Characteristics as Fundamentals	64
3-10	Product or Service Characteristics as Basic to Strategy Design	65
4-1	Example of a CAP Profile: Bull Machine Works	88
4-2	Example of a CAP Profile: Mildew Molding Company	89
4-3	Market Characteristics as Fundamentals	90
4-4	Market Characteristics as Basic to Strategy Design	91
5-1	The Learning Curve (or Experience Curve)	107
5-2	The General Electric Stoplight Matrix	109
5-3	The BCG Portfolio Planning Matrix	110
5-4	The Arthur D. Little Portfolio Matrix	111
5-5	Charles Hofer's Portfolio Matrix	112
5-6	Stages of Business Growth	113
5-7	Naylor's Strategy Matrix	116
5-8	Business Characteristics as Fundamentals	119
5-9	Business Characteristics as Basic to Strategy Design	120
5-10	The Strategy Tripod	121
6-1	Examples of Leadership Strategies	139
6-2	Examples of Opportunity Strategies	140
6-3	Examples of People Strategies	140
6-4	Examples of Public Strategies	142
6-5	Examples of Resource-getting Strategies	143
6-6	Examples of Desirability Strategies	145
6-7	Examples of Managing Strategies	145
6-8	Examples of Belonging Strategies	146

6-9	Examples of Credibility Strategies	148
6-10	Examples of Risk/reward Strategies	149
6-11	Examples of Master Business Strategies	150
6-12	Components of Enterprise Strategy	152
6-13	Two Tablets of Stone	153
6-14	Enterprise Characteristics as Basic to Strategy Design	154
7-1	Strategic Control as Key to Successful Action	174
7-2	Strategic Control as a Key Management Process	188
8-1	The Management of Social Impact	211
9-1	Opportunity Management and Strategy Design	230
10-1	The Excellence Model	252
10-2	Excellence Model Enterprise Strategy Requirements	253
10-3	People and Performance	256
11-1	Operations, Day by Day	284
12-1	Leontiades' Organizational Change Matrix	299
12-2	Self-renewal as a Survival Requirement	301
12-3	Management of Strategic Action and Control	302
13-1	Strategy Design Fundamentals—Step by Step	315
13-2	How to Build a Strategic Model	320
13-3	Strategy Design Fundamentals	325
14-1	The Three Levels of Primary Strategy	334
14-2	Matching Product, Business, and Enterprise Strategies	338
15-1	Outline of a Strategic Plan	357
15-2	Strategic Management and Value-driven Planning	362
15-3	The Strategy Design Process	362
16-1	Policy Makers as Key Actors in the Strategic Management Process	383
17-1	Strategic Management as a Requirement in Public and Not-for-profit Organizations	401
18-1	Strategic Management as a Small Business Requirement	419
19-1	International Strategic Management	433
20-1	Political Relationships as a Component of Strategic Management	447
21-1	Strategic Management: From Planning and Strategy to Action	459

CONTENTS

PART I
STRATEGY, POLICY, AND THE BUSINESS FIRM 1

CHAPTER 1

THE NATURE AND ROLE OF BUSINESS POLICY 2

The Mission, or Social Role 3
Goals and Strategies 5
A Business as a Corporation 5
Achieving Social Ends by Economic Means 6
Making Up Rules 7
Business Policies 8
Creating Resources 8
Organization Competence as a Strategic Variable 10
Examples of Business Strategies 11
Business Firms Versus Other Sorts of Organizations 11
Strategy, Policy, and the Business Firm 13
Questions for Analysis and Discussion 13
For Further Information 14
CASE 1 Weaker Services, Inc. 15
CASE 2 The Carnegie Clinics 21

CHAPTER 2

STRATEGY, POLICY, AND ACTION 25

Habits and Policies 26
Emerging Issues as Problems and Opportunities 26
Carrying Policy into Action 28
Mission, Goals, and Strategy 29
Primary Strategy 32
Strategy Summary 33
Questions for Analysis and Discussion 34

Examples of Primary and Contributing Strategies   36
For Further Information   37
CASE 3   Adams Enterprises   38
CASE 4   Jones Joints, Incorporated   41

CHAPTER 3

THE PRODUCT AS BASIS FOR A STRATEGY   44

Elements of Product and Business Strategy   45
Differentiating the Product   52
Product Life Cycle   55
Sources of Profit from a Product of Service   58
Elements of Strategy and Sources of Profit   61
Linking Strategy to Product   63
Questions for Analysis and Discussion   64
For Further Information   66
CASE 5   Random Gardens   67
CASE 6   Assured Inspection Service   70

PART II

FOUNDATIONS FOR PRODUCT AND BUSINESS STRATEGY   73

CHAPTER 4

THE MARKET AS BASIS FOR A STRATEGY   74

The Nature of the Market   75
Market Life Cycles   77
Market Structure   79
The Nature of the Competition   81
Competitive Action Potential (CAP)   87
Linking Strategy to Competition and Market   90
Questions for Analysis and Discussion   90
For Further Information   92
CASE 7   The Brussels Bowl Company   93
CASE 8   The Paper Trap Company   99

CHAPTER 5

THE BUSINESS AS BASIS FOR A STRATEGY 104

The Nature of the Business 105
Learning Curves 106
Life Cycles and Businesses 107
A Classification of Business 108
Portfolio Management 115
Shareholder Value 117
Linking Strategy to the Nature of the Business 119
Questions for Analysis and Discussion 119
For Further Information 121
CASE 9 The Peoples Potions Pharmaceutical Company 122
CASE 10 Ruction Resources, Inc. 128

CHAPTER 6

STRATEGY FOR THE ENTERPRISE: THE GOVERNING STRATEGIES 136

Enterprise Strategy and the Building Blocks 137
Enterprise Choice Criteria 143
Master Business Strategy 149
Enterprise Strategies and Achievement Strategies 151
Questions for Analysis and Discussion 153
For Further Information 155
CASE 11 Monarch-United Service-Tribulations/Incorporated 156
CASE 12 The Decision Process at Gumdrop Holdings 166

PART III
STRATEGIC ACTION AND CONTROL 171

CHAPTER 7

STRATEGIC CONTROL 172

Enterprise Choice Strategies 174
Strategic Control as an Ongoing Process 179
Enterprise Strategy Problems 181
Strategic Blindness: Cause and Cure 181
Perceptual Barriers and the Means to an Overview 183
Strategic Overview Management 184

For Good Management: Strategic Control
   with a Clear View Ahead   187
Questions for Analysis and Discussion   188
For Further Information   189
CASE 13   The Oaken Box Company   190
CASE 14   Organic Resources Corporation   196

CHAPTER 8

MANAGING SOCIAL IMPACT   200

Costs and Benefits   201
Business Impact on Society   203
Anticipating and Understanding Social Impact   204
The Social Impact Areas   204
Social Balance Failure   205
Managing Social Impact   206
Profit Maximization and Social Cost Avoidance   210
Questions for Analysis and Discussion   210
For Further Information   212
CASE 15   Toxic Threads   213
CASE 16   Goliath Data Processing   215

CHAPTER 9

MANAGING OPPORTUNITY   217

Constructing the Opportunity Plan   218
The Role of Restructuring   223
Master Strategy and the Master Builder   224
Opportunity Management   225
The Plan for Course Correction   228
Opportunity Management   230
Questions for Analysis and Discussion   231
For Further Information   231
CASE 17   The Hungry Harvest Corporation   232
CASE 18   Righteous Chemical Company   235

CHAPTER 10

MANAGING PEOPLE AND PERFORMANCE   237

Leadership Strategy   238
The People Component   240
Competence Requirements for Success of a Strategy   243

The Management Operating System   252
The Excellence Model and Its Alternatives   254
The People Component in Enterprise Operations   257
Questions for Analysis and Discussion   257
For Further Information   258

CASE 19   High Velocity Enterprise   259
CASE 20   Mom's Pantry Industries   261

CHAPTER 11

MANAGING OPERATIONS   267

Organizing the Enterprise   268
The Role of the Public Strategy   271
Operations Strategy   272
Bigness as a Problem   276
Third Wave Management   279
The Role of the People Versus Efficiency and Achievement   280
Management of Operations Strategy   283
Questions for Analysis and Discussion   285
For Further Information   285

CASE 21   The B.W. Weevil Company   286
CASE 22   Arcane Industries   289

CHAPTER 12

SELF-RENEWAL MANAGING ORGANIZATION CHANGE   291

The Risk of Organization Atrophy   292
Open System Requirements for Organization Vitality   292
Competent Managers and Incompetent Systems   293
The Management of Organization Self-Renewal   294
Organization Culture   295
Society's Need for Business Self-Renewal   300
Self-Renewal and Change   300
Structure Follows Strategy   301
Questions for Analysis and Discussion   303
For Further Information   303

CASE 23   United Unlimited Universal Company   304
CASE 24   The Incredible Telephone Company   307

PART IV
HOW TO DESIGN STRATEGIES   311

CHAPTER 13
DESIGN OF A PRODUCT OR BUSINESS STRATEGY   312

The Strategy Design Process   313
Competitive Advantage   314
Creating Leverages   318
Strategic Models   319
Effective Strategies   321
Understanding the Requirements of a Strategy   323
Strategy Design   324
Questions for Analysis and Discussion   325
For Further Information   326
CASE 25   The Executive Buzz Saw at Upquick, Inc.   327
CASE 26   The Quick-Time Cement Company   330

CHAPTER 14
MATCHING PRODUCT, BUSINESS, AND ENTERPRISE STRATEGIES   332

How the Enterprise Strategies Govern   333
Design and Redesign of Master Strategy   335
Finding the Boundaries   336
Working Out a Design   337
Integrating Strategies   337
Questions for Analysis and Discussion   338
For Further Information   339
CASE 27   Adventures with the New Central Marken-Spackler   340
CASE 28   Limits to Business Growth   346

CHAPTER 15
STRATEGIC MANAGEMENT AND VALUE-DRIVEN PLANNING   349

Long Range Planning   350
Strategic Management   350
Planning as a Process for Organizational Learning   352
Quality, Customers, and Strategy   353
Time as a Strategic Variable   355
What Is a Strategic Plan?   356

Strategic Management and Value-Driven Planning   361
Questions for Analysis and Discussion   363
For Further Information   363
CASE 29   Seawing Industries   364
CASE 30   Value-Driven Planning at Unified Industries   367

PART V
PRACTICING STRATEGIC MANAGEMENT   375

CHAPTER 16
POLICY MAKERS—AS TOP MANAGEMENT, AND AS PEOPLE   376

The Strategy and Policy Environment   377
The People Who Work in This Environment—Their Backgrounds   377
Interaction with the Public   381
Global Horizons   381
The Role of the Master Builder   381
The Management of Strategy and Policy   382
Questions for Analysis and Discussion   383
For Further Information   383
CASE 31   Firefly Computers   385
CASE 32   The Master Builder   393

CHAPTER 17
MANAGING IN PUBLIC AND NOT-FOR-PROFIT ORGANIZATIONS   397

Building a Constituency to Support the Organization   398
The Public Face of Public Business   399
Designing Public or Not-For-Profit Strategy   400
Public Management   400
Questions for Analysis and Discussion   401
For Further Information   402
CASE 33   Lands and Forests Department   403
CASE 34   The Dungy Museum   407

CHAPTER 18

SMALL BUSINESS AND ITS SPECIAL PROBLEMS   413

Managing Without Staffs and Specialized Resources   414
Entrepreneurship: Starting New Businesses   415
Regulations, Government, and the Bias Toward Bigness   417
Assistance in Finding Markets and Growth   418
Small-Business Management Strategy   419
Questions for Analysis and Discussion   420
For Further Information   420

CASE 35   The Growth Company   421
CASE 36   The Drip-Drop Paint Co.   424

CHAPTER 19

OTHER COUNTRIES AND OTHER CULTURES   427

Universals   428
Local Requirements and Differences   429
Different Legal and Social Systems   429
People and Their Culture   430
The Multinational Federation   431
Strategy for International Management   432
Questions for Analysis and Discussion   433
For Further Information   434

CASE 37   The Plant in Taspotamia   435
CASE 38   The Chocolate Machine Company   440

CHAPTER 20

THE POLITICAL WORLD AROUND THE ORGANIZATION   443

Economic Power Versus Political Power   444
Relationships with Government Power   446
Business Policy for a Political World   447
Questions for Analysis and Discussion   448
For Further Information   448

CASE 39   The Green Emerald Company   449
CASE 40   Nerdly Electric and Gas Company   454

CHAPTER 21

FROM PLANNING AND STRATEGY TO ACTION

Creating Resources   458
Power for the Strategy   460
Substance Governs Strategy   462
The Entrepreneur as a Rent Collector   463
Policy, Strategy, and the Business Firm   465
Designing Effective Strategies   466
Strategy and the Excellence Model   467
Conclusion   468
CASE 41   Growth for the Ithilien Chemical Company   469
CASE 42   The Month Manufacturing Company   478

SUPPLEMENTAL CASES

CASE 43   Modern Medicines, Inc.   490
CASE 44   The Byte-So Software Company   494
CASE 45   Swinging Genes   497
CASE 46   The Loose-Leaf Tobacco Company   500
CASE 47   The Upscale Suits Company   502
CASE 48   Watch Display Chemicals   504
CASE 49   Modeling a Specialty Chemical Business   509
CASE 50   Promises for the Future, Incorporated   511
CASE 51   The Medical Meter Company   513

Glossary   515

Index   520

PART 1

STRATEGY, POLICY,
AND THE
BUSINESS FIRM

CHAPTER 1

THE NATURE AND ROLE OF BUSINESS POLICY

KEY IDEAS IN THIS CHAPTER

Chapter 1 begins the presentation of strategy design fundamentals:

- **The mission, or social role** – of a business, together with a series of **examples of mission statements.**
- **Goals and strategies** – as an introduction to business goals and objectives and their translation into strategies.
- **A business as a corporation** – with many strategic and other consequences of this legal form.
- **Achieving social ends by economic means** – as the challenge with which business and other managers must learn to live.
- **Making up rules, creating resources,** and **organization competence as a strategic variable** – as an introduction to a trio of key strategy design concepts.
- **Examples of business strategies** – to help make the presentation more concrete.
- **Business firms versus other sorts of organizations** – to point out the universality of this strategy framework.
- **Strategy, policy, and the business firm** – as a chapter summary and an introduction to the balance of Part One.

THE MISSION, OR SOCIAL ROLE

A business exists for a purpose—for a social role, or mission—because its continuation depends on making a profit. Profit can be earned only if the business sells goods or services for more than they cost to produce. This means the goods or services have a sufficient value to the customers to result in a profit. Otherwise the purchasers spend their money on something else, and the business ceases to exist.

The social role, or mission, of the business is to provide some type of goods or services to fill a need—goods or services in which customers find sufficient value to justify paying the necessary price. Otherwise the purchases will not be made, and the business will disappear.

A mission of a specific business is its purpose, which is its attempt to satisfy a specific set of society's needs. Society will pay to satisfy its needs, so that a firm defining such a social role is establishing a potential equation. It hopes to earn a profit by satisfying society's needs at a cost less than it is able to charge. The social role becomes a hunting license for a territory within which management hopes to generate a profit, as shown in Figure 1-1.

Newman[1] and Ackoff[2] relate the concept of mission to a much broader statement of purpose; but while their examples are crisp and concise, many of the mission statements developed from this approach become listings of what the organization hopes to be like in a variety of social and operational dimensions. The result can become too general to be the basis of concrete programs. By narrowing the purpose to the specific social role that the organization seeks to fulfill, as emphasized here, a tighter and more concrete base for action is created. It is much easier to understand how to create and maintain a close-to-the-customer, market-driven organization if the mission is aimed specifically at customer needs to be satisfied, with goals defined within the scope of this mission and a strategy aimed at progress toward those goals.

In brief, the mission of a business is the social role it will fulfill by satisfying certain needs of customers or society well enough so that these customers will pay more for the necessary goods or services than it costs the business to deliver them.

---

[1] William H. Newman and James P. Logan, *Strategy, Policy and Central Management*, 8th ed. (Cincinnati, Ohio: South-Western, 1981).

[2] Russell L. Ackoff, Elsa Vergara Finnel, and Jamshid Gharajedaghi, *A Guide to Controlling Your Corporation's Future* (New York: John Wiley & Sons, 1984).

FIGURE 1–1 THE MISSION, OR SOCIAL ROLE. WHERE TO HUNT FOR PROFITS?

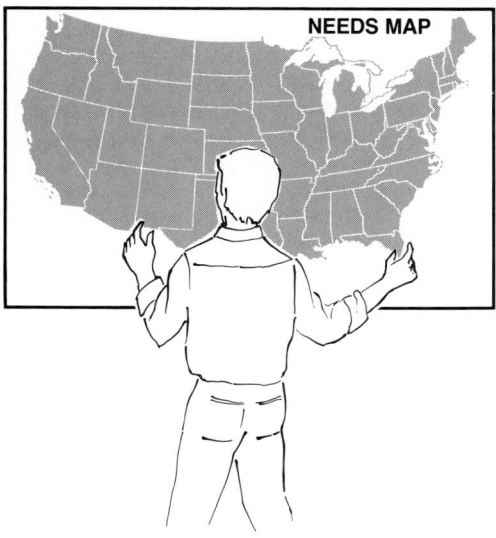

EXAMPLES OF MISSION STATEMENTS

- **For a full-line automobile manufacturer:**
  Our mission is to provide automobiles to satisfy the personal and business transportation needs of the American public.
- **For a sports car manufacturer:**
  Our mission is to provide automobiles to satisfy the high-performance, personal transportation needs of the American public.
- **For a pharmaceutical company:**
  Our mission is to supply the newest and best ethical pharmaceutical products, thus providing for that part of the health-care needs of the American public.
- **For a packaged food manufacturer:**
  Our mission is to supply tasty and attractive, branded-quality, packaged-food products for the pleasure, nutrition, and good health of the American public.
- **For a newspaper:**
  Our mission is to fulfill the public need for fast and accurate reporting of current events together with their background and interpretation.

GOALS AND STRATEGIES

The goals of an organization are specific targets within the area defined by its mission. Goals and objectives are treated as roughly equivalent here, although goals are more likely to be larger or longer term, and the very specific and short-term targets are more likely to be called objectives, in the "management-by-objectives" sense. The mission provides the framework; the goals define targets within the mission that, when achieved, should lead to significant progress toward achieving that mission; and the strategies are the basis for action plans aimed at achieving the goals.

A BUSINESS AS A CORPORATION

The large majority of businesses function as corporations; a corporation is an economic entity made possible by the law. In a famous Supreme Court decision, Chief Justice John Marshall wrote:

> A corporation is an artificial being, invisible, intangible, and existing only in contemplation of the law. Being the mere creature of the law, it possesses only those properties which the charter of its creation confers upon it. . . . Among the most important are immortality and . . . individuality; properties by which a perpetual succession of many persons are considered the same, and may act as a single individual.[3]

The importance of this definition is the emphasis on the corporation as the artificial creature of the law, limited by its charter and by the laws that govern it. The corporation has a legal framework that is also economic in nature. Survival requires economic performance, and the corporation is conditioned to react in an economic dimension.

It has been said that money is the language of the firm. Essentially all significant businesses are corporations, and corporations by their nature must behave according to economic constraints. Yet many of the considerations that influence management actions are social and ethical in nature, and they are often difficult to accommodate within an economic framework. There is an inherent contradiction here. Even in charitable and other not-for-profit corporations, the basically economic nature of the legal structure often causes conflict with the social role or mission of the organization.

---

[3] The Trustees of Dartmouth College versus Woodward, *4 Wheat,* (U.S.) 518, 636 (1819).

ACHIEVING SOCIAL ENDS BY ECONOMIC MEANS

The mission is a social role, but the firm is an economic entity whose survival depends on economic performance. In spite of potential conflict between its mission and its economic nature, the business strives for social ends by economic means. A business strives for social ends by persuading customers to buy products or services for the social role they perform—as a radio manufacturer sells radios that allow the purchasers to listen to radio broadcasts, an important aspect of contemporary social interaction. To succeed, the manufacturer must achieve a level of sales and profits sufficient for the business to operate. And if a business sells those quantities of its products necessary to achieve a level of economic performance permitting survival and growth, then those products are—as evidenced by the continuing purchases—sufficiently beneficial to society. Given the fact of purchase as an endorsement of the product's value, the business is making a social contribution as well as an economic profit.

This argument assumes (1) that society regulates the marketplace sufficiently to ensure that products contain value on which customers base their continuing purchase and (2) that purchase of a product by customers is evidence of that product's worth.

While our society attempts to restrict sale of illegal products and to protect customers against deception and fraud, it also endorses a system by which product value (or service value) is a matter of individual decision rather than collective judgment. Tobacco products, alcoholic beverages, adult literature, and firearms are products whose continued sale is strongly opposed by significant elements in society; but the overall social judgment has been that the purchase endorsement of these products by specific customer groups justifies their existence, even in the face of intense disapproval by others. Society's position is that any legal product not misrepresented or defective in some way is a good product if people want to buy it; a business makes a social contribution by supplying these products so long as society as a whole does not impose restrictions.

The mission of a business is to satisfy a specific type or class of customer need. Mission statements, as need oriented and market connected, tend to describe only one sort of business or relationship; they often are so specific to an individual business that an enterprise consisting of several different businesses has difficulty in stating a single mission that unifies them.

The scope of a mission statement is defined by the range of needs that the business finds it practical to attempt to serve. Usually the missions of a group of related businesses can be unified into a single statement covering all of them. One definition of a conglomerate is as a multibusiness enterprise without a single mission unifying the thrust of its businesses. This characteristic makes a conglomerate more difficult to manage, and it loses some of the potential for synergism between its businesses for lack of this unifying relationship.

MAKING UP RULES

Management of a business enterprise—of an economic entity attempting to make profits and survive by achieving a social purpose—establishes rules of behavior as a part of its function in directing the enterprise. A striking difference between the corporation as an individual created by the law and all other types of individuals is that other types of individuals are born into a social framework laying down rules for individual behavior. In many human societies the rules are so detailed that a person can go through life by following them, with almost no need for individual thought or decision. But the corporate society has no such rules, beyond the bare requirements for filing certain reports and paying taxes.

Society has created "Thou shalt not!" rules to prevent price fixing and other disapproved business behavior, but there is almost no positive guidance. The management of each corporation must create and establish its own rules of behavior for the business; and while management may choose to follow a general pattern, strict imitation of other businesses is usually unwise.

A management has the task of studying the needs of its own specific business, in the light of the mission it has selected and the competition it faces, and devising rules for its operation that will yield satisfactory results. This task is never complete because the business continues to change and the problems and challenges evolve. As new situations arise, new rules are required. Management must create them as they are needed.

Business is always competitive, currently or potentially, so that as one management faces new situations and makes up new rules by which to operate, the managements of its competitors are doing the same thing. If business is a competitive game, then it is a game where the players each make up their own rules within a framework established by law. The players most ingenious in creating new rules are likely to achieve the best profits.

When Tom Watson, Sr., of IBM Corp., began to lease systems of office equipment in the 1920s rather than to sell individual machines as his competitors did, he created a new market environment. By leasing he removed customer equipment-financing problems and costs and the business risk of the equipment investment. IBM representatives designed installations to fit business needs and then helped with startup. IBM service kept the system running, so that the customer business was assured of an operating system tailored to its needs; there was no investment, only a monthly fee.[4]

No one else marketed systems of equipment this way, and IBM's competitors did not seem to know how to respond as IBM steadily increased its market share. Watson made up new rules for office equipment marketing, made these rules effective through the supporting organization he had built, and benefited greatly at the expense of his competitors. Because Watson was so much better at making up new rules than anyone else in that marketplace at that time, IBM grew toward the preeminence it has enjoyed ever since.

BUSINESS POLICIES

The rules that a management sets for itself as it manages the business become policies. When management has selected a mission or social role, it then chooses specific targets or goals within this mission and focuses the energy and resources of the organization toward these goals by the strategy it defines. That strategy is put into effect by laying out guidelines for this action. These guidelines are the policies for conduct of the business as discussed above.

This book deals with the process by which the strategy is set and the pattern of conduct is defined in the areas of action in which the organization engages. This process is most effective when its components are considered explicitly, but the ingredients of any pattern of management action implicitly generate such rules. Any business has a strategy and some rules of conduct for the enterprise as a whole and also for specific areas within it. Strategy is defined and policy established by management decisions for research, capital expenditures, hiring and firing, pay increases, and the multitude of other actions necessary as an organization exists, conducts its businesses, and deals with the outside world.

CREATING RESOURCES

A part of any strategy is the wise use of available resources. The art in games of strategy, such as checkers and chess, is to use resources skillfully. As with most military strategy, the objective is to win by defeating a

---

[4] Robert Sobel, *IBM: Colossus in Transition* (New York: Bantam Books, 1981), pp. 91–110.

specific opponent. In game-theory terminology, these are "zero-sum" games. One player wins and the other loses.

Business strategy is different because neither the resource pool nor the payoffs are clearly spelled out in advance. The competitive process is often a very personal one, sometimes involving many players. One or all of the players can augment his or her resource pool and change the potential payoffs by properly selecting a strategy to confront the others more effectively.

Peters and Waterman[5] used the Frito-Lay distribution system as an example of organizational excellence, and others have praised this system also. Frito-Lay built and trained a distribution team to an unusual level of effectiveness in support of its retailers. Frito-Lay created this resource as a part of its strategy for rapid growth in snack foods in the same way that IBM service was a necessary resource created by Watson to make possible the success cited earlier. Both served to increase the profit that could be earned from a specific marketplace beyond any profit possible before the new resource was created.

Forbes once profiled Time Energy Systems,[6] a then fast-growing service company specializing in energy-saving control of heating and air conditioning in large buildings. Time Energy Systems liked to sell "free" control systems—no up-front cost to the building owner, with Time Energy taking a share of the energy savings as its profit. This made a very profitable but very capital-hungry growth plan. David Brown, the founder, was fresh from bankruptcy of an unsuccessful startup in a different field. How could a newly bankrupt entrepreneur get startup capital? Much of the early growth was funded by limited partnerships created building by building as the company grew, each secured by a specific contract with that building owner. Later, after it had established a track record, Time Energy raised about $20 million in two stock offerings. With an attractive idea in creative hands, money flowed to the idea, and Brown got Time Energy off to a rapid start. This is another example of an entrepreneur creating needed resources, here by an imaginative approach to financing.

When a few Americans became fascinated with small European automobiles after World War II and began to import them privately, the idea caught on. Many manufacturers saw the potential of the U.S. market, and they began shipping cars to the United States. Of the various British, French, Italian, and German manufacturers, Volkswagen seems to have understood the U.S. market best; it began immediately to create a dealer service network. For lack of similar support, most of the other entrants

---
[5] Thomas J. Peters and Robert H. Waterman, Jr., *In Search of Excellence: Lessons from America's Best-Run Companies* (New York: Harper & Row, 1982).
[6] Robert H. Bork, Jr., "He Who Laughs Last," *Forbes,* July 15, 1984.

failed and withdrew from the market, leaving Volkswagen as the preeminent automobile importer until the Japanese entered. The VW cars were good, but so were some of the others. Only Volkswagen had created the service-support resource necessary for survival in the market.

The underlying argument is that business success requires a sound strategy, and a part of that strategy is in obtaining or creating the necessary resources. Whether this means assembling, motivating, and training a superbly effective distribution team, as in the Frito-Lay case, or obtaining financing by novel means, strategies are founded in part on the creation of resources needed for the desired accomplishment.

Just as a colonial cabinetmaker often made new and specially shaped tools to build each new type of furniture, business strategy sometimes requires creating the tools needed for a specific accomplishment. Resources are among management's tools for accomplishing its goals. The art is to know which resources can be created and how to accomplish this on a timetable and within a budget.

ORGANIZATION COMPETENCE AS A STRATEGIC VARIABLE

Some strategies are easy to execute, and some are hard to execute. Organizations and related people costs are a major expenditure area, and a good management will not hire expensive, overqualified people for simple tasks or attempt difficult tasks without first building an organization with the necessary skills. And because organizations, organization cultures, and the roles and relationships of the individual employees are usually reshaped only slowly, a given management often finds itself committed in the present to a pattern of motivation and expenditures inherited from past practices. While expenditures can be raised or lowered rapidly, motivation and skills levels take much longer to change. At present, and in spite of major efforts by the current president to change the situation, General Motors management appears seriously hampered in its efforts to shift to newer styles of production management by the inertia of an organization still evolving from a motivation and skills base established in the 1940s, 1950s, and 1960s.

A given strategy calls for an appropriate organization to carry it out—an organization appropriate in skills and motivation and therefore in cost-effectiveness. In creating resources, as discussed in the preceding section, often a more competent organization must be created. This requires an investment of management efforts and other resources over time. Further, this investment carries with it a commitment to that created organization, and the value of the organizational investment is likely to be lost if that commitment is violated, as discussed in a later chapter.

An organization is a strategic variable, therefore, because (1) different levels of cost-effectiveness and competence are required by different strategies, (2) improvement in competence or cost-effectiveness often requires significant time, expense, and management effort, and (3) an investment in a high level of organization cost-effectiveness and competence is a somewhat fragile asset requiring careful management.

EXAMPLES OF BUSINESS STRATEGIES

- Our strategy is to develop innovative new electronic products for new markets, concentrating on areas where success can lead to a major new business.
- Our strategy is to build a broad line of health-care products for use in doctors' offices, adding any products that make appropriate contributions; our line should fill, as completely as possible, the needs of doctors for products used in office procedures.
- Our strategy is to seek a "second supplier" relationship in our markets by offering, at 10 to 20 percent lower prices, products and supplies as similar as possible to those of the market leader.
- Our strategy is to offer customized services (or products) to those customers willing to pay a little more for a service (or product) that is easier to use and more specifically fitted to their individual needs.

BUSINESS FIRMS VERSUS OTHER SORTS OF ORGANIZATIONS

This book emphasizes the problems and challenges facing for-profit businesses, as does most of the literature in the business policy and strategic management field. There are several reasons for this, starting with the tremendous numbers of business organizations, the widespread interest in their troubles and successes, and the tendency for new developments to occur first where business is under acute pressure from problems or opportunities. It is easy and convenient to talk first about businesses, and the number of available examples tends to be higher.

But there are many other sorts of organizations that have policy and strategy problems too; and in spite of the differences in organization funding or purpose, their policy and strategic management needs are remarkably similar. As discussed in later chapters, charities, not-for-profit corporations, government agencies, and museums—a wide variety of different types of nonbusiness organizations—have similar needs. They must each have a clear understanding of their mission, goals, and strategy, and they must achieve their social ends through economic means by operating

FIGURE 1-2 FUNDAMENTALS

Define the mission—the key social role.
Create economic means—yield social ends and profits.
Make up your own rules—but be good at it.
Match strategy with available talent—don't accidentally demand the impossible.

ABOVE ALL, LEARN HOW TO CREATE RESOURCES.

FIGURE 1-3 MISSION, GOALS, AND STRATEGY AS PART OF STRATEGY DESIGN

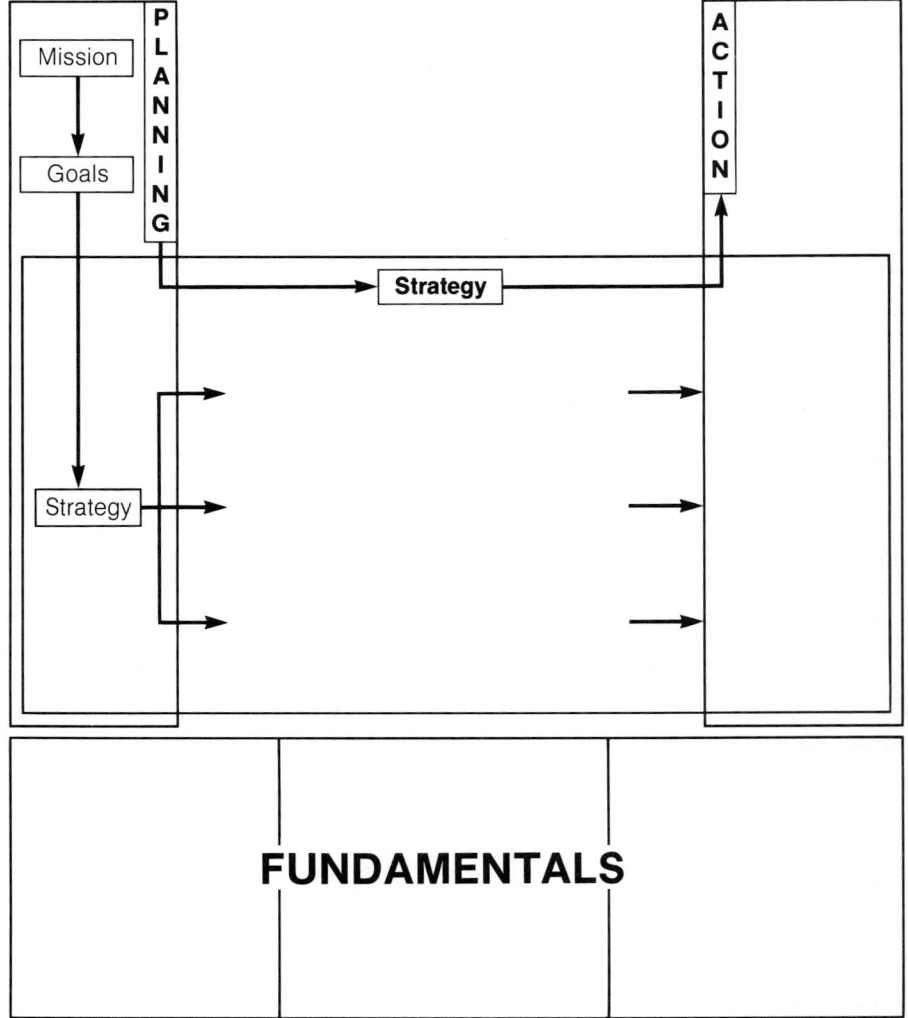

within a budget framework. These institutions also fit the analytical pattern developed here chapter by chapter.

Business examples will provide the basis for most of the discussion in the next several chapters, therefore, but the framework is a more general one, as developed in Part Five.

STRATEGY, POLICY, AND THE BUSINESS FIRM

Strategies are basic approaches that management selects for designing actions to solve a problem or accomplish a goal. A strategy says, "This is how we will carry out our business" in some specific action area. Policies are guidelines or rules that management sets for itself in the operation of the business. These rules can arise by specific decisions, as when management chooses a new direction for the business, or they can grow out of habitual operating patterns. Management has complete freedom in making these rules so long as no laws are broken; the success of a business often depends on the creativity of its management in making up rules and creating resources to enhance the strategic and competitive position of the enterprise.

The three chapters in Part One of this book provide an overall picture of strategy, policy, and the business firm as summarized in Figure 1-2, with the underlying flow moving from planning to strategy to action and the specific links progressing from mission to goals to strategy. Both of these concepts are illustrated in Figure 1-3. Building on the foundation provided in Chapter 1, Chapter 2 deals with the way habits become policy and with the formulation of strategy as the basis for both. But strategy has different parameters at different levels, and Chapter 2 also introduces the concept of primary strategy, which guides product, business, or enterprise development, and the need to design each of these three levels of primary strategy differently. Then Chapter 3 presents the components of product and business strategy, leaving enterprise strategy to be discussed in Part Two.

QUESTIONS FOR ANALYSIS AND DISCUSSION

1. Choose three different business units and develop a statement of the mission of each as you see it.
2. For the businesses you used in question 1, list some of the specific goals toward which these managements seem to be working.

3. Give examples of contemporary business behavior that illustrate the functioning of the legal framework on which it rests.
4. Find your own examples of social ends achieved through economic means by different sorts of businesses.
5. Do any of the examples you chose in question 4 also illustrate the process of making up new rules for the business to run by? If so, explain. If not, find three suitable examples not from the text.
6. Do any of the examples you chose in question 4 or question 5 also illustrate the process of creating new resources for the business? If so, explain. If not, find three suitable examples not from the text.

FOR FURTHER INFORMATION

Ansoff, H. Igor, *Corporate Strategy* (New York: McGraw-Hill, 1965).
  An important, basic book that has helped shape the field.

Drucker, Peter, *The Practice of Management* (New York: Harper & Row, 1953).
  A management classic because it helps to make many strategic management dimensions clear.

CASE 1
WEAKER SERVICES, INC.

John Brown had always wanted to make a lot of money. From business school he went into a brokerage firm; he joined the staff of a merger and acquisitions specialist two years later and a venture capital firm a year after that. Five years out of college he was doing well—he had a good record, much good experience, and a better salary than most of his classmates, but no immediate prospects for making a lot of money. This frustrated him. In another five years he might reach a level where he could begin to accumulate equity in startup companies in addition to the normal fees for his services. Over time this process had brought sizable fortunes for some of the senior people he contacted, but John was young and impatient.

WEAKER SERVICES

One day John got a call from his wife's favorite uncle, an upstate lawyer. A client had died, and the uncle was now the executor of the Weaker estate. A part of the estate was D. E. Weaker Services, Inc., a profitable accounting and financial services business that had been leaderless since Daniel Elijah Weaker's death. The estate needed someone to take charge; the salary was only a little more than John was already making, but the package included 10 percent equity in Weaker Services and options to buy more stock later.

John was intrigued. He investigated, saw the potential for future growth, and accepted a position as president and chief executive officer of D. E. Weaker Services, Inc. Weaker Services' sustaining activity was accounting and related financial services for a large number of small businesses, including medical and professional groups. The company also did a great deal of pension and personal financial planning for the principals of these firms and groups. John Brown spent six intensive months during which he worked, in turn, in each of the four branch offices, met the clients, and learned the details of the operation. Daniel Weaker had been ill for several years before his death; the growth of the business had continued despite the lack of strong direction, but there had been lapses that John began to repair. Billings responded rapidly to the energy of the new chief. By the end of John Brown's first year, revenues were up 75 percent and profits had more than doubled. In the eyes of the trustees and directors who voted the balance of the stock as representatives of the estate, John Brown was a hero.

At the beginning of the second year, John engineered the purchase of a family-owned machine tool company, which became Weaker Machine. He persuaded the directors to create a holding company called DEWS, Inc., with D. E. Weaker Services as one wholly owned subsidiary and

Weaker Machine as another. John had never liked being a "weaker" chief executive officer, and it was good business sense to keep the established financial services business separate anyway.

Then DEWS acquired a small furniture factory and an established regional truck line, and John's vision began to take shape. During his first year he had found a suitable successor as president of Weaker Services; this allowed him to give his attention to corporate growth. A part of the reason he bought the machine tool company was that Silas Elmer, the man running it, was superbly qualified once freed of interference from the family.

John Brown's management pattern was simple and straightforward. In each case he put a subsidiary in the hands of a capable executive with a very adequate base salary and generous bonuses based on the growth and profitability of that business. John was interested only in buying sound businesses at bargain prices. In the case of the machine tool company, a family disagreement had almost paralyzed the firm, and it soon would have failed. But the organization was still sound; it recovered immediately once Silas Elmer was free to operate it properly, and it began to grow rapidly.

Weaker Services had a strong balance sheet and no debt when John Brown took over. In addition to this, an extensive portfolio of real estate and stock in client companies had accumulated over the years as partial payment for services. In several cases the clients had since been acquired by larger firms. John found holdings of listed stock exchanged for shares of local companies many years earlier but still carried on the Weaker Services corporate books at the original price and under the name of the original company. One block of Fortune 500 stock that was acquired in exchange for services valued at ten thousand dollars, thirty years earlier, sold for enough to pay for the furniture factory, the truck line, and a new warehouse. In another case DEWS exchanged a piece of property, valued at one thousand dollars when it was acquired in 1947, for a 30 percent interest in a major shopping center built on the property site. DEWS then traded this equity for a very attractive company that sold peat moss and nursery supplies.

The Weaker Services (now DEWS) board of directors continued to believe that John Brown could almost walk on water, because the DEWS financial performance was so good. Net profits had doubled in the third year, then doubled again in both the fourth year and the fifth year, to about sixteen times the level when John took control. The directors (and trustees of the estate) arranged a public offering of DEWS stock to consolidate the gains for the heirs, and John began to borrow money and exercise his own stock options. The directors had pushed the dividend rate up until John projected that, with expected continued growth, his dividends would pay the interest on his loans and something on the principal and tax liability, to the point that the stock his options entitled him to buy would pay for itself in ten years. He would own 25 percent of the equity free and clear, and he would have a *lot* of money, even more than in his college dreams. DEWS was a major listed company now. John's favorite speech, "The DEWS and Don'ts of Business Success," was in great demand; almost every month, someplace in the business press, a fresh profile appeared of the thirty-two-year-old wonder boy who had built DEWS.

After the offering, 50 percent of the stock was in public hands, with 25 percent still held by the estate and 25 percent controlled by John Brown. This gave him a much freer hand in setting policy, the directors already tended to favor anything he proposed, and acquisitions had continued at a steady pace. The DEWS cash flow after dividends was good, the hidden assets John had found paid for some purchases, and the other purchases had been financed by borrowing money eventually secured by the assets of the particular business being acquired. John and his controller both kept personal contact with all of the individual businesses, but there were thirty-two of them now, six reporting to each of five senior vice presidents, and Weaker Services and Weaker Machine still reporting directly to John.

STRESSES AND STRAINS

One Monday morning John got a call from the secretary of the president of Weaker Services, to tell him that her boss had died of a massive heart attack during the night. John called the widow with condolences, sent flowers, appointed one of the vice presidents at Weaker Services as acting head of the business, and told his secretary to revise his schedule as soon as the funeral arrangements were set. Then he pondered. This had been his first and perhaps most successful executive appointment, except that the departed Weaker Services president had never properly groomed a successor. That could be a problem.

Monday afternoon was devoted to a presentation by a machine tool business consultant. Silas Elmer was clearly the best old-fashioned machinist around and a superb manager, but John had begun to worry about shrinking margins in the business. When a major order was lost because a Japanese firm producing in Kentucky underbid Weaker Machine by a large margin, John, over the opposition of Silas Elmer, had commissioned a consultant study. The report was devastating. The consultant said that Weaker Machine should have been out of business long ago, based on its equipment and work methods, and that the company had been sustained only by the excellence of Silas Elmer's utilization of obsolete machines. Yet another stage in machine improvement was just coming into general use by the competition. These improvements would surely wipe out the remaining Weaker profitability. The consultant spoke of robotics, computer control, and massive investment and then admitted that the business would need ten times the present turnover to repay it. John had a full day scheduled Tuesday, and by then the funeral had been set for Wednesday, so he scheduled Thursday at Weaker Machine for a long, hard session with Silas Elmer on what they would do next.

John had reserved Tuesday morning for a meeting with Smith White, senior vice president of the auto parts group, and the presidents of the six companies that reported to him. They were concerned about the future of the auto parts industry. All six companies had been hurt by the last recession and were in various stages of recovery; but the thrust of the meeting was that DEWS would have to make large new capital investments in order to have a sound, long-term position. The morning was spent on the need for computer controls and automated manufacturing steps, the high cost of developing effective robotics, and the sophisticated manufacturing logistics necessary to support "just-in-time" auto production systems. Over lunch the talk shifted to the future of the auto industry, and John was left with the picture of a competent, concerned group of executives trying very hard to build a more viable relationship with a changing auto industry.

John finally told the group to begin to flesh out the specifics of their ideas and to see how much capital would be needed and what the returns might be, but he had the feeling of having crossed a watershed. Up to this point the DEWS businesses had each funded themselves or had arranged and secured their own borrowings without building up any major debt load. The six auto parts companies had much more than paid for themselves, relative to the initial investment by DEWS. But a major infusion of DEWS capital would change this relationship and make the success of the auto parts businesses a keystone of DEWS' future, which they never had been in the past.

After lunch John had a long-scheduled meeting with Arthur Minor, the DEWS controller, for a first look at next year's budget. While the prospects were for gains in overall sales and profits, John knew that Arthur Minor was also concerned about a possible downtrend in several of the DEWS businesses. They spent most of the afternoon on these potential trouble spots, which were more numerous than John had expected.

Wednesday morning was the funeral. After the services and condolences to the family, John spent the rest of the day talking to Weaker Services people, renewing acquaintances and freshening his contact with the business. That evening a quiet dinner with the acting president left John with the feeling of a sound operation without any immediate crisis, but badly in need of the sort of leadership he himself had brought to it eight years earlier.

Thursday morning's meeting at Weaker Machine opened with Silas Elmer trying to resign. John refused to discuss the resignation until they dealt with the future of the business, and a long and stormy morning followed. Silas was still angry because the consultant had been brought in, and he was fiercely resistant to the new ideas. Yet he acknowledged that the business could not go on as it had. John saw Silas as a strong, proud man, embarrassed by the way he had let change get ahead of Weaker Machine but not yet able to deal openly with his failure; John also saw Silas as deeply committed to the business, concerned for its future, and anxious to secure its future somehow.

By lunchtime Silas had got most of his pain behind him, and they were discussing possible tactics for rebuilding the Weaker Machine business. John told him to get out into other people's plants, to see for himself the best practices and the newest machines in the United States, Japan, and Europe, before committing to any specific program. By the time John left at seven o'clock that evening, Silas Elmer had made his second in command acting head of Weaker Machine so he could work full-time on the necessary planning. When Silas asked if he could call on the same consultant again for ideas and suggestions, John began to feel hopeful for the first time; but he told Silas to get a second opinion also. And he knew that, in Weaker Machine, DEWS had a business in deep trouble, led by a friend who would have very hard work in the adjustment before he could design and operate a truly state-of-the-art, competitive plant.

Friday John got back to his own office to find that the Environmental Protection Agency (EPA) had banned a pesticide made by a DEWS business and that two other DEWS businesses had reported loss of significant contracts to Japanese and German competitors. As John gathered details by phone, he learned that in both cases the awards had been made at prices below DEWS' costs.

Late Friday afternoon John called in Arthur Minor to review the impact of a very hard week. By six o'clock they were back to the grand plan, which Arthur Minor had helped John to build and to execute. DEWS was planned to consist of a group of businesses, each with a proven ability to make money, each under the leadership of an able president with strong personal incentives for financial success. Any business that could make money was a candidate, so long as it could be bought well and run well. DEWS' acquisition record was excellent, and DEWS' operating results were excellent too, up to that point.

But John was disturbed by the lack of management depth in the businesses. At Weaker Machine the business had gotten out of date and no one had known it until now; at Weaker Services one man had died and the spark of the service business needed to be relit again. Then there was also the uncertainty John sensed in how his business heads were going to deal with the EPA problem or with the fresh challenges from import competition. Where he himself could help two or three businesses in grappling with their problems, who else could?

In this respect it had been difficult to get what he wanted from the senior vice presidents. Smith White was the exception, in that he was really coming to grips with the long-term needs of the auto parts group—but then he was the only one whose assigned businesses were all in the same field. Of the five senior vice presidents, John had found it necessary to replace three within the last two years, and he was still doubtful about two of the incumbents. It seemed to take a different sort of manager to live with five or six different types of businesses at the same time.

As the discussion became more philosophical, John Brown got out a special bottle he had hidden away, and he and Arthur shared bourbon and philosophy. Both of them had wanted wealth and success very badly. The building of DEWS was a superb achievement, started by John, carried on together, and capable of rewarding both of them beyond their dreams or needs. But might it fail in operation because they couldn't keep all of those businesses going? They couldn't and wouldn't let that happen! But why should this be a problem? Their business choices had been good, and their success in picking good subsidiary company presidents had been far above average. Why shouldn't growth go on forever?

John Brown put it this way: "Arthur, all we have ever asked of these businesses was that they make money—to make their presidents and key executives rich, to make the stockholders rich, to make us rich. Was that wrong? What else could we have asked?"

QUESTIONS

1. Do you think there is a problem at DEWS? Or is it just a run of bad luck that will all work out as John Brown and Arthur Minor add managers and emphasize training of replacements?
2. Would DEWS be different if there were an overall purpose to unify the business?
3. Can you find any evidence of problems due to the lack of corporate emphasis on mission and purpose?

CASE 2 THE CARNEGIE CLINICS

Andrew X. Carnegie had reached a point in his life where he wanted to do something important with his money. His family company had received a takeover bid that turned into a fierce bidding war between giants. Andrew had not wanted to sell, but he had no family to leave the firm to anyway, and the price had reached a level that no sane businessman could refuse. Then, as a rich, restless chief executive officer with no company to run, Andrew was next persuaded to try the oil business. He became part of a group buying undervalued reserves on which to build a major oil company. The group borrowed heavily to leverage its assets, and bought well. The success of the group came to the attention of certain European and other offshore investors who made a very attractive offer and bought the entire package. Andrew more than tripled his capital in the oil deal. He hadn't really liked the oil business anyway; what should he do next?

His wife wanted him to retire, and Andrew was ready for a change of pace. So he decided to do something worthwhile with all of his money. If he reserved a few million to live on, the rest could go to a worthy cause. Because his name was the same as the earlier Carnegie, he had heard the story of the Carnegie libraries many times. When the Carnegie Steel Company was sold, the first Andrew Carnegie looked for good things to do. Universities were benefited, foundations were created, and many, many towns got new libraries. Andrew X. Carnegie began to visit charitable foundations to see what was accomplished with money from other large fortunes, but he did not see any pattern he wanted to follow. He commissioned two consultant studies on the ways in which his capital could be used to do good. Still he was unsatisfied; there should be something he could do that would have a greater impact.

One day a doctor friend asked him why he did not use the Carnegie fortune to give the world a cure for cancer. Andrew was immediately interested. It turned out that the doctor had seen a demonstration of some advanced laser technology, and so Andrew went in pursuit. He found a group of enthusiasts trying to adapt the computer control systems of a magnetic resonance scanner to laser cancer treatment. Success required use of the following: (1) a dye system selectively absorbed by cancer cells; (2) lasers operating at wavelengths that would penetrate tissue and be absorbed by the selected dye; and (3) controls such that the amount of laser energy absorbed by a given cell could be precisely controlled. The theory was that individual cells could be heated just enough to destroy them; a temperature of 40° C would be enough (normal body temperature is 37° C). The requirement was that only the cancer cells be heated. The system was elaborate because of the extensive controls needed for safe operation; it faced many unknowns, such as the rate at which cancer cells can be destroyed without overtaxing the body's ability to remove the waste.

Andrew was impressed. He called in experts in the various technologies to confirm the viability of the approach, and he concluded that the group had designed a first-rate but technically elaborate approach to the treatment of almost any cancer. He wrote a check for $500,000 to take an option and to give the group some cash to buy equipment. Then he started to study how to give cancer treatment to the world.

Six weeks later Andrew was acutely frustrated and very discouraged. He had talked to a lot of people in U.S. and United Nations health organizations about how to give cancer treatment to the world. They were all interested on a "Yes, but . . ." basis. That is, the idea had the same appeal to everyone once Andrew proved that it could work. Until then, it was shelved with all other hairbrained schemes. Because it dealt with cancer it got more discussion time, and Andrew got a picture of the hurdles to be overcome. To begin, since the treatment involved a dye material to be injected into the body, the dye material would require approval as a new prescription drug. Someone from a drug company told him that this would cost $10 million for each dye. Further, because the treatment system would involve new types of lasers and new sorts of control systems, these would require approval as new medical devices. Several technical people rejected the whole concept as unworkable, because the control requirements were extremely precise if only the desired tissue were to be heated: "Murphy's law says you will have equipment failures. If the equipment failures kill patients, they won't let you play around any more, regardless of the cures."

Andrew began to have a picture of a very long and demanding technical path leading to the successful treatment of people. He got enough expert advice to satisfy himself that the system was theoretically sound and that it could be made safe and reliable with the proper instruments and operating controls. He received a proposal that he fund a $5 million project to build an instrument for treating rabbits, in order to demonstrate the validity of the approach. He told the designers that, if he were going to spend that amount of money, they should come back with a proposal for an instrument that would also treat people when the experimental work reached that point.

Concurrently he was still looking for a way to give the eventual cancer treatment to the world. One of his consultants advised setting up a nonprofit foundation for this purpose, which the consultant offered to head for a six-figure salary. This foundation would have trustees from the World Health Organization and several other international bodies. Andrew was already uncomfortable about the viability of the proposed effort; so when he came to the proposed list of trustees, several of whom he had met and classified as noncontributors in the course of his own inquiries, he got so disgusted he threw the report in the fireplace.

The next day he had lunch with Tom Thompson, one of his partners from the oil deal. After they had settled their business, he began to vent some of his frustration with the health establishment. To his surprise Tom laughed: "Andy, when you were in the oil business you weren't so soft in the head."

"What do you mean?"

"We did have some good luck on some of those oil reserves, but most of what we bought anybody could have bought, and you know it. We were the only ones who could see the value before all of the pieces were put together. So we put it together and made out like bandits selling the package. Why should the cancer business be any different?"

"You mean . . ."

"I mean that if you are as serious about this cancer business as you say, you are going to have to carry it all of the way through to a clinic with tile walls and a receptionist that greets the patients. Then if it works, everyone will believe you, and you will be seven kinds of a hero. But if the whole procedure has to be done as carefully as you say, you are going to have to keep control of the way the machines are run so that some quack doesn't get one, run it wrong, kill a lot of people, and give your treatment a bad name.

"Why don't you form a company? I've got some cash too, from the oil deal. I might want a piece of this, because I bet it will pay off pretty well."

"Tom, you miss the whole point. I want to do something good for people, not just make money again."

"Andy, you are going soft-headed again. Look at what you told me before. You mentioned the first Andrew Carnegie and Henry Ford. The real contribution both of them made was in the work they did, not in the money they gave away. Carnegie really helped with the growth of the country because he made good steel rails at the right price when the country needed them for railroads. The steel technology came from Europe, and anybody else could have gotten it just as well. But old Carnegie made it work, cut the price, and sold as much as he could make. His competitors didn't like him much because they had to learn to make steel better just to stay in business. Meanwhile, he put away enough money to build a lot of libraries later.

"And Henry Ford—when he took off, the automobile was a rich man's toy. He learned to make the Model T and he cut the price. He built cars a working man could afford. He made a lot of money building cars, but he did more good for the country than the Ford Foundation can ever equal, good as it is.

"In both cases other people had an equal shot at the technology. The contribution was in making it work. And that's always the way that it is. If this cancer thing is any good, the fastest way for it to bring treatment to the world is by building a good company to deliver it. That way you have the quality control and control over the way the treatment is operated. And capital—if one of these clinics costs five or ten million dollars, how many will it take for the world? You probably need at least a thousand clinics scattered across the United States, to be able to treat the millions of people who get cancer. That means you need between five and ten billion dollars in capital just for the United States. For the world you probably need more thousands of clinics, and it will take agencies and governments years to find all of the tens of billions of dollars in capital, regardless of how many lives it saves. But a private firm making money can raise as much capital as it can get a good return on—no limits.

"The best way is for you to go into the cancer treatment business, get the system going, and then expand. Cut the price of the treatment if you want to be a philanthropist, but I predict that will turn out just the way it did when Ford cut the price of the Model T. So many more people bought them that his profits went up.

"That's the end of my lecture, but I really do want a chance to buy stock in the Carnegie Clinics."

QUESTIONS

1. What do you think? Given the facts of the case, what is the best way to give cancer treatment to the world?
2. How does all of this fit with the concept of accomplishing social ends by economic means? Discuss.

CHAPTER 2

STRATEGY, POLICY, AND ACTION

KEY IDEAS IN THIS CHAPTER

Chapter 2 discusses the policy process and introduces the three levels of primary strategy:

- **habits and policies** – the way policies develop.
- **emerging issues as problems and opportunities** – as the driving force for many policy and strategy changes.
- **carrying policy into action** – or it is not worth creating.
- **strategic management** – as a key emphasis for effective executives.
- **mission, goals, and strategy** – and the way these three concepts fit together.
- **three levels of strategy** – for three different levels of management challenge.
- **primary strategy** – as the central thrust, with many **contributing strategies** in support.
- **strategy summary** – relating the types of strategy to each other.
- **examples of primary and contributing strategies.**

FIGURE 2–1 ACTIONS LEAD TO POLICIES

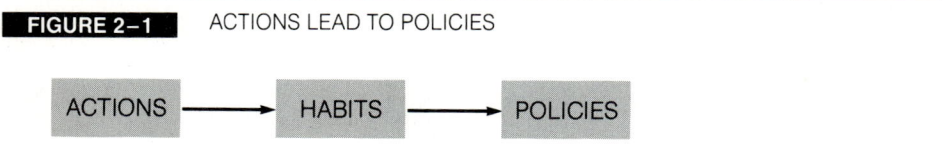

Strategy and policy develop spontaneously as a business operates, with or without conscious guidance of the process. This chapter starts by considering the strategy and policy development process and then moves through mission, goals, and strategy to a more formal definition of the levels of strategy and the relationship between them.

HABITS AND POLICIES

An organization, like a person, develops habits that govern its actions. A firm decides not to penalize an employee for missing work on an occasional day, and from this decision, a personal-leave policy evolves. In another company the bank balance falls dangerously low, and the treasurer conserves the firm's cash by telling his staff to "age" all invoices before paying them. This pattern of action quickly becomes a habit. Actions become operating habits, which in turn become the policies by which an organization runs, as illustrated in Figure 2-1. They may develop as informally as a person's habits, similar to the way a firm's vacation policies and bill-payment policies evolve.

Employees occasionally become ill, and companies sometimes arrange for paid sick leave on an individual basis. To control costs and to avoid discrimination through helping one employee and not another, it becomes necessary to define, publish, and enforce a sick-leave policy. In some sales areas accepting small orders or creating special products for individual customers raises costs; the need for cost control may lead to a special-order policy limiting such sales. The larger the organization, the more likely that these policies will be put in writing and issued officially.

EMERGING ISSUES AS PROBLEMS AND OPPORTUNITIES

In an established business the organizational habit patterns are usually well established, whether or not they have been written down; the habit and policy-formulation process deals largely with refinements unless major changes are being considered. Many of the possible reasons for major policy change relate to emerging issues in the outside environment, and some firms have established issues-tracking systems to watch for indications of future problems and opportunities. *Emerging issues* is a shorthand term for impending changes that will affect a business or its opportunities as society struggles with new technology, makes new rules and requirements, and learns to use new products and services.

Social change has become more rapid than ever before during peace time. Year by year society imposes new controls to limit use of toxic materials, to curb unacceptable business behavior, or to establish penalties for actions against the public welfare. Where society sees the need to use this rule-making power, the process leading to a new rule is usually visible and its outcome at least partially predictable.

At the same time society's needs are changing with surprising rapidity. Life-styles evolve, population groups age, people move to new areas, and new products and technologies are adopted. Hispanics are becoming the second largest ethnic group in the United States; single-parent families are a large and growing market; the complex of communication and information industries is becoming the nation's largest employer. These trends suggest opportunities that some companies find attractive; they are samples of a pattern of major changes in the structure of our society. One man's synopsis of these change patterns is John Naisbitt's *Megatrends*, organized around ten trends now changing our society:

- from an industrial society to an information society
- from forced technology to high tech/high touch (instead of mass production of standard products, use of high technology to improve the quality of life)
- from a national economy to a world economy
- from short-term to long-term decisions in our businesses
- from centralization to decentralization of our society
- from institutional help to self-help (a return to self-reliance)
- from representative democracy to participatory democracy (a voice for everyone)
- from hierarchies to networking (replacement of the management pyramid)
- from north to south (restructuring of the United States)
- from "either/or" choices to multiple options (a broader horizon for our lives)[1]

---

[1] John Naisbitt, *Megatrends* (New York: Warner Books, 1984).

In a parallel view of the same process, Alvin Toffler argued in *Future Shock*[2] that the rate of change in our society had become so great that there was a risk that our culture would be paralyzed by the shock induced by the change. In *The Third Wave*[3] he carried this analysis forward, picturing an emerging world with new institutions and an emerging new culture shaped by the changes.

The need to anticipate impending change varies from one type of business to another; different firms view this need in different ways. For the business-policy area this means that some businesses are anticipating issues and opportunities not yet at hand in a forward-looking policy process; other businesses react to rules and needs as they are defined by society. In either case a large fraction of policy changes arise as a result of emerging issues, and these changes are becoming increasingly urgent as the rate of change accelerates.

This book deals only briefly with the emerging-issues area itself, which is the subject of a growing literature of its own. In considering the wide variety of situations and problems affecting business policy today, however, it is important to be aware of how many of these issues arise directly or indirectly out of the rapid social change processes now active.

CARRYING POLICY INTO ACTION

The purpose of a policy is to guide action. The span of possible policy problems is large, ranging from issues over equal opportunity and proper handling of people in the organization to the central thrust of the business and the selection of appropriate areas and strategies for new ventures. In each case the payoff comes only at the point of management action—action taken or action avoided.

Action results from strategy and policy only when the results are communicated. Then line management must act on the desired policies and enforce them. Often when a new policy is announced, experienced managers will wait for a clear indication that the company is serious about the change. Only when they see that the new policy has solid top-management support will they begin seriously to put it into action.

STRATEGIC MANAGEMENT

Before it is effective, strategy must be created, translated into policy, communicated as appropriate, and made to work. In making it work, the effective integration of a well-conceived strategy with management of the

---
[2] Alvin Toffler, *Future Shock* (New York: Random House, 1970).
[3] Alvin Toffler, *The Third Wave* (New York: Morrow, 1980).

ongoing business process is now being called strategic management. The term *strategic management* came into general use as a result of conferences in 1973 and 1977 and the books that followed,[4] plus the continuing work of Ansoff, Hofer, Schendel, and others.

The original and continuing concept of management itself includes planning, or *prevoyance*, in Fayol's terminology,[5] and it therefore includes strategy formulation and execution. Some have attacked the term *strategic management* as redundant, because the concept of management already includes strategy or strategic planning as a component part. But much actual management practice has not been effective in integrating strategy into operating routines, so the extra emphasis carried by the designation "strategic management" is well justified. Also, recent studies of strategy and the strategy formulation process have led to new insights, and the integration of strategy into management as it was practiced by Fayol and other management pioneers can be enriched and increased in effectiveness today.

The concept of strategic management also allows a useful and proper emphasis on resource creation and on an action output from the strategy and policy process. Strategy must be translated into action to have meaning, and the proper action arises from a given set of strategies and policies as the result of effective strategic management.

Test Question

MISSION, GOALS, AND STRATEGY

A business organization can gain profit only by a commercial transaction in which it sells goods or services for more than they cost to deliver; the difference is the profit. When a person or a business buys, this is accomplished by exchanging purchasing power—whether cash, check, or credit—for that good or service. The exchange takes place because the buyer finds the good or service more valuable than the purchasing power that must be surrendered. Thus the buyer is, in terms of his or her own personal value system, better off for having made the purchase, subject, of course, to fair representation of the products or services and no unexpected consequences from their use, as discussed in Chapter 1.

---

[4] Based on the 1973 conference, H. I. Ansoff, R. P. Declerc, and R. L. Hayes (eds.), *From Strategic Planning to Strategic Management* (New York: John Wiley & Sons, 1976); and based on the 1977 conference, Dan E. Schendel and Charles W. Hofer, *Strategic Management: A New View of Business Policy and Planning* (Boston: Little, Brown & Co., 1979); continuing interest led to foundation of the Strategic Management Society and the *Journal of Strategic Management*; also, see H. Igor Ansoff, *Implanting Strategic Management* (Englewood Cliffs, N.J.: Prentice-Hall, 1984).

[5] Henri Fayol, *General and Industrial Management*, trans. Constance Storrs (London: Pitman, 1949); first published in French in 1916.

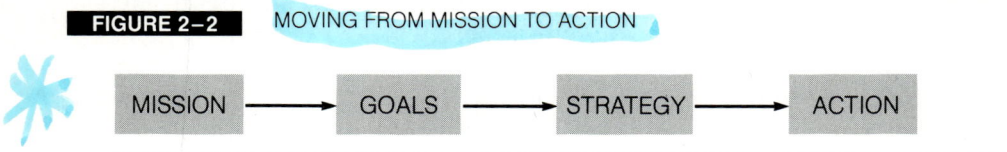

FIGURE 2-2 MOVING FROM MISSION TO ACTION

MISSION → GOALS → STRATEGY → ACTION

This excess of value that causes the buyer to be better off as a result of the purchase means that society as a whole should be better off because the business is operating—the business is fulfilling a beneficial social role. The survival of a business presupposes this beneficial social role, which is its mission.

By performing its mission, the business creates the opportunity to sell goods and services at a profit. It if does not perform its mission well, too few will buy and the business will cease to exist. The profit incentive is crucial to business performance, but underlying the concept of the business must be a beneficial social role sufficient to create the profit opportunity.

Within the scope of the mission, tangible targets are necessary; these are the goals. The mission is the basic social role, and the goals are the specific targets, within the framework of that role, that management is working to achieve. Thus the mission of a brewer may be to supply the light-lager-beer needs of a region; as its goal, the management may strive to increase sales, until the brewery runs at 90 percent of capacity, and to raise profitability to a target level.

Some managers put goals in personal terms: "I want to reach $100 million in sales before I retire." If this retirement date is a number of years away, such a goal could lead to a long-term plan for building the business. If this retirement date is close, the resulting actions could be short-term and not geared to future needs. Where the major management goals are for very near-term achievements, such as profitability for the current quarterly report, the future of the business may be neglected. Long-term goals often require investments that achievement of short-term goals will not allow, and the reconciliation of long-term and short-term goals is an urgent and recurrent problem for any management group.

In working to achieve goals, it is necessary to have some sort of a plan of action, whether formal or informal. The core and directing element of such a plan is the strategy, the basic approach to the problem. The basic flow of the entire process, from mission to goals to strategy to action, is shown in Figure 2-2.

Strategy has been called the road map to the goals because it lays out how progress toward those goals will be achieved. Here strategy is the art or science of using available and newly created business resources with maximum effectiveness in moving toward specific business goals. The execution of a strategy often involves competitive confrontations, and the analogy to a military battle plan or to the competitive strategy of a game is apt. Lessons both from game theory and from battle strategy are very useful in certain business situations. Any strategy should answer a "how" question—that is, how progress is to be made toward achieving goals. The specific goals that are relevant vary because there are many different sorts of strategy, but the resulting strategy should be a clear statement of how goals are to be accomplished within the appropriate organizational context.

THREE LEVELS OF STRATEGY

Strategy, and the "how to accomplish a goal" question that defines it, comes in many shapes and sizes. It may deal with the whole of a given accomplishment—designated as a primary strategy here—or with only a piece of an accomplishment—the contributing, or support, strategies. Primary strategies are classified according to the level at which the accomplishment is intended: (1) the level dealing with an *enterprise* as a whole, (2) the level dealing with the operation and development of a *specific business*, and (3) the level dealing with the *individual products* and product strategies.

Primary strategy is aimed at creating a pattern of action that results in a specific accomplishment, whether for an entire firm, a particular business unit of that firm, or an individual product of that firm. Contributing or support strategy however deals only with the pattern of action by which a specific function, department, or other unit contributes toward the accomplishment of a primary strategy that is usually also requiring actions by other units. Primary strategies establish goal requirements for contributing strategies.

Occasionally it is also necessary to deal with a group of products or services handled under the same primary strategy; this is often called a *program strategy*. These may be related products within a product line. For example, Coca-Cola might group several light, diet, and other cola variations together under a program strategy coordinating the handling of all products using a Coke or Coca-Cola brand name. Or, a program strategy might be defined for a major cluster of activities in a service department or public agency. In either case, program strategy is a potential intermediate level between the product and business strategy levels, and it can be accommodated easily when the need occurs.

The two basic types of strategy, primary strategy and contributing strategy, are summarized in Figure 2-3. Primary strategy varies by levels, according to the scope of the business considerations that govern it. Contributing strategy varies by purpose, according to the function or unit that strategy is designed to guide. Primary strategy guides how some portion of the business process of the enterprise will be carried out, and contribut-

FIGURE 2-3	THE TYPES AND LEVELS OF STRATEGY	
Types	Levels	Purpose
Primary Strategy	• Enterprise as a whole • Specific business • Individual Products or product strategies	• How to make progress toward mission and goals
Contributing strategy	• Specific function, department, or other unit	• How best to support the primary strategy

ing strategy guides how a specific function or unit of the business will operate in support of the primary strategies.

Many organizational units may need to define a contributing strategy. Such strategies include all of the normal functions and components; some examples are research strategy, marketing strategy, department strategy, night-shift machine shop strategy, and executive-dining-room-staff strategy. Units needing to define contributing strategies include any unit capable of planning, since any plan has a chosen or implied strategy at its core.

Many strategies are named after the organizational unit or function they are designed to drive. An effective production strategy, for example, may be an essential component of a business strategy and will form the basis for the planning of the production unit and the other units of the company whose activities synchronize with production.

PRIMARY STRATEGY

The three levels of primary strategy define the business potential that the various functional strategies work to optimize. Product strategy—or service strategy, in the case of a service business—sets forth how progress will be made toward the product or service goals, and it drives the plan for the product. The limits of its achievement, whether due to the product or the strategy, set limits on the potential that the functional strategies can realize. That is, without good products and a good product strategy, functional performance is limited, as is the performance of a business built on such functions.

Business strategy is the next-higher level. It sets forth how progress will be made toward business goals, and it sets the limits of achievement of a business unit that may be made up of large numbers of products or services. It uses the product or service strategies as a base and integrates them into a whole whose potential may be greater or less than the sum of the individual product or service strategies, depending on the nature and effectiveness of the required integration. Poorly matched, the strategies for different products can cause interference with each other's performance. Or, synergy can arise among good products and increase the total value of the products because of the skill with which business strategy integrates them.

The highest of the primary strategy levels is that of the enterprise strategy, the key framework controlling the general plan of accomplishment for the enterprise as a whole. This is discussed in more detail in Chapter 6. Enterprise strategy governs how the firm will move toward overall goals and apportion its assets and capabilities; business strategy will provide the core for the planning and action in a specific business area; and product strategy will provide the same core for the planning and action programs for a specific product or service.

When this hierarchy of three primary strategy levels is matched against the various functional or contributing strategies to which it relates, the linkages are as required for results. That is, a production strategy or a research strategy must be based on specific types of products (and therefore should support those product strategies) and must also be based on the strategy of each business of which those products are a part. Each functional strategy should be compatible with the resource and other enterprise strategies governing these products. Thus a functional strategy, such as a production or research strategy in this case, will form the core for the action plan for the appropriate functional units after it is properly related to the requirements of the higher-level strategies.

STRATEGY SUMMARY

By defining the mission for each business and for the enterprise as a whole and by selecting the goals within the scope of the mission or missions, management lays the groundwork for clear-cut definition of strategy.

The three primary strategy levels (product, business, and enterprise) require both a bottom-up approach and a top-down approach. Product and business performance are built on customer purchases in the face of competition; therefore, the business and the total enterprise must be built up on the basis of products or services successfully sold. From this point of view, each product plan is an element that must aggregate into a business and into the total for the enterprise.

The top-down approach interacts with these product and business plans in two ways. In the first place, investments are usually required in order to achieve the full potential of a product or a business. Therefore the attractiveness of each product or business to top management (and ulti-

---

FIGURE 2-4 LINKING STRATEGY TO ACTION

Actions
                Lead to habits
                                          Lead to policies

Emerging issues
                Ask when to change
                                          Make change a habit

Defining strategies
                By level
                                          By types

Strategic management
                                          TURNING STRATEGY INTO ACTION

---

mately to the owners of the firm) must be sufficient to merit that investment. Further, a given enterprise sets out to operate within a pattern and establishes a corporate personality. Each operating unit contributes to that pattern and personality, and when management wishes to reshape, some products and businesses are added and others are sold or withdrawn from the market. Thus the bottom-up building approach mentioned earlier is subject to management guidance as to the types of products and businesses that should receive attention and resources.

Subordinate to the primary strategies are the functional and unit strategies as different organizational components define the requirements for their contribution to accomplishing these primary strategies. Program strategies represent an intermediate level between product and business strategy levels that are used whenever a group of products, services, or other activities have characteristics making coordination of their strategies worth the additional effort. The concept unifying and directing these types and varieties of strategy is the fundamental flow from mission to goals to strategy and action that centers around these types and levels of strategy, as summarized in Figure 2-4 and illustrated in Figure 2-5.

QUESTIONS FOR ANALYSIS AND DISCUSSION

1. Find two or three of your own examples illustrating how habits turn into policies in an organization.
2. What are some of the emerging issues you see as those most challenging for business firms in the next several years?

FIGURE 2–5 ACTION AS THE OBJECTIVE

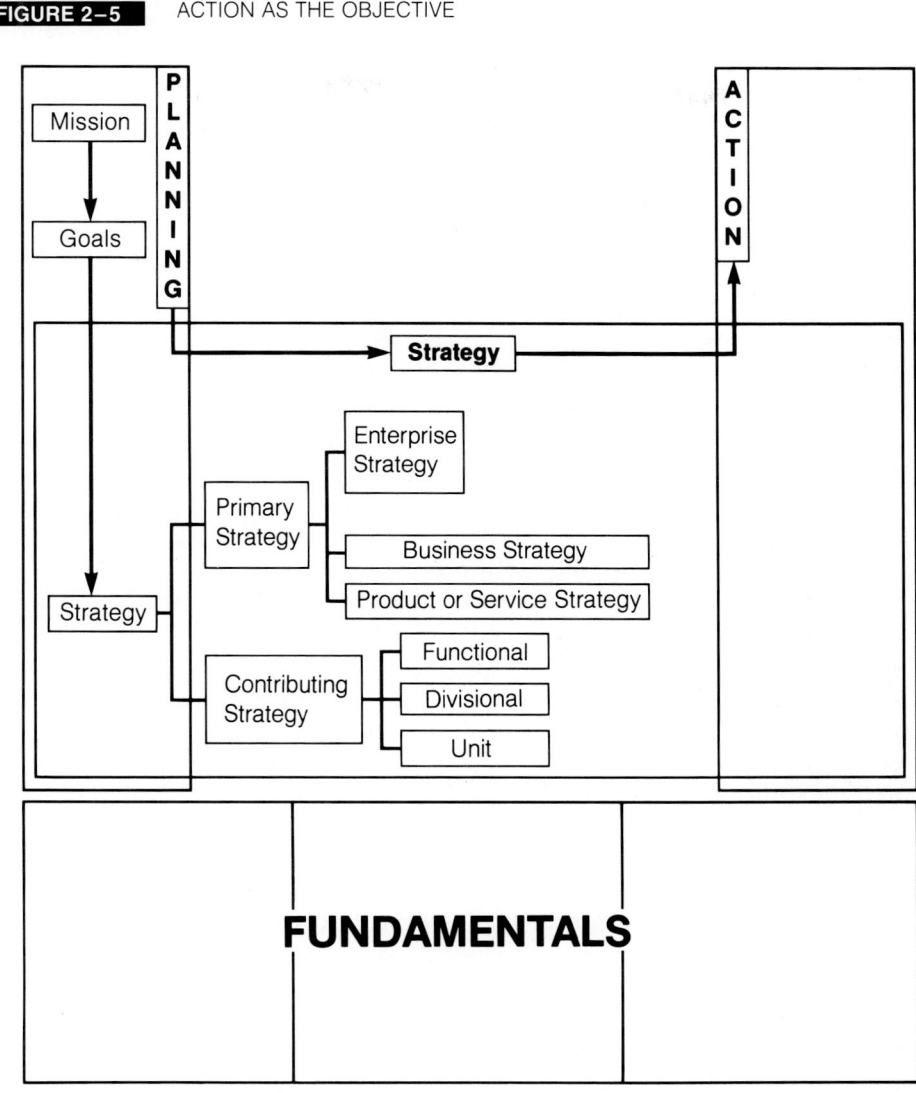

3. What sorts of changes might a wider practice of strategic management bring in the business world of today?
4. Find examples where several related products or services from the same company might benefit from the development of a program strategy.
5. In some fast food restaurants all of the products are logically related, and this relationship would be described as a part of the business strategy. Other chains have a more complex menu, with several

separate programs (e.g., breakfast menu) that must be considered individually, but whose nature and relationship are governed by the business strategy. Find specific examples of both.

6. The way the kitchen is operated in a fast food restaurant is governed by the production strategy, one of the key functional contributing strategies that makes the individual product (and program) strategies effective, so that the overall business strategy will work. Describe some of the different production (contributing) strategies these chains use.

EXAMPLES OF PRIMARY AND CONTRIBUTING STRATEGIES

Note to remember: a strategy is an *action statement.*

- It states in a direct manner *how* you or your company plan to *act* in order to reach your action targets.
- It states in clear, future-oriented terms *what* you will *do.*

PRIMARY STRATEGY FOR A BUSINESS

We will expand our market position as a chemical supplier to textile companies by aggressive marketing of a family of specialty products providing superior solutions to technical operating problems for our customers.

Marketing Contributing Strategy. We will develop superior effectiveness in learning the detailed operating needs of textile industry customers, establishing the necessary technical service relationships, designing the family of specialty products best suited for the needs of these customers (with the help of Product Development), and convincing these customers that we can serve their needs better than any other potential supplier, all within the bounds of a sound long-term business with healthy profit flows.

Production Contributing Strategy. We will improve our ability to produce a variety of high-quality custom products for on-time delivery, often on short notice, and to keep a competitive cost position in spite of small batches and frequent schedule changes.

PRIMARY STRATEGY FOR A BUSINESS

We will become the largest and lowest-cost producer of our family of quality commodity chemicals, thus building a major, profitable, long-term market position.

Production Contributing Strategy. We will continue to refine the economics of large-scale operation in order to maintain the lowest-cost position in quality output of our family of commodity chemicals.

Marketing Contributing Strategy. We will tailor our efforts to the requirements of moving the quantities of output required for the necessary production-cost position or of finding the best possible compromise if market conditions should require output restriction.

FOR FURTHER INFORMATION

Fayol, Henri, *General and Industrial Management,* trans. Constance Storrs (London: Pitman, 1949).
   The first good book by a strategic manager.

Naisbitt, John, *Megatrends* (New York: Warner Books, 1984).
   One clear view of the way our society is changing.

Schendel, Dan E., and Charles W. Hofer, *Strategic Management: A New View of Business Policy and Planning* (Boston: Little, Brown & Co., 1979).
   The first authoritative view of the scope of strategic management.

CASE 3 ADAMS ENTERPRISES

Adams Enterprises was a profitable subsidiary of ATL, Inc. ATL had been American Track Layers until the nation's railroads stopped building new lines. The then president of ATL liquidated the dying machinery business, changed the name to ATL, Inc., and began to use the ample corporate reserves for acquiring businesses in more promising areas. As a conglomerate, ATL had a very active involvement in the management of some of its subsidiaries—the troubled ones—and a much more passive relationship with the successful ones. Adams Enterprises was very successful, and ATL left it totally alone, ordering the corporate staffs to stay away as long as the rapid and profitable growth continued.

Adams Enterprises started as a combined travel, insurance, and real estate agency that somehow broadened into souvenirs and gifts. It had only limited manufacturing facilities, buying most of its merchandise from others, and it sold to gift shops in the region and directly to customers by mail-order catalog. Such a diverse business worked because Joe Adams, the founder, found an able, young manager for each of the component areas of activity. Individual managers were in charge of the travel, insurance, real estate, gift-merchandising, mail-order, and manufacturing areas, all under the direction of Manuel Pope, the president since ATL acquired the business from Joe Adams.

The mail-order business was growing rapidly and the gift-merchandise line also. Manuel Pope and his subordinates put their energies into encouraging this growth. The travel, real estate, and insurance managers were ambitious also, but these businesses were more local by nature. They began to open branch offices, however, so that a chain grew up across the region. Manuel Pope had almost a free hand in this growth, for each year's sales and profits were more than the year before, and the capital investment requirements of these sorts of growth were small enough so that their funding required only a part of the cash flow of the business. The branch office space was leased, most of the manufacturing was done by others, and the largest investment expense was in the growth of working capital as the business grew. Conscious of this, Pope emphasized careful control of inventory and receivables, including an excellent computer inventory-control system for the mail-order business. ATL saw the growth, applauded it, and approved Pope's small capital requests more or less automatically.

Fifteen years later Adams Enterprises had over 3500 employees, and it had become the largest single contributor to ATL consolidated profits each year. One day when the President of ATL was called away for a funeral, Sven Williams, ATL vice-president for finance, had to speak before the securities analysts in the president's place. The speech had been written in advance, but no one from ATL except the president had ever spoken to the securities analysts before, and they were pleased at the chance to pose questions to a new face. Most of the questions were about Adams, and Williams answered them; but he went back to the president later with a request that he be allowed to spend time at Adams—without in any way disturbing the operation—because the hands-off policy had left him knowing so little about an important part of ATL.

The visit was easily arranged, and after spending a week absorbing the details of Adams Enterprises, Sven asked for an appointment with Manuel Pope to report and to ask questions. The two had a pleasant lunch in an alcove off Pope's office, and Williams asked his questions and complimented the operations at length, because they were well run. At the end, however, he had some questions about details. One concerned the reason for paying different sorts of bills on different schedules. Manuel Pope was puzzled. He called data processing and in a few minutes had confirmation that the computer programs controlling accounts payable treated different bills differently, so that some creditors were paid faster than others. The next call was to the accounts payable manager; she reminded him of a fuss involving three major packaging and paper goods suppliers: "You said that if they were going to treat us that way, they could wait an extra week for their money. And, wherever there is no prompt-payment discount, those bills sit for an extra week automatically. When the system was put on the computer, the extra week was built in. Isn't that what you wanted?"

After Manuel Pope had hung up, he turned back to Sven Williams, "She's right, you know. I did say that, and I meant it. But that must have been twelve years ago, and I had forgotten it completely!"

Williams next asked about the sorting of customer complaints and why some complaints automatically went to the marketing vice president's office rather than to the office set up to handle complaints. This called for another phone call, and Manuel was reminded of the origin of another old policy. "I think it's time to review that routing," he told Sven, "but we once had a problem with some of the major stores that handled our gift items, and any complaint related to those sales was routed directly to the vice president for more rapid handling."

Finally Williams asked why the company used a meal-ticket system for compensating overtime workers. "I don't have to make any phone calls on that one," Manuel Pope laughed. "That is an inheritance from Joe Adams. In the beginning whenever anyone had to work unscheduled overtime, Joe sent out for a meal so the employee would not have to go hungry. If the worker had a lunch or did not want to eat, he gave them the money value instead, in order to be fair. Then when he tried to stop all of this after the cafeteria was built and food was available in the plant, he got a grievance from the union. An arbitrator told him he had made this benefit a part of overtime compensation and couldn't take it away without negotiating a change in the contract. It has been in the contract ever since."

"You know," he told Sven Williams later as the two men parted, "it's awesome the way my people have kept some of those details, like the delay in payments to the paper suppliers. That is a policy I established once upon a time. I meant it to be temporary, but I never told them that, and it just kept going on. The divided routing of the complaints is another leftover, created because I wanted it that way once upon a time and never changed it. How do we keep these habits from going on forever?"

QUESTION

1. What do you think? How do operating executives keep their habits from being built into the company system and carried on forever?

CASE 4 JONES JOINTS, INCORPORATED

Jordan Jones was a plumber's son and a master plumber in his own right. He worked summers to earn his tuition, and since he had his own truck and tools, he operated a weekend plumbing business during the college year to make spending money. Those parts of his engineering classes that related to pipes and plumbing in any way were of particular interest to him, and he did especially well in them. As a strength-of-materials project, he studied stress patterns in pipe joints, and he spent his time in the machine design course trying to improve the stress profile in threaded fittings. During spring vacation of his senior year, he started on a design project of his own, borrowing university computer time here and there for stress analysis. The result was a new concept of how pipe elbows, couplings, and other joints should be designed.

In June Jordan was hired into an engineering training program at Smith Tools that kept him very busy, but on weekends and after work hours he refined his designs and then applied for a design patent on the Jones Joints. The patent examiners found that he had greatly reduced the weight of material required to obtain a specific strength and that this was true for a wide range of different piping materials. They recognized this in the range of claims they allowed him to make in the patent when it was granted and issued two years after the application.

Jordan had discovered along the way that he had a very good patent attorney. He was especially impressed on the day the patent was issued, when the patent attorney told him that this was an important, basic patent on a new type of pipe fitting. He also advised extensive patent filings in other countries. Jordan was not in a position to pay for this, but the attorney had a proposal which pleased Jordan very much. In exchange for a 10 percent interest in the patent, the attorney waived the fee for the now-completed U.S. patent work, and he agreed to do the necessary legal work and to pay all of the necessary fees to get protection for Jones Joints in all countries that recognize and respect patents.

Of course Jordan Jones wanted to commercialize his invention. He organized Jones Joints, Inc., to make and sell couplings, elbows, and other fittings; he resigned from his engineering job; and he went into business. Financing was not a problem because the necessary investment was not large and a number of uncles who were master plumbers also wanted a chance to buy shares in the business. Initial sales, however, were slow.

Jordan had read several books on marketing strategy—the need to have something to offer to the customer and the importance of establishing a large enough sales base to achieve a favorable cost position through production volume. He realized that, even with the raw material and fabricating cost advantages of his improved design, his costs at low volume were not better than those of his larger competitors. He found that customers were impressed with the idea of an improved design, but not willing to pay extra. After all, once the joints had been made to meet a given set of specifications, most contractors really did not care whether they were a little lighter or not. As a result Jordan found that Jones Joints, Inc., was breaking even and earning a small salary for him, but nothing more. He had to look for ways to make the business more viable.

To bring in more revenue, the patent attorney suggested a licensing arrangement with an existing manufacturer of pipe and fittings, preferably one not competing directly with Jones Joints, Inc. Jordan explored the possibilities. He found the various manufacturers interested enough so that it was easy to reach the right people, but nothing came of the discussions. Finally the vice president of one competitive company said: "Look, you have a system that could save us quite a lot of money. But to use it, we would have to retool our plant. We have a good competitive position now and no need to rebuild. We like your system, but not enough to lay out a lot of capital, let alone pay you a royalty."

Shortly after that Jordan had a special meeting with his board of directors—the patent attorney, the uncles, and others who had invested in Jones Joints, Inc. "We have some decisions to make," he said. "This business is not going any place, and it never will unless we develop it more seriously. The way to show the advantage of Jones Joints is to offer a complete line of pipe and fittings in two or three different materials. The pipe ends need to have a special smoothing anyway, so I can take full advantage of the design. We don't need to do very much of our own manufacture, at least initially, but we have to market the full line and that will take more investment. Otherwise we should stop spinning our wheels."

After a good deal of discussion and several more meetings, the financing requirements were worked out, money raised, and Jones Joints, Inc., began to sell a full line of pipe and fittings. On this basis it could compete better, and volume began to grow. The cost advantages inherent in the improved design were realized at higher volumes, and Jordan discovered that he knew a lot about how to market to the plumbing trade. But the business questions began to move farther and farther from the simple piping design issues, as Jordan realized when he had to spend almost a month planning and organizing a line of fluxes and joint compounds he needed to offer for use with the pipe and the fittings.

Then Jordan began to get questions about the enterprise he headed—such as whether the hiring policies gave men and women equal opportunities, whether Jones Joints, Inc., should establish a pension plan, and whether he should set up an engineering and development department. State and federal inspectors were due next month to check on working conditions in the plant. He had to decide whether to subscribe to a regional salary survey so that he could compare the company's wage rates with other local employers. His uncles had advised him to run the sort of a company where the workers did not need a union to protect them, and Jordan was trying to do that. At the same time, he was trying to sell in a product area where the craft unions are strong. If he could operate so well that his employees did not need a union, could he avoid appearing anti-union to his union customers?

One evening after a difficult day of trying to guide the enterprise, his father asked him how he liked running his own company. "You know, Dad," he answered, "I came out of school knowing a little about how to design a good product and sell it, and I thought that was enough. I no sooner got started than I found out that I had to have a whole line of products to have a business that would go. Now I find I can't run a business based on the products and markets by themselves. I have to deal with every angle of hiring and employing people; and I have to live with all of the rules and regulations. If I ever really get control of how to set strategies for the products, for the business, and for the firm as a whole, I know I will enjoy it. But sometimes at night when I'm tired, I wonder if I just should have stayed in the Smith Tools engineering department."

QUESTION

1. Find and analyze the three levels of primary strategy at Jones Joints, Inc. What contributing strategies can be found in the case?

CHAPTER

THE PRODUCT AS BASIS FOR A STRATEGY

KEY IDEAS IN THIS CHAPTER

Chapter 3 lays out some of the key considerations in framing a product or service strategy:

- **elements of product and business strategy** – such as deliverables, resources, leverages, focus, positions, display requirements, cash flow; together with exercises in applying the elements.
- **differentiating the product** – showing a continuum ranging from unique products, strong specialties, and weak specialties to commodities.
- **product life cycles** – and their effect on strategy.
- **sources of profit from a product or service** – and the way they change.
- **elements of strategy and sources of profit** – interrelated for best results.
- **linking strategy to product** – as a summary relating the different components of product or business strategy to each other.

The first two chapters presented an overview of the strategy/policy process. After definition of mission, goals, and strategy, the three levels of strategy were laid out, together with the components of each and the links required from strategy to policy to action, so that strategy will have practical meaning.

Among the keys are the elements of a product or service, the life cycle of a product or service, the way products or services can be differentiated, and the sources from which a product or service generates profit. These concepts are discussed in this chapter, starting with the elements of product and business strategy.

ELEMENTS OF PRODUCT AND BUSINESS STRATEGY

Some strategies succeed while others fail. These successes and failures are attributable to a variety of factors, but failures often result from incompatible choices among the components from which such strategy is constructed. Both product and business strategy are built up, piece by piece, from a series of elements.[1] These are the (1) deliverable(s), (2) resources, (3) leverages, (4) focus, (5) positions, (6) display, and (7) cash flow, as illustrated in Figure 3-1.

DELIVERABLE(S)

The deliverables are products or services (or the catalog of related products or services) for which the strategy is designed, and that, in a cost-effective manner, must meet and satisfy customer needs in the opinion of that customer. Product and business strategies aim at generation of revenues through sales of products or services. In order for this result to be achieved, the business must have something to sell. A given deliverable may be positioned and promoted in a wide variety of different ways, but at the end of the sales process it must transfer to the customer and fulfill a reasonable portion of that customer's expectations, or no sustainable commercial activity will result.

RESOURCES

The necessary combination of technology, equipment, time, talent, money, and position required to put a strategy into action successfully constitute the resources. These are the available array of assets relevant

---
[1] George C. Sawyer, "Elements of Strategy," *Managerial Planning*, May/June 1981, pp. 3–5, 9.

FIGURE 3-1 ELEMENTS OF PRODUCT AND BUSINESS STRATEGY

Deliverables: The product or service (for the catalog of related products or services) for which the strategy is designed, and which, in a cost-effective manner, must meet and satisfy customer needs in the opinion of that customer; the deliverable must be an effective satisfier of those needs.

Resources: The necessary combination of technology, equipment, time, talent, money, and position required to put a strategy into action successfully.

Leverages: The specific incentives to buy a given product or service, *as perceived by the buyer;* the reasons why the customer sees the deliverable product or service as a satisfier of his or her specific needs.

Focus: The defined relationship with the customers and the market place upon which a strategy is based.

Position: Any consequence of past operations that can become a resource providing leverages for strategies. Valuable positions include those based on brand names and other market success; unusually effective production, service, distribution, or selling organizations; raw material costs or control; superior or protected processes and technology; cost advantages; unusual management or organizational competence; and strong ties to customer need and habit patterns.

Display requirement: The arrangements necessary so that potential customers can become sufficiently familiar with a product or service and how and where to buy it. Because it can bring additional interaction with the customer, display is often coordinated with focus, and with advertising of the leverages.

Cash flow: A progress measure and control element, to predict and track the action pattern of a strategy and to gauge its vulnerability to sudden failure or success.

Product line (Business Strategy Only): Choice of the line of products or services best to achieve the potential of the business.

---

to a specific strategy. Money is included because it is necessary for obtaining other resources, but it is not directly productive. Some resources are used up and disappear, as money is spent, and other resources—such as IBM service—are created by a strategy and increased in value by its success.

LEVERAGES

Leverages are the specific incentives to buy a given product or service, *as perceived by the buyer;* these are the reasons why the customer sees the deliverable product or service as a satisfier of his or her specific needs. Leverages are the factors which persuade a customer to buy a specific product or service. These may range from tangible elements, such as price and product superiority, to product image and the symbolism of ownership and usage. Researchers suggested a few years ago that a man bought a powerful convertible as a substitute for a mistress, and automobile advertising was keyed subtly to evoke this as a product leverage.

With this and all other leverages, the operative truth is what the customer believes, since these beliefs lead to the purchase. The art of using leverages as a part of a business strategy is the art of causing the customer to see a given product or service as a desirable or essential purchase. A sales executive once explained leverages as the way to pry the customer's wallet open. This is a crude image, but conveys the importance of leverages very clearly.

FOCUS

The defined relationship with the customers and the market place upon which a strategy is based is known as the focus. In many retail product lines the relationship with the customer is entirely impersonal, as with cosmetics sold in a variety store. Some manufacturers want a closer relationship with the customers, and use beauty consultants in department stores to give assistance in choice and use of the various cosmetic products in the line. Yet other manufacturers sell cosmetics to stylists who perform at least part of the product application—selling a beauty service as well as cosmetic products—and give careful and repeated guidance on how the products are to be used.

All three approaches succeed. The products sold impersonally, as in the variety store, must be the simplest and most foolproof. With the personal demonstration and the personal application can come increasingly complex products, but the price must rise also to cover the cost of adding an expensive personal element to the product delivery system.

The importance of the focus component of strategy is that as management defines the relationship with the customers it intends, it also needs to learn (1) the support costs and product line requirements this relationship requires, (2) the prospects for profit after paying these costs, and (3) the way that competitive product lines and support systems fit into the market place. Thus, a manufacturer would probably not attempt to develop a personal relationship with variety store cosmetic customers because the cost of the necessary beauty consultants would be hard to support, considering the relatively low-priced product lines such stores carry.

POSITIONS

Position refers to any consequence of past operations that can become a resource providing leverages for strategies. Valuable positions include those based on brand names and other market success; unusually effective production, service, distribution, or selling organizations; raw material costs or control; superior or protected processes and technology; cost advantages; unusual management or organizational competence; and strong ties to customer need and habit patterns.

Positions are the customer and market franchises, the images, the production cost advantages, the reputation, and the other factors that can build up in the market place or inside the firm as a result of a successful business or product, and that make that success easier to sustain in the future. Coca-Cola built a valuable market image and brand franchise that brings repeat sales. Or, in a commodity market a commanding cost position can follow from the economies of scale attained by achieving a dominant market share.

In another type of dominance IBM established a position in computers such that new professionals entering the field need training on IBM equipment more than any other, and the fact of having this training makes their subsequent purchase of IBM equipment more natural than that of its competitors. Thus there is a tendency for the breadth of IBM equipment usage to give it a position as an industry standard that can perpetuate itself.

Because they are such a large factor in maintaining the success of a company or product, an important part of a strategy is to use the thrust of present efforts to build the strongest and most durable positions possible. This requires an understanding of the nature, strength, and value of various types of positions and how they may be built. If current sales also build long-term positions, this can bring a significant increase in the total long-term return from the strategy being employed.

DISPLAY REQUIREMENT

The arrangements necessary so that potential customers can become sufficiently familiar with a product or service and how and where to buy it are known collectively as the display requirement. Because it can bring additional interaction with the customer, display is often coordinated with focus, and with advertising of the leverages.

The display requirement is the group of actions necessary to bring customers to whatever relationship with a specific product or service is required for them to make a purchase decision. As necessary, they can learn about the product, see it demonstrated, handle it or try it, and gain sufficient familiarity to buy it. Sometimes display involves establishing a distribution network, so that the product will be widely available in showrooms or on counters. Or display may require only the type of promotion that makes the potential customers aware that the product exists. Display activities often overlap with efforts aimed at establishing a specific focus, or with advertising to create the leverages and cause the customer to buy.

CASH FLOW

A progress measure and control element, cash flow is used to predict and track the action pattern of a strategy and to gauge its vulnerability to sudden failure or success. Cash flow is a key element of strategy because cash is a resource regulator. Businesses go through stages of growth, and some of these stages are typified by cash requirements and others by cash return. Cash flow should be predicted in the planning, and deviations from cash flow projections can sometimes be the most sensitive indications of the true progress of a plan and its strategy. Cash flow must be managed especially carefully during the investment phase when cash shortage is chronic. Later, as the business begins to generate more cash than its current needs, this is the beginning of the return on that investment representing true long-term profit.

While profits are the overall measure of success, the rate at which cash must flow into a new and growing business is a critical factor, and larger-than-expected requirements can be a danger signal. Bankruptcy occurs when a profitable small company allows its sales to increase too fast relative to its cash resources and then cannot pay its bills. And if a business does not begin to generate excess cash after it becomes well established in the market place, the initial investment may never be recovered.

PRODUCT LINE STRATEGY (Business Strategy Only)

A company's product line strategy involves its choice of the line of products or services to achieve the potential of the business. In building up a product strategy, the effort is always to get that combination of elements that will give the best possible results, given the nature of the product and of the available resources. Similarly, a business strategy will be designed to get the maximum potential from the available or obtainable products and resources. Under best conditions this potential will be more than the sum of the individual product potentials, but it could be less if the products do not fit well together. Therefore the considerations in designing a business strategy include the nature and design of the line (or grouping) of products or services that will be sold together, as well as a judgment as to whether the proposed product strategies are adequate. For examples of product and service strategy, plus product line and service line strategy, see Figures 3-2 and 3-3.

By understanding the need for and availability of resources and the strength and value of the potential leverages, and by defining a strategy that focuses the resources and leverages on the customer and displays the product or service in the desired and effective way, the business or product should achieve profitable current performance in minimum time. From profitable current performance it can also construct long-lived positions which make this success easier to continue in the future.[2]

---

[2] Pankay Ghemawat, "Sustainable Advantage," *Harvard Business Review*, September–October 1986, pp. 53–58.

FIGURE 3-2 EXAMPLES OF PRODUCT AND SERVICE STRATEGY

Product Strategy

Deliverable: A small, variable-speed electric motor.

Focus: Close working relationship with the customers, who are primarily original equipment manufacturers.

Display requirement: Technical brochures mailed to inquiries from technical advertising and trade show presentations, with personal follow-up and demonstration of prototypes.

Positions: Our reputation, established relationships, and technical advantages due to design patents, plus faster and better response to technical inquiries.

Leverages: Better motors, made by our company, customized to your need, sold at a competitive price, with quality and performance guaranteed.

Resources: Our reputation, advertising and promotion support, design and technical service groups, and good sales support.

Cash flow: Positive after the first year; on the average, one out of four inquiries worth taking to a prototype stage results in a quantity sale, in most cases with reorders over several years.

Service Strategy

Deliverable: Personal checking account.

Focus: An area saturation direct mail and media promotion personalized insofar as possible by careful tailoring of mailers according to demographic classifications, and by face-to-face contact with the representative opening the account.

Display requirement: Widespread promotion of account features, plus rack literature in bank and limited personal support from tellers and platform personnel.

Positions: Reputation of our bank.

Leverages: • Competitive interest rate and account features; advantages over not having such an account.
  • Willingness of present customers to recommend us to their friends.
  • Lower charges than competitors on some services.

Resources: Bank reputation and computer processing system. Bank's teller network; promotional budget.

Cash flow: Negative initially due to promotion costs; breakeven estimated after 9 months with steadily growing profit contribution thereafter.

FIGURE 3-3 EXAMPLES OF PRODUCT LINE AND SERVICE LINE STRATEGIES

Product Line Strategy

We will develop and maintain a line of performance-oriented specialty chemical products that will fulfill all significant requirements of the major textile processes of the major mills in our sales area. For major customers only, we will customize products and extend the line in order to supply their total needs; for minor customers we will apply existing products to their major needs. We will attempt to keep our total product line confined to fifty or fewer products by pruning old products and by reformulating as custom product requests signal changes in need.

Service Line Strategy

We will offer customized data processing services to each major type of small business, but with a careful control of the program design to keep the data records generically similar, and thus convenient for our CPA clients who service these businesses and recommend their use of our programs.

ELEMENTS OF STRATEGY

A product strategy or business strategy is built from the elements profiled above in an iterative, interactive process. Usually this process starts with a specific product or service, or with its concept. To sell that product or service, leverages must be found or created, and the nature and potency of these leverages will vary with the chosen focus, the nature and strength of the existing positions, and the most feasible alternatives for display. Often a slight redefinition of the deliverable will make it fit better with a given focus and positions and create stronger leverages. Underlying all of this is a need for resources, and the balancing of all of these elements results in projections of cash flow suggesting the degree to which the projected strategy meets management criteria and goals set at the enterprise level, as will be discussed in Chapter 6.

EXERCISES IN APPLYING THE ELEMENTS OF STRATEGY

1. Choose a food product and define at least two different levels of focus that could be used to market it. What difference would this make in the resource requirements?
2. Make two lists of specific products and services: (a) those that seem to have specific display requirements (what are these requirements?), and (b) products that can be displayed successfully in a number of different ways.
3. List the leverages (based on *buyer perception*) for three different types of products. Can you find examples of important leverages not

created by the seller? (For example, you might eat in a really poor restaurant if you were hungry enough and nothing else was open.)
4. List some of the major established positions that may cause you to buy certain products, and give examples of these positions in the market place.
5. (a) List the assortment of goods and/or services sold by specific business units and (b) discuss the probable reason for their being sold together. (For example, fast food restaurants find it desirable to include both food items and beverage items in their product line. Why?) (c) To what extent are these required combinations, because otherwise the customers may not buy, versus optional additions that attempt to increase sales volume?

DIFFERENTIATING THE PRODUCT

Products vary in uniqueness, from generic grocery offerings that position themselves as completely standard and faceless to famous gemstones that would be recognized immediately by jewelers all over the world. Products can be found at all points between these two extremes, but a classification into four principal stages highlights the shift in product or service characteristics and guides the strategy design process. These four stages of differentiation are (1) unique products, (2) strong specialties, (3) weak specialties, and (4) commodities, as summarized in Figure 3-4.

UNIQUE PRODUCT

A product for which there is no substitute at any price in the opinion of the buyer is termed a unique product. Whether there is a substitute for a product is a matter of customer opinion, and different customers will have different opinions. Where one person looking for a painting will accept anything attractive within a certain price range, another customer may insist on an English landscape, and a third on a specific scene by Turner. With the increasing specificity of the request the range of choice is narrowed more and more toward a unique product. Most purchasers will accept a substitute at some extreme of price differentiation, thus validating the generalization that every product has a substitute, but in some cases the price differentiation may be extremely large, as when an art collector bids a record auction price to obtain a specific painting.

When Loctite first offered its line of adhesives as a replacement for metal lock washers, comparable adhesives were not available commercially from other sources. A metal washer could still be used for most applications, but the properties of the adhesive made possible some assemblies where a metal washer could not be used. For these specific uses the

---

FIGURE 3-4   DIFFERENTIATING THE PRODUCT OR SERVICE

Unique product: A product for which there is no substitute at any price in the opinion of the buyer.

Strong specialty: A product whose substitutes are sufficiently inferior so that the buyer will willingly pay a premium price to get it.

Weak speciality: A product sufficiently better than its substitutes that the buyer will always select it, if price and other considerations are equal.

Commodity: A product normally bought from the seller with the best price or delivery among those able to meet the product specifications.

Loctite product was a unique product whose only substitute was through use of a less desirable assembly.

STRONG SPECIALTY

A product whose substitutes are sufficiently inferior so that the buyer will willingly pay a premium price to get it is classified as a strong specialty. The Loctite adhesive was originally priced to cost about the same as the metal lock washer it replaced, but as its properties were recognized, users developed a strong preference for it and used it even where it did not replace a metal washer, paying more to get a better result. This is the normal situation with a strong specialty product. Almost every product has obvious substitutes, but strong specialty products give performance sufficiently better than their substitutes so that the purchaser will willingly pay the difference.

The marketer needs an awareness of the price limits of this preference, since significant volume may otherwise be lost to admittedly inferior substitutes. Valium, a tranquilizer with strong specialty product characteristics, was even considered to be a unique product by some doctors because of superior results in treating patients. At one point the State of California made a major issue over its cost, and insisted that California doctors use phenothiazine tranquilizers instead for public assistance patients. The phenothiazines were inferior treatment for some conditions, but the price of Valium was farther above the price of phenothiazines than the State felt that its advantages justified, and California insisted on the less preferred medication. This is an example of a strong specialty product losing market because one customer felt the price premium was too large.

WEAK SPECIALTY

A product sufficiently better than its substitutes so that the buyer will always select it if price and other considerations are equal is a weak specialty. That is, a weak specialty is a superior product whose degree of superiority is too small to justify a price premium. A weak specialty can be used to gain market share very effectively, so long as the price is the same as that of the competitors.

Many businesses with custom formulas, special blends, or other special-for-the-customer offerings are attempting to create weak specialty positions. These businesses usually incur extra costs in the customizing and must recover these by increased sales if they cannot increase the price. Technical service support for a mature product line can also help to give it weak specialty characteristics for customers who buy the product at least partially to get access to the service.

Sometimes these strategies succeed. Hoffmann-La Roche strengthened its sales position in bulk vitamins by a series of special blends and formulations with weak specialty product appeal—one example would be the family of products designed for direct compression into tablets, introduced to simplify that type of processing for the purchaser.

Sometimes these strategies fail, with the extra costs of the specialty cutting margins and not yielding extra sales—either because the special properties were not appealing enough, or because competitors matched with an alternative weak specialty equally attractive to the buyer. A group of competitors can sometimes find themselves all paying for similar extra product features or technical service support without gaining any competitive advantage at all.

COMMODITY

A commodity is a product normally bought from the seller with the best price or delivery among those able to meet the product specifications. Commodities are available from many vendors and are reasonably well standardized. Many metals, grains, and chemicals are commodities, and skillful purchasers often attempt to convert specialties into commodities by establishing a clear set of specifications and inducing competitive bids.

DIFFERENTIATION AND THE ELEMENTS OF STRATEGY

Commodities, available in essentially identical form from many vendors, are unlikely to support differentiated elements in the product strategies of different producers. That is, all producers are likely to use the same focus, display in about the same way, and concentrate on about the same leverages, except to the extent that their differing positions bring cost and market share advantages. Expensive focus and display strategies advantageous for some strong specialities are unlikely to be chosen for commodities because of competitive pressures on all but the dominant firm, and the dominant firm will have minimum need for these higher expenditure levels. Therefore the level of differentiation chosen for a product may determine which elements of strategy are most advantageous; and where a particular focus or other product strategy element must be used for other reasons, this may make the profits uncertain unless the product can be differentiated into a specialty.

PRODUCT LIFE CYCLES

Products have life cycles. New products become old and may be replaced by still newer products. The markets for these products expand, contract, or change in other ways as the product demand is affected by economic and social variables.

Product life cycles are of many types; Figures 3-5 and 3-6 show two of the extremes. Figure 3-5 is a life cycle typical of a capital goods item with a fixed total market, or of a consumer product that will be replaced by a better product or a newer fashion. The product is brought to market as an innovation, goes through a period of evaluation and testing, wins market acceptance, and begins to sell rapidly. As its potential market begins to saturate, sales first peak and then fall to a replacement level, which may be too low for the product to stay in the market. Or, when a product is replaced by a better product, this cuts off the expansion of the market and causes sales to fall.

Figure 3-6 shows a product life cycle that starts in the same way, but differs in that the product finds a permanent place in the market. As it matures, the sales shift from a growth curve to some other curve governed by variables affecting demand in its markets. This life cycle might be typical of a commodity such as polyethylene or vitamin C, or a consumer product such as Listerine or Jell-O, that wins and holds a market franchise over a long period of time.

These two life cycles are defined in simple terms, and many intermediate forms exist, as well as subtleties including the effects of changes in promotional support or modifications of the product. However these simple cycles provide the basis for suggesting that the optimum strategy for any particular business is very much related to the sort of products and product life cycles, or services and service life cycles, on which that business is based, and to anything that may extend these life cycles.

A business based on short-lived capital products such as new instruments, or on one-time service projects such as the construction of new plants or completion of R&D projects, determines its size and growth characteristics largely by the size and effectiveness of the development effort that tries to bring in new products or projects faster than the old ones are completed or fade away. The toy business requires about 60 percent per year of new product sales to replace lost volume as older products shrink, and some analysts feel that the maximum potential size of a toy

FIGURE 3-5 A SHORT-LIFE-CYCLE PRODUCT

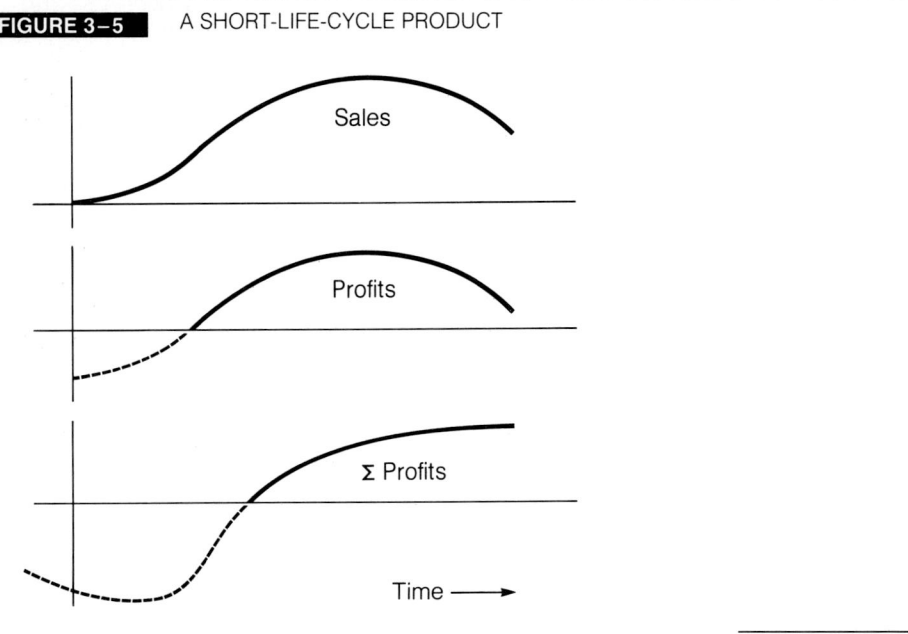

company is about $1 billion in annual sales because the necessary new products cannot be developed fast enough to support a larger sales volume at this product turnover rate.[3]

As a business with long-lived products grows, the management will become increasingly concerned about maintaining acceptable profit margins as a larger and larger fraction of sales come from mature products in the later phases of their development; therefore that management may become relatively less interested in new products. Thus, established businesses with major long-lived products are less likely to have a major new-product emphasis.

In both Figure 3-5 and Figure 3-6 the profit curves show initial losses as a product or service is first marketed, with a breakthrough into profitability at some point early in the rapid growth of sales. The curve for the summation of profits reflects the premarket costs and after-launch losses as investments, with start of repayment as the product becomes profitable, breakeven as the product approaches maturity, and finally the beginning of a return on the investment.

---

[3] "How Hasbro Became King of the Toy Makers," *Business Week*, September 22, 1986, pp. 90–92.

FIGURE 3–6 A LONG-LIFE-CYCLE PRODUCT

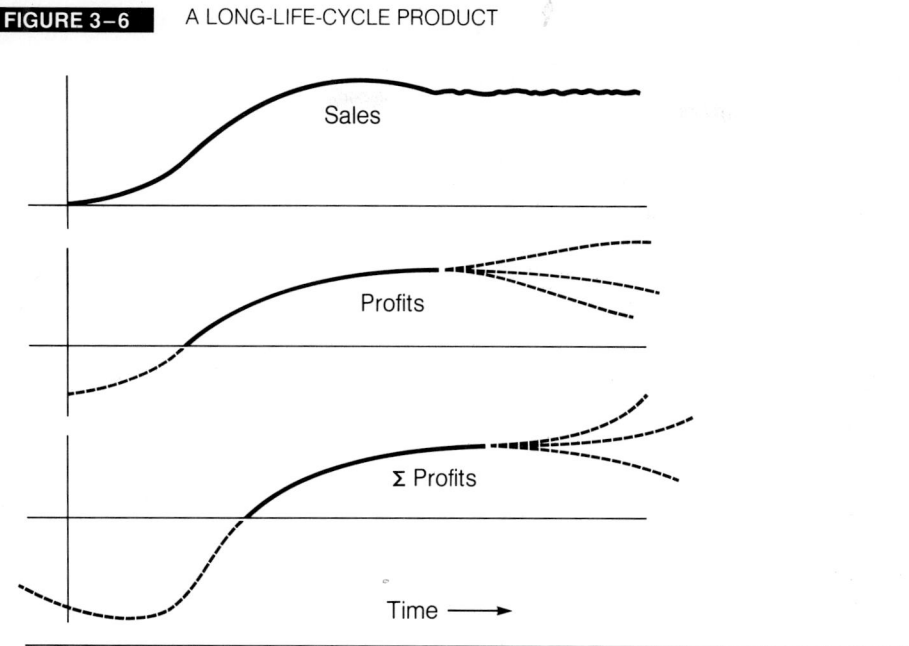

The short-product-life business must be a high-innovation business, in that it must develop new products or sell new projects at least as fast as the old ones fade away if it wishes to exist over the long term. Such product or project development is normally a significant expense, and an important fraction of the resources of such a firm tends to be devoted to this activity.

While the products or projects that result need to be profitable on a current basis, it is equally important that, on the average, the resulting profits exceed the initial investment in the product or project. A frequent difficulty is failure of a series of individually profitable projects or products to earn enough profit fully to repay the development costs, so that the firm consumes an element of its capital as each successive new activity moves through its life cycle and fades away.

The business with long-life-cycle products has a second type of product strategy to manage. Initially each product passes through the same stages of development. Then as the product matures, it assumes different profit and market characteristics, and the product strategy should shift to reflect the changing basis for its competitive strengths.

SOURCES OF PROFIT FROM A PRODUCT OR SERVICE

Profit has many possible sources, and it is important in designing a strategy to understand the sources of profit upon which it depends. In his *Theory of Economic Development*[4] Schumpeter argued that the only true profit was from innovation. He emphasized the importance of the innovation process and the economic and public benefits of its high early rewards. Then others are attracted by these high profits, enter, and compete the profits away. When Schumpeter was asked to explain the money earned and reported as profit under other circumstances, he suggested that those so-called profits often included interest, rent, and other types of earnings; he did not want to consider these earnings as true profits, although accountants include them in the profits reported to management and the shareholders.

A broker or trader performs a service by making a certain type of transaction possible, and this is the basis for a trading profit or fee. A wholesaler who buys in bulk and resells in smaller quantities earns a fee by this service. A retail merchant or industrial distributor performs a service by financing, distributing, and promoting merchandise so that it can be located and purchased by the final consumer. For this service the merchant is entitled to be paid, and the payment must compensate for the cost of the capital employed, including a proper allowance for risks in the transaction and a fee for the distribution service itself. Another type of profit would be the return to speculation or to gambling, as in the commodity markets, where the essential element is the skill or luck in playing against risk or uncertainty.

Where a high apparent profit level continues over a long time, often the nature of the money stream changes. If established initially as the return to innovation, this is a profit that will dwindle with time. For the same level of earnings to continue, other factors must begin to control. These other factors are those that describe an advantage in cost or access to customers, justify a fee for a service, or represent barriers preventing the entry of competition.

The return that these other factors may properly earn is not an innovator's profit, but often a form of rent. Rent was first defined as the return to the owner for the use of land. Ricardo's classic analysis started with land of differing levels of fertility. The poorest land—whose income would cover the direct cost of production—would be farmed, but would earn no rent. On richer land the production costs would be essentially identical but the yields higher, and the extra revenue from the larger harvest would

---

[4] Joseph Schumpeter, *Theory of Economic Development* (New York: Oxford Press, 1961).

FIGURE 3-7   SOURCES FOR BUSINESS PROFIT*

True Profit

    The *returns to innovation;* usually fading away after a few years.

Fees

    For *distribution services:* making merchandise conveniently available for purchase.
- retailing of all sorts, mail-order outlets, industrial distributors, and supply houses.

    For *production services:* the assembly and testing of the final product.

    For *trading services:* bringing together interests of buyer and seller.
- securities and real estate brokers, trading between countries.

    For *breaking bulk:* reselling lesser quantities not otherwise available.
- odd lots of common stock, small packages of coal, or potting soil for plants.

    For *use of capital:* a return on the investment required for the business pattern.
- financing of retailer via trade credit from wholesaler, maintaining the inventory level necessary to guarantee same-day delivery.

    For *insurance:* protection against inventory and other business risks carried in the customer's interest.
- spoilage and obsolescence of inventories, hedging of commodity and currency risks.

    For *specialized services:* customs processing, personal shopping, custom design.

Rents†

    Earned by *differential productivity of resources:* such as a superior cost position.

    Based on *brand names,* reputation, customer habits, or other market franchise.

    Due to *patents,* trade secrets, control of natural resources, or any other sort of monopoly position.

    Due to *economies of scale* in purchasing, production, distribution, or marketing.

---

*Where profit is the net return from a particular business activity after direct and allocated costs and taxes.
†A further separation could be made between rents on land and quasi-rents on other factors, but this seems unnecessary here.

---

be the amount of rent the owner could obtain for the opportunity of farming his rich land.

    The relevance of these distinctions to business and product strategy is that the money streams reported as profits in most businesses include other types of income (see Figure 3-7). In economic terms these reported profits are a mixture of (1) true profits from innovation, (2) fees for making a market, for distribution and other services, and as interest on the capital employed, and (3) rents based on entry barriers and advantageous posi-

> **FIGURE 3–8** EXAMPLE OF SOURCES OF PRODUCT PROFIT
>
> **How much profit is there?**
>
> | | | per unit |
> |---|---|---:|
> | Sales price | | $10.00 |
> | Cost | | 5.00 |
> | Profit before taxes & corporate overhead | | $ 5.00 |
>
> **Where does the profit come from?**
>
> | | | |
> |---|---:|---:|
> | *Innovation profit* (now estimated to be declining at the rate of 25% per year) | $1.00 | |
> | | $1.00 | |
> | *Rents* | | |
> | patent (3 years of life remaining) | 2.00 | |
> | brand name and reputation | .50 | |
> | scale economies | 1.00 | |
> | | 3.50 | |
> | *Fees* | | |
> | manufacturing service | .25 | |
> | distribution | $ .25 | |
> | | .50 | |
> | | | $ 5.00 |
>
> *Comment:* Of $5 profit per unit, the $2 contributed by scale economies, brand position, and manufacturing and distribution services appear relatively secure. The $1 per unit profit due to innovation and the $2 per unit rent on the expiring patent will disappear over the next few years. Conclusion: to keep substitute products from eroding our market position, we will need (1) further innovations or specialty product varations, (2) new promotions substantially enhancing the value of the brand image, (3) $3.00 per unit in programmed price cuts, or (4) some combination of the above.

tions in the market place. Here are definitions of these sources of product, service, or business profit:

- **innovation profit** the true profit from having something new or different to sell that is not available anywhere else.
- **rent** any payment for the use of intangible or tangible property.
- **fees** any payment for a service corollary to the product or service being purchased.

While the stockholders normally will not care what the source is so long as the product brings in the money, the management of products and businesses generating these different sorts of income require different strategies. When a product comes to maket as an innovation and then continues to generate a return after the innovation has lost its newness, this occurs because the management of the product has caused, or at least allowed, continuation of the high return on the basis of different sources of profit. For an example of sources of product profit, see Figure 3-8.

ELEMENTS OF STRATEGY AND SOURCES OF PROFIT

Starting with leverages as the specifics encouraging purchase at a given price, the source of these leverages must be in the deliverable, based either on the innovations that it represents or the positions that protect it, always recognizing that these positions are likely in their turn to be based at least in part on other available resources. To the extent that the leverages leading to the sale and resulting profit are from innovation, the profit is pure in the Schumpeterian sense. As other elements emerge also, other considerations enter.

General Foods has a valuable market franchise in the Jell-O product and trade name. Long past the innovation stage, the product is believed to return an attractive profit. That profit includes a fee for distribution services—in that General Foods makes the Jell-O product widely and conveniently available—but whereas generic pudding products intended to serve the same customer need are available at one price, Jell-O commands a somewhat higher price. The difference is a profit of another sort—rent, in the economic sense, as a price premium earned by the strength of the franchise for Jell-O, which good marketing of a good product has established over the years. And, if General Foods' cost of goods is less than for the generic competitors due to higher volume, this cost difference represents a separate sort of rent earned by the production and distribution position, and adds to the total reported as profit.

In managing a product such as Jell-O, the nature of the different sources of profit is a proper part of the framework of the product strategy, and as these sources change with the evolution of the product life cycle, optimum product strategy will shift correspondingly.

When Librium was first marketed in 1963, it represented an important innovation, soon followed by the parallel but somewhat different innovation of Valium. These two products had utility as tranquilizers not possessed by predecessor products, and both seemed to have a permanent place in tranquilizer therapy. Both products are known to have been profitable for the company that brought them to market, and the initial profits were clearly a return to innovation. But as these products matured, the continuing profits were no longer innovator's profits.

Generic chlordiazepoxide, the Librium substance, has been available for years at a fraction of the Librium price, but has been slow to penetrate because of the strength of the Librium market franchise. Traditionally the prescription drug market is willing to pay a very high rent—again in the economic sense—to the holder of an established product franchise, in part because of continuing concerns about quality differences in generic products, and more because the doctors who prescribe the product find it easier to practice good medicine by keeping constant the drug, which is a small part of the cost of the treatment, and varying other factors in search of better health response from the patient. Therefore they will continue to use a drug that has given good results and concentrate their energies on other aspects of their practice, rather than turning aside to check out a cheaper generic drug.

Not all pharmaceutical companies seem sensitive to the inevitable shift of a new product profit base from innovation, where Librium profits were initially derived, to rent based on accumulated positions and franchises plus a distribution fee, as have since become the basis for Librium profits. Failure to understand this shift could lead to errors in product management.

More dramatic is the consistent shortfall of the recurrent activist and public-sector attempts to establish generic prescription products as a means of cutting pharmaceutical company profits—where the cause of the failure is, in part, a fundamental misunderstanding of the nature of the franchise upon which the use of the higher-priced products depends. Had the drug companies and their opponents each developed clearer insights as to the source of the profits they have been quarreling over, several companies might have fared better competitively in the transition from managing innovative products to collecting rents and distribution fees, but also the generic prescription efforts might have gained market share faster.

The central point for product and business management is to identify the different sources of profit on which a given product or business depends, and then to develop a strategy to make best use of this potential, using leverages based on the positions that earn each sort of actual or potential profit.

When Xerox launched its major early leasing program, it was choosing to sell a copy service on a per-copy basis rather than to sell copy machines. While the final consequence—making Xerox copies—was the same, the copy-service concept brought in other sources of profit, in addition to adding a major leverage by bypassing the customer's need to invest capital in copy machines.

Or, in its period of early growth American Hospital Supply removed a large part of the hospital-supplies inventory risk from customer hospitals by guaranteeing quick delivery of a wide variety of items, so that the hospitals need not order until the product was actually required, allowing the hospital to operate with minimal inventories. The distributor was paid for these services, but was much better able to manage inventories and inventory risks, so the resulting distribution pattern was both economically efficient and profitable.

In the same way insurance companies make a good business out of underwriting fire insurance and many other risks they can manage more economically than client companies, and commodity speculators by their speculations permit the hedging of grain purchase prices—where this hedging allows producers to enter into contracts for future delivery of meat or processed foods that would otherwise be too hazardous.

The number of examples could be multiplied further, but the underlying point is this: there are many sources of profit in commercial transactions, and innovation is only one of them. Good strategy often involves using several sources of profit, but this diversity can be managed effectively only if the different profit elements are recognized, because each is earned by specific positions and leverages, many of which required significant investment to create. With a clear understanding of the sources of the profit, the resulting cash flows can be measured on a return-on-investment basis for the strategy as a whole and for its component profit sources.

LINKING STRATEGY TO PRODUCT

Product differentiation of commodities into specialties favors higher prices; Levitt argued that a skillful marketer can differentiate anything,[5] and Peters predicts that those marketers unable to differentiate will not survive.[6] However, (1) the inherent nature of the deliverable in a specific case may make it easier or harder to make that product or service into a specialty, and (2) the nature of the positions providing the leverages for the product or service suggest whether rent is possible, as from a superior commodity cost position or a patent blocking competition. Further, the stage in the product life cycle and other circumstances under which the specific product or service will be carried to the buyer will suggest whether a distribution fee, return on risk or inventory investment, or other special income source may be a proper addition to the income stream that product or service is designed to generate. A well-conceived product strategy will integrate the choices among its various elements with an appropriate degree of differentiation, after considering the poten-

---

[5] Theodore Levitt, "Marketing Success Through Differentiation—of Anything," *Harvard Business Review*, January–February 1980, pp. 83–91.

[6] Tom Peters, *Thriving on Chaos: Handbook for a Managerial Revolution* (New York: Knopf, 1987), pp. 23–24.

FIGURE 3-9   PRODUCT OR SERVICE CHARACTERISTICS AS FUNDAMENTALS

Building product or service strategy from its elements
- deliverables
- resources
- leverages
- focus
- positions
- display
- cash flow

Choosing the best degree of product differentiation
- unique product
- strong specialty
- weak specialty
- commodity

Adding up the sources of profit from a product
- innovation
- rents
- fees: for distribution, production, trading, risks, use of capital.

BUILDING SOUND PRODUCT STRATEGY

---

tial sources of profit from that product and the best short-term and long-term approaches to generating them.

The elements of product and business strategy are governed by the enterprise strategies that will be discussed in Chapter 6. Then, as indicated in Figure 3-9, considerations of the basic product or service characteristics, and of the life cycle characteristics, both reviewed in this chapter, are foundations for an effective linkage from planning to strategy to action, as illustrated in Figure 3-10.

QUESTIONS FOR ANALYSIS AND DISCUSSION

1. Make a list of *unique* products (remember, in the opinion of the customer a unique product has no substitute, regardless of price differential). How many can you find?
2. Make a list of *commodities* which have been successfully converted to specific *weak specialties*. Have any of them become *strong specialties* (meaning that the customer will pay extra to get them)?
3. Make a list of specific products and classify them as to their positions in their life cycles. (Try to find products at all stages in their life cycles). Classify each product as to whether it is likely to have a *short* or *long* product life.
4. Repeat question 3 by making a list of specific services and classifying them in the same way.

FIGURE 3–10 PRODUCT OR SERVICE CHARACTERISTICS AS BASIC TO STRATEGY DESIGN

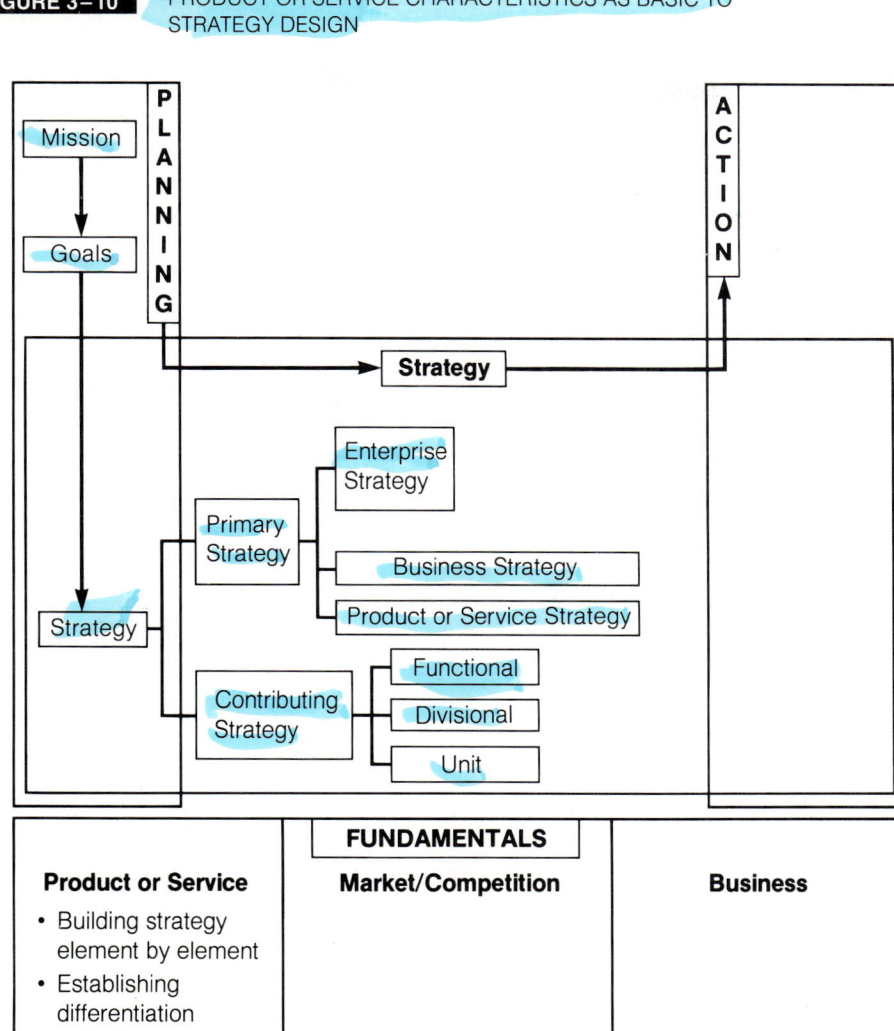

5. List products depending on more than one source of profit and list the sources. Try to find examples of as many different sources of profit as possible.
6. Trace typical products through their life cycle to see how their sources of profit have changed. Not all follow the same pattern—try to find several different patterns.

FOR FURTHER INFORMATION

Sonder, William E., *Managing New Product Innovations* (Lexington, Mass.: Heath, 1987).
   An authoritative review of the new-product-development process.

Schumpeter, Joseph, *Theory of Economic Development* (New York: Oxford Press, 1961).
   The classical analysis of profit from innovation.

CASE 5 RANDOM GARDENS

Isaac Warren built Random Gardens as a country house a century ago and lived out his life there. The old house burned the year after Isaac's death, but his son Joe stayed on in what had been the caretaker's house, down near the highway. Then as the area began to build, the town put in streets and services, and Joe's taxes were raised. He considered selling his house and land to a developer, but it was the old family home, and besides, where would he go? His dilemma began to resolve itself one day when the town road commissioner stopped by to ask about gravel.

Random Gardens was a plot of rolling hills, and where the town road passed at the back of the property it cut across the toe of a gravel bank that interested the town. The result was an agreement that the town could dig at Joe's gravel bank and pay him for what it took. The income was not large, but it did help with the property taxes. Then a contractor stopped one day to ask about taking out fill at the side of the gravel bank. Joe sold it, load by load, and was surprised at the way the money added up. He looked at the hills he had, did some calculating, and borrowed enough money to buy a larger truck and a front loader. Joe had always been in the landscaping business, although he had never worked very hard at it. Now he shifted into higher gear, began to develop the business potential, and the family fortunes improved.

Joe Junior worked for his father evenings, weekends, and summers from the time he was large enough to hold a shovel, and he came home from college in the late spring and worked through to September to help carry the warm-weather peak in the business. But after he graduated he took a highway engineering job in another state, and his father hired local help in his place. Eight years later his father was ill for a couple of weeks, which was unusual for Joe Senior, and later when Joe Junior heard about it he spent a weekend at home, to see how his folks were.

Joe was back at work but things seemed different. Saturday afternoon his dad stopped Joe Junior after they parked the truck for the night, to talk a bit. Joe Senior told how he had had a mild heart attack. It had frightened him more than it injured him, but the doctor strongly suggested a change in life-style. "I have done pretty well in this business," he said, "and I've got enough saved to live on. Your mother and I are going to buy a little place in Florida for the winters and travel a little. I don't need this land and business any more, and you can have it if you want it. It was your granddad's, and I'd be pleased to give it to you. But if you don't want it, I have to sell it. And I will need a decision in a couple of weeks, because if I stay too long on the same routine I'll work until I get another heart attack. Besides, there is a possible buyer, but I put him off for a while."

Joe Junior went home and talked to his wife, thought a little, quit his state job, and moved back to run the family fill and landscaping business.

He started with some careful estimates of the gravel and fill situation, since most of the profit came from there rather than from the landscaping work. He found that he had around twenty years of reserves at the present rate of mining, and little chance of getting more. The area had become much more residential and the zoning did not permit quarrying or soil mining, except that Random Gardens was exempted because the business had existed before the law was passed. And Joe Senior had always operated very carefully, so as not to create any nuisance his neighbors might complain about, because there were people in the neighborhood who would welcome any reason to challenge the Random Gardens exemption from the zoning ordinance.

If the quantity of soil to mine and sell was limited, as it was, then Joe thought he should look at where it went, and what could be done to get a better price. First he began to limit some of the bulk sales, where his dad had given a large contractor a special price on very large quantities of fill. Without any sudden changes or disruption of relationships he reduced the discounts and limited the quantities, step by step. He also looked to see where he got the highest prices. The best prices were for topsoil, of course, although only a part of the Random Gardens hills would qualify.

One day in a supermarket Joe noticed a bag of potting soil. It seemed to be rather ordinary topsoil sterilized and packaged in a small bag, with a high price that caught his instant attention. He inquired in that store and many others and conducted a personal market survey of the region. There was a good market for packaged potting soil. He bought the necessary equipment and began to bag and sell some of the better Random Gardens topsoil in small bags. He encountered competition, starting with the brand he had first seen; the supermarket and garden store buyers tried to use the competitive threat to persuade him to cut his prices, but Joe took a different tack. He got an attractive printed bag and began to emphasize the Random Gardens name, and its local origin: "Home soil for your home plants." He started to advertise occasionally in the local newspaper, to support the store displays, but this also brought inquiries to him at home. He put up a sign and a small sales booth on a convenient corner of the property where his wife also sold a few plants, and he got display racks made for use in the stores that carried his product.

Joe had also seen packages of gardenia soil, African violet soil, and four or five varieties of English-style garden soil, and began to investigate their market potential. He made a visit to the state university and got acquainted with some of the professionals in the agricultural experiment station. They bombarded him with pamphlets and references on houseplant nutrition, and after he had read a little and got better acquainted with them, they began to help him understand how to formulate potting soil for various plants and conditions, and the way in which this could lead to healthier plants and more flowers. From this grew the Random Gardens specialty plant soil line and the slogan "Be kind to the roots of your flowers."

Joe found that the more he worked to develop the specialty plant soils, the more he earned, to the point that two years later he suspended all sales of bulk fill and turned the landscaping business over to a nephew. On one corner of Random Gardens he now had an attractive salesroom and showplace for plants, and the plant soil line was retailed all over the region. The other stores had at first objected to Joe's selling at Random Gardens in competition with them, but as he built up its attraction and advertised the name, their sales increased substantially also. Joe was now buying small quantities of some special soils for blending, to get specific mixes, but he could well afford to do this. In fact, some of the banks his father had been selling for bulk fill made an excellent base for a premium blend, once the right materials were added. And the rate at which he was using up the hills at Random Gardens had dropped, to the point that Joe's children and grandchildren could well continue the business if they wanted to.

QUESTIONS

(*Note:* Answer (a), (b), and (c) for each of the three questions.)
For the sale of soil from Random Gardens:

1. List the seven elements of the product strategy used.
2. Classify the product according to the degree of differentiation.
3. List the sources of the profit from the sale.
   (a)   as Joe Senior sold it
   (b)   as Joe Junior first sold potting soil
   (c)   as the Random Gardens Specialty Plant Soil line was sold

CASE 6 ASSURED INSPECTION SERVICE

Frank James was a professional engineer with spare time and not enough income. When a local realtor asked him if he did house inspections, he decided on the spot that he did, and added a new corner to his professional practice.

Many buyers of existing homes worry about hidden flaws in the construction, as do the mortgage bankers and brokers, and a demand had grown for a knowledgable professional evaluation of a property that is on the market. Frank had not been aware of the extent of this demand, but a little checking showed him that it was significant. Although the fees were relatively low, this was good fill-in work, so Frank refined his inspection routine, had some cards printed, and began to call on real estate brokers and mortgage officers to generate referrals. As he gained experience, Frank became aware of a wide range of different techniques and degrees of competence among the numerous people who offered this inspection service. Because he was licensed as an engineer, he had an advantage, and he discovered that those without an engineering license charged less but got fewer calls.

Then one day an insurance agent proposed that Frank buy malpractice insurance, on the basis that, if he missed a defect in a house, the buyer might sue him for engineering malpractice. Frank was interested. "But what about the buyer?" he asked.

"I don't know what you mean."

"If I need malpractice insurance, in case I miss a defect, then doesn't the home buyer need insurance, too, to fix any unexpected defects?"

"Oh," laughed the agent. "Yes, he or she does, and we sell that, too."

Frank asked a lot more questions. A day or two later he called the agent again: "If you sell someone insurance against defects in a house, their premium should be lower if they have had a good inspection first. Do you take that into account?"

"No, but we should," answered the agent, and he and Frank began to work on a proposal.

Out of all of this evolved the Assured Inspection Service. Frank did the inspections, and the fee, which was substantial, included half of the cost of insurance against defects in the house after purchase. If the buyer looked at more than one house, Frank would credit the same insurance fee to a second and third inspection also. And the prices were planned so that the buyer would have an inspection plus purchase insurance at an attractive total cost, because the insurance company could afford to write policies for much less after Frank's inspection. Frank's inspection volume began to build, because he had acquired the reputation for doing the best work. He and his wife planned their first vacation in years, and he bought a new convertible.

QUESTIONS

1. As Frank first entered the inspection business, what were the elements of strategy, the degrees of differentiation, and the sources of profit from the strategy?
2. For Frank's Assured Inspection Service, answer the same three questions.

PART II

FOUNDATIONS FOR PRODUCT AND BUSINESS STRATEGY

CHAPTER 4

THE MARKET AS BASIS FOR A STRATEGY

KEY IDEAS IN THIS CHAPTER

This chapter reviews the nature of markets and the competitive process:

- **the nature of the market** – as organization, information, geography, boundaries.
- **market life cycles and structure** – and some of the ways these may change.
- **the nature of the competition** – between companies, between warriors, and in today's competitive process.
- **competitive action potential** – as a simple and useful tool.
- **linking strategy to competition and market** – a summary of key market factors.

Chapter 4   The Market as Basis for a Strategy

No strategy will stand alone. It needs careful grounding in fundamentals, and the purpose of Part Two is to present some of its foundations. The next two chapters summarize basic areas in which any strategy should be firmly grounded because the strategy depends on them. These areas relate to the product or service, already discussed in Chapter 3, to its markets as discussed in this chapter, and to the characteristics of the business offering the product as discussed in Chapter 5. Over all are the governing enterprise strategies, discussed in Chapter 6.

Just as the nature of the product or service has dimensions that condition the choice of an appropriate strategy, so does the nature of the market in which it will be offered. This chapter considers the market and its life cycle, and the competition in that market.

THE NATURE OF THE MARKET

A market is the forum in which a product is exchanged for money or other purchasing power; the forum in which the buyer and seller or their agents meet, negotiate, and execute the exchange. Markets vary widely in their characteristics—in organization, information flows, geographic size and homogeneity, and the degree and nature of competition.

ORGANIZATION

Is the market in one place or in many places and linked by a communication network? Who can participate, and how is this controlled? Does any agency or organization oversee the functioning of this market? Some markets are rigidly and formally organized, as in the case of the New York Stock Exchange, where only securities approved and listed in advance can be traded, and the trading can be conducted only by the members of the exchange and only in accordance with a very specific pattern of trading rules. Most markets are less organized and less formal. In the case of the markets for residential real estate and for clerical employment, the transaction process is more individual and less publicized, but still a part of a broad competitive pattern. Yet other markets, such as the market for idle steel mills or the market for construction of a new electric power complex, differ so much according to the circumstances surrounding each buyer and seller that every transaction tends to be a unique event.

AVAILABILITY OF MARKET INFORMATION

In terms of sales dollars or units sold, how large is this market? What are the market shares of different companies or products? How much of different sorts of product are sold? How much do different types of customers buy? Good market information is an important competitive tool, and information availability varies widely from market to market. The New York Stock Exchange requires that the price and volume of every transaction be reported, and the day's trading is summarized and published in newspapers all over the world. While few markets build in such detailed reporting, specialized information services usually spring up, and one characteristic of a market is the extent and caliber of the information services available. Real estate prices and clerical wages are estimated by area surveys, which may be purchased from the organizations conducting the surveys. In the same way audits of major consumer goods, drug, and other markets may be purchased from firms that provide this information as a service. Information on special transactions, such as the sales price for a used manufacturing plant, may or may not be readily available; in this as other specialized market areas accurate market information may be difficult to obtain.

GEOGRAPHIC SIZE AND HOMOGENEITY

Are all of the product or service offerings in this market essentially identical? Or are there different types or grades? What determines the geographic limits of the activities of individual competitors and for the market as a whole? A market such as the U.S. market for new Cadillacs seems quite homogeneous, because General Motors makes one basic line of Cadillacs and sells them to distributors nationally on a reasonably uniform price schedule. Yet the market is organized around a system of local dealerships, each with an advantage in its local area because it is closer to those customers and can serve their needs more conveniently than more remote agencies.

Many markets subdivide geographically. In the case of Cadillacs, the subdivision is according to dealerships supported by groups of customers. Cement and sulfuric acid are heavy industrial products whose freight cost is high relative to their market value. They tend to be manufactured regionally and shipped a minimum distance, with competition primarily at the margin of their territory or against other manufacturers within economical shipping distance. The markets for fresh vegetables were once entirely local, but their shipping radius has been extended repeatedly by improvements in refrigeration and handling, to the point that California, Texas, and Florida growers now ship to the rest of the country.

Other factors determine market homogeneity, which is based on the degree to which most of the customers will buy the same product. The typewriter market was once relatively homogeneous, since all offices equipped with typewriters had available essentially the same sort of machine. Then development of portables opened different home and college markets; electrics brought higher-priced, higher-performance office applications; and now the evolution of word processing has further fragmented the market, with a wide variety of different configurations linking a typewriter or printer with a large or small computer.

In this case the different classes of customers always had different needs, but the market did not recognize the differences, and some needs went unsatisfied. The actual market was relatively homogeneous until a range of machines filling more of the customer needs was developed and made available; the market expanded as a consequence. Now analysts predict narrowing of this range of products, as computer/word processing applications evolve into a pattern that can serve the present range of customer applications with a smaller number of printers/typewriters than at present.

In many markets the lack of homogeneity of customer needs is extreme. One manufacturer found it necessary to create separate sales and technical service forces for food industry and animal feed marketing of the same bulk vitamin products, in order to compete effectively for the business of customer companies with different and specialized needs for the same group of products.

MARKET BOUNDARIES

What factors limit the market activities of individual competitors? Veterinary product manufacturers need separate clinical support for treatment of each species of animal, and their sales promotion is limited to those species for which the expense of gathering this data is justified. Many limitations of this sort impose boundaries on where individual companies compete and on the scope of a given market.

The important market characteristics relative to business strategy and policy are those that determine how the market should be approached. These begin with the market size, boundaries, patents and other competitive barriers, and the nature and extent of present and predictable competition. Then it is important to examine these market characteristics to see how susceptible they may be to change as new products are developed and marketed—as the typewriter market changed and grew under the impact of successive innovations—and to make judgments as to how likely significant innovations may be and their most probable sources.

MARKET LIFE CYCLES

A market comes into being when an area of customer need is discovered and matched with specific goods and services that have the potential for satisfying that need. Other sellers join the activity and compete for buyer interest. Other buyers discover the market and come to make purchases.

CHANGES AS THE MARKET GROWS

The nature of the market can be changed, as the development of word processing expanded and developed the different needs formerly served by typewriters. Boundaries of a market can change, as when U.S. drug and chemical companies accepted the idea of buying chemicals from other countries, and competition in certain specialty chemical markets became international for the first time. The nature of the demand can change, as customer industries pass through periods of prosperity and retrenchment; and the nature of the competition can change, as when oil producers first entered petrochemical manufacturing and marketing in large numbers.

A market may come into being when a major customer need appears; for example, Sears' entry into retailing markets outside of the U.S. required an aggressive purchasing effort to obtain local supplies of the necessary goods. Sears assisted some local firms in entering specific lines of manufacture, so that the national capability to manufacture certain consumer goods was greatly increased and eventually supplied markets other than through the Sears buyers.

A market may come into being as the result of successful commercialization of a discovery. When the potential for making office desk calculators smaller and less expensive was discovered, an aggressive, competitive new portable electronic calculator market resulted. A market may come into being as a result of new rules and regulations; environmental legislation created opportunities for laboratories to perform required animal and chemical testing for the market participants. It also created opportunities for specialized disposal firms treating difficult wastes for the waste-producing firms.

EVOLUTION THROUGH THE MARKET LIFE CYCLE

A newly created market is usually disorderly. The market participants have not yet learned to work together smoothly, the pace of innovation leads to changing and imperfect production processes, and the new market attracts new participants, each entering at a different state of readiness and with a different competitive effectiveness. As a market becomes less new, the service and the relationship between buyers and sellers becomes more orderly. As the market grows, often the sellers overexpand. A shakeout is common, as more successful firms outdistance the others and the number of competitors begins to drop.

Typically the rate of innovation in a market is highest at the beginning, declining later. Competitive barriers limiting entry to a new market are often short-term only. Know-how and trade secrets diffuse across the industry, patents are bypassed or expire, and the special advantages of one firm become less and less. The market is said to mature, as the competitive offerings become less differentiated, price competition sharpens, margins shrink, and demand becomes more cyclical. Perhaps the market will move on into a period of decline, as the growth of the auto industry caused the carriage and buggy-whip markets to decline.

CHANGING THE PRODUCT AND MARKET LIFE CYCLE

The concept of different stages of a market life cycle is useful in the strategy formulation process. The caution, and the problem in strategy design, is that the structure and stage of development of a market is the consequence of the forces bearing upon it, in terms of innovation, competition, and consumer need. Any good strategy will be effective because it strengthens the position of the company applying it. This has the potential for changing the situation in the market to a degree proportional to the effectiveness of that strategy.

Those who were around Elmer Bobst at the time tell of the acquisition of the Lambert Pharmacal Company to form the Warner-Lambert of today, which Bobst long headed. Lambert had one very important but obviously mature product, Listerine. When Bobst agreed to acquire Lambert for a price that stunned his subordinates, the Lambert family was very happy; they had sold at a very good price before the inevitable decline.

Bobst had a different view, and began to promote Listerine as it had never been promoted before. Sales and profits skyrocketed, more than validating the purchase price. By an aggressive change in marketing strategy Bobst had rejuvenated an apparently mature product into a new growth phase, at the same time revitalizing and expanding the mouthwash market in which it competed.

The point is that the useful, necessary classification of markets and life cycles before a strategy is defined is only tentative; all of these things can be changed. Changes as dramatic as Bobst's success with Listerine are uncommon but not unparalleled. Because innovation and profit margins are low in a mature market does not mean that either *must* stay low; a product with sufficient leverages and a well-chosen focus can break open a static market situation, bring new sales and profits, and permit the building of enduring positions, as the Warner-Lambert Listerine position still endures in today's market.

MARKET STRUCTURE

After a market becomes established, it tends to divide into the hands of a number of competitors with widely different market shares. Over time the number of competitors tends to shrink. Many analysts have studied this evolution of market structure.

One interesting approach to analyzing market structure was that of Reith at DuPont. Reith's Generalized Distribution Rule,[1] based on a statistical analysis developed by Kendall,[2] was intended to describe the equilibrium between competitors in any market, given the number of competitors. Kendall's analysis was based on the size distribution of random numbers, so that in effect Reith treated markets as if the distribution of ability, innovation, resources, and therefore market success among competitors were a result of random processes. In the auto industry the Rule predicted that the largest of four competitors should have a 52 percent market share, exactly General Motors' 1960s share of a U.S. auto market effectively divided amongst four companies. The remarkable fits Reith found between actual versus theoretical structure of the auto industry in the 1960s and in several other industries suggests that a random process could often be used for a first approximation of industry division between competitive firms.

This allows construction of a useful model of the market and industry evolution process. In the early days of an industry if a relatively large number of firms have market shares randomly distributed as to size (but totalling 100 percent, of course), when the industry has good and bad years, the effects will be uneven. Typically the larger firms have more ability to withstand adversity, more margin to survive blunders, and intrinsically better profits because of scale economies at various stages in the development/production/distribution process. As an industry operates, therefore, the normal fluctuations tend to jeopardize the small firms more, and occasionally one falls by the wayside.

New entrants are possible, but typically as a market evolves toward maturity, it becomes more difficult for a newcomer to enter, and profit incentives for entry decline. The general pattern is of a process where firms fall out of an industry from time to time as conditions change, fewer new ones enter, and older industries with reasonably homogeneous markets tend to drift slowly into a few strong hands.

The U.S. auto industry was highly fragmented in its early days, but many of the companies failed or were absorbed by their competitors. After General Motors decisively overtook Ford to establish its market leadership in the early 1930s, the auto industry moved toward a more stable situation, with GM, Ford, and Chrysler followed by smaller producers such as Studebaker, Packard, Hudson, Nash, and Willys. Studebaker was an effective competitor before World War II, but industry eco-

---

[1] John E. Reith, "Generalized Distribution Rule," unpublished manuscript, Dupont Textile Fibers Department, Wilmington, Delaware, April 1967.
[2] M. G. Kendall, "Ranks and Measures," *Biometrica*, Vol. 49, pp. 133–139 (1964).

nomics changed. After the war the required break-even volume had increased above Studebaker's prewar sales rate. Even after the merger with Packard, Studebaker did not succeed in achieving volume adequate to make it a viable competitor in the postwar market, and eventually it dropped out. Nash, Hudson, and Willys evolved into American Motors, then became a U.S. base for Renault, and now a part of Chrysler. GM, Ford, Chrysler, and American Motors were the remaining firms in the 1960s study Reith reported.

THE NATURE OF THE COMPETITION

Markets differ significantly in whether the competition is local, national, or international, whether it is from other sellers of the same product, of comparable but different products, or from entirely different material or service patterns. Two Cadillac agencies in adjacent territories compete, at least for the business of those customers who live near the boundary between them. But the Lincoln/Continental competition with Cadillac is of an entirely different nature, as is that from the agency promoting on-call limousine service as an alternative to owning a Cadillac or Continental.

Cadillac and Continental have competed for years, within boundaries set approximately by the competition of their respective parent companies, General Motors and Ford. Then Mercedes-Benz intruded, starting with a small but annually increasing percentage of this segment of the automobile market, to the point that an increasingly European design emphasis for the other two became a competitive necessity.

In a more extreme example, Polaroid broke into the strong Kodak home photography market franchise by offering instant developing, effectively segmenting the market to create an area where only Polaroid could supply the demand.

COMPETITION IN THE MARKET

In any particular market, what is the nature of the competition? All businesses have actual or potential competition. Also, all strategy must be viewed as competitive, considering the number of claimants there are for every available dollar of purchasing power.

In the simplest cases, competition is a more or less direct issue between several business firms. Since General Motors was created, Ford has been a key competitor, and so long as these two firms are important in the U.S. auto market, a strong rivalry seems likely to continue. In other cases the competition has a harsher character—where one party is a government-subsidized company, or where the national interest of a country is clearly linked with the success of a specific company—because it becomes less likely that a simple economic struggle in the market place can resolve the competitive issues.

Sometimes a market is dominated by competitors who are not in it but could decide to participate, because their potential for entry conditions margins and competitive bids. Or, a market may be held primarily by a few firms and yet suffer low margins because entry is so easy that potential garage operators limit the price.

In planning a strategy it is desirable to characterize the nature of the competitive situation as clearly and objectively as possible. Who is in the market, and why? Who is likely to enter and who is likely to leave? Why don't more people enter? Is this a national or an international market? Who has a political stake in the division of market shares? Are there public policy considerations in any of the relevant countries or political jurisdictions that will override success in the market place?

COMPETITION: PEOPLE, PRODUCTS, AND BUSINESSES

Competitors are people and firms. But even the firm is an individual both legally and actually, and competition is a process based on the confrontation of individuals. Too often this emphasis is lost in the impersonality of systems and approval processes, but competition is won or lost according to success against other individuals. Some individuals may not care very much if they lose, and others may respond fiercely; this is an individual matter.

Competition is a very personal process. One of the advantages the Japanese have in international business is that they have been trained to think of competition in personal terms. Many western managers see competition as institutional and impersonal, and sometimes get left behind when competitive issues between individual managers and individual firms become important to the outcome of a given strategic situation.

WARRIORS AS COMPETITORS

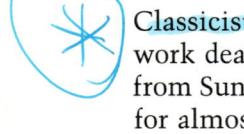

Classicists start with Sun Tzu's *The Art of War*,[3] an interesting early work dealing largely with the psychological aspects of war. A quotation from Sun Tzu can be found that will provide an apt and colorful backdrop for almost any competitive business situation. Musashi applies to modern competition more directly.

---

[3] Sun Tzu, *The Art of War*, trans. & intro. by Samuel B. Griffith (Cambridge: Oxford University Press, 1971).

Musashi was a seventeenth century Samurai warrior in Japan. The supreme swordsman of his day, he lived out a turbulent life and died undefeated. These were not ceremonial conflicts; they ended with one combatant dead or disabled. But after establishing his mastery Musashi stopped using a steel sword at all; his skill was such that the Japanese wooden swords were sufficient for him to kill his opponents. Then as an old man he taught a few disciples, and one of them recorded his philosophy as *The Book of Five Rings*.[4]

Swordsmanship is irrelevant in most business situations, but Musashi's focus on the spirit and behavior of an opponent is not. He offers useful insights into the way one gains a psychological advantage over a competitor, the way to make direct action most effective, and how to read the response a particular action is likely to bring.

TODAY'S COMPETITORS

Ohmae's *Mind of the Strategist*[5] is more immediately useful. In addition to an interesting approach to strategy, hidden behind his insights was the same viewpoint as Musashi's, that the competitor must be specifically identified, confronted, and defeated for success to follow. Ohmae separately analyzed the position of the corporation offering the product, of the customers, and of the competitors, in each case looking for a key factor for success on which to build. Together the corporation, the customer, and the competitor form Ohmae's strategic triangle. Given a key factor for success, such as a superior cost position or a product advantage, a strategy should be developed to capitalize on it. This may be based on exploiting a position of relative superiority, on aggressive initiatives, or by finding new strategic degrees of freedom. Ohmae gave several examples of redefining the presentation of a product to overcome a competitive disadvantage, creating new leverages for its purchase and changing market segmentation.

Michael Porter's *Competitive Strategy*[6] focused on market structure, competitive interaction, and the way that this causes an industry to evolve over time. He related these ideas to products with specific positioning, and to interaction between products, competitors and market, and the underlying business. Market approaches could be based on cost

---

[4] Miyamoto Musashi, *A Book of Five Rings*, trans. Victor Harris (Woodstock, N.Y.: Overlook Press, 1974).
[5] Kenichi Ohmae, *The Mind of the Strategist: Business Planning for Competitive Advantage* (New York: Penguin Books, 1983).
[6] Michael Porter, *Competitive Strategy* (New York: Free Press, Macmillan, 1980).

leadership, differentiation of the product, or focus[7] on a market niche. Much of the book was devoted to typical response patterns, with price leaders and followers, and changes in industry structure, integration, and maturity.

A step farther in the same direction was Sammon's *Business Competitor Intelligence*,[8] with each chapter by a successful practitioner in one of the different aspects of industry, market, and company analysis, and with suggestions for the organization and control of a competitor intelligence activity. Sammon focused on gaining a detailed understanding of the strengths and behavior patterns of specific competitors to predict what they will do next or how they may respond to a specific challenge to their sales or profitability.

A competitor, in the sense of the specific business unit with which a given firm competes, is often a part of a larger enterprise, and the relation between the two is important in assessing competitive strength. Multinational companies often gain a part of their competitive advantage in a given market by the sharing of development expenses between subsidiaries in many countries and by sales into many different markets to give them full world-scale economies of scale in manufacturing, and their competitors are at a serious disadvantage if they respond to a competitive attack in only one country.

Hoffmann-La Roche, the Swiss chemical and pharmaceutical company, has long been the world's largest producer of vitamin C. Takeda, the Japanese chemical and pharmaceutical company, makes vitamin C also, and at one point a few years ago began to expand its production capacity in a way that suggested a potential challenge to Roche dominance of the world market. The result was a competitive confrontation, not in Switzerland or even in Europe, but in the Far East, in all of the Pacific Rim Countries—in Takeda's natural markets, therefore—until Takeda decided not to expand its production capacity any further and the competitive pressure relaxed. This is what Porter and others speak of as multipoint competition, and many European and other multinationals try always to keep themselves in a position where they can attack or respond to a particular competitor in many different markets, including that competitor's home market.

Multipoint competition need not be multinational, and the same sort of competitive confrontation is played out again and again as fast food chains expand from neighborhood to neighborhood, and as regional

---

[7] Porter uses "focus" as concentration on a restricted portion of the market; here "focus" is used in the broader sense of *choosing* the desired relationship to customers and market, as one would focus a camera on a near or distant objective.

[8] William Sammon (ed.), *Business Competitor Intelligence* (New York: Wiley, 1984).

THE COMPETITIVE PROCESS

Products or services are offered in the market place as a part of a particular mission; that is, to fill certain customer needs, and at a price that permits a profit for the seller. To accomplish this, the deliverable itself must be created, which may be simple or may be the result of a long innovation process. Once created, the deliverable must be displayed according to its specific needs, a focus must be established creating a relationship with the prospective customers, and leverages must be established in the minds of the customers sufficient to lead to purchases. From a pattern of related purchases, a sale stream grows up and the seller begins to prosper. Competitors observe the success and make offerings aimed at the same customer needs.

The issue then shifts from the simple *ability* of a product to satisfy a customer need, to the relative cost-effectiveness of different product offerings to the same customer. Classically the number of product offerings multiply and become more alike in character and cost, and the product then becomes a commodity the customer can purchase from the lowest priced or most convenient vendor. Some companies do well in a commodity market because they have cost, distribution, or other advantages over their competitors, based on their positions, of course. Learning curve theory, discussed further in Chapter 5, suggests that such a vendor may be able to increase the relative advantage from year to year as a result of greater production and sales volume than its competitors.

To avoid the shift to a commodity market, marketers seek differentiation—to separate the identity of their product or to fit it specifically to the needs of a group of customers in one niche in the market. In this way they create specialties, maintain higher prices, and achieve a better competitive position than in a pure commodity market. Such firms also seek to improve their fundamental positions, whether by product innovation, vertical integration, or in any other way in which relative competitive advantage can be increased.

To succeed in a commodity market, a firm must have a competitive advantage over other firms supplying the same product, usually a cost advantage. Porter summarizes[9] the alternatives as (*1*) obtaining a cost advantage, (*2*) differentiating the product from those offered by others, and

---
[9] Michael E. Porter, *Competitive Advantage* (New York: Free Press, 1985), pp. 11–19.

(3) concentrating on the needs of a narrower segment of the market. This concentration may permit those narrower needs to be served more cheaply, thus establishing a cost advantage for this market segment, or this concentration may permit development of products more closely suiting the needs of this segment; this then becomes differentiation aimed at that segment only, the most frequent route for a niche strategy. Porter then goes on to point out a common strategic dilemma of being "stuck in the middle," where a company is attempting both to pursue a commodity strategy and to establish some superior product features, but lacks either the cost advantage or the advantage in product features necessary to gain market share.

Porter also discussed the value chain at some length,[10] where this is a strategic analysis of value-added stretching from the basic raw materials to the final consumer. Every company has a value added—based on the difference between the prices it pays for its inputs and the prices it receives for the products or services it sells. Different competitors in the same industry have different value chains—that is, different value-added profiles, based on what they make and what they buy, and to whom they sell and at what stage in the distribution process. How much of the value-creation process a firm carries out and how skillfully, and how well that firm has positioned itself in its purchasing and selling arrangements can go a long way toward explaining its competitive position.

The day-to-day action as these processes unfold is complex and personalized between specific customers and against specific competitors. Many markets are at an in-between stage, where various participants have successfully differentiated weak or strong specialties out of the central commodity area, and yet the differentiation is small enough so that they must adjust prices relative to a central commodity price. And the central commodity price may be set by one or more leading participants and with varying degrees of homogeneity in the industry pricing that results. A common scenario unfolds when the market weakens, with various competitors discounting below posted prices but trying to keep appearance of price maintenance to get competitive advantage from the cuts. Such discounting spreads until one of the major participants cuts posted prices "to restore discipline to the market," the other competitors follow, and the situation continues to evolve from that point.

The essence is that while the customer need sets a ceiling on the price, competitive action sets the floor. Purchasing agents for manufacturers and buyers for retailers become highly expert at sensing and taking advantage of the competitive interplay based on the circumstances and the personalities of the key people and the key firms. Thus the products

---

[10] *Ibid.*, pp. 33–163.

or services, the customers and markets, and the selling/producing businesses form a set that continually interacts, and this interaction is an essential part of the framework that should be considered in designing the strategy.

COMPETITIVE ACTION POTENTIAL (CAP)

For a given business under specific conditions, who are its competitors, what are they planning to do, and how will they react to a new strategic initiative? These are key questions, not always easy to answer, and crucial to the planning and action for any strategy. Most businesses and most products have existing competitors, potential competitors are everywhere, and both should be considered in the strategy design. The start is to list present and potential competitors and profile each. A simple competitive action potential (CAP) analysis is an effective beginning.

Competitive action potential can be derived rather easily by most groups, and in a very short time. Usually there are not that many important competitors; most businesses can narrow the field rapidly to between two and six other firms that are the ones to watch. And these firms are not unknown. Usually the management people, particularly in the marketing area, are acquainted with the managers and aware of the personality of the competitive firm, and of some of its strengths and limitations. Given this familiarity, it requires only a brief group discussion to develop a profile of a given competitor and how that firm is likely to behave.

If the group has decided on an exciting strategy that will have a major impact on the market, when will each of the competitors learn about this, and what will they do? The "when" can be guessed by the nature of the trade relationships—does "everybody" know that a major promotion is in preparation, even though they may not know what the product is? Will competitors see product approval notices, or hear reports on field tests? Most groups can guess rather accurately when their competitors will first hear of a new product or promotion.

What can they do about it? Cut prices? Introduce their own new product? Design their own new promotion? The number of action options a given competitor has are not that large—rarely more than five or six possibilities and usually fewer. And from the profile of the firm, coupled with the impressions of the group, it will be possible to rule out some of these options as unlikely or impossible. For example, if a competitor's plants are already on overtime due to production troubles, that firm will probably not choose a response that requires rapid manufacture of new merchandise.

Normally a CAP analysis results in a list of two or three possible

FIGURE 4–1 EXAMPLE OF A CAP PROFILE: BULL MACHINE WORKS

One of our major competitors; no authoritative sales figures are available, but from credit and industry sources we believe Bull Machine sales are comparable to our own, but have been at about the same dollar level for many years. Old Bill (Bull) Bull apprenticed there under his father, the founder. He was already a master machinist when he inherited the company at 21, in the depths of the depression. He immediately put all the rest of his father's money into expanding and modernizing the business, and by 1935 he had one of the best and most modern shops in the country. Ever since then he has run a lean, efficient business with low overhead, little staff and only a modest sales effort; he is in apparent good health, active and alert, looking at least twenty years younger than he is, and still doing some specialty machining himself; he tells visitors he needs two or three hours a day of shop work to keep his own machinery going. Bull has several very capable foremen who substitute for him when he is away; no one knows if he has retirement plans, but the business can easily go on in his absence.

As a competitor, Bull Machine is a force to be reckoned with. Bull has an excellent reputation, especially in handling difficult jobs. Costs are good on routine work; although he pays his machinists very well, productivity is good and his overhead low. His disadvantages are due to a weak sales effort—he may not always hear about jobs where he could submit the lowest bid—and work requiring newer and more sophisticated machines. Bull has moved slowly in numerical control and other newer areas; as a consequence he is no longer competitive on repetitive, high-volume jobs. There have been rumors that he is about to spend $4 million to completely re-equip the shop, but there is no confirmation to date.

In competing with Bull it is important to study past bid patterns closely, as his newest bid on a similar job is likely to be similar. Also, it is important not to price or bid a job in such a way that it appears to be a direct challenge to Bull or a slur on Bull quality, because Bull may rise to the challenge. Three years ago he found that a complex gear design had not been executed correctly in the shop and had the gears remade, but missed the delivery commitment by two weeks and lost money on the order. When the customer put the same gear out for bids again with a penalty clause for late delivery, Bull bid 33% less and may have lost money, just because he wanted to prove that he could deliver on time. Bull's wife died forty years ago, he has no close relatives, and lives modestly and for the business, which has been very profitable during most of the last fifty years; Bull can afford to lose money on a job if he wants to prove a point.

Summary: Bull Machine is a tough competitor, particularly for difficult and custom work, but less formidable for large-volume routine jobs. Bull Machine often doesn't hear of new work unless it comes from existing customers; our marketing is better and we have often taken new jobs where Bull would probably have underbid us if he had heard about the work. It doesn't bother Bull to be underbid, because he has always been able to keep his shop busy; but when bidding against him it is important not to allow the bid to appear as any sort of a challenge. Purchasing agents have been known to bait bidders into saying something that would get Bull angry when he heard it, because they knew he might take the job away with a very low bid.

FIGURE 4–2   EXAMPLE OF A CAP PROFILE: MILDEW MOLDING COMPANY

Mildew is a division of Acme Telegraph and Land, a conglomerate with very strict financial performance requirements. Mildew's business is in custom molding powders and directly competitive with our own plastics division; in the regional market we rank second in dollar volume and Mildew ranks third. Mildew's management has changed rapidly, due to turnover of various sorts, an Acme plan for rotating executives from division to division, and an occasional discharge when quarterly profit objectives are not met. The managers tend to be good but not thoroughly enough acquainted with the business to be formidable competitors. John John, the current General Manager, appears to be very able and could begin to challenge us if Acme leaves him there for two or three years.

Mildew delivers custom colors by blending, as we do, and has a very good blending plant, except that it is somewhat harder to clean out between colors than ours; a thorough cleanout costs them two days' production time unless they use overtime very heavily in order to accomplish this in one day. To minimize the cost impact of the cleanout, Mildew is now running a three-week color cycle, since no cleanout is necessary in going from white to successively darker colors ending with black and a thorough cleanout. In contrast, our color cycle is only two weeks because of our lower cleanout costs and the desire of sales to be able to take orders for quicker delivery. Mildew's line is good and their product costs at least as good as ours, but most of our customers want rapid delivery. When an order fits the Mildew routine cycle, they are likely to win it; but they are very reluctant to schedule special cleanouts even for a large customer, so that we win most of the orders that would require them to change their schedule.

---

responses per competitor for a small number of key firms. This is a small enough total number of possible responses for someone to analyze each briefly to see whether any of these competitive actions have the potential for upsetting the planned campaign and, if so, whether some slight modification might make the chosen strategy better able to withstand attack.

The initial CAP profiles are usually surprisingly accurate, because an effective product and marketing team knows much more about its competitors than it realizes. But key factors can be missed, and these profiles merit circulation amongst those connected with the business from time to time, plus thoughtful consideration of the picture they present. Sometimes an information gap will become obvious and suggest further investigation. Also, familiarity with the profiles will sensitize the group to the strategic significance of specific bits of competitive information as they become available.

Competitive intelligence is important, and in some large firms its gathering becomes a major staff activity. For at least an initial approach however, a simple CAP analysis is a useful part of a sound product and market planning exercise. For examples of brief CAP profiles, see Figures 4-1 and 4-2.

> **FIGURE 4-3   MARKET CHARACTERISTICS AS FUNDAMENTALS**
>
> **The nature of the market**
> - organization
> - information
> - size
> - homogeniety
> - boundaries
>
> **Market life cycles**
> - changes as the market grows
> - evolution through the life cycle
> - changing life cycles
> - structuring the market
>
> **The nature of the competition**
> - competition in the market
> - competitive action potential
>
> **Competitors as people**
> - understanding the opponent
> - differentiation, and the competitive process
> - product and market competition
> - prices: needs set the ceiling competition sets the floor
>
> LINKING STRATEGY TO COMPETITION AND MARKET

LINKING STRATEGY TO COMPETITION AND MARKET

This chapter has discussed the nature of the market, the stages in the market life cycle, the nature of the competition, and competitor analysis. Its purpose has been to suggest a series of market-related dimensions that need integration into product and business strategy for it to be effective, as illustrated in Figure 4-3, and as related to the overall planning-strategy-action strategy design framework in Figure 4-4. Especially, this chapter focused on the existence of competitors as an inevitable reality, and the need to understand and confront specific individual competitors as a personal reality for anyone active in strategic management.

QUESTIONS FOR ANALYSIS AND DISCUSSION

1. Choose a market, other than the examples from the text, and describe it as to organization, market information, homogeneity, approximate number of participants, boundaries, and other basic characteristics.
2. List several markets and characterize them as to the stage in their market life cycle. Try to find markets at several different stages.

FIGURE 4–4 MARKET CHARACTERISTICS AS BASIC TO STRATEGY DESIGN

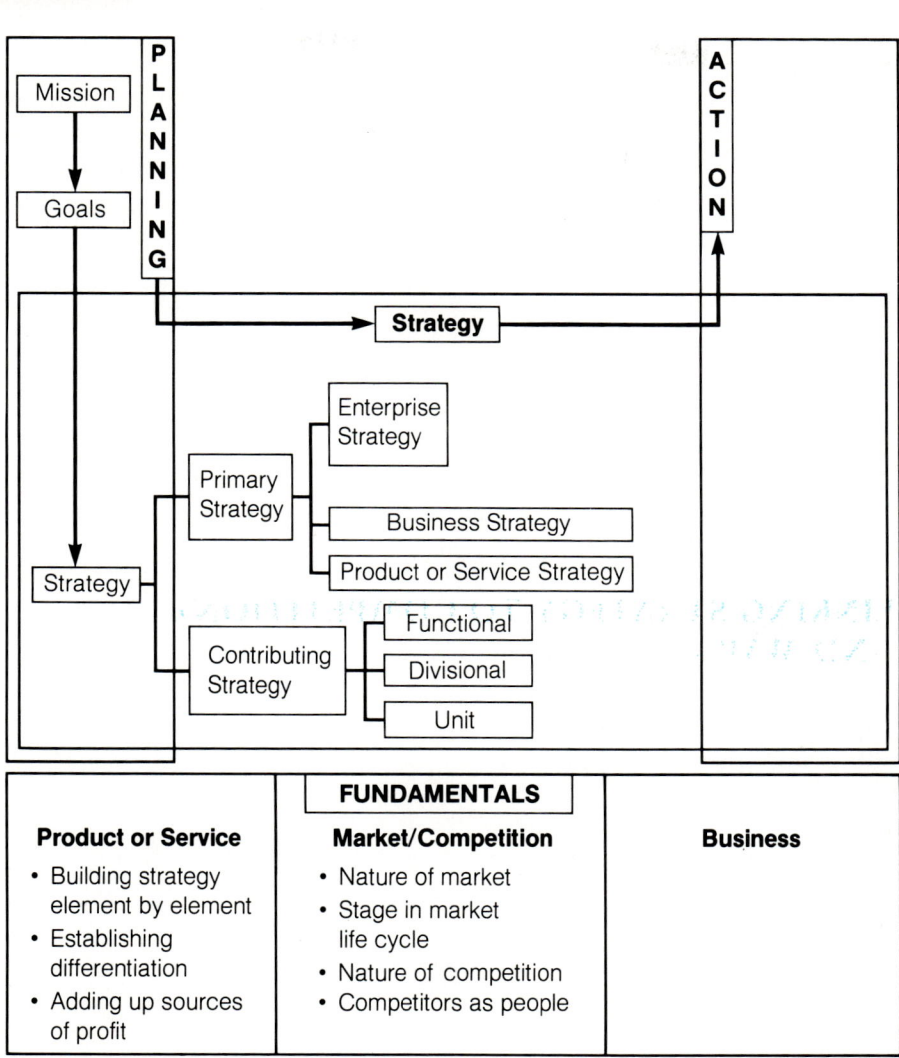

3. For the markets in Question 2, what is the market structure (approximate number of participants and degree of concentration)?
4. For the markets in Questions 2 and 3, characterize the ease of entry and exit.
5. For the markets in Questions 2, 3, and 4—are there any indications as to whether the competition between companies is personal or impersonal, and why?

FOR FURTHER INFORMATION

Musashi, Myamoto, *A Book of Five Rings,* trans. Victor Harris (Woodstock, NY: Overlook Press, 1974).

    An incisive competitive analysis from the viewpoint of a master swordsman.

Ohmae, Kenichi, *The Mind of the Strategist* (New York: Penguin Books, 1983).

    A good analysis of competitive strategy by a leading Japanese consultant.

Porter, Michael E., *Competitive Strategy* (New York: Free Press, 1980), and *Competitive Advantage* (New York: Free Press, 1985).

    Useful, authoritative analyses of competitive forces.

CASE 7
THE BRUSSELS BOWL COMPANY

The market for salad bowls suddenly exploded. It was the opportunity that helped the Brussels Bowl Company out of a tight spot.

One of the founders of the town of Brussels, Maine had built a dam across the river and used the water to drive a sawmill. The dam had been repaired and the mill rebuilt many times since then, but both had continued to operate. Today the water power drove an automatic generator that fed electric power into the utility network, and in turn the woodworking machinery was powered with electric motors. Where the first sawmill had been primarily a means to make logs from the local pine forests into lumber to build houses, the pine forests had retreated rapidly as the country grew; they were growing back now, but the Brussels sawmill had long ago been converted, first to a furniture factory, and then back and forth amongst the variety of cabinetmaking, millwork, and other wooden products that gave hope of employing people and making a profit.

Since colonial times the mill had had a lathe for making wooden bowls, and when the previous proprietor managed to get all of the lobstermen angry at him just when he was beginning to gain a worthwhile share of the lobster trap market, his nephew took over the company, renamed it the Brussels Bowl Company, and started to make a place again for Brussels in the world of wooden bowls.

Wooden bowls were a colonial and frontier alternative to glass and china bowls. They had aesthetic advantages to some people and for some purposes, but one of their original attractions in a world of large trees was that they were very inexpensive. The frontier days were long past, and the primary demand for wooden bowls was long gone, but many people still liked them. The Brussels Bowl company had an old but good bowl lathe, milling equipment to cut its own bowl stock out of logs, dry storage space in the old mill building for seasoning, and access to a nearby dry kiln as needed. The company reactivated its line of bowls, and began to work to expand sales.

Wooden bowls were mostly purchased in quantity, unfinished, by buyers with sharp pencils and little humanity. The Brussels Bowl Company could get a good share of the business rather easily by bidding at its cost. A lot of bowls were sold that way, just to keep the machinery running and the people employed, but the company could not go on without profits. The nephew even thought of trying the lobster trap market again.

Then the tourist industry discovered wooden bowls and demand soared. If you sanded a bowl, put a clear finish on it and a figure of a lobster, or a pine cone, or the name of the resort, the summer visitors bought the bowls in large numbers. Bowl orders increased. The Brussels Bowl Company put the bowl lathe on two shifts and cleared a floor in the old mill for a finishing room where twenty women lacquered and stenciled bowls. The demand was seasonal, but only in February and March did it slacken enough for the mill to turn bowls for bulk sale to the quantity buyers who had sustained the business before.

The next year demand expanded even more, and the Brussels Bowl Company ordered the very best and newest in high-speed bowl lathes. During the hectic season that followed, the old lathe ran 24 hours a day, seven days a week, and the thought of the beautiful new high-speed lathe that was coming helped to sustain the morale of all of those connected with bowls. Not only did the Brussels Bowl Company run its bowl lathe at capacity, so did every other woodworking mill in New England that had a lathe and the bowl stock to turn on it. Good maple and other woods suitable for bowl turning rose sharply in price, and less careful operators turned bowls out of wood that had not been properly selected and seasoned. As the market cycle continued, some gift shop operators, hungry to buy bowls to sell, also began to find they had bought cracked or otherwise imperfect bowls they could not sell.

The buyers became more selective just at the time when the supply had finally expanded beyond the demand. The following year will be long remembered in the bowl business, because it was the year when it seemed to snow wooden bowls. Everyone had finally got enough good turning stock, and it was as if every bowl lathe in eight states had run without stopping all winter. In the spring when the buyers began to stock for the season, they were bombarded with offers for bowls. Those who had not ordered in advance had the widest range of choice they had had in years, and as early as April some of the vendors were giving very attractive quantity discounts.

By the middle of June it was clear that bowls were in surplus, to the point that many inventories would be carried over into the next winter. Some of the small manufacturers were pressed to reduce their trade credit, and of course had to sell their bowls for what they could get. Almost every other week from the middle of July until after Labor Day a bankruptcy liquidator cleared out the trade inventory of one or another failed bowl company. None of these inventories was very large, relative to the size of the market, but they supplied cut-rate merchandise to many retailers. Tourist sales of bowls were good, and encouraged by special prices, so the carryover of unsold bowls was much less than it might have been otherwise.

The Brussels Bowl Company was less hurt by all of this turmoil in its market place than it might have been, although it received delivery on the new automatic bowl lathe and had to pay for it at a time when the number of bowls to be turned had gone down rather than up. The president made the best of the situation by scheduling the year's output of unfinished bowls for the bulk buyers as a break-in run for the new machine. Fortunately, Brussels had encouraged season contracts at a substantial discount with its retail outlets, because the nephew expected some sort of cycle in the market and wanted to build long-term relationships rather than get the highest possible price for every bowl. Thus the Brussels Bowl local business was not much hurt by the turmoil, although it seemed wise to make further price concessions to the contract purchasers in token of the general fall in the market, and this hurt profits.

The bright spot was that the Brussels Bowl Company, concerned about the stability of this promising new market, had been looking for ways to extend its business to new areas, and was beginning to establish sales through city department and specialty stores, with a special "big apple" design for New York, and so forth. This was new, high-profit business that partially offset the pain of the shakeout in the local tourist market. Altogether Brussels Bowl had a good year, with profits only a little under the year before and volume up, but the cost of the new lathe and some related modernizing of the milling and sanding equipment strained the cash flow.

By the next spring the tone of the bowl market had changed. The shakeout had eliminated some small operators and discouraged others. Prices were still soft due to unsold inventories remaining from the year before, but the number of firms offering bowls had shrunk significantly, the price of good logs for bowl stock fell with the drop in the number of producers, and the Brussels Bowl Company found that most of its customers renewed their season purchase contracts rather eagerly, after they had bargained a little to see if they could get any more price concessions. Bowls were still available from inventory liquidators in June, but as some of these buyers had sensed, they were in short supply by August, and the Brussels Bowl Company had to run both the old and new lathes until the middle of September to keep current with orders.

In the fall when the Brussels Bowl Company began to add up the results for the season and to plan for the next year, it became clear that this had been an extremely good year. Volume was up substantially and costs were down. Even with the lower prices, profits were very good indeed. Even unfinished bowls sold in bulk showed a respectable profit margin. Painful as it had been to finance the new lathe during the shakeout in the market the year before, it had put Brussels Bowl in a very good cost position. "If this is the kind of market it is going to be, we had better see what else we can do to cut costs," said the president, and the key people at Brussels Bowl did a careful review of the operation and began to spend money very carefully, in the spirit of a thrifty clan. They improved log handling, found better sanding equipment, put in new air filtration and ventilating equipment to control fumes and reduce dust defects in the finishing room, and worked to make their bowl production operation the best it could be.

The next year was another one of good volume and competitive prices, and the Brussels Bowl margins rose again as a result of the work on the production system. That winter the company invested in improvements again, this time in better storage and handling for the incoming logs, and in a new packing room, to make the finishing area more of a "clean room," and to make the order handling and shipping more efficient.

Development of department and specialty store sales had continued as a successful and profitable diversification, and Brussels Bowl's stenciling equipment had been modified also, to make it easier and faster to run custom designs for a specific city or store. In the course of the sales development work the Brussels people had attempted a market survey, to get some idea of the size of the wooden bowl market, the number of firms selling into it, and the number of buyers. The marketing manager said that she could not yet put much confidence in the final numerical estimates—there are too many potential sources of error in this sort of a study until it has been checked in different ways—but the survey did show several important things.

In the first place, the market still appeared to be expanding but not as fast as Brussels Bowl production records would have suggested, because the number of bowl manufacturers was continuing to shrink and part of Brussels' growth was at the expense of companies leaving the market. Prices had settled out at a level where the market was not attractive to any manufacturer who did not have good equipment and a significant volume, and some of the marginal producers strong enough to have survived the earlier market shakeout had stopped making bowls and shifted their energies to other fields, presumably because the bowl market was no longer profitable for them and they could make more money elsewhere.

While there was no good way to estimate the exact market shares held by the different producers from the data available so far, Brussels Bowl was clearly one of the leaders. The company had discovered that only two of the other bowl manufacturers still continued to bid against it for the unfinished bowl sales. Enough was known about the other leaders to suggest that Brussels Bowl probably had the best production costs, because no one else had invested in the same sort of automated turning equipment, and the Brussels plant in total was really very well set up and operated at this point.

The market survey also showed that Brussels Bowl had been by far the most aggressive in developing outlets through department and specialty stores out of the tourist area. This was a higher-margin business, and the company continued to look for ways to improve the service and widen the variety of special designs it could offer to the department store buyers.

The president circulated a memo, which was then posted in the work areas:

"The demand for wooden bowls seems steady, very competitive, and growing slightly from year to year. We hope and believe that this market will continue its growth. To make our future secure here at the Brussels Bowl Company by supplying this market:

"(1) we need to make the Brussels Bowl Company the lowest-cost and most efficient manufacturer of wooden bowls in the world, if it is not the best producer already, and to keep improving our operations to maintain this advantage.

"(2) we need to send out only top-quality bowls, bowls that we can be proud of when we see them in stores and in the homes of our friends. We must make our "made in Brussels, Maine" imprint a mark of top quality, stamped only on the best bowls in the world.

"(3) we need to serve our customers so well, by quick and efficient service, a wide variety of sizes and designs, and friendly, respectful handling of their orders, that they will never feel the need for comparison shopping with our competitors."

QUESTIONS

1. To what extent is the life cycle of the wooden bowl market, as described above, a typical market cycle? To what extent is it different from a typical cycle?

2. Discuss the degrees of product differentiation in this market at its different stages, and the degree to which weak or strong specialty products were developed.

3. At the time the case ended, the president of the Brussels Bowl Company asked the marketing manager for an analysis of whether they should make any special effort to increase their market share in the wooden bowl market. What would you advise, and why would you advise this?

CASE 8 THE PAPER TRAP COMPANY

Ephraim had a dream. He had helped on lobster boats from the time he was big enough to stand in a small boat in rough water, and operated his uncle's boat for two years after high school. Then in 1977 his uncle died, and the will specified that the boat and gear be sold and the money used to send Ephraim to college.

Now twelve years later, the Acme Corporation, which could never resist a bargain, saw a small paper company in financial distress and bought it for very little. Afterwards Acme discovered that the paper company also had had a new ventures department, and Ephraim's boss, the Director of Development for Acme, suddenly had to decide what to do with a group of leftover new ventures Acme had inherited. One was the Paper Trap Company, set up to make lobster traps out of paper. The boss remembered Ephraim had once caught lobsters and called him in: "Ephraim, here is your first company. We acquired it by accident, it makes lobster traps out of paper, and that is about all we know. Go up and look it over, spend a few weeks there if you need to, and make a recommendation. If you think it makes sense to run it, you will be the president, and I will ask you to prepare a business plan. Otherwise bring back a proposal for selling or liquidating the venture. Good luck."

Ephraim had now spent two weeks in Harbor Center, where the plant was, and the Paper Trap Company did make some sense. His enthusiasm was beginning to catch fire. His dream was to do something good for the lobstermen, and also to come back home, figuratively at least, as the president of an important local company.

One problem he would have was with the name of the company, which could have been chosen only by a paper company, but the name could be changed. The product was actually a plastic laminate with a recycled paper fiber base. It made a good lobster trap, and looked and felt enough like a wooden trap so that it would probably find more acceptance than the molded plastic creations that had been proposed. He needed information on the production economics, because recycled paper fiber was cheaper than new wood fiber, but the best place to buy it was not in lobster country, and no one had worked out what a dependable fiber supply delivered to a plant in Harbor Center would cost. Meanwhile it seemed reasonable to assume that Paper Trap could afford to sell a laminated lobster trap for about the same cost as the conventional wooden traps. The product would look and feel a great deal like the conventional wooden product, and would last essentially forever, where wooden traps break and wear out.

Ephraim started a series of inquiries on paper fiber costs and then began to do a market analysis while he waited for fiber quotations. He felt that the paper traps, or whatever they were finally named, had a good chance for market acceptance if properly presented. But they would face competition. Historically lobster traps had been built locally since the wood they required was generally available and lobstermen had never liked to pay for someone else's labor. But now that wood was getting more expensive, the better economics of factory cutting and assembly had come into the picture, and factory-made traps had begun to come into general use. Lobster trap assembly did not justify automation, however, and experimental use of hot-melt adhesives in place of nails had been instantly rejected by the lobstermen, who wanted to be able to see the nails. Thus the pattern was of factory assembly of precut lobster trap parts, where the worthwhile economies were in the quantity purchase and precutting of the wood. Yet while one could buy precut traps in kit form and nail them up in a few minutes, surprisingly few lobstermen did this. Either they built the trap entirely, or they wanted it preassembled and ready to use.

Ephraim had spent a number of hours at the computer terminal searching databases and calling up information on the lobster market and the companies in it. A few days later reports he had ordered began to arrive, and as he read them they brought out new questions. He analyzed the competition, gathered what figures he could, and began to build up a picture of the lobster trap market:

TABLE 1   ESTIMATED DIVISION OF LOBSTER TRAP MARKET

Product Form			Percentage of market	
Wooden traps				96%
locally made			27%	
purchased in kit form			5%	
Forest Pine		2%		
Builder's Supply		2		
Harborbottom Trap Company		1		
purchased fully assembled			64%	
Forest Pine		21%		
Block Warren		13		
Builder's Supply		12		
Harborbottom Trap Company		8		
South Central Lumber		5		
other		5		
Plastic traps				4%
molded thermoplastic			3%	
Central Chemical & Plastic		2%		
Molded Products		1		
assembled panels			1%	
Modern Fabrications		1%		
TOTAL				100%

Ephraim looked at the analysis he had assembled and decided that Paper Trap's target should be the 64 percent of the market now supplied by fully assembled wooden traps. The 27 percent of locally made traps was declining year to year and would probably fade away to a lower figure over time, but this part of the market seemed relatively inaccessible to a new entrant like Paper Traps. Similarly, the purchase of precut kits had failed to win any significant share, and probably would continue to decline as the purchase of locally made traps declined. And, while the plastic traps were still in the market, they had been very badly received and were losing the share they held. Neither type stacked or handled as well as the wooden traps, their price was a little higher due to the cost of the plastic, and Ephraim felt that, unless there were some unexpected innovation in economy or design, the plastic traps would disappear from the market over the next few years.

Since the fully assembled traps were the key competition from which Paper Traps had to take market share, the key competitors were the present (and potential?) sellers of fully assembled lobster traps. But since three of them also sold kits, he would have to count the contribution from the kits to their total sales volume in assessing their strength as competitors. On this basis he added the kit and fully assembled trap sales together and constructed the following market profile:

TABLE 2   COMPETITIVE PROFILE—LOBSTER TRAP MARKET

Competitor (assembled trap + kit sales)	Market Share of Total Market	Market Share of Available Market*
Forest Pine	23%	34%
Builder's Supply	14	20
Block Warren	13	19
Harborbottom Trap Company	9	13
South Central Lumber	5	7
other	5	7
TOTAL	69%	100%

*Assuming that the 27% of locally made traps and 4% of plastic traps were not available.

From all that he knew at this point, entry of other companies into the market seemed unlikely, but this was a matter of opinion rather than certainty, and Ephraim knew that he had not yet learned the nuances of the lobster trap market. He had a page of tentative conclusions he was beginning to define. He noted: "No indication of other new entrants to the market" and also "How would we know if other companies were considering entry?—check further."

Ephraim constructed a competitive profile, based on the available information. The "other" participants in the market were small and of no immediate importance. Except for more checking for any signs of major new market initiatives from these or other companies, he could concentrate his attention on the five competitors listed above.

Forest Pine, the largest competitor, was a subsidiary of a major forest products company. It had no obvious linkages to lobstermen or marine products, except that it had been the first company to start manufacturing and selling lobster traps, years ago, as a part of a program to broaden the utilization and sales of its forest products. Its marketing did not look especially formidable, but it was in a very good manufacturing position because of its integration into the larger forest products company. More than that, Ephraim found a feature article about Forest Pine and its lobster traps done several years earlier, with many pictures of the manufacturing process. The reporter had made much of the fact that most of the wood Forest Pine was using to make its lobster traps would otherwise have been wasted, as it was too short or too small for normal lumber sales. To Ephraim that meant that Forest Pine could afford to cut prices a long way before giving up any of their market to someone else, and the management of their company had the reputation of being very good at choosing the approach to their markets that would bring in the greatest overall revenue. Ephraim wrote on his page of tentative conclusions: "Let's be very careful never to get into a price war with Forest Pine."

Builder's Supply was the second largest competitor, but it was not a manufacturer of lobster traps at all. This was primarily a sales company that contracted with others to manufacture the goods it needed, including the lobster traps. There was no reason to think that Builder's Supply had any unusual cost advantages, but it had an excellent distribution system, with lumber and building materials stores in almost every town. Near the seacoast each of its stores also had a well-stocked marine department, and Builder's Supply was obviously trying to increase the volume of supplies and fittings it sold to lobstermen, scallop dredgers, and fishermen. The fact that it had done relatively well with the lobster traps and kits showed that quite a few lobstermen were trading in its stores. "This company wants the sales dollars and will fight for them," noted Ephraim, "but it may not really care whose lobster traps it sells or what they are made of."

Block Warren had been an interesting company. Block and Warren were lobstermen who sold their boats and set up a store to supply the trade. Both had since left the business and a former variety store manager had taken it over. The company appeared to have only a narrow product line and to be losing ground year by year. It had an interest in a sawmill in a coast town, and its lobster traps were made in a shed there. Ephraim noted: "not an important competitive factor, or likely to be, without new management."

The Harborbottom Trap Company was the only company Ephraim had heard of, before the Paper Trap Company, that had been set up specifically to make lobster traps. Harborbottom had been founded a long time ago by an inventor with a new and patented lobster trap design. The new design didn't work very well, but the company had already been set up, so after the inventor gave up and went off to other things, the man who was actually building the traps for him continued to make and sell good, conventional wooden lobster traps, which is what Harborbottom did still. It was probably holding its own in the market and no more, and doing as well as this only because the proprietor had distribution agreements with two smaller store chains that competed with Builder's Supply. Neither was a particularly effective outlet, but the only lobster traps they sold were Harborbottom, and they accounted for essentially all of the output of the company. "A company standing still," noted Ephraim, "probably with a good operation but no special advantages."

South Central Lumber Company was the fifth of the competitors, and represented only 7 percent of the market. It was a large regional millwork company that had started making lobster traps in an attempt to enlarge its wood products sales volume, and sold only through its own four millwork outlets. It sold mostly to gift shops, and used the roofs of its lumber sheds and other buildings to age the traps, so that they would weather to a suitable silver grey before being offered to the tourists. Ephraim noted: "No reason to believe they sell any significant number of traps to lobstermen, or are likely to be a competitive factor in Paper Trap's future business."

Ephraim had begun to receive quotations on the supply of waste paper fiber Paper Trap would need to operate, and the potential production costs began to look better and better. Paper Trap had already made a small quantity of very good traps and he began to visualize the testing and market introduction process. He listed the leverages he would use to sell the product, and the display process necessary before the lobstermen would believe in it. Paper Trap had had a quiet test under way, and Ephraim had access to a number of five-year-old traps in daily use that looked almost new. Perhaps he could establish a strong enough entry so that he could interest Builder's Supply in distributing his traps; he could afford to give them a very healthy trade discount—but he must not forget a double check against any other possible market entrants. . . .

Ephraim drifted off into detailed product and market planning. He hadn't told his boss yet, but obviously he had decided to become the president of Paper Trap and direct its entry into the market.

QUESTIONS

1. Choose an industry with which you are familiar and profile the competitors in the way that Ephraim did.
2. How could Ephraim minimize the risk of Paper Trap's being surprised by another new market entrant?
3. For Paper Trap—summarize the elements of strategy for the product.
4. For Paper Trap—what is the degree of differentiation of the new lobster trap? What are its sources of profit?
5. Do you think Ephraim should find a new name for the product or let it be Paper Trap as it goes to market?

CHAPTER

THE BUSINESS AS BASIS FOR A STRATEGY

KEY IDEAS IN THIS CHAPTER

This chapter discusses basic business characteristics and some of the major techniques for comparing different business units:

- **the nature of the business** – and the way it varies with different sorts of firms.
- **learning curves** – as a tool for relating potential cost reductions with business strategy.
- **life cycles and businesses** – a process of change to different growth and cash flow characteristics as a business ages.
- **classification of businesses** – GE stoplight matrix, BCG portfolio planning matrix, Arthur D. Little matrix, refinements by Charles Hofer, stages of business growth, PIMS = profit impact of marketing strategy.
- **portfolio management** – strategic business units and the strategy matrix.
- **shareholder value** – profitability, market appraisal, debt/equity ratio, managing for shareholder value.
- **linking strategy to the nature of the business.**

The two previous chapters developed product and market concepts that are important as strategy is designed and put into action. This chapter will extend this discussion to differences between businesses as an additional dimension in strategy design and strategic management, beginning with the nature of the business and business life cycles and learning curves, and then considering portfolio techniques and related management tools.

THE NATURE OF THE BUSINESS

Not all businesses are the same, and not all strategic alternatives apply equally well to all businesses. The differences between different sorts of businesses are large enough so that for many years *Dun's Review* (now *Dun's Business Monthly*) published an annual summary of typical financial ratios for a great many categories of firms, to aid those who needed to analyze these financial statements.

Accounting practices differ significantly in some business areas and can confuse the casual business observer; for example, by the way that some public utility construction expenses increase current income. Or, American Express and several other major diversified corporations have acquired insurance companies and had difficulty integrating them into their operating pattern—and insurance company accounting practices are so very different that some have suggested this as the reason for their confusion. As discussed further in Chapter 6, Air Products, with a highly regarded management, decided to divest Adkins-Phelps, a prospering subsidiary, because the unusual seasonal financial flows were so unlike anything else in Air Products as to make controllability of the subsidiary uncertain.

More central to the issues of strategy design are the differences in functional emphasis in some businesses. A good commodity manufacturing strategy is often based on aiming for the lowest manufacturing cost with the greatest possible economies of scale, and then trying to achieve sufficient market dominance to permit both a high profit rate and an unchallengeable cost and price position. But in a consumer marketing business low costs would not guarantee success; effective promotion would be at least as important. And a market-oriented company such as Procter & Gamble can build an important cost position for its promotion by achieving advertising price discounts based on the total advertising budget for all of its products together.

These are only examples, but the point is that each type of business has its own requirements and quirks. Successful strategy design requires an understanding of these requirements of a particular business, as well as insight into the degree to which these requirements could be modified if a particular strategy required it.

LEARNING CURVES

An important measure of different operations and businesses is their position on the learning curve. The learning curve concept sprang from the observation that after the first prototype of a fighter plane was completed and then the same vendor built a second and third plane from the same plans, the cost tended to decline in a regular manner as learning accumulated.

From this type of initial observation and a great deal of additional study came the generalization that cost declines in a predictable way as more and more items are produced; specifically, that the logarithm of the cost of almost any operation *potentially* declines in direct proportion to the logarithm of the total accumulated production volume. This generalization has been confirmed on a great many different sorts of operations. A learning slope of 0.8 is common, and both steeper and flatter slopes have been reported in specific cases, after correcting the data for inflation and changes in material costs. As illustrated in Figure 5-1, this would suggest that if a factory built 100 automobiles or produced 100 batches of chemicals, it would achieve a certain cost level, but that its costs would then fall to 80 percent of that level by the time that 1000 cars or 1000 batches of chemicals had been produced, and would decline again to 80 percent of the 1000-unit cost by the time that 10,000 units had been produced.

The power of the insights springing from this learning curve concept are very great, but there are limitations. The power is in visualizing the advantage of the leader in a market, who by having the largest sales volume could achieve the lowest production costs, and who should be able to increase this cost advantage steadily by continuing to manufacture and sell faster than its competitors, and therefore to move down a learning curve faster. From this a powerful argument can be made for gaining market share at almost any cost, in order to get into a position where cost advantages might appear inevitably to follow.

The problems in applying the learning curve concept are four: (1) the cost gains are not automatic. Intelligent, aggressive management is required to keep costs falling at the predicted rate, and, particularly in the dominant company, it is easy to get less gain or none at all. (2) Learning is based on making the same thing repeatedly. Where model changes are small, the impact may not be serious; but where major changes are necessary in design and technology, these may wipe out learning curve advances entirely. (3) Learning is accomplished by a combination of innovation and teamwork, leading to a steadily improving production system. But once a system has developed to a given level, it may also be achievable by others who cancel the competitive advantage by copying its features. Also, such a system may become obsolete if technological advances change

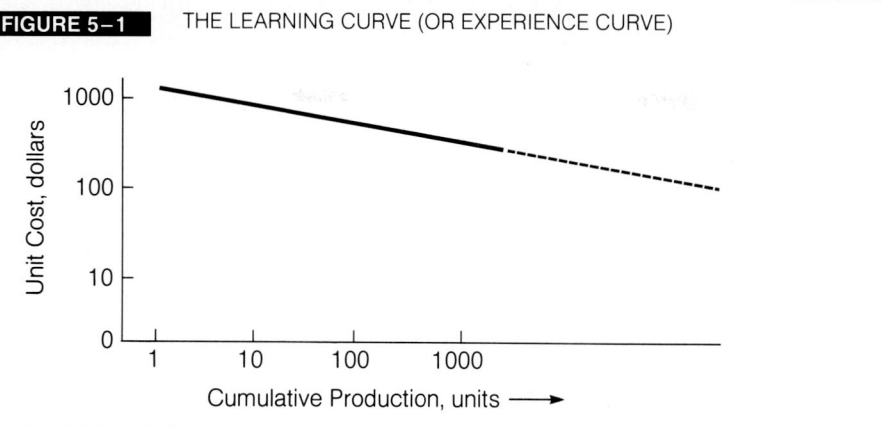

FIGURE 5–1 THE LEARNING CURVE (OR EXPERIENCE CURVE)

the foundations on which the process is based. (4) The data supporting the learning curve effect is based primarily on single operating units. When an organization grows to the size that it requires numbers of plants operating more or less in parallel, the potential for learning curve gains is at least partially offset by the inevitable inefficiencies of a larger organization.

The learning curve concept is a highly valuable management tool, but major blunders have been caused by its careless application. Although it predicts product costs, management applications of the learning curve have primarily been as a part of an overall business philosophy, often coupled with an extreme emphasis on achieving market share. The learning curve is valuable and should be used, both in operations management and strategic management, but as only one of a series of factors controlling choice of strategy.[1]

LIFE CYCLES AND BUSINESSES

Businesses are based on sale of products or services, and businesses have life cycles, in part based on the underlying product and market life cycles and in part as a life cycle of the organization itself. A research department

---

[1] Because some people used learning curves only for labor costs, and to differentiate the services of the Boston Consulting Group, Henderson used the term 'experience curve' instead and developed many business applications; see Boston Consulting Group, *Perspectives on Experience* (Boston: The Boston Consulting Group, 1970), and also Bruce D. Henderson, *Logic of Business Strategy* (Cambridge, Mass.: Abt/Ballinger, 1984).

is created to find replacements for a business's products, and its success moves that business beyond the limitations of individual product life. Markets have life cycles, however; and as markets mature, they change. Often they yield lower margins with fiercer competition and a lower rate of major product innovations, and the businesses serving them must change. Often there is a shift from a market evolution guided by creative sellers to one with a stronger and stronger role for the aggressive buyer.

New and fast-growing businesses tend to be profitable but to have high investment requirements. Often the cash flow burden of financing growth in an exciting new market is a heavy one, and high-growth companies are traditionally cash-poor in their early years. The reason that deficit financing in these years is widely practiced is that, as the products and markets begin to mature, investment requirements usually diminish and cash can flow back out of the business, repay the investment, and provide a return.

Business life cycles are no more fixed than product life cycles. A business ages as it develops and matures internally, and as its relationship with customers and the outside environment becomes less dynamic and more stable. But if new markets open and internal growth resumes, the business can effectively shift back to an earlier stage in its life cycle and develop from that point. Business life cycles are guides, therefore, but subject to change under the impact of an appropriate new strategy.

Several large firms have based a major part of their approach to enterprise strategy on the recognition that the different businesses in a diverse corporation tend to be at different stages in these cycles, and need to be evaluated and managed accordingly. This concept of a business life cycle is one of the key elements in the portfolio management approach to comparison of businesses and business opportunities in a diversified enterprise.

A CLASSIFICATION OF BUSINESSES

From the observed differences between businesses at different stages of their life cycle in different markets and with different shares of their markets came the appealing concept of a simple system to classify businesses so that the best could be selected. A variety of classification systems has been tried, with varying success. No universal system has been accepted, but several approaches merit review.

THE GE STOPLIGHT MATRIX

General Electric, aided by McKinsey & Company, is credited with developing and applying the simple matrix shown in Figure 5-2. Divided into nine squares, this required the classification of the industry as high, me-

FIGURE 5-2 THE GENERAL ELECTRIC STOPLIGHT MATRIX*

	Industry Attractiveness		
Relative Business Strength	High	Medium	Low
High	(Go)	(Go)	(Caution)
Medium	(Go)	(Caution)	(Harvest)
Low	(Caution)	(Harvest)	(Harvest)

*Adapted from *Putting It All Together* by William E. Rothschild, Amacom 1976. Reprinted by permission of the author.

dium, or low in attractiveness, and the classification of that business as high, medium, or low in strength.

Businesses with high- and medium-strength positions in high-attractiveness industries, and high-strength positions in medium-attractiveness markets should have good profit prospects, and these three squares were colored green. The yellow squares, for caution, started with a business with an excellent position in an unattractive market, plus the business with a medium position in a mediocre market, and the business with a poor position in an attractive market. Those businesses with a medium or poor position in an unattractive market, or a poor position in a medium market could have a doubtful future; the squares were colored red, for "stop," and the idea was that either the business should find a way to move out of the red area, or GE should put it on the "harvest/divest" list and move out of that business.[2]

This simple matrix provides an excellent quick comparison, but deals with almost none of the subtleties of the business positions. It is a

---

[2] William E. Rothschild, *Putting It All Together: A Guide to Strategic Thinking* (New York: Amacom, 1976), pp. 141–162.

FIGURE 5-3 THE BCG PORTFOLIO PLANNING MATRIX*

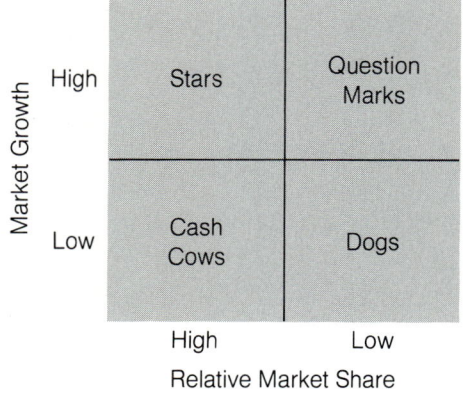

*Adapted from *The Product Portfolio Matrix*, © 1970, The Boston Consulting Group, Inc.

good summary device for highlighting areas needing attention, but does not provide an immediate guide to action.

THE BCG PORTFOLIO PLANNING MATRIX

Another well-known classification matrix is shown in Figure 5-3. This is a four-cell matrix widely publicized by the Boston Consulting Group. It classifies all markets according to high or low growth, and all businesses according to high or low share, with the four squares named for the most likely financial outcomes based on standard assumptions.[3] High-share businesses in high-growth markets are Stars, building importantly for the future, although investment requirements for their growth could be a cash drain in the present. High-share businesses in low-growth markets are Cash Cows. Investment needs should be low if market growth is past, profits should be good if share is high, and a substantial cash flow can be milked out of the business for use elsewhere.

Businesses with a low share in a high-growth market are Question Marks. At some point they would become too small to be viable relative to market growth; therefore their future is uncertain without a change in

---

[3] Malcolm B. Coate, "Elementary Portfolio Planning Models," in Thomas H. Naylor and Michele H. Mann (eds.), *Portfolio Planning and Corporate Strategy* (Oxford, Ohio: Planning Executives Institute, 1983), pp. 1–23; also, see Henderson and BCG books cited previously.

FIGURE 5-4   THE ARTHUR D. LITTLE PORTFOLIO MATRIX*

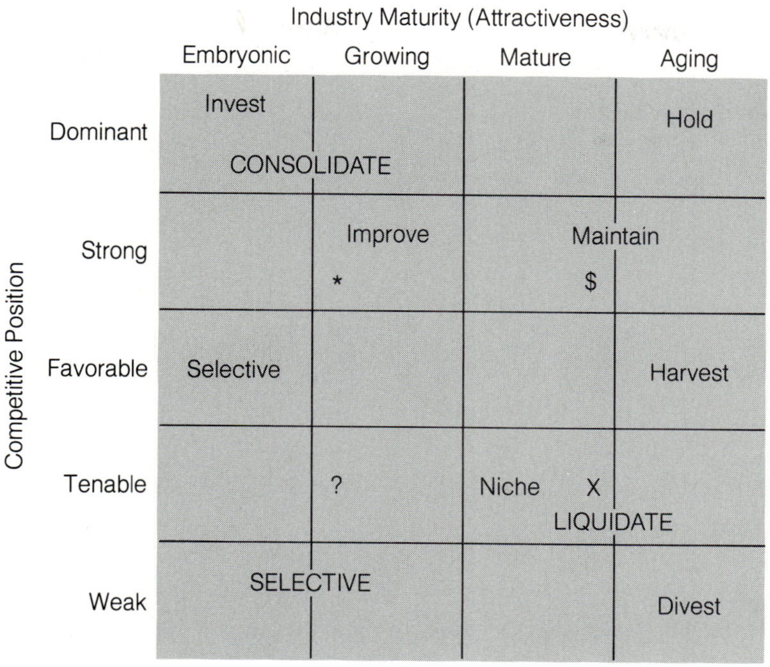

	Industry Maturity (Attractiveness)			
Competitive Position	Embryonic	Growing	Mature	Aging
Dominant	Invest	CONSOLIDATE		Hold
Strong		Improve *	Maintain $	
Favorable	Selective			Harvest
Tenable		?	Niche X LIQUIDATE	
Weak	SELECTIVE			Divest

*Quoted from "A System for Diversity" (Cambridge: Arthur D. Little, undated).

position, and very heavy investment is often required to build a major market share. Businesses with a low share in a low-growth market are the Dogs; they are unlikely ever to be very profitable; better to get out of the business if that is truly the outlook.

BCG has applied this matrix widely, and with success. Like the GE Stoplight, it provides a quick classification that can be very helpful, and it flags a standard group of management problems. Also like the GE Stoplight, it does not reach to fundamentals, and while it suggests problems, it does so only crudely and with standardized assumptions. Judgments based on this matrix alone could go astray.

ARTHUR D. LITTLE MATRIX

In reaction to the simple classification used by BCG, Arthur D. Little developed a somewhat more complex matrix for the same purpose, as shown in Figure 5-4. This matrix classified the market/industry into four categories: embryonic, growing, mature, or aging; and the competitive position of the business as weak, tenable, favorable, strong, or dominant.

FIGURE 5-5 CHARLES HOFER'S PORTFOLIO MATRIX*

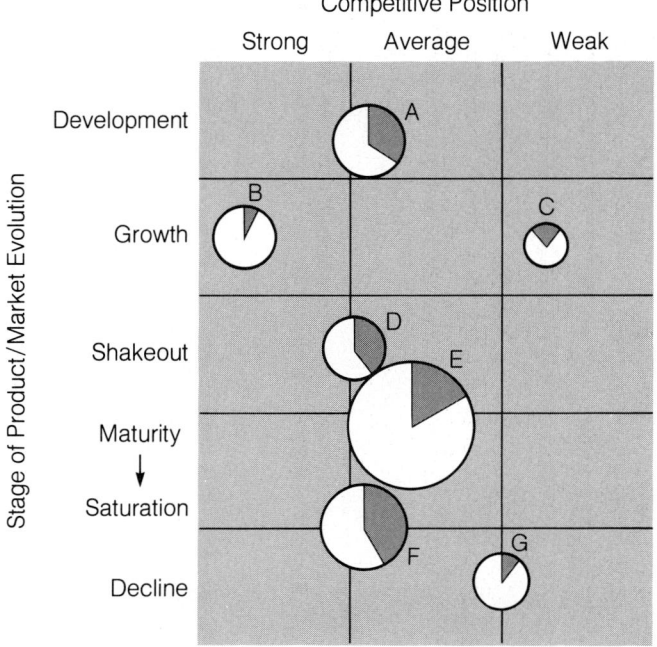

*"A Product/Market Evolution Portfolio Matrix" adapted from *Conceptual Constructs for Formulating Corporate and Business Strategy* by Charles W. Hofer, Case Publishing, #BP-0041, 1977. Copyright © 1977 by Charles W. Hofer. Reprinted by permission of the author.

Businesses then can fall into one of $4 \times 5 = 20$ boxes, and the follow-up action alternatives are more finely classified also. ADL has found the result useful, but it could still be the basis of premature action if underlying dimensions are not examined also.[4]

REFINEMENTS BY CHARLES HOFER

To use these matrix approaches for sound management decisions requires a great deal of separate analysis of the specific business and its strategic alternatives. Even so there are potential problems, and to remedy one class of them, Hofer developed an alternative matrix much richer in information, as illustrated in Figure 5-5. It is a 3×5 matrix with the competi-

---

[4] Coate, *ibid.*

FIGURE 5-6 STAGES OF BUSINESS GROWTH

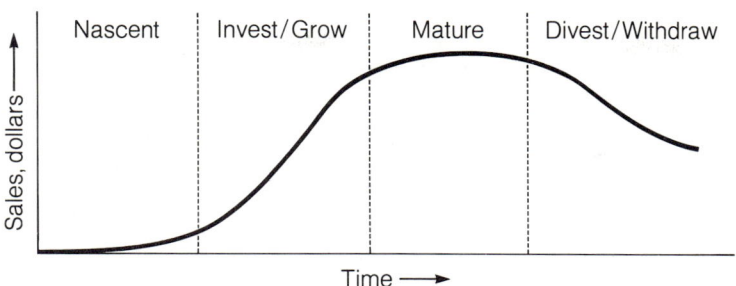

tive position classified across the top as strong, average, or weak, and the vertical axis classified according to stage of product/market evolution as development, growth, shakeout, maturity/saturation, and decline. The additional information comes from plotting each specific business within the enterprise as a circle proportional to the size of the market it participates in, with a wedge inside of the circle indicating market share held. Thus the users of the matrix see not only the square into which the business or product is sorted, but how large the market is and what share the entrant holds.[5]

STAGES OF BUSINESS GROWTH

Another approach to classification of businesses is according to where they are in their life cycles. In one such system, also developed for General Electric, new businesses start at the **nascent** stage, move into an **invest/grow** phase, then into a **mature** phase, and finally into a **divest/withdraw** phase, as shown in Figure 5-6. In the first two phases they normally represent a cash drain. Even though the invest/grow stage is normally one of high profit margins, current asset requirements grow rapidly with the business, and good development of the overall potential usually requires high fixed-asset investment also.

During the mature phase investment requirements normally drop, profits continue, and the business generates cash that can begin to repay the investment and fund new ventures. Then as the stage of maturity advances, profits begin to fall and the future of the business becomes less and less attractive. At some point the harvest/divest stage is reached,

---

[5] Coate, *ibid.*

where the management attention shifts to recovery of as much of the invested capital as possible, whether by liquidation or divestment.

These stages are real, recognizable, and useful in managing the businesses. However, a given stage has no fixed time span, so that one business may stay in the same stage of development for many years while another moves to the later stages rapidly.

PIMS = PROFIT IMPACT OF MARKETING STRATEGY

Another interesting comparative tool is PIMS, a system developed for General Electric under the direction of Sidney Schoeffler, who then continued it as an independent effort.[6] It is not a classification, but a comparative measure often used with the classification systems summarized here. Subscribers give PIMS confidential sales and other financial data from their operations. By compiling and compositing this information for specific lines of business, average industry data not otherwise available is produced and distributed back to the subscribers as a comparative yardstick. PIMS is widely used, particularly in the longer-established and more mature business sectors. It can help in evaluating a business by giving the management a specific measure of the difference between current industry average sales and profit performance and performance of their own individual business.

Purpose of a Classification. The idea of classifying businesses into some sort of taxonomy is either to discover which ones to invest in, as will be discussed in the next section, or to manage individual businesses better. As businesses go through stages of growth, and as their financial characteristics change from stage to stage, both those directly in charge of a business and their superiors could benefit from understanding the subtleties of each situation.

General Electric once made a point of the fact that a different sort of manager is required to build a fast-growing business effectively, versus maximizing the cash flow out of a mature business, and that these different types of managers must be measured against different performance standards in order to provide adequate performance incentives for each. This is a difficult, frontier area, of using different standards for performance under different business conditions, but the need is real and a number of firms are attempting measurements and rewards on such a basis.

---

[6] PIMS services are offered by the Strategic Planning Institute, 955 Massachusetts Avenue, Cambridge, Massachusetts 02138.

PORTFOLIO MANAGEMENT

Portfolio management is named for the investment analogy, since management of a diverse enterprise can look at its various businesses as a portfolio of investments. Just as a mutual fund manager sells and buys securities, management can shift its investment according to the relative promise of the various alternatives. When an enterprise consists of a wide variety of distinct business units, the management can use this diversity as the basis for investment and divestment decisions, shifting its portfolio of businesses in the direction of maximum opportunity for growth and profit.

This is exactly the way that a closed-end investment fund and many holding companies operate, except that an operating company also can redirect the energies of the individual businesses rather than just buying or selling their stock. This could give the operating management a substantial advantage over an outside investor, but requires a considerable degree of involvement with each business to achieve that advantage.

STRATEGIC BUSINESS UNITS

If a management is going to judge its businesses independently according to their individual investment merit, this requires that the businesses be organized as independent entities. General Electric was credited with the modern launching of this process when it broke its organization into a series of strategic business units, or SBUs—each intended as a free-standing and more or less independent entity within GE. The SBUs were to be given full profit responsibility based on their approved plans, held accountable for the outcome, and funded or divested according to their relative promise as an investment opportunity for the parent corporation, as discussed further in Chapter 11. Top management guidance was to be accomplished through the interaction as the business plans for each strategic business unit were prepared, discussed, and approved, and through the overall management operating system and reward structure.

The stages-of-growth type of analysis described above was one of the tools for gauging where in such a portfolio of businesses money should and should not be invested. These growth stages are valuable tools, because they help to emphasize the necessary shifts in business and investment management from stage to stage. Where rapid investment in an invest/grow business is normal and its absence suggests mismanagement, a mature business normally requires little capital, and the reasons for significant investment should be examined with care.

Portfolio management or some equivalent is a logical part of the overall resource allocation process in any diverse business, and portfolio management techniques are a distinct advance. However, they have made it easy for some managements to become very remote from the underly-

FIGURE 5-7 NAYLOR'S STRATEGY MATRIX

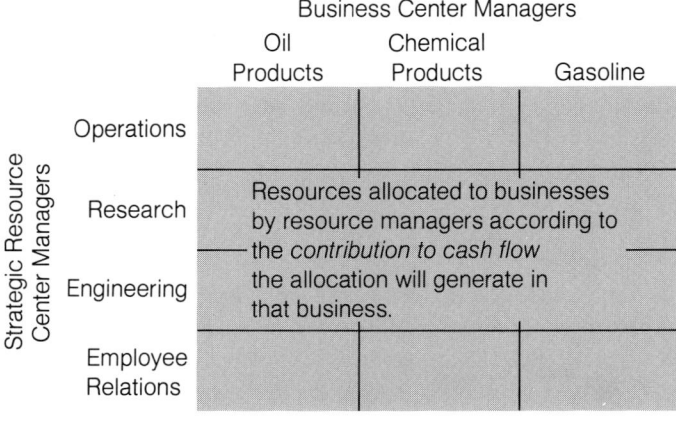

ing businesses, and the relatively poor stock market evaluation of highly diverse companies appears to reflect disappointment with the results.

A practical problem in applying portfolio management concepts in a large enterprise is the difficulty in tracking performance of large numbers of business units. Haspeslagh reported the tendency of major companies to reduce the number of units considered by top management to an average of 30 by grouping them together. To a degree this defeats the purpose, since the resulting top management judgments are based on a composite of several underlying strategic business units that may have quite different profit and market characteristics.[7]

THE STRATEGY MATRIX

In some large enterprises separate strategic business units cannot be created, because of interdependencies between them, use of common facilities, and joint economies of scale. This means that these businesses cannot use the standard portfolio management approaches, because these do not recognize such interdependencies. Naylor developed a strategy matrix technique for such applications[8] that applies some of the concepts underlying matrix management to the planning problems of a diverse enterprise, as illustrated in Figure 5-7. In such a company business centers

---

[7] Phillippe Haspeslagh, "Experience with Portfolio Planning: The Results of a Survey," in Thomas Naylor and Michele H. Mann (eds.), *Portfolio Planning and Corporate Strategy* (Oxford, Ohio: Planning Executives Institute, 1983), pp. 42–82.

[8] Thomas H. Naylor, "The Strategy Matrix," in Thomas H. Naylor and Michele H. Mann

are defined to manage specific components of the marketing activity and any other easily associated activities, as well as resource centers. The resource centers manage joint resources, such as a petroleum refinery, that send outputs to several businesses, and allocate the output according to which business can achieve the greatest profit contribution as a result. The system of allocations is reviewed by top management during overall planning and in case of any dispute.

SHAREHOLDER VALUE

The owners of a firm are very concerned about what their investment is worth. Shareholder value, as a measurement standard, is a simple development of this ownership concept based on the profitability of the firm, how investors view it, and its debt/equity ratio.

PROFITABILITY

For most shareholders the simplest measure of shareholder value is what they can get by selling their stock. The stock of many major corporations is owned by members of the investing public and is routinely traded on the various stock exchanges at a price based on a day-by-day equilibrium of supply and demand. The present and anticipated corporate profits often influence this price significantly. Therefore the success of a particular management strategy can be measured, at least in part, by its success in producing these profits, and success in increasing these profits is normally reflected through a higher price. Unfortunately stock prices are affected by very many other things, so that the correlation between corporate earnings and stock price is often imperfect.

MARKET APPRAISAL

Not all profits are valued by stock market investors in the same way; some groups of stocks are valued highly in relationship to their earnings and other groups valued less. Also, the stocks of individual members of an industrial grouping are bid up more or less. Investors see different

---

(eds.), *Portfolio Planning and Corporate Strategy* (Oxford, Ohio: Planning Executives Institute, 1983), pp. 31–41. Also see Thomas H. Naylor, *The Strategy Matrix* (New York: Basic Books, 1986).

companies and industries as having different potential and value them differently.

DEBT/EQUITY RATIO

Most successful corporations can increase profits for shareholders in the near term by borrowing money and using it to buy back a part of their stock. Under present tax laws dividends to stockholders must be paid out of after-tax profits, but interest costs can be deducted directly from the business income. Thus, a 10 percent interest rate costs the business 10 percent, but a 10 percent dividend rate costs the business 15 percent to 20 percent, depending on the state and federal income tax rates then in effect since the income taxes must be paid out of a sum large enough to leave 10 percent after taxes. A debt-free corporation can make its stock more attractive, and therefore higher priced, by borrowing and using the money to buy back its stock, up to the point where investors begin to worry that the firm might have difficulty meeting interest payments in case of a downturn. Dividend payments are optional for management but interest payments are not, and a firm unable to pay its creditors goes bankrupt. Therefore any risk of an interest payment default will concern investors and depress the price they are willing to pay for the stock.

MANAGING FOR SHAREHOLDER VALUE

The shareholder value management concept is that the management should create value in the firm by each investment of its capital, manage its portfolio of businesses for strong profit growth and in such a way as to be perceived favorably by the investment community, and use debt to the extent that it will help increase earnings per share without jeopardizing the favorable appraisal of future prospects. The targets of many corporate takeovers in the past several years have been firms whose would-be acquirers believed that their breakup or restructuring would bring a substantial increase in the stock price. In many cases large profits resulted from these takeovers, takeover attempts have multiplied, and many other managements have become sensitive to the need to manage for shareholder value. Management can not prevent its firm's stock price from moving up or down with the broader market, but it can influence the way its own stock is compared with others in that market by the way it directs the firm, so that managing for shareholder value is becoming an important business strategy dimension.

| FIGURE 5-8 | BUSINESS CHARACTERISTICS AS FUNDAMENTALS |

Learning curves
- marching down to lower costs
- pitfalls in application

Business life cycles
- stages of growth
- changing stages

Classification of businesses
- GE stoplight matrix
- BCG matrix
- ADL matrix
- Hofer's matrix
- Stages of business growth
- PIMS

Portfolio management
- strategic business units
- troubles with SBUs
- Naylor's strategy matrix
- shareholder value

LINKING STRATEGY TO THE NATURE OF THE BUSINESS

LINKING STRATEGY TO THE NATURE OF THE BUSINESS

This chapter has examined the nature of the business and its life cycle, of learning curve and portfolio management concepts as a part of the necessary considerations in strategy design, as illustrated in Figure 5-8, and as related to the planning-strategy-action sequence in Figure 5-9.

The purpose of all of this is as a prelude to the strategy design process that follows. As developed in the first three chapters, strategy design requires a fitting together of different types and levels of strategy itself, as related to the mission and goals. But before discussing design of strategy and the sources of energy on which it draws, it is important to be clear on its foundations; a sound strategy rests on three points like a tripod, supported by the fundamentals of the product or service as discussed in Chapter 3, in its correctly calculated relationship to the competition and the market as discussed in Chapter 4, and to the business itself, with which this chapter has dealt. This tripod is illustrated in Figure 5-10.

QUESTIONS FOR ANALYSIS AND DISCUSSION

1. If the learning curve slope for a chemical product is 0.8 and the cost after the first 100 batches is $100 per batch, *approximately* how many batches will have to be produced before a good management can be expected to bring the cost down to $50 per batch?

FIGURE 5–9 BUSINESS CHARACTERISTICS AS BASIC TO STRATEGY DESIGN

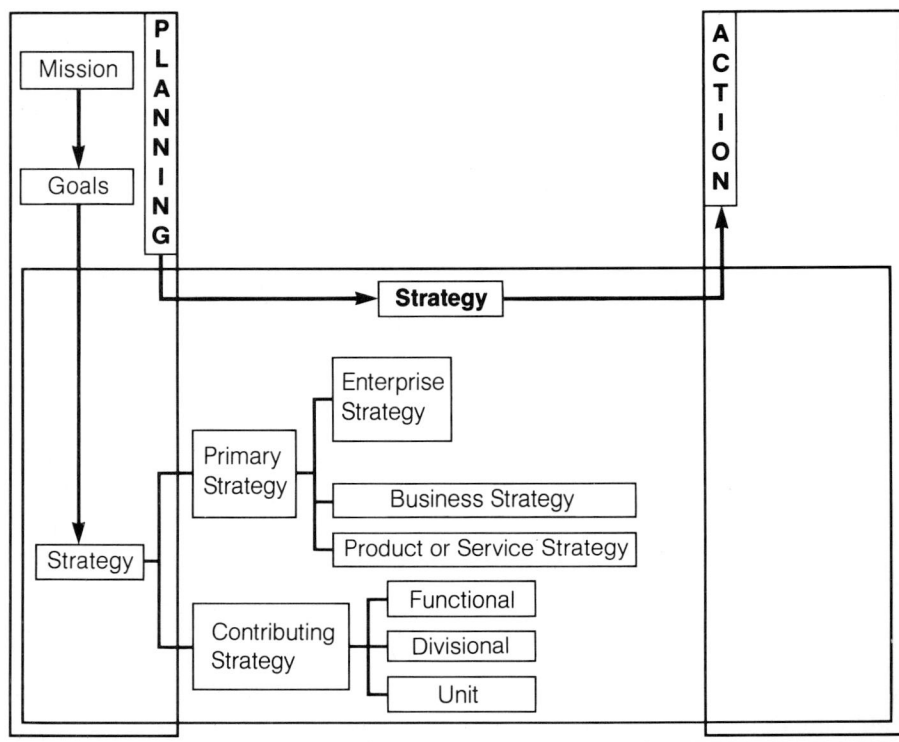

2. List five or six individual business units (independent companies or SBU's within larger companies) and classify them as best you can:
   (a) in the GE stoplight matrix
   (b) in the BCG portfolio planning matrix
   (c) in the Arthur D. Little portfolio matrix
   (d) in the Charles Hofer portfolio matrix
   (e) according to the stage of growth of the business

FIGURE 5-10 THE STRATEGY TRIPOD

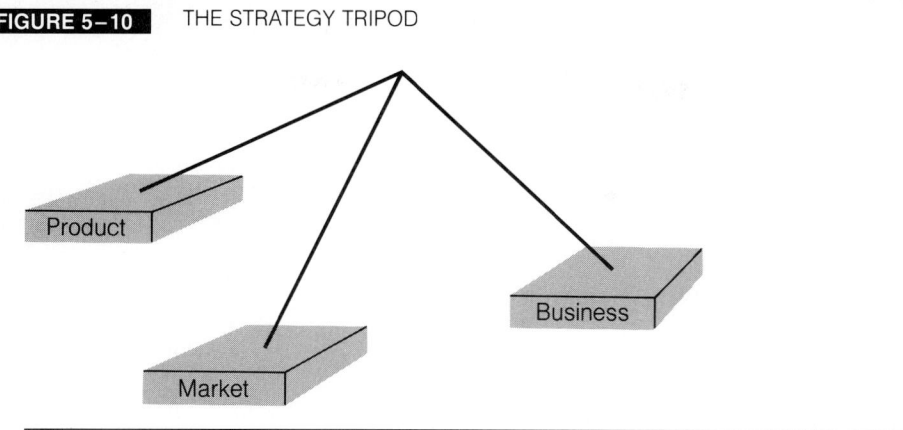

3. List two or three businesses within large companies and explain how the Naylor strategy matrix might be useful to corporate management in that case because of the difficulty in defining a separate strategic business unit.

FOR FURTHER INFORMATION

Naylor, Thomas H., & Michele H. Mann (eds.), *Portfolio Planning and Corporate Strategy* (Oxford, Ohio: Planning Executives Institute, 1983).

An interesting summary of different portfolio planning techniques.

Reimann, Bernard C., *Managing for Value* (Oxford, Ohio: The Planning Forum, 1987).

Basic techniques of managing in such a way as to increase shareholder value, with reference to the writings and approaches employed by the major factors in this field.

"Strategies for Value-Based Planning," *Planning Review* special issues: January-February 1988 and March-April 1988.

Current contributions from the major writers in the field with references to their previous works.

CASE 9
THE PEOPLES POTIONS PHARMACEUTICAL COMPANY

The Peoples Potions Pharmaceutical Company had been founded long ago by a group of successful doctors and other professionals who felt that the cost of pharmaceuticals was too high. The company they founded succeeded and won a place in the market, but had never fulfilled its founders' dreams of offering low-cost products. Peoples (or 3Ps, as it was nicknamed in the marketplace) had a modest generic drug line competitive with other generic drugs, but for products of its own development the rising costs of regulatory compliance and of the research activity itself had prevented any real breakthrough to lower prices. But when 3Ps started to manufacture niceomycin, the directors thought they finally saw a place where the company could cut the cost of prescriptions.

Niceomycin was a broad spectrum antibiotic with a remarkably wide range of effectiveness, few if any side effects, and the potential for replacing many of the older antibiotics with a newer, safer product. It was very expensive, because it was a fermentation product very difficult to manufacture. The product itself had been known for many years and could not be protected with patents, although its medical importance had only recently been recognized. Several pharmaceutical companies were manufacturing niceomycin already, in each case by a process of their own development which they protected with process patents.

An independent researcher had approached 3Ps with an idea for a better process for niceomycin manufacture. The fermentation pilot plant had confirmed the potential and added improvements of its own. 3Ps and the researcher agreed on a fair payment for the ideas. The legal department found that the proposed niceomycin process was not covered by any existing patents and believed that 3Ps could protect several features of it with patents of its own, so that the company would be able to recover the investment necessary to build a manufacturing plant. The investment was a large one for 3Ps, but the project was very attractive both financially and as a chance to bring down the cost of a very important drug. 3Ps did not have a good enough pharmaceutical product sales and distribution system of its own to handle the output of a full-sized plant, but there was a good market for the bulk antibiotic, and 3Ps would primarily supply this market.

Even though some use could be made of existing equipment, and even with intensive expediting by 3Ps engineering and purchasing executives, it was 18 months before the first production could start, and another year before the new plant could be really complete and ready to run at capacity. During the interim the pilot plant had found yet other improvements in the proposed niceomycin process, the use of the drug had expanded beyond the capacity of the companies already producing it, and 3Ps' management became more and more anxious to have niceomycin to sell.

The startup itself was, by industry standards, a good one. Incomplete as it was, the plant was intended to operate initially at 35 percent of its design capacity, and it reached this output rate after only three months. There had been lost batches, imperfect process steps, and equipment that failed to work properly, but for a totally new process and a difficult product, the startup was an achievement which earned the respect of those who knew about it.

Niceomycin sales were easy, because the product was in short supply. At the going price it began to repay the 3Ps investment. "Let's wait until we have the plant finished," said the president, "before we talk about cutting the price."

At the same time production management began a sustained drive to increase output. This was not according to the engineering timetable, which showed that the next 30 percent of plant capacity would not be ready for another 6 months. But even though the new equipment was not ready, why not try to get more out of the old? And to make those engineers hurry!

More workers were hired, and overtime began to be used in the niceomycin plant as 3Ps had never used it before. In a market begging to buy more of a very expensive product, the marginal return was so large that if an increase in antibiotic output resulted, the extra labor costs were lost in the rounding. At that point the president calculated that every extra milligram of niceomycin they produced brought in an extra dollar.

One day an engineer came to the plant manager with an idea for installing a duplicate centrifuge at one step to increase yields. It would produce one more gram per cycle of niceomycin from fractions now going to waste. The plant manager made the engineer go through the yield calculations three times, and then called in the head of the development lab to check the yield data. It looked entirely sound. The whole group trouped into the 3Ps president's office, interrupting his appointments without any apology; he reviewed the proposal, gave his verbal approval, and sent them to purchasing. The centrifuge was ordered by phone a few minutes later, it happened to be available, and a truck was sent to pick it up. The necessary tanks and piping were standard equipment. Some of the accessories were made in the machine shop, because they would not otherwise have been available for six weeks. With round-the-clock overtime the construction moved rapidly, and the new centrifuge was ready for startup in two weeks.

The plant manager had been following the job closely and when he went out to watch the new unit going through its paces, he called aside the project engineer who had started the whole thing. "John, this idea of yours just cost us $100,000, and accounting says we could have done it for half if we hadn't been in such a bloody hurry. But the idea was to get an extra kilo of niceomycin, and it's worth it. I want you to keep track and send me a report when this thing has saved the first 100 grams. At $1 a milligram, that will be $100,000, and your toy will have paid for itself. Once it is in the black, I'll put in a recommendation that something appropriate be added for this when your next bonus is calculated."

Engineering managed to gain two months on completion of the next 30 percent of plant capacity, and by that time the output from the first 35 percent of the plant had already reached 50 percent of the original design, due to process improvements and extra people and equipment to raise yields. Startup was smooth, since the process was already running in the other equipment, except that the training of the necessary new staff caused minor delays. The final increment of plant capacity was not delivered early, because there had been so many process changes that it was all that engineering could do to fit them in without being late; but by the time that the full plant was running, output was at 150 percent of the original design and rising. As with many other things difficult to manufacture, good operators found ways to improve on the original concepts. And as with many other fermentation products, the development group began to find ways to raise the yields significantly.

A year later the president and the vice-president of marketing were wondering about price cuts. The market had shown no sign of saturating; niceomycin was still being sold as fast as it could be made and shipped. And, as a by-product of its process improvements, many doctors preferred the 3Ps product because it was much purer than the product from its competitors. With improvements in the fermentations and another $1 million invested in the refining equipment, the plant was just shifting over to a new process that would double its output. The president took the pricing problem to the next directors' meeting, and they decided on a 10 percent cut due to the increased efficiency of the new unit, which was fully on line by then, and authorized another 25 percent cut at the discretion of the president, when he felt that the plant was running smoothly at its new capacity.

The second price cut was put into effect three months later. The first price cut had been immediately matched by 3Ps' competitors, as everyone had expected, and the second cut was matched also, except for one company that cut 35 percent; 3Ps and the rest of the market then matched the cut, and the 3Ps president called for a briefing by marketing, marketing research, and the technical people on the competition and the competitive processes. It turned out that competitive intelligence was difficult because each competitor used a different process, and because the rapid flow of process improvements had increased plant capacities and (presumably) reduced costs. But 3Ps appeared to be the largest single producer and clearly had the best product. The competitor with the aggressive pricing policy was another large producer, and there were unconfirmed rumors of inventory buildup there because doctors preferred the 3Ps product. Except for this, the market was still expanding as fast as the producers could increase their output.

The 3Ps president then had a meeting with the plant manager, chief engineer, and chief accountant. "We have the first hints that this will become a competitive market," he said, "And we should be thinking about how we will bring our costs down so we can compete better." They talked for two hours about alternatives, and each went away with a work assignment. The plant manager and the chief accountant each had undertaken studies related to cutting costs, and the chief engineer was to find out what the economies would be if 3Ps doubled its capacity again, to give it a commanding share of the total niceomycin output.

A big increase in capacity did not show the expected additional cost savings, and 3Ps' directors did not feel comfortable investing more in this one product line. The engineering and accounting reviews of the operation did show worthwhile economies, however, and the savings began. The operation had been staffed for startup, including normal startup troubles, so that fewer operators were needed for smooth operation, even at the higher capacities that had been reached. Further, the emphasis on output at any cost had brought a few bad habits. Corrections occurred, excess people were quietly reassigned, and costs improved even as output continued to increase with more process improvements.

Near the end of the next year 3Ps' marketing saw real signs for the first time that there was more niceomycin in the market than doctors wanted, although 3Ps had not yet felt any slackening of its demand. The president of 3Ps announced another 25 percent price cut, justified internally by the large savings of his cost improvement program, and the price stayed at this level for some time. While some competitive products were offered for less, the difference in product quality was now well enough recognized to bring a difference. But also, someone had found another way to match the quality of the 3Ps product without violating its patents, and the industry rapidly re-standardized at this quality level except for the two smallest producers, who could not achieve the quality increase and dropped out of niceomycin manufacture.

3Ps had a hard decision, which took many months. The head of its fermentation pilot plant and the technical people responsible for the rapid development of the new niceomycin processes proposed a $10 million expenditure for a new pilot plant. They justified this on the basis that they had done essentially all they could with conventional equipment, and that large additional improvements might be just out of reach. They wanted new and special equipment and an increased development budget to keep up the improvement of the process. Development costs were and always had been a significant share of niceomycin costs. With the proposed budget these costs would rise noticeably, just when 3Ps was becoming concerned about price competition in the market. A $10 million expenditure was a big investment for 3Ps, which was not a giant company like some of its competitors, and there had been an argument for several years about how long the rapid improvement of the niceomycin process could be maintained, even by the best development group; some of the outside directors asked how there could still be room for any more yield improvements.

The end result, after many stormy meetings, was that 3Ps decided it could not justify investing another $10 million in development equipment just then. The director of development announced that there was nothing else he could do without new equipment and resigned. Within the next few months several other key development people left also, program planning became less clear, and top management lost confidence in the effort. 3Ps decided to suspend efforts at major improvements in the niceomycin production process, and cut staff and budgets accordingly. Plant operation became easier and more routine because there was less experimental work, and as the routine was refined, further cuts in production staff became possible.

When price weakness again appeared in the niceomycin market, the president looked at his cost position and cut prices another 25 percent, and 10 percent a few weeks after that. At this level the market seemed to stabilize, and 3Ps continued to operate essentially at capacity. Costs had stopped falling with the end of development, but they were good, and margins were good. There were rumors about process improvements elsewhere, but nothing anyone could substantiate.

Then the president of 3Ps got an offer from the former development director of another company to develop a better process for 3Ps. In exchange for a generous employment contract he would guarantee certain results that happened to be about twice as good as 3Ps was getting in its routine production; and it was quite clear that what he was really offering to do was to give them someone else's production process. This offer was highly unethical and probably illegal. 3Ps would not deal with such a man, but the indications that the competition had got so far ahead were very disturbing. 3Ps sought in every way it could to get a clearer picture of the competitive situation, and as the months passed it became more definite that its process was no longer the best.

The president asked for proposals from his own people, and also from several outside consultants, trying to find a sound course of action. But several of the proposals boiled down to a large pilot plant investment such as the $10 million that had been turned down, plus the need to rebuild the development staff and regain lost time. And the niceomycin market had begun to get soft again. A price war started, and while 3Ps matched several successive 10 percent price cuts without cutting its margins dangerously, 3Ps' costs had begun to creep up a bit with inflation, and the niceomycin market began to look less attractive.

3Ps' management decided it was not wise to try to catch up in niceomycin development at this point in time. The company did not have the excess resources to risk, and the market was now growing less profitable. And, predictably, the niceomycin market became less and less profitable for 3Ps, as costs crept up and prices either held stable or fell during the occasional confrontation between companies as competitors improved their processes. Soon 3Ps' plant was running below a breakeven basis as prices continued to fall—that is, making more running than shut down, but losing money according to the accounting statements. When the first major capital improvements were needed, it was shut down for good, just over ten years after its startup.

As the 3Ps president reflected on the flow of events, he regretted that they had not plunged, and doubled capacity at the peak of their success—although it had looked very risky at the time. But he reminded himself that they had contributed a lot toward cutting the price of niceomycin, even at the expense of being driven out of the business.

QUESTIONS

1. Define the various stages of growth through which the 3Ps niceomycin business passed.
2. A bulk antibiotic is normally a commodity product. How did 3Ps manage to establish a specialty position, and what happened to it?

CASE 10 RUCTION RESOURCES, INC.

Edward Ruction III had just drawn a tough travel assignment. He was an up-and-coming young assistant controller in the headquarters group of Ruction Resources, a major conglomerate enterprise. The first Edward Ruction was a blasting contractor whose E. Ruction Excavators became known for the most ingenious and creative use of explosives in the world of construction, until the firm had grown into general contracting and chemical plant design. The business continued to prosper and Ruction Senior found that the cash flow generated by its success was very substantial. A trader at heart, he used the cash as opening stakes, and began to buy and sell companies. Finally, five years earlier, he had changed the corporate name to Ruction Resources, promoted himself to Chairman of the Board, and turned over the operation of the construction company to his son.

A number of Ruction relatives worked for Ruction Resources, but Ruction Senior was very anxious that there be no favoritism, to the point that it was harder to make progress in the company as a Ruction relative than otherwise; of Ruction Senior's four sons, one had been fired by his father, and two had left voluntarily after several years in the ranks. The remaining son, Edward Ruction Junior, by all reports an extremely able executive, had risen slowly through the ranks to head the construction company. His son, Edward Ruction III, was one of five of his generation of the family working in various parts of Ruction Resources. He had worked three years as an engineer before going back for an MBA in finance, where he was high in his class at a prestigious school and had many offers. One of the best was from Ruction Resources financial staff. He talked to his father, who told him: "The controller's staff is one of the best and hardest training grounds for a young executive that I know of. And it will be 25% harder for you because of the family name. But if you like the idea of being in the family firm, and are willing to work a little, try it for a while. And after a year or two you will start getting calls from recruiters, because they are always looking for a Ruction graduate to fill a top spot for a demanding client."

Edward III spent two very hard years in a very competitive financial analysis group, survived with honors, and had been promoted to assistant controller almost a year earlier. There were a number of assistant controllers, because the controller needed always to have a trained assistant to send on an important mission, or to substitute for him if he had to be in two places at once. But Edward Ruction III drew the difficult travel assignment—what the staff called the annual review of misfit capital requests.

Ruction Resources consisted of the construction firm, the only company directly operated by Ruction, and several layers of executives who served as reporting points for the various businesses Ruction had acquired over the years. These executives were responsible for those businesses, but the corporate staff also was required to profile the needs and behavior of each business, and the line and staff views were aired together in a series of meetings Ruction Senior chaired every August. The strong opinion of Ruction Senior was that capital appropriations should be related to the stage of development of the business that requested them, and proposed capital budgets were reviewed from this perspective. Wherever the requests did not fit these expectations, the business went on the controller's Misfit List.

When the list was complete, the controller gave it to one of the assistant controllers, who then had three months to visit the companies involved, do any necessary background work, and return with a recommendation to the controller (and to Ruction Senior) as to why that business should or should not be making capital requests outside of the pattern the growth stage suggested. Ruction Senior had been an early disciple of the BCG portfolio analysis approach, and still used it as one of several ways of looking at a business. But he had seen mistakes, some of them his own, from rote application of the analysis; hence the Misfit List and several other cross-checks in the corporate strategy process. The misfit report would be reviewed very carefully, and in the presentation meeting Edward would have to defend his conclusions to the responsible General Managers, Ruction Senior, and the other management levels in between. His being chosen for this assignment was a large compliment from the controller and a larger personal challenge.

BUILDING MORE LEGS ON A CASH COW

Edward decided to allow time to visit each business twice, and set off almost immediately on the first round of travel. He had to go to the Far East, and decided to learn about retailing in the southwest on his way. One Ruction subsidiary was a major established regional department store. It was the leader in its metropolitan region and had made a successful shift with earlier suburban growth; today it had the original downtown store, still the largest single retail outlet in the region, another downtown store on the industrial side of town, and five suburban stores in shopping malls around the outside of the metropolitan area. The stores were all doing well individually, as was the business as a whole. The business volume was growing year to year just a little faster than the area grew, even though outside consultants kept saying that the store, already dominant, was unlikely to raise its market share any further.

The business was generating a great deal of cash every year, and had all of the characteristics of a cash cow. It had a good physical plant which was being kept modern and attractive, a stable and growing business, no reason for significant investment, and appeared able to generate a significant stream of cash indefinitely. But the president of the subsidiary was suddenly proposing to build three more stores, opening one in each of the next three years; a cash cow should not need that sort of investment, and that got the business on the Misfit List and on Edward's travel agenda.

The president of the subsidiary was not surprised to see Edward. His friends in the controller's department had reminded him of the misfit capital routine (all Ruction managers had been exposed to it) and told him to get his ammunition ready, first for an assistant controller, and later for Ruction Senior. Edward got to the point very directly: "I am sure you have good reasons for wanting to build new stores. Please help me to understand them; I have to make a recommendation to Mr. Ruction, and if I agree with you, I will help support the request."

This led off into a discussion of shifts in the demographic base of the region. Edward wanted to see the data and spent three days talking with the analysts who had prepared the proposal and with city, state, and local officials, and in visiting various parts of the area. The president's argument was that the metropolitan region was growing geographically, primarily to the southwest, as a result of a new expressway, several new industrial plants, and traffic generated by a new theme park. To maintain its historic role and market share, the store would have to serve this new area; hence the proposal to build more stores.

The expansion proposal itself was very well organized and executed, as might be expected from a very well-run business. The demographic shift seemed well established, as something already occurring that would have its impact on shopping habits very soon; the proposal seemed timely. The major issue Edward found was whether this growth was expansion of the metropolitan area beyond that which had been expected, or a simple population shift. For the business this meant the difference between new people and new business to pay for the new stores, and adding more capital just to follow the old business to a new site. He was pleased that the local analysts had worked very hard to get an answer to this, but was not convinced by their data. Together they planned a further study, with the encouragement of the president of the store chain. As Edward told him: "You have a good case for needing new stores, and if they will bring in new business, then the return on this capital is attractive and not many years away. But if all of this is just to keep up with present customers who are moving, you will cut the cash flow from the store almost to zero during the expansion and be no better off at the end."

AN ELECTRONIC STAR WITH GROWTH PROBLEMS

Edward's next stop was at a semiconductor plant in South Korea. The plant manager spoke perfect English, as did enough of the staff so that Edward could get along; he had learned only a little Korean, and was very concerned about whether he could get to the heart of business problems he might find.

The situation was that Ruction had made a very timely investment in a firm then building its Korean plant. This firm had found a new niche in the semiconductor market, the plant was to serve it, and all had worked out according to plan so far. Edward found a busy, bustling place, as he expected, for he knew that the plant was running at capacity. The capital requests had included plant expansion, to double output within two years, but with back orders already building, a much higher rate of expansion was needed if the firm was going to maintain its place in the market. Any star business should expand faster than the market it is in, and this one was not; hence it was on the Misfit List and Edward stopped to see what was going on.

He spent a busy week watching the operation, talking with the engineers and managers, and getting a sense of the pace and progress. It was a good operation, but under great pressure. Many people were working at the edge of their abilities, as measured by training and experience. The plant manager put it this way: "We have to expand as fast as we can, and we will. But if I push too fast, it might all fall down. I will bring the output up as fast as I can. My forecast says how fast I think I can do it, and I am willing to be judged by whether I meet it. But we have so few well-trained people to do the training, and so many that are still learning themselves, that we just can't expand any faster."

WHEN DOES A STAR BECOME A DOG?

Edward next visited the only Australian subsidiary Ruction Resources had at that moment. This was an electronic thermometer company, which could have been anywhere in the world but happened to be in Australia. Ruction Senior had met the principals sometime during a visit to a major plant construction job the firm was completing. He had become fascinated with the concept of an electronic thermometer, which needed only a bit of capital before it took over the medical world. That had been sometime ago, and the intervening years had been busy and, for Ruction Resources, expensive. The thermometer prototypes had come through only a bit behind schedule, had gotten a very good reception from doctors and nurses, and the decision had been made to go ahead and build a plant. Unfortunately, the plant had not been able to make anything like the prototypes. The equipment had been rebuilt twice, but the market the business had developed so far was being supplied with handmade thermometers that cost approximately three times the sales price—as a temporary measure, of course, until the plant got going.

Edward spent two weeks in the thermometer works. He wanted to get thoroughly acquainted with the situation, the equipment problems, and the outlook for solving them. As an engineer, he wanted to understand how the prototype manufacture could have gone so well and the plant startup so poorly. He was not able to establish the facts about the prototypes well enough to make a public conclusion, but he went home suspecting that they had all been handmade, and that someone had lied to Ruction management about this. In any case, he was not impressed with the plans to modify the machinery a third time to get into production; it sounded very much like what had been tried before. This subsidiary was a problem! He started inquiries to get additional data on competition and the market, so it would be waiting for him when he got back to Ruction Resources headquarters.

TENNIS QUESTIONS

Edward's first U.S. stop as he came back around the world was a tennis racquet plant in southern Florida. This was a prosperous small operation slated for rapid growth. It got on the Misfit List because the capital requirements were far too small for the projected growth rate. Edward found a neat, well-run operation, except that it was small. He asked the plant manager about expansion plans, got an evasive answer, and then pulled out a copy of the expansion plan the manager had submitted to corporate headquarters two years earlier.

The plant manager blushed, avoided the question, and they sparred some more. Finally Edward asked: "Do you want me to report that you have no plans for expansion?" The manager did not. "Then you will have to tell me what they are and how they will work out." The manager wanted to talk about this over dinner. They had dinner, and an after-dinner drink, and then another.

Finally the plant manager said: "You don't look like the sort of chap who will go away without an answer, and you know, that's really what I have been hoping for." Then he began to talk about tennis racquets, how they are made, why the Ruction Racquets were so special, and finally got to the point. "Our secret is in the core of the handle. My father made racquets with a piece of Jackson Elm in the center of the handle. Then one day he and I discovered that Mission Elm is even better, and you are now only the fourth person in the world who knows what that last piece of wood is. It really makes a difference—that's why there is a waiting list for the racquets we build, and we could sell ten times as many. But Mission Elm is hard to get. When I planned that expansion, I knew where to buy a grove that we could cut on a sustained yield basis—but then there was a brush fire that killed the elms, and somebody bought the site for a shopping center. And I have scoured the whole range of the Mission Elm without finding another grove to replace it."

"Then you either have to find another material, or keep the racquet production at the present level?"

"Yes."

"What hopes for another material? Wood? or plastic? or a laminate?"

It turned out that essentially all of the natural woods had been tested and most of the commercially available plastic materials. No one seemed ever to have tried to build a laminate to match the specific characteristics of Mission Elm, however, and no one at the plant seemed to know very much about the newer plastics materials technology. The next morning when he and the plant manager resumed the conversation over coffee, Edward put it this way: "There is an unexplored potential for making a plastic material or plastic laminate to your specifications, and I want to recommend that someone very good in plastic materials technology spend some time on the problem, to see if he or she can help you. Otherwise, you can't expand to compete in the mass market for tennis racquets, which is what top management thinks you are doing. And if you can't expand, you should start raising the price of the best racquets in the world, until the order backlog begins to shrink a bit. This would be only a little specialty business on that basis, but it could make a lot of money."

THE MISFIT REPORT

Edward had a total of eight businesses on which to report, with the four discussed here the most difficult. In each case he started with background from the corporate files, added from personal observation and questions, and then looked for additional facts to fill any gaps. The additional studies of the developing demographics of the area took him back to the southwestern department store for the results, and the additional information about the Australian and world thermometer market soon reached him at headquarters. As he drafted his report, here is how the discussion of each of these four businesses started:

Southwestern Department Store

Present Classification: Cash cow
Proposed Classification: Cash cow with calf
Recommendation: Fund
Discussion: This metropolitan region has a new area of population growth. The store expansion is the logical way to maintain historic market position in this market. Independent studies of the regional development confirm that the observed area of growth represents growth to the region instead of internal migration. Undoubtedly there will be some internal migration, however, and its net effect is hard to project. However, if the population served by the new stores is only 75 percent new to the area, rather than 100 percent as assumed in the expansion proposal, the new capital required for the new stores will be repaid by new profits in less than three years. While this does interrupt some funding of other Ruction businesses from this source, the expansion seems both justified as a project and important to the future of the store chain. Approval is recommended.

Korean Semiconductor Plant

Present Classification: Star
Proposed Classification: Star
Recommendation: Find another way to expand, quickly.
Discussion: This appears to be a good operation but running under as much strain as it can be expected to sustain. More rapid expansion is needed, but pushing these people too hard might result in less instead of more. This calls for a second nucleus of production, and probably a second plant site, with action needed quickly before the potential for rapid market penetration is lost.

Australian Thermometer Plant

Present Classification: Question Mark
Proposed Classification: Dog
Recommendation: Liquidate/Divest
Discussion: This plant is still unable to manufacture the product except by hand at three times the sales price; I am not convinced the prototypes were actually made by machine, and am not impressed by the plans for a third rebuilding of the machinery. Meanwhile the market, virgin when the prototypes were made, is getting crowded with other electronic thermometer entrants, to the point that a new market survey will be necessary to find out if the Ruction thermometer still has a competitive advantage that justifies worldwide marketing when we finally learn how to make it. Nothing has worked for us here; any money that can be recovered is better invested in another area.

Florida Tennis Racquet Plant

Present Classification: Question mark
Proposed Classification: Question mark
Recommendation: Materials development
Discussion: The trip uncovered the fact that the production barrier is actually the shortage of a critical natural material, and discovery of other sources seems unlikely. No one with contemporary materials knowledge has looked at the problem to see whether a plastic or laminate substitute seems feasible, and this should be done. If the outlook is promising, a materials research program should then be funded. Otherwise the business should recognize that it is already at production capacity, can serve only a small niche in that market, and should raise prices to maximize the return from the small number of world-class racquets it can produce.

QUESTIONS

1. Discuss each of the four cases, to justify (or not) the original classification of the business.
2. Did Edward Ruction play a constructive role in assisting Ruction Resources management? If so, describe it briefly.
3. Comment on the Ruction Resources management process, as it is reflected in the case.

CHAPTER

STRATEGY FOR THE ENTERPRISE: THE GOVERNING STRATEGIES

KEY IDEAS IN THIS CHAPTER

Chapter 6 describes the overall governing strategy framework that management sets for the enterprise as a whole, and within the boundaries of which its business or businesses must function:

- **enterprise strategy** – consisting of building block, choice, and master business strategies.
- **building block strategies** – for leadership, opportunity, people, a public strategy, and a resource-getting strategy—determining what kind of an organization this will be, and the way in which it will direct the energies of the enterprise.
- **choice criteria** – for desirability, managing, belonging, credibility (of proposals), and risk/reward balancing of decisions—determining the sorts of things that will be approved day-by-day and that will shape the enterprise of the future.

- **master business strategies** – a unifying strategic theme or themes tying together the activities of different components of a complex enterprise.
- **enterprise strategies and achievement strategies** – a unifying summary of enterprise strategy considerations.

An enterprise has a strategy of its own, as differentiated from the strategies of the businesses it contains. Ansoff[1] recognized the difference between the strategy for a specific business and for the enterprise as a whole. This recognition was carried forward by Newman[2] and Steiner[3] in the concept of master strategy for a firm; as "developing a distinctive competence at the corporate level," by Berg;[4] as institutional strategy by Naylor;[5] and as strategic intent by Hamel and Prahalad.[6] It is important to make a clear-cut distinction between the enterprise strategy, which governs and limits the one or several businesses of a firm, and the subordinate strategies within that firm.

Resources are created and applied within the realm of the individual businesses. But the ability of an individual unit to undertake a specific business or product strategy is determined largely by the nature of the enterprise of which it is part. Even in a one-product firm the nature of the resulting enterprise becomes a reinforcement to or constraint upon the strategies of the business and product managers.

ENTERPRISE STRATEGY AND THE BUILDING BLOCKS

Enterprise strategy is different in nature from the strategy for a specific product or business because at the enterprise level the firm sells nothing and meets no customers; such activity is all at the business and product

---

[1] H. I. Ansoff, *Corporate Strategy* (New York: McGraw-Hill, 1965).

[2] William H. Newman and James P. Logan, *Strategy, Policy, and Central Management*, 8th Ed. (Cincinnati, Ohio: South-Western, 1981).

[3] George A. Steiner, *Strategic Planning: What Every Manager Must Know* (New York: The Free Press, Macmillan, 1979).

[4] Norman A. Berg, *General Management: An Analytical Approach* (Homewood, Ill.: Richard D. Irwin, 1984), pp. 147–149.

[5] Thomas Naylor, *The Strategy Matrix* (New York: Basic Books, 1986).

[6] Gary Hamel and C. V. Pralahad, "Strategic Intent," *Harvard Business Review*, May–June 1989, pp. 63–76.

levels. Enterprise strategy is of a different quality and more global. Instead of product or business positions and profits, enterprise strategy deals with what sort of an enterprise the firm wishes to be, and what the criteria should be for directing its energies.

The enterprise uses five types of **building block** strategy to shape its own nature, and five types of **choice criteria** in its resource decisions. In addition, a complex enterprise may need a **master business strategy** to direct and integrate the strategies of its component businesses. The building block strategies are basic organizational characteristics, set largely as a result of management preferences, that determine the nature of the enterprise and the sorts of businesses in which it can succeed. The five types of building blocks are the (1) leadership, (2) opportunity, (3) people, (4) public, and (5) resource strategies. The choice strategies are the decision criteria used by management in allocating resources as it receives resource requests and makes choices among them. The five choice criteria for individual management decisions are the (1) value, (2) managing, (3) belonging, (4) credibility, and (5) risk/reward strategies. The five building block strategies will be discussed first.

LEADERSHIP STRATEGY

The strength, style, and intensity of management direction of the organization's activities, and the manner and formality or informality with which the management group chooses to work among itself and with the organization as a whole constitute the leadership strategy. This strategy determines the extent to which an enterprise will undertake long-range programs to improve its strategic position, or not.

An enterprise can be run in many ways. A management group can interact informally and across organizational levels, or it can use formal structure and organizational protocol to govern its actions. It can choose ambitious goals for building and strengthening the enterprise, or only attempt to hold the present position in its markets. It can organize with heavy staff support of all line activities, or minimize staff in favor of developing less specialized and more autonomous line managers. No single way is right for all organizations or all situations, and alternative approaches are almost always possible. The choice defines a leadership strategy, and the selection of this strategy has profound implications for the way the total organization will perform over time. For examples of leadership strategies, see Figure 6-1.

OPPORTUNITY STRATEGY

The aggressiveness or passiveness of the opportunity search and the way in which detected opportunities are evaluated and developed, or not, make up the opportunity strategy. Any enterprise will assume a posture

Chapter 6 Strategy for the Enterprise: The Governing Strategies 139

FIGURE 6–1 EXAMPLES OF LEADERSHIP STRATEGIES

The statement of the leadership strategy of an enterprise tells how the management of that enterprise by its manners, emphasis, and style of operation will create the desired degree of motivation, compliance, coordination, initiative, and enthusiasm among those who follow its direction.

A. Our leadership strategy is to give the organization clear guidance as to the desired types of actions and activities, plus quick feedback on problems and accomplishments; within this framework subordinates will be measured for their initiative and amply rewarded according to the results they achieve.

B. Our leadership strategy is for management to put its best thinking into the formulation of the annual budget and to expect all members of the organization to do likewise, to be sure that all appropriate activities are properly funded. Then all energies should be directed to meeting and exceeding the performance standard on which the budget is based, with further ideas for different or additional activities reserved until the next budget is prepared.

C. Our leadership strategy is to welcome action initiatives from subordinates, provided that they are properly documented and substantiated, receive support within the organization, and are submitted by managers willing to take personal responsibility for the outcome.

Discussion: If put into action as written, strategy A will develop individual initiative and encourage rapid progress anywhere within the boundaries management sets, where B will enforce participative development of a carefully programmed pattern, and strategy C will shift the risks of all new initiatives onto the proposers, thus forcing all managers to be much more cautious and conservative.

---

toward opportunity and innovation, and this will become a limiting condition influencing operations. Opportunity is unpredictable in its occurrence. Some enterprises maintain a separate stock of resources in order always to be prepared to move quickly—toward a purchase, an acquisition, or other sudden chance for advantage. Other firms keep opportunity in its place, taking no initiative until management is sure the time is absolutely correct. Usually such firms forgo unscheduled chances for advantage. Still other firms define the need for an opportunity, arrange for the necessary resources, and then set out to create that opportunity if it does not occur spontaneously. For examples of opportunity strategies, see Figure 6-2.

PEOPLE STRATEGY

People strategy involves the kind of employee community and the nature of the teamwork and of the long- or short-term relationships the organization builds and maintains. An enterprise has a posture toward its people,

FIGURE 6–2   EXAMPLES OF OPPORTUNITY STRATEGIES

The statement of the opportunity strategy of an enterprise tells how the management of that enterprise will react to, use, seek, or create opportunities as it works to achieve its goals.

A. Our opportunity strategy is for all new product and business ideas to be reviewed by the director of research, except that those from outside the company must first clear through the law department.

B. Our opportunity strategy is for new product and business ideas falling outside the areas of present marketing activities to be considered by the management committee after one of the major executives has reviewed the proposal for completeness and agreed that there is a sound potential justification.

C. Our opportunity strategy is for the management committee to select the product and business areas into which growth is desired and appoint a task force, under the direction of the director of development, to propose a specific proposal for entry into each area for presentation to and approval by the management committee.

Discussion: If put into action as written, Strategy A will tend to stifle innovation or other development of opportunities except for any active innovation processes internal to the present businesses, strategy B will define a much more receptive but basically passive opportunity climate, and strategy C a more active, opportunity-seeking approach.

FIGURE 6–3   EXAMPLES OF PEOPLE STRATEGIES

The statement of the people strategy of an enterprise tells how the management of that enterprise will recruit, train, motivate, and reward the people it employs and who make up its organization.

A. Our people strategy is to hire people fully qualified for their initial assignments at the salary rates necessary to attract high performers; and to reward high performance well, with individual job security depending on continued high performance.

B. Our people strategy is to hire the best graduates, pay them well and give them the opportunity to make meaningful life-long careers working to build our joint future, with all possible assistance in relocation and retraining when company needs change.

C. Our people strategy is to seek out team players, recruiting well-prepared graduates of minor schools; to create a fair but demanding work environment to maximize the return from the salary cost, and to continue employment for each work team as long as their efforts win reasonable profits in the current market environment.

Discussion: If put into action as written, strategy A will result in an organization of individual high performers, but with a minimum of organizational cohesion and teamwork, where B will build strong, high-morale teams, and C a sound organization but with less group spirit and loyalty.

both workers and managers, a philosophy regarding their efforts, and a degree of commitment to them that has profound consequences for the other aspects of its operation. Some corporations make a specific effort to keep salaries and fringe benefits above or below salaries paid by other companies. Some businesses make a major effort to help their employees to achieve meaningful and rewarding careers.

A firm such as IBM attempts to create a sense of employee security and an implicit guarantee of lifetime employment, where other firms feel free to lay off and rehire workers with every shift in demand. Delta Air Lines, which has a long-standing no-layoff policy, performed surprisingly well during a bad period for airlines, compared with competitors who used heavy layoffs to cut costs—and some analysts attributed this good performance to the extra enthusiasm and spirit of Delta employees partially as a result of this no-layoff policy. For examples of people strategies, see Figure 6-3.

PUBLIC STRATEGY

An enterprise needs a strategy for its public role, and for the image it hopes to project to each of its many publics. Such a public strategy involves how the organization relates itself to the public, the degree to which the impact of enterprise actions on the public is emphasized or minimized, the extent to which organization actions are open and visible, and the way in which the contact of the organization with the public and the media is organized. It can decide to be aggressive with its opinions, as Mobil is, or quiet. It can attempt to build and promote a strong philanthropic image, as Norton does. It can court the favor of the stock market, the securities analysts, and its shareholders as many large corporations do, or ignore them all and concentrate on the business. By accident or design this strategy will be created, and will color and condition the other actions of the enterprise. For examples of public strategies, see Figure 6-4.

RESOURCE-GETTING STRATEGY

The money-spending and money-obtaining policy, the adequacy of the resource supply it can tap, and the way in which it interrelates with the other strategies constitute the resource-getting strategy. Some firms have money to spend and others do not, because of the nature of the business and its assets, and because of the management attitude toward investment, debt, and sources of funding. Hoffmann-La Roche long avoided debt, keeping sufficient balances on hand so that new buildings, new manufacturing plants, acquisitions, and other current needs could be funded out of current assets. Most businesses rely on borrowed money, but differ widely as to the size of the debt burden they will consider carrying. Some firms borrow only with difficulty and by mortgaging their physi-

---
FIGURE 6–4   EXAMPLES OF PUBLIC STRATEGIES

The statement of the public strategy of an enterprise tells how the management of that enterprise will achieve and maintain the relationship with the public that management wants.

A. Our public strategy is to make the minimum necessary compliance with all regulations but no more, and to avoid public statements by its executives except to the extent made necessary by the immediate needs of the business.

B. Our public strategy is to keep the legislators, government, and public fully informed on all issues material to our business and to make a consistent effort to provide research studies, press releases, legislative testimony, and executive speakers as appropriate.

C. Our public strategy is to try to shape laws, regulations, and public opinion in areas of interest to our business—by an organized lobbying effort, issue-oriented advertising, personal executive efforts, and supplemented by employee letter-writing campaigns and other activities as appropriate.

Discussion: If put into action as written, strategy A defines an attitude of passive compliance without any attempt to anticipate issues or explain company actions, where B is a quiet but much more pro-active strategy, and strategy C an aggressive effort to guide the public process wherever it touches the interests of the business.

---

cal assets, while others develop skill at resource creation and an aura of success such that almost any need for funds can be accommodated.

Many corporations will sell common or preferred stock to raise additional capital from equity investment whenever market conditions are favorable. But some firms, particularly smaller ones, fear the dilution of ownership and control by selling stock, and suffer delays in growth instead. For examples of resource strategies, see Figure 6-5.

BUILDING AN ENTERPRISE

By its planned and unplanned choices in the five building block areas management fixes many elements in the character and nature of the enterprise, more even than they are fixed by the nature of the businesses in which the enterprise participates. By the choice of its leadership strategy, of a posture toward opportunity, of a people strategy as evidenced by its employment practices, of a public strategy, and in the way it obtains the resources it needs, the enterprise sets boundaries that often determine the types of businesses in which it is likely to do well or badly. While too few managements have taken the time to define these strategies carefully, they provide a powerful constraint on the actions of the firm and its individual managers.

Chapter 6 Strategy for the Enterprise: The Governing Strategies   **143**

FIGURE 6–5   EXAMPLES OF RESOURCE-GETTING STRATEGIES

The statement of the resource-getting strategy of an enterprise tells how the management of that enterprise will obtain the flow of resources necessary to achieve its mission and goals.

A. Our resource strategy is to cultivate the securities analysts and attempt by all reasonable means to translate our good performance into a high price/earning ratio, so that our stock can be advantageously used for acquisitions and sold to fund all corporate programs.

B. Our resource strategy is to pay generous dividends to make our stock an attractive investment vehicle, selling additional stock as appropriate to fund our growth so long as this can be accomplished without significant dilution of earnings.

C. Our resource strategy is to retain the major share of our earnings for growth and grow as rapidly as we can without incurring any debt that cannot be fully repaid within two years.

D. Our resource strategy is to leverage our growth program as heavily as can be supported at anticipated interest rates, confident that this is the best way to obtain maximum return on our equity.

Discussion: If put into action as written, strategy A aims at tactics designed to bring maximum pricing of the equity, which then can be sold or exchanged to provide more resources, where strategy B aims at a more modest equity price justified by the yield from the dividends to provide a basis for selling additional equity as more resources are needed, strategy C limits the firm to the resources its earnings provide, and strategy D expands corporate resources as aggressively as the firm's borrowing power will permit.

ENTERPRISE CHOICE CRITERIA

The management preferences in the five building block areas largely determine the basic nature of the enterprise, but the firm is created in actuality by a flow of allocation decisions, as support is given to some proposals and refused to others. This is the area of enterprise choice strategy. Its decisions are based on standards for (1) desirability, (2) managing, (3) belonging, (4) credibility, and (5) risk/reward.

DESIRABILITY STRATEGY

The standards used to determine the degree to which a specific project is a good kind of undertaking for this firm, according to the standards set by the organization's mission and goals, define its desirability strategy. How worthwhile or how important is this activity in the light of our mission and goals, and what are the personal and organizational dynamics of this opportunity? Major companies often enter a new field by acquiring a good small company from which the business can be expanded. Often this makes the management willing to pay much more for the initial acquisition than it would have otherwise, because of its desirability as a starting point for a major program. For examples of desirability strategies, see Figure 6-6.

MANAGING STRATEGY

Managing strategy determines how diverse or how homogeneous the enterprise should be, how many types of management challenge should be compounded, and how complex the overall management task should be permitted to become. Manageability is a primary basis for management choice in almost every case where investment in more than one business area is being considered. Some managements feel that they should limit themselves to one or two types of business, but others are very casual about moving into any area where the financial returns appear attractive.

During its early growth phase U.S. Industries made much of its desire to acquire any company in any business, so long as it had good prospects for growth and profitability. W. R. Grace, a successful company that made diverse acquisitions until it was considered a conglomerate by many analysts, changed course and divested many of these businesses and rearranged into a chemical and consumer sales company in order to have a more identifiable and manageable business pattern. Avon Products long concentrated its energies on continuing successful growth in the direct sales area, and then began to broaden into other marketing. William Wrigley, the leading chewing gum company, has continued to concentrate its energies in that one product area. These represent different managing strategies pursued by different firms. A management's choice among different investment opportunities is heavily conditioned by its own feelings about the span over which its management will be most effective. This is a key element in enterprise choice strategy. For examples of managing strategies, see Figure 6-7.

BELONGING STRATEGY

A set of criteria determining the degree to which a given product, business, or project will mesh into the fabric of the enterprise define its belonging strategy. This element of choice strategy is closely related to manageability. It includes a judgment of the comfort of management with a proposed project, its fit with the rest of the enterprise, and the controllability of that activity within the organizational framework. Management should be able to manage each area in which it puts resources, and it

FIGURE 6-6   EXAMPLES OF DESIRABILITY STRATEGIES

The statement of the desirability strategy of an enterprise tells how the management of that enterprise will choose among the alternatives available to it in order most effectively to concentrate on activities consistent with its mission and goals.

A. Our desirability strategy is first to consider the degree to which each activity merits investment and support in its own right, and then to choose new activities and continue investment in old activities in proportion to the degree to which these activities (a) help to form a pattern we desire for the company, and (b) add to the strength and manageability of the enterprise as a whole.

B. Our desirability strategy is to judge each activity on its own merit and without consideration to other parts or activities of the enterprise.

Discussion: If put into action as written, strategy A requires that all activities fit together in a self-reinforcing pattern, where strategy B is based on a totally conglomerate approach to growth.

FIGURE 6-7   EXAMPLES OF MANAGING STRATEGIES

The statement of the managing strategy of an enterprise tells how the management of that enterprise will choose among the alternatives available to it in order to keep the difficulty of the management task at a level that will not jeopardize the desired quality of managerial performance.

A. Our managing strategy is only to manage manufacturing businesses making complex products for industrial users.

B. Our managing strategy is to concentrate on businesses selling packaged products requiring sophisticated marketing support and moving through distribution channels in which we are already established.

C. Our managing strategy is to acquire and operate any business that meets our criteria for return on equity.

Discussion: Strategy A requires that all businesses the company manages have a specific type of manufacturing activity and a similar customer base and B requires a similar focus around marketing and distribution commonalities, where strategy C requires managing a very large variety of different sorts of activity.

should feel comfortable about the process, lest discomfort lead to hesitation and mistakes. Several of the leading ethical drug manufacturers did not invest in research on birth control products because they did not believe they would feel comfortable marketing these products; then after society accepted the oral contraceptives and made them respectable, some of these companies belatedly joined the product development race.

FIGURE 6–8 EXAMPLES OF BELONGING STRATEGIES

The statement of the belonging strategy of an enterprise tells how the management of that enterprise will choose among the alternatives available to it in order to maintain a grouping of activities that fit together well, with which management is comfortable, and over which top management feels that it has adequate control.

Comfort strategies

A. Our belonging strategy is to publish and sell only books and magazines that emphasize the importance of traditional moral values.

B. Our belonging strategy is to confine ourselves to businesses where marketing is a small fraction of the total expense, and where cost and quality are more important to success than promotional skill.

Discussion: Strategies A and B represent two sorts of limits on the types of activity a given management is *comfortable* with operating.

Fit strategies

A. Our belonging strategy is to obtain scale economies in every distribution system in which we participate, seeking out and adding additional products reaching the same customer group through the same channel.

B. Our belonging strategy is to develop as many profitable end uses as possible for each of our patented technologies, to maximize our return on that research success.

Discussion: A and B are two strategies for adding compatible activities to maximize return on a position or discovery—where the extra profit comes because these activities *fit* well together.

Controllability strategies

A. Our belonging strategy is to confine ourselves primarily to variety store products, because we have a proven ability to maximize return from low-margin products and have done less well in controlling the pricing and promotion of higher-margin product areas.

B. Our belonging strategy is to confine ourselves to businesses where we can minimize the number and type of credit accounts we must carry more than sixty days, since control over large outstanding consumer credit balances is not one of our strengths.

Discussion: Strategies A and B represent two sorts of limits on the type of business that belong within a given enterprise in the view of its management, in order to maintain proper *control*.

Fit is the relationship of one business element or activity to the others around it. It can be a significant consideration both because good fit helps with comfort, and because sometimes there is an economy of scale—where several similar activities can be carried on jointly better than any one of them alone.

Controllability represents the management judgment as to how well a particular activity would fit into the management operating system, and how well the present control system or a modified system would allow management to stay current with the events in that area.

Air Products & Chemical, a diversified industrial gas and chemical company, acquired Adkins-Phelps, a strong regional herbicide and pesticide distributor, as a first step in a major diversification that was not carried any further. The acquisition was a compatible one; Adkins-Phelps continued profitable growth and related well to Air Products management.

As a seasonal business Adkins-Phelps accomplished almost all of its annual sales in a six-week period, with correspondingly wide swings in inventory and cash requirements. While Air Products had managed it very adequately, the concern was whether anyone at the corporate center really understood the Adkins-Phelps business well enough to detect anomalies or to react if it began to get into trouble. Management decided that the risk was too great, that Adkins-Phelps did not belong within Air Products, and that it should sell the subsidiary and invest in more familiar areas instead. For other examples of belonging strategies, see Figure 6-8, although this area is sufficiently complex so that in some firms more than one type of belonging strategy may apply.

CREDIBILITY STRATEGY

For each request for resources, management's credibility strategy determines the specific requirement management sets for the quality of the underlying plan and the ability of the managers proposing to make it work. In any choice between alternative uses of resources the credibility or quality-of-plan issue should be an important one. Regardless of how large or exciting the potential opportunity may be, is the specific plan being proposed a sound and workable one? And can the specific manager or group carry out the plan, to turn the invested resources into the expected returns? Unless the plan is sound and the chosen managers capable of making it work, the project should not be approved. While most managements react intuitively against a weak plan in a familiar area, they do not always ask enough searching questions, particularly about operations in unfamiliar areas, so that explicit treatment of this element of choice strategy is important. For examples of credibility strategies, see Figure 6-9.

RISK/REWARD STRATEGY

A risk/reward strategy deals with management's risk/return criteria and the way these criteria change with specific circumstances—for a specific project, the acceptability of the projected payoffs and the likelihood that they will or will not be achieved. This element of choice strategy is included automatically in most financial systems, at least to the extent of

> **FIGURE 6-9** EXAMPLES OF CREDIBILITY STRATEGIES
>
> The statement of the credibility strategy of an enterprise tells how the management of that enterprise will choose among the alternatives available to it in order to apprcve only those sufficiently soundly designed and managed to have a reasonable chance of being put into action successfully.
>
> A. Our credibility strategy is to approve any request from managers whom we like.
>
> B. Our credibility strategy is to approve any request from managers with good political connections within the management group.
>
> C. Our credibility strategy is to review all otherwise acceptable requests to be sure their structure and concept are sound, the timetable specific and realistic, and the responsible managers have the ability to carry out the assignment.
>
> *Discussion:* Companies sometimes seem to follow strategies like A or B, even though they are unlikely to say so. Strategy C is widely endorsed although actual management practice may fail to follow it.

some calculation of return on investment or discounted cash flow for the project. The actual dimensions of the choice are larger; few projects are truly certain of achievement, and the actual probability of success can be estimated only approximately at best. A management's investment decisions will be based on some composite of the projected returns and the apparent risks, and this judgment process should be made as open and uniform as practical, so projects of equal attractiveness are uniformly funded or rejected. For examples of risk/reward strategies, see Figure 6-10.

CHOICE STRATEGIES

The flow of decisions based on the value, managing, belonging, credibility, and risk/reward strategies go a great distance toward determining the long-term nature of the enterprise. These strategies are based on simple questions: (1) Is this a good step in the development of our business? (2) Can we manage this project or business? Is it good use of our talent to try? (3) Will we be comfortable operating this? Will it fit with our other operations? Will we be able to control it? (4) Is this a sound plan presented by managers who can make it happen? (5) Are the potential rewards large enough to justify the risks?

The purpose of the choice strategies is to guide the ongoing process of analysis and decision among alternative projects and ventures. The building block strategies define the capabilities and shape the public perception of the enterprise, but its actual nature is determined by its product and business activities, and the choice strategies determine what these activities will be in the future.

Chapter 6   Strategy for the Enterprise: The Governing Strategies   **149**

FIGURE 6-10   EXAMPLES OF RISK/REWARD STRATEGIES

The statement of the risk/reward strategy of an enterprise tells how the management of that enterprise will choose among the alternatives available to it in order to approve proposals with an acceptable risk/reward balance and reject the others.

A. Our risk/reward strategy is to fund investments relatively certain to achieve our target rate of return, except that some other projects will also be funded if necessary to the health of one of our base businesses.

B. Our risk/reward strategy is to compare projects on an expected-value basis (estimated return-on-investment times estimated probability of achievement), and fund those with the highest expected value plus a few of the low-probability projects with high potential impact.

C. Our risk/reward strategy is to fund projects we get excited about, so long as the financial projections show a reasonable return.

Discussion: Strategy A is a common old-style approach to investment that assumes the certainty of most project returns without specific probability estimates. Strategy B calls for probability estimates that are inherently difficult to make but can refine the choice if achieved; the decision to include a few low-probability projects is a mark of a more risk-taking management. Strategy C is an intuitive approach to project selection without clearcut payoff standards.

MASTER BUSINESS STRATEGY

Master business strategy is a pattern defining how to build a business or complex of businesses; this may include integration or coordination of different components of the enterprise or changes in these components, including creation of new units, restructuring of old ones, and acquisitions or divestitures—actions planned with a perspective longer in range or broader in scope than the self-interest of the managers of the various components would dictate. A master business strategy deals with the relationship between the different activities of the enterprise wherever these relationships have strategic importance. An enterprise may develop several related business units because of the potential for integration, synergy, or collective competitive advantage of the resulting business grouping. Several business units may use the same product or the same service, allowing economies of scale in purchasing carload quantities of a raw material, qualifying for a corporate discount on advertising costs, or justifying backward integration into manufacture of a key part or intermediate. The volume of merchandise moving through a specific distribution channel from several different business units may permit efficiencies and a competitive advantage for the enterprise none of the component businesses could support alone. Different businesses may each offer re-

> **FIGURE 6–11**   EXAMPLES OF MASTER BUSINESS STRATEGIES
>
> The statement of the master business strategy of an enterprise tells how the management of that enterprise will add to and articulate the activities of its component businesses as they develop and expand so that they reinforce each other and enhance their competitive effectiveness.
>
> A. Our master business strategy is to give discounts for volume purchases based on the total volume purchased from any of our subsidiaries any place in the world.
>
> B. Our master business strategy is to allow our appliance service profit center to increase the warranty service cost it charges our appliance business center to maintain the desired level of service readiness in the face of declining service volume due to improved reliability.
>
> C. Our master business strategy is to build a significant position in all of the major markets for our products worldwide, committing our resources cautiously but entering each new country market when the first viable commercial opportunity can be found and suffering through as many years of initial losses as may be necessary to establish ourselves.
>
> D. Our master business strategy is to include in our evaluation of our portfolio of businesses a careful analysis of their interrelationships so that our allocation of resources will be based on the needs of the future pattern we are trying to build as well as on current profits.
>
> *Discussion:* Strategies A and B may be to the corporate advantage but require steps the individual profit center may be reluctant to take without top management encouragement, where strategies C and D are possible only at a corporate level. Master business strategies can be very diverse because of the many possible business interrelationships, within one country or worldwide, so the four strategies above are only a sampling.

lated elements to a particular group, as the business selling the appliances and the business providing parts and service.

Diverse businesses often have complex relationships with similar competitors, in which they buy a variety of different materials from each other, and management often reviews the overall buying and selling pattern with a given competitor at times of competitive stress, as when a Hoffmann-La Roche business launched an aggressive promotion to expand its Zestab chewable vitamin sales at the expense of its competitors, and a corporate-level concern developed that this might jeopardize important bulk vitamin sales to Bristol Myers, a major chewable vitamin competitor, by another Hoffmann-La Roche business.

Several studies of the success of Japanese companies in the United States have noted the fierce competition between Japanese companies in the Japanese home market, and the way that products have been refined and perfected in this environment and the best brought to the United

States after Japanese success had repaid the development costs. The offset in multinational business strategy and the long-standing practice of some international companies is to build a significant presence in the market of each major country, in part because this allows confrontation with any major competitor in many different markets, including his home market. And of course a master strategy is required to articulate the operation of the individual businesses in the different countries as such a competitive confrontation evolves.

A single-business enterprise has no need for a master strategy apart from its basic business strategy, and for a diverse enterprise such as De-Kalb the seed and energy businesses may be so different and so independent in their operation that there is no need for a master strategy to relate their function. But many enterprises do need master strategies, particularly in building a complex of related businesses. For examples of master business strategies, see Figure 6-11.[7]

ENTERPRISE STRATEGIES AND ACHIEVEMENT STRATEGIES

There are three levels of primary strategy. Enterprise building block, choice, and master strategies, summarized in Figure 6-12, are governing strategies at the highest level, with business and product strategies subordinate. Enterprise strategies largely determine both the nature and capabilities of the firm as a whole. The product and business strategies drive the action in the market place, and the functional and unit strategies make possible accomplishment of the primary strategies they support.

Each business is driven by a mission and a set of goals, so that business and product strategies are goal-oriented achievement strategies. Enterprise strategy is less consciously designed, sometimes developing spontaneously or as an extension of the style and capabilities of the executive group.

Many managements have never thought seriously about the value systems they mandate for the organization through the governing building block and choice strategies they practice and enforce. Therefore enterprise strategy tends to be less results-oriented and can be achievement-limiting in its consequences. Market action starts with product or service strategies assembled from the appropriate elements. These product strategies become a part of an achievement-oriented business strategy, but the

---

[7] For another development of the concept of master strategy, see James M. Higgins, *Strategy: Formulation, Implementation and Control* (New York: Dryden, 1985), pp. 92–93.

> **FIGURE 6-12** COMPONENTS OF ENTERPRISE STRATEGY

Building Block Strategies—basic organization characteristics, set largely as a result of management preferences, that determine the nature of the enterprise and the sorts of businesses in which it can succeed.

Leadership strategy: The strength, style, and intensity of management direction of the organization's activities, and the manner and formality or informality with which the management group chooses to work amongst itself and with the organization as a whole.

Opportunity strategy: The agressiveness or passiveness of the opportunity search and the way in which detected opportunities are evaluated and developed, or not.

People Strategy: The kind of employee community and the nature of the teamwork and of the long- or short-term relationships the organization builds and maintains.

Public strategy: How the organization relates itself to the public: the degree to which the impact of enterprise actions on the public is emphasized or minimized, the extent to which organization actions are open and visible, and the way in which the contact of the organization with the public and the media is managed.

Resource-getting strategy: the money-spending and money-obtaining policy, the adequacy of the resource supply it can tap, and the way in which it interrelates with the other strategies.

Choice Strategies—decision criteria used by management in allocating resources as it receives resource requests and makes choices among them.

Desirability: The standards used to determine the degree to which a specific project is a good kind of undertaking for this firm, according to the standards set by the organization's mission and goals.

Managing: How diverse or how homogeneous the enterprise should be, how many types of management challenge should be compounded, and how complex the overall management task should be permitted to become.

Belonging: The degree to which a given product, business, or project will mesh into the fabric of the enterprise.

Credibility: For each request for resources, the specific requirements management sets for the quality of the underlying plan and the ability of the managers proposing to make it work.

Risk/reward: Management's risk/return criteria and the way these criteria change with specific circumstances; for a specific project, the acceptability of the projected payoffs and the likelihood that they will or will not be achieved.

Master Strategies—A pattern or patterns defining how to build a business or complex of businesses; this may include integration or coordination of different components of the enterprise or changes in these components, including creation of new units, restructuring of old ones, and acquisitions or divestitures; actions planned with a perspective longer in range or broader in scope than the self-interest of the managers of the various components would dictate.

FIGURE 6-13 TWO TABLETS OF STONE

Building Blocks
- Leadership strategy
- Opportunity strategy
- People strategy
- Public strategy
- Resource strategy

Choice Criteria
- Desirability strategy
- Managing strategy
- Belonging strategy
- Credibility strategy
- Risk/reward strategy

Ten commandments for your organization—written by accident or written by design?

governing enterprise strategies may or may not encourage or permit development of the product and business strategies to their full potential.

As governing strategies, the five building blocks and the five choice strategies are as important, and sometimes as rigid, as if they really were ten commandments written on two tablets of stone, as illustrated in Figure 6-13; but they are an essential link in the flow from planning and strategy to action, as shown in Figure 6-14.

QUESTIONS FOR ANALYSIS AND DISCUSSION

1. Give an example of a leadership strategy, not from the text, based on a specific business organization.
2. Give an example of an opportunity strategy, not from the text, based on a specific business organization.
3. Give an example of a people strategy, not from the text, based on a specific business organization.
4. Give an example of a public strategy, not from the text, based on a specific business organization.
5. Give an example of a resource strategy, not from the text, based on a specific business organization.
6. Give an example of a desirability strategy, not from the text, based on a specific business organization.
7. Give an example of a managing strategy, not from the text, based on a specific business organization.

FIGURE 6–14   ENTERPRISE CHARACTERISTICS AS BASIC TO STRATEGY DESIGN

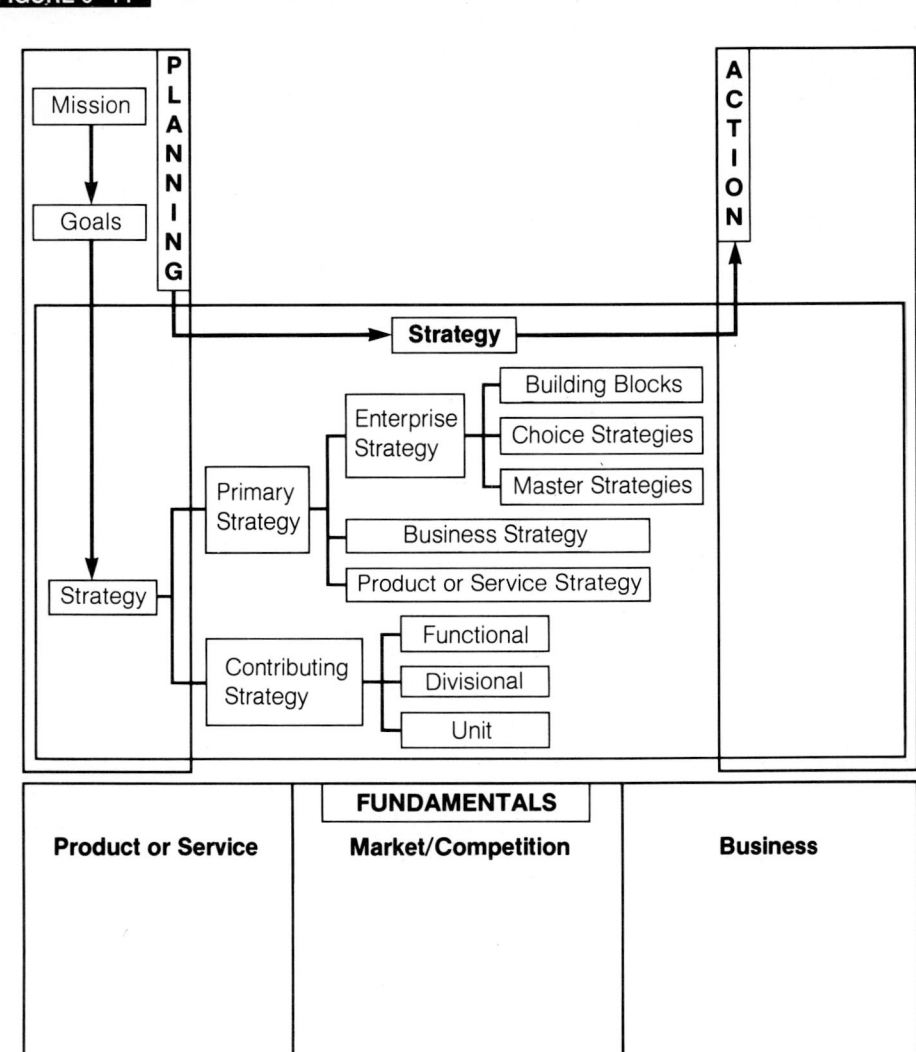

8. Give an example of a belonging strategy, not from the text, based on a specific business organization.

9. Give an example of a credibility strategy, not from the text, based on a specific business organization.

10. Give an example of a risk/reward strategy, not from the text, based on a specific business organization.

11. Give two examples of a master strategy, not from the text, based on a specific business organization.

FOR FURTHER INFORMATION

Berg, Norman A., *General Management: An Analytical Approach* (Homewood, Ill.: Irwin, 1984).
    A good traditional view of this process.

Buzzell, Robert D., and Bradley T. Gale, *The PIMS Principles: Linking Strategy to Performance* (New York: Free Press, 1987).
    Important data on the relationship between performance and profits.

Goold, Michael, and Andrew Campbell, *Strategy and Style: The Role of the Centre in Managing Diversified Companies* (New York: Basil Blackwell, 1987).
    Contribution of corporate management and central staff to success of the business units.

CASE 11 MONARCH-UNITED SERVICE-TRIBULATIONS/INCORPORATED

The chairman and chief executive officer returned from a three-month trip around the world to a backlog of papers. M-US-T/I (Monarch-United Service-Tribulations/Incorporated) was in the midst of an effectiveness survey of its operations, and on his desk the chairman's secretary had neatly stacked reports that had come to him during his absence. He separated out five of them for immediate reading:

1. A summary of the latest employee attitude survey.
2. Report to the Chairman from Acme & Fitch, Corporate Culture Consultants.
3. Highlights of the Arpam and Arpam consultant report on M-US-T/I as a corporate innovator.
4. Monarch-United Service-Tribulations/Incorporated public image evaluation by the advertising agency.
5. The corporate treasurer's analysis of problems in raising the capital required for the next steps in the growth of M-US-T/I.

The chairman's secretary also had a folder full of issues requiring his consideration as chief executive officer, and quietly suggested that he might want to give first attention to some of them, as a number of weighty decisions had awaited his return. "No," the chairman said, "I think that I will read these other reports first. The place has managed without instant response from the C.E.O. for three months; the problems will keep for another hour or so until I am ready for them. Hold my phone calls." He asked for coffee and pastries, and a uniformed waiter brought them immediately. With a large crumpet in one hand the chairman began to read the employee attitude report. Here is the executive summary from that report:

THE WEEBLY WEEBLY CONFIDENTIAL SURVEY OF EMPLOYEE ATTITUDES AT MONARCH-UNITED SERVICE-TRIBULATIONS/INCORPORATED

Executive Summary. As in past years, this survey was commissioned by the Vice President, Personnel and carried out jointly by Monarch-United Service-Tribulations/Incorporated personnel staff and Weebly Weebly Surveys. To preserve the anonymity of the employees, all interviews were conducted by Weebly Weebly workers, and all questionnaires tabulated at Weebly Weebly World Headquarters. This report has been prepared by Weebly Weebly to summarize the findings.

I. *A good place to work.* Again this year more employees find

Monarch-United Service-Tribulations/Incorporated a good place to work. Specifically, 42 percent of the interviewees rated working at Monarch-United Service-Tribulations/Incorporated "a minimum-adequate existence" or better, a distinct improvement over 41 percent last year and 39 percent the year before. 38 percent of the questionnaire respondents gave a similar rating, as compared with 36 percent last year and 34 percent the year before. The Tribulations Insurance Division got the highest ratings again this year, with approval from 57 percent of the interviewees and 54 percent of the questionnaires, while the Monarch Disposable Diaper Division again got the lowest ratings, with approval from 21 percent of the interviewees and 19 percent of the questionnaires.

At the very top of the rating scale, 6 percent of the interviewees considered M-US-T/I "a good place to work." This compares with 7 percent last year and 6 percent the year before, showing no clear trend.

II. *Accomplishment.* We are pleased to report that the percentage of employees characterizing a day at M-US-T/I as "a day of accomplishment" rose to 15 percent from 10 percent last year and 7 percent the year before. But this is still short of the goal of the "every day a worthwhile day" advertising campaign directed at employees over the past three years, and Appendix 1 of this report details a proposed expansion of the "worthwhile day" advertising campaign from a $15 million dollar budget to a proposed $25 million level in the next year.

III. *Purpose.* As suggested by M-US-T/I executives, for the first time this year's questionnaire included questions about the purpose of the work. The suggestion was an excellent one, and a problem has been uncovered. Only 5 percent of employees said that they understood how their work contributed to the operation of the company, and most of these were janitors, cafeteria, and other service workers. Most of the production workers do not seem to know why their jobs are needed, except in the most general way, and this has negative implications for motivation on the job. Appendix 2 of this report presents a suggested $15 million budget for an employee-focused advertising program to help each member of the M-US-T/I organization understand how his or her work contributes to corporate progress.

IV. *Quality attitude.* This variable was also measured for the first time at M-US-T/I executive request and showed that most employees do not care very much about the quality of the output; a typical response was "that's what Quality Control is paid for, and I am not going to get involved." This is a potentially serious problem, but rather than propose another increase in the corporate advertising budget, Weebly Weebly suggests that the program described in Appendix 2 to sell employee purpose will have secondary benefits in the quality area over the next year. Then a specific quality-focused campaign can be designed to build on this foundation.

V. *Leadership.* Unfortunately, there is little progress to report in this area. Again this year the employee group showed very low recognition of the names of their corporate leaders and little interest in what they did. While the Employee Communication Division campaign over the last year to personalize the executive group to the employees was based on well-conceived communications tools, there is little sign of its impact. As a next step it is recommended that members of the executive group actually begin to visit the various M-US-T/I facilities on a regular basis and meet a few of the employees.

VI. *Desires and Complaints.* As in past years, the Weebly Weebly workers were asked to assemble a composite picture of employee desires from the interviews and questionnaires. "More Money" led the list, as in past years, but seemed more strident. It is disturbing that this was frequently linked to mention of new union initiatives and new efforts to organize M-US-T/I workers not now represented by unions. In anticipation of possible management interest in gathering more information here, Weebly Weebly has prepared a proposal for a separate $100,000 study of this problem. This proposal is included as Appendix 3.

Other issues important to the work force were more vacation, better health benefits, better supervisors, and "a muzzle on those meatheads in personnel." This last issue comes from the M-US-T/I campaign to control excessive tardiness and absenteeism, a major effort over the past year. The apparent problem is that the employee group sees personnel as the police force here, and a great deal of vindictiveness has been generated. Practice elsewhere would suggest a more active role for the immediate supervisors in control over their subordinates; this would relieve what appears to be unfair pressure on the personnel staff.

VII. *Conclusions.* This survey appears to have been a valuable extension of the work of past years, and should be useful in guiding Monarch-United Service-Tribulations/Incorporated management. The detailed analysis in the sections that follow shows how these responses differ in different parts of M-US-T/I and in different types of work. Together they show a picture that is evolving steadily and in the desired directions, but which clearly will require several more years of effort to achieve the types of employee attitudes M-US-T/I management has set as an objective.

After the chairman had finished the report, he paged back through it reflectively. On the cover page he wrote a note to his secretary: "Terrible attitudes—who do we think we are fooling—we have to do better—can we think of better things, or do we approve the Weebly Weebly proposals? Please draft a 'who do we think we are fooling' memo along these lines for me to send as a confidential memo to the Management Committee." He threw the attitude survey into the out box, poured more coffee from the pot on the tray, and reached for the corporate culture report. Here is its executive summary:

REPORT TO THE CHAIRMAN AND CHIEF EXECUTIVE OFFICER, MONARCH-UNITED SERVICE-TRIBULATIONS/INCORPORATED FROM ACME & FITCH, CORPORATE CULTURE CONSULTANTS

Executive Summary. As requested by the Board of Directors of Monarch-United Service-Tribulations/Incorporated, Acme & Fitch has carried out a detailed survey of the M-US-T/I corporate culture; the scope and methodology of this study are detailed in Chapter 1; the findings in each of the various subsidiary companies are detailed in Chapters 2 through 11; these findings are summarized in Chapter 12 and analyzed in Chapter 13; and a major culture modification program is proposed in Chapter 14.

The purpose of the study was to characterize the culture within which Monarch-United Service-Tribulations/Incorporated operates and to determine the value systems that characterize it, their uniformity and strength, and the degree to which this culture and its value systems contribute toward continued M-US-T/I progress. Based on interviews of a random sample of 2,000 of M-US-T/I's employee population, in-depth interviews with 99.3 percent of the managers at or above the third executive level and the equivalent staff grades, and repeated computer consistency checks using the patented, exclusive Acme & Fitch system of culture determinants, Acme & Fitch has reached the following conclusions:

I. M-US-T/I has less evidence of a uniform corporate culture than any other organization that has ever been studied. Several M-US-T/I units, such as the integrated steel works at Inclusion, West Virginia have cultures of their own, and some of the major subsidiaries, such as the SoftWall Tire Division, apparently had very strong identities in the past, but these have tended to weaken year by year since their acquisition by M-US-T/I. A culture springs spontaneously into being as a result of the pattern of habitual actions of the employees and managers, and the situation at M-US-T/I suggests that only a very weak pattern of habitual actions links across the corporation as a whole. This would be characteristic of an investment company with only stockholder ties to its units, but is unusual in a large operating company such as M-US-T/I.

II. The lack of a strong culture is reflected in the lack of uniform corporate value systems or a sense of corporate identity. Many interview incidents illustrate this. One manager identified himself immediately as a SoftWall man, even though he had moved from SoftWall to the M-US-T/I corporate staff five years ago. Because of the lack of unifying value systems and behavior codes there is little grounds for the corporate concern about the risks of submerging employee identities; Acme & Fitch could find no evidence of any impact.

III. The absence of M-US-T/I corporate level impact on employees and their value systems is not the whole story. As usually happens in the absence of a central culture, subcultures develop, some more intense than others. As indicated earlier, the preexisting cultures in the companies M-US-T/I has acquired are not a problem. The climate within M-US-T/I is such that these have each tended to decay slowly. While core values remain, for instance at SoftWall and at the Inclusion plant, they have lost the vigor they must have had when these were growing, independent companies, and are actually much weaker now than the local allegiance component in a major corporation with a strong culture.

A potential problem is developing with counterproductive local subcultures. Several small staff units have developed a degree of internal cohesion and teamwork that produces admirable results not necessarily in the corporate interest. For example, last year the convention arrangements for the SoftWall annual sales meeting were so confused that three vice presidents had to sleep on furniture pads in a rented moving van, and this led to the immediate discharge of the responsible staff. There were rumors another staff unit had engineered this fiasco, and Acme & Fitch found several departments with the sort of subculture that would encourage this sort of dirty trick on rivals. While this situation does not represent a broad corporate problem at present, it would be better checked before such incidents become more common.

IV. Acme & Fitch believes that a strong corporate culture is a valuable asset to any management. Acme & Fitch strongly recommends that M-US-T/I seek to strengthen its culture.

Acme & Fitch has had a record of success in aiding corporate managements in modifying cultural values and building towards the culture and value systems that management desired. A proposal for Acme & Fitch participation in a three-year culture-building program is included as an appendix to this report; it would begin with a retreat for key M-US-T/I managers, to formulate more clearly the sort of value systems and culture they would like to build. But, since this area has received relatively little attention at M-US-T/I in the past and there is no evidence of an indigenous culture developing spontaneously, Acme & Fitch would present brief summaries of several viable culture and value patterns, and suggest one that could be adapted for M-US-T/I use as a culture transplant, without the time and effort required for a totally independent design.

If the Acme & Fitch proposal is found to be acceptable, with or without modification, it should be put into motion very soon. But if M-US-T/I management prefers to approach building a stronger culture and value systems in a different way, then that different way should also be given a high priority. Acme & Fitch believes that M-US-T/I will have increasing difficulty in operating in a coordinated manner if it does not develop more cultural cohesion, and this cannot be done in less than several years.

When the chairman finished the Acme & Fitch report, he swore softly to himself and took another sweet roll from the tray. On the face of the report he wrote: "Schedule a full presentation of the Acme & Fitch proposal to the Management Committee ASAP," threw that report into the out box also, and reached for the report on corporate innovation.

EXECUTIVE SUMMARY OF ARPAM & ARPAM REPORT TITLED "MONARCH-UNITED SERVICE-TRIBULATIONS/INCORPORATED AS A CORPORATE INNOVATOR"

(Note to the executive group: The attached 793-page single-spaced report on corporate innovations at M-US-T/I is a very valuable work, in the opinion of those who have read it, and should be studied with care by top management, as was the authors' intent. However, the report has no introductory summary, and was written in such a way that careful reading of the entire document is required in order to gather the meaning. As a convenience to the executive group the following summary was prepared.)

Summary. M-US-T/I has some important accomplishments but overall a very mixed innovation record. Arpam & Arpam has analyzed this record under three categories: (1) innovations of the same generic nature as existing M-US-T/I activities, (2) innovations not of the same generic nature as existing M-US-T/I activities, and (3) breakthroughs new to M-US-T/I and to the industry. For innovations related to present activities, M-US-T/I performance correlates with the size and caliber of the various research and development staffs. Arpam & Arpam found little sign of innovation in the M-US-T/I operating areas although it is common in other companies. Where a research department has been established, it generally has a good track record for new products; because of the orientation of these departments, the new products are always of product types already being marketed.

For innovations not close to existing activities, whether just different sorts of products or true breakthroughs, Arpam & Arpam found no organized M-US-T/I effort. Two hundred fifty pages of the report are devoted to substantiation of this point; the essence is that there are a variety of internal organizational mechanisms that reject any idea outside of proven areas; in an organizational sense the consultants "prove" that M-US-T/I cannot innovate, so that the only ongoing innovation process is the proliferation of existing product types through divisional research and development.

There are obvious exceptions to this generalization because M-US-T/I has been the source of several important breakthrough innovations. The consultants analyze all of the well-known cases and some others that have not been publicized before. The general conclusion is that they happened by accident. For example, SoftWall Tire is known through the industry for its nonwoven tread reinforcement breakthrough. Yet the idea came from Winky Rubber, a customer not able to pay its bills whose assets were acquired by Soft-Wall as a part of a bankruptcy settlement. The SoftWall manager who reviewed the Winky operation ordered immediate abandonment of the tire tread work and sale of the related fixtures and machinery as part of the liquidation. But the memo containing these instructions got lost because intercompany mail routes linking Softwall and Winky had not been set up correctly. No one noticed that the memo was lost, and the work at Winky continued. Nine months later Winky sent four sample tires to the SoftWall test center for evaluation, the breakthrough showed in the test results, and the rest is history.

The consultants deal with these cases of accidental success in innovation very delicately, so as not to upset M-US-T/I sensitivities, but each of our publicized innovation successes has a history like this, where the idea survived in spite of the clear intentions of our managers to discard it. The conclusion, related to the questions that Arpam & Arpam were asked to address in the report, is that M-US-T/I has no demonstrated ability to innovate outside of its existing product areas, and must develop such a mechanism if it wishes to accomplish innovations of this sort.

The last hundred pages of the report deal with alternative innovation mechanisms that have succeeded in other companies. The report is a sound and sobering one. To those of the M-US-T/I managers who wanted an impartial analysis, it should provide the basis for further specific action.

After reading through this summary, the chairman swore again. "No choice—I have to read the whole report. And then we have to do something about this—I'd better make sure the Management Committee reads it too." He thumped down the massive manuscript on a clean corner of

Chapter 6   Strategy for the Enterprise: The Governing Strategies   **163**

his desk, picked up his phone, and buzzed his secretary. "A note to the members of the Management Committee, please, as follows: I have asked my secretary to schedule a half-day Management Committee discussion of the Arpam & Arpam report with the consultants on (find a date about two weeks away). By next week please give me a memo indicating which of the various mechanisms for encouraging innovation outside of existing product areas is the best candidate for installation at M-US-T/I."

He hung up and reached for the public image report; here is its summary:

THE PUBLIC IMAGE OF MONARCH-UNITED SERVICE-TRIBULATIONS/INCORPORATED: AN ANALYSIS PRESENTED WITH THE COMPLIMENTS OF THE BULLZ & BULLZ ADVERTISING AGENCY

Executive Summary. The public image of Monarch-United Service-Tribulations/Incorporated is less of a distinct identity than a faint kaleidoscope. That is, the public at large has little picture of the corporation as a whole, and those with such an image may have any one of several, according to which facet of corporate operation is visible to them. One image comes from the Monarch disposable diaper line—the "king of the baby bottoms" promotional image. Others know the company from Tribulations/Incorporated and the flamboyant "take away your cares" insurance promotions of times past. Almost no one associates M-US-T/I with the various retail chains United Service operates, and even the investing public seems little aware of the Inclusion Steel subsidiary, the western coal developments, or the oil and energy properties.

A survey of newspaper mentions gathered by the Bullz and Bullz nationwide clipping services suggests that the largest fraction of reporters see M-US-T/I as an ominous conglomerate of unknown nature. The only window in the overcast is the bit of humor the press made when certain executives attacked a financial writer for translating M-US-T/I to MUSTY. This is a sore subject with M-US-T/I management, but it helps to make a point. If the corporation wants a better public image, it needs a name people can remember and a planned public identity; at present it has neither.

Bullz & Bullz' recommendations are as follows:

1. Choose a new name. Either change the name of the corporation into something people will remember, as Monarch helped give an identity to the diaper company, or choose a catchy nickname—but "musty" has entirely the wrong connotations, even if M-US-T/I management could live with it.

2. Build an image around the name. Bullz & Bullz would like to help, and attached is a proposal for a two-phase program; first to find a name, and second to establish this name in the public mind through a multiyear public image advertising campaign.
3. Build the image inside the company, too. We see a situation where the employees don't have a clear image of the company either—and no one can do a good job selling the image to the public until it exists clear and bright inside the company.

The chairman turned past the executive summary and browsed the supporting data in the body of the report. Several of the sections on newspaper references to M-US-T/I made him grit his teeth; somehow M-US-T/I had come to be used as a proxy for all bad, large corporations by certain midwestern newspaper editors. On the face sheet he wrote: "On the next Management Committee agenda: "Corporate name: Shall we be 'Musty' to the world or pick something else?" He threw the report into "out" and moved on to the capital requirements memo.

FUELING THE GROWTH OF M-US-T/I

The corporate treasurer had written a long analysis of capital needs, little changed from the last projections. The chairman skipped through to the last part, where the treasurer finally came to grips with where money might best be raised:

M-US-T/I has its problems in the capital markets. In spite of a good earnings growth pattern it has so weak an investor identity that the price/earnings ratio is significantly below that of other conglomerates. This makes any financing through sale of common stock very unattractive and raises takeover risks.

The bond and commercial paper markets are not closed to M-US-T/I, but the company is not known to investors and must pay a premium interest rate until it establishes a track record. . . . (The treasurer went off into a ten-page program to establish a presence in the commercial paper market over a five-year period; the chairman skipped it.)

Other possibilities include secured loans, sale/leaseback of real estate, and sale of limited partnerships in certain specific projects. . . . (It boiled down to the fact that M-US-T/I would have to finance by privately negotiated secured borrowings, or else pay an exorbitant interest rate.)

The chairman shut the report abruptly, called for more coffee, and began to review the picture the five reports made as a group. He pulled out a yellow pad, wrote, crumpled up the paper, and discarded it. The second and third sheets met the same fate. Finally he wrote:

M-US-T/I Status:
1. We have been making money, more each year.
2. The corporation isn't very impressive, in any of these five reports.
3. Can we keep it going in the future?

QUESTIONS
1. How would you state the five building block strategies for M-US-T/I?
2. Do you think any of them should be changed? If so, how?

CASE 12 THE DECISION PROCESS AT GUMDROP HOLDINGS

The Director of Corporate Planning at GumDrop Holdings needed to know the decision criteria the Gumdrop Management Committee members were applying in their operation of the company. Gumdrop Holdings had originally been an investment company named Gumeraeai Dropephani Holdings after its founder. Few people could manage the founder's name, and it had been contracted to GumDrop in common usage. The current president had accepted the inevitable and had changed the name to GumDrop when the corporate charter had been revised to convert it to an operating company some years earlier.

The change in name had come at a turning point in the GumDrop fortunes, just before a chance to take handsome profits by selling several of its earlier investments. Then GumDrop invested in three computer area startup situations that developed very well, the cement division began to profit from capital expenditures to lower production and distribution costs, and a toxic waste treatment subsidiary increased its profits rapidly in spite of a difficult regulatory climate.

GumDrop was a relatively large and complex corporation operating primarily in the United States. Its managers insisted that it was not a conglomerate, and in spite of the gap between computers, waste treatment, and cement, GumDrop turned down many growth opportunities as too far afield. The Director of Corporate Planning had an excellent relationship with the president and the various vice presidents who made up the Management Committee, except they wanted no theoretical discussion. The Director was supposed to bring in acquisition candidates and new business projects they would like, and to know what they would like and accept without wasting a lot of their time with questions beforehand. This was not really fair, but the Director decided that since they would not take the time to tell him directly, he could learn their goals and decision criteria by studying what they did. He collected notes on major decisions as they were made. Here is a summary:

> When the computer software company asked for ten million dollars, GumDrop had already received several million in profits on an original investment of a hundred thousand dollars. If the Management Committee had refused the request, GumDrop would still have received a steady stream of profits, diminishing over time, but probably several more millions in total. Instead they approved the request in the face of clear evidence that it was a long-shot gamble on the future of that business. They told the software company: "You are an effective, productive group that has made a lot of money for GumDrop. We believe you know what you are doing and have a good chance to succeed in spite of the odds. Prove us right!" The

Chapter 6   Strategy for the Enterprise: The Governing Strategies   **167**

gamble worked out and they got the ten million back twice in the next three years.

In another case the Management Committee refused a request to put more capital into the cement business to increase reserve capacity; the management of that business wanted more spare capacity so as never to be in short supply, for fear that that would invite a competitor into the market. The Management Committee told them to transship from another mill or even buy from a competitor to keep their customers supplied, but not to tie up their capital in new capacity until they had enough new demand to generate a good return on the new investment.

Yet when the same cement company management hesitated even to ask for funds to convert a kiln for experimental incineration of toxic chemicals that required the careful control of combustion conditions the kilns provided, the president called to ask why the request had not been submitted, and the Management Committee approved it immediately when it came in: "Here is a chance for low-cost energy plus environmental benefits; why hesitate?"

When the toxic waste treatment company management proposed an expansion into operation of toxic waste dumps, the Management Committee refused the request, in spite of exciting profit projections, feeling that the rules under which toxic waste dumps are operated were too changeable for a sound estimate of the long-term economics of the business: "If you stick to 100% disposal of the waste you handle, then it's gone; you never have to treat the same waste twice. But in a dump, it is still there, and if the standards change, some court or government agency may make you resurrect the waste and treat it again."

Undismayed, the waste treatment company management developed a proposal for disposing of sludge from city sewage plants by using it as fertilizer, with controls and safeguards sufficient to guarantee against all public health hazards and environmental damage. The profit projections were almost too good to be believed and the expansion possibilities almost infinite, because so much sewage sludge is produced. Again the Management Committee said: "No, this is too uncertain an area. It is true that you are permanently disposing of the sludge, recovering fertilizer values, and solving a nasty sludge disposal problem that is really giving society fits. But while you have dealt with all of the obvious problems, this is too emotional an issue; the American public is so concerned about recycling human waste as fertilizer for food crops that they will find something else wrong with your proposal—they will not accept an operation like this for at least another generation; let's put our capital where the risks are less."

Then the computer software company got a proposal from a

distributor to invest in bringing its own identity to the consumer market. The idea was to package with the software a good small personal computer and printer made by a Korean vendor anxious to reach the U.S. market. The package appeared fully competitive in features and could be priced 30 percent below competition. But the Management Committee said, "No! This is a fast-moving, tough competitive market we don't know anything about. If you are right, you might do very well until the next new generation of competitive products comes out. When will that be? What would you do in the face of a 50 percent price cut by a competitor? You shouldn't enter a market like this without having plans on the shelf for two more campaigns after your entry and the money to carry them out. We can't back you that far in a consumer market where the company has no experience or expertise, and we can't really tell in advance whether you know what you are doing since you have no experience marketing there either."

But when the computer software company got a proposal from one of the CAD/CAM companies that it set up a dedicated software group to do fast adaptations of its programs for individual customers of a major new automated drafting and design system, the Management Committee was quick to approve the necessary expense and capital investment: "These are industrial customers whose revenue potential should be obvious, and you are already good at judging when to spend development money on custom applications. This takes you into a new field, but the skills requirements seem to be exactly those you have. Move quickly, and good luck."

A sudden opportunity to acquire another regional cement producer came to the cement company. With the acquiescence of the president of GumDrop, the president of the cement company began to negotiate seriously, assisted by attorneys from his own and the corporate legal group. As an attractive proposal began to take shape, the president of the cement company and the president of Gum-Drop, available members of the Management Committee, and the various GumDrop lawyers met to talk over the prospects. After the first half hour the cement company president called in two market development engineers who had been helping in the negotiations. The acquisition package looked very good because it added steady, profitable cement sales, the price was extremely favorable, there were no antitrust or market concentration issues, and GumDrop was in a position to move rapidly.

The president of GumDrop kept coming back to the operating situation after the acquisition: "You say that this company is sound but poorly managed and that's why it's on the block at a bargain price. But after the acquisition you will still have the same people running it, and they want a commitment to stay on for three years.

Where would you get the right people to run the plants if the jobs were vacant?" The discussion went on for another hour, and it turned out that the cement company president had plenty of talent available to run the acquired plants. "Then," said the president of GumDrop, "I think you have to rearrange the package to ensure that you have the freedom to put in good managers any time you want to. Otherwise I don't see how we can give you a green light."

After the meeting the senior GumDrop lawyer pointed out to the cement company president that the proposed agreement need not require that the acquired executives run the plants; only that they be paid for three years. With this as the keynote they reviewed the list of minor points in the agreement that had not yet been resolved. At the next meeting they won just enough additional concessions from the cement company so that they could show the GumDrop president they had saved the guaranteed salary cost of the acquired executives, while the cement company president was free to use whomever he wished to run the plants. The acquisition agreement was approved almost immediately.

QUESTION

1. From these notes on the decision process at GumDrop Holdings, what do you think the choice criteria are? List all five of them, and note any contradictions in the supporting data.

PART III

STRATEGIC ACTION
AND
CONTROL

CHAPTER 7

STRATEGIC CONTROL

KEY IDEAS IN THIS CHAPTER

- **enterprise choice strategies** – for desirability, managing, belonging, credibility, risk/reward—keeping the different activities of the enterprise within the strategic framework.
- **strategic control as an ongoing process** – adjusting operations or strategy for changes in competition, technology, market structure, and organization vitality.
- **enterprise strategy problems** – when enterprise strategies do not fit with the desired pattern of product and business activity.
- **strategic blindness, perceptual barriers, and the means to an overview.**
- **strategic overview management** – of social impact, opportunity, course correction, operations, and self-renewal.
- **strategic control with a clear view ahead** – integrating summary.

Strategic management requires carrying out the sequence from planning to strategy and action in such a way as to achieve the desired results—through actions keyed to the specific requirements of the enterprise and of the environment in which it operates. Part Three of this book, Strategic Action and Control, is devoted to six areas where strategic overview-level management of the strategies for the enterprise is required, because in today's increasingly dynamic business environment frequent but usually small changes are needed in these areas. As a first step, the present Strategic Control chapter deals with the overview-level extension of the management control processes. Succeeding chapters deal with (1) managing social impact, and the challenge of avoiding injuries to society and confrontations that could reduce business freedom of action, (2) managing opportunity, and the guidance of the opportunity-finding and creating processes a given firm may want to use, (3) managing people, and the way that the work is structured and the structure knit together, and (4) managing organization change, to keep organization functions and processes modern, rejuvenated, and effective.

Just as control is a key function of management, strategic control,[1] as illustrated in Figure 7-1, is an essential element in strategic management. The function of strategic control is to ensure that the policies put into action and the results generated represent real progress toward the selected goals. The control component of the normal management process focuses on how competently a plan is being translated into action, but strategic control looks also at how appropriate these actions are for getting the desired results in the environment as it now exists and as it will become tomorrow.

The distinction between "control" and "strategic control" can be challenged on the same ground as the distinction between "management" and "strategic management," because a full and rigorous definition of "control" would have included all of this in the first place. But actual practice has so frequently left the strategic control elements unfulfilled that the extra emphasis on a control function for strategy as well as for performance is well justified. In particular, strategic control is necessary to ensure that strategic decisions are made from the necessary overview perspective, and to exercise control over the enterprise choice strategies that themselves govern the evolution of the enterprise.

---

[1] The importance of strategic control was argued by Hofer and others; e.g., Charles W. Hofer, et al., *Strategic Management: A Casebook in Business Policy and Planning* (Minneapolis, Minn.: West, 1980), pp. 19–25.

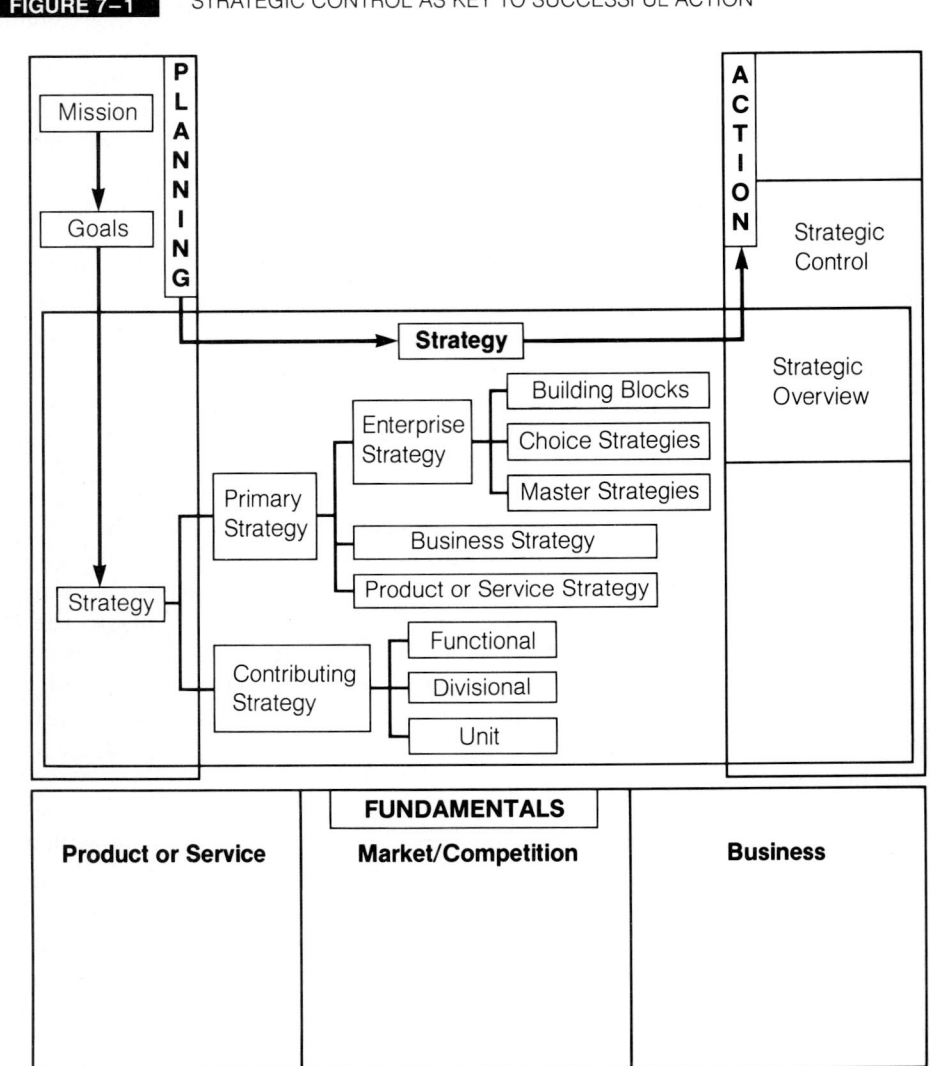

FIGURE 7-1 STRATEGIC CONTROL AS KEY TO SUCCESSFUL ACTION

ENTERPRISE CHOICE STRATEGIES

As outlined earlier, the enterprise choice strategies set criteria for decisions in five key areas. These governing criteria are specified by the desirability, managing, belonging, credibility, and risk/reward strategies.

DESIRABILITY STRATEGY

While it seems obvious that the organization should engage only in what management regards as desirable activities, this area needs conscious, careful review. Sometimes executives are tempted to approve individually interesting or profitable projects without considering their relationship to the enterprise as a whole. The real importance of the desirability strategy, therefore, is in keeping a consistency among the various interests and efforts of the firm—to be sure that the firm obtains the desired reinforcement and synergy among related activities, plus multiple uses of important skills, assets, or positions to maximize the rent they yield.

Strategic control over the desirability strategy is based on confirming that management's pattern for intended integration, diversification, and growth is being achieved through the choices made as this strategy is applied in project approval or rejection. Ongoing activities of the firm should also be reviewed in the light of this strategy as it has evolved, to see if any require redirection or discontinuance. Most ongoing activities also evolve, changing their nature over time as technologies change, customer needs change, regulations change, and as other pressures from the firm's environment increase or diminish. When General Electric sold its small appliance business to Black & Decker, this appeared to some as a major change in GE direction; but in announcing the sale GE management pointed to fundamental changes in the small appliance business that now made it fall outside of the range of activities GE saw as desirable for its future. Good managers must follow the needs of their customers and markets, and this can cause the activities of the firm to scatter outside of the pattern originally intended. Strategic control over desirability strategy helps to ensure that either the strategy is modified to accommodate the business evolution, or the diverging activities are modified or spun off, as in this case the GE small appliance business was sold.

MANAGING STRATEGY

One important question about any proposed new activity is its manageability versus the level of management difficulty the firm has decided to attempt. This judgment is based on a managing pattern for the sorts of things this enterprise can and should attempt to manage. Strategic control is achieved by evaluating the way this strategy is working out, and recommending any necessary changes in the strategy or its application.

The pressures on the managing strategy are the contradictory forces of concentration and diversification. Diversification would seem to reduce risks, but good arguments can be made for improving results by focusing management attention narrowly on business areas that can be managed very well. Although it is proven that some managements have operated several different businesses successfully, others have not, and some hazard accompanies increasing diversity.

To the extent that management is a science, it should be possible to map out the requirements of managing many businesses, plan for the necessary information and support, and operate that variety of businesses successfully from one management center. But some businesses have elements that are not clearly understood, or that change over time in a way not clear in advance. For instance, the requirements for success in the steel business in the United States changed over the decades since World War II in a way that the major steel companies did not foresee, as evidenced by their present situation. Because the management of some businesses is not entirely a science, managers who have been deeply immersed in a specific business sometimes sense problems and take corrective action that could not have been taken by a more distant manager relying on the programmed art of managing that business. For lack of this personal immersion, therefore, a more distant management suffers some disadvantage.

Conglomerate companies are now less favored in the stock market, and tend to bring price/earnings multiples less than their component parts would bring separately. Peters and Waterman[2] cite errors through excessive diversification as a performance-limiting component largely absent in their sample of excellent companies, and list recent studies showing that financial performance of diverse enterprises tends to be lower than for their less-diverse counterparts.

The issue for any enterprise is that of balance. Good management of an enterprise seems more likely, all other things being equal, if that management concentrates on areas where it has substantial knowledge of the underlying business. But businesses and markets have life cycles, external conditions change, and the future of an enterprise may require diversification into unfamiliar territory.

For example, the area of financial services is a dynamic and changing one at present. Banks, brokerage firms, and insurance companies individually have felt that their future was not secure unless they could broaden into a much wider range of services, and consequently their managements have decided to enter different and very unfamiliar financial services businesses. Merrill Lynch moved into real estate, Prudential bought Bache to establish a base in the brokerage business, Bank of America bought and then resold a discount broker, and so forth.

These and many other managements have attempted to move out beyond their own present knowledge of the business because this seemed

---

[2] Thomas J. Peters and Robert H. Waterman, *In Search of Excellence: Lessons From America's Best-Run Companies* (New York: Harper & Row, 1982).

to be a future requirement for continuing success. Some of these moves will probably not work out well, and most studies show that the failure rate in diverse acquisitions is quite high. Yet the management decided to take this risk, and it may be that the future of some of these firms depended on taking such risks and succeeding.

In selecting its criteria for managing, enterprise management is balancing at least three factors: (1) the familiar is safer, and disaster due to management error is less likely; (2) a given management group has a strength and an individual and collective competence; only projects this group can manage should be undertaken; new managers can be hired to strengthen the group, but group cohesion and overall control will weaken dangerously if they are brought in too rapidly; and (3) the future of the enterprise requires growth plans more than offsetting shrinkage as products and markets age, and obtaining this growth may require moving into new areas that then must be mastered and managed.

BELONGING STRATEGY

This choice strategy for comfort, fit, and controllability is a close companion of the managing strategy. All new activities should fit the standards top management sets for belonging; that is, management should be able to feel comfortable overseeing the operation under discussion, it should mesh in an acceptable manner with the other activities of the enterprise, and it should be controllable by top management.

These are subjective standards. Comfort will relate closely to the managing standards, except that a particular executive group may have a blind spot or an area of discomfort that makes management of a specific business unusually difficult. If this is not recognized, the resulting mistakes may cost heavily. One pharmaceutical management was unable to adjust to the way that a successful cosmetics and toiletries business must spend money on advertising and promotion, and yet made several attempts to diversify into this business area. But top management could not bring itself to make an adequate delegation of the major promotion expenditure decisions to the successive general managers. As a result the execution of business strategy was uneven, with action stopped from time to time while senior management debated whether to approve the continuing marketing effort. Within the cosmetics and toiletries unit energy focused more on selling each step of its program to top management than on defeating competition, and the business made little progress. Eventually top management tired of the resulting losses, liquidated its unsuccessful venture, and concentrated its energies in other fields.

Fit may bring positives to a program, if a project has the potential for sharing costs or otherwise benefiting another operation. Controllability is a subjective measure of whether management feels it can keep track of progress so that it understands what is happening and knows when and how to intervene if trouble develops. A part of the strength of an enterprise with more than one business is the potential for a business in difficulty to get help. But to make this strength real, top management must be aware of a problem and able to help the business solve it. And with all three facets of the belonging strategy, the function of strategic control is to review the strategy, its application, and the results it is yielding, and to recommend any changes that may be necessary.

CREDIBILITY STRATEGY

This is a simple strategy. No investment should be made unless the top management feels confident of the quality of the plan on which the proposal is based, and of the ability of those responsible to make this plan work. But sometimes the obvious is overlooked; hence it is desirable to confirm approval for quality of plan and management explicitly and reject proposals lacking the necessary credibility. Strategic control will confirm whether this strategy is being consistently applied.

RISK/REWARD STRATEGY

Most managements will have in mind a basic rate of return necessary for new projects; this may be the hurdle rate necessary to match the desired return on assets, or an estimate of the company's return on capital. But beyond this is a more subjective judgment of risk and reward which becomes personal to the management group; firms sometimes fund projects with major uncertainties, and this is a matter of management temperament and strategy.

Many examples and contrasts are possible. The troubles of the steel industry in the 1980s have been traced by some to management reluctance to consider new technology in the first round of post-World War II expansion; these were large existing businesses but management feared that ventures into new technology might jeopardize their profitability, and left the experimental installations to the Japanese who have never given back this leadership. In contrast, Compaq Computer, a successful manufacturer of IBM-like personal computers, moved ahead of IBM with the first major system to use the new Intel 80386 microprocessor.[3] This gave Compaq a temporary leadership, but at the risk of being wiped out if the IBM counterstrategy eventually shifts the market to products with greatly different features, since Compaq is not in a position to challenge IBM dominance directly up to this point. Compaq had succeeded by establishing itself as a quality alternative to IBM with its own set of special features, and several analysts felt that this new high-risk strategy was

---

[3] "Compaq Is Trying to Steal a March on IBM," *Business Week*, September 22, 1986, p. 30.

forced on Compaq, which needed a major innovation because it was rapidly losing its advantage over the lower-priced IBM clones.

For each enterprise there must be risk standards and profitability standards. If these have not been developed explicitly, they will be hiding in the minds of the decision-makers and influencing decisions in ways that seem obscure to observers. Hidden standards may be producing risk/reward decisions and results counter to management's conscious desires; the role of strategic control is to be sure that this does not occur. There is nothing wrong with subjective standards for things difficult to make objective, but for something as basic as enterprise choice strategy it is helpful to the rest of the organization to make the standards explicit.

STRATEGIC CONTROL AS AN ONGOING PROCESS

As decisions move through the management operating system, the strategic control emphasis is on evaluation of the strategy put into action, versus the situation as it exists or will become under the impact of some new competitive development. The action of strategic control is to monitor and approve so long as the flow of strategic actions is in the desired direction, or to question and review when the results fall short, or when the environment appears to be changing beyond the range of management assumptions. This questioning and review cycles the process back to reevaluation and reformulation versus reaffirmation of the strategy, actions continue to flow under the new instructions, and strategic control continues to match results against them.

COMPETITION

A first focus of strategic control is on competitive action and inaction, plus changes influencing the number and nature of potential participants in a given competitive arena. The number and strength of the competitors in the personal computer field changed rapidly in a few months, with Osborne and Texas Instruments fading from prominence and numerous new companies entering the market. Or, the textile industry maintains a profound and continuing interest in U.S. relations with China, since China itself, Taiwan, and Hong Kong all compete in the U.S. market on terms determined in part by the persuasiveness of the U.S. government in obtaining competitive restraint, for instance through voluntary quotas for textile exports to the United States from each country. And, the failure of the first well in a new North Slope drilling area suggested that the importance of this oil source area might diminish as existing fields begin to mature. In any of these fields any competitive shift might require a recast of strategy, and the role of strategic control is to signal such a need.

TECHNOLOGY

In the same way, any developments representing new technology or new use of available technology could foreshadow major changes, and strategic control should track them closely. For example, solar energy is not a factor in many energy applications because of its present high cost, but several sources report important progress with amorphous silicon systems. As this progress is carried through into commercial products, and as concurrent progress in storage battery development is achieved, solar systems could become the competitive choice for many uses near the fringe of electric distribution systems. The question is how fast these developments will occur; some predict substantial near-term progress and others do not, and the difference could be a critical strategic control variable for companies potentially affected.

MARKET STRUCTURE

Another key strategic control area is that of market structure. As product sectors grow, mature, and shrink, as competitive energies shift from one part of the market to another, and as new technologies impact, the underlying structure of a market tends to shift.

Kodak has long dominated home photography in the United States, and neither the Polaroid instant camera nor Japanese competition in films invaded this central core significantly. New technology brought video cameras. Kodak decided to offer a home video camera, thus accelerating the adoption of these new cameras, and chose to enter through a joint venture with a Japanese partner. Success will shift the structure of the home photography market, and some analysts think the shift will permit the first real competition in the central area Kodak has dominated for so long, because Kodak will not control this application of video technology. This is the sort of market structure shift the strategic control function should follow carefully, for the strategic options available to the participants in this market might change significantly as home photography broadens into video technology.

ORGANIZATION VITALITY

One of the most important strategic control areas concerns the management operating system and the overall vitality of the organization. The management operating system and the organization it serves should be a lean, responsive, effective network of linkages aiding each member of the organization in performing individual and common tasks at top effectiveness. As discussed further in Chapter 12, the management operating system will atrophy and degrade spontaneously unless managed, and effective strategic control accomplishes this management.

ENTERPRISE STRATEGY PROBLEMS

The leadership strategy of any given organization seems often to have arisen more or less by accident from the habits and behavior patterns of key managers. Also, the management posture regarding the opportunity strategy and the people and public strategies often seem to arise by chance. Only resource strategy tends to get routine review, as successive generations of top managers look for ways to acquire the resources necessary to accomplish all of their projects. In that way, resource strategy is more like the five choice criteria, because choice decisions must be made routinely. The criteria for the choice decisions represent a difficult area for managers of any diverse enterprise, and portfolio management and many other approaches have been suggested.

When an enterprise is formed, its management group quickly develops a style and habit patterns for their enterprise-level strategic decisions. Building block and choice criteria developed informally become institutionalized for the future from these initial habit patterns. And since institutional change in an organization requires effort by management, these initial values are likely to remain imbedded as organizational decision criteria almost indefinitely. Change occurs only when the Chief Executive Officer or another major executive becomes concerned enough about one of the enterprise-level values to make an issue and a campaign out of changing it.

Enterprise strategies are not examined as carefully and frequently in most organizations as product and business strategies, and sometimes they misdirect effort as a consequence. Management neglects enterprise-level strategy for three reasons: (1) the questions from below usually do not force reevaluation of building block and choice strategies, (2) top management tends to be very busy on other things, and (3) review of enterprise-level strategy inevitably also involves a certain amount of introspection, to consider how well the top management itself is doing its job in that particular area. Operating executives are not very introspective by nature and tend to put off self-examination. One of the major contributions of an effective enterprise-level planning activity is that the process requires these difficult areas to be considered.

STRATEGIC BLINDNESS: CAUSE AND CURE

Business management does not always succeed in its endeavors. General Motors, Ford, Chrysler, International Harvester, U.S. Steel—a long list of major corporations have had heavy losses and gone through major trauma in the recent past, and the frequency of troubles and even disasters among large organizations is surprisingly high. In some cases individual managers may have made mistakes. In many other cases the leaders appear extremely able based on individual performance, yet their firms got into deep trouble under their leadership.

Security analysts and other outside observers often conclude afterward that such troubles were caused by the choice of a wrong strategy. This raises questions about the process by which management makes strategic decisions, and why this process sometimes goes astray. Even in large corporations with able managers, capable staffs for the gathering of information, and a massive pool of resources at their command, this decision process goes wrong from time to time, yielding answers resulting in bad decisions and calamity.

The easiest way to explain some of the failures in major firms is to assume that, for some reason, management did not see or did not understand the problem. For example, it would seem that the U.S. automobile industry should have shifted to smaller, more fuel-efficient cars two to three years earlier than it did. Yet, even though many people outside of the auto industry were saying this at the time, the executives concerned with this decision did not see a compelling reason to change—as evidenced by their actions, and their subsequent competitive disadvantage versus the Japanese. If the auto executives had had a clear vision of the present reality, they would probably have managed their companies differently in earlier years.

While the auto industry is a convenient target, the problem is a broader one, and the same lack of perception is quite common elsewhere. The invention that became the Xerox copier was offered to a large number of leading U.S. industrial companies, all of which turned it down. They saw a difficult and demanding technology without enough potential to justify development. Yet after Xerox demonstrated this potential and began to enjoy the profits, some of these and many other companies sought to enter this market and compete for a share.

U.S. technology led to the invention of the transistor and to its mass production for defense and aerospace applications, and the use of these transistors to make better and less expensive radios was considered and dismissed by companies who were then the leading producers of radios for U.S. and world markets. These companies convinced themselves that the transistor was not yet ready for use in consumer products.

The Japanese bought transistors in quantity from Texas Instruments and other U.S. manufacturers, took these transistors to Japan, assembled them into radios, and brought the radios back again to the United States. The public was enthusiastic about the performance, light weight, and low price of transistor radios. The Japanese began to manufacture their own transistors, their radio assembly work overflowed to other far eastern countries, and they took over the U.S. radio market. The former industry leaders were so far behind by the time they became convinced that change was necessary that they were not able to stay in the mass market for radios at all.

The available evidence suggests that these executives, like many other executives before and since, suffered from a condition of strategic blindness. This is an occupational consequence of the concentration necessary for successful operating management. It arises because most operating executives condition themselves to function from a limited viewpoint, considering only events and data with proven relevance to daily decisions. From such a viewpoint a new transistor or a potential Xerox copier is invisible—it can have no proven relevance because it never existed before.

Strategic blindness is an operating management viewpoint limited to routine considerations and blind to everything else. Strategic blindness is not unusual. It is the *normal* condition of the operating management of any organization, until the problem is recognized and a deliberate effort made to shift viewpoint from time to time to get the perspective required for strategic decisions.

PERCEPTUAL BARRIERS AND THE MEANS TO AN OVERVIEW

One of the necessary attributes of a manager is the ability to concentrate. Concentration is the process of blocking out external distractions in order to be able to give full attention to a specific problem or situation. If a manager did not have the ability to concentrate, he or she would be shifted to a new thought or task by each interruption, and would have great difficulty in finishing anything at all.

Most managers develop a considerable power of concentration initially that then increases further as they learn to function in the increasingly hectic maelstrom of responsible operating management. This concentration is desirable, and allows them to do the job.

But concentration is also an act of exclusion. By narrowing the span of attention to the issue at hand, the rest of the world is excluded. By concentrating many hours per day, per week, and per month for many years, the operating executive loses touch with most parts of the world beyond those of proven relevance to the business operation. The manager has a personal life outside of the business, but indications are that many of the concentration habits are carried along as an unconscious element and applied to nonbusiness issues also.

These concentration habits are based on a personal shorthand of assumptions and approximations that allow instant discard of the irrelevant, and assign a specific relationship to peripheral matters so that no break in attention to the central areas is necessary to deal with them. These assumptions and approximations are usually constructed with care initially, but they are not reviewed—this would be a distraction—unless some external event breaks the concentration pattern and the manager is caused to formulate it over again. For example, early in their careers many of today's older managers formed assumptions about the relevance of minorities and females to business management, and some continue to use these assumptions without realizing how much society has changed.

Strategic blindness as described here is not uncommon behavior. Many managers suffer from it, sometimes chronically. But it is a disease whose treatment is well advanced when the afflicted manager recognizes the problem, because the solution is not difficult and most managers are anxious to avoid making stupid strategic decisions.

While concentrating on operating matters, a manager erects a system of barriers that prevents sound strategic judgement. That manager is strategically blind, and risks monumental blunders by making decisions with strategic dimensions. Either these decisions should be deferred to an executive with a strategic overview of the situation, or else the operating executive should drop those concentration barriers temporarily and seek a strategic overview before attempting to make or evaluate strategy.

STRATEGIC OVERVIEW MANAGEMENT

A strategic overview is a vantage point from which an executive can recognize and evaluate the full range of considerations, both inside the organization and in the surrounding society, that could be relevant to the present or future significance of a particular decision. A strategic overview requires a considerable understanding of the business of the organization, and also of the society around it. Much of the information necessary for the understanding of the external factors can be obtained from staff and other reports, so long as the mind that will do the evaluation has an understanding of the background plus the necessary analytic and synthetic ability.

In a major shift in the upper management organization pattern, for a number of years General Electric was divided into sectors each responsible for several billions of dollars of annual sales. Each sector dealt with all of the GE businesses in one area, such as consumer products. The sector executive level was announced as a necessary step in getting better formulation of corporate strategy. At this point GE management felt that its individual business strategies were being well formulated, but that all of the higher-level executives were too much involved in the day-to-day operation to give attention to corporate strategy. The sector executives were given this missing strategic component as a primary assignment.

A few other very large corporations created sector executives also, but for most firms the extra overhead of another top management level is not justified—GE has again eliminated this level—and the operating executives must continue to make the strategic decisions. This does not mean that strategic blindness and strategic calamities are necessary, since it is not difficult for most managers to learn to put operating problems aside briefly and to shift perspective as necessary. If this shift in perspective is accomplished once a year routinely and when strategy problems arise, and if someone has anticipated the issues well enough to gather most of the information necessary for the appropriate strategic decisions, strategic overview management can be accomplished effectively and efficiently by capable operating managers.

Strategic overview management is best given a certain discipline, because it is normally performed under time pressure by operating managers with other preoccupations. A simple pattern calls for review of the enterprise choice criteria, as discussed earlier, plus a set of five brief plans. These five plans,[4] dealing with social impact, opportunity, course correction, operations, and self-renewal, are described briefly below.

MANAGEMENT OF SOCIAL IMPACT

This plan deals with the consequences, the impacts on society, as the business makes decisions that affect its people, its operations, its raw materials, products and wastes, and its resources. The underlying insight is that society is profoundly affected by these decisions, and is beginning to hold each business responsible for injury or disruption its actions cause. Smooth and profitable operation of a business requires a largely harmonious relationship with society, as discussed further in Chapter 8. Maintaining this harmonious relationship requires anticipating what the firm's actions will mean to society, the likely public reaction, and the alternatives, before these actions are taken, and either moderating high-impact actions or balancing them in some way to prevent adverse public reaction.

THE MANAGEMENT OF OPPORTUNITY

This is a plan for the utilization of the resources of the firm, first in support of the present types of products and services, then in the further evolution of its present businesses, and finally in the shift into new business areas as necessary to meet the firm's goals. Important work in the opportunity area may be performed in a research department, but a strategic overview is needed for opportunity planning, and research like any other operating department often loses this perspective. A principal variable bringing new opportunities is social change, and the challenge is to track the emergence of the change processes and develop the resulting oppor-

---

[4]For further discussion of strategic overview management see George C. Sawyer, *Corporate Planning as a Creative Process* (Oxford, Ohio: Planning Executives Institute, 1983).

tunities at the correct time. The management of opportunity is discussed further in Chapter 9.

THE MANAGEMENT OF COURSE CORRECTION

This is a plan to keep programs from being derailed by nonstrategic changes in the world around the business. It represents the effort to steer activities so that a regulatory decision to ban a material or change a rule will not cause unnecessary cost or delay. It is also discussed in Chapter 9.

THE MANAGEMENT OF OPERATIONS

This plan adds the insights available from a strategic overview so that ongoing operations are adapted as necessary to keep them sound and competitive year after year as the future unfolds. Emphasis is on the human component of the enterprise, and the several enterprise-level strategies related to people and output. Management of operations is discussed further in Chapters 10 and 11.

THE MANAGEMENT OF SELF-RENEWAL

This is the plan for shifting the people and modifying the organization so that the organization can continue to operate successfully decade after decade. This is a difficult area. The normal operating pattern already provides for qualified replacement of individual managers and other employees one by one as the need arises. The strategic overview contribution is the insight as to when people should not be replaced, when they should be replaced by people with different qualifications, or when the organization structure and its operating pattern should be changed. The process is hard to manage because the critical changes directly affect the top managers who must make the plan; someone has compared this to the surgeon taking out his own appendix. But the organization can be prepared only if its present management attempts to anticipate the future, and future requirements will probably differ from the requirements of today. Management of self-renewal is discussed further in Chapter 12.

Information Requirements. Line management tends to live in the present, and to decide today what should be decided today—with a hundred-year perspective, if the decision seems to require it. Few line managers are willing to spend time worrying about decisions that do not yet have to be made. On the other hand most know that when a decision is due, it must be made, and they will proceed with inadequate information rather than let operations suffer for lack of direction.

When line operating managers take the time and apply the effort to

4. Give at least one example of actions showing the sort of desirability strategy in use in an organization you have observed or read about.
5. Give at least one example of actions showing the sort of managing strategy in use in an organization you have observed or read about.
6. The text suggests that conglomerate management is more difficult and less likely to succeed. Do you agree or disagree and why?
7. Give at least one example of actions showing the sort of belonging strategy in use in an organization you have observed or read about.
8. Give at least one example of actions showing the sort of credibility strategy in use in an organization you have observed or read about.
9. Give at least one example of actions showing the sort of risk/reward strategy in use in an organization you have observed or read about.
10. Discuss the way in which a firm could set up effective monitoring of competitive action.
11. Discuss the way in which a firm could set up effective monitoring of new developments in technologies affecting its operation.
12. Discuss the way in which a firm could set up effective monitoring of changes in market structure.
13. Discuss the way in which a firm could set up effective monitoring of shifts in its own organizational vitality.

FOR FURTHER INFORMATION

Hofer, Charles W., et al., *Strategic Management: A Casebook in Business Policy and Planning* (Minneapolis, Minn.: West, 1980).
    Strategic management as seen by an early proponent.

Sawyer, George C., *Corporate Planning as a Creative Process: Action Laid Out in Advance* (Oxford, Ohio: Planning Executives Institute, 1983).
    Further background on some of the concepts from this chapter.

CASE 13 THE OAKEN BOX COMPANY

Among other things, Carl Oaken was an old-style machinist who could build almost anything if he set his mind to it. A California friend who knew only that Carl was a good mechanical engineer asked for help with a maintenance problem on a coding machine in his packaging plant. Carl looked at the offending machine and exclaimed: "It won't work right because it's built all wrong." He solved the maintenance problem with a minor change in the design of a part, but scolded his friend for the crude equipment he was using. "Anyone could build a better machine than that."

"Carl, that is one of the newest machines; it was featured at the last packaging machinery show. I know it's clumsy, but it's the best there is. If you really can build a better one, you could make a lot of money. I'll buy the first one. If you're serious, let's talk about price and delivery."

Carl had just sold a profitable consulting business. The vacation he had planned faded from his mind. "Tell me some more about what you want that machine to do," he asked. He had never worked with packaging machinery. It intrigued him, and he decided to learn more about it. The next day he made some phone calls, and then began to tour packaging plants. A machinery show was opening in Chicago; he spent three days there. Two weeks later he arrived in Germany just in time for a packaging machinery show. Everywhere he went he studied the packaging machinery, and asked endless questions about the way it worked, and the maintenance and adjustment problems. After two weeks more of plant visits in various European countries he went to Australia and Japan to renew acquaintances and see equipment there, and then back to California.

He called his friend and they scheduled a lunch the following week. Carl had decided that his first idea, for an improved bottle coding machine, was a good one. He had also decided that the packaging industry was ripe for a lot of new machinery.

But first he had to build the coder. As a convenient source of standard parts he bought a used coder of an obsolete design for almost nothing. He also bought a better drive motor, and took the old coder, the motor, and a few parts to his machine shop, where he cleared off a large table and went to work, making other parts as he needed them. In two days he had built the first Oaken Coder. As soon as he was satisfied that it worked, he thought for a while about how such a machine should be manufactured and how it should be maintained, tore it apart completely, and rebuilt it again with new parts here and there. By the evening of the third day he had a much more attractive machine, and one that could be manufactured in quantity.

The Oaken Coder was a very simple little machine. Carl called his friend and suggested that he come an hour early for lunch to show him something; in half an hour they had clamped the Oaken Coder in place on the packaging line, plugged it in, put it into routine production, and had it working perfectly.

Carl's friend was properly impressed, and Carl invited him to invest in the Oaken Box Company. "That coder is a good little machine, and I want to start producing it as soon as I can get my patent attorney to file for some patent coverage. But what I really want to build is a good automatic box machine. I know how to do it, and the ones I see running really demand improvement."

The Oaken Box Company was soon organized and began to build machines. Carl Oaken found a distributor to handle the Oaken Coder and it sold well, providing a welcome income stream to cover expenses and finance the development of the box machine. In the course of time the box machine was also marketed, and soon became the centerpiece in a line of Oaken packaging machinery.

The box machine took flat stacks of cardboard boxes one at a time, opened up each box, folded in the bottom tabs and closed the bottom of the box, inserted a bottle and perhaps also a leaflet (or whatever else was to be sold inside the box), folded in the top flaps and closed the box, and then discharged the finished boxes in groups of six or twelve that slipped into a larger carton. Other companies had built box machines and continued to build them, but the challenge was to have sufficient simplicity and versatility in a complex machine to cope with the inevitable variations in the cardboard boxes and the filling process, to operate at the high speeds necessary in a modern packaging plant, and yet to suffer only momentary interruptions from the inevitable jam or mistake. During his travels Carl had seen a really elegant box machine that was so delicate it had been put out of service for three weeks when the neck fell off of a glass bottle as it fed into the box, the bottle turned sideways, and the resulting jam required a team of factory representatives to restore the internal alignments of the parts.

The Oaken Box Machine distinguished itself because Carl Oaken had the art of building complex things simply and robustly. It soon became the industry standard and held this position for many years. As time passed, the design of the Oaken Box Machine was further improved, and Carl Oaken brought out new models. He found ways to simplify setup and adjustment, so that the box machine could be adjusted to run a different size box in a few minutes. He added adjustments that compensated for differences in the texture and condition of the cardboard boxes, so that there would be fewer interruptions in the product flow. He improved the feed of the bottle into the box, so that the machine speed could be raised still further. Each significant improvement became a new model, and Carl had marketed the Mark XII box machine before he had his first significant failure.

The speed of a packaging line was limited by the speed of the individual machines that made it up, and every machinery builder wanted to build machines that would run faster. Carl Oaken had decided to at least double the speed of the box machine for the next model, the Mark XIV. This was a major development task because the problems of variations in the boxes and in the feeding process were compounded by each speed increase. Further, the penalties of downtime increased with higher-speed equipment because of the time required to bring the whole line up to speed, and the potential confusion and pile-ups from each breakdown. Carl decided that the Mark XIV had to set new standards for operating reliability, or else no one would gain any advantage from the speed. To get this reliability, he decided that he had to have more automatic adjustments, plus the ability to change some of the key settings while the machine was in operation.

The Mark XIV project resulted in seven patentable improvements in design, but the machine did not meet Carl Oaken's specifications, and he never marketed it. The difficulty was that in going to a more sophisticated adjustment and control system a more elaborate electronic system also became necessary, and with the vibrations and debris inside a packaging machine running at high speed the failure rate of the sensors, vacuum tubes, and control components cancelled out the advantages inherent in the higher speed.

Carl Oaken kept the Mark XIV in a corner of the shop as a reminder, and went back to the challenge of making his present machines simpler and more reliable. Then, because he was still frustrated with his failure on the Mark XIV, he turned away from box machines and designed an important new capping machine and two high-precision liquid fillers.

The Oaken Box Company did well, of course, with its steady flow of improved designs, and Carl Oaken thoroughly enjoyed his role as chief designer. He was not interested in the routine of running a bigger and bigger company, and had never given enough attention to marketing, particularly in other countries. But Carl Junior (or Young Carl, as the organization called him) was an astute businessman and a good manager even though he had little of his father's mechanical aptitude. With the passing of time, Carl turned over more and more of the day-to-day details to Young Carl, and about a year after the failure of the Mark XIV Young Carl became President and Chief Executive Officer of the Oaken Box Company, with his father continuing as Chairman and Chief Designer.

One of the first things Young Carl did as president was to persuade his father to spend a few weeks on the Mark XV box machine, because three of the inventions Carl had made to build the Mark XIV were of equal value on the slower machines. Although the Mark XV project was a brief one, it was an important one for the company, because competitive box machines were being improved steadily also. The Mark XV, the first new Oaken Box Machine marketed in four years, quickly reaffirmed the company's ability to build the best and most reliable box machines available. More Mark XV machines were sold than of any previous model.

Carl Oaken continued to apply his talent in other parts of the product line, and Young Carl continued to worry about the competitive position of the Oaken Box machine. At one point he assigned a good young engineer to do a careful market survey of all of the different automatic box machines, comparing their features and analyzing customer experiences and complaints about their performance. The Oaken Mark XV continued to lead the list, but the ranks of the competitors had changed since a survey ten years earlier. Two Japanese machines, a German machine, and an Israeli machine were stirring new interest in the industry. All had problems, but there were new features here and there, and signs that the box machine industry was becoming more competitive again.

Young Carl gave the survey to his father, and then suggested that the two of them lay out a plan for a Mark XVI machine. Carl Senior agreed, spent some time in the shop and some time in travel, to get his own view of customer interests, and then gave Young Carl a list of the features he proposed to add to the Mark XVI. It was a good list, development started immediately, and six months later the Mark XVI Box Machine was announced. Again, it was a successful model.

But Young Carl noticed that his father had made no further attempt to increase the speed of the machine, where some of the competition now claimed to be as fast as the Oaken machine. Two years later Young Carl asked the same young engineer to repeat his study of the competitive box machines. The survey again confirmed Oaken Box leadership, but showed another new list of competitive features and new European and Japanese competitors. Several of the newer machines claimed top operating speeds higher than the Oaken Box machines.

Young Carl and his father talked about a Mark XVII machine, and this time Young Carl pushed the speed issue a bit harder: "Dad, it seems to me there is too much smoke here not to mean something." Carl Oaken made a point of looking at several of the new and higher-speed machines and talking to the people that operated them in the course of his next trip. He came back with an attractive list of new features to build into the Model XVII and started it into development. But he proposed no basic change in operating speed: "Son, I'm not convinced that those other machines are actually any faster. We always could have claimed another 15 percent on the speed, and I once saw one of our old Mark IV machines jury–rigged to run 40 percent faster than my design rate. That old Mark IV was doing a good job, too, but I had to remind the packaging engineer that I was not responsible for the jams he had when someone made a mistake in feeding it at that speed.

"We still have the old Mark XIV prototype, and we could always dust it off, bring it up to date and market it. It will run three to four times as fast as the Mark XVI or the Mark XVII I am designing—but it just isn't reliable enough to put the Oaken name on it and turn it loose."

"Dad, I know that the problem on the Mark XIV was in the electronic controls, and that you had some of the best brains in the electronics industry trying to help you solve that. But a lot of new things have been done in electronics since you fought with the Mark XIV. Any chance the same problem would have a new solution now?"

They continued to talk about the speed of box machines off and on during the development of the Mark XVII, but to no real conclusion. Meanwhile the work on the Mark XVII went smoothly, the first prototype outperformed all expectations, and Young Carl ordered a complete rearrangement of the Oaken Box Company booth at a major international packaging show three weeks away so the Mark XVII could be a feature of the show. The advertising agency and a local print shop went onto emergency overtime to get the necessary sales releases, product brochures, and supporting literature ready in time.

Both Young Carl and his father were pleased with the booth, the literature, and the trade reaction. But questions kept turning up about a Japanese machine neither of them had ever heard of, and on the third day of the show Carl Oaken broke away from the booth to try to track down the rumors. In a small booth in a corner on the top floor of the exposition hall he found the machine in question. The booth was an awkward shape, the sales literature was crude, the attendant spoke imperfect English, and the whole display had the appearance of a last-minute addition to the show. But the machine spoke for itself; while Carl Oaken could have faulted details, the concept was of an automatic box machine that could be adjusted while running, in almost the way he had attempted to design the ill-fated model XIV. Carl immediately began to ask about the controls, and to look at the machine, to see what he could see. He challenged the attendant as to whether the machine could operate reliably in a production situation, and was invited to see one in operation.

"Mr. Carl Oaken!" He heard himself hailed by name and turned to meet a young Japanese who introduced himself as an electronics engineer. "We are most pleased to see you here, because we have a great debt to you. In the text of some of your patents you talked about a machine to be controlled in this way, and we wondered why no one had ever built one. That idea was not patented, it seemed to be a good one, and here is the machine. You asked about seeing one operate. We have one running in a customer plant ten miles away. I would be greatly honored if you would let me take you to see it."

By the time Carl Oaken got back to the booth, Young Carl was beginning to wonder what had happened to him. When he saw his father's face, he wondered even more. "Carl," Carl Oaken Senior said, "let someone else take over for you here, and let's go someplace where I can tell you what I just saw."

They found a quiet corner in the coffee shop. "Son," Carl said, "I just saw a box machine a lot like the Mark XIV running routine production. I never saw a box machine run so fast, except the Mark XIV between breakdowns. The examples in my improvement patents described the Mark XIV in a very general way, those Japanese read about it in the disclosure statements and examples, built the machine with solid state controls and microchips, and it runs like a dream. And I don't think they violated any of my patents.

"They are latecomers here, with a poor booth and no literature, and no one is paying much attention to them. But that machine speaks for itself, and by next year they will be center stage. We have to find a really good electronic systems designer, and I have to get the covers off of the Mark XIV and start to bring it up to date. I want to call it the Mark XX, because it's good enough to skip numbers for. And I have kept my own file of improvements for the Mark XIV, in case I ever got it built, and I have some good ideas there—with a little luck we can have a better machine in service and announced for sale before these latecomers start to take the whole business away from us. But I can't imagine how anyone got so far ahead, the way we both watch the industry."

QUESTIONS

1. How did the Oakens get behind the frontier of box machine development?
2. What could have been done to prevent this?

CASE 14 ORGANIC RESOURCES CORPORATION

THE FLORIDA ACQUISITION

Aram Aram had just finished his presentation to the Management Committee of Organic Resources. He had proposed the acquisition of Southeastern Data, to extend the network of regional data processing companies owned by his division of Organic. He had a good case, presented it well, the questions were largely friendly, and approval seemed certain. Then John Samuels, the research vice president, began to speak: "Aram, you have made a persuasive case. If we are going to go ahead in this business of acquiring data processing companies, you seem to have a good candidate. But you know I thought that we really should have invested in more research instead of in buying data processing companies . . ." (Visible thunderclouds appeared on the brow of the Chief Executive, and John Samuels quickly changed his tack.) "But what I really wanted to say, Aram—Florida is a logical place for expansion, but I keep getting the feeling that we would be acquiring this company mostly because it fits well with the way you want to live. You like Florida, and you can go down there in the company plane as much as you want, once you have a subsidiary there."

Aram Aram swore to himself. John Samuels had fought and lost the same battle to get the acquisition money transferred to research time and time again, and he would scuttle the data processing program any way he could. But he had asked a fair question, and Aram tried to give it a fair answer. "John, we spent several hours here in the Management Committee not too long ago talking about the data processing business and the need to make it into a national network. Our present operating base is here in the midwest, with a really good satellite operation in New York and another in Boston. We decided then that the next step before we started to acquire regional companies rapidly was a good nucleus either in California or Florida. Ever since then we have been looking very hard for a good company to acquire in either place, and they aren't easy to find. The best California operation we were offered is too expensive and has real operating troubles, even if we could negotiate the price down. I don't think my bunch has enough experience yet to handle a turnaround, solving-the-troubles acquisition yet, although they should be ready to do that in another six months or a year.

"We found a good company to acquire in Miami, the one we are talking about. And, yes, I have a house there and a boat, and I fly down as often as I can. For that matter, the reason we found the company is that I know a lot of people in the local business community because I spend time there. A friend of mine down there heard that these people might sell and persuaded them to talk to me. But the company is a good one, Florida was one of our targets, and I'm not ashamed of the fact that I go there. So long as it is part of building the business for Organic Resources, why shouldn't I build in a place I like to go?"

The president reserved decision, ended the meeting, and asked John Samuels to stay for a few minutes for a private chat. The two of them discussed John's habit of trying to knife Aram's project in spite of previous Management Committee decisions. The discussion was brief, because the Chief was a man of a few well-chosen words. John Samuels left feeling cut off at the knees, and the president told his secretary to find Aram Aram. "Aram," the president told him, "you made a good proposal, and you are in the process of building an important business for us. You have full approval to go ahead with the acquisition as soon as possible. And don't worry about this business about the trips to Miami. You are responsible for the results you are getting and the results you have promised to get for us in the future. I could care less if you get them in a comfortable place. I just want that national network of yours to take shape on the schedule you set, if not sooner. Good luck, go with my blessings, and bring us back results."

THE PEST MANAGEMENT COMPANY

Organic Resources was about to launch into the pest control business with the acquisition of the Pest Management Company; or so it seemed from the discussion. Ray Green, the assistant controller, had the floor. He had just summarized for the Management Committee the feelings from the financial area about the proposed new business area, and they were all positive. Organic Resources had mapped out a growth strategy based on building new nationwide service businesses, preferably with a high-technology or proprietary technology base; in most cases the entry would be by buying one or more good regional companies and using them as a base for a national business. Pest Management fit the model exactly, the company was extremely profitable, and seemed to be an ideal candidate to use as a model for developing similar businesses in every city in the country.

The Management Committee was clearly intrigued. Even John Samuels, who was normally against everything that did not start with an idea in his own department, was clearly favorable to the idea. The president saw that he could get unanimous approval, if he polled the group. But he wondered, and he waited, listening to the discussion. Finally he asked, "Would we put the pictures and progress report from the Pest Management Company at the beginning or the end of our Annual Report?"

Everyone looked surprised. The question seemed trivial, and the Chief never asked trivial questions. The controller ventured first: "We always have put the businesses in alphabetical order—that would put Pest Management right after Personal Health and right before Restaurant Services."

A vice president spoke up: "If you do that, there shouldn't be any pictures of rats or cockroaches right before Restaurant Services."

Another answered: "Personal Health would get upset about that, too."

A third suggested: "Maybe we could get Pest Management to agree never to show any pictures of pests."

The president had been listening to the interchange. He interrupted: "Suddenly the bunch of you don't seem so brotherly towards having Pest Management as a member of the family. But if we go that way, we are going to have to embrace and defend the business just like any other Organic Resources business. You all sound like a bunch of politicians offering to integrate someone else's school district. This Pest Management Company sounds like a really good growth opportunity for us—but are you all willing to embrace it like a brother?"

The discussion went on for another hour. Everyone was in favor of Pest Management, except for a few restrictions here and there, but the more they talked, the more barriers they put up. Finally the president said: "It seems to me we have two choices. One is to grab the opportunity, and then I'll have to replace any Management Committee member who gets too uncomfortable. Or the other choice is to say that we aren't really comfortable being exterminators, and go on to look for a new opportunity in its place. I suggest we turn down Pest Management and look for other green pastures."

Not surprisingly, the Management Committee agreed.

OPTICAL TECHNOLOGIES

The Organic Resources Corporation Management Committee struggled with the proposal to invest in Optical Technologies. The proposal was to acquire a 35 percent interest for $950,000 with an option to acquire the rest of the company within two years. Optical Technologies had developed a new data transmission system that would greatly improve and extend communications capabilities between automatic teller machines and the bank or office managing their operation. The plan was to use the new technology as the basis for a national chain installing and servicing these machines, and such a business would be a very profitable growth opportunity of the type Organic Resources was seeking. However, while Optical Technologies had a good chance of getting patent protection for its machines, Organic Resources experts had pointed out that there were other ways to accomplish the same result, and that Optical Technologies would probably have direct competition from either one or two Japanese firms soon after it entered the market.

The Management Committee had been back and forth over the options, but there really did not seem to be much choice. To invest at all would require almost a million dollars. There was no point in acquiring the rest of the company until the system was proved out, and if it didn't prove out, the initial million would be lost. Finally one of the Vice-Presidents said: "What we are all skirting around is that this is a long-shot investment. But the odds aren't that bad, and the payout is good if it works. I think we should take a chance."

The discussion went on for another half an hour, as the president carefully drew a position out of each Management Committee member, but all of them felt about the same—the opportunity looked worth the risk. The president felt that way, too, and they approved the $950,000 investment.

QUESTIONS

1. Which choice strategies could you see being considered as Aram Aram, John Samuels, and the president discussed the Florida acquisition?
2. What choice strategies entered into the Pest Management decision? Explain your answer.
3. What choice strategies entered the Optical Technologies decision? Explain your answer.

CHAPTER

MANAGING SOCIAL IMPACT

KEY IDEAS IN THIS CHAPTER

- **business costs and benefits to society.**
- **business impact on society** – and the need for freedom to operate.
- **anticipating and understanding social impact.**
- **the social impact areas** – of direct impact and systemwide impact.
- **social balance failure** – management choices.
- **managing social impact** – principles and guidelines to guide management action.
- **profit maximization and social cost avoidance** – chapter summary.

Business is a part of society. It is a part that has won a certain independence and freedom of action because society has benefited by the employment opportunities, new products and services, and the broad rise in living standards brought about by business growth. Society needs a healthy business sector, in order that these benefits may continue and increase.

What does business owe to society, and society to business? These questions are important because the strategies and policies defined by a management will also assume or define relationships with society and with the governments society has established; success depends, among other things, on the soundness of these relationships. Business depends on society and needs its members as customers. It needs society as a rule maker to oversee the markets, to set a pattern of laws and customs, and to give business freedom to operate within this pattern. This allows a business to plan its investments, production, and commerce in hopes of reaping the fruits of a successful venture, where it might not receive these fruits if there were no social control or law enforcement.

As a business operates, its actions affect society and society's members in many ways. Not all of these impacts are favorable. Past unfavorable social impacts have brought confrontations causing society to pass restrictive laws and create new regulatory agencies. To avoid wasting business energies in confrontations with society, its social impact should be managed. This chapter is devoted to social impact management, and the way that policies and strategies should reflect it.

COSTS AND BENEFITS

A business can expect, within limits, to benefit society by its operation. This benefit comes because the business makes available goods and services for purchase, gives employment, and otherwise contributes to economic activity. The limits are defined by its cost-and-profit equation, and by the value built into its products.

The cost-and-profit equation is simple in concept. A business can continue to exist only if it makes a profit; otherwise it consumes its resources and goes out of business. This profit is calculated by subtracting the costs of operation from the revenues received by sale of the goods or services. But the costs subtracted are the private costs of the firm. Business operation sometimes brings other costs to society, and any difference between the private costs and the total costs to society is a potential flaw in the claim of benefit to society.

The revenues of the firm from sale of goods or services are set by the quantity sold and the price. While the price is defined by the seller and may or may not be influenced by competitive forces, the actual transaction is a free one—that is to say, the customer is not forced to buy, and could keep the money or spend it on something else. A free transaction will occur only if the good or service is worth more to the purchaser than the money which must be surrendered to obtain it.

If the good or service is worth more to the purchaser than must be paid for it, the consumer benefits by the exchange. This benefit is one of the sources of the increase in living standards accompanying the growth of industry. But this benefit exists only if the worth of the good or service purchased is greater than the value of the money the consumer gave up to make the purchase—that is, the product must live up to expectations. A business benefits society by its operation, if the merchandise it sells gives the value the purchaser expects to find, and if there is no discrepancy between the costs the firm has paid and included in its profit calculation and the costs of that merchandise to society. But over the history of the industrial system, business has left many unpaid costs that fell on society, and has not always represented its merchandise fairly. In the beginning the benefits to society from industry were so large and so obvious that no one looked at the costs, such as the costs of pollution or injury to workers. The importance of these costs was not fully understood, and these problems were accepted as a part of the cost of progress.

As various elements in society began fully to comprehend the extent and the source of these social costs, a movement began to force business to behave more responsibly. Restrictive laws were passed, regulatory agencies were created, and the modern system of business regulation began to evolve, largely because of the need to get business firms to pay the full costs caused by their operation.

Today the rules under which business operates have been modified. The fringe benefit package offered by the modern employer covers many expenses of employees that are a part of the cost of living but that business formerly did not pay. Laws govern safety in the work place and workman's compensation for injuries. More treatment of industrial wastes is required than formerly, and pollution is being reduced. Society has begun to look very critically at business and corporate actions; it often assumes that social ills are due to unpaid business costs, and looks for ways to restrict business behavior and eliminate these costs.

This has created a business environment where a management faces the additional challenge of operating its business in a way that is acceptable to society and to the governments society has created. This challenge adds significant additional complexity to strategy and policy, requiring an awareness of social needs and a sensitivity to social change processes. The benefit from this additional challenge is that most new business opportunities also arise out of these changes in society. Thus a more socially sensitive manager is also better able to guide business growth.

BUSINESS IMPACT ON SOCIETY

As management operates any business, it proceeds through a series of decisions. These are the decisions that deploy the firm's resources in support of specific strategies and in pursuit of specific goals. In the dynamics of most businesses many strategic decisions are needed, and the withdrawal, shift, or redeployment of resources is frequent.

Each business decision has an impact on society, because each change in work schedules has consequences for employees, their families and friends, and each change in products or the way work is performed has similar consequences for suppliers, customers, neighbors, or community. These impacts will not all be significant, and more will be seen as favorable than will be seen as injurious. But where the firm, through its freedom to operate, has the authority to make a change, society is more and more insisting that it is responsible for correcting or compensating any unfavorable consequences.

The customs, laws, and regulations governing this insistence on business responsibility for its actions are evolving unevenly, and society is not equally sensitive to all of the different sorts of impacts that a firm's actions may have. But the pattern is set; society is likely to demand the right to review any business decisions it views as adverse to some element of society, and when it chooses to do so, society is well able to block business actions and restrict a firm's freedom to operate.

The management of a business has a simple problem, although the solution may be complex. It is in business to make a profit through selling goods and services. It needs a harmonious relationship with society. It cannot afford to fight with society—such confrontations consume massive amounts of executive time, and expenses are high. Society, having the greater power, will prevail in the end anyway if the issue seems important to its members.

For management to pursue the sale of its goods or services and make a profit, and to avoid getting distracted into confrontations with society, that management needs to examine its decisions before they are put into action, to judge the social impact and consequences of each. Before it starts to act, management has much more freedom to modify an action likely to create undesirable issues. Also it can work to develop a pattern of relationships in any critical social areas, such as the relationships with the local community and with the regulatory agencies. This will also open channels for comfortable negotiation of issues that may arise, before the fact if possible, so that the business can continue to benefit society, and to maintain maximum freedom to grow in sales and profits.

ANTICIPATING AND UNDERSTANDING SOCIAL IMPACT[1]

The management of corporate social impact requires a strategic overview perspective, deals with the anticipated direct or systemwide impact of a firm's actions in each of twelve areas of operation, and attempts to achieve a social balance in each area. A social balance is a condition such that, in any one area of operation, the business does not harm society. This condition is often easy to achieve, since the business contributes positively in so many ways—through its employment, its products, and its payment of taxes, for example.

THE SOCIAL IMPACT AREAS

DIRECT-IMPACT AREAS

One business impact is through its sale of goods and services. This sale should benefit society, unless there has been misrepresentation, side-effects or injury results from the product use, or there are after-sale product support requirements that are not met.

The second impact area is from the use of physical resources by the business, and the third area is from the use of human resources. Physical resource usage often involves issues of scarcity, and potential resource exhaustion, where the human resource considerations relate to the continuity of employment, career paths, hiring and layoff patterns, and the way that the employment policies relate to life-cycle needs of employees and their dependents.

The fourth direct impact area is from the wastes discharged by the business, and the fifth from the business' impact on the local community. In the handling of wastes, the requirement is that the business operate in such a way that the environment is not damaged by its discharges. Similarly, the community should not be harmed by business impacts; and business has a positive interest in a healthy and well-managed community—its employees need and use the community services, and a significant share of the costs of running the community are paid by the business or with funds originating in it.

---

[1] This and the following sections are summarized from George C. Sawyer, *Business and Its Environment: Managing Social Impact* © 1985, pp. 326–329, 344–347. Reprinted by permission of Prentice-Hall, Inc., Englewood Cliffs, N.J.

SYSTEMWIDE IMPACT AREAS

The first of the systemwide areas concerns the public issues in which the firm becomes involved. No longer is it possible for a major firm to avoid involvement in public issues. Society is likely to make an issue out of any significant decision, and a pattern of constructive involvement is required. The second systemwide impact area is the natural involvement of a self-interested business with ethics and social value systems as it both meets and shapes the requirements placed on it by society. The third area deals with loyalties and allegiances, both the umbilical ties of every corporation to the law-making political entity that gives it life, and the requirements for and limits on the loyalty the organization can expect from its employees.

The fourth area is that of governance, as the enterprise attempts to fit itself into a social control system, and to call attention to the economic and technological needs of that system so overall social governance can evolve constructively. Because of increasing interdependence of different regions and between industries, steadily increasing social control over business actions seems inevitable, but the present regulatory pattern is so clumsy and expensive that more efficient governance processes will be required for continued economic progress. The fifth area is that of regulation itself, as a firm lives under and works with the regulatory system society has already imposed, and the sixth area is the impact of the use of technology by the firm. The final systemwide impact area deals with the impact of the resource policies of the enterprise, as assets or employment are shifted from one region to another.

SOCIAL BALANCE FAILURE

The above treatment of social impact areas builds in the presumption that a business can and should recognize and pay its full costs of operation, whether required to do so or not. This requirement is a sound beginning, but not the final word. It represents a reasonable starting point because, in very many cases, the business that recognizes it might create a large social cost can avoid doing so. If another means can be found to the same end and no social cost is created, then no payment is necessary, no burden is placed on the business, and the business remains free to sell and make profit.

Where maintaining a social balance would require payment of a real additional cost not legally required to be paid, a new problem arises. The logic of the interaction with society dictates payment, for society's reprisals for costs left unpaid are often very expensive—but a competitive market place may leave little money for these costs. The business that would prefer to pay its full costs but cannot because of competitive pressures can propose legislation such that all of the competitors will also have to bear these costs—arguing that, by helping to bring the issue to the surface it can shape a more reasonable requirement than angry activists will try to write in later. Or, a business can simply continue to operate, hoping that it will become better able to pay its full costs before society becomes angry enough to shut it down. Such a business is receiving a subsidy, at least implicitly, in being allowed to continue to operate with society paying part of its costs—costs caused by environmental damage or injury to workers, for example.

MANAGING SOCIAL IMPACT

Management of social impact starts with a set of principles and guidelines suggesting the course of action most likely to minimize a given problem and also to leave the business maximum freedom of action in the long run. The principles of social impact management are summarized here:

PRINCIPLES OF SOCIAL IMPACT MANAGEMENT

I. RESPONSIBILITY: A business bears responsibility for the consequences of its actions in proportion to its freedom to take those actions.

II. SOCIAL COSTS: A business must either avoid or balance social costs, or face the social stress they cause.

III. LAW: A business depends on respect for the law, in its own operations and from others, since the law is the principle bulwark upon which the existence, success, and security of the business depend.

IV. RESOURCES: A business must use natural resources wisely or risk challenge of its right to use them at all.

V. CONTINUITY: A business must balance any costs it causes when it breaks ongoing relationships whose continuity it has allowed to become implied.

VI. OPPORTUNITY COSTS: A business must consider the opportunity costs it has created for the other parties when breaking ongoing relationships.

VII. COMMUNITY: A business should concern itself with the community and its services by ensuring that the total of the contributions it has made—directly or indirectly—or encouraged from others represents a fair share of the total requirement.

VIII. ETHICS: A business by its actions and words shapes the ethics and culture of the community, and will be judged according to those ethics in the long term.

IX. PUBLIC: The social impact of its actions precipitates any significant business into an important public role, and self-interest requires careful management of that role.

Nine Principles. These principles generalize the way business and society work together. The *responsibility* principle is based on society's tendency to hold the creator responsible, almost regardless of later circumstances—as in the anti-litter laws enforced against beverage companies, and, by many people, the immediate assignment of responsibility for the Bhopal accident to Union Carbide simply because it was responsible for the plant's being there. Similarly, the *continuity* principle recognizes the human tendency to assume without proof that such a week-by-week relationship as employment will last forever, and then to react against the "breach of contract" when that relationship is broken off. Just as society now awards legal status to squatters' rights and common-law marriages, it appears to be evolving a "property right" concept for a worker's job. In both the responsibility and continuity cases, the stated principle could sometimes be unfair to a business—but that is not the point. The purpose of the nine principles and the guidelines that follow is to guide action according to the most likely direction of reaction from society, fair or not.

GUIDELINES FOR MANAGING SOCIAL IMPACT

1. QUALITY: On the whole, goods and services fulfill the expectation of the purchasers.
2. SERVICE: Reasonable requirements for after-sale and continued support of routine use patterns are met.
3. SAFETY: Goods and services are free of danger and unexpected side effects in normal use, attempt to ensure the safety of predictable types of product misuse, and do not cause unacceptable environmental aftereffects from the goods and services or their packaging.
4. CONSERVATION: A firm whose operation is using or consuming scarce resources manages its operations with a sensitivity that minimizes the risk that its right to use these resources will be withdrawn.
5. VALUE: Each member of the organization receives fair compensation, including adequate provision for dependents and for retirement, works under conditions that do not impair health, and in return is expected to deliver full productive energy during the time allocated to the job.

6. OPPORTUNITY: Meaningful tasks, challenging career paths, and equality of opportunity to pursue these tasks and paths are maintained with minimum possible disruption.
7. POLLUTION: Wastes discharged from the business operation do not cause any measurable detriment to the environment.
8. DUMPS: Wastes go to land, ocean, or other dump sites only with society's consent to the permanent loss of resources the dump site represents; but such use of dumps is best avoided because of the magnitude of later cleanup costs.
9. WASTE: Energy and resource content of waste streams is minimized by recovery or recycling as an operating economy that also reduces environmental burdens.
10. DEPENDENCE: A firm recognizes the degree to which it is dependent on and served by the health of the local community and encourages this health wherever possible.
11. CONTRIBUTION: A firm operates in such a way that it and its employees support their fair share of the costs of community services, including those used by the business and needed by both the employees and the fringe of the community.
12. NEIGHBORHOOD: A firm recognizes its own effect on the nature and character of the neighborhood around it and minimizes adverse effects insofar as possible.
13. SELF-INTEREST: In public processes a firm recognizes and pursues its own self-interest and cultivates an understanding of this self-interest as it relates to the social and political processes so that neither the anger of society nor its political power will be aroused.
14. SOCIAL CHANGE: The business power to mold and reshape society is used wisely by selecting areas where social forces supporting such change have already been set in motion and by not encouraging attempts at change that will be rejected by society's governance processes.
15. STANDARDS: Wherever a firm encounters areas where social standards are needed but do not yet exist, it creates appropriate standards, begins to live by them, and offers them for broader adoption as appropriate.
16. ALLEGIANCE: A corporation gives its primary allegiance to the society that makes the rules controlling its existence. In the view of that society, it must blend in as a sound corporate citizen to have hopes of long-term acceptance and survival.
17. FEDERAL MANAGEMENT: A business with operations in many different nations or other rule-making social units encourages each subsidiary to become a part of the local society, recognizes the

divergent allegiances of the several subsidiaries, and develops economic and managerial unity in a framework consistent with these local ties.
18. POWER: A business uses its economic power and its political influence carefully to avoid presenting a threat to the society or alarming the political power of that society.
19. LOYALTY: A business expects and requires allegiance from the members of its organization within the legal scope of its business and within the personal scope of the employees' normal growth and progression as individuals, and recognizes the likelihood of unrest or defection if it attempts to require illegal or unethical actions, or actions detrimental to an employee's self-interest.
20. WEALTH PRODUCTION: As a wealth producer, and in the interest of its own economic soundness and that of society, a firm attempts to make its productive processes as efficient in the use of materials, energy, and labor as competitive circumstances will permit.
21. SOCIAL CONTROL: As a regulated wealth producer, a firm strives to build public information about the basic issues underlying the choice of the most efficient pattern for regulating it and its industry.
22. REGULATION: A firm learns the network of rules and regulations applicable to its operations, determines which are relevant, viable, and under enforcement, and works quietly and constructively with the various regulatory authorities, confronting them only as business self-interest truly requires.
23. TECHNOLOGY: A business dependent on long-term processes for generation of new technology develops an understanding of this dependence and seeks opportunities to encourage the replenishment of this technology.
24. NEW PRODUCTS: When goods and services that change lifestyles and cultural patterns are introduced and promoted, an effort is made to minimize the social stress caused by the change, to hasten adoption, and to avoid challenge of the right to introduce such goods or services.
25. CAPITAL: A business conserves and expands its resource base to maintain and increase the level of opportunity, in its own interests and in the interests of its employees and the dependent community.
26. PROFITS: A business handles its profits in such a way as to minimize the economic, social, and political impact of their use, particularly the impact from movement of profits across borders to a parent corporation or stockholders.
27. SEVERANCE: When evolution of the business creates a surplus of plants, people, or community services, the firm makes a serious

effort to find alternative profitable uses for these dependent resources, or at least to cushion the severance so that the long-term economic health of the community and of former members of the organization will be preserved.

27 Guidelines. Where the nine principles are quite general, the 27 guidelines are intended to be much more specific. Their individual derivation is discussed in *Business and Its Environment*. The idea is that management should have a set of comprehensive, flexible norms to suggest the most desirable course of action; this can then become an anchor point in the list of alternatives actually being considered. While the suggested actions may not in all cases be possible, the process serves two purposes: (1) if a proposed action of the firm will have a serious impact that cannot easily be offset, perhaps the action should be reconsidered or replanned to have a less severe impact, and (2) if an adverse impact cannot be balanced, its severity will provide a basis for considering whether a backlash, in terms of regulation or other social action, is likely to be provoked.

PROFIT MAXIMIZATION AND SOCIAL COST AVOIDANCE

The plan for the management of corporate social impact is a plan for a healthy business to use to build and maintain a sound, harmonious relationship with society, so that it will have more freedom to pursue profitable growth in sales of goods or services, as summarized in Figure 8-1. By avoiding creation of social cost, it furthers this relationship, and increases its own ability to maximize profits. Profit maximization is a familiar goal, and the one for which the corporate structure is best suited. However, the interests of society do not permit it to allow corporations to pursue profits until their responsibilities to society have been discharged. A management that recognizes this can quietly devise the most effective route toward operating in a satisfactory balance with society, and then pursue profit goals with full energy.

QUESTIONS FOR ANALYSIS AND DISCUSSION

1. Do you agree that a business that gives fair value benefits society by its existence? Discuss.

FIGURE 8–1 THE MANAGEMENT OF SOCIAL IMPACT

Maintaining social balance
Direct impact areas
- sale of goods and services
- physical resources
- human resources
- waste streams
- community

Systemwide impact areas
- public issues
- social value systems
- loyalties and allegiances
- governance
- regulation
- technology
- resource policies

Principles and guidelines for social impact management

PROFIT MAXIMIZATION AND SOCIAL COST AVOIDANCE
---

2. Give examples of social costs caused by a business.
3. Give an example of a business action with a social impact in the area of:
   - (a) sale of goods and services
   - (b) use of physical resources
   - (c) use of human resources
   - (d) waste streams
   - (e) the community
   - (f) public issues
   - (g) social value systems
   - (h) loyalty and allegiance
   - (i) governance
   - (j) regulation
   - (k) technology
   - (l) use of business resources
4. Give an example of social balance failure and discuss possible remedies.
5. The text argues that by avoiding harmful impacts on society a business can gain more freedom in its pursuit of profits. Do you agree or disagree? Discuss.

FOR FURTHER INFORMATION

Buchholz, Rogene, *Fundamental Concepts and Problems in Business Ethics* (Englewood Cliffs, N.J.: Prentice-Hall, 1989).
    Ethical aspects of business behavior.

Sawyer, George C., *Business and Its Environment* (Englewood Cliffs, N.J.: Prentice-Hall, 1985).
    Further information on management of social impact.

CASE 15 TOXIC THREADS

Toxic Threads was a large producer of synthetic fibers. These included a wide variety of blends using acrylic fibers. Acrylonitrile monomer, used in making these fibers, is a gas comparable in toxicity to cyanide gas. It is synthesized from natural gas and then stored or shipped as a liquid under pressure. Acrylonitrile is used in many processes and is a routine part of tank car shipments between U.S. chemical plants. Toxic Threads made its own acrylonitrile, which was then polymerized and spun into textile fibers in a large chemical complex. This plant complex, which had an excellent safety record, was located in the industrial district of a large eastern city.

During a foggy summer night a large object fell from the air, striking a storage tank inside the Toxic Threads plant. This was a large tank in which acrylonitrile was stored. The falling object, later identified as an airplane engine, broke open the tank and released the contents. An alarm sounded in the plant security station and one of the guards immediately told the local police emergency center that one of their sensors showed a toxic substances leak. This was the first step in the area safety routine established earlier; the warning sensors in the plant were set to extremely low levels, and approximately once a month this led to a minor alarm of some sort, but there had never been a leak serious enough to cause any concern to the area. The police emergency center followed its established procedure, which was to send out an alert to all units, and to start the timer for an area alarm in 15 minutes if they had not had a further report from the plant.

The portion of the plant where the main acrylonitrile storage was located was not operating at night, this area was across the plant from the control room where the night plant security station was located, and the fog was so dense that driving was difficult. It took almost 15 minutes for security to discover that there was a major leak. Immediately a disaster alarm was sounded in the plant and also in the police emergency headquarters. But the acrylonitrile cloud was indistinguishable from the dense fog at night, and no night disaster in a fog had been foreseen. Shortly after the disaster alarm was sounded the gas cloud reached the control building, killing the three security guards and four chemical operators, the only people in the plant at the time, and the only people who knew what the problem was.

The local authorities tried to discover the specific reason for the alarm but without success. Two volunteers who entered the plant in a patrol car died suddenly but gained no information. Meanwhile the gas cloud drifted slowly over the nearby inner city area; as the pattern of fatalities became obvious, evacuation was started; but it was not very effective because of the fog, the darkness, and uncertainty about a safe direction to go. Because of the earlier alert to the local emergency services, large numbers of emergency units came into the area and their casualties were correspondingly high.

Daylight showed several hundred people dead, and by then the toxic gas was gone. No one could explain where the airplane engine that started the trouble had fallen from; it had not been from a commercial plane, and none of the private planes passing over the area reported the loss or were implicated by later investigation. The model and manufacture of the engine were established from the wreckage but nothing else, and thousands of this model had been made and sold over many years. The final investigation report speculated that a private plane had been carrying a spare engine which somehow came loose and fell. While no one was satisfied with this explanation, no better one was ever put forward.

Toxic Threads had an excellent safety record, its safety procedures had been cited as a model in a major national survey, and even after the disaster the routine precautions stood re-examination well. The recrimination later focused on the fact that none of the company, local, and state disaster drills (of which there had been many) had considered the possibility of a fog at night or of all of the plant personnel being killed before they could tell the local authorities what was wrong. Of course, many people felt that this plant, or even the synthetic fiber industry, should not be permitted to operate. The company was not found to have been negligent in any way, but lawsuits totalling $47 billion were filed based on the doctrine that having toxic chemicals on the premises made the company liable. The company took the position that the random fall of an airplane engine fit within the "act of God" interpretation and that they should not be liable. It was predicted that the matter could not be settled except by the Supreme Court, and that it would require many years of litigation to get a Supreme Court verdict.

QUESTIONS

1. Who was responsible, in your opinion?
2. Several legal experts predicted that, if Toxic Threads were held responsible, it would force a shutdown of much of the textile, chemical, and plastics industries, including most oil refineries, because no private company could afford the risks of processing hazardous materials. This would be bad, and many of us would miss being able to buy gasoline, but the public should have some protection. How can these conflicting needs be reconciled?

CASE 16 GOLIATH DATA PROCESSING

Goliath Data Processing was a fast-growing and prosperous data processing company. It was in the stage of its growth where it could hardly build plants and hire people rapidly enough. Goliath had decided on another new plant which would employ 4000 people initially and expand from there. It was not looking for handouts from the local development authorities—just a good site with transportation, utilities, and access to a good labor pool. Goliath liked to hire and train local people for its work, paid well, and tried to be a good corporate citizen.

Acme Realties was a firm that specialized in assembling urban building sites, usually secretly, and its management knew all of the ins and outs of city politics. Acme learned that Goliath was looking for a plant site and picked one out. This was a 20-block site of badly deteriorated housing. About half of the buildings were still occupied, with the other half empty and abandoned by the former owners. Acme satisfied itself that it could deliver the site and approached Goliath on an exploratory basis.

Goliath was interested but cautious. The Goliath real estate people knew it was not easy to acquire and clear such a site. But as Acme sensed an interest, it began to step up its campaign. It persuaded the local utility to offer electric rate incentives. It persuaded the city to offer real estate tax abatements. Acme told the local members of Congress, who made personal appeals to Goliath and asked for help from the governor and the mayor. When both the governor and the mayor told Goliath how welcome they would be, and that it was Goliath's duty and responsibility to employ all of those inner city people, the president of Goliath told his legal and real estate people to go ahead, if they could protect the company. After all, it really was a very good site, even without the incentives they hadn't asked for; it was just a matter of trying to be cautious about Acme's ability to deliver.

The final agreement was that Goliath would buy on a package basis. That is, Acme was to acquire the site, remove the buildings, and rough grade, so that Goliath could come in and start to build. Acme promised to deliver the site in six months, the mayor called Goliath again to urge it to go ahead, and the deal was signed. Goliath gave Acme $2 million as a down payment, with the balance to be paid when the site was delivered. The next day Acme sent eviction notices to all of the 4000 tenants in the occupied buildings and started six wrecking crews knocking down vacant buildings on different parts of the area. But the 4000 tenants had not been consulted, did not like the idea of being evicted, and the demonstrations and protests escalated rapidly. No one could find the Acme Realty offices, so they firebombed the local Goliath headquarters instead. The site demolition was stopped by a court order. The city council passed a resolution condemning Goliath, and the mayor could not remember that he had ever encouraged Goliath to locate there.

Goliath had a problem because it needed a new plant operating on schedule. The production vice-president asked the president to let him build on a South Carolina site instead. The legal vice-president said that he would try to get the two million back from Acme, but that this was the sort of firm where he might spend $500,000 in legal fees in order to get $100,000 of their lost money back. The president said: "You know, I really wanted to build there and employ those inner city people. I think it would have worked out very well."

The marketing vice-president told the president it was still his social responsibility to build in the inner city. The president said: "I really would like to, but unless there is some way to clear that site immediately, we have no choice but to go to South Carolina, because we have to get a plant built and the products out."

QUESTIONS

1. What do you think Goliath should do now?
2. Everyone would have been happier if Goliath had built in the inner city. But considering that they had to move so rapidly, was it a waste of time even to consider it?
3. The president of Goliath also was considering a proposal for fighting through the clearance proposal, knowing that it would take several years. Meanwhile Goliath would have to go ahead in South Carolina and would probably not need the plant site by the time it was available, in which case it would sell the property. This course of action would have recovered the $2 million already invested, since the site could easily be sold at a profit when it was finally cleared—but some of the people who were expecting a Goliath plant there would say they had been deceived. Should Goliath fight to finish buying the site and get its money back by selling at a profit? Or walk away with a $2 million loss?

CHAPTER 9

MANAGING OPPORTUNITY

KEY IDEAS IN THIS CHAPTER

This chapter discusses the overview-level management of opportunity, within the scope of the enterprise opportunity strategy and in order to obtain the desired level of new opportunities:

- **constructing the opportunity plan** – for new products or services, for the base business, for the relevant technologies, to maintain the optimum level of integration or dis-integration.
- **the role of restructuring** – as a continual or a cataclysmic process, often with takeover, leveraged buyout, or stock buyback.
- **master strategy and the master builder** – for enterprise-level opportunity management.
- **opportunity management** – of diversity, innovation, and by creating the desired future.
- **the plan for course correction** – steering the business around potholes.
- **opportunity management** – chapter summary.

Opportunity is a key strategic component. Its shifts and evolutions are difficult to track. They require a careful overview of the social, technological, competitive and other factors that influence opportunity change. As discussed in Chapter 6, one of the five key enterprise building blocks is the opportunity strategy. By deciding how passive or how aggressive to be in seeking out and developing innovations, how much to lead versus how much to follow others in changes in the market, and how much or how little of the available talent and money to stake on new developments, an enterprise determines a major part of its organizational personality and culture. It also establishes boundaries on the types of profit opportunities it will pursue, and the opportunity strategy that is selected becomes a governing element to which other primary and contributing strategies must relate.

CONSTRUCTING THE OPPORTUNITY PLAN

The opportunity plan—for the next generation of products and businesses—deals with (1) the evolution and life cycle of the present line of products and services and of the markets into which they are sold, (2) the growth and maturity of the present businesses, including any shifts in the underlying technology, and (3) investment in new businesses as required to achieve enterprise goals.

The need for an overview level of opportunity planning seems at first to be a reflection on existing research or development units, but it is not. Rather, it is a realistic evaluation of the way that these and most other innovation-focused departments are formed, staffed, and operated. Normally such a unit is created to achieve a specific set of product or business objectives and staffed with people with the capabilities required for the specific tasks. As the routine operation of the unit goes on from month to month and year to year and the unit performs the work for which it was created, these operating managers also develop their wall of concentration barriers, and lose any breadth that their initial perspective may have had.

When the technical or social frontiers shift—the kind of development for which an overview perspective is often required—the busy operating manager of a research unit is as likely as any other operating manager to miss the significance of the shift. But as a key member of a planning team with an overview perspective, the same manager can make major contributions as the group recognizes and develops resulting opportunities.

THE PLAN FOR NEW PRODUCTS OR SERVICES

What new products or new services will there be? Products and services have life cycles, and Chapter 3 discusses typical patterns of sales, profits, and investment. As products or services move through the life cycle appropriate to their nature, the research or development unit is normally asked to find replacement products to maintain and extend the market success. The element of overview planning in this is to try to anticipate changes in the market place that will receive these new products, since many markets evolve at a significant rate.

This anticipatory element needs emphasis. It is more common for good technical people to talk to good marketing people and then concentrate on improving the present good products. Too often this has led to successful development projects lasting several years and producing products already obsolete—because the market changed while the work was in progress. The planning should look forward, to develop products for the markets into which the products will actually emerge, and to estimate the degree to which these products will replace volume lost as old products decline and whether they will also provide new growth in sales and profit.

THE PLAN FOR THE BASE BUSINESS

Here the overview is focused on the evolution of the central business concept. From this central point the nature of the required products or services can be compared with what exists. As businesses change, it is sometimes necessary to find other customer need areas, to redefine the mission and goals, and to approach the business opportunity in a different way, as did AT&T. AT&T promoted and accepted divestiture of its local telephone operating subsidiaries to settle the Justice Department antitrust suit because this expanded its growth targets to include the national network of data transmission and related services. The need for such shifts occurs in most business areas, but not frequently. The question for opportunity planning, then, is whether the basis for this particular business is shifting or should be shifted. Overview-level planning provides a forum in which the mission and goals of the business can be routinely reviewed, so that when a time does come that they should be changed, managers will take notice, make a plan, and act.

A PLAN FOR THE TECHNOLOGY

Is our firm making full use of its technology and developing the strongest positions it can? Any enterprise investing in innovation processes will achieve new positions based on proprietary technology from each success. The value of such positions is reflected by the return they can generate. Management of such a position means realizing this return—that is, receiving the rent it can earn in all of its potential areas of application: sales to different customers, in different markets, and in different geographic areas. The management process, market by market and opportunity by opportunity, is to examine each potential application, decide where the value is sufficient to justify development, select a development route, and get action started.

This does not mean that a firm must enter every business area, and some can be developed better through other firms. Boots, a large English pharmaceutical company, discovered and developed ibuprofen. To get sales in the U.S. market, it licensed the product; Upjohn marketed ibuprofen under the brand name Motrin as a prescription drug for the treatment of arthritis. Later, having established a more credible marketing presence in the U.S. prescription pharmaceutical market, Boots began to market a similar ibuprofen product under the brand name Rufen, in an attempt to get more profit from direct sales than it could through its royalties from Upjohn.

At about the same time the Food and Drug Administration became convinced that ibuprofen could be sold for other purposes without a prescription. Boots, not ready for so fiercely combative a part of the U.S. drug market, licensed the product to Whitehall Laboratories, a Division of American Home Products, for over-the-counter sale as Advil. Upjohn, also aware of the potential of this market but not wishing to be identified with a product promoted in this way, licensed its U.S. rights to Bristol-Myers who sold it as Nuprin. Whitehall's and Bristol-Myers' intention was to obtain a substantial share of the nonprescription drug market for pain relievers dominated by aspirin and Tylenol. To the extent that they succeeded, through royalties they would add to the return of the Upjohn and Boots-U.S. technical positions, and ultimately to the return to the technology position of the parent Boots organization, which had the basic rights to the product.

This situation arose because Boots was not content to earn a return from its research success only in the markets in which it was then active. It saw the potentials and obtained successful development, through Upjohn and Whitehall (and indirectly through Bristol-Myers).

In the same spirit of seeking out maximum rents from any worthwhile position the research yields, new pharmaceuticals are routinely screened for additional potential as veterinary products. Substances affecting life processes of humans could also have favorable or unfavorable effects on insects or plants, and many new drugs are screened there too. Some of the pharmaceutical companies developing these substances have no veterinary sales route, and many sell no insecticides or plant control chemicals, but the possible license fees are still an attractive incentive.

INTEGRATION AND DIS-INTEGRATION

Is the present degree of horizontal and vertical integration correct? A key strategic business variable is what Silver called the scope of the firm [1]—that is, how far the activities of a given business unit extend into preparation of parts and raw materials, to marketing of the products or services at different levels, and the extent of the territory in which the business carries out these activities. Two dimensions of this scope are the horizontal and vertical integration. *Horizontal integration* deals with the extent to which similar activities in other areas should be added, *backward vertical integration* with the degree to which a business produces its own raw materials, parts, and components, and *forward vertical integration* with the degree to which a business sells to the ultimate consumer rather than to retailers, distributors, or other intermediaries.

Horizontal integration has the potential for important scale economies in purchasing, production, and marketing, where automobiles, appliances, and many other sorts of consumer goods require national markets to compete effectively. Hospital chains are growing because hospitals can be run at lower cost this way, and the pharmaceutical industry is moving toward global leadership by a handful of major firms because the heavy research costs can be recovered from sales in many countries. But horizontal integration does not always bring advantages, and these may shift with various competitive and economic changes.

Backward vertical integration is often necessary for a new industry, a business needing unusual raw material quantities or qualities, or a stability of supply not ensured by the open market. In the thrust of rapid early growth the Ford Motor Company built its own steel mills, arranged for its own supplies of coal and iron ore, and made as many of its own component parts as possible. It was attempting to become fully integrated backward toward its raw material base. Today in a different and more mature automobile market Ford has sold its steel mill and buys a much larger fraction of its parts and components from others; its degree of backward vertical integration is much less. In most cases the first major industry in a less-developed country must backward integrate not only to provide a large share of its own raw materials, but also its own maintenance and other specialized support services. Yet in industrialized areas where service firms have developed, it is often much more advantageous for similar companies to purchase specialized services such as crane and other services requiring major equipment or unusual skills.

Forward vertical integration moves a firm toward its customers. In

---
[1] Morris Silver, *Enterprise and the Scope of the Firm* (Oxford: Martin Robinson, 1984).

introducing their products in developing countries, major appliance manufacturers have sometimes found it necessary to open their own retail outlets to get the necessary demonstration of the product to consumers unfamiliar with its use, and to obtain the required quality of service support. Then later, as the appliance market has developed and local entrepreneurs have learned how to sell and service washing machines and refrigerators, the manufacturers have drawn back, leaving the local retailing and support function to be performed by local entrepreneurs in a way that has proved more efficient and economical elsewhere.

The optimum degree of horizontal and vertical integration changes as a business changes, and as the markets and the society evolve. Where dependable and efficient markets develop, firms find little incentive to integrate across them. Integrated oil companies still have an advantage over nonintegrated competitors because the crude oil markets and markets for the various petroleum factions still are not free enough to provide a dependable basis for nonintegrated operations. Grain markets are further developed, and even though grain prices fluctuate substantially, these fluctuations can be hedged with futures contracts, and firms needing to buy quantities of wheat or corn have minimal incentive to integrate into wheat or corn production. Although integration may have economic benefits, the vertically integrated firm tends to be less flexible in its response to changes in raw material economics or customer needs, so that its economic advantage could fade and leave the nonintegrated competitor better positioned.

Patterns of vertical integration and the way they change have been studied,[2] and it is frequent to find vertical integration earlier in the development of a business, with a decline in vertical integration as the business approaches maturity and decline. In general, (1) the various integration alternatives often give the opportunity for positions and leverages critical to the success of a strategy, (2) economics of vertical and horizontal integration positions shift significantly as conditions change, so that integration patterns need routine review and adjustment, and (3) shifts in integration patterns often require significant changes in the governing enterprise strategies, particularly desirability, belonging, and managing, and changes in the degree of vertical integration may be possible only if top management will allow review and possible revision of the governing strategies.

---

[2] Kathryn Rudie Harrigan, *Strategies for Vertical Integration* (Lexington Mass.: Lexington Books, 1983; see also Kathryn Rudie Harrigan, *Strategic Flexibility* (Lexington, Mass.: Lexington Books, 1985), Chapters 4–5, pp. 63–102.

THE ROLE OF RESTRUCTURING

Does our firm need restructuring? U.S. Industry has undergone a wave of restructuring in the last several years. Basically this is a process of rearrangement of operations and assets following from the discovery that a particular firm has lagged in adapting its strategies to changed conditions and perhaps failed in the quality of its management, to the point that rapid retrenchments are required to ensure economic health and stockholder support. At the cutting edge of this trend have been developments in acquisition and buyout financing, making it relatively easy for a management generating weak earnings or poor security prices for its stockholders to be turned out and a new management installed.

Two major mechanisms for replacing the present management of a firm are by tender offer, where a premium price is offered for the stock, and by leveraged buyout, where an investment group buys the stock and forms a private company. In both cases the process is normally accompanied by a large debt increase, as money is borrowed to finance the process. This debt increase normally brings an earnings increase for the remaining stockholders because debt capital costs less on an after-tax basis. But the shift also greatly increases the fixed cost the business must pay—due to the added interest costs—making the firm more vulnerable to any economic downturn.

To avoid such a takeover, the incumbent management also may borrow heavily and buy back stock to give the stockholders the same sort of improvement in earnings, and whether the shift from equity to debt capitalization is triggered by takeover, leveraged buyout, or buyback of stock, it is normally accompanied by divestment of nonproductive assets, layoffs, simplification of top-heavy organization structures, and the other elements of a typical restructuring process. The restructuring trend is healthy. However, those firms that were managed well from year to year accomplished this process in small and relatively painless steps by making orderly change a way of life, thus avoiding the organizational cataclysm and turmoil of a major restructuring.

ADDING BUSINESSES IN OTHER AREAS

Will our firm need to shift to other business areas to achieve the growth it needs? Another contribution of the overview analysis is in estimating the future of the present business areas, and matching the outlook for sales and profits with the business goals and with the returns being generated elsewhere. It is not automatic that an enterprise should diversify since this increases the burden on the management, but it is important that the adequacy of the future prospects of the present business be considered. If diversification offers higher returns or if the returns from the present businesses may decline, management has good reason to reexamine its opportunity strategy and its managing and belonging strategies, to see where entry into other business areas should be considered.

However, as competitive pressures continue to increase, a multibusiness enterprise will more and more have to justify its costs, including any bureaucratic hindrances the central organization represents, as being less than its contribution to the success of each business unit. Just as conglomerates are now being challenged as to whether their business units would be better as independent companies, the central contribution and efficiency of all multibusiness enterprises will face similar questions. Reimann[3] uses the Phillip Morris acquisition of Miller as an example of the importance of skills transfer. Phillip Morris' marketing skills were new to the beer market and propelled Miller to a strong second position in the market before its competitors responded effectively enough to check its advance. But that was several years ago, and today's question would be whether Miller is stronger as a subordinate unit under Phillip Morris management and paying its share of the central administrative costs, or whether Miller would be better off on its own again. Phillip Morris made a large contribution to Miller success and could realize its profit through a leveraged buyout or sale of stock. The logic that seems to be emerging from today's restructuring is that, in a case such as this, Phillip Morris should keep Miller if it believes it can really contribute substantially to Miller's further success; but if Miller is to be just one more business unit paying a share of central management costs, Phillip Morris should take its profit and let Miller go on alone.

A firm may need to shift to other business areas to find the opportunities it seeks, and it should look for areas where its skills can make a contribution, as Phillip Morris marketing skills did at Miller. And that firm's management should also look at the contribution/cost ratio as such a relationship continues, to be sure that all parts of the firm continue to return better as part of it than otherwise.

MASTER STRATEGY AND THE MASTER BUILDER

What are our master strategies? Or, what master strategies are needed in the opportunity area? In Chapter 3 the concept of master strategy for the firm was mentioned as a superordinate strategy over the business strate-

---

[3] Bernard C. Reimann, "Corporate Strategy: From Portfolio Planning to Value Building," 1988 FAR "Best Paper in Corporate and Organizational Planning" winner.

gies. Part of the master strategy idea is that of the master builder, with building blocks and choice strategies in place, to craft a major enterprise out of the complex of businesses and the pattern of investments assembled. Complex enterprises are built out of component businesses. If the governing strategies permit, a management able to do well in one business could build another in a related area, and another—and thus families of businesses are created, perhaps with still others added by acquisition, subject to choice strategies determining how similar or diverse they can be, and subject to the management skill in picking attractive areas to enter. 3M or Johnson & Johnson have each built a large family of closely related businesses, with the close relationship of the businesses making their management easier and increasing the chance for common use of resources or for synergism in the market place.

At the level of overall direction of the enterprise a management desiring to build a major multibusiness company can and should be thinking about how the businesses fit together and where the family of businesses might expand advantageously. This is a most proper and important part of the opportunity management plan and concept, and the tools presented here could aid greatly in the work of an entrepreneurial master builder.

OPPORTUNITY MANAGEMENT

Each management needs to consider how to develop the opportunities it has and needs. This involves a management strategy for the firm as a whole, and an innovation strategy to guide investment in research and other creative activities.

DIVERSITY

How diverse should this enterprise be? The managing strategy at the enterprise level specifies the degree to which the firm will attempt to manage different types of businesses.

Too often unless a specific plan for managing a diversity of businesses has been developed, a firm tries to manage many businesses as if they were all the same. General Motors failed in its entry into the aircraft engine business even though it had accumulated a backlog of successful aircraft engine production experience during World War II. This failure has been attributed to the fact that the typical new product development cycle for aircraft engines is many years longer than for other General Motors products. In other ways the aircraft engine business was very like the existing family of GM engine businesses, but the longer new product development cycle required a different pattern of management, and the engine business did not prosper.

The area of veterinary products with its attractive total dollar volume has represented a frequent diversification failure for pharmaceutical companies. In spite of the obvious applicability of human drug products to animal care, the market is different—remarkably fragmented by the need to treat each individual animal species in a different way. Company after company failed because it treated the veterinary area as a simple extension of the human pharmaceutical market rather than as a family of overlapping smaller markets, each requiring separate service.

The track record of the conglomerate companies that have bought and sold subsidiaries based on financial information alone is very mixed, and several of the former highfliers have come to disaster. The indications are that there are times when top management needs to know a good deal about the businesses it is managing, and to the extent that such knowledge is required it limits the range of businesses with which one management can work successfully.

There is no clear agreement on how diverse an enterprise can safely be, and many different degrees of diversity are being tested by major firms currently. With these different degrees of diversity are a variety of different control philosophies that attempt to minimize the handicap of a conglomerate company. Each management should consider the degree of diversity it is willing to attempt, or needs to attempt, and include this judgment as a parameter in its planning through reaffirmed or restated enterprise choice criteria. The higher the degree of diversity, the greater the risks, at least in terms of challenges to control systems and management ability, so that the safer course is to minimize diversity as long as this does not limit growth and profitability, or introduce other risks through dependence on specific markets.

INNOVATION

How much innovation is needed and how will this be accomplished? Are there specific, critical innovation targets? A part of the management challenge is the challenge to innovate. Drucker defined an innovation as a useful new combination of resources, and any management activity deals with potential gains from innovation continually. In the plan for managing opportunity the innovation needs and innovation plans should be laid out clearly. Many innovation plans will consist largely of decisions to fund certain research projects, and the details can well be left to research functional planning, except for a composite judgment by which different projects are compared for potential payoff and potential success.

Other innovations first require a new concept of a product application, a potential service, a means of distribution, or some other market or use parameter, so that the first challenge is to generate a creative insight.

Many techniques exist for accomplishing this, by structured group approaches to creativity, and by use of consultants and other outside experts. At the level of the strategic overview and the plan for managing opportunity nothing limits a management group to existing inventions. A part of the overview-level planning process is to define needed innovations, and with surprising frequency they can be achieved if management decides to pursue them seriously.

CREATING THE DESIRED FUTURE

Are there places where our firm needs to create the future? The plan for the management of opportunity deals with the present and more with the future, because in the time required to accomplish any of its plans the business will have moved into that future. The first overview specification is based on projecting the evolution of this future, but Drucker also spoke of "creating the future," meaning that a management has a very real power to design a future and make it come true.

This does not mean that anything at all can be made to happen. But it does mean that new types of products and systems can be built, introduced, and established in the market, and that distribution systems and customer habits can be shifted. Color television became physically possible soon after black-and-white television, but development stalled. There was no market for color TV sets because there were no color broadcasts. No one could afford to broadcast in color because there were no sets to receive the signals. RCA decided to hasten the adoption of color television by starting color broadcasting and offering color sets at the same time, even though it sustained heavy losses in both for some time, and its efforts made color television a public reality very rapidly. Long ago the tobacco industry launched an advertising campaign aimed at making it respectable for women to smoke cigarettes. The campaign succeeded and effectively doubled the size of the cigarette market. In neither case were the companies making people do something they did not want to do—viewers wanted color television, and women wanted the option of smoking cigarettes—but the campaign altered the timetable and the resulting reality very substantially.

The potential still exists for a business to influence the direction and rate of development of a particular trend, by choosing the desired branch and evolution of that trend and hurrying its development. Thus, the market is changed and the future created, to the advantage of the change agent if the campaign is carefully and thoughtfully planned. The plan for the management of opportunity starts with the momentum of existing lines and existing businesses, then looks at alternative businesses and at the future, with the challenge to management to shape that future, to create in it the opportunity it wishes to find.

THE PLAN FOR COURSE CORRECTION

Just as the driver of a car or the pilot of a ship must watch for obstacles ahead and steer around them, so must the management of a business steer through a variety of changes in laws, materials availabilities, and waste treatment requirements. Changes directly affecting the components of the business or the essence of its strategy must be considered instantly when they arise. But many changes are essentially nonstrategic, except that affected businesses must react or conform. Yet they can stop a major program as abruptly as a broken axle stops a car. They are the business equivalent of the potholes drivers learn to dodge in late winter; even though they are completely impersonal and unrelated to a particular car or its occupants, they can break a tire or a wheel if the driver is not alert. A change in the equal employment regulations could result in severe sanctions against a noncomplying business, but has little or no effect on a business with an effective compliance process. Or, when a hazardous chemical is banned, only those using it are affected by the ban, and only those without good alternatives are affected seriously. The plan for enterprise course correction is a systematic, overview-level review of where the various corporate programs are directed and the business terrain through which they must move, in search of potential pothole-type hazards business managers need to steer around.

One consultant's success story dealt with Red #4, one of the later members of this family of coal tar food dyes to come under attack as a possible cause of cancer. On noting the first signs of suspicion, he prejudged the outcome and advised General Mills, his employer at the time, to take Red #4 out of all of its products. This was not difficult since other colors were available, and routine marketing continued during the necessary development work. The change was made, thus moving General Mills programs away from this particular pothole. Some of its competitors still had products containing Red #4 in the market place when the official ban came, and they suffered lost sales, embarrassment, and bad publicity.

The entire field of hazardous materials, starting with nuclear materials and highly toxic chemicals, has become a field of difficulty and rules changes. Even "safe" and familiar materials such as benzene showed potential for causing cancer and became subject to severe new restrictions. Safety rules must be followed, of course, and the course correction issue concerns new rules, usually created because of a new hazard or a new awareness of a previously unrecognized hazard. Anticipating the changes is frequently possible because the trends of investigation which produce them are well known.

The banning of Red #4 cited above followed logically from the banning of several of its chemical cousins; that it would be tested was obvious. All of its cousins that had come under suspicion had later been banned—and from the first evidence of cancer in the test animals the probability of an eventual ban justified the immediate action that was taken. In the same way, benzene use was not restricted at the first hint of a problem; confirmatory testing was needed and performed; alert observers knew that this testing was going on, and that it was likely to lead to restrictive action long before the restrictions were put into effect.

The entire field of regulatory action is a potential source of new rules and requirements that stop programs until the firm finds a way to comply. Such new rules rarely come without warning, and a part of the effort required for the course correction plan is a foresight-type review of developing regulatory themes, to see where potential threats may be emerging.

When a social issue is building in a community, this will be obvious. Its potential impact on a specific business may also be discernable. A few years ago activists in several cities lost patience with the pace of federal enforcement of integration rules and instituted a series of boycotts. The targets of the boycotts were firms convenient to reach and surround, rather than conspicuously bad actors; several supermarket chains were chosen, for example, because they were so vulnerable if a boycott kept their customers away. A foresight diagnosis of this vulnerability might have led their managements to take extraordinary steps, not just to comply with the law, but to establish a sufficient rapport with the activists that the firm no longer would be a target.

OPEC caused a shortage of oil in the United States and shortages of petrochemicals soon followed. One small biological products business was heavily dependent on acetone, a familiar solvent used in many laboratory and production procedures for biologicals. Acetone was made from corn—at least, so the head of this business believed. It truly had been made from corn in the past; more recently it had become a petrochemical. In a small business without staff to look at the outside environment, it is not surprising that no one realized that the acetone from the local laboratory supply house was not being made from corn any more, and the petrochemical shortage caused a brief shutdown of the plant.

The whole point here is to look around the margins of the operation, to see where real but less obvious vulnerabilities may be. It is unlikely that a business would be shut down by a paper clip strike, but if there were no paper for the copy machines, it would hit some firms hard.

Not all eventualities can be anticipated, and most of the time and attention should go to the strategic variables. But a little time every year is well spent if it keeps Red #4 or an activist boycott from becoming strategic by shutting the business down unexpectedly. A large fraction of these external events that disrupt the business are of such a nature that

---

FIGURE 9-1   OPPORTUNITY MANAGEMENT AND STRATEGY DESIGN

Managing opportunity
- new products or services
- the basic business
- the technology
- shifting to other business areas

Opportunity
- diversity
- creating the future

The opportunity building block
- governing the innovation plan

Keeping the business out of unnecessary trouble
- regulations and recalls
- safety rules
- social stress
- material shortages

OPPORTUNITY MANAGEMENT: TOOL OF THE MASTER BUILDER

---

their likelihood, if not the specific event, is predictable; the purpose of the plan for course correction is to reduce these interruptions of the business flow to the few truly unpredictable events.

OPPORTUNITY MANAGEMENT

Management really does have a choice in the way in which it deals with opportunity; this is a key component of enterprise choice strategy. But operating managers in the grips of strategic blindness are at their worst in the opportunity area because of the frequency with which the route to large advances by the enterprise or by its competitors emerges in unseen new dimensions of familiar problems.

    Once a strategic overview is established, and once the enterprise and the business have established a basic posture toward opportunity—whether one of waiting for others, waiting for opportunity, seeking out the opportunity, or creating it—preparing and acting on a plan for managing opportunity is not difficult, although it requires a thorough understanding of the technical and social evolution of the surrounding environment. A sound opportunity strategy to govern the development effort determines the relative aggressiveness or passiveness with which a given firm will build its plans and put them into action, as shown in Figure 9-1, as it continues to develop the dimensions of strategic action and control.

QUESTIONS FOR ANALYSIS AND DISCUSSION

1. For an organization you know or have read about, speculate about the possible contents of the opportunity plan:
   (a) for new products and services
   (b) for the base business
   (c) for the technology
   (d) for shifting to other business areas
2. How can the management of a given firm decide how diverse that firm ought to become?
3. What will determine the innovation strategy a specific management selects?
4. Give an example, not from the text, of a business that has created some part of the future it wanted to have.
5. Give your own example of a course correction problem created by a development in the area of:
   (a) regulations and recalls
   (b) safety rules
   (c) social stress
   (d) material shortage
6. Give two or three examples of business programs that have been halted by course correction problems for which the business was not prepared.

FOR FURTHER INFORMATION

Day, George S., *Strategic Market Planning: The Pursuit of Competitive Advantage* (St. Paul, Minn.: West, 1984).
   Opportunity planning from a strategic marketer.

Hax, Arnoldo C. (ed.), *Planning Strategies That Work* (Oxford/New York: Oxford Press, 1987).
   Opportunity planning from a planning perspective.

Waterman, Robert H., *The Renewal Factor: How the Best Get and Keep the Competitive Edge* (New York: Random House, 1987).
   In order to survive, U.S. business needs to shift to a new organization and opportunity base.

CASE 17 THE HUNGRY HARVEST CORPORATION

John Swain, the president of the Hungry Harvest Corporation, spent much of his time on the corporate diversification program, and he approached different fields in different ways. When he decided to go into the data processing service field, he picked Steve Moran, then a member of the acquisition analysis staff, and said: "Steve, you have been doing good work as a member of the team, and I think you are ready for an individual assignment. Effective immediately, you have a $5000 raise, you report to me, and your job is to find a good way for Hungry Harvest to get into data processing services."

Steve asked a few questions to be sure he had the boundaries clear, and went to work. He bought subscriptions, read widely, visited plants and trade shows, and tried to learn as much about regional data processing as possible. John Swain approved. But when John Swain sent down some literature on a data processing firm he had heard of, he got no response. A few weeks later a finder (business broker) sent in a prospectus on a firm that looked very appealing. John sent the prospectus down to Steve. Nothing happened, and after a few days John picked up the phone: "Steve, did you get that last prospectus I sent down?"

"Yes."

"What did you think of it?"

"I'm not sure, sir. It looked rather good in several areas, but there were two places where I haven't got clear criteria yet."

"What do you mean, criteria?"

"You asked me to find a good way to get into the field, so I decided to find out what a good way is, and I think I'm almost there. You didn't say I had to pick a company immediately—but to find a good way to enter."

John accepted this grudgingly, because that was what he had told Steve. And a few weeks passed.

A college classmate of John's called, as he sometimes did: "John, if you are interested, I've really got a deal for you." It was a regional data processing company, John's friend was really good at picking companies, and the figures sounded too good to be true. John had all of the information sent to Steve by special messenger.

A day passed. Nothing happened. Another day passed, and John gave himself a lecture on respecting his delegations. On the morning of the third day he stopped by Steve's office: "What is happening with the information on that data processing company I had sent to you?"

"It looks rather good, sir, and I'm just confirming the last four of my criteria. Can I have another two hours?"

In two and a half hours Steve appeared and the secretary showed him in. "This is the best one yet, sir," he began. "I think we should double-check some of the facts here, but if they hold up, this might be the right company for us."

John was not a waiting type of man. He picked up the phone and called his friend, to see what was going on. "Sorry, John, the company's gone. Word leaked out, two people started to fight over it, and its just been sold at twice the price I quoted."

Steve didn't seem much bothered: "At least we didn't make a mistake, sir; there are a whole world of companies out there, and I am really learning to evaluate them."

"Steve," said John quietly, "my job is to act. I wanted you to help me take the right actions, and we haven't anything to show for three months and a lot of my time. I don't think you and I think enough alike to ever acquire a company together."

John transferred Steve to internal auditing and picked Fred Brown to replace him. Fred Brown had had two years as a junior manager in a data processing company, and enough experience in the acquisition analysis group to do a good job of sizing up a company. In a week's time he had a tentative definition of the sort of company he thought they should acquire. It was a good definition. He began to learn more about the industry and sharpened the definition. He contacted brokers and finders, letting anyone who was interested know that Fred Brown at Hungry Harvest was looking for a good regional data processing company to acquire.

Companies came in in large numbers. He got the same company from three different brokers, which could have created a legal tangle, but the company was of no interest anyway. John Swain had never seen so much action, but nothing was happening. He asked Fred Brown. Fred put it very simply: "I have screened more moth-eaten and doggy companies than I thought existed. I am not going to recommend a dog; but it seems to me that if I can keep the candidates coming in at this rate, sooner or later there has to be a good one."

John Swain went back to his office and thought quietly for five minutes—a long quiet time for him. Then he picked up the phone and called Bill Warren. Bill was a young, restless, aggressive no-nonsense marketing executive looking for a better job. "Bill, do you know anything about regional data processing?" The phone call turned into a lunch together. Bill did not know a lot about regional data processing, but he knew more than a little, and he had sold successfully to those companies for several years. John's proposition was simple: "Bill, I want Hungry Harvest to get into the regional data processing business, and I have a good analyst who knows how to evaluate and screen data processing companies. But he doesn't know how to find them, unless someone brings them in. You know where the companies are. Hungry Harvest is going to have a national chain, and we will need some good managers. Why don't you come over here and work at finding companies until we get a business going, and then you can have a good national marketing job, or something in the division management, depending on where you and I see your greatest potential."

Bill said "Yes" and Fred Brown began to see companies he had never heard of, because no one knew they could be bought until Bill Warren walked in and started to sell the idea of a deal with Hungry Harvest. Several of these were very attractive prospects, and John Swain got into the serious negotiations himself. The first acquisition was at a handshake in a month, and, as word got out, it became easier to contact some of the good companies that knew how fast the business was shifting toward national operation. Hungry Harvest acquired six regional companies the first year and twenty the second, before Bill Warren switched into management and John Swain let the pace cool a little so that the data processing division would have time to consolidate.

QUESTIONS

1. What posture towards opportunity did each of the men who helped John Swain typify?
2. When would one posture be better than the others?

CASE 18 RIGHTEOUS CHEMICAL COMPANY

The Righteous Chemical Company had always attempted to be a model employer. Located on the outskirts of a small southeastern city, Righteous produced and packaged a wide range of chemical products in its bright, modern plant. Many of its employees were women, and the company had been established long enough so that it was now hiring a significant number of the sons and daughters of its first employees. Management was very pleased with the "happy family" image this gave the operation.

Across the industrial district from the Righteous Chemical plant was Instant Organics, a chemical company that had been developing very rapidly and with less regard for employees and community. Many of its operations were improvised, and pollution complaints were frequent. Finally the bad working conditions (Occupational Safety and Health Act and Environmental Health Act violations) brought OSHA and EPA fines and legal action at the same time that the birth defects of several children were traced to toxic chemical exposure of their mothers in the Instant Organics plant. Also product liability claims were flooding in from Instant Organics customers, and the company filed for bankruptcy. As the financial records were examined, payoffs to city employees were uncovered, a political scandal erupted, and the incumbent city administration was swept out. The new mayor, Oral Rector, was a fiery conservative fundamentalist who promised to return the city to the old ways that had made the country great. While his direct backing was from only a small splinter of the population, he had gained almost 100 percent endorsement from the nonwhites, the women's groups, the environmentalists, and most of the rest of the citizenry due to the misdeeds of the previous administration.

Oral Rector came into office with total control of the city council, a strong mandate for action, and a package of programs ready to be written into law. One of them was a new city employment act aimed at eliminating the sort of working conditions Instant Organics had created. Among other things it mandated that any employer using chemicals of any sort maintain careful records showing the degree of chemical exposure of all pregnant women, as well as the way in which the company ensured that pregnant women suffered less chemical exposure than other employees.

Righteous Chemicals was in trouble immediately, even though its working conditions were considered close to ideal, because it could not show that pregnant women had less chemical exposure. It was a violation of federal law to try to find out who was pregnant, but the new city ordinance specified a heavy daily fine for not maintaining the required records and required shutdown after 30 days if the company did not come into compliance with the city ordinance. The president of Righteous Chemicals met with Oral Rector, but the mayor was not one to compromise. The chairman of the Righteous Chemicals Board of Directors had lunch with the Congressman from their district, but the Congressman did not want to get involved; "Give me a year," he said. "After this demagogue begins to discredit himself, I can help. But right now the people think he walks on water, and there is nothing I can do."

Righteous Chemicals management began to consider shutting down its plant and moving to another area, because it could not operate where it was without violating either federal or city rules.

QUESTIONS

1. What would you do if you were president of Righteous?
2. Could the company have foreseen this?

CHAPTER 10

MANAGING PEOPLE AND PERFORMANCE

KEY IDEAS IN THIS CHAPTER

Chapter 10 deals with why one aspect of the enterprise leadership and people strategies—the way that an enterprise decides to select and to manage its people—is such a key strategic variable, in that it largely determines potential productivity and organization performance potential for demanding tasks:

- **leadership strategy** – how will the people of the organization be motivated and led? with respect for the individual? with shared goals?
- **people strategy** – are the people here to contribute, or just to do what they are told?
- **the competence requirements for success of a strategy** – 7S framework, In Search of Excellence, TEAM, the Five-Fold Way, the excellence model— how to build high competence if you need it, and what it costs.
- **the management operating system** – a key and spontaneous embodiment of how management manages.
- **the excellence model and its alternatives** – a demanding route to major economies and accomplishments.
- **the people component in enterprise operations** – a weaving-together of the ideas from this chapter.

As a component of strategic overview management, the plan for the management of operations deals with the strategy of those operations, discussed in the next chapter, and the strategy for managing the people on which these operations depend, discussed here. This chapter emphasizes the special importance of the leadership and people building block strategies in shaping the organization, and in determining its performance potential and that of the management operating system governing it. High levels of organization performance are often desirable, and review of the characteristics of high-achievement organizations is followed by presentation of an excellence model defining the requirements for their creation.

LEADERSHIP STRATEGY

Leadership strategy determines the nature of the organization more than any other enterprise strategy. The key components of leadership style are the management attitude toward the people of the organization, and the manner in which top management chooses to work with the management group and the organization as a whole.

A business organization is a group gathered for a purpose the leadership has a key role in defining or interpreting. Andrews spoke of the chief executive as the architect of that purpose,[1] and Selznick called the resulting organization "a technical instrument for mobilizing human energies and directing them toward set aims."[2] As management directs the energies of its group toward its purpose, it uses an organizational structure whose major requirement is that it aid the group in its accomplishments.

A part of the structure will be an organizational hierarchy or chain of command, with those at the top directing the efforts of those below. This is not a democratic process, for each level has a basic responsibility for the functioning of the subordinate group, but there are many ways in which each manager can choose to work with peers and subordinates.

FORMALITY AND INFORMALITY

A formal style of leading an organization tends to result in a more uniform, rational, and controllable operating pattern, and is common in very large organizations, especially major government agencies and bureaus, because it minimizes the effect of individual people on organization func-

---

[1] Kenneth R. Andrews, *The Concept of Corporate Strategy*, Revised Edition (Homewood, Ill.: Richard D. Irwin, 1980), p. 5.

[2] Philip Selznick, *Leadership in Administration* (Evanston, Ill.: Row, Peterson & Co., 1957), p. 5.

tion. For some purposes it is desirable to minimize variation created by the differences between individual people. In police and fire protection systems, for example, great emphasis is placed on a completely standardized response to an alarm, so that there can be no hint of bias or unevenness. For other purposes, as in some research work, individual performance is required, and complete standardization would be avoided. A formal and standardized pattern of operation is less effective where operations change at a significant rate. Peters and Waterman found that one of the characteristics of the excellent organizations they studied was a high degree of informality, coupled with a less elaborate organization structure and much more flexibility; instead of organizing for every contingency, a much smaller and simpler structure was changed every time conditions changed.[3]

RESPECT FOR THE INDIVIDUAL

Many years ago McGregor created the opposing organizational prototypes he called Theory X and Theory Y.[4] The Theory X prototype was based on the concept of the lazy, undependable worker; management style and control procedures assumed this. Theory Y was a more optimistic appraisal of workers as basically desiring to do good work, cooperative, and dependable if given the chance to demonstrate what they could do.

One of the most interesting things about McGregor's Theory X and Y prototypes is the degree to which a given management attitude becomes a self-fulfilling prophecy, guiding worker behavior into the pattern assumed in advance. A work group usually has a good understanding of its supervisor's attitude toward them, because this attitude shows in so many small ways. A supervisor who believes that he or she has a Theory X work group will show this in his or her attitude, and workers believing they are viewed as lazy, dishonest, and needing very close supervision react angrily to the disrespect in the viewpoint. In so reacting, they tend to behave as badly as the Theory X image forecasts. Workers treated as valuable, cooperative, and with worthwhile opinions tend to respond favorably, and are much more likely to behave according to the Theory Y prototype if other conditions permit this.

The fundamental ingredient here is respect from one individual to another. Where respect is given and received, the basis is laid for productive teamwork. Peters and Waterman found that respect for every individual was a cornerstone of management philosophy in their sample of ex-

---

[3] Thomas J. Peters and Robert H. Waterman, *In Search of Excellence: Lessons From America's Best-Run Companies* (New York: Harper & Row, 1982).
[4] Douglas McGregor, *The Human Side of Enterprise* (New York: McGraw-Hill, 1960).

cellent companies.⁵ Certainly there are wide differences from one firm to another in the way individuals are treated. The differences in the pattern and pace of their businesses are to some degree a factor, and the key leadership and people strategy definitions by top management have a large impact on operating results.

SHARED GOALS

In designing an operation, management must decide how much to share with the people in that operation. Some managements tell those people only what they are required to do to earn their pay, but it has been observed many times in the past that the people of an organization wish to know what their work accomplishes, and what the goals of the overall effort are. Given the opportunity, they will identify with these goals and attempt to contribute to them, sometimes to a much greater degree than management has any right to expect.

Peters and Waterman identified this factor as "shared values," and reported that it was a uniform characteristic of the excellent organizations they studied. That is, excellence was found linked with a leadership style in which the key values underlying the enterprise goal structure were fully shared throughout the organization, and became a part of the way of life of its members.⁶

THE PEOPLE COMPONENT

Another of the five enterprise building block strategies is the people strategy. This is the general specification by top management of what sort of people will be brought into the organization and how they will be treated, and several aspects of this strategy deserve consideration.

COMPENSATION AND HIRING

In its approach to paying and staffing the organization, top management puts a coloration on all that follows. The key decisions set the level of salaries versus competitors, the level of hiring, the internal promotion practices, and the degree of enterprise commitment to the career and security of the individual employee.

How much to pay is a key and continuing question. There is no

---

⁵ *In Search of Excellence*, p. 277.
⁶ *Ibid.*, pp. 279–291.

single best way, and good organizations have been built with different approaches. The Hoffmann-La Roche U.S. organization once established a policy of paying above-average base salaries as a part of its rapid organization-building, and used regional salary surveys and other comparative data as the basis for internal adjustments if it found that competitive salaries for sales representatives, executive secretaries, or other payroll categories were rising in the region. The rationale was that, with base salaries at least 10% above industry average, plus a good bonus and benefits structure, the organization had a better choice in its hiring, got a select group from the job market as a result, could retain its people better against competitive bids, and built a better and stronger organization as a result.

Each year at graduation time a competition develops for the top MBA graduates and the top law-school graduates from the most prestigious schools, and the salary differentials these "top-of-class" graduates get are surprising enough to receive feature-article coverage in the business press. The successful bidders, often management consulting firms and major law firms, justify paying almost a double salary to the top member of the Harvard class, etc., by the way that this enhances their image with clients.

Other firms have observed that many students with sound personal and academic credentials have difficulty in placement; perhaps they do not know how to write a resume, or they freeze during interviews. These firms believe that, after the premium-wage offers have been made, there will still be many capable graduates who will work for less if the job sounds attractive, because they don't have better offers. Such firms make a policy of paying a little less, and perhaps spend more effort on their screening process in an attempt to ensure the quality of the result.

PROMOTION POLICIES

Firms hiring many fresh college graduates often do this because they prefer to train these graduates within the firm and then promote them to higher job levels as needs occur. Other firms who wish to minimize training costs almost never hire a college graduate directly. They look instead for someone who has worked for another firm for several years, gained experience, established a track record, and can contribute immediately in a more responsible job when hired. Many employees become restless, want more rapid advancement at about this point, and can be lured away by such a firm.

An organization recruited person by person from good jobs in other firms does not have the same internal ties and team spirit as a group hired and trained together. For the maximum in team-building and organizational cohesiveness, an organization usually hires at the entry level and then promotes primarily from within. For organizations with more emphasis on individual performance, less emphasis on teamwork, less career commitment to the employee, and less concern about turnover, hiring of individuals pretrained elsewhere is more common.

There is no simple answer on how much to pay or at what level to hire, but from each of the above alternatives comes a different pattern of internal dynamics in the resulting organization. But pay alone is only part of the story, and the selected compensation pattern must be matched with compatible choices in the promotion and commitment dimensions and in the general character of the enterprise, in order to get the best results from the pay level selected.

COMMITMENT

Different organizations take different views of the commitment between employer and employee. In the past automobile firms routinely laid off workers whenever the assembly line was not to be run, and when an automobile plant was closed, it was more or less automatic that the workers were out of a job. IBM is an example of a different sort of firm that has taken the view that its employees should feel secure in their jobs; it goes to great length to retrain and relocate employees when an operation is closed, so that continued similar employment with IBM is available to the worker.

While the nature of IBM's business may have made job security easier to provide than for Ford or General Motors, the auto workers objected strongly to the frequent layoffs. Step by step the auto unions won salary guarantees such that the auto workers now have excellent near-term protection against loss of wages. The economic burden of providing this job security is nearly the same for the auto companies as for IBM, but the resulting internal relationship between company and employee is entirely different. IBM is doing something IBM management commited to years ago because this was the way IBM wanted to treat its people, and its employees know this. The auto company guarantees were won only because the United Auto Workers made a strong stand for them in collective bargaining; the worker's *union* allegiance was strengthened as a result, even though the companies paid the cost.

Each organization evolves a policy of people-treatment, based on the beliefs and experiences of the management and the specific circumstances of the business. This policy becomes a part of the framework of the organization and colors the other actions as organizational cohesion is built and the business functions. If an organization wishes to make a commitment to job security—as IBM has—to make this commitment effective, most of the promotions must be from within except in times of very rapid expansion, to provide the necessary opportunities for growth for the existing employee group; and the company and employee must join in career planning so that employees will be ready to move up when openings occur.

ACHIEVEMENT LEVELS

Pay, promotion, and career planning presume an organization making progress in achieving its business purpose, and in theory each employee should be contributing to that progress. The people building block strategy defines job performance standards that the organization will impose and accept. Peters and Waterman found that their list of excellent companies had high internal performance standards, and that peer pressure generated as a result of the sharing of values and the informal leadership style was a greater factor than demands for performance from line superiors.

The intent of the leadership and people strategies is to guide the development of the organization into a motivated and effective team. The motivation of people, whether workers or managers, is based on the value they can be made to see in the effort; that is, on the incentives they see. The management purpose is to cause each member of the organization to develop what Herbert Simon called an "organizational personality," in which that person focuses on accomplishing his or her role in the success of the organization;[7] Chester Barnard long ago discussed economy of incentives, emphasizing the desirability of a blend of financial and personal motivations for best results.[8] Constructing a high-performance organization normally requires a mixture of both types of rewards, and the leadership and people strategies govern both reward systems.

COMPETENCE REQUIREMENTS FOR SUCCESS OF A STRATEGY

Beyond the product, market, and business foundations on which a successful strategy rests are a number of other considerations determining the best way to design it. Some strategies are relatively easy to execute, and others require higher levels of organization performance. Therefore the collective competence level at which a given organization can be expected to perform becomes important when selecting a strategy. This requires an understanding of the relationship between the way a company is organized and managed and the way its people work together. If a strategy requires a higher level of performance than the organization is pre-

---

[7] Herbert A. Simon, *Administrative Behavior*, 2nd Ed. (New York: Macmillan, 1961), pp. 198–199.

[8] Chester I. Barnard, *The Functions of the Executive* (Cambridge, Mass.: Harvard University Press, 1960), pp. 139–160.

pared to achieve, that strategy will probably fail unless management improves organization performance first.

THE 7S FRAMEWORK

The McKinsey 7S framework, as presented by Pascale and Athos[9] and recapitulated by Peters and Waterman,[10] was an interesting probe into the determinants of organization performance. As a part of an internal study the McKinsey staff reexamined business basics in an attempt to account for the success levels achieved by some Japanese and U.S. companies. The conclusion was that preoccupation with **strategy, structure,** and **systems** (the so-called hard S's) had dominated U.S. management thinking. This preoccupation had caused a weakness in many U.S. organizations relative to Japanese and other competitors because it caused **superordinate goals** to be neglected, as well as the so-called soft S's (**staff, style,** and **skills**)—all of the strategy components related to the people. The concept of the 7S framework was of seven different areas all deserving emphasis and defined as follows:

- **Strategy:** Plan or course of action leading to the allocation of a firm's scarce resources, over time, to reach identified goals.
- **Structure:** Characterization of the organization chart (i.e., functional, decentralized, etc.).
- **Systems:** Proceduralized reports and routinized processes such as meeting formats.
- **Staff:** "Demographic" description of important personnel categories within the firm (i.e., engineers, entrepreneurs, M.B.A.'s, etc.). "Staff" is *not* meant in line-staff terms.
- **Style:** Characterization of how key managers behave in achieving the organization's goals; also the cultural style of the organization.
- **Skills:** Distinctive capabilities of key personnel or of the firm as a whole.
- **Superordinate goals:** The significant meanings or guiding concepts that an organization imbues in its members.[11]

---

[9] Richard Tanner Pascale and Anthony G. Athos, *The Art of Japanese Management* (New York: Warner Books, 1981).

[10] Thomas J. Peters and Robert H. Waterman, *In Search of Excellence: Lessons from America's Best-Run Companies* (New York, Harper & Row, 1982).

[11] *Art of Japanese Management*, p. 125.

Pascale and Athos used the resulting 7S framework as the basis for business comparisons. Their book is valuable, many of its conclusions about past management neglect of key areas are correct, and the present analysis can be considered as a parallel development of the same general field.

The 7S framework treats its seven elements as essentially equal, but the present focus on strategy as permitting creation of resources and also forming the basis for their allocation requires broader definitions. Strategy is a preeminent variable. Structure becomes a derived variable except in the very short run, as Chandler[12] and others suggested long ago, with systems also tailored to the strategy. The mission is the genesis of a central purpose providing superordinate goals or **shared goals** (after Peters and Waterman). Staff and skills become two aspects of the people strategy, and style equates to a considerable degree with leadership strategy. To design a strategy that not only directs but creates resources to achieve its goals, the 7S framework must be respectfully rearranged so that mission and strategy are dominant, with the other key components of successful strategy design and execution as essential but subordinate.

IN SEARCH OF EXCELLENCE

The need to rearrange the 7S framework to fit the pattern of this analysis returns the discussion to the enterprise-level strategies, and their effect on business and product strategy. More broadly, the issue is the way in which the governing enterprise strategies limit the performance of the organization, and therefore limit the strategies it can use successfully. Peters and Waterman approached this from a different direction by looking for the causes of high performance. As they were careful to point out, theirs was a descriptive study of organizations based on a sample too small for statistical validation of the conclusions. The intent was to select excellent organizations based largely on objective performance criteria and then study them in search of commonalities that might explain their high performance, as summarized below.

The eight attributes that emerged to characterize most nearly the distinction of the excellent, innovative companies go as follows:

1. **A bias for action,** for getting on with it. Even though these companies may be analytical in their approach to decision making, they are not paralyzed by that fact. . . .

---

[12] Alfred D. Chandler, *Strategy and Structure* (Garden City, N.Y.: Doubleday, 1961).

2. **Close to the customer.** These companies learn from the people they serve. They provide unparalleled quality, service, and reliability—things that work and last. . . .
3. **Autonomy and entrepreneurship.** The innovative companies foster many leaders and many innovators throughout the organization. . . .
4. **Productivity through people.** The excellent companies treat the rank and file as the root source of quality and productivity gain. . . .
5. **Hands-on, and value driven.** Thomas Watson, Jr., said that "the basic philosophy of an organization has more to do with its achievements than do technological or economic resources, organizational structure, innovation, and timing." Watson and HP'S William Hewlett are legendary for walking the plant floors. McDonald's Ray Kroc regularly visits stores and assesses them on the factors the company holds dear, Q.S.C.&V. (Quality, Service, Cleanliness, and Value). . . .
6. **Stick to the knitting.** . . . while there were a few exceptions, the odds for excellent performance seem to favor the companies that stay reasonably close to businesses they know. . . .
7. **Simple form, lean staff.** As big as most of the companies we have looked at are, none when we looked at it was formally run with a matrix organization structure, and some that had tried that form had abandoned it. The underlying structural forms and systems in the excellent companies are elegantly simple. Top-level staffs are lean; it is not uncommon to find a corporate staff of fewer than 100 people running multibillion-dollar enterprises. . . .
8. **Simultaneous loose-tight properties.** The excellent companies are both centralized and decentralized . . . they have pushed autonomy down to the shop floor or product development team. On the other hand, they are fanatically centralized around the few core values they hold dear. . . .[13]

In Search of Excellence is important reading. The wide sale of the book speaks for its favorable reception, but the study has been criticized, in part because it does not prescribe a specific pattern of organization. Heller reviewed the data presented, defended the study, and suggested that Peters and Waterman had omitted a ninth factor at least as important as the other eight, that a serious **determination to achieve market leadership** was equally characteristic of their excellent companies.[14]

---

[13] *In Search of Excellence*, pp. 13–15.
[14] Robert Heller, *The Supermanagers* (New York: E. P. Dutton, 1984), pp. 175–180.

TEAM

The Atlanta Federal Reserve Bank asked a group of economists and analysts to look for common factors among 22 high-performing companies in that region. The findings substantially paralleled those of *In Search of Excellence*, to which they referred. The authors used the acronym TEAM to describe the four common factors they found:

- **Technology/innovation:** A major emphasis on innovation, particularly in the area of technology.
- **Entrepreneurial management:** An entrepreneurial management style that keeps the company lean and flexible for prompt action and willing to take risks that promise high returns.
- **Affiliation of employees:** A view of employees as associates or affiliates—the company's most valued long-term asset—rather than as adversaries.
- **Market strategy:** An ongoing attention to marketing strategy that sharply defines the company's comparative advantage.[15]

Again the approach was by analyzing the behavior patterns of companies meeting other favorable criteria, and without prescribing a positive course of action. This is a defensible approach. Any sample of top-notch companies deserves careful study, and these companies are obviously doing a lot of things correctly.

But suppose that all of these companies were using the same brand of copy machines; what would that prove? Because one or all of the excellent companies do some specific thing does not prove that it is necessary to do that to be excellent. In addition to the common characteristics of high-performing companies, other information is necessary in order to synthesize a prescription for high performance, even though these studies may correctly foreshadow most of the requirements.

THE FIVE-FOLD WAY

Independent of the Peters and Waterman study there have been a number of attempts to specify the pattern in which a successful company should operate, such as Allio's Five-Fold Way:

---

[15] Donald L. Koch, Delores W. Steinhauser, Bobbie H. McCrackin, and Kathryn Hart, "High Performance Companies in the Southeast: What Can They Teach Us?" *Economic Review: Federal Reserve Bank of Atlanta*, April 1984, pp. 2–24.

Successful organizations appear to endure and prosper if they develop and promote five attributes:

- **A dominant theme:** A guiding vision, driving force, or organizational strategy toward which resources are allocated.
- **Organizational commitment:** An endorsement of the dominant theme by all members of the organization.
- **Congruent managerial systems:** Measures of performance, reward systems, information systems, and managerial selection procedures that fit the needs of the organization.
- **Functional competence:** Managers and staff who are good at their trade, be it manufacturing, finance, marketing, or any other necessary skills.
- **Adaptability:** The sensitivity to change as new demands are imposed by the environment or the stakeholders.[16]

Strategy Requirements. Central themes in the above studies are the importance of people and of goals. As business processes have become more and more complex, it has become more and more important to have all of the people in the organization as participants in designing and improving its programs, products, and performance. This participation comes only as a part of an equation based on mutual respect, mutual interests, and shared goals. For an enterprise management that will attempt complex achievements, particularly over a span of years, such a broadly motivated and participating organization is an essential management tool.

People work best under simple arrangements based on direct human contact. The more elaborate and indirect forms tend to degrade into a deadening bureaucracy. A simple, personal management effort can accomplish at least as much cross-coordination as a matrix structure if the contact matrix is kept small and the managers are energetic. Organizational devices permitting this sort of direct, hands-on management then become a design requirement.

These concepts are summarized in a set of principles for creation and management of a highly effective organization based on (*1*) purpose, (*2*) leadership, (*3*) commitment, (*4*) relevance, (*5*) learning, and (*6*) excellence, that make up the excellence model.

The excellence model describes an organization with peak internal and external effectiveness of function, and therefore it is the desired form

---

[16] Robert J. Allio, "Doing Well—The Five-Fold Way," *Planning Review*, January 1984, p. 4.

wherever effectiveness of a strategy depends on superior organizational performance. Such performance is achieved, enterprise strategies permitting, when a skilled and dedicated management brings about the transformation of an organization to the excellence level of operation.

THE EXCELLENCE MODEL

The excellence model can be described as a pattern for management of a group or of an organization in a manner that can lead to maximum organization competence, individual contribution, and effectiveness in executing strategies. This pattern sets requirements for purpose, leadership, commitment, relevance, learning, and excellence.

Purpose. A clear mission for the enterprise as a whole or each part of it. Each member of the organization must come to feel a personal purpose contributing to fulfillment of that mission, and toward which that person can devote full energy and enthusiasm.

When each member of the organization feels a personal purpose derived out of and contributing to the mission of that organization, this provides a natural basis for the integration and synergy of their joint efforts springing out of their joint commitment as guided by their leadership.

Leadership. Active and effective leadership based on integrity and trust, with mutual respect plus sharing of ideas and enthusiasm throughout the organization.

An effective effort needs effective and competent leadership exercised by leaders their followers respect, and whose decisions they trust. A climate of participation must underlie the shared commitment, and requires a sharing of ideas and enthusiasm between leaders and followers as a group. Such a sharing requires mutual respect—not necessarily liking or friendship but sincere respect—for the rights and dignity of each individual by the others.

The required climate of participation should not interfere with decisive management action as circumstances require, and should not compromise the decision-making authority of the responsible managers in any way, but this participation does require free and open discussion of what the group is trying to accomplish, including alternatives its managers may not prefer. Because of the internal dynamics of an excellent organization, the group will have large numbers of ideas. Managing such an organization requires the patience to deal respectfully with bad and mediocre ideas, but is also rewarded with a surprising number of good ones. A good manager will want to let the group settle many of the details of its own role in the joint effort because of the strong motivating value—in a management-by-objectives setting-and-meeting-my-own-goals sense—but enough good ideas surface so that this sharing is usually quite rewarding.

Commitment. Work built on the shared efforts and successes of all of the members of the organization, with (1) high standards of performance demanded by the group more than by the leaders, standards met and exceeded by most of the participants, and (2) a level of job security, opportunity, and family security adequate to minimize distraction of group members from the organizational purpose by personal matters.

Everyone in the group works together, as a consequence of the shared purpose, presses toward the same goals, and shares the common desire for achievement that only an effective collective effort can bring—leading logically to collective impatience and dissatisfaction with any parts that are lagging behind, and with the laggard individuals, if weak individual performance is holding back the progress of their joint efforts. The leadership role is to guide this individual and joint effort, to be sure the group has the opportunity to pursue its shared purpose with full enthusiasm.

Guiding the effort includes creation of a sufficiently secure atmosphere in the work place that the members of the work group will not be distracted from the desired commitment to the task by procedural, work place, and job security concerns.

The sharing of efforts and successes on which the commitment is based includes some sharing of the fruits of this success. This sharing can take many forms, but the requirement is that each member of the group truly believes that his or her efforts will be recognized, appreciated, and rewarded in some tangible way.

Relevance. A sharp and perceptive sense of customer need now and as it changes day by day, so that the company's products or services will continue to satisfy those needs effectively.

The work effort must be sharply focused on valid and viable targets—real customer needs in the present and future, in the case of a business organization. That their joint effort is truly important and relevant and therefore worthwhile is an essential belief that reinforces the commitment of all of the members of the group to their joint purpose. That the effort truly be relevant in the marketplace is necessary to keep the group convinced of the importance of their commitment, and to produce the sales and profit results required for the organization to continue.

Learning. Mastery and use of all appropriate techniques, tools, and technologies.

As a dimension of the effort related to a different aspect of relevance, the equipment, techniques, and technologies through which the efforts of the group are employed must represent a wise and adequate choice; to ensure this outcome a broad knowledge of relevant tools, techniques, and technologies is needed, so that the most appropriate combination can always be employed.

Excellence. A continuing drive for excellence—in the quality of output, in the efficiency and effectiveness of operations, and in the determination further to improve each part of the organization every day.

As a state of mind in an organization dedicated to being the best, each member needs to keep trying to find and achieve improvements, individually and collectively. The objective is that each person try to find something to improve every day, and an excellence model organization will try seriously and sincerely to achieve this result.

The excellence model describes an achievable level of group performance, but such performance does not develop spontaneously. It must be created by the responsible managers by providing the leadership, the purpose, and the climate, by working with the group to build the participation—to help it find higher and higher performance levels—and by insisting on the importance of the joint purpose and of the individual efforts to achieve it.

Excellence model organizations often spring into being when a group faces major challenges, as during the initial growth of a struggling new company, a product launch succeeding against major obstacles, or a process startup required to overcome major technical and other difficulties. Such organizations are created under the drive of good leaders who know how to employ the full range of abilities of all of their subordinates; an operation largely according to the six principles of purpose, leadership, commitment, relevance, learning, and excellence comes into being, and the performance of the group rises to the excellence level. But often as success is achieved, performance pressure fades, top management attention shifts elsewhere, the organization grows and management levels are added, and a more normal and more bureaucratic pattern of delegation and control begins to dominate. The specialness of the effort and of the group itself fade little by little, and output capabilities drift toward the dependable mediocrity more common in large organizations.

The excellence model requirements are summarized in Figure 10-1. In addition, the leadership and people building blocks and the choice

> **FIGURE 10-1** THE EXCELLENCE MODEL
>
> **Purpose:** A clear mission for the enterprise as a whole or each part of it. Each member of the organization must come to feel a personal purpose contributing to fulfillment of that mission, and toward which that person can devote full energy and enthusiasm.
>
> **Leadership:** Active and effective leadership based on integrity and trust, with mutual respect plus sharing of ideas and enthusiasm throughout the organization.
>
> **Commitment:** Work built on the shared efforts and successes of all of the members of the organization, with (1) high standards of performance demanded by the group more than by the leaders, standards met and exceeded by most of the participants, and (2) a level of job security, opportunity, and family security adequate to minimize distraction of group members from the organizational purpose of personal matters.
>
> **Relevance:** A sharp and perceptive sense of customer need now and as it changes day by day, so that the company's products or services will continue to satisfy those needs effectively.
>
> **Learning:** Mastery and use of all appropriate techniques, tools, and technologies.
>
> **Excellence:** A continuing drive for excellence—in the quality of output, in the efficiency and effectiveness of operations, and in the determination further to improve each part of the organization every day.

strategies must be such as to permit the excellence model to function, as summarized in Figure 10-2. Such an organization is a powerful and necessary resource for some strategies, and often worth the effort of constructing for the added strength and profitability of the positions it creates.

THE MANAGEMENT OPERATING SYSTEM

The management operating system is that network of linkages by which a management group communicates among its members, gathers information from organization and environment, and directs the performance of its operation. Its nature is defined by the accumulated impact of all of the policies, rules, and procedures laid down by management plus the habit patterns developed during past operations. Usually there is little formal design of this system; it springs up as units begin to operate and management to manage, and incorporates each new directive and procedure as the enterprise evolves.

This casual and agglomerative system assembly procedure serves well, because it captures decisions and occurrences and builds a library of experience that can be recalled for the handling of similar problems in the future. There is a degree to which routine operating matters can be guided

---

FIGURE 10-2   EXCELLENCE MODEL ENTERPRISE STRATEGY REQUIREMENTS

The individual enterprise strategy requirements for creation of the excellence model can be summarized as follows:

Leadership strategy: An active strategy based on respect for the individual.

Innovation strategy: Opportunity-seeking; not passive.

People strategy: Fair, caring, challenging, and creating a secure environment.

Public strategy: No specific requirement.

Resource strategy: Relaxed; organizational effectiveness makes the enterprise relatively easy to fund.

Desirability and **Credibility:** Carefully conceived and enforced standards, although not necessarily rigid or formal.

Managing and **belonging:** Emphasis on areas where the group has high confidence in its ability.

Risk/reward: No specific requirement, except not excessively conservative.

---

and decided without thought, and to this degree the automatic response of the management operating system is invaluable as it recalls and applies standard solutions to recurring problems. But this system is not sufficient unto itself; like the autopilot in an airliner, it serves only to free human intelligence for larger or less routine problems. Management intelligence is needed to handle the nonroutine, and also to evaluate and modify the management operating system itself.

The management operating system has a set of major characteristics determined by the policies top management establishes and practices consciously or unconsciously, particularly those based on the leadership and people strategies. This system should be a dynamic, directed entity orienting day-by-day operations to today's and tomorrow's problems. Yet by its nature, the system captures and stores yesterday's intelligence for reuse tomorrow.

The bridge, to keep the system alive and current, is the management redirection it often fails to receive. Any management operating system left to itself assumes a strong self-direction as lower-level people invoke the proven wisdom of past successes; it becomes increasingly rigid in its procedures, and resistant to change. While many of its characteristics are desirable and help to keep a well-planned operation running smoothly, the system becomes obsolete as problems change and the stored solutions do not, unless a constructive and evolutionary pattern of change is planned and directed by top management. The task of continually redirecting the management operating system requires a strategic overview for its effective planning and execution, and is itself a key element of strategic overview management; but the management spirit that drives this task when it is well performed is another manifestation of the make-every-thing-better-every-day ethic of the excellence model.

THE EXCELLENCE MODEL AND ITS ALTERNATIVES

The people and the leadership strategies must be coordinated to be effective, and the requirement of the excellence model is that they be oriented toward involving every individual in a collective goal-oriented effort. This type of involvement is remarkably easy to achieve but has its price.

Most people would very much like to believe in the importance of the effort of which they are a part, and in their own ability to contribute to this effort even in a minor way. This gives meaning and justification to their days at work and allows a greater sense of personal satisfaction and self-worth. This desire for identification and involvement is so great that this loyalty will be given instead to a professional or fraternal organization or to a union, if the management makes it difficult for the employee to identify with the company. But with guidance and reinforcement from management a very substantial group involvement is rather easy to generate.

To make such an involvement effective,

1. the members need a clear understanding of the firm's mission, at least in the dimensions where it relates to them,
2. each individual needs to find a personal purpose within that mission; that is, to find a way in which he or she can contribute toward the overall progress,
3. the group collectively needs to press against the boundaries limiting its performance and seek to improve; by their efforts and enthusiasm they create pressure for group performance that acts as a remarkable catalyst for creative solutions from the group as a whole.

This involvement of the group requires constructive leadership from the supervisors and a reduction in the distractions that otherwise block it. The keys here are a sense of security for the contributors and their dependents, rewards and opportunities as earned, and scrupulously fair treatment for all individuals. This bypasses issues that otherwise preoccupy many individuals, preventing their whole-hearted involvement and diluting group effectiveness. It also reinforces the image of the company and mission as being worth all of the dedication: "I take care of the Company and it will take care of me."

Such a group becomes fiercely loyal, and expects the same loyalty in return. It sets high performance standards, sometimes higher than management would suggest, and even encourages discipline or discharge of individuals who fail group or company standards after they have had a fair chance. It expects to contribute to and to share in the firm's success, at least to an extent that shows its contributions were truly valued.

The excellence model, then, tends to produce a highly effective, highly motivated work force requiring management care and protection—in part because the potential of such a group results in positions capable of earning significant rents, and in part because the involvement equation has obligated management. This obligation can be a problem or an opportunity. Management freedom of action is limited by its commitment to its people because any default can shatter the value systems around which the group has organized. This commitment is also an opportunity because of the range of achievements this kind of organization makes possible.

Alternative consequences from different sorts of leadership and people strategies vary from a Theory X "police the lazy rascals" approach, or a depersonalized bureaucratic system, to the value-driven excellence model. These choices represent a negative, a neutral, and a positive approach to the membership of the organization. Any of these patterns can get most jobs done, but both the efficiency and the involvement of the members of the organization will vary from one to another, changing costs and rates of progress.

Firms in highly technical work or needing closely coordinated long-term relationships tend to gain the greatest premium from the excellence model. But McDonalds, not in a high-tech business and with a large force of young people subject to high turnover, was high on the Peters and Waterman list of excellent organizations. As at McDonalds, this management style can be carried over into almost any sort of organization, but the competitive advantage it yields seems likely to be higher at a firm like 3M, where a significant fraction of the employees involve themselves in design of new products and businesses.

The alternatives to the excellence model all involve lower levels of organizational efficiency or effectiveness, but require a correspondingly lower level of commitment to the organization by management. The difference is acceptable if the resulting strategy still has needs-leverages linkages better than competitive offerings, and the firm is still able to prosper. Sometimes a management astute in its grasp of the market situation will make rules well enough and find needs-leverages linkages good enough so that it can prosper without having a good organization at all—someone who is smart enough or lucky enough does not have to do everything right. But unless one can plan on never meeting a smarter or luckier operator, in the long run it seems wise to build the best possible operating unit to gain as many advantages as possible.

> **FIGURE 10-3** PEOPLE AND PERFORMANCE
>
> **Leadership strategy**
> - formality and informality
> - respect for the individual
> - shared goals
>
> **The people component**
> - compensation and hiring
> - promotion policies
> - commitment
> - achievement levels
>
> **Organization requirements for successful strategies**
> - 7S framework
> - In Search of Excellence
> - TEAM
> - The Five-Fold Way
> - The Excellence Model
>
> **The management operating system & resource strategy**
>
> **The excellence model and its alternatives**
>
> PEOPLE AS A KEY COMPONENT IN ENTERPRISE STRATEGY

Now with a prescription for building a highly motivated organization—how does this relate to strategy design?

1. Not every business can or should attempt to build an organization in the excellence model. There are reasons why the U.S. Army needs a much more rigid structure, including possible rapid expansion around the organizational nucleus in times of emergency. And many organizations are temporary; a construction contractor may draw together a crew of union members from the local building trades council whose allegiance is to the union that places them in job after job. This makes it difficult for the contractor to create a cohesive organizational unit for a job lasting only a few weeks.

2. Not every management is able to or would wish to manage in the excellence model fashion.

3. Not every business needs this caliber of organization in order to function effectively.

4. The excellence model describes an organization that is a valuable management tool in the pursuit of specific accomplishments. For less demanding tasks other organizational performance levels will serve, although sometimes less profitably.

THE PEOPLE COMPONENT IN ENTERPRISE OPERATIONS

The enterprise is managed by a management operating system, and many of the most important decisions top management makes concern the nature of that system and the sorts of linkages between groups and between people on which this system is built. These decisions will be an expression of the leadership style that has been selected and of the people strategy of the enterprise. Together they will determine much of the character of the resulting organization, perhaps including the sorts of businesses it can and cannot enter successfully. The way people and performance are managed are key inputs for strategy and action design, as shown in Figure 10-3. By choices of the governing enterprise strategies therefore, and in its oversight of the management operating system, management can establish a level of effectiveness from its investment in people that can be a critical variable in design of certain business and product strategies, and therefore a key component of strategic action and control.

QUESTIONS FOR ANALYSIS AND DISCUSSION

1. Develop your own example of the way that the management operating system of a specific organization stores past experience and guides the functioning of the operation.
2. When would an organization work better if the leadership process were very formal? Very informal?
3. The text argues strongly for the importance of respect for the individual, but many organizations do not practice it. What do you think?
4. If shared goals help an organization so much, why do so few managers manage this way? What do you think?
5. Is it better to be tied closely to one organization? Or free-floating to change jobs (or be laid off) at any time? What would you prefer?
6. Describe any high-achievement organization you have seen. Why did it achieve so much?
7. From annual reports, business magazine feature articles, and any other available sources, build up a picture of the enterprise strategy characteristics within which a given company operates. How many of the specifics from the characteristics lists from the 7S framework, In Search of Excellence, TEAM, The Five-Fold Way, or the

Excellence Model can you identify as being *followed* or *not followed* by that management?

8. For the organization in Question 7, does its operation suggest that it had adequate enterprise strategies or not, and why?

FOR FURTHER INFORMATION

Peters, Thomas J., and Nancy Austin, *A Passion for Excellence* (New York: Warner Books, 1985).
    Good examples of how successful high-performance organizations work.

Peters, Thomas J., and Robert H. Waterman, *In Search of Excellence* (New York: Harper & Row, 1982).
    Essential reading for anyone interested in this field.

CASE 19 HIGH VELOCITY ENTERPRISES

Carmela Veloz, the controller of High Velocity Enterprises, was calling Ryan Borsch, Vice President, Personnel: "Ryan, you really have to do something. I have been waiting two weeks since Elan Ahab left, and we had two weeks' warning of that—so it's a month now and I haven't even seen anybody to interview. I need a new head accountant *instantly* and your people don't seem to understand this!" The conversation went on in this vein, until Ryan finally managed to slow Carmela down, and to sort out a few facts.

Ryan knew that Elan Ahab had obtained a good job as controller of a smaller company and left High Velocity with two weeks' notice—a little too short really, but everyone wanted an executive who was leaving to be out of the executive group quickly, and there had been no complaints. Elan had been hired from outside to head the accounting group ten months earlier. The group was weak because several senior accountants had left about the same time to work for a rapidly expanding defense electronics firm, and personnel had been working with him to find good senior accountants to strengthen it; three had been hired, but they were not at a level to be candidates to replace Elan, and Carmela also said that she knew of no good candidates in the company to head the accounting department itself.

Ryan called Sam Swede, the personnel man who was trying to find job candidates for Carmela to interview. Sam confirmed that there was no one in accounting worth serious consideration "and really no one in the company." The High Velocity personnel group had a good personnel skills computer search system, Sam had used it, and the only qualified people in the company were already at levels higher than the job Carmela was trying to fill. The position had been advertised and the ads had produced 400 resumes, with a few more still coming in, "but we missed the target, Boss. Either they have no solid management experience, or there is something obviously wrong in the resume. I know the caliber of person Carmela wants, and I don't see anybody worth a serious interview. We still will check out a few of the better candidates as fast as we can and I've got preliminary interviews set up, but I've already asked a couple of search firms to help steal a good head accountant from wherever."

Ryan encouraged him on: "Good. Let's try to get someone promising for Carmela to look at as soon as possible." Ryan called Carmela to tell her something was happening.

Just as he put down the phone, the president came in: "Ryan, yesterday afternoon I went to the monthly meeting of the Young Presidents Club, and through 18 holes of golf I listened to the virtues of executive teamwork. You know I've never been that much of a team player, but when I came back here this morning, I found a great new expansion proposal from Charlie Savage; when you read it carefully, he is trying to cut Barney Jones' throat again, and the two of them should be helping each other. Am I missing something, by not pushing this teamwork thing harder?"

"Of course you are, J.R.," Ryan laughed. "You are missing the chance to brag about all of the teamwork at High Velocity.

"But seriously, how could you really expect Charlie Savage and Barney Jones to work together? Charlie has been with the company for maybe 18 months, and Barney about 9. They run two divisions that compete with each other, both can make a better bonus if the other stumbles, and so far as I know they hadn't even met each other until 2 months ago when they both made presentations to the Management Committee on the same day. You wanted a company of hot-shot high performers, and I don't think any other CEO in the country has as good a group as you do. But they aren't team players and never will be.

"I could shift gears in the hiring and screening and in five years' time we could begin to build work teams like the ones you heard about. But I don't think you would be very happy with that sort of a group."

The Chief was not very pleased with the answer, and the two men talked for fifteen minutes more. Finally he got up: "Ryan, you're right, I have the kind of organization I wanted and I'm proud of it. If it were different I'd be yelling. But I'll have to admit that teamwork stuff sounds good sometimes when I hear it." He left. Ryan wondered for a moment if he should have tried to persuade the Chief to change his ways, and then realized again that almost nothing would ever change that management style. For as long as J.R. was CEO, High Velocity would continue to staff with high performers stolen from other companies at the moment of need, and teamwork never would be a religion, the way it was elsewhere. And High Velocity had good earnings and was growing rapidly; what more could anyone want anyway?

Ryan called Sam Swede again, to ask for a progress report on the search for a new head accountant on the 15th, which was 6 days away. "I have to begin to put some pressure on getting that job filled," he thought to himself.

QUESTIONS

1. Do you see any reason why High Velocity Enterprises cannot go on indefinitely hiring and staffing in this way?
2. List the advantages and disadvantages of building an organization in the way that High Velocity Enterprises has done it.

CASE 20 MOM'S PANTRY INDUSTRIES

MPI, Inc. had grown into a major food company. It had begun when Eldridge Clayton, a local grocer, decided one of his great-grandmother's recipes had potential and started the Mother's Orange Marmalade Company as a sideline. The business grew until Clayton's daughter Jane, who made and canned the marmalade in the beginning, had 30 employees at MOM's, as it was called, in a converted barn. John Greystoke, Jane's son, superintended the building of the first proper factory building. He added blackberry jam to the product line, and a full line of other jams and jellies soon followed. His wife suggested pies, tests were successful, and a growing line of pies and pastries followed. John's daughter Lucy became president when John retired; she added a successful new line of cookies and changed the name of the company to MOM's Pantry Industries, to reflect the increasing diversity of the product line.

Lucy wanted time for her many grandchildren and turned direction of the company over to her son Eldridge Yokum, whose fresh energies then brought ten years of unprecedented growth. The company was owned by the Claytons, Greystokes, and Yokums, all large families, and with the rapid increase in the value of the shares came estate problems. Eldridge solved these by a stock offering that established a public market value for the shares and provided cash for acquisition of a troubled cookie company with a good national distribution system. Soon MPI, Inc., as the company had been renamed for the public offering, was recognized as a growing force in the food industry and listed on the New York Stock Exchange. Eldridge was succeeded by Elmer Rafael, MBA-trained and with an excellent record over many years as the MPI Marketing Vice President, and almost a family member since he had married a Clayton girl. Elmer carefully maintained the family-company atmosphere of MPI, and built up a good, professional management team at the same time.

MPI had started in a small town. To a large extent it was still a family company, and although it had marketing, distribution, and some production in many other parts of the U.S. and Canada, its major activities were still concentrated in the home area. But the small town it started in had since become a suburb of a major, growing metropolitan area, so MPI no longer seemed to others to be a small-town company.

☐   ☐   ☐

Fred Inman had been with MPI for four years. He had just come back from a vacation trip home and was restless and uncertain about his future. William Williams, his section manager and immediate superior, asked him to talk to Biddle Bean, the management development advisor assigned to their section of MPI, and then come back. Fred's problem was that he and his cousin Sam Winter had both interviewed for jobs with

MPI at the same time four years ago. Fred got a good offer and accepted. Sam got turned down and finally found a job with a smaller company at lower pay. However, Sam had been able to use the first two years of his work experience to get a section manager job at another small company. Then six months ago he was approached by a recruiter for High Velocity Enterprises and hired away to fill a better section manager job there. Sam was clearly ahead of Fred now, both in pay and position, as Fred had learned when his uncles told him how proud Sam was making the family. Fred had had four good years at MPI, liked the company, and enjoyed the work, but he did not like to see a less able person making more rapid progress.

Biddle Bean was a seasoned, friendly man, well respected around the company. He listened carefully to Fred, asked a few questions, and then began to review Fred's record at MPI, which was a good one. Fred had spent the first year in a training program, and then a year each in a series of responsible junior-level assignments. Fred knew his work was well regarded, that he was considered "promising," and that his raises, while not dramatic, had been above average. "Fred," Biddle began, "you have a problem that comes out of the nature of our company. We passed over your cousin to hire you. Your record confirms our good judgment, but your cousin is a section manager now and you aren't and you're upset. But we don't look at a section manager's job the way High Velocity Enterprises does, or the company before that did either. We want a more seasoned and mature section manager because we see that as the real first step in our management progression.

"If you have looked at the company, you know our section managers move around a good deal—because MPI wants section managers to have broad experience, and to move up in management as fast as they can grow. It is rare for MPI to appoint a section manager who does not have five years of good performance with the company—in spite of how fast MPI is growing—and yet we have general managers now who were first appointed as section managers only five years ago. Not many section managers get fired, either, but the performance standards are high, and any who can't move up get moved aside, into areas of lesser responsibility where they can continue to contribute.

"Most other companies, including High Velocity, hire a lot quicker and fire a lot quicker, because they don't care about getting the breadth in their managers that we are after. Your cousin knows enough to manage a section in one area, and I am sure you do too, but we are also building toward the next promotion, and High Velocity doesn't bother; they would just as soon hire a manager from some place else to be your cousin's boss, and MPI doesn't like to do that. We want to grow our own top management out of managers who understand the company and its traditions and know how to work together.

"Your cousin is ahead of you, you don't think he is as able and neither did we, and you don't think it is fair. I sympathize, but that doesn't help you much. Here you have built an excellent base for the future with a company that really cares about such things, and with a company where the higher-level managers are advancing very rapidly. Your cousin has a better job, but in an environment where there is not much safety net if he missteps, and no real concern about whether he ever gets another promotion. I can't tell you what that is worth to you, because you are probably better able to look after yourself than he is. The long-run question is where you will get the most reward and satisfaction out of your career. We try to make MPI the kind of place where you will, but I can't make any guarantees and neither can Bill Williams. You may not know that he recommended you for a section manager's job last month. That job isn't filled yet, but it is really too soon for you in the MPI view of things, and I wouldn't want you to get your hopes up."

Fred Inman thanked Biddle Bean for his time and went back to talk to Williams, who gave him another view of much the same ground. By the time Fred left for the day he was convinced that there were reasons for the slower progress at MPI, but uncertain how the long-run picture would work out. Sam Winter's quicker progress still bothered him, until he got the mail that evening and found a letter from Aunt Susan; something had happened at High Velocity, Sam would have to find another job, would Fred be a darling and find him a section manager's job at MPI? Now Fred was sorry for Sam and had an impossible letter from his Aunt to answer. He still had the question: could he make a better career on his own, bouncing from company to company, or as a part of an aggressive management team at MPI?

☐ ☐ ☐

Elmer Rafael, the president of MPI, had found the trap of getting desk-bound early in his management career and avoided it better than most managers. He had made a point of learning a great deal about the rest of the company even as a part of his marketing assignments, and as president he felt a special need for broad contact. This he accomplished through a "random" schedule of visits to the out-of-town facilities his secretary programmed as side trips whenever he travelled, plus two hours twice a week in the headquarters complex itself. MPI had a 500-acre main plant, two smaller plants, a distribution center, a research center, and two office buildings at various spots on the western edge of town; twice a week Elmer would appear somewhere in this complex, usually unannounced, visiting people and asking questions. He knew most managers and many other employees by name and had sufficient knowledge of company operations and programs that he rarely needed to carry reports with him. Because of his style of managing he found that his subordinates also maintained a much greater familiarity with the details of their own operations than they might have under another president.

Elmer had just finished a quick tour of the jam and jelly area. He stopped in the section manager's office and complimented him on the cleanliness of the area and how smoothly the lines seemed to be running. The section manager was obviously pleased at the recognition and gave good, clear answers to two or three quick questions before Elmer left. Elmer was as brief as possible because he found that he had interrupted a discussion with Frank Ripley, the food products superintendent. But Frank looked either very troubled or ill, and three quarters of an hour later Elmer came back by Frank's office, and Frank was in. "Frank, I'm sorry I interrupted you out there in the jam and jelly area—but it really did look good and the lines were humming the way they should—and since I say what I think when things are bad, I wanted to mention the good things, too."

"You don't have to apologize for a compliment, Chief."

"No, but it looked as though you had worn your own thunderstorm to the meeting, and I thought I must have come in at a particularly bad time."

"It wasn't in the jam and jelly area, Chief. I had some papers to drop off there, and frankly I was glad to sit for a couple of minutes in a well-run office. I had just sent the pie and pastry manager on three weeks of vacation he didn't want, and now I have nobody to run that area."

"You suspended him?"

"I wouldn't want to put it that way—he is a good, long-service employee, and I hope we can work something out for him. But he has got all tangled up in his personal life, he has let it interfere with the way he is running his operation, and now he is trying to shift the blame on his employees. He was trying to fire three employees for three different mistakes, and in each case the fault seems to be his and not theirs. It's messy, and I've asked the personnel boys to assign a senior-level manager to listen to the same story to be sure I didn't miss anything. But he had to be off the job before we had an explosion there, and I took care of that. And, if I have this together right, he can't ever go back to pies and pastries again. He may need a few months in some sort of off-line assignment and some counseling to get his personal life under control again before he can go back to any sort of responsible work. That leaves me with a key area without a manager, and I haven't got a good candidate at the moment, even on a temporary basis."

"Whew, that is a hot one. I'm glad you are sending this out for a second opinion before the final verdict; but if he is really the kind of man to fire someone else for his own mistakes, I wonder what we can ever do with him. We can talk about that later, but I see why you didn't look bright and cheerful. Where are we going to find a manager for you quickly?"

"Chief, I don't know. I've asked Biddle Bean in personnel for a review of all of the trainees and juniors. I know that there is no one that is really ready, in terms of years and experience, but I don't want to go outside for a manager except as a last resort. The lid only blew off of this whole mess earlier this morning, and that's as far as I've had time to go."

On his way back to his office Elmer stopped in the cafeteria for a sandwich. He saw Biddle Bean and sat down with him. "Biddle, I hear we are running low on good managerial candidates just now."

"Chief, you are right as usual. But you must have been talking to Frank Ripley, because he's the only one I have told that just recently."

"It was Frank. But what I really wondered was how our training program was meshing in with our needs."

"Better than we expected, except that when Top Management did the plans, you guys didn't level with us on how fast this place was going to grow. We have developed a few more good candidates than we promised—as evidenced by good performance in the jobs they have gone into—but the organization needs more than we have."

"How are we going to fill the openings?"

"By tomorrow my boss will have a proposal for expanding our training, and hopefully that will quickly find its way up to you. But it takes five years or so to develop a good section manager, and that won't help Frank Ripley or the others who will be needing people sooner. We have also asked for a fresh "best estimate" on MPI growth rates, that planning should give to us shortly, and we will look at the gap between supply and needs to see if we have to hire managers outside, although no one wants to do that. We can place some of the juniors a little ahead of schedule, but we can't go too far without defeating the purpose of the training. I should be able to give you a better answer on the near-term solution in about a week, and the long-term depends on expanding the training program. Meanwhile we have a very promising junior manager named Fred Inman who has been getting a little restless anyway. I figured Frank Ripley had had enough interviews for one day, and that first thing tomorrow morning I would send Fred's folder over and suggest an interview."

"Great—but do one thing this afternoon, please. Call Frank and tell him you will send him a candidate. You're right not to go any farther; I told him to take the afternoon off and unwind—and he probably won't do it. But he will sleep better tonight knowing that you have someone for him to look at."

☐   ☐   ☐

Elmer Rafael's afternoon was normal CEO routine, with calls, appointments, meetings, and reports. One item in the controller's monthly report struck him. Norma Daniels, the controller, put together her monthly report by asking each of her section heads to write a page or less, with her own summary on top. The result was a bit informal but fresh and interesting. Susan Salsun's page for her accounting area had a line about "the difficulties in maintaining accurate cost standards when the production departments campaigned to discredit them." Elmer called her, and found that the problem was the cost standards for the jams and jellies: "This is our oldest product line; you'd think we would know how to set standard costs by now."

Of course Elmer agreed. "But we no sooner set a cost than the department upsets it. We used last year's standard adjusted for cost increases as a starting point, and the department beat it so much we had a big positive variance to explain, and of course we revised the standard to reflect the first quarter, and they did the same thing to us again in the second quarter; and can you believe that it happened again in the third quarter!"

"Have you asked the section manager about this?"

"Yes, and he says they are just learning how to run the department, and when they get it all figured out he will tell us what to set as a standard! Can you believe that!"

Elmer thought of the clean, busy production area he had complimented that morning. "Yes, I can believe that. I think you will find that the manager took charge of that department late last year, and probably they are just learning to run it!"

"You mean, after all of these years?"

"Yes. We keep talking about excellence here at MPI, and we have some truly excellent spots in our organization—but somehow since the new machinery came in, this must be the first time we have had the kind of manager in jams and jellies who could make the excellence model work. I'm sorry he has made your work harder, but think of the savings. And some of those old jellies that were beginning to look marginal will have a secure place in the product line again."

QUESTIONS

1. Some companies emphasize a "company" way of doing things and expect employees to learn and to follow it, on the basis that it makes other things easier if certain standards are followed. This is a part of what MPI was doing. To what extent is this "company way" good or bad? Discuss.

2. Many companies would simply have fired the manager caught trying to blame mistakes on a subordinate. MPI did not. Wisdom or weakness? Discuss.

3. Discuss how you view the personal equation of moving from company to company frequently in order to get rapid advancement, versus a more stable career in one organization.

CHAPTER

MANAGING OPERATIONS

KEY IDEAS IN THIS CHAPTER

The ability of a firm to make a given strategy work depends in part on the way in which its operations are structured and managed, and this chapter outlines some of the fundamentals:

- **organizing the enterprise** – reasons for creating separate businesses or profit centers and some of the considerations in doing so.
- **the role of the public strategy** – organizationally and strategically.
- **operations strategy** – productive and service units, structure and work planning, keeping the structure flexible, the role of functional strategies.
- **bigness as a problem** – as shifting economic factors bring scale economies to smaller and smaller units.
- **third wave management** – the excellence model plus a more effective structure, where a high-performance organization is needed.
- **using people in the operation** – the labor, contributor, and manager models, for increasingly higher productivity and achievement levels.
- **strategic management of operations** – summary of key factors.

For the enterprise to operate, it must be given a structure, jobs must be designed, and an operating apparatus must first be created and then modified as the firm, its customers, and the environment change. This chapter will examine the subdivision of the enterprise into operating units as an aspect of the firm's ongoing operations, the design philosophy underlying the structure of work, application of that philosophy to white-collar and blue-collar operations, and options for the contributing strategies as various functional elements define their support of the primary strategies.

ORGANIZING THE ENTERPRISE

A firm with many products usually must separate their management. Control over different processes, different technologies, and different customer groups often calls for separate management responsibilities within the firm. The intricacy of this management problem varies from company to company, and the managing and belonging strategies establish how complex and diverse a given company's operations may become.

Firms operating in several business areas often organize their operations into profit centers called strategic business units or SBUs, following the pattern once set by General Electric. Each SBU is normally intended to be an independent business controlling the resources necessary for its function and operating more or less autonomously under the oversight of upper management.

The SBUs may be gathered into groups, with a convenient number of SBUs reporting to a group executive, a convenient number of group executives reporting to a more senior executive, and so forth, until all of the SBUs of a large enterprise are assembled into a hierarchy. This model has limitations as discussed in Chapter 5, because senior management can give proper attention to the fundamentals of only a limited number of businesses. Also, the assumption of total independence of the SBUs is weak, with the weakness hard to compensate. Many firms assembled the grouping of businesses they have because of common technologies, common customer groups, or other relationships, one to the other. Yet the pressure of the SBU framework tends to prevent SBU general managers from acknowledging these relationships and acting on the commonalities unless this specifically improves short-term profits of their individual SBUs. Left to itself this pressure for individual performance destroys the synergism between the businesses.

And many SBUs cannot be given full control of all of their resources. A major plant complex or refinery may need to be run as an integrated unit and yet may supply products for several businesses, a distribution system may serve several businesses selling in the same region or to the same customers, or there may be other good reasons to use shared resources. This resource sharing to a degree defeats the performance measurement concept of the SBU, and Naylor suggested a strategy matrix system of product centers and resource centers to be used where SBU definitions become artificial, as discussed in Chapter 5.

A key consideration in selecting an organization pattern for the firm is the cost and contribution or profit expected from each part, including the central structure. SBUs or other business units are expected to generate a profit. Corporate staffs, central management, and central services are a corporate expense, often a large one, and this cost must be recovered from the various business units. Each central service is intended to have a contribution/cost ratio advantageous to the businesses it serves; that is, its contribution to the functioning of a business unit should be sufficiently greater than its cost so that the business unit is strengthened by that service.

The central structure of a firm can contribute to the success of its subordinate units in many ways but brings two kinds of costs. A fair share of the expense of the central activity is an obvious cost to the business units. The hidden cost is the degree to which added central functions make the business process slower and less market-responsive. That some conglomerates were sold in parts, business by business, for more than the market value of the whole is an indication that investors believed that the cost of the central structure exceeded the benefits. As the possibility that some large firms are not efficient is more clearly recognized, strategic management will examine the contribution/cost relationship with each subordinate unit, to make this ratio as favorable as possible. An increasingly efficient market for individual business units has developed, and provides management the opportunity to recover the fair market value of any business unit whose earning power is being depressed by continued membership in a large firm. Therefore in selecting a structure, it can and should be one mutually beneficial to all of its parts.

The central organizational requirements of the enterprise are actually rather simple, in spite of complexities in applying them. Separate business operations should be under the control of executives who plan and execute the strategy for these operations, and are accountable for and rewarded according to the outcome. Each of these separate operations should be within the personal oversight and control of a more senior manager, and the resulting enterprise hierarchy requires sufficient organizational cohesion to ensure coordination and common purpose.

Within the business units, and to a degree at the enterprise level, structure must follow strategy. In the short term a given structure limits the strategies a unit can execute, but in the long run either strategy prevails and the structure evolves, or the unit will lose competitive effectiveness as conditions eventually change.

But the major structuring alternatives of large organizations all fight the same dilemma:

1. To organize in a way that *guarantees* the desired coordination and control as an automatic part of the management operating system also creates a formal structure that then becomes bureaucratic and impersonal.
2. To maintain the necessary personal relationships between managers also leaves the coordination and control on an informal basis that usually fails eventually in a large organization.

The solution to this dilemma and the pattern required by the excellence model is to keep the effective size of the organization small enough so that personal control can be maintained. The variety of mechanisms for keeping the organization small all break it into parts and coordinate the parts. The Johnson & Johnson solution is perhaps the most elegant structurally, in that the parent corporation keeps its organization small by creating a new subsidiary for each business entity. This subsidiary has its own officers and board of directors to run it, so that it needs no other reporting relationships. It either owns its own resources or obtains them by negotiated contracts with other corporations. Those chosen for the board of directors of a subsidiary are usually officers of related J & J subsidiaries. The directors then coordinate these different businesses and have a personal interest in making the coordination effective.

Other firms keep units small by subdividing operations when they reach what is viewed as a critical size, and by avoiding almost entirely the central staff functions typical of a large firm. This lack of central staff enforces decentralization of routine decisions to lower management levels, and top management needs extensive personal contact to maintain control without heavy staff assistance. But these tend to be "management by walking around" types of companies anyway, where senior executives do spend heavily of their time in keeping contact with the people and operations reporting to them.

Not all firms will choose to create units small enough to be managed in the pattern of the excellence model. Not all managers could or would be comfortable to manage in this style, many organizations are operating strategies now sufficiently effective and profitable that they are under no pressure to change, and some managements believe that there are other routes to success. General Electric, as an example, would appear to be too large in its central functions and in some of its operating units to fit the norms suggested by the *In Search of Excellence* study. Yet General Electric has had a long, uninterrupted period of growth, as successive managements have experimented quite successfully in search of the best means for the central planning and control of a very large and diverse enterprise. It is not yet clear that GE has succeeded because of its management training and its management system, which has been altered repeatedly, or whether the good performance derives from a level of experimentation with the management system sufficiently intense to prevent the solidification and potential decay of the management bureaucracy normal in so large an organization.

Where a management chooses a more elaborate and more formal central means of coordination than one based on human contact, there is normally a trade-off, in that such a management no longer can be so personal, and the impersonality normally is followed by poorer coordination and some loss of organizational effectiveness. GE is fighting against this loss, with considerable success so far.

THE ROLE OF THE PUBLIC STRATEGY

As a business operates, its decisions will each have a social impact, and this social impact makes necessary some ongoing dialog with various elements in society. From time to time the business needs approvals from governments or other elements of society. Or perhaps the business wishes to influence legislation, or in other ways to induce society to assist the business.

The strategic element is management's decision on the form and posture through which necessary dialog with society will be conducted. Some firms take a humble, passive role in such matters, largely relying on the administrative structure of the regulatory bodies, complying with requests, and accepting the rulings that result. Other firms approach these relationships with a stronger posture, attempting positively to expedite the process and influence the outcome. Still others will dispute an outcome that does not please them, as the textile industry has sought protection against imports, carrying the issue into political and public discussion, and attempting to stir support that will resolve any issue in their favor.

A wide range of options is available to any enterprise and to the individual businesses within an enterprise. The management task is to select an option compatible with the needs and desires of the firm and with the time and talents of those who must carry it out, plus a routine pattern for this interaction with society so that the organization as a whole can play the desired role. Creation of a specialized public relations or public affairs function is common; sometimes this includes the community relations function and sometimes not. Frequently separate staffs charged with specific regulatory relationships are created, such as for liaison with the Food and Drug Administration, where a firm has extensive dealings with a particular agency. The general counsel sometimes oversees necessary interaction with legislative bodies and government officials, or there may be a separate organizational unit charged with all lobbying and related activities.

According to the functions the management wants performed as part of its public strategy, a corresponding organization structure will be created. The rest of the organization needs to know how it relates to this structure and what its own role should be. More and more often now some unexpected public issue puts a minor manager in the position of having to speak for the enterprise, and that manager needs advance guidance.

OPERATIONS STRATEGY

Each of the major functions of management—planning, organizing, staffing, directing, and controlling—has its component elements and procedures, as does the management operating system itself. Each of these procedures should be (1) considered for its potential vulnerability to outside events, (2) compared with parallel procedures and processes elsewhere, and (3) examined for potential application of new technology from any source.

The plan that is needed, for the management of corporate operations, should adapt the operation to any impact from these external change processes. By doing so it continually redirects the inertia of the organization as it rolls forward into the future, shifting direction and emphasis in the way most appropriate to keep the firm's operations current, effective, productive, and competitive.

PRODUCTIVE AND SERVICE UNITS

One major distinction between various operating units comes from their difference in function, where some have a productive purpose, and others provide a service. Units with a productive purpose exist to make or process something; the need for the unit and the evaluation of its performance can be based on the quantity, quality, and cost of the output. Inside an industrial company the service units function in support of the productive efforts, so that the demand for their services is a derived demand. The evaluation of their output is also derived, from their contribution to the functioning of the whole.

Production, distribution, and sales are productive functions, in each case with a tangible output through units produced, orders handled, or sales achieved. All three depend on personnel services, but personnel can measure only derived contributions. Even though employee turnover ratios and personnel staff cost per employee may be calculated, it can never be entirely clear how much the personnel function contributes to overall profits.

Maintenance has a similar service role. Individual maintenance tasks can be measured against engineered performance standards, but the intangibles of the way that the service benefits the output from the productive units have much more to do with the real contribution of maintenance to the operating whole.

Research is justified by productive output of new products, even though time lags may be long and measurement difficult. But most corporate staffs are service units and have little tangible output. They can be measured only by estimating a contribution to making the total enterprise function effectively.

Whether a unit is primarily of a productive or a service nature may not be determined by its location in the organization. Inside an administrative staff division a printing and duplicating function may be a productive unit in cost, delivery, and quality competition with outside vendors. Yet the scheduling office of a major production unit often has no performance measures other than its service in providing workable schedules.

The importance of the distinction between productive and service functions is in the different management processes as the managers respond to their performance measures. Productive processes are measured by their ability to generate a profit or a profit contribution. Service processes are measured by comparing their costs with the benefits perceived by the rest of the organization. The management tasks of the two types of units are almost exactly parallel. The difference is in the way that the management control process affects the behavior of the managers in charge of particular units.

A productive unit justifies resource requests by its ability to produce more or to produce for less. It can often get more resources than it really needs if results are favorable, but may be denied even critical priorities when the bottom line looks bad. A service unit must deal entirely with management perception of benefits from its services compared with their cost. Due to the intangible nature of the benefits, the process inevitably becomes somewhat subjective and even political.

The management processes of the two different types of units must focus on achieving two fundamentally different types of objectives. One is a bottom-line output measure and the other a politically acceptable cost/benefit ratio. This difference is pervasive and affects the whole psychology of the management. The management process gears itself for a political/budgetary control in the case of the service processes, versus a market/economic control for the productive processes.

An organization focused on service must emphasize the benefit/cost ratio of these services, and promote them as effectively as possible to keep the constituency supporting the services convinced that these benefits exceed their cost. The response desired from this constituency is one of belief and perception, so that the arguments are generally framed on subjective grounds, and presented or lobbied in that way which will have the greatest impact on these beliefs.

By contrast, an organization whose primary purpose is productive has a bottom-line measure from which it is difficult to escape. Its internal processes orient around the revenues that will be generated, the profits that will be received, and the best way to present and defend them.

STRUCTURE AND WORK PLANNING

The performance of the business process is carried out through a large number of routine operations. Routine operations deal with the combination of current requirements and accustomed habit patterns. The habit patterns are a part of the building of a sound, productive routine. Also, these habit patterns become central to the operation and must be respected.

One key element in work planning for any group at any level in the organization is the choice of what will be fixed, and what variable. Most managements work out a pattern of things that are usually the same—these are the elements of the routine procedures—and design this pattern to accommodate variable elements as they most frequently occur. The human personality has keyed into it a certain requirement for structure, and a certain resistance to change; both traits were survival requirements for the primitive tribes from which human civilization later developed. In a modern organization the same traits are still important factors governing behavior.

An automobile assembly plant once developed a smooth, repetitive procedure for the painting of automobile wheels—the operator purged his spray gun, connected a paint hose, sprayed four wheels, purged the spray gun again, reconnected a paint hose, and repeated the procedure. The procedure design, with a built-in clean-out and reconnection after each four wheels, meant that the operator could change color for each car by connecting a different hose without varying the preset routine. Because color was designed into this procedure as a variable, a possibility for a change in color with every car had been included within the routine procedure.

In the same way an automotive engineer planned the wheel-painting routine, almost every white collar or blue collar job has elements where change is automatic and accepted, and others that seem always to stay the same. A shipping room has a fixed order-picking, packing, and handling routine—but bases it on the assumption that no two orders will be the same; and each can be shipped to a different address because this flexibility is built into the standard procedure.

KEEPING THE STRUCTURE FLEXIBLE

Operating management has always a set of routine procedures with built-in variables, as the address was left as a variable in the shipping room example. Changes in these variables are assumed as a part of the operation. Changes in the procedures themselves must be made with care and planning, because the procedures become a part of the familiar structure that the group clings to and protects.

To build a high-performing operation in a changing field, it becomes important to structure the routine around those elements likely to change but little, allowing rapid or even radical change in the other elements without disturbing the routine. Because the routine procedures were built on changes in both packing materials and addresses, the shipping room could easily ship to the moon—just one more type of packing materials, one more address, and delivery to a different carrier. And while the first shipment to the moon would be a lively topic of discussion, it would not threaten the familiar procedures, where a much smaller change outside these familiar procedures could cause stress or pain, and invoke the challenges of managing organizational change.

Operating management also has familiar procedures to which it clings. And, within the normal concentration barriers of operating management, reasons for changes in management's own familiar procedures almost never assert themselves. This is why a strategic overview is so essential here, to ensure that operations do not lose relevance for lack of changes in management's own process as new factors emerge.

FUNCTIONAL STRATEGIES

Contributing strategy, introduced in Chapter 2, is the strategy underlying the operating plans and actions of a department, function, or other organizational unit. Such a strategy directs the way a specific organizational function will be performed, and the way this function contributes to the performance of one or several product, business, and enterprise strategies.

The subordinate position of a functional strategy does not reduce its importance, for it may provide the cutting edge, in terms of leverage, position, or another element, that gives a product, business, or enterprise strategy potential for success. Each functional area is itself a separate major area of study and will be treated only briefly here to relate it to the various components of the strategic management sequence.

Marketing strategy determines the product focus, defines and conveys the leverages, arranges to fulfill the display requirements, and strives to make best use of available positions and resources. It also attempts to build enduring positions in the market place that will yield rent in the future, and to establish effective distribution to aid in selling and as a source of an ongoing distribution service fee. This increases protection against competition and adds to the total that can be reported as profit.

Research & development strategy is designed to guide an effort that is the source of potential new products or services, and the vehicle by which the businesses it serves keep their desired relationship to new technology and participate in its application.

The production strategy accomplishes the desired output of goods or services, whether by emphasizing economies of scale, the learning curve, and continuing productivity increases for a basis manufacturer, or by extensive subcontracting in a business less concerned about building a proprietary, long-term manufacturing position.

Distribution, grouped here with marketing, is often recognized as a separate function. Engineering, finance, purchasing, personnel, and each of the other specific functional units needs and will have a functional strategy. The importance of specific functions varies greatly from one business to another, but the key is that each function works toward effective performance, and effective support to the primary strategies.

BIGNESS AS A PROBLEM

The U.S. business community has been taught to worship bigness—and not without cause—but based on facts and technology that are now changing rapidly. As business firms learned to do things on a larger scale, products became less expensive. Bigger plants and equipment were more efficient, a bigger firm had superior access to financing and other resources, and large firms first applied modern financial and management systems to their operations.

General Motors acquired already successful school bus and diesel locomotive companies and greatly amplified their success by applying the GM pattern of management and control. It seemed that medium-sized companies benefited by being incorporated into a larger company, and conglomerate acquisitions demonstrated this benefit. By acquiring smaller enterprises, applying modern management systems and financial controls, and supplying resources as required to maximize their profitable growth, early conglomerates greatly increased earnings. But then the conglomerate advantage seemed to fade away. Some of the leaders suffered reverses, and now financial analysts speak of a conglomerate discount in stock prices—meaning that investors will pay only a stock market price less than the earnings appear to justify. Several takeovers have been based on the desire to sell off the component businesses of a conglomerate individually and recover the conglomerate discount as a profit.

Disappearance of the conglomerate advantage was due to business system changes.[1] Many markets are so large now that most, if not all, of the scale economies of bigness can be achieved while serving only a fraction of the market. Modern management systems are widely applied to large and small enterprises, and financial services have increased in availability and sophistication so that a giant firm no longer has a significant advantage over the medium-sized firms.

But the market has put the conglomerate earnings at a discount, saying that it is a *disadvantage* for a medium-sized firm to be part of a larger firm rather than independent. The suggested explanation is that the bigger organization is less efficient in management and more bureaucratic in its central processes. This leads to a new theory of organization, that it should run with a minimum of formal central processes, that it somehow be kept small enough not to suffer from the organizational limits to corporate growth.

A discounting of bigness also appears to result from important changes in manufacturing and related technologies. Two areas of rapid change are in the technologies determining the economies of scale in manufacturing and setting the size of the central organization needed to run a given facility. Economies of scale are based partly on the size of reactor vessels, machinery, and plants, where big continues to be better, but new capabilities and flexibilities are changing the variables in this equation. Big equipment has often been single-purpose because its disadvantage has always been the time and cost of changing over to another product. With new setup systems and modern control systems, setup and changeover times are falling rapidly. For some types of products the entire changeover can be accomplished by computer, making the changeover instantaneous and opening the door to large savings by running small amounts of some products on the largest and most efficient machines; this also makes it possible for smaller firms to use the most efficient machines. More and more plants are reaching the point of being able to run whatever variety of products the incoming orders specify, and in almost any order; that is, to manufacture to order. A plant running on a manufacture-to-order basis needs no finished inventory. Orders can be received electronically, made, and shipped the same day in many cases, and the necessary organization becomes much smaller and simpler.

In an old-style large manufacturing organization the necessary staff

---

[1] Bernard C. Reimann, "Corporate Strategy: From Portfolio Planning to Value-Building," FAR "Best Paper in Corporate and Organizational Planning," winner, 1988.

support functions were large and elaborate, but the large scale economies of the larger plant paid for this overhead, including any loss of staff and management efficiency due to the size of the organization. Now these scale economies are becoming available without the heavy central staff requirements—together with large savings in inventories, handling, and overhead costs. The conclusion is that the economic logic of the organization with a large central management apparatus is disappearing rapidly.

In *Thriving on Chaos*[2] Peters pursues the "small is beautiful" theme, perhaps to excess. But the balance point has really shifted, and it has not yet come to any determinate equilibrium. Major conclusions at this point include the following:

1. The old automatic advantages of any very large organization are largely gone because so many of the traditional sorts of assistance a corporate center could provide to its businesses are readily available to almost any well-run medium-sized corporation.
2. Smaller and more flexible organization units are more effective in fitting to customer needs, as seems to be crucial in today's competitive markets, and large enough to run modern, efficient, and fully cost-competitive plants of the newer types.
3. There are still many ways in which membership in a larger organization can be beneficial to a business unit, but these benefits must arise out of specific circumstances, usually as a result of good strategic management of the large organization, and the contribution/cost ratio resulting from this membership must be beneficial to the subsidiary if it is to remain competitive in the long run.
4. Where the strategies a business pursues require a highly effective organization for their successful execution, the smaller organization has a clear-cut advantage, because it is more difficult to establish the personal relationships necessary for excellence-model levels of performance in a large organization.
5. Truly competitive organizations will become smaller and more flexible as these trends run their course. These may be independent organizations, or smaller units of larger firms, depending on how ingenious larger firms are with organizational devices minimizing the true cost of membership in the firm for their subordinates and allowing an excellence-model operation to be developed.
6. In terms of strategic management of operations, the subject of this chapter, it becomes essential that management estimate the rate at

---

[2] Tom Peters, *Thriving on Chaos: Handbook for a Management Revolution* (New York: Knopf, 1988).

which its operations will have to change to meet the new requirements outlined here, use that estimate to manage this change process, and review its progress in accomplishing these changes versus the competitive forces it faces on a routine basis.

THIRD WAVE MANAGEMENT

Between chapters about John Sculley's career at Pepsico and Apple in his *Odyssey*[3] are short studies of the forces he saw at work in both organizations and across U.S. industry. Using Alvin Toffler's second wave and third wave concepts[4] as a base, he classified Pepsico, IBM, and most of U.S. industry as second wave corporations. These were traditional top-down organization, pyramid types of companies—Pepsico and IBM being excellent performers and very successful, most of the rest less so. In third wave organizations such as Apple, the various managers work in a participative network, and each individual is highly self-directing. Little is said about control structure, but Sculley was in charge.

Paralleling Sculley's commentary are ideas in Peters' *Thriving on Chaos*.[5] One of Peters' fundamental points is that workers at all levels must become self-directing, even though this takes a lot of training and support, because self-directing workers are more productive, respond better to the real needs of customers and the business, and need much less oversight; the corporate pyramid shrinks radically, and both levels and staffs disappear, with massive savings in overhead. Peters does not describe the organization structure that results except to emphasize that it must be much more flexible and informal. But Peters and Sculley seem to be studying the same phenomenon, and their ideas integrate well.

The work of the people of a firm can be defined and controlled in more than one way. Traditionally people are each employed to do a specific job that has been defined for them in advance, are judged on how well they do it, and are expected not to think beyond the requirements of that specific assignment. This behavior pattern matches what Sculley called a second wave organization, where workers at each level, including knowledge workers and managers, are expected to perform within preset boundaries and within a system that supervises and directs their performance.

The alternative, common in startups, some small firms, and now developing in third wave corporations, is for each individual to be

---
[3] John Sculley with John A. Byrne, *Odyssey* (New York: Harper & Row, 1987).
[4] Alvin Toffler, *The Third Wave* (New York: Morrow, 1980).
[5] Tom Peters, *Thriving on Chaos: Handbook for a Management Revolution* (New York: Knopf, 1988).

self-directing. Self-directing? This requires a starting point, an assignment well-enough designed and integrated with the rest of the organization to provide a sound foundation. It also requires a great deal of training, both initially and as on-going support; but the result—a work force essentially self-directing at all levels—has been achieved in very many organizations, a number of which are described by Peters. A truly self-directing work force requires a different organization structure; most or all of the first-line supervisors disappear, middle managers spend most of their time coordinating and facilitating work of subordinates, middle management spans of control increase radically, and the organization structure shrinks to a nearly flat pyramid.

Conventional organization theory contrasts a mechanistic and an organic model; as described, the second wave corporation could be fitted into the mechanistic model. The third wave corporation has internal flexibility and informality in common with the organic model, but they do not fully correspond. One way of visualizing a third wave organization is within the mechanistic model but under the premise that all workers are self-directing and that the mechanistic pyramid and control structure have been modified accordingly. Strong, active upper management and real strategic management control over all activities are clearly needed, but applied in a manner consistent with a largely self-directing subordinate role.

The relevance in this chapter on strategic management over operations is that the third wave organization is an additional strategic alternative. The excellence model, to obtain a high level of organization motivation and competence, can be applied in either a second wave or third wave structure, given the necessary conditions and investment of management energy to build it. A third wave structure then represents a further step, again with additional management energy required to create and control it. The result, according to Sculley, Peters, and many others, is an organization that can achieve remarkable things, in terms of high accomplishments and low cost. Peters argues strongly that no other sort of organization is going to be competitive in major industrial areas in the future. And the shift toward smaller organization units, discussed earlier, is an important parallel development because these highly flexible organization forms are at their best in smaller organizations and most difficult to install successfully in extremely large ones.

THE ROLE OF THE PEOPLE VERSUS EFFICIENCY AND ACHIEVEMENT

From the different ways of looking at an organization discussed in this chapter, one conclusion is that the strategy that management defines for its internal processes and handling of people is critically important. What an organization expects of its employees makes a substantial difference in (1) staffing—the number and types of people needed to accomplish a given amount of work; (2) overhead—the structure required for direction and control over that work; (3) commitment—the degree of commitment management must make to the members of the organization; (4) management—the caliber of management the organization requires; and (5) achievement—the degree to which the organization can accomplish tasks whose challenge rises above the routine. There are at least three basic approaches to using people in an organization:

1. Every employee is hired to do a specific job and is expected to do it well, and it is the task of the supervisor to see that the job is done properly. This is the *laborer* model, the traditional structure—to define a job, fill it, and expect quiet performance within the assigned duties. Whether the employee is a janitor, a lawyer, a machinist, an engineer, or the head of the medical department, the attitude of management is "Don't tell me how to run the company. Do your job and be quiet—that's what you are getting paid for." The laborer model leads to traditional "tall" organizations with relatively narrow spans of control, much supervisory attention to subordinates, and extensive staffs to help with the details of the operation and of its management.

2. Every employee is hired to do a specific job and to contribute his or her ideas about "how we all should work together"—the *contributor* model. Supervisors have to work to build the relationships—and ultimately the trust—in which real participation can occur. It is harder to manage a participative group effectively and without undue use of time in discussion, but the reward is in lower overhead requirements—span of control can be greater and fewer details need to be handled by staff—and higher productivity because of higher motivation. Because of their culture, the Japanese seem to move almost spontaneously into contributor-model organizations, where U.S. companies must work to build them. Some Japanese organizations have substantially smaller overhead pyramids than comparable U.S. organizations. Experience over the past ten years suggests that, without some other comparative advantage, laborer-model organizations cannot compete successfully with contributor-model organizations.

3. Every employee is hired not only to do a job but to manage himself or herself—the *manager* model. These are the organizations in which the first-line supervisors disappear and middle management spends much of its time coordinating and integrating the efforts of its subordinates. Corporate-level staff work almost disappears, spans of control become very large, and the management pyramid shrinks radically. A partial offset is the necessity of a training/support activity

so that every employee really can manage his or her own work. These are radical-sounding ideas, but companies are doing this; Lincoln Electric has been oriented this way since before World War II, and Peters[6] lists some of the more recent converts to this approach. The result is extremely high motivation and high productivity among a self-managing group, and impressive results that the Japanese will have more trouble matching because their culture does not emphasize the individual responsibility and initiative this model requires.

STAFFING

Frederick W. Taylor showed that the amount of work a person can be required to do can be calculated; legions of industrial engineers refined his calculations; and good management expects and requires output at 80 percent of the engineered standard rate where such standards are used—this is work in the laborer model. Taylor also demonstrated that, given suitable incentives, most employees would choose to work at much higher rates than could be required; he developed piecework incentive systems to get this higher performance. Modern motivation theory carries this further—Drucker's management by objectives concepts and Maslow's concept of self-actualization and the motivation for achievement it can call forth are two examples. The salient points are that people can decide to work much harder than they can be required to work, there is a synergistic effect when an entire group works in this way, and output can rise substantially—certainly to twice the level of output that could be required, and probably higher. Except where piecework pay scales are practical the laborer model does not lend itself to incentives for performance beyond the standard rate, but both the contributor and manager models do, starting with the self-motivation resulting from the personal involvement. The contributor model, well implemented, should achieve a substantial increase in productivity, and the manager model still more.

OVERHEAD

The overhead staffing and costs in an organization should be based on the work that has to be done to keep the operation running smoothly and under management control. This work is greatest in a laborer-model organization because people who are not directing their own work need more upper-level guidance, and because the contributor-model and manager-model organizations make successively greater delegation of authority to lower levels, decreasing the work of the overhead group accordingly.

---

[6] *Ibid.*

COMMITMENT

A laborer-model organization requires minimum commitment by the employees to the company or by management to the members of its organization. This gives management maximum short-run flexibility but sometimes leads to the formation of very strong unions. A contributor-model or manager-model organization requires respect and trust among its members in order to function; an excellence-model organization is required for either to achieve its potential, and, as discussed earlier, this commits management to maintain the environment such an organization requires.

MANAGEMENT

The easiest to manage is a laborer-model organization, because procedures are clearly prescribed and questions from subordinates are discouraged. A contributor-model organization requires greater interpersonal skills and more real ability, and both requirements escalate further in the manager-model organization. Both of these models encourage suggestions and challenges from subordinates, and the manager-model organization also calls for a pattern of guidance of subordinates best described as coaching, to build the necessary self-management skills.

ACHIEVEMENT

Achievement is a combination of productivity that rises due to the greater motivation and lower overhead of the contributor and manager models and the increased ability to accomplish difficult tasks, as stressed earlier in the discussion of the excellence model.

These three models are prototypes chosen from an almost infinite series of gradations between extremes achievable by competent management after suitable adjustment of the enterprise strategies. The challenges in using them come in maintaining the very real control needs of management and in understanding the costs and commitments required to build any organization that will work at a higher level of effectiveness than the laborer model achieves.

MANAGEMENT OF OPERATIONS STRATEGY

Management should establish that all procedures are open to change; that reevaluation from a strategic overview is constant and ongoing; that the threat of change will be moderated by wise management action; and per-

---

FIGURE 11-1   OPERATIONS, DAY BY DAY

Organizing the enterprise

Public strategy

Operations
- productive versus service units
- structure
- work planning
- keeping the structure flexible
- functional strategies

Avoiding the disadvantages of bigness

Third wave organization
- to use where appropriate

Laborer, contributor, and manager models
- different uses of people for different operations results

EXECUTING STRATEGY AND BUILDING PROFITS, DAY BY DAY

---

haps that organization members can participate in planning changes and redesign of those procedures affecting them directly—but that the organizational norm is one of active change in preparation for moving into the future.

To plan the management of enterprise operations, and to accomplish the dynamic management pattern suggested above, the services of the foresight function discussed earlier are again invaluable. Someone must track events in the outside world, making the bridge to establish relevance when it exists, and calling the event or trend to the attention of the operating managers concerned with this component of strategic overview planning. Operating management could do its own environmental search, but usually does not, for lack of time in the face of the normal operating pressures. The key is to gather the information for operating management to use to make a plan and act on it, with the key linkages as shown in Figure 11-1.

By building toward a more effective and efficient pattern of operation, the firm strengthens all present and potential positions based on costs, delivery, and service, thus reinforcing many of its needs-leverages linkages and adding force to the strategies these leverages drive. Strategic management effectiveness in maintaining and increasing the basic strength and effectiveness of the operation is a key strategy and action component.

QUESTIONS FOR ANALYSIS AND DISCUSSION

1. Find organization charts for one or more major businesses (sometimes they are summarized in the annual reports) to see whether that firm subdivides itself into SBUs or into some other sort of product or geographical divisions.
2. Choose firms with several sorts of public strategies (as evidenced by their actions), and state what those strategies appear to be.
3. In an organization with which you are familiar or about which you have read, look for both productive and service units. Find two or three of each, and state approximately what their role is.
4. Look at the structure of the work in any routine operation and list the things that are fixed and the things that are left variable (e.g., because of different work structures it is easier for some fast food restaurants to handle special orders than others).

FOR FURTHER INFORMATION

Peters, Tom, *Thriving on Chaos: Handbook for a Management Revolution* (New York: Knopf, 1988).
  A strong, authoritative call for a new style of management based on smaller and more flexible organizations as a necessity for long-term survival of most significant businesses; buttressed by multitudes of examples from personal contact with key U.S. companies.

Sculley, John, with John A. Byrne, *Odyssey* (New York: Harper & Row, 1988).
  The contrasts between second wave and third wave management from a man expert in both.

Toffler, Alvin, *The Adaptive Corporation* (New York: McGraw-Hill, 1985), and *The Third Wave* (New York: Morrow, 1980).
  The shift in our society, from an industrial second wave that is losing its force, to a new third wave that will change the face of our society.

CASE 21
THE B. W. WEEVIL COMPANY

Old John Weevil made his mark on his sons. He was a man who believed in a set approach to problems. A man should work out his own way of keeping things standardized, and he did. His sons were named Ben, Bill, and Bob. He tried very hard to be equally strict with all of them, but this fell hardest on the oldest; Ben was a big, burly lad with a mind of his own who got tired of being beaten; when he was 13 he knocked his father down, picked up some clothes, and left. As B. W. Weevil (he told people that that was all the name he had), he worked his own way, for he was a strong, personable, ambitious lad. At one point he worked in a grocery store. The owner discovered that B. W. had a natural gift with numbers, and encouraged him to develop it. B. W. learned to keep the store's account books, got help from the grocer's wife with his reading, and started on a self-study course in basic accounting. Then he worked as clerk for an accountant for a while and began to read real estate and commercial law at night. When he was 20 he worked for a year in a brokerage firm where he met some men who had organized a new business and were trying to get it started. It was quite clear to him that they were doing everything wrong and would fail, but no one had asked him. He did point out to one of the brokers that if he had a business like that, he could make a lot of money, even if the other fellows were going bust.

A week later B. W. was called into a meeting and asked about this. He repeated his statement, they challenged him, and he started to list the things he would do and why they were better. They questioned him for two hours, made him wait outside for fifteen minutes, and then offered him a half-interest in the business if he could make it pay back its debts and make money. He accepted, and succeeded. He had saved the firm a serious embarrassment and a good deal of money, since that business had been about to fail. He soon arranged to buy the other half of the business also, so that he could be independent, and the B. W. Weevil Company was born.

B. W. had a gift for business; that is what they said. And that must have been right, for the Company grew and grew. First its basic merchandising business expanded, and then B. W. began to acquire companies; he had a knack for this also. Again and again he bought a company that was bankrupt or otherwise in distress, worked a few weeks to get it back into shape, and then turned it over to one of his managers to add into the Company. He did well in selecting managers and in delegating responsibility to them, and even though the Company was getting large and complex, he had it in capable hands and under excellent control. Without working very hard at all he could be a very successful owner and president. But he did work very hard, because the Company was his life. Remembering his own childhood, he had sworn never to bring children into the world, and had never married. He ran the routine operation of the Company on a leisurely, half-time basis—and spent the rest of his waking hours on plans and schemes for making it larger and better. He continued to do much of the acquisition search, and to spend a couple of weeks with each new business to make it ready to join the others; this was very successful. But then he began to spend some of this extra time on new approaches to marketing, and this was disastrous.

The problem was that, in the image of his father, B. W. wanted a standard system for doing things. His system for management and financial control worked well on the variety of businesses he applied it to, but as he developed a system for marketing and applied it uniformly, not all businesses responded the same way. B. W. decided that selling and promotion expense should be better standardized. But requiring that marketing expense as a percent of sales or advertising as a percent of sales be the same for grocery, wholesale, plumbing supplies, cosmetics and toiletries, and the variety of other Weevil businesses gave strange results, and profits for almost all of these businesses went down. Then B. W. read about corporate identity as a reinforcement to sales, and decreed that all of his companies sell only under the Weevil name. In some cases, like plumbing supplies, this was a reinforcement because the trade knew that B. W. was the driving force but couldn't always remember the name of his company. For other businesses, like the feed business, the association was very bad; sales of animal feeds dropped badly, and the baked goods business was hurt because no one would buy packaged "Weevil" cookies.

Then one day a vaguely familiar-looking stranger walked into the office and said: "You must be Ben Weevil." This itself stopped all conversation, since B. W. had always said that "B. W." was all the name he had. "You probably don't remember me," the stranger continued. "I am your brother Bob." Bob Weevil was 50; he had been 8 the day that B. W. had knocked down their father and left home. B. W. was silent. Bob continued: "I never would have found you except for that crazy advertising. I have been using your farm supplies for years. But when you changed the name and began to advertise "B. W. Weevil, the Farmer's Friend" all across cotton country, I figured nobody but my father would be foolish or stubborn enough to do that, and I know he's dead. So I guessed it had to be you, like a chip off of the old block."

Presently B. W. took Bob into the inner office where they could talk, but the office staff could see that he was shaken. It turned out that it was not because his brother had turned up—they had been on good terms and B. W. was rather glad to have met him again—but being compared to his father for stubbornness or foolishness had hurt B. W. deeply, particularly as he began to realize that it was true.

The Weevil Company changed. B. W. began to include his key managers in decisions and planning. He began to listen more to their ideas for the company, which soon recovered from his ill-advised attempt to make all of the businesses the same, although some of the harder-hit businesses had to put forth extra effort for several years to regain lost ground. As soon as the firm was running better again, B. W. sold a large block of his stock in a public offering, arranged for the stock to be listed on a major exchange, and established a stock option plan and a financing plan that made it easy for his key managers to earn a share in the company. The business needed him less, so he located his other brother, began to get acquainted with his nephews, and slowly reestablished a life outside of the B. W. Weevil Company. The company didn't acquire more businesses so rapidly without B. W.'s energetic assimilation process, but the existing businesses did much better because no one was trying to force them all to be the same without a reason.

QUESTIONS

1. To what extent is it, or is it not, sound to use the same financial approach to assimilating and managing all businesses, regardless of their nature? Discuss.

2. To what extent is it desirable for a company to sell all of its products under the same name? What sort of limitations on such a policy suggest themselves?

3. To what extent have other companies found that one uniform sales name everywhere has disadvantages? What are some of the examples?

CASE 22 ARCANE INDUSTRIES

When Arcane Industries, long neglected by the public, began to receive recognition for its growth rate, the chairman wanted still more public praise. The growth had come initially from astute acquisition of undervalued properties, but now within the company he felt that management strengths must be developing also. He commissioned a major study of the corporate operations by a prestigious business school, confident that this would result in the overdue recognition of Arcane management.

The business school professors were not quite sure what they were getting into, but they did not want to turn down a generous corporate grant that would certainly lead to publications and more corporate consulting. To minimize their own exposure they decided to limit the initial survey to the corporate process for allocating resources, and chose two graduate students with obvious ability whose conclusions could be disavowed if necessary. These "pilots" each chose a division and spent a month there. They had open access to everybody and everything, according to the directive from the Chairman, and actually the organization did cooperate very well. The two of them understood why they had been sent first and decided to coordinate their reports. The divisions they were studying were in different parts of the country, so they arranged to spend Sunday together comparing notes before the Monday when they were both due back at the University.

Jim had been in the Works Division of Arcane, and he had found a simple if cynical resource allocation process. He had got quite well acquainted with the assistant controller, who put it this way: "The official standard for approval of capital projects is that they have to show a return of 20 percent, but you know how playing with the numbers moves those calculations around. What happens is that no one submits any projects that are not returning at least twenty percent according to their calculations. Then our unit audits the calculations, and the result depends on how critical we are. What boils out is that a business that is making good profits can get more resources, because we don't look too hard at their estimates, but a marginal or losing business gets almost nothing because we and everyone else attack the basis of their justification and usually push the projected profits down too far to pass. That is the corporate process: them who has gets; they are the heroes and can write their own tickets. The losers are second-class citizens and get almost nothing. In the Works Division resource allocation is according to who already has a good bottom line."

Joe had been in the Half-Wing Airways Division and had an entirely different story. "Jim, Half-Wing is just one big profit center, the way they run it. That means that expenses are budgeted unit by unit and can't be matched against revenues, except for the Division as a whole. I have a whole notebook full of stories about how the different units justify—and get—their budget allocations. The most imaginative one I found was the training director. He knows how hard the value of training is to measure and he doesn't even try. Instead he concentrates on building a constituency inside the Half-Wing management group. No one can attend one of his training classes unless they are nominated by one of their superiors, and that superior is the target.

"Everytime an employee is sent to a training session, one week after the employee gets back to work, the boss who nominated him gets a followup questionnaire, and usually returns it carefully filled out, because the training director is believed to be very close to the Half-Wing General Manager and no one wants to offend him. The questionnaire asks for an evaluation of the effectiveness of the training, but of course after one week there is no way to tell. Therefore most managers scribble something favorable because they have to justify their own decision to send the employee on company time, and they don't want trouble with the training director. And this gives the training director a file of written endorsements from almost every member of the management group, and he keeps adding to the file week by week. If anyone said anything about him, all he would have to do is to pull out the quotes from that person's reports and ask which was the story-telling. While I was there he did a statistical analysis of these reports and used it as justification for a supplemental budget request for three more trainers and another series of programs. He got it approved because no one wanted to buck him and then have him pull out all of those comments. In the Half-Wing Airways Division resource allocation is according to the political skill of the requestor, at least now when Division profits are good."

Jim and Joe looked at each other. "Do you think anybody back at school will believe either story?" Jim asked. "Or are we going to end up on the outside trying to finish graduate school somewhere else?"

QUESTIONS

1. How can you explain the resource allocation processes Jim and Joe described?
2. Do these two stories sound like a realistic description of an actual decision process? Discuss.
3. From these decision process characteristics, should either be improved? How?

CHAPTER 12

SELF-RENEWAL: MANAGING ORGANIZATION CHANGE

KEY IDEAS IN THIS CHAPTER

- **the risk of organizational atrophy** – the structure can age and deteriorate.
- **open-system requirements for organization vitality** – for preventing the aging process.
- **competent managers and incompetent systems** – strategic blindness at its worst.
- **the management of organization self-renewal** – with wisdom, luck, and a steady hand, to keep the organization young forever.
- **organization culture** – as the product of the leadership and people strategies.
- **society's need for business self-renewal** – to continue service and support to society.
- **self-renewal and change** – renewing to create what should be, rather than reproducing the past.
- **structure follows strategy** – summarizing the way that strategy calls for building and renewing an organization structure appropriate to the needs of that strategy.

Self-renewal is the process by which an organization stays young and vigorous, as is required if it is to continue to design and execute effective strategies. To manage this process, the executive group must understand the scope and nature of the self-renewal need, and plan for its accomplishment.

THE RISK OF ORGANIZATION ATROPHY

Organization self-renewal is the process by which an organization maintains its vitality and effectiveness beyond the tenure of its human components, to a theoretically infinite life span. Just as a given molecule of the body is rebuilt with new materials through a continual exchange of specific chemical entities, so the specific human elements of an organization change with the hiring, firing, promotions, retirements, resignations, and all of the other reasons why one person may replace another in a job. In spite of the biochemical interchange process, people go through a life cycle because this process is not sufficient to keep all elements of every molecule renewed. The total biological structure matures, ages, and ultimately dies.

Unfortunately, and in spite of the replacement of its human components, an organization ages in almost the same way. The organization self-renewal task is to recognize the ways in which an organization can age, as its elements become less relevant and less effective, and to overcome this aging process.

An organization ages in part by formalization, as the connective procedures become over-rigid. It ages also in problem-solving. As problems recur and become familiar, they can be fitted into categories, with a solution for each. As the categories become known and accepted, problem-solving becomes more and more routine and less cerebral. This routinization is satisfactory so long as the nature of the problems does not change, but over time their nature always changes, at least in details. One consequence of organizational aging is the tendency to continue to use standard problem solutions after they cease to fit the problems exactly.

OPEN-SYSTEM REQUIREMENTS FOR ORGANIZATION VITALITY

An organization and its management operating system together form a complex open system, with all of the normal open system characteristics.[1] One of these characteristics is the requirement for energy input from outside of the system boundaries, to prevent function and performance from degrading.

In the specific case of an organization and its management operating system, this energy input requirement is the management intervention necessary to keep the system functioning at peak efficiency against changing requirements. A well-run enterprise rarely has major reorganizations, because it does not need them. It does not need them because the need for change never accumulates. Management is continually making small adjustments in response to need, so that over a period of time significant shifts in structure or in personnel are accomplished quietly and almost unnoticed.

This requires a steady input of management energy from outside of the system—that is, from outside of the routine components of the operation. When a management gains a strategic overview, it attains a position outside of the operating routine from which such adjustments can be made.

COMPETENT MANAGERS AND INCOMPETENT SYSTEMS

One of the characteristics of an operating manager lacking a strategic overview is the way in which such a person can become embedded in the management operating system and subject to its requirements.

A competent manager will attempt to manage all controllable job elements in an optimum manner. However, as in any system with many elements, evolution of the different elements of the management operating system must be coordinated if the efforts of individual managers are to build toward a condition optimum for the whole. But the management operating system, as a total system, normally is not managed; it grows spontaneously as its components are developed individually; the functioning of the system as a whole is no one manager's responsibility since it links between managers, and primarily at a level of detail beyond the view of the chief executive. The linkages from manager to manager may get attention in a few specific areas such as materials flow, where some organizations have a separate system of coordinators or expediters. But with the larger part of the management operating system of linkages

---

[1]Daniel Katz and Robert L. Kahn, *The Social Psychology of Organizations* (New York: Wiley, 1966), Chapter 2.

effectively unmanaged, these local efforts will at best represent an expedient solution rather than optimum performance.

If unmanaged, the management operating system degrades with time as uncoordinated changes are made in its individual components. The harder the individual managers work to optimize their components, the less optimum the composite operation is likely to become. As the management operating system degrades, its linkages become less effective and its guidance to individual managers less appropriate. But inside the system, operating managers are not able to see this. With the passage of time the individual managers become more and more competent as they gain experience, and the system that links them becomes less and less competent as it loses relevance to the environment for which it was designed. The endpoint is an incompetent organization staffed with highly competent managers, all strategically blind and unable to see why their hard work yields so little.

THE MANAGEMENT OF ORGANIZATION SELF-RENEWAL

The self-renewal needs and the risks are highest at the upper levels of management. The people in these positions directly determine the enterprise future through day-to-day decisions as the business evolves, as well as indirectly determining that future through hiring decisions and through design of business systems and procedures. With the same decision makers governing both processes, failures in their perceptions often result in compounded errors.

If a missed variable unexpectedly disrupts current programs, it is likely to make demands for managerial knowledge and experience the firm has also failed to acquire. The onset of heavy financial penalties for Equal Employment Opportunity compliance failures caught some companies by surprise, even though the requirement was not new and compliance pressure had been building. These companies were forced into immediate creation of a significant, acceptable program in an area where none of the management group knew the requirements of the law, how an effective program should be designed, or how to manage it without disrupting relationships with the existing employee group. Strategic blindness, in not perceiving that this was a new law that had to be obeyed, caused these companies to pay severe penalties for past behavior and also to disrupt their current operations through a disorderly attempt at instant compliance. They had defaulted in timely consideration of this problem as well as failing to gather the competence to deal with it when it became a crisis.

The largest difficulty in dealing with needed change in the organization and in the management operating system is in the area where top management itself is both the judge of the need for change and the factor in the system that is being evaluated. It is hard for the members of a top management group to be objective about the efficiency and effectiveness of their own individual functioning, or about future requirements that could call for experience and knowledge they do not possess. In some cases the only way in which a management can accomplish a sufficiently detached strategic overview is by delegating this analysis to an outside committee. Sometimes members of the board of directors have sufficient knowledge and sufficient detachment from the operating routine to carry out this portion of the planning. In other cases it is necessary to turn to outside professionals.

In any case this is a task whose delegation must be handled with care, in spite of the urgency of getting the job done well. No management will be comfortable in creating a review committee to make self-renewal recommendations involving its own future; it will wish to keep control over the committee. Yet the professionals with this assignment will not feel comfortable in making forthright recommendations which could be adverse to some of the managers who will judge the report and authorize payment for it. The most viable compromise can be supervision of such a self-renewal evaluation by a committee of the board of directors, preferably a committee strong enough to guide the task well and sufficiently removed from routine operations to judge from a reasonably neutral position.

ORGANIZATION CULTURE

Organization culture has become an issue, a challenge, and a focus of self-renewal discussions, particularly since books such as *Theory Z*,[2] *The Art of Japanese Management,* and *In Search of Excellence* pointed out the potential strategic differences between competitors due to differences in their organizations' cultures. In the nomenclature of this book, organization culture is a certain sort of position built by the cumulative impact of the enterprise or governing strategies on the organization. The way the management operating system accumulates past practices and repeats them is a basic culture-building process, and the various impacts of the governing strategies are captured in the same way.

---

[2] William G. Ouchi, *Theory Z: How American Business Can Meet the Japanese Challenge* (Cambridge, Mass.: Addison-Wesley, 1981).

AMERICAN SPIRIT

One recent analysis of organization culture was Miller's *American Spirit*.[3] After restating the need for changes to restore U.S. industrial strength, and building on themes from *In Search of Excellence* and from his own experience, Miller proposed a list of eight necessary attributes for a new and competitive American corporate culture:

1. **The Purpose Principle**

    The distinction between the leader and the manager can be summarized by the word "purpose." Leaders have a noble vision of their purpose. Leaders create energy by instilling purpose in others.

2. **The Excellence Principle**

    Excellence is not an accomplishment. It is a spirit that dominates the life and soul of a person or a corporation. It is the never-ending process of learning that provides its own satisfaction.

3. **The Consensus Principle**

    The successful manager of the future will make full use of the collective wisdom of those within his jurisdiction and he will learn to derive pleasure, not from the making of decisions, but from assuring that the best possible decision is made.

4. **The Unity Principle**

    The workers no longer want to be separated from responsibility. They want to participate in the business game and they want to play to win. Let's make them all managers, now!

5. **The Performance Principle**

    The primary law of human behavior is that behavior is a function of its consequences. That which is rewarded increases. When we learn to reward performance, we will have performance.

6. **The Empiricism Principle**

    The primary task of the manager is to think. The future success of the corporation is dependent on his ability to think clearly, critically, and creatively.

---

[3] Lawrence M. Miller, *American Spirit: Visions of a New Corporate Culture* (New York: Morrow, 1984).

7. **The Intimacy Principle**

    Intimacy is the thread between the inner person, his manager, and the organization they serve. It is intimacy that permits trust, sacrifice, and loyalty.

8. **The Integrity Principle**

    Leadership requires followership and following is an act of trust, faith in the course of the leader, and that faith can be generated only if the leaders act with integrity.

Miller's eight attributes sum to a specific picture of internal organizational processes. For the reasoning leading him to these conclusions, *The Art of Japanese Management, In Search of Excellence* and his *American Spirit* make an excellent trilogy. But whether Miller's picture is the ultimate or only a proximate description, he proposed a condition very different from the operating pattern in many firms. He then devoted the second half of the book to change processes by which, with careful management, the culture of an organization could be shifted in the direction of the one that he recommends.

Reinforcement for Miller's thesis came from Pascarella's *The New Achievers*,[4] a somewhat parallel study of the way that, given the opportunity to participate and share in the goals, the organization will come alive, unify around its purpose, and rise to new levels of achievement.

Davis addressed this same area in *Managing Corporate Culture*.[5] After developing the importance of corporate culture in determining whether a given business strategy can be carried out, he laid out the necessary change processes. These parallel the organizational change processes Miller outlined, except that Davis came to grips more specifically with the way strategies are paralyzed. It is as if he discovered obstructions to business strategy that the present work would attribute to improperly defined enterprise strategies, and then persuaded management to exert the effort necessary to remove the obstacles so that its business strategies could operate.

CHANGE AND AT&T

No organization change processes are easy, and orderly changes in organization culture are among the more difficult. This point needs reemphasis. A position, whether of a brand name in a market place or the sort of position that organization culture represents, is built piece by piece over time. In a large organization, building the organization culture is like building a

---

[4] Perry Pascarella, *The New Achievers* (New York: Free Press, 1984).
[5] Stanley M. Davis, *Managing Corporate Culture* (Cambridge, Mass.: Ballinger, 1984).

glacier, and its inertia is almost as great when there is need to change it in an orderly way. But unlike a glacier, the culture of an organization is built on basic beliefs and trusts, and it can be shattered like glass if inappropriate management action destroys these basics.

It will be some time before the organization dynamics of the breakup of the Bell system are fully analyzed. It is already clear that the basic strategic concepts of AT&T management in proposing the breakup were good, but the system experienced culture shock and difficulty in learning to function as a federation of independent companies. Pessimists who predict that AT&T will not do well in the next few years do so largely on the basis of arguments translating to a belief that AT&T cannot change its organization culture fast enough to make its new strategy work. Like AT&T, many other managements will have to change their organization's culture to permit strategies their survival requires, and such changes must be managed skillfully if they are to yield a better rather than a worse outcome.

LOGICAL INCREMENTALISM

James Brian Quinn[6] made an excellent case for an incremental approach to change in large organizations. That is, instead of mapping out all of the steps in some global shift, a management should decide on the direction and take the first small step. Another step should follow, and another, until ultimately the change is accomplished. The advantages are twofold: (1) the small steps do not create an undue threat to anyone and the organization has time for orderly adaptation, and (2) each step is planned from the present at the time that it is taken; thus, the variations between expectation and achievement are accommodated, and the inevitable zigzagging as other pressures fall on the organization does not prevent a reasonably straight ultimate course to the objective. Quinn's contribution was his realistic approach to the dynamics of change in large organizations, and his analysis provided a powerful insight into the change process.

THE ORGANIZATIONAL CHANGE MATRIX

Leontiades analyzed organizational growth and change processes and developed a useful matrix, shown in Figure 12-1, contrasting a steady-state and an evolutionary management style as a firm moves up or down the scale from a **single business** to a **dominant single business** to a **multi-**

---

[6]James Brian Quinn, *Strategies for Change: Logical Incrementalism* (Homewood, Ill.: Richard D. Irwin, 1980).

FIGURE 12-1 LEONTIADES' ORGANIZATIONAL CHANGE MATRIX†

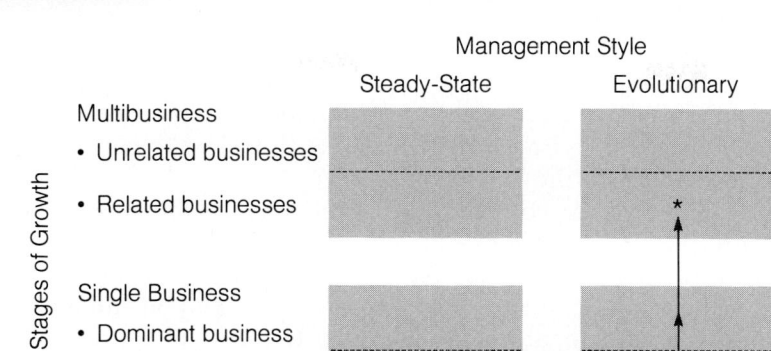

*Illustrating a move from a nondominant single business, first to an evolutionary management style, and then (by acquisition) to a multibusiness with a grouping of related businesses.
†Adapted from *Strategies for Diversification and Change* by Milton Leontiades, Little, Brown & Co., © 1980, p. 74. Reprinted by permission of the author.

business with related or **unrelated activities.**[7] The management problems and organizational requirements change quite significantly as the firm moves from one box to another—or attempts to move, fails to accomplish the necessary changes, and falls back. From this matrix and from other dimensions of the shifts in requirements for structure, planning, and management, Leontiades provides another series of insights into the nature of the organizational transitions that successful strategy changes require.

Culture summary. Organization culture is important and requires careful management in times of change, but it is a dependent variable whose nature is determined by the cumulative impact of the major strategies of the enterprise over time. Some of the great entrepreneurs of the past would undoubtedly argue that, given a top management with sufficient integrity, respect for the individual, clear shared goals based on real customer needs, and firmness of purpose, the culture would take care of itself. And it would, although some of today's techniques might aid a management in changing the culture of its organization more rapidly and more smoothly than in the past.

---

[7] Milton Leontiades, *Strategies for Diversification and Change* (Boston: Little, Brown & Co., 1980).

SOCIETY'S NEED FOR BUSINESS SELF-RENEWAL

The corporation as a legal form through which business is accomplished is essentially eternal. It need never cease to function if its parts are kept up to date, well-integrated with each other and with the customers, suppliers, and others on which the business depends.

Not only is the business corporation theoretically capable of eternal life, but the enterprise assumes a role in society that should require it to function indefinitely. The community depends on the business—not only this year and next year, but forever. The employees depend on the business for continued employment; while individually they will age and retire, others will take their places, and the dependency will go on—either forever, or until the business defaults on maintenance of the expected ties. And the same is true of customer expectations for continued supply of their favorite products, of supplier expectations that the firm will continue to buy the products that were tailored to fit its needs, and so forth. Society needs and hopes for business firms that last forever.

The stockholders and managers have an even larger stake in a continuing business. And the means to long business life is through careful planning, by constructing a plan for organization self-renewal and then putting this plan into action—not as a one-time exercise, but as a steady, gentle paring and reshaping to keep the organization and the management operating system always current, lean, and effective.

SELF-RENEWAL AND CHANGE

As discussed in Chapter 11, many firms will need to evolve into smaller and more flexible units if they are to self-renew and continue successfully. This is a part of a surprisingly rapid evolution of the business environment as U.S. industry feels real pressure to regain at least its competitive parity. Because of these changes, the guiding framework of mission, goals, and enterprise strategies of a firm will need review. Any enterprise that set this framework a decade or two ago risks the possibility of its being obsolete or irrelevant. Today's is a rapidly changing world. General Motors, once the world's premier organization, is struggling. It is not that GM has failed to change—it has changed considerably—but apparently not so rapidly as the world around it.

The point here is that the external framework that does and should influence management when mission, goals, and enterprise strategies are set is changing at a more rapid pace than ever before, and these changes

FIGURE 12-2	SELF-RENEWAL AS A SURVIVAL REQUIREMENT

The risk of organizational atrophy
Open-system requirements for organizational vitality
Competent managers and imcompetent systems
The management of organizational self-renewal
Organization culture
- American Spirit
- change and AT&T
- logical incrementalism
- the organizational change matrix

Society's need for business self-renewal
Emerging issues in business strategy and structure

STRUCTURE CHANGES WITH STRATEGY TO KEEP THE BUSINESS ALIVE

will need to be reflected in the enterprise strategies and the other primary strategies of more and more firms.

STRUCTURE FOLLOWS STRATEGY

When Chandler wrote that structure followed strategy, he referred to the way that major changes in enterprise strategy at Dupont, General Motors, and Standard Oil required complete redesign of the organization structure. But the same principle applies in this area of organization self-renewal.

If the management strategy does not include organization and management operation system changes as the business changes, then the organization will degrade slowly in routine performance of the policies set down when the governing strategies were last thoroughly examined. At least the details of policies usually require modification as external circumstances change, or else the organization will drift from its chosen strategy. Certainly if the operating details of the action flowing from the strategy are not reexamined and modified as necessary, they will not trigger necessary changes in the organization structure.

A good organization changes almost continually, as management adapts to changes in requirements, and cataclysmic reorganization is rarely required. But the organization also needs a self-renewal strategy, as summarized in Figure 12-2, so that its structure evolves as its strategy shifts. Then because the overall evaluation and evolution process keeps the strategy and structure vital and effective, the individual operating

FIGURE 12-3 MANAGEMENT OF STRATEGIC ACTION AND CONTROL

```
PLANNING                                                    ACTION
┌─────────┐                                              ┌──────────────┐
│ Mission │                                              │  Strategic   │
└────┬────┘                                              │  Management  │
     │                                                   └──────────────┘
┌────▼────┐                                              ┌──────────────┐
│  Goals  │                                              │  Strategic   │
└────┬────┘                                              │   Control    │
     │                                                   └──────────────┘
     │        ┌──────► Strategy ──────────────────────┐
     │        │           ┌─────────── Building Blocks │  Strategic
     │        │  Enterprise ─────────── Choice Strategies  Overview
     │        │  Strategy   └────────── Master Strategies
     │  Primary
┌────▼───┐  Strategy ─── Business Strategy              Management of
│Strategy│─                                              - social impact
└────────┘  └─────────── Product or Service Strategy    - opportunity
            Contributing ─── Functional                  - course
            Strategy    ─── Divisional                     correction
                        ─── Unit                         - people
                                                         - output
                                                         - self-renewal
```

	FUNDAMENTALS	
Product or Service	**Market/Competition**	**Business**

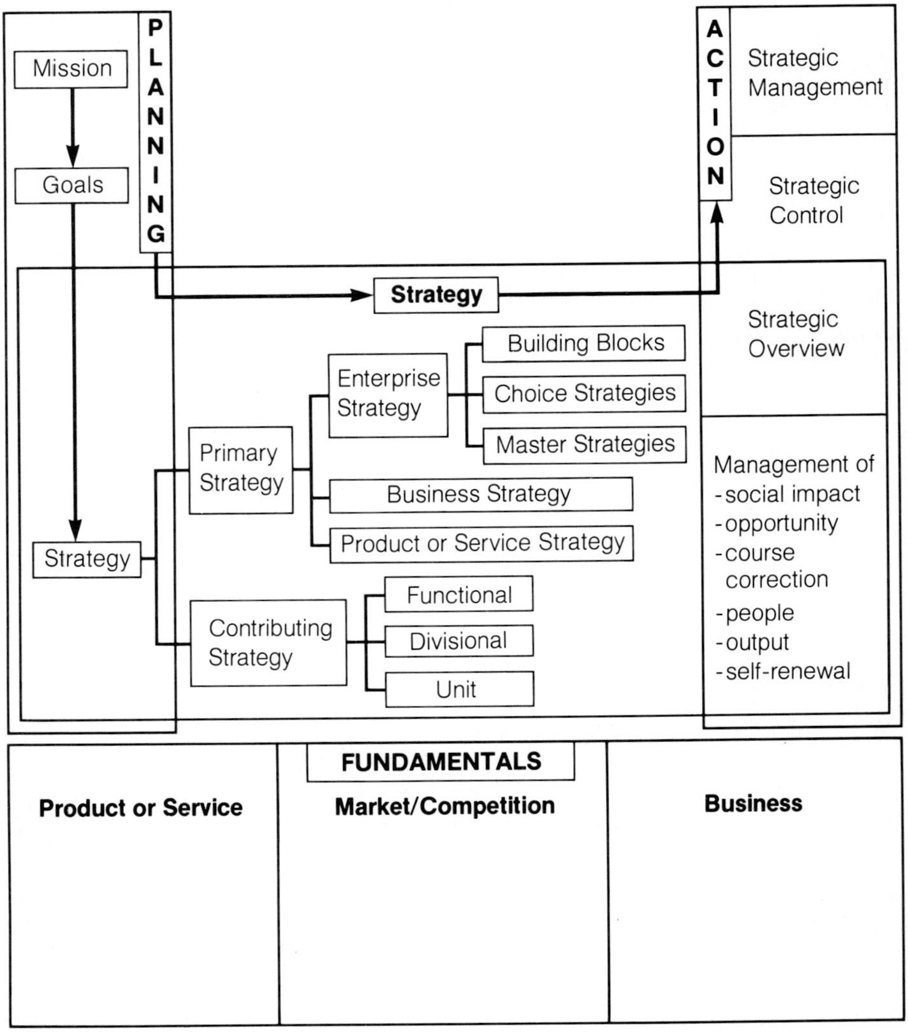

managers are effectively linked. Their individual competence adds up to a competent and effective system more likely to prosper and survive. The strategies dependent on their efforts are more likely to be correctly executed and thus more likely to succeed in the market place, making this self-renewal management area another key strategic action and control component.

☐   ☐   ☐

This chapter completes Part Three: Strategic Action and Control. The six chapters of this part of the book have summarized the overall strategic control processes, the management of social impact, opportunity, course correction, people, operations, and self-renewal, all key strategy areas requiring a strategic overview and shaping the evolution of the firm according to the quality of management strategy and action in each. Together these form a key strategic management component in the flow from planning to strategy to action, as shown in Figure 12-3.

QUESTIONS FOR ANALYSIS AND DISCUSSION

1. Find an example of an organization that seems to have suffered from organizational atrophy. What are the symptoms you see?
2. Look for an example of an organization that has maintained its organizational vitality over a long period of time. How can you tell? How did the management accomplish this?
3. Look for an example of a top management having difficulty with the necessary self-renewal management (e.g., no qualified management replacements, or key people who should retire but do not). Describe the situation briefly.
4. Compare Miller's list of cultural attributes with the present practices in any organization with which you are familiar.
5. Find an example where the community, or society as a whole, has suffered because a business could not manage its self-renewal and faded away.

FOR FURTHER INFORMATION

Davis, Stanley M., *Managing Corporate Culture* (Cambridge, Mass.: Ballinger, 1984).
    Corporate culture, and how consultants help managers manage it.

Miller, Lawrence M., *American Spirit: Visions of a New Corporate Culture* (New York: Morrow, 1984).
    A vision of what corporate culture should be, and how management might accomplish this transformation.

Quinn, James Brian, *Strategies for Change: Logical Incrementalism* (Homewood, Ill.: Irwin, 1980).
    Management of organization change from a general management perspective.

CASE 23 UNITED UNLIMITED UNIVERSAL COMPANY

The official corporate history was summarized in an elegant little booklet on the reception room table in the main lobby, and elaborated in a great, flowing mural that stretched across 60 feet of the west lobby wall, with dates and events footnoted. The opposite lobby wall displayed pictures of the successive chief executives, all smiling, with a plaque listing the major accomplishments of each. In an animated showcase in one corner was an illuminated working cutaway model of the original "unlimited" universal joint the founder had invented. The total effect on a first-time visitor was not quite that of a museum, for it was brighter and more elegant, but the lobby was calculated to give a sense of viewing sacred history, and to imbue a touch of awe at being so close to the center of such a vast and important company.

This was as it should be, for United Unlimited Universal, familiarly known as UUU, had grown greater, into a pillar of U.S. industry. Its stock was a component of the key stock market averages, and its sales slogan "We work for U!" was familiar in every home. UUU had long dominated several key industrial sectors. The current management had launched a massive lobbying and public relations campaign encouraging import restrictions, to help make the basic UUU businesses competitive again, and turned the balance of its energies into acquiring financial service businesses and several chains of recreational vehicle campgrounds, to increase profits if the lobbying effort did not succeed.

Ralph Urban had come to UUU on business. He had never been to the headquarters building before, and he had come a few minutes early just to have a chance to look at the place, to get the feel of the establishment before he was announced for his appointment. Ralph had come to see the sales manager of the small engine division, who had his office high in the building, just below the executive levels. Up there the offices were elegant, as might have been expected from the lobby, but showed more clearly that the decor had been established in the 1920s and not changed much since. It was all marble and oak, but gave a feeling of being back in time, and without the smiles and dynamism of the lobby mural. Ralph found the sales manager actively interested in seeing him—as he had expected, since he had come to make final arrangements for a large quantity of small engines his company needed for a new lawn mower it was about to market.

UUU had the best engine for this purpose, but the engine case needed a few minor modifications and the price was above the budget Ralph's design group had been told to achieve. The purpose of the meeting was to discuss the changes in the case design, and to see what sort of price concession Ralph could get by doubling or tripling the size of the initial order.

The meeting went well until Ralph discovered that UUU was planning to add a design charge for the necessary changes in the motor case—although Ralph was supplying the final drawings, and production of 100,000 engines would require new molds anyway, which could be made at the same cost in the new design. Ralph protested over being charged extra for something that was no extra cost to UUU, and discovered that this was a matter of UUU policy. Also a matter of UUU policy was the pricing of an order for 100,000 (when Ralph had used only 30,000 as a basis for the preliminary quotations); yes, there would be a lower price, but the difference was so small it did not even compensate for the price increase for the case design change, leaving Ralph in the position of being asked to pay more for the motor on a project for a very cost-competitive sector of the mower market.

Ralph was upset and said so. The sales manager wanted the order very badly—according to Ralph's intelligence it represented a solid three-month production run for a half-idle factory, and it was probably the only hope the sales manager had for getting any Christmas bonus at all. The man did what he could, which was to call the marketing manager, who called the operating vice president, who called the executive vice president, who called the president of the small engine company—and Ralph ended up in a meeting in the executive conference room of the small engine division with twelve of the top executives of the division, all anxious to save a large order. But it turned out that all were rigidly bound by UUU corporate-level pricing policy.

Ralph went through the economics of the order, predicting almost exactly the savings to UUU in making 100,000 rather than 30,000 engines and asked for a price concession in proportion to the savings. The manufacturing vice-president was there; he made a few phone calls while the meeting waited and then shamefacedly conceded that Ralph's estimates were pretty good. But they could not change the policy, the price would have to stay high, and Ralph stood up to go. Someone said something about "patriotism" and "buy American," and Ralph exploded: "That was uncalled for—I never threatened you with anything, or said where else we might buy—but as a matter of fact, I came to this meeting with firm quotations from a Korean vendor and an Italian one; both are 30 percent below your price. I came here anyway, because if you cut your price to show the economies from an order of 100,000, you would only be 10% above the competition and we were willing to pay that premium. I didn't even ask you to shave your profit margin! But UUU is such a hopeless corporate dinosaur, that all I've accomplished is to waste half a day in talking; next time I will place the order with the lowest bidder in the first place."

In the course of time the president of the small engine division wrote a memo asking for more freedom to change corporate pricing policies, and used the loss of Ralph's company's order as support. The memo stirred enough interest to get on the agenda of the Management Committee, right after a review of the continuous steel casting machine's economics. The Southern States Steel Division of UUU had modernized; a major portion of the massive capital investment was for conversion to 100% continuous casting, the equipment was now operating, and costs were no better than before. The works manager of that division had been discharged for insisting that corporate scheduling and distribution procedures had to be altered in order for the continuous casting unit to be profitable; now, six months later, the cost picture was no better and the new works manager and his four principal assistants had again alleged that they could do no better without more freedom to make and sell according to the rhythm of the business. They had been discharged also, of course, leaving the division losing money and without any seasoned top managers, and the Management Committee was considering the problem. But the discusson got so acrimonious that the president recessed the meeting without reaching a decision, and the problem of pricing freedom for the Small Engine Division was left unresolved. Anyway, Ralph Urban's company had long since placed its engine order with one of the overseas competitors.

QUESTIONS

1. What was wrong at UUU? Discuss.
2. Why is this a common problem? Discuss.
3. What can be done about this type of problem? Discuss.

CASE 24 THE INCREDIBLE TELEPHONE COMPANY

As the amazing invention of the telephone spread across the United States, entrepreneurs in almost every city and town organized a local telephone company; then as long-distance service improved, these local companies began to merge to create regional networks; the larger phone companies continued to grow, learned to cooperate, and finally a national telephone system evolved. The Incredible Telephone Company (ITC) took its name from the first public reaction in a small rural town to talking over electric wires, and its leadership from the genius of a local businessman who saw the need for a regional phone system earlier than anyone else in the territory. ITC stopped expanding when all of the local companies in that area had been acquired, but it had built a large business base by then.

ITC had become a major company largely able to take care of its own needs as the business expanded. It had a local telephone office in every town it served, its own long-distance subsidiary that handled the switching between offices and the cross-connections with areas served by other telephone companies, and its own manufacturing subsidiary, Tinker Bell Phones (or TBP), to manufacture the telephones and other equipment required for the continued growth and prosperity of the ITC system. Regulation was established in state after state, and ITC faced control by a new regulatory commission in every state where it operated.

ITC management analyzed the regulatory atmosphere that was being created, to define their strategy more clearly. But the regulators were mostly pressing for good public service and not looking very hard at telephone rates so long as they were not higher than the independent small companies had established. This was a very favorable environment for ITC because it was getting substantial economies of scale as it learned how to run its network better and better, and it had already started to emphasize good service as a means to getting more people to install telephones. To a degree the regulation was helpful therefore; it was apparently unavoidable anyway, and ITC cooperated enthusiastically. The entire ITC network was pushed to develop the best possible grade of public service, and TBP was told to develop and build the best, most serviceable telephone equipment that could be designed.

With good equipment and good service the number of subscribers within the service area skyrocketed, and profits soared. ITC began a carefully publicized series of rate reductions—in each case with public hearings and a maximum of publicity during preparation and processing of the necessary filings with the regulatory commissions. The strategy was simple. ITC costs were falling rapidly and ITC knew it would have to reduce rates, so it made a specific proposal based on current costs; but the proposal took two years to move through preparation and formal consideration to approval, and by then ITC would have achieved a new series of cost reductions to be reflected in a new rate reduction proposal which would also take a couple of years to get approved. The publicity was great and requests for new telephones continued to soar; ITC was making more profit than it really should have been allowed by the regulatory commission, and yet who could criticize when ITC again and again took initiative to cut its own rates?

Finally the savings from the expanding network began to flatten out, and the rate reduction process slowed down. TBP did help quietly by developing successive new generations of telephones and switching equipment, but ITC did not adopt these immediately because it did not want to lose its investment in the older equipment; as old equipment was retired, however, TBP's newest and best replaced it. Operating costs dropped, as well as the numbers of operators and technicians required. Thus, cost savings continued, even though they were less conspicuous, and when rising costs and wages moved ITC and the other major phone companies into the position of needing rate increases, ITC could continue to argue that its increases were less than the inflation rate. ITC people had been well schooled in giving the public the best service, and ITC management had become expert in always giving the public a generous share of any savings, and yet retaining excellent profits for the shareholders.

One day ITC lost its monopoly on supplying telephone equipment. Up until then, if Tinker Bell had not made it, ITC would not connect it, and would confiscate any non-Tinker Bell equipment it found anywhere in the system. But then a court said that any piece of telephone equipment compatible with the system could be used, and that ITC had to connect and service it. Suddenly someone was running a marketing blitz for designer phones, the supplier could not make enough to fill the demand, and Tinker Bell did not make designer phones at all. Business firms began to buy office phone switching equipment with capabilities not available from the units TBP offered, and then to connect this "foreign" equipment to the ITC local office.

Then ITC lost its long distance monopoly. Other companies gained the right to connect to the local ITC office and handle long distance service if they could persuade individual subscribers to sign up for it. Worse yet, some business firms began to install connections from their own company switchboard to the competing long distance firms, bypassing the local ITC office altogether. The rules for the telephone business had changed almost completely, and ITC had quickly to find a new way to operate in order to hold on to its business.

☐ ☐ ☐

The president of Tinker Bell Phones was meeting with his key staff on the manpower problem. As a beginning he summarized the situation: "For years we manufactured for a captive market, and ITC decided how fast to bring in each new development after looking at their own replace-

Chapter 12 Self-Renewal: Managing Organization Change 309

ment economics and our manufacturing economics. Then we were stampeded; when ITC had to accept "foreign" equipment on the system, everything that wasn't truly competitive had to be replaced as fast as possible; we ran "too fast," in terms of our long-term planning, to make up the gap, and ITC took some heavy writeoffs on old equipment retired before it was fully depreciated. At the same time we had the most aggressive process development effort in Tinker Bell history, to get ready to compete on a cost basis with outside phone suppliers.

"The program succeeded better than we could have hoped, and we have it in routine operation now. But now our orders are cut back. We were running at an artificially high rate before to replace our own obsolete equipment, we are getting less than 100% of system demand now due to competition, and the new manufacturing methods almost doubled our labor productivity. Our early retirement incentive campaign was successful, and our marketing of telephone equipment outside of the ITC system has started better than we thought. But even so, we have 30% excess hourly staff, and have to do something. TBP and ITC have never laid people off and I really don't want to start, but we can't afford to pay them to sit on their hands. What are we going to do? That is what this meeting is about."

☐ ☐ ☐

Jane Waller was an ITC system supervisor. Quality of service in her area had fallen 3% according to the performance reports, and she had talked with all of her supervisors to see why they thought the quality was off. The problem they pinpointed was imperfect compatibility between TBP switching equipment and some of the local businesses' phone equipment. She had discussed the problem with her technical contacts at Tinker Bell; some modification of their switching equipment appeared necessary, but the key TBP department head didn't want to do the work: "We built the Tinker Bell equipment right, and I'm not going to mess it up because you folks are letting a lot of foreign (non-TBP) junk onto the system now." Jane wrote an urgent memo to her boss asking him to intervene, and called him to tell him it was coming. She knew he was still upset about connecting "foreign" equipment too, and hoped he wouldn't take the same attitude as the department head at TBP: "Boss, two of the companies having the switching trouble have been investigating microwave ties from their rooftop to some other long-distance carrier. If I can't personally assure them that ITC will solve their problem *very soon*, I am afraid we will lose their business altogether." She sighed when she put down the phone, because she knew she was fighting against the traditional ITC system.

☐ ☐ ☐

Bruce Johnson was sharing a second can of beer with some buddies after a very hard shift. He had spent most of the day running between the Carmel Soup Company office, the local ITC office, and the Long Distance

Division center that served the area, trying to solve problems in the soup company's long distance service. "You know," he said, "the trouble is all in that strange switching system they use. I fought with it all day, I couldn't accomplish a thing, and I am going back tomorrow with an "expert" from Tinker Bell to start over. If they had just put in a Tinker Bell board in the first place, the connection would be automatic and the service perfect. But when I told them that, I got yelled at because of how much Tinker Bell charges for switchboards, and all of the features this one has that TBP doesn't offer. Then one of the managers told me that if I didn't think I could solve the problem, just to say so, and they would connect to a long distance carrier that could. You get no respect any more—it used to be that all people wanted was phones that worked, and now I don't know what they want. But I want another beer."

☐   ☐   ☐

Stewart Michaels was a consultant hired by the president of ITC. He was in the president's office summarizing a long report he had presented: "Over the years you folks at ITC have built one of the most cohesive and best-motivated organizations I have ever encountered, but you built around a tradition of quality and service that essentially disregarded everything else. Now ITC faces very many other demands, and your people don't really know what to do. No one has said that quality and service aren't important, and of course they still are. But where do all of the new demands fit in? They make a stress that is almost tearing the organization apart."

QUESTIONS

1. How would you define the problem at ITC?
2. How would you tell the president of ITC to get the company back to the organizational performance level it had had in past years?
3. Are there any realistic alternatives to wholesale layoffs at TBP? What effect would "the first layoffs in ITC history" have on the ITC and Tinker Bell organizations?

PART IV

HOW TO DESIGN STRATEGIES

CHAPTER 13
DESIGN OF A PRODUCT OR BUSINESS STRATEGY

KEY IDEAS IN THIS CHAPTER

Chapter 13 outlines the process of designing a product, service, or business strategy, weaving together the various components presented earlier:

- **the process of strategy design** – selection of strategy components, checks for their compatibility, and comparison with alternatives.
- **competitive advantage** – and back to the drawing board, if a strategy doesn't show it clearly.
- **creating leverages** – to make a strategy strong enough to use.
- **strategic models** – a quick technique for testing strategies before taking them to market.
- **effective strategies** will make profits – is your strategy good enough?
- **understanding the requirements of a strategy** – the support it needs, as the action flows on.
- **strategy design** – a summary of the chapter and the process.

The purpose of careful definition of the elements and levels of strategy, and of the many considerations in their strategic management and control, is to define a process for making better strategies and making them work in the market place. The three chapters of Part Four: How to Design Strategies are devoted to the steps necessary in creating effective strategies. This chapter defines a system for product or business strategy design, Chapter 14 relates the considerations in such a design to the limits set by the enterprise strategies, and Chapter 15 discusses the strategic management and planning systems many firms use in managing their strategy and action process. That is, a strategy should be fitted well into customer needs, optimized for the business framework in which it will operate, made consistent with overall enterprise direction, and fitted into the strategic planning and management system in use in that firm.

The process of creating a strategy superior to the competition is challenging. With a clear framework the design process seems simple, but the many interacting variables challenge the designer. This chapter will outline the process of product or business strategy design and discuss some of the different sorts of challenges in using it.

THE STRATEGY DESIGN PROCESS

The strategy design process is a series of steps listed briefly below, and then repeated with an illustrative example for each step:

1. Confirm the goals of the desired strategy.
2. Define the deliverable; what is its most likely life cycle? Where is it now in that life cycle?
3. Define the other elements of the strategy, starting with focus, leverages, positions, display requirements, and nature of the product line.
4. Define the intended degree of differentiation.
5. List the anticipated sources of profit from the strategy.
6. Project the financial returns; estimate cash flow and resource requirements.
7. Review to be sure all of the projections and assumptions are mutually consistent, with changes as necessary, to ensure this consistency, and then complete the financial return, resource requirements, and cash flow projections.
8. Review the strategy design for promising alternatives and develop them also.
9. Use the pattern of profit response to differences between alternative strategies in guiding design of still more alternatives, until an apparently optimum strategy has been constructed.

Steps 1–7 outline a process that will describe a specific strategy, assuming that the components of the design are adjusted until they are mutually compatible. Then by reviewing the resulting strategy design for promising alternatives, a series of related strategies can be developed and compared. Different choices of focus, different degrees of differentiation, different positioning, differences in design of the deliverable, and development of different sources of profit—all are possible and sometimes advantageous—except that a change in one of these variables requires changes in many of the others, and so many combinations are possible that the actual flow of the design process is guided by a combination of judgment and trial-and-error, to see which changes in the initially defined strategy bring improved results.

Because of the numbers of interacting variables the strategy design process normally starts with a first approximation based on the context. The environment surrounding a product, service, or business, the competition, and the market is rich in habitual patterns of how things should be done. From judicious use of this context the first tentative strategy is formulated—based on everyone's knowledge of how things should be done in this market.

This context is valuable but dangerous. The value is in providing a workable first approximation. But a strategy based only on this context will normally lead to failure, because it will have no competitive advantage unless by accident. This first draft can only provide a starting point; from a strategic overview and by incorporating competitive advantages the purpose is to reshape the strategy until it becomes effective.

In practice, then, the strategy design process consists of establishing a strategy based on current norms of practice, and then departing from these norms wherever the deviation seems advantageous. The strategy design process discussed above and summarized in Figure 13-1 provides the discipline necessary to mold each specific strategy variation into a workable alternative, so that these variations can be compared and the best selected.

COMPETITIVE ADVANTAGE

A key direction-finder in the evolution of a strategy is competitive advantage. That is, how is our offering to these customers' needs better than the other choices our customers have? Our leverages must be superior or we are unlikely to sell the product. Specifically, where are our leverages better?

There are a number of types of business strategies based on particular sorts of leverages. They all work if the leverages are good enough, with potential results according to the market targets selected. A commodity

Chapter 13 Design of a Product or Business Strategy

FIGURE 13–1   STRATEGY DESIGN FUNDAMENTALS—STEP BY STEP

1. *Confirm the goals of the desired strategy.*

   For a watch company:

   Mission: to supply the needs of the public for attractive and reliable wrist watches at a moderate price.

   Goals: improved sales, improved market share, and improved profitability for our wrist watch line.

2. *Define the deliverable; what is its most likely life cycle? what is its position in that life cycle?*

   Deliverable: A line of attractive wrist watches with an inexpensive battery-powered movement. Wrist watches are a long-established product with a continuing demand. Inexpensive battery-powered watches sell into a well-established market. Individual watches last only 2–3 years; but as a product-type they are long-lived, and the market mature but still growing.

3. *Define the other elements of the strategy, starting with focus, leverages, positions, display requirements, and nature of the product line.*

   Focus: Remotely personal. That is, no personal contact with customers except through nonspecialized salespeople in retail stores—but in advertising, in our company image, and in any written or other contact we may have with customers, we convey personal interest and awareness, and attempt to build a personal, caring image for our firm over a period of years.

   Leverages:
   - a good watch
   - attractive
   - economical
   - well-styled
   - convenient
   - dependable
   - made by us

   Positions: our name and reputation for quality (both are good, but we are not yet well enough known to gain much leverage here).

   Display requirements: Store display. People seem to want to see a watch before buying. Catalog pictures work, but an attractive presentation in a store display works better; we consider this a requirement.

   Nature of product line: 30–40 styles each for men's and women's watches, with continual design and introduction of new styles to replace those whose demand is tailing off. The cases group in three price ranges that we can adjust as new styles are offered. We keep our line competitive at the low end, with a premium for better styling and case that can vary with changing conditions.

4. *Define the intended degree of differentiation.*

   Watches are not commodities, but competition is very strong. Our basic offerings we view as weak specialties—that is, we try to build a preference for our

   continued

> **FIGURE 13–1** STRATEGY DESIGN FUNDAMENTALS—STEP BY STEP (CONTINUED)
>
> product at about the same price as competition, and for the higher-priced portion of our line we add a premium for better case and better styling, but without charging more than for comparable cases and styling elsewhere.
>
> 5. *List the anticipated sources of profit from the strategy.*
>
>   The bulk of our profit comes from a steady flow of small innovations in styling plus some rent on our reputation and brand name. We also get manufacturing and distribution service fees, but these are quite small in our industry.
>
> 6. *Project the financial returns; estimate cash flow and resource requirements.*
>
>   To mount this strategy we need to increase our advertising budget and enlarge our styling and design group. Cash flow will be negative the first year and we will show losses. The second year will be about breakeven, we will be back at the present level of profitability in the third year, and will earn back the additional investment in the fourth year, with additional profits thereafter.
>
> 7. *Review to be sure all the projections and assumptions are mutually consistent, with changes as necessary to ensure this consistency, and then complete the financial return, resource requirements, and cash flow projections.*
>
> 8. *Review the strategy design for promising alternatives and develop them also.*
>
> 9. *Use the pattern of profit response to differences between alternative strategies in guiding design of still more alternatives, until an apparently optimum strategy has been constructed.*

strategy is based on supplying essentially the same product as the competitors. Little room remains for leverages establishing competitive advantage within a commodity strategy other than by selling cheaper or in some way giving superior service. Most successful commodity strategies are based on selling at lower prices, building up market share, improving costs with increasing volume, and establishing profitable market leadership. But without a cost superiority or some other commanding competitive advantage, a commodity strategy cannot succeed.

Niche strategies are based on serving some particular segment of the market better than anyone else—by somehow specializing in the service of the needs of those customers—usually by differentiating the product or service and creating a group of specialties with superior appeal to that specific customer group. Differentiation to create specialty products is normally part of an effort aimed at a niche market, although a niche strategy can succeed equally well if circumstances permit a cost advantage in supplying the specific needs of those customers.

A part of strategy design is choice of sources of profit, as discussed earlier. Each source of profit must be based on a need of the customer, and these additional needs may also represent a further segmentation of the market and an increase in competitive advantage. McKesson, the drug wholesaler, offers its customers a variety of inventory management and other services allowing direct electronic ordering with guaranteed rapid delivery. These extra services have reinforced the competitive position of independent pharmacies that otherwise might have disappeared, and reinforced the competitive advantage of McKesson in serving these customers because the pharmacy has become so integrated around McKesson services that it would be more difficult to buy from a competing wholesaler. Not all McKesson customers have wanted or needed these services. What McKesson has done is to develop a part of its customer base into an important niche market. It has made these customers stronger and therefore larger customers, increased its own competitive advantage in serving them, and gained additional sources of profit.

Sears long ago developed its appliance service as a necessary adjunct to appliance sales as well as an additional source of profit. More recently it discovered that many of its customers greatly prized the security of an appliance service contract. Sears sells such contracts at prices high enough to have brought criticism from consumer advocate groups, thus gaining an additional source of profit but probably without any significant increase in competitive advantage.

McKesson and Sears found customer need areas closely allied to the primary business with potential as additional sources of profit, and both developed these areas aggressively. Sears chose to harvest this profit directly. McKesson has taken little additional profit, choosing to use the thrust of these new services to strengthen its customer group competitively while bonding them more closely to McKesson, thus gaining additional profits on its base business.

Sears and McKesson both had sound businesses. Both added new resources of profit—Sears for the additional revenue, and McKesson to strengthen its base business. Whenever a firm wants more profit, it can either attempt to increase the margins on its present sales or to develop new sources of profit, as Sears did. Whenever a firm sees its present business threatened and needs stronger leverages, it can attempt to add new sources of profit, as McKesson did—and greatly strengthened its customers' businesses at the same time.

Many companies do valuable design and technical service work for customers, sometimes as an additional source of profit, and more often without charge as a part of the sales service package intended to increase the competitive advantage of a specialty product. As a customer service a container manufacturer once designed a special bottle for a soft drink and copyrighted the design, of the classic wasp-waisted Coca-Cola bottle, and at some later time the Coca-Cola Company discovered that it could not buy these bottles from any other vendor, until it finally paid the price necessary to buy the rights to the design.

Special services for customers—such as design, appliance service, data processing support, leasing, inventory management; the list can be made very long—often provide the basis for a profitable additional relationship. These services add leverages to buy, or add strength to the existing leverages. They tend to increase differentiation and encourage development of niche markets because of their differing appeal to different groups of customers. They can increase competitive advantage, or profits, or both.

In developing additional sources of profit, as this chapter on strategy design strongly encourages, a time comes when each additional source of profit must be priced to the consumer, directly or as part of a package. Sears appears to have maximized the profit flow from its service contracts, the company that owned the Coke bottle design used this ownership to ensure an exclusive supply position, and McKesson has emphasized the close bonding to a strengthened customer group more than current profits from the additional services. All of these are defensible strategic choices in a given set of circumstances. The overall objective is a sound and relatively secure market position—requiring sufficient competitive advantage to defend it, possibly with differentiation and development of one or many market niches, and, consistent with market reality, with as many soundly conceived sources of profit in each as managerial ingenuity can generate.

CREATING LEVERAGES

A competitive advantage means giving our customers a clear reason to buy from us rather than from the competition—by creating leverages, in the language of Chapter 3. How to create leverages? As a small pharmaceutical manufacturer Alcon chose to concentrate on special needs of ophthalmologists not fully served by the major pharmaceutical firms. The Alcon products initially had little novelty in a world of wonder drugs, but they were superbly fitted to the way in which ophthalmologists wished to practice, and Alcon grew. A by-product of this success was Conal, a sister division that developed a similar relationship with urologists. With rapid and profitable growth in both areas Alcon soon became large enough to begin to discover and develop its own new pharmaceuticals. Lacking a functional product advantage or a meaningful cost advantage in the beginning, Alcon started by creating leverages from a focus relating closely to ophthalmological practice and tailoring its products to fit the needs of these doctors better than any others available. From essentially generic products Alcon created specialties that ophthalmologists preferred over competitive offerings. Alcon prospered.

How to create leverages? A study of possible new consumer appliances once led to a proposal for an electric carving knife. The deliverable could be built and the costs seemed acceptable. There was no established market because the product had never existed. No one seems to have demanded its development, and many commentators ridiculed it when it was announced. Yet the developers were right; when the electric carving knife was presented as a convenience for elegant dining, it found a ready market. Starting from the possibility of the deliverable, the marketers judged correctly that needs-leverages linkages could be created, and then proceeded to create them successfully.

In each of these cases someone analyzed the potential deliverables and customer needs, and then put resources into creating that which was necessary to make the needs-leverages-purchases relationship effective in the market place. How do you design strategy? Within the limits the organization imposes, find potential needs-leverages linkages that could bring the level of purchases necessary to achieve the desired goals—by matching possible deliverables against customer needs. Sometimes this requires redefinition of the deliverable and resegmentation of the market to find a specific product or service with sufficiently strong needs-leverages linkages.

The key to a sound strategy is that it be built on an effective, fulfillable system of needs-leverages linkages. And for long-term success the excellence model demands a steady effort to make those needs-leverages linkages stronger, year by year, week by week, and day by day.

STRATEGIC MODELS

It is useful to evaluate a simple conceptual model of the proposed strategy as a means of maximizing its effectiveness and value. Such a model can aid in improving the action plan or in choosing between alternatives. It aids discovery of inconsistent elements in a particular strategy or unexpected consequences from its execution.

A strategic model is an exercise in decisions and consequences, as outlined in Figure 13-2. Given that a certain strategy is to be put into action, what will be the consequences? As the action moves onward, who will be affected? Who will react, and in what way? A specific approach toward developing a business should lead to a product line of a roughly predictable size and number of products, and with a roughly predictable range of sales volumes; how will this work out? A given program for launching a product will lead to sales to some types of customers at the expense of others who are likely to buy from someone else; is this acceptable? The idea in strategic modeling is to take the consequences of the planned actions a step or two farther than is normal during the initial design of the strategy, to see if there are surprises or inconsistencies. It is a

> **FIGURE 13–2** HOW TO BUILD A STRATEGIC MODEL[2]
>
> I. Define the proposed strategy for a product, service, or business as outlined in Figure 13–1.
>
> II. Catalog the consequences of the action the strategy requires, and particularly the evolution of events as the strategy has its impact, sales grow, and competitors respond:
>
>   A. How will your potential customers and competitors respond to your strategy? How well do you know your customers? And how sure are you of the way they will respond? What are the major options for response for each of your competitors?
>
>   B. How much freedom of action do you have to shift your approach once the strategy is in motion? Or, how tightly are you locked in? Can you use extra resources to get extra leverages if you need them? As your focus succeeds and your sources of profit flow, what will be the consequences, for you and for the market place?
>
>   C. What kind of business are you building?
>   1. Will your continuing success provoke additional competitive action?
>   2. What sort of a product line will you build? (number of products, distribution by size, by uniqueness, by maturity, and by market position?)
>
>   D. What will your product or business look like in five years?
>   1. Briefly develop each element of a business plan,[3] and characterize each, especially the background, environment, and functional plans.
>   2. Review this rough plan for feasibility, consequences, and surprises (e.g., if you expect your business to double every year for five years, you could have difficulty in finding the resources or in building soundly and fast enough to support such a strategy).
>
> III. Turn the proposed product or business over and around, and look at it from as many points of view as possible. The purpose is not to pick the strategy apart—but to understand it thoroughly, and particularly to avoid the kind of surprises later from which business disasters are born.
>
> IV. Keep the whole process within the boundaries of common sense.
>
> ---
> [2]Please note that Cases 46 and 47 deal with strategic modeling of business.
> [3]Discussed further in Chapter 15.

quick, effective exercise, and can show unsuspected weaknesses in a strategy while still at the design stages.[1]

---
[1] For further discussion of strategic models see George C. Sawyer, *Corporate Planning as a Creative Process* (Oxford, Ohio: Planning Executives Institute, 1983), pp. 125–132.

Strategic modeling is a useful tool for examining, testing, and perfecting the strategy of a business: (1) to aid in the choice between alternative strategies, (2) to develop a complete understanding of the chosen strategy, (3) to aid in defining the problems and challenges in making it work, and (4) to aid in determining whether that strategy is consistent with the other efforts of the firm. A given strategy has a logical set of consequences; the challenge is to recognize them in advance.

EFFECTIVE STRATEGIES

The need and the challenge in designing strategies is to plan the right actions and execute them. The necessary standard of performance is set by the customers and the competition; a strategy resulting in a product or service more effective in meeting customer needs than its alternatives is likely to be successful. Goliath rose among the Philistines and became their champion. His individual combat strategy was highly successful and he reigned supreme. Like Goliath, many ongoing strategies could be defeated. But they stand as proven effective because they are succeeding in the market place, unless some David mounts a successful challenge.

The point is to underscore the difference between effectiveness and efficiency. Successful strategy starts by being effective; it focuses on real needs of customers and satisfies these needs. When a strategy is effective in meeting customer needs, it returns a profit to the producer who would otherwise go out of business. But many successful strategies are not efficiently executed, and at the time it may matter very little. If sales and profits are good and growing, who cares?

When competition moves in, the situation can change. A strategy is no longer effective if it ceases to yield profit. Firms not able to regain effectiveness disappear. It has been suggested that the problem with U.S. basic industry is that life was too easy for twenty-five or more years after World War II, that competition was largely between unimaginative domestic producers, and that whole industries were able to generate steady profits without real need for competitive efficiency, to the point where the industrial base must now be rebuilt to reestablish U.S. competitive parity.

In any case, the requirement of strategy design in the short term is for a strategy that yields a profit, whether the resulting operation be efficient or not. In the longer term good management demands at least a competitive level of efficiency, and excellent management demands excellence—in terms of the best current operation and a steady rate of further improvement. Against an excellence standard, strategy design becomes more demanding, more effective, and more likely to generate long-term sales and profits.

IS YOUR STRATEGY GOOD ENOUGH?

An effective strategy is a strategy that is better, in terms of needs-leverages linkages, in fulfilling a specific role in the market place than any competitive strategy. There is no theoretical or practical limit to the amount that the competitive strategies can be improved, since each is based on the ingenuity of a more or less hungry management in devising new approaches and new rules for their competitive challenge. The history of competition is that any strategy sooner or later loses effectiveness because others find ways to narrow its advantages and then surpass it. Patents expire or can be bypassed, know-how diffuses across an industry, and even the best technology or process ceases to be the best as innovation continues.

For a given firm to seize the lead and keep it, it must start with an effective strategy; that is, one sufficiently better relative to its market targets so that it can win a profitable share. It must then improve its position until its leadership is established. Such a strategy must be based on superior leverages to succeed. Many good leverages can be made into enduring positions. Market leadership itself is a position, and the scale economies and learning curve potential of the market leader usually can be made into cost and distribution positions. The market leader should be able to accumulate positions reinforcing its initial strategy. This makes maintenance of that strategy easier, and makes the leadership more profitable. This is a little like the old king-of-the-hill game, where, everything else being equal, the boy on the hilltop had the advantage and could stay there. Thus, the market leader often can hold market share with little effort. Reinforced by the leader's various positions, its products or services may not need to be as good as the competitors', yet success continues.

But the differential between the established leader and its competition is based on a relatively fixed level of rent earned by the leader's positions, and any inferiority in the leader's products or services uses up a part of that differential. Often this means that the margin between the leading strategy and a competitive strategy narrows over time. Then a competitor devises a new approach—an innovation that in some way increases the effectiveness of its strategy even temporarily—and draws ahead of the leader. But the leader has become dependent on rent from positions based on leadership; those positions melt if leadership fails. Either the leader mounts a successful counterattack or leadership shifts and the former leader fades away.

A more difficult and more effective role for a firm that has won a position of leadership is to continue a steady and unrelenting effort to improve its products, leverages, and positions still further. This has four internal justifications: (1) Many product or service markets have significant price elasticity; better operations mean lower costs; and if the leader can cut prices, the market may grow and profits increase. (2) It helps profits a lot to keep improving the costs. (3) "Someone else will do it if we don't—

just keep making things better." (4) "If they really are trying to gain on us, it will give them fits when we cut the price."

This is the excellence model again, of course. Create a good operation based on an effective strategy, and keep every person sincerely involved in making the products, operations, and customer services better every day.

UNDERSTANDING THE REQUIREMENTS OF A STRATEGY

A number of years ago several major companies attempted to improve their marketing positions in the fertilizer industry with a new, close-to-the-customer focus. By building large numbers of local blending stations they would be able to provide custom fertilizer blends for each user and create a secure local market franchise reinforced by sales of pesticides and other farm chemicals to the customers trading at the blending station. Most fertilizer was then being sold in bags by farm stores, and this new strategy, while capital-intensive, seemed quite attractive because these stations handled fertilizer in bulk and therefore had a cost advantage over existing farm stores in the local area around each station. A nationwide chain would require a very large investment, but it seemed practical to spread this investment over a period of years.

But when several different companies began to develop the same strategy, their blending stations began to compete with each other. Where each station in a given chain had a bulk cost advantage over nearby farm store competitors, its operating costs were about the same as for other bulk stations. It could gain a competitive advantage only if the overall purchasing and cost position of the chain gave it an advantage, and at best its profits would be less. To improve its competitive position each chain now needed to expand, to preempt more local markets by building in each suitable area before the others did. Each chain needed to increase its overall market share, its production, and its purchasing volume faster than the others. Capital investment requirements escalated and profit margins fell. American Cyanamid and W. R. Grace had both started to build chains of bulk stations. Both abandoned their strategy after several years, stopping expansion and eventually selling off the stations they had already established.

These companies had selected a close-to-the-customer focus for fertilizer blends that were undifferentiated commodities. This strategy generated profit primarily from rents based on the bulk cost advantage over fertilizer in bags, plus small fees for blending and distribution services, plus any rent earned by the chain's basic commodity cost position. The nature of the market opportunity for blending stations forced these companies to compete to build stations in each territory before the others did, and this competitive acceleration of the investment escalated the cash demands and reduced the potential profits until it defeated the strategy. A close-to-the-customer focus usually requires a specialty product that opens additional sources of profit to pay for the extra resources such a focus requires. In this case the rent from the local supply position would have supplied the profit instead, if competitive action had not erased it. As it was, any competitor building in the same locality duplicated the local cost advantage and could also earn the blending and distribution service fees.

Just as in the fertilizer case, a commodity strategy whose source of profit depends on market-share-related economies of scale can strain corporate resources when the market expands rapidly. In the late 1940s a now-forgotten company called Commercial Solvents was one of the first to invest in modern methanol synthesis capacity, and it became the market leader. As low-cost producer it successfully integrated forward into the consumer market for methanol antifreeze. But the national market for methanol was growing very rapidly, and Commercial Solvents' management was not prepared to fund a commodity strategy that would have required investment in enough new plants to maintain market leadership. Commercial Solvents did not expand but the market did, and soon others had newer and larger plants with lower costs. No longer in a strong cost position, Commercial Solvents sold its consumer brands to better-positioned companies and continued to supply methanol to industrial customers. Then as the market leaders continued to improve their production costs and lower their prices, the Commercial Solvents plant became too marginal to operate and shut down.

It is generally unwise for a company to invest in a commodity strategy unless it is prepared to fund the growth required to maintain this position, just as it is unwise to depend on rents vulnerable to competitive action as a primary source of profit, and a strategic model will often aid in understanding the vulnerabilities in these and other situations. The different elements in the strategy design interact, and can lead to problems of the sort that occurred in the fertilizer and methanol markets. The important thing is to recognize these interactions and anticipate their consequences before the first investment in the strategy.

STRATEGY DESIGN

Strategy design is a straightforward but demanding pattern of laying out all of the known guidelines and constraints, choosing elements for the desired strategy and then iterating through the elements until a consistent set is derived that can become the basis for an effective strategy. This usually involves generation and evaluation of a series of alternatives, and the

FIGURE 13–3 STRATEGY DESIGN FUNDAMENTALS

The process of strategy design
- elements of the strategy
- differentiation
- position in life cycle
- sources of profit

Competitive advantage and creating leverages

Needs-leverages linkages

Strategic models

Is your strategy good enough?

BUILDING AND TESTING A STRATEGY DESIGN

strategic modeling technique can assist in selecting the best design to be put into action.

Taken altogether, strategy design is a key and basic process. Obvious in some respects, this process is not always carefully practiced, and the result may be faulty if the design is not carefully considered and balanced in its elements. Careful strategy design is a fundamental for the successful action that is its objective, as summarized in Figure 13-3.

QUESTIONS FOR ANALYSIS AND DISCUSSION

1. Discuss the way in which the degree to which management is able to devise new rules and create new resources for the business will make the strategy design process (a) more difficult, and (b) much easier.

2. Choose a product (or service) in a business that interests you, and list a set of possible answers to the strategy design questions posed in the chapter.

3. For a flamboyant advertising campaign—analyze the copy and list the leverages the advertising attempted to create. For the key leverages, to what extent do you think this effort either failed or was successful?

4. For products or services successful over a long period of time, (a) list some of the key needs-leverages linkages on which this success was built. (b) How do you think these linkages were created?

5. For some of the successful products or services in question 4, what sort of supporting strategies are required for these leverages to succeed?

6. For a given business and strategic decision you know about or have read about, make as complete a list as you can of *all* of the non-ridiculous alternatives the decision makers had. How many can you find?

7. For a business with which you are familiar (a) list the sources of profits as you see them, (b) suggest two or three additional sources of profit that could be added, and (c) for each of the added sources of profit, explain whether the price increase it justifies is likely to be significantly larger than its additional cost.

FOR FURTHER INFORMATION

Ansoff, H. Igor, *The New Corporate Strategy* (New York: Wiley, 1988).
  Corporate strategy revisited, over twenty years after Ansoff's landmark analysis.

Bogue, Marcus C., III, & Elwood S. Buffa, *Corporate Strategic Analysis* (New York: Free Press, 1986).
  A different view of strategy, incorporating more on production and other considerations.

CASE 25: THE EXECUTIVE BUZZSAW AT UPQUICK, INC.

Ronald Reames, the President and CEO of Upquick, Inc., was an unusually successful and colorful industrial executive. Ronnie, as he liked to be called, enjoyed publicity, but the feature writers had trouble in capturing the essence of his style. One business magazine wanted to try a different approach, and the result was that Jill Patak, one of their best feature writers, got permission to observe Ronnie through the annual series of business plan presentations. When Jill told a friend in Upquick middle management about this, he said: "Oh, you're going to get a demonstration of the corporate buzzsaw." When she asked what this meant, his explanation was very vague. She also heard of two Upquick executives who had a bet over whether Ronnie would change his style with an observer present.

The first meeting started out as a carefully rehearsed if somewhat formal corporate presentation, with Ronnie and the rest of the executive group listening intently. The general manager who was presenting his plan laid out the prospect of an exciting and very profitable extension of his business. When he was finished, Ronnie asked him to explain again what his competitive advantage was. He did, and detailed leverages easily sufficient to justify choice over the competition. "Let's go back to the basis of the competitive advantage," said Ronnie.

They did, and it was a clever and original way of organizing the display unit. "I'm really impressed," said Ronnie, "but how do you keep everybody else in the business from copying this, once they see it?"

—dead silence—

Finally, from the general manager, who was almost trembling: "Chief, I guess I don't know."

Suddenly Ronnie's voice was hard and cutting: "Then go find out, and don't come back until you do!"

Everyone left the meeting very quickly. Ronnie quietly confirmed the scheduling of the next presentation with Jill, and went on to his next appointment.

The next presentation was from the office machine division. Its feature this year was a new combination facsimile and copy machine the general manager described with color slides and a video demonstration of the machine features. Ronnie led off the questions: "I'm very impressed with the machine and worried about whether your competitive advantage is enough to get you the price you have to charge. Let's go through your leverages again, and match them against the competition." Under his questioning the picture emerged more clearly. "Now let's review your sources of profit." They did.

"As you have it, this product will fall flat on its face. Great product, premium price. Not enough leverage to move it against the competition at that price. You have two choices—price competitively and position it as a weak specialty; it will sell but you'll go broke unless you can cut the cost a lot more than I think you can. Or leave it a strong specialty and add enough new leverages to make it go. The easiest way to beef up your leverages is to add sources of profit that add more to customer appeal than to cost. It'll take more than just a leasing plan, but you might try to build around one.

"You have spent a lot of R & D money and got 95 percent of a great product. Go and reposition it to get the other 5 percent. Lower prices, better leverages, more sources of profit, or whatever else; do the rest of your homework and come back in about three weeks." He looked at his pocket calendar. "Let's make it the 24th at 7 A.M. Then we will have as much time as we need to work this over and get it right." He had picked a Sunday morning, of course; Jill heard a faint groan from a management committee member who saw another weekend slipping away.

"Meeting adjourned—but come back on Sunday the 24th with something that will work in the market place."

The third presentation was a little like the first, in that the business was building a major program around an important competitive advantage—but it emerged under Ronnie's questioning that this was an advantage that would be rather easy for a competitor to copy. This time Ronnie fired the general manager on the spot, as this was the third time he had put forward a strategy without seeing obvious defects in it.

At the beginning Jill had made an appointment with Ronnie for the day after the third presentation to talk about the process these presentations represented, and she found him feeling rather defensive. "You have drawn a sad lot of businesses to observe so far, Jill. I know the troops call me "Buzzsaw" for chewing up bad work the way I do. But I can't let weak strategies by, and I haven't much tolerance for managers who try to get me to approve programs without first understanding them themselves. I usually assume that half of these presentations will have to be recycled for mistakes to be fixed, but I can't remember drawing three bad ones in a row before.

"It all seems so simple, to fit the parts of a strategy together. I just don't understand how otherwise good general managers can miss their own mistakes so often."

QUESTIONS

1. (a) Restate in your own words the problem with the first strategy that upset Ronnie. (b) Do you think he was correct in being severe with such a mistake?

2. (a) Restate in your own words the problem with the second strategy that upset Ronnie. (b) What are some of the other sources of profit

you would test, to see if they could be worked into this product strategy? Which do you think would add leverages more than justifying their cost?

3. (a) Why do you suppose that Upquick general managers are proposing defective strategies so often? (b) What would you advise Ronnie to do about it?

CASE 26 THE QUICK-LIME CEMENT COMPANY

The Quick-Lime Cement Company had grown to prominence in its region, and when Alonzo Bird, son of the founder, became president, he looked for ways to continue its growth. His father had already extended the business geographically into the territories of other cement companies until lower freight costs closer to the competitive cement plant eliminated Quick-Lime's competitive advantage. Alonzo decided to look for growth closer to home by adding related and compatible product lines. His first venture was into a line of low-temperature cements that could be used in the fall and spring when ordinary cement might freeze and disintegrate before it had a chance to set. The technology of these products is demanding, but Alonzo was able to make an arrangement with a Scandinavian firm that had a full line of frost-resistant products. The products were not that much more expensive than ordinary cement, even after adding the royalty to the Scandinavian company, but Alonzo had discovered that these frost-resistant cements carried a substantial price premium. He asked his marketing consultant: "Have I found a gold mine? Or is there something I am missing here?"

The consultant investigated and reported back: "These are strong specialty products, with the premium based on the superior frost-resistant performance of the products. Contractors need help in delivering that performance, in the form of technical service from you. You haven't figured in those costs—you will need good people on call to help—and this is a problem with such a seasonal product, because you have to find something else for these people to do the rest of the year."

The Quick-Lime Technical Service Department was formed, and the frost-free cement line achieved even more new sales than Alonzo Bird had expected. The profit contribution was discouragingly small, however, and Alonzo asked his marketing consultant if all of this was worth the trouble.

"That depends on you," said the consultant. "To add these products you had to shift from commodity to strong specialty marketing. That meant creating a different focus, more personal and with good technical service support. The move succeeded, but the cost of creating focus ate up the profit. This took you to a new plateau. Now to get more profits you have to add more specialty products without increasing the sales and technical service costs too much."

Alonzo added high-strength cements, light-weight cements, underwater cements, and quick-setting cements. Sales grew in a very pleasing way, and profits grew in proportion. "Where do you think we are now?" Alonzo asked the consultant.

"Successful, but almost at the end of additions to the standard type of cement line. To go further you have to begin to offer special-purpose cements for special uses, in each case with additional costs for extending the focus to embrace a new group of users."

Alonzo continued this line of development, blocking out cement specialty after cement specialty, calculating the cost of obtaining the necessary focus and display, and going ahead wherever the leverages were sufficient to offer real hope of a profit. Soon Quick-Lime found itself also supplying a variety of other cement products made from other materials. Alonzo organized the industrial cement division, and the construction cement division; by then Quick-Lime was a leader in hot-melt adhesives. Then later when Alonzo Bird, Jr. became president, one of his first acts was to organize the household cement division, for all of the products for household use—but he recognized that his father had really laid the groundwork for it.

"Where," he wondered, "will I be able to extend the Quick-Lime Cement business farther, and what kinds of resources must I add, to keep the focus consistent with the needs of each specialty and give it the leverages necessary for success?"

QUESTIONS

1. Describe the evolution of the Quick-Lime business, explaining the shifts in focus and the increased resource needs of each.
2. If Alonzo had simply added the specialty products without changing the focus, what would have happened?
3. At the end of the case Quick-Lime had four different cement businesses (cement, industrial cement, construction cement, household cement) formulating very different sorts of cement from very different materials for very different customer groups. In terms of managing strategy, is Quick-Lime getting too diverse? Discuss.

CHAPTER 14

MATCHING PRODUCT, BUSINESS, AND ENTERPRISE STRATEGIES

KEY IDEAS IN THIS CHAPTER

- **how the enterprise strategies govern** – and control product and business strategies by the types of activities these governing strategies encourage or permit.
- **design and redesign of master strategy** – changes necessary due to the evolution of the firm that may reshape business and product strategies.
- **finding the boundaries** – other sorts of organizational limits that a product or business strategy may encounter.
- **working out a design** – fitting the needs of a strategy within the constraints set by the organization.
- **integrating strategies** – a summary of the process of designing a product or business strategy within the governing strategy framework.

As discussed in earlier chapters and summarized in Figure 14-1, there are three different levels of primary strategy—for the enterprise, for the business, and for the product or service. Chapter 13 dealt with the process of designing product or business strategy, but without considering the limitations placed on these lower-level strategies by the enterprise or governing strategies. The role of the governing strategies is to establish the sort of organization that the firm is and will become. As a result they often narrow the area within which business and product strategies can be effective. This chapter examines these limitations, and the process of integrating product or business strategy with the enterprise strategies.

HOW THE ENTERPRISE STRATEGIES GOVERN

Strategy design is governed by the series of enterprise-level decisions about the type of enterprise the firm chooses to be, the kind of operations it will engage in, and the sorts of risks it will accept. The building block strategies, the choice criteria, and the master strategy determine the nature and to an extent the capabilities of the enterprise, as has been emphasized several times. Characteristics controlled by these enterprise strategies may be success requirements for certain businesses; that is, a business based on development of new short-lived, high-technology products could not prosper in an enterprise with a passive innovation strategy, because this would not stimulate the necessary new product flow. In a given strategy design situation the course of action is to establish as clearly as possible what the relevant enterprise strategies are, and go on from there. For example, the leadership and people strategies together determine the degree to which the resulting organization could or could not achieve the effectiveness inherent in the excellence model if a strategy requires this level of performance.

Desirability strategy is directly related to the tightness and intensity of the goal pattern of that specific firm, managing strategy defines the extent and nature of the diversity whose management may be added to the management task, and belonging strategy accommodates other sorts of organizational preferences and barriers that should influence decisions. For a conglomerate these three strategies set a rather loose pattern focused on financial return, and the head of a business within a conglomerate might pay very little attention to these three enterprise strategies, confident that any sufficiently profitable proposal would be approved by top management. The same three choice criteria could define a much tighter and more subjective constraint for an enterprise concentrating on one or two business areas, and a general manager wishing support

FIGURE 14–1 THE THREE LEVELS OF PRIMARY STRATEGY

Enterprise Strategy	Business Strategy	Product Strategy
Building blocks	Resources	Resources
Leadership Strategy		
Opportunity Strategy	Leverages	Leverages
People Strategy		
Public Strategy	Focus	Focus
Resource Strategy		
	Positions	Positions
Choice criteria		
Desirability Strategy	Display	Display
Managing Strategy		
Belonging Strategy	Cash Flow	Cash Flow
Credibility Strategy		
Risk/reward Strategy	Product Line	
Master strategy		

for a resource request might check first to see if the proposed activity would be acceptable before fully exploring its profit potential.

Public strategy is the most independent of the five building blocks and rarely limits the growth of a firm, although the market profile set by the impact of the business on society tends to set a minimum level of public exposure. Management may choose to escalate this public role as Mobil did after the oil embargo or as Manville did by its bankruptcy strategy, or it may choose a quiet role, as American Home Products and Beatrice Foods did for a great many years.

The resource strategy is somewhat independent of the others, but determined in part by the firm's attitude towards debt financing and the financial community. However, resource strategy is also heavily influenced by the outcomes of the leadership, people, and innovation strategies, inasmuch as the excitement and reward of successful resource creation attracts funds to a dynamic business. Individual business units are limited by enterprise resource strategy only when a firm suffers an internal resource shortage so severe it prevents otherwise-profitable investments.

The managing and belonging strategies can be specific strategy constraints. If management insists that its managers know how to run a business before attempting to acquire it, as Johnson & Johnson did in the past, this limits possible acquisition areas. Or if management rules out product areas because it does not like their connotations, as Dupont once refused to consider rest-room sanitation products, this is another sort of limit.

Credibility strategy presents a different constraint related to the way

Chapter 14 Matching Product, Business, and Enterprise Strategies   335

that management makes decisions. The better managements require well-thought-out proposals with capable managers to execute them, but organizations differ widely in the formality and nature of the process by which they establish project credibility.

Risk/reward strategy is also a constraint. It may be necessary only to show that a project will meet a minimum return level, but better risk/reward strategies are based on a balancing of risk with the potential for reward, although this is more difficult and inevitably somewhat subjective.

Master strategy can also be a constraint on product and business strategy. If a specific unit is outside of that master strategy's thrust, the firm may take away resources in order to fund the master strategy, for example. Or if local business objectives must be shaped to an overall purpose, management may cause a local business unit to sell at lower or higher prices than it would otherwise have chosen, because of the needs of the master strategy—as in the case of multipoint competition with a multinational competitor, where the master strategy guides the actions of the profit centers in different countries. But not all large firms and fewer among smaller firms have active master strategies, and the great majority of business units can make product or business strategy without concern for master strategy constraints.

Enterprise strategy accommodates the interests and abilities of the management group that designs and must operate it, and should also relate to the market requirements for effectiveness of the resulting business and product strategies. To formulate sound product and business strategy, the organization must be such as to permit personal and responsible strategy design and execution, with accountability of the key managers, whether through use of strategic business units or in some other way. Business strategy and product or service strategy are all based on needs-leverages linkages, and as the requirements for establishing such linkages are defined, the innovation, cost-cutting, market positioning, and promotion potentials can be cataloged and explored. If the enterprise prospers, then enterprise, business, and product strategies are proven adequate. If profits falter, often all three levels of strategy must be recast.

DESIGN AND REDESIGN OF MASTER STRATEGY

The primary emphasis here is on product and business strategies, with enterprise strategies guiding and limiting, and possible reconsideration of these linkages when appropriate. Master strategies override many of these considerations, are unlikely to be formulated or reviewed except by the very top levels of management, and can cause profound changes throughout the organization when they are revised. During his tenure as chief executive officer Peter Grace has recast his master strategy for Grace several times, with acquisitions, divestitures, and major shifts in emphasis following. Or Caterpillar, a multinational company supplying worldwide markets primarily from the United States, was hard-pressed by cost problems in overseas markets due to the high foreign-exchange price of the U.S. dollar, and by Japanese competition, and shifted to more of a worldwide production pattern to put it in a stronger position for future currency fluctuations. This was not just a matter of building an overseas plant, but a recast of the production functional strategies and therefore the business strategies for the entire Caterpillar product line.

When master strategies need change, because of external changes or because top management emphasis changes, other enterprise strategies often require corresponding changes, with all of the business and product or service strategies potentially modified by any shift in enterprise strategy limitations and emphasis.

FINDING THE BOUNDARIES

Strategy design starts with a mission, and targets goals within the span of that mission. What is this specific strategy intended to accomplish? Will the proposed strategy challenge any organizational boundaries? Check the division lines between assignments, between delegations of authority, between the activities of different organizational units, between the zones of interest or control of specific executives, or any other sort of boundary that management may once have established or decided to tolerate. Innovative strategies very often challenge boundaries, and many failures in obtaining approval or in operations afterwards are traceable to unintended challenges to them. It is wisest and safest to start with a full view of the boundaries and sort out the implications of any boundary challenges before deciding on a strategy and putting a challenge forward formally.

If a strategy does not fit within the boundaries already set by the organization, its approval and successful execution will become more difficult. Key boundaries come from the enterprise-level strategies and the territory lines around division and individual interests. These boundaries are set by the parent enterprise, and often are firmly fixed. But because they limit performance, they are sometimes challenged, and properly so. An organization needs a routine for reexamining its overall pattern of operation, starting with the enterprise strategy. But this is sensitive territory, involving feelings and preferences of the top executives.

Business or product strategy design may be poorly executed if limitations caused by enterprise-level strategies are not discussed openly. Open discussion keeps the perspective clearer, as well as the significance of these limits to strategy. This does not necessarily mean those limits should be changed, as they may represent appropriate boundaries on specific types of growth.

WORKING OUT A DESIGN

For a proposed product, business, contributing, or enterprise strategy, consider other strategies that may be relevant and make a list of them; hopefully this will be a short list, but many strategies get snagged either in approval or in action because of unrecognized linkages to other programs.

When Pillsbury decided to market Betty Crocker ice cream bars, this automatically linked the ice cream bar strategy with the strategies for the cake mixes and other products marketed under the Betty Crocker brand. While the linkage does not appear to be a bad one, this sort of tie between product strategies reduces the freedom of product and business managers on both ends of the linkage. In a case where the commonality is a key resource or customer group rather than the brand name, the linkage may be just as important without being so obvious. Such a linkage is usually intended to take advantage of leverages based on an established position, and may be based on joint use of a brand name, of manufacturing or distribution facilities, of a sales force, or a variety of other factors. After looking for such linkages, list any other strategies that may be affected by the strategy being proposed, so that the degree of the potential effect can be considered.

The next check is against all of the boundaries recorded before, of other products, in the organization, and from the enterprise level. If there are no boundary problems, fine; the time has come to propose the strategy formally. If there are boundary problems, what are they, and how serious?

Every day managements make basic changes in boundaries they laid down in the past—but more managements adhere to the status quo and decide not to change. In general this is the process: define all boundaries in advance, do the best design possible, look again at the boundaries, and then go ahead according to best judgment; that is, not taking a boundary challenge to top management unless the challenge makes enough sense to be worth any turbulence it may cause.

INTEGRATING STRATEGIES

A sound strategy is based on an effective, internally consistent set of elements well integrated with the enterprise strategy, as summarized in Figure 14-2; that is the thrust of this chapter. The difficulty in applying all of

---

FIGURE 14-2   MATCHING PRODUCT, BUSINESS, AND ENTERPRISE STRATEGIES

How the governing strategies govern
                        Finding boundaries
                                          Working out a design

Making up rules
                        Creating resources
                                          Power to the strategy

Strategy and the excellence model
                            PRODUCING EFFECTIVE, WELL-INTEGRATED STRATEGIES

---

this is that the enterprise strategies are often more informally and subjectively conceived, to the point that their ability to limit and prevent business and product strategy performance too often goes unrecognized. The lesson is that sound strategy design requires an open internal management climate where these issues will be surfaced for review and then decided according to the level of results management is willing to accept. This is a critical part of the overall strategy design process in which planning and strategy lead to action.

QUESTIONS FOR ANALYSIS AND DISCUSSION

1. Find your own example of a commodity product strategy in a rapidly growing market requiring expansion faster than the market to build market share.
2. Find your own example of a commodity service strategy in a rapidly growing market requiring expansion faster than the market to build market share.
3. From organizations with which you are familiar, give examples of the sort of organizational boundaries that limit strategy design.
4. Find other examples of product or business strategies whose effectiveness has been limited by conflict with the enterprise strategy of that firm.

FOR FURTHER INFORMATION

Buzzell, Robert D., and Bradley T. Gale, *The PIMS Principles: Linking Strategy to Performance* (New York: Free Press, 1987).

    Strategies matched against profits, a unique correlation from the PIMS data base.

Hammermesh, Richard G., *Making Strategies Work: How Senior Managers Produce Results* (New York: Wiley, 1986).

    An authoritative view of strategic management from the top of the organization.

CASE 27: ADVENTURES WITH THE NEW CENTRAL MARKEN-SPACKLER

Steve was the able young product manager for the new central marken-spackler, and he became so enthusiastic about the prospects for this machine that his wife thoroughly tired of hearing about it. Product strategy had been settled some time ago and preparations for launch were under way, although the actual launch date was still several months away. Allen Frankel, the general manager and Steve's boss, was largely responsible for the successful development of the marken-spackler and had personally guided its evolution from concept to prototype to customer endorsement. Now it was moving toward national marketing; Steven and Allen had projected that it would triple the sales volume of their little new division and make it into a worthwhile and profitable business for the first time.

Allen had asked for another review of the product plan. Steve was puzzled: "I thought this was completely OK with you after the finishing touches you asked for on the last round of reviews."

"Yes," Allen responded, "but it's time to spend some time on the next level, on the way the enterprise strategies and organizational boundaries in this corporation relate to our planned product and business strategies. Translation: Are we sure the organization will let us do what we have to do to make this product strategy work?"

ENTERPRISE STRATEGIES

They started on the list of enterprise strategies, as well as they had been able to work them out from the pattern of management actions. Allen liked to start from the end of the list and work back. For example, their company had only a few master strategies and these did not relate to Allen's division's business area at all; therefore there was no problem with the master strategies. Risk/reward strategy was no problem because the projected profitability was high and the risks very small. As to credibility strategy, Allen felt they had a good plan and enough personal stature to convince management they could make the plan work, and the earlier management reviews of their plan for the marken-spackler seemed to confirm this. Desirability and belonging strategies seemed OK—this was the sort of product the company really wanted, and there weren't any awkward connotations or controllability problems that might cause concern. Managing strategy was not a problem—as a management challenge, this product was like many others the company had marketed successfully. Or perhaps there was a problem?—because the company used a very structured approach to marketing, and marken-spackler customers would have to have much more individual attention initially.

Resource strategy raised no issues; their resource demand was modest, and the corporation had a generous cash flow from retained earnings just now. Public strategy did not relate to the marken-spackler at all, they were well within the umbrella of a good overall people strategy, and the opportunity strategy had pointed them towards the development of the marken-spackler in the first place.

The leadership strategy was generally quite open and aggressive, except that the corporation did have a fondness for standardizing the way things were done—such as the marketing approach that had caused the earlier concern. Allen concluded: "Steve, I can only see one potential enterprise strategy problem. Make a note: 'Will the managing and leadership strategies make it hard for us to give the individual customer attention marken-spackler customers require?'"

ORGANIZATION BOUNDARIES

Then the two of them began to talk through the steps of marken-spackler manufacture, distribution, and shipping, and all of the purchasing, order-flow, accounting, and other linkages they could think of, to see how the marken-spackler would move through the corporate system, and whether there were potential organization boundary or territory problems.

One potential problem was with spare parts. "Allen, how are we going to manage spare parts when the corporate controller is pushing so hard for a standardized inventory system? His system will keep us from carrying extra parts in stock for alternative settings as we calibrate each machine to the customer's conditions during startup." Steve looked worried.

"You are talking about the gauging and setting elements?"

"Yes."

"Any reason why the drives and gear train and the rest of the machinery won't be OK in the standard system?" There was none.

"We can't afford the time and energy for a fight with the controller, so I think we will have to bypass part of his system. Please calculate the cost of this and let me see how it looks—but in addition to putting all of the parts into the corporate parts-control system in the way we are supposed to, I think we need to ship a complete kit of all of the different gauging and setting elements to the sales office responsible for the installation every time we ship a machine. Then they will have anything they could need for changes during start-up, and they can return the kit afterwards so whatever they used can be added before it is shipped out again. Then after we have some experience with what the start-up needs really are, we can look at the whole thing again and decide. Hopefully by the time the corporate watchdogs discover our bypass, we will have clear justification for whatever extra parts we really need."

They continued their review of procedures. Suddenly Allen stopped: "Wait a minute—we are going to have an accounts receivable problem I didn't think about."

"You mean the standard collection procedure?" Steve asked.

"Yes! Your product plan is laid out on the basis that if the customer installs the machine immediately, each new central marken-spackler will be in full operation before that customer is invoiced—this is part of your guaranteed performance package. The standard corporate receivables control won't let us do that, and I don't think a little division like ours could get that changed. We will have to reroute the shipping papers, so that the corporate system gets the date of first successful operation as the date of sale. That should be only two weeks' difference anyway for most installations—and this is a tremendously profitable package that justifies the change."

Steve hesitated, then spoke: "Sounds good for now. But a big fuss could break out later, when this all comes out. Someone could get fired for not following corporate procedures."

"Not 'someone.' *Me*. Nobody else has to take my falls for me. But if the product goes well, this will all be forgiven; and if it doesn't, they will want a new general manager anyway. This corporation desperately wants new products and growth, but no one upstairs seems to realize how much their corporate procedures limit them to products like the ones they already have. To have any chance of making our little division succeed, I have to push the boundaries. I might get fired for it, but I won't be here long anyway if I don't build sales and profits."

Steve and Allen completed their review without finding any more boundary issues. Allen summarized: "We found two boundary problems, and ways of bypassing them for long enough to get started. We found one enterprise strategy problem, where the leadership and managing strategies mandate a standardized marketing approach we may not be able to live with. Except for that the strategy will run like clockwork. What are we going to do about marketing?"

THE CUSTOMER SERVICE PROBLEM

The corporation had worked out a marketing system whereby the businesses calling on a particular group of customers shared a common sales and technical service force. It was a well-worked-out system, with allocations of sales and technical service time established in advance and enforced from day to day, and provision for training of specialists for customer problems such as Allen and Steve were expecting during each central marken-spackler startup. The difficulty was that the standard system did not allow an intense enough response. Allen and Steve wanted a start-up team to spend their full time around the clock for three or four days with each new machine, to see it properly adjusted and into smooth operation. Steve had built the cost of this support into the product plans already, but they had not found any way the corporate system would let them deliver the necessary support service.

They talked through the problem again, and could think of only two possible solutions. The direct solution was to try to change the corporate system. The indirect solution was to add three or four "market engineers" who would be "aiding marketing research" and "studying changing customer needs" by rolling up their sleeves and acting as start-up crew for each new machine. Allen tried very hard to get approval to hire these "market engineers," after explaining to his boss and his boss's boss exactly what he was doing and why. Both men understood the need and agreed to support his request, even though it was a bypass of the corporate system. But all of this was to no avail—it took two months of arguing, and still the corporate system gave Allen a final and definitive "no market engineers" decision.

ASKING FOR A CHANGE

Allen, Steve, and the rest of the marken-spackler team reviewed the situation a number of times. Allen's final question: "Is there any way we can make the product go, considering the amount of support we can get through the standard marketing system?" The group talked about alternatives for two more hours. The conclusion was that they could not make the product go.

"OK," Allen said, "fur is going to fly somewhere. The only other choice is to try to get management to let us change the standard system." And he tried, very hard, starting an appeal process that culminated when Allen, his boss, and his boss's boss, and the whole marken-spackler team appeared before the management committee to discuss the problem.

The management committee listened patiently to Allen's presentation and asked a number of questions. Finally the president summarized: "No, we have worked out our marketing procedures rather carefully and they have served the organization well. I don't see the need to change these procedures for your product. This is a very exciting product that should make a lot of money for the corporation, and the management committee gives you full credit for guiding its development. But I'm not convinced that its requirements are that special. I think we should leave the marketing system the way it is and go ahead."

"With all due respect, Chief," Allen responded, "I wouldn't have asked for this meeting if I thought there was any other way we could succeed with this product. A change of marketing strategy is necessary in my view, or we will fail. In the existing system I have to recommend that the product not be marketed at all."

"I can't accept that," responded the president.

"I thought you would feel that way," said Allen grimly. "And I think you should get someone who believes that the program can succeed this way to direct it, so you and the management committee will feel that it had a fair trial. I'll clear out my desk and be gone by the first of the month."

As they came out of the meeting, Steve looked very badly shaken.

Allen took him aside. "What you do is your business, but don't feel any obligation to quit because I did. I am the only one who stuck his head up; it needn't hurt the rest of you.

"If I were in your shoes, I would follow orders quietly and see what happens next. If the program succeeds, you are the product manager and its your product that has succeeded. If the program fails, it won't be your fault if you stay out of the line of fire. If you stay, be sure my successor has a chance to make his own decisions about the parts and receivables things, where I told you not to follow procedures exactly. And if the launch goes the way I expect, perhaps you can help pick up the pieces afterwards."

TO MARKET

The central marken-spackler was welcomed by the market, but when the first customers had difficulty getting it into routine production, orders fell off. Eighteen months later sales were only 20 percent of forecast and the product only marginally profitable when the general manager resigned—or was fired? No one was quite sure. Steve found himself in the office of Allen's old boss being asked for his ideas about how to revive the product. Steve suggested a team of market engineers, to give supplemental help at start-up, a kit of gauging and setting elements for start-up adjustments delivered to the sales office every time a machine was shipped, and a sales incentive plan where the customer would not be invoiced for the machine until it was in routine operation. The boss said that these were exciting new ideas, Steve found himself as acting general manager with approval to try all three, and the sales of the central marken-spackler began to revive, although it took almost a year to live down the bad reports from the launch. The corporation was ecstatic over the profit flow, Steve was confirmed as general manager, and he and the rest of the team got bonuses, but Steve knew the product would never reach the full potential it had had originally.

QUESTIONS

1. Do you think it was right or wrong for Allen to plan to violate corporate procedures? What would have been a better way to get the corporation to change internal boundaries and enterprise strategies?
2. Do you think Steve reacted correctly when Allen told him not to follow corporate procedures exactly? Do you think Steve should have quit when Allen did? To a certain extent Steve profited because Allen got himself into a position where he felt he had to resign—should Steve feel guilty about this?

Chapter 14 Matching Product, Business, and Enterprise Strategies 345

3. The net result of the central marken-spackler launch program was a small change in some organizational boundaries and in the managing and leadership strategies. Describe these changes.

4. To what extent do you think the changes you identified in question 3 will help other product strategies? If you look at this as a part of a process for the slow change of enterprise strategies, what do you think of the process?

CASE 28 LIMITS TO BUSINESS GROWTH

Roger, the CEO, was impressed but not convinced: "This enterprise strategy thing is really impressive, and I can see where it would cause problems in a lot of corporations. But here—I can't believe we have that problem. Have you seen any evidence of it?"

This last was a question to the strategy consultant who had just completed the third in a series of weekly strategy discussions with the management committee. The consultant hesitated, because CEO's do not always welcome frank answers, and then decided he might as well speak his mind: "Roger, you know I haven't been around your organization very much to look for that sort of thing. But I did hear you fellows talking about the uphill battle your facsimile division is having trying to establish a firm base in a very competitive market place. That sounds like the kind of job that calls for organizational excellence, but that part of your company has been restructured twice in the last six months, with either three or four 10% across-the-board personnel cuts—and there is no way you could have organizational excellence with the amount of stress and turmoil those cutbacks cause; which is to say that the facsimile effort is probably being held back by a people- and leadership-strategy problem.

"I'm guessing, of course, and I'd welcome the chance to collect some facts so I could put this all together more carefully—but yes, I think I can find some places where your enterprise strategies are holding back your businesses. That in itself is not important because you may have businesses you want to deemphasize—but you should always know where the business is being limited and make a decision as to whether you want it that way. For instance, if my guess about the facsimile business holds up, you should either change the strategies that are limiting it, or phase that unit out and approach the market some other way."

The facsimile troubles were a sore spot, the consultant had scored his point, and Roger turned out to be reasonably open to criticism, for a CEO. In the next half hour it developed that he and the management committee would very much like to know where their enterprise strategies were holding back specific businesses, and then to discuss what to do about each case. Better yet, various management committee members had candidates for him to check—businesses not doing as well as it seemed they should, and other sorts of sore spots. When the meeting broke up, the consultant had several pages of notes, a lot more work to do, appointments with the planning director, personnel director, and chief financial officer to talk about the way the organization functioned, and a week-away date with the CEO to talk about what he had learned by then.

At the next week's meeting with Roger he started with a question:

Chapter 14   Matching Product, Business, and Enterprise Strategies   347

"Roger, how do you feel about the progress of your biotechnology business?"

"Good but not comfortable. I like what I hear but I don't understand it very much."

"That fits. The man in charge of it is really uptight and on edge, worrying about whether he has executive support. If he were sure he didn't, he would leave. If he were sure he did, I'll bet he would turn out twice as much."

"You came in to talk about enterprise strategy. How is this thing in biotechnology an enterprise strategy problem?"

"This corporation has always had a very structured approach toward opportunity—picking targets carefully and then working out ways to get there. This biotechnology business is different and you know that—his new discoveries could come anywhere. You suspended the old opportunity strategy, at least in this area, when you made the commitment to biotechnology, but you haven't ever dealt with what you would do with some of his possible discoveries. He knows this, and he's not convinced you would develop a cure for cancer, or a procedure for doubling the number of eggs a chicken lays, or for making pine trees grow three times as fast."

"But of course we would develop any of those things."

"I know that, and you know that, but he only knows that your corporation never did any of these things, is inexperienced, unprepared, and hasn't thought about the problem. Going back to enterprise strategies—what I mean is that when you decided biotechnology was an exception from the old opportunity strategy, somebody should have thought just a little about an opportunity strategy for biotechnology. As it is, the uncertainty is slowing down the work, just because he doesn't know how serious you are.

"Another example is the way some of the general managers and corporate staffs treat the solid waste management business. It used to be that your corporation turned away from 'other people's garbage.' You had a strong barrier set up through your belonging strategy. No problem with that, or with the fact that three years ago corporate management decided to change it. But most of the organization doesn't seem to know about the change. I'm sure you told them—but no one has said 'The solid waste management people are your brothers and sisters; welcome them into the corporate family' either. And the solid waste management business is spending a lot of money to buy services outside the corporation that could be better provided by your staffs, because the solid waste managers are so angry over the treatment they get from the staffs inside. Your new belonging strategy is OK, except that no one brought the organization up to speed in the new direction when you changed it.

"Roger, this is only an update, and I have a lot more work to do. And it's not a bad report, because no business is seriously hurt and you can remedy these problems easily any time you choose to act. But don't be surprised that I found problems—management of enterprise strategy is a neglected area, and I've never looked at a large corporation without finding worse problems than I have found here so far."

QUESTIONS

1. In your own words, restate the enterprise strategy problem that was hampering the facsimile business.
2. In your own words, restate the enterprise strategy problem that was hampering the biotechnology business.
3. In your own words, restate the enterprise strategy problem that was hampering the solid waste management business.
4. How would you go about reviewing the enterprise strategies of a diverse corporation to see if they were consistent with all of its businesses? Discuss.
5. How would you go about discovering whether all of the businesses of a diverse corporation felt they were adequately guided by the enterprise strategies? Discuss.

CHAPTER

STRATEGIC MANAGEMENT AND VALUE-DRIVEN PLANNING

KEY IDEAS IN THIS CHAPTER

This chapter discusses strategic management's planning system, why it is and should be value-driven, and its position as a vehicle for carrying strategies into action:

- **long-range planning and strategic planning** – the recognition of the need.
- **strategic management and value-based planning** – line managers planning, and value for the shareholders.
- **planning as a process for organizational learning** – a management team finding new strategies together.
- **quality, customers, and strategy** – extending the planning to multifunctional teams coordinating design, development, and production with customer needs—and finding competitive advantage effectively.
- **time as a strategic variable** – making competitive advantage and lower costs out of quicker response to customer needs.

- **outline of a strategic plan** – with discussion of the parts and of the planning process.
- **strategic management and value-driven planning** – summary of the integration of the elements of value-driven planning, and of the strategy design process.

A recurrent criticism of the strategy process in many firms is that it is too short-term. Normally several years may elapse after a decision to start a research project or to build a plant before the business can reap the profits; and to make the strategy process effective, an adequate time perspective is required. For long-term investments this means long range planning, and starting early in the 1960's Long Range Planning appeared as a discipline, a battle cry, and in the titles of many books.

LONG RANGE PLANNING

Long range planning meant planning actions ahead far enough to show the return from necessary investments. Long range planning got good results and some not-so-good results. As times passed and the process was analyzed more deeply, the complaint was that too many of the things that had been planned were details, and too little attention had been given to the underlying strategy. Strategic planning—that was the thing—and the development of corporate planning systems continued even more rapidly under the strategic planning banner.

Strategic planning protagonists suffered similar disillusion and setback, because major strategic planning efforts in a number of firms did not improve corporate financial results. A corporate planning process can be very elaborate and expensive, and to match the total organizational investment in an impressive 200-page printed and bound corporate plan, investors wanted to see a corresponding step-up in sales and earnings. But the linkage between the plan and action was not always clear, and retrospective reviews showed that too many managers managed in exactly the same way as they had before, regardless of what was written in the plan.

STRATEGIC MANAGEMENT

Strategic management became the new standard, because it is not enough to make a strategic plan. Strategic action is necessary, line managers take the action, and to get better results they must be taught to manage strategically. Strategic management became and continues to be the key theme—in the title of this book, for example. Strategic management still requires a strategic plan. Strategic planning systems had been overextended and overformalized in large segments of U.S. industry, and as the present wave of restructuring and overhead reduction swept across the country, planning staffs were among the many targets and formal planning was severely trimmed. Strategic management requires strategic planning, but line managers are the only true planners, because only they can link plan and action. The reappraisals and cutbacks reinforced this—that strategic planning must be carried out by line managers. With the true planners planning and a substantial reduction in paper and formality, planning became a more valid and justifiable organizational process, a process including an important but much smaller role for planning staff in assisting line managers in their planning.

At about the same time that strategic management and strategic planning were working toward their present equilibrium, the wave of corporate takeovers began. The question was, in whose interest does management manage? And, because the public stock market price of the stock was being used by raiders to select takeover targets, management seized on the idea of managing for shareholder value in hopes of gaining a higher price for its stock to make the company a less attractive takeover target.

Of course, most managements argue that they always have managed in the interest of their shareholders, and most managements learned long ago that public market stock prices move up and down in response to market phenomena no one business firm can control. But as the market rises and falls, some companies and some industries are valued higher than others, and management does have a degree of influence here. For example, because of their earnings history many conglomerates have been valued so low that the component businesses were worth more separately—and as Chapter 6 points out, a shift to at least a modest amount of debt has made some firms more attractive to their shareholders. A management unhappy with a conglomerate stock market appraisal can restructure itself to emphasize a more basic business theme, as W. R. Grace has done, and many managements have used debt to buy back stock.

Managing for shareholder value now has come to represent a set of management tools. At the same time its limitations are being criticized, and the underlying management approaches are still evolving. One recurrent theme at present is that management decisions should always be aimed at creating value within the firm; by creating value they are likely eventually to lead to a more favorable stock market appraisal. Value creation—a sound and sensible concept. The planning should be value-driven, so that the action that follows will be value-creating.

As with any important and rapidly evolving field, emphasis shifts as new ideas are put forward. But strategic management and value-driven planning are valuable core concepts around which these ideas should center for some time:

1. Planning is action laid out in advance. The only members of an organization who can make action commitments are the line managers; they must validate every step of a plan for it to have meaning. Logically they are and should be the planners, and they must plan and manage strategically, to have any hope of long-term success.
2. Management actions should be aimed at creating value. Shareholder value in general and stock prices in specific are both important, and better measures for this value-creation will continue to evolve. But retrospect shows numerous past management actions that did not create value and many examples of management carelessness about such things. It appears that the general standard of management can and should be raised, by more attention to creating value and to value-driven planning and action.

A strategic plan comes from a process through which the members of a management group formulate and share their plans. In a management process requiring the cooperation of a large number of managers the specific action plans of each must be meshed, and these managers can often find ways to make their actions reinforce each other, thus adding to the impact and synergy of the total process. Assuming that the leadership strategy permits this, the process will also become participative, with the whole group searching for ways to make their actions more effective.

PLANNING AS A PROCESS FOR ORGANIZATIONAL LEARNING

In a study of companies that had been in business for more than 75 years, the planning group at Shell found that one common characteristic was an ability to live in harmony with the changing business environment, even when this required major changes in strategy. This ability to adapt to changing requirements appears to be rare, relatively few major companies seem to adapt successfully, and repeated studies of past industrial leaders show that most have remarkably short spans of success.

The Shell group attributed the ability of some companies to adapt to changed conditions to a collective learning ability of the management teams—an institutional learning process. In "Planning as Learning,"[1] de Geus tells how Shell used its planning system as a forum for reexamination of their established and successful business strategy. Shell had em-

---
[1] Arie de Geus, "Planning as Learning," *Harvard Business Review*, March–April 1988, pp. 70–74.

Chapter 15   Strategic Management and Value-Driven Planning   353

phasized vertical integration as key to profitable growth until this became an automatic part of the thinking process of Shell managers; after the OPEC embargo this strategy came into question. Introduction of scenarios for alternative future oil prices into the planning system led eventually to an open discussion of whether vertical integration would still be a correct strategy. After intense discomfort about beginning this discussion, the management team began to sense the depth of the strategic changes that had occurred, began to develop the implications of these changes, and in a space of about eighteen months shifted its viewpoint and adopted a fundamentally different basic strategy.

A planning system may take many forms, but its essence is as a participative linkage through which a group of managers can share and coordinate their planning so that the company as a whole and its individual units are working toward the same ends. This sharing and coordinating requires a common value system and overall strategy, and when shifts are necessary in either the shared values or the basic strategy, the group must shift together, if the change is to be effective. This means new values or new directions developed into new fundamentals for the organization, adopted, and put into action. In the world of more and more frequent change into which we appear to be moving, fundamental adaptations such as the successful shift in strategy at Shell will be needed much more frequently than in the past, and those companies with an effective shared planning system linking their managers will be much more likely to make these shifts successfully.

QUALITY, CUSTOMERS, AND STRATEGY

Quality means, among other things, that the customer should get exactly what he or she wants, and "The House of Quality" starts with the now-classic quality function deployment (QFD) system originated at Mitsubishi's Kobe shipyard[2] and discusses its extension and adaptation by a significant assortment of U.S. companies. This system is based on careful, thoughtful analysis of what customers really want—both their requests, and the reasoning lying behind these requests—and a much more careful tailoring of product design, development, and manufacture to fulfillment of customer needs. The relevance here is that this system, as well as other less formal approaches to the same ground, require a major and unprecedented level of cooperation and coordination between the different

---

[2] John R. Hauser & Don Clausing, "The House of Quality," *Harvard Business Review*, May–June 1988, pp. 63–73.

elements in a firm—to design, develop, and manufacture products in such a way that customer satisfaction can be maximized and cost minimized at the same time. This requires a certain sort of a planning system. In the Hauser and Clausing article, planning is achieved through design teams whose members represent all elements of the design and production process—teams that deal directly with the consumer needs, and work for best fulfillment of customer need and cost at the same time.

The planning emphasis in this chapter stems from the "Strategic Management and Value-driven Planning" title—on the substance of an effective planning linkage among the management group as a part of the management operating system. Formality should be minimized, but in part that is determined by the style and leadership strategy of a specific management. More important, the shared planning function should be extended as far as serves the strategic management purpose, and many companies are using cross-functional teams, such as the 'house of quality' teams cited above, as an extension of this planning.[3] These teams may include nonmanagers or reach outside of the firm, often including distributors, purchasing agents, or individual customers, depending on the specific function of the team. The point is that value-driven planning should extend as far as necessary to find the value toward which it is directed. In the past some firms limited planning to a few high-level executives, and thus cut themselves off from some of the sources of the value their planning systems should be seeking.

Another limit on planning systems is a lack of creative imagination. In a recent article Ohmae[4] challenges the tendency of many managers to rush out and do battle with their competitors without stopping to think first about what they are doing. His point is not that competitors should be ignored, but that they should be attacked as skillfully and strategically as possible; he quotes Sun Tzu on the wisdom of avoiding unnecessary battles. Often it is possible to approach the competitive ground from a different direction that minimizes the advantage the competitor may have created; such a change in direction is often more efficient in use of resources and more effective in overcoming the competitor, as shown in his examples. A part of the role of strategic management, and a part of the purpose of a value-driven planning system, is to accomplish just this shift in ground, to put the competitor at a disadvantage. This book has emphasized making up new rules for the market, and creating new resources to support a strategy, in order to accomplish these same ends.

---

[3] Tom Peters, *Thriving on Chaos* (New York: Knopf, 1988).
[4] Kenichi Ohmae, "Getting Back to Strategy," *Harvard Business Review*, November–December 1988, pp. 149–156.

TIME AS A STRATEGIC VARIABLE

Of course, time is important. And time is money, in many different ways. Just-in-time production is no longer a new idea, but not yet widely applied. Its implications are the first example in a fresh call[5] for more attention to time as a strategic variable. Just-in-time production eliminates raw material inventories, and saves the investment these inventories represented, but requires closer coordination between a firm and its suppliers. It also has led to major investments in improved tooling, to allow more rapid changeovers from one production item to another, and to major internal studies of where the time really goes in the typical multi-month production process, or multiyear design and development process. The uniform conclusion is that a great deal of the elapsed time is waiting time lost because of the difficulty of coordinating the sequential steps.

Now imaginative use of computer power for scheduling has given an organization potential control over these delays, and multifunction teams, such as the House of Quality teams mentioned above, have begun to study the flow from stage to stage. The result is that production cycles and development cycles have been radically compressed without impairing their function and usually with a significant reduction in overall cost. More important, the responsiveness of the organization to outside needs is greatly increased. A shorter production or development cycle formerly brought a competitive advantage, but the move toward more rapid response is becoming so widespread that firms not moving in this direction are finding themselves disadvantaged.

After a simple streamlining of a process to take out the delays, the next step is an analysis of what can be done to shorten its intrinsic nature. Numerically controlled tools are not new; but with the next steps, in computer control and computer-aided design, the process moves toward much faster flow. Sometimes this means manufacturing to order; Allen-Bradley moved a large line of industrial contacts to a manufacture-to-order basis in a new flexible manufacturing facility, shipping most orders on the day received, eliminating all finished-product inventories and a great deal of overhead, and greatly improving its competitive position.

The relevance to planning and strategy is that technology available now is erasing many of the time barriers that make many processes slow and costly. The cost-saving itself would be an adequate incentive for seizing the opportunity to save time. But the stakes are much larger, because

---

[5] George Stalk, Jr., "Time—The Next Source of Competitive Advantage," *Harvard Business Review*, July–August 1988, pp. 41–51.

quicker operations become simpler and respond to market needs faster. The real and commanding competitive advantage is in quicker response to customer needs, and a key challenge to value-based planning is to find new ways to use these time-saving technologies and build them into the strategic management action by the firm.

WHAT IS A STRATEGIC PLAN?[6]

A strategic plan is action laid out in advance, a snapshot of a strategic planning process. A useful outline is shown in Figure 15-1 and discussed below. Other outlines may be used, but these same components will be found in some form in any good strategic plan.

EXECUTIVE SUMMARY

Each plan should start with a brief section designed to give the essence of the plan and its recommendations in a quick capsule for the busy reader. Those few who have great interest or something at stake will read the plan carefully. They may read it as a means of learning about the business, as the basis for their approval, as a means to prepare a brief in its support, or as critical opponents searching for flaws. The body of a good plan will receive serious and critical readership from only a relatively small group of friends and enemies. This body should be substantial if it is to withstand analysis, and honestly supportive of the statements the summary contains.

BACKGROUND

A plan starts from a context growing out of the history of the enterprise. The firm is controlled by managers with individual personalities, some have taken positions on issues, and any ongoing business has a history of successes and failures. The Background section briefly states the context in which the plan is being presented. If a manager feels that his planning is heavily constrained by the need to make use of available plant capacity, it is important to say so. If shortage of cash requires delay in previously established plans for increasing inventories, this should be stated. Stating this context will also refresh the memories of those who may not have thought about this business as an entity since the previous plan was pre-

---

[6] Adapted from George C. Sawyer, *Corporate Planning as a Creative Process* (Oxford, Ohio: Planning Executives Institute, 1983), pp. 10–19.

FIGURE 15-1   OUTLINE OF A STRATEGIC PLAN

1.	Executive Summary	9.	Forecast
2.	Background	10.	Functional Plans
3.	Environment	11.	Resource Requirements
4.	Business Appraisal	12.	Financial Analysis
5.	Mission	13.	Realism
6.	Goals	14.	Alternatives
7.	Strategy	15.	Recommendations
8.	Product or Service Programs		

---

sented. Thus, each reader will start the plan with an awareness of the boundaries and limitations used by the planning group and built into the structure.

ENVIRONMENT

Businesses are affected by recessions, earthquakes, wars, disasters, social stress, market conditions, competitive actions, inflation, taxes, and a host of other external factors. Obvious though many of these factors may be, they are often missed by managers so involved in the day-to-day routine that they do not have the time to stop and think about the world in which their business functions. A brief Environment section provides the discipline of an organized statement in a context appropriate to the plan.

The Environment section should survey the environment briefly and comprehensively, devoting time to careful development only where a particular factor is likely to affect corporate decisions now or in the near future. A survey of environmental factors often starts with the likely impacts on the business (1) of developments in the political and regulatory environment, (2) of social forces and economic trends, (3) of changing technology, and (4) of developments in the competitive environment. Also, it often includes (5) a profile of the actual markets in which the business operates. In some cases the ecological factors influencing the business also require separate discussion. The Environment section highlights the most critical sensitivities and vulnerabilities of this business to the world around it.

BUSINESS APPRAISAL

This is a short summary of the business situation. Given the background as stated and the present and projected environment as the planning group sees it, what is a realistic assessment of the business outlook? The purpose is to sharpen and converge the analysis drawn out of the background and environment, and to underscore those key questions that provide a backdrop for the plan that will follow.

MISSION

The mission is a statement of the role in which a business hopes and plans to serve society. As a profit-seeking entity, a business unit can survive only by providing goods or services to some segment of society at a price greater than the cost. In order for the necessary price to be paid, the purchasers must see value greater than the purchasing power that must be surrendered to obtain these goods or services. The business must perform some valuable role, through offering goods or services in which buyers see value greater than the cost, or it cannot survive. This role, in which it can find the basis for its pursuit of profit, is its mission.

GOALS

Goals—or objectives—are a necessary precursor to any serious plan for accomplishments. The Goals section in a plan should be a concise statement of what the following programs of action are designed to accomplish.

STRATEGY

From a set of goals, the next step is to their means of achievement. Given that market share is to be increased, how will this be done? Through a major advertising campaign? A different method of distribution? A radical price cut? A basic approach to achievement of the market share goal must be selected for the planning to proceed. This major approach is the strategy this business will follow in striving to achieve its goals, as developed in Chapters 13 and 14.

PRODUCT OR SERVICE PROGRAMS

When a strategy has been selected, the next step is to block out the major areas around which the action plans should be organized. These may represent groups of products or services—hence the term Product or Service Programs. It is common to find that products in a product line occur in families that should be related in their planning and marketing. For example, in a mail order catalog the products are grouped together, and the buying staff can plan for appliances, televisions, power tools, or women's shoes as groups of products in such a product line.

FORECAST

From the product or service programs as developed from the strategy, what will the revenues be, product by product? The Forecast section is intended as a simple statement of the revenue the business can be expected to generate in each time period as a result of the plan.

FUNCTIONAL PLANS

The strategy, as broken into product programs and developed into a forecast, is a projection of results that can be achieved only if the necessary components of the organization function together in a coordinated way. This means that each of the functional areas must itself develop a plan for this role, with its own set of goals and strategy. This section of the strategic plan is intended to present these functional plans in their relationship to the strategy and forecast.

Detailed functional planning is often necessary. However, the corresponding component of the strategic plan—whether it be for production, marketing, manufacturing, distribution, research, engineering, or another function—is usually limited to a brief summary supported elsewhere by a separate plan detailed to any required extent.

RESOURCE REQUIREMENTS

The functional plans become real and meaningful to management only when they also are related to a statement of what the effort will cost. If an expanded program requires more people, or new capital commitments, or some other change in resource needs, the Resource Requirements section is designed to show this as well as the planned use of existing resources. The resource requirements of all of the functional plans should add together to a statement of total resources required to accomplish the strategic plan that is being presented.

The Resource Requirements section will largely be cast in financial terms, but it is useful also to include other statements of the demands on scarce resources. Many managements want tabulations of the numbers and levels of people required to staff each function, or the loading on a key item of equipment.

FINANCIAL ANALYSIS

From the resource requirements, which show a full statement of the costs of the business, and from the forecast, which projects its revenues, an income statement and balance sheet can be constructed. The Financial Analysis section presents and analyzes this income statement and balance sheet, in terms of rates of return, resource demands, and general soundness of the approach.

REALISM

A plan is of necessity built on assumptions. These assumptions should be chosen with care and presented as made. At the end of the planning process it is useful both to the group doing the planning and to those who must approve the results if the composite of those assumptions is reviewed. Given that the best assumptions have been made at every stage, this is a judgment as to whether the probabilities of a plan working out well are good or bad, due to the risk of events from outside of the plan interfering with its progress. The Realism section gives the next levels of management an appraisal from the planning group, particularly since others will raise these same uncertainties as issues. For control of the discussion process, it is best to identify and address known uncertainties openly, to show that they have been considered, and to present them from the perspective the planning group prefers to use.

ALTERNATIVES

Almost every strategy and almost every plan is based on the choice among alternatives. In establishing the credibility of a plan it is important to establish that other alternatives are known to exist and were in fact considered. The purpose of an Alternatives section is to catalog some of these briefly and to mention the reasons for their discard. Often a proposed course of action is strengthened by such a review, because the alternatives are so unpalatable.

RECOMMENDATIONS

The energy and exposure required in laying out a plan and circulating it to top management is a part of a program for accomplishment. The plan should be a means to obtaining top management endorsement of the action program. The Recommendations section summarizes briefly the specific actions that should be taken and requests their approval. If the plan has been well constructed, these recommendations, which were presented briefly in the Executive Summary, will have developed from the logic of the plan, and will stand out as good candidates for executive approval when the plan is reviewed.

The Strategic Plan. The preceding sections presented fifteen elements a strategic plan should include. These elements were presented in a natural order, and could become fifteen separate sections except that it might grow in length, where in most cases a short, well-conceived plan will fit the need better, and the savings are very great. A good, short plan is more likely to be read and used, and as such is better able to return the value on which a value-added planning process must be justified. The elements recited here can easily be combined in a number of ways, and should be combined where this aids in achieving a more effective presentation. But the discipline of carrying out planning effectively requires that the concept of each element be adequately included.

The planning process is a continuum, a flow process that cycles through its various articulations as decisions occur, sales are made, and new facts are gathered. As such, the planning is an essential component of the management operating system, and should be made to flow as simply and naturally as possible.

STRATEGIC MANAGEMENT AND VALUE-DRIVEN PLANNING

Management needs to look ahead—with a strategic overview, of course—and to plan for a reasonable number of years. The planning process is a means for the management group to share ideas and coordinate the necessary flow of action. A valuable staff role exists—the foresight function mentioned earlier, in addition to clerical assistance—but the primary strategic planning role should be carried by line management. This then becomes a strategic management effort focused on the selected goals, including appropriate measures of the values management action can create—strategic management and value-driven planning—to design strategies as discussed in earlier chapters and summarized in Figure 15-2, and turn them into effective action, as illustrated in Figure 15-3.

□   □   □

This chapter is the third and concluding chapter of Part Four: How to Design Strategies. Chapter 13 outlined a deceptively simple strategy design process, with elements of strategy, degrees of differentiation, sources of profit, and so on—"choose the right one from each box and create a winning strategy." The process appears simple; but the simplicity is deceptive because of the consistency required among the different choices, and the care with which some of the variables must be defined. In concept, strategy design would make a great video game. In practice, available information does not yet allow rigorous programming of such a game, or computer optimizing of the strategic choices, but nonetheless it is useful to have the strategy design components in a logically consistent array to use as a basis for judgment and for further refinements of the process.

Chapter 14 suggests that each new product, service, or business

FIGURE 15–2 STRATEGIC MANAGEMENT AND VALUE-DRIVEN PLANNING

The process of strategy design
- elements
- differentiation
- life cycle
- sources of profit

Competitive advantage and needs-leverages linkages

Matching product, business, and enterprise strategy

Strategy and the excellence model

Strategic planning and shareholder value

CREATING STRATEGY, ACTION, AND RESULTS

FIGURE 15–3 THE STRATEGY DESIGN PROCESS

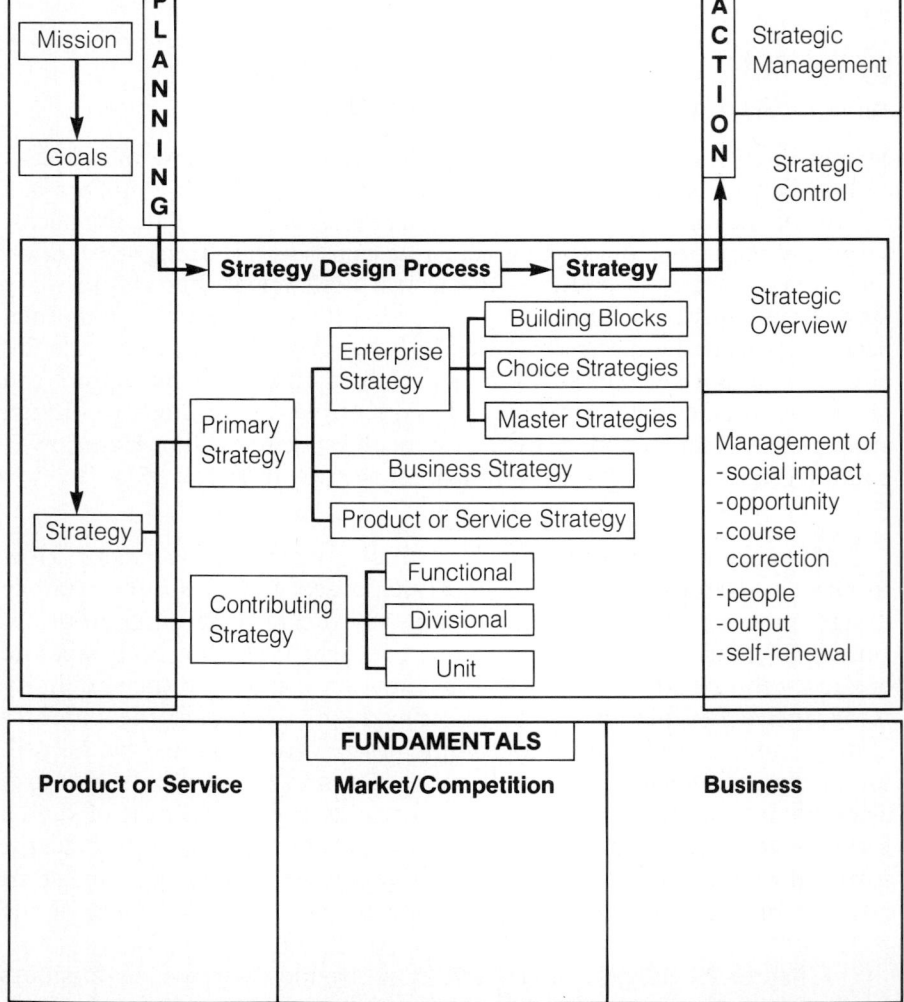

strategy be reconciled with the overall enterprise strategy framework of the firm. Because top management desires to operate in one way rather than in some other way eliminates some product, service, and business strategy choices and may either increase or reduce the chances of success of others. Top management runs the firm, of course, and its preferences should be respected; but enterprise strategy choices made casually and for other reasons sometimes limit product and business strategies in unanticipated ways that are harmful to the enterprise as a whole.

Chapter 15 brings in the firm's planning system—not part of the strategy but key to strategic management—because a strategy becomes action only as part of a plan that must be conceived and shared among the responsible managers and communicated to the others directly concerned. How formal or improvised this planning system is will depend on the leadership strategy and the corporate environment, but there must be a conception, sharing, and communication of plans or there will be no action. It becomes a part of the strategy design process, therefore, to ensure that the strategy is conceived in a way that links it into whatever planning system may be operating and confirms that the selected strategy will add value to the firm as a result of the strategic management action it requires.

QUESTIONS FOR ANALYSIS AND DISCUSSION

1. Find an example of a corporation that has improved its earnings per share by buying back stock and calculate the increase in shareholder value that resulted.
2. Find an example of a company whose parts were worth more than the whole and calculate the increase in shareholder value from breaking it up.

FOR FURTHER INFORMATION

Sawyer, George C., *Corporate Planning as a Creative Process* (Oxford, Ohio: Planning Executives Institute, 1983).
  Further information on the corporate planning process and its operation.

Steiner, George A., *Strategic Planning: What Every Manager Must Know* (New York: Free Press, 1979).
  A good overview of strategic planning from one of the senior figures in the field.

CASE 29 SEAWING INDUSTRIES

The division managers at Seawing Industries accused the corporate planning department of operating an alarm system. And in a way, they were right. At an earlier point in the development of the planning system the president had asked Planning to develop a routine for monitoring the progress of the plans; Planning wisely invited the financial area into partnership, and the two departments worked out a division of responsibilities that the president approved. Each time a business or department plan was approved, Planning and Finance examined the projected accomplishments to look for milestones or checkpoints to use as a basis for measurement as the operation went forward. If the financial results fell outside of those projected in the plan, Finance brought this to management attention in the same way it reported variances from the approved budgets, and the variance got management attention. If the nonfinancial measures got off of plan, the planning department brought this to management attention; this was the planning "alarm system." The president paid a good deal of attention to the planning "alarm notices" and often inquired to see what the problem might be.

Most of the planning alarms were reports on specific events, such as new products delivered early or late, as the case might be, or other specific actions forecast in the plans. Today's alarm was a report that a new air pollution monitor being developed at Seaside Research Center was behind schedule. The Research functional plan had predicted that a production prototype would be released to the Air Systems Division, which was funding the development. Air Systems was counting on the sales volume from the introduction to meet its financial projections, and the favorable reaction to the new concept of the monitor to help it win two large government contracts. The planning staff member assigned to the research plan had already gathered some background information for the alarm report, but Jane Wales, the director, wanted comments from a higher level. She called Dr. Peter Wells, head of Seaside Research Center: "Peter, we have to report routinely on plan progress, and we are about to send up a bulletin saying that the air monitor prototype is not on time. This will cause a fuss because Air Systems is counting on rushing it to market. Is there anything you would like us to say about the circumstances? Or would you like to commit to an alternate date?"

Peter Wells asked for time. He promised to call back in half an hour. Forty-five minutes later he called: "Jane, there's no good reason for the delay. We owe Air Systems an apology, and I am going to call the general manager as soon as you and I have finished. Air Systems will have the prototype in a week." Planning reported that the Research Division had committed to deliver the prototype within a week, and they did. Jane

Wales learned later that Peter Wells had fired a technician on the spot when he learned that the delivery was delayed because the technician had hidden the fact that he had lost the final test results on the prototype when there still had been plenty of time to do the testing over. Therefore the machine, which was actually ready, could not be delivered on time.

Another planning alarm was based on the reject rate in the Seattle lab. The production plan had projected that component output would rise and cost would come down rapidly, and they had. In fact, they had come down so fast that the plant was meeting its cost objectives in spite of 35 percent rejection of its finished products. Rejects had been a problem earlier, but when the last plan was prepared, the division had projected that its reject rate, which was averaging about 20 percent then, would fall to 5 percent at this checkpoint. Again Jane Wales called, this time for the plant manager. He was unsympathetic. "We are meeting really ambitious cost targets. When we get the rejects under control, the costs will be still better."

"And we will report it that way," Jane answered. "But the Japanese will probably soon be getting the same production rates that you are, and they usually get reject rates down faster than we do. The jump in reject rates could mean something fundamental has changed in the process—have you considered getting a consultant to look at your process and quality control system?"

The only other significant alarm on this week's list was generated because the water systems group had missed its introductory sales goals for the new water monitor. Routine sales fluctuations were covered in other reports, and planning picked up only the major steps in sales growth and market penetration. Jane Wales called the director of marketing: "Ray, the new water monitor sales didn't take off the way that the marketing plan predicted, and we are supposed to report that to the brass. Is there anything you would like us to add?"

The previous president had spent a lot of time working with corporate planning and the various members of the executive group to set up the plan monitoring system in the best way. The so-called planning alarms on product sales were supposed to be based on large enough deviations from plan to suggest that the marketing strategy was not working the way it was expected to—that it was significantly above or below plan, probably due to some change in the product or market. The alarm on the water monitor sales would cause the executive group to ask, "What is wrong with the water monitor marketing strategy?" and this is exactly what the president had intended.

The marketing manager knew this and had been expecting Jane's phone call. "Jane, this is a situation I am very upset about. I spent the last two weeks in the field with water monitor sales representatives. I spent a day making sales calls with each of ten representatives in nine states and had the field representatives from the region I was in brought together for an evening meeting eight of the nights I was out there. The water monitor is basically a good product, but we have a serious problem with it at present, and I will be recommending a change in strategy within a week.

"Don't put this in your bulletin, but we have not been telling the customers about the most important single advantage of the product, and a good Japanese product we have been ignoring is developing into the key competition. We are getting some good new sales aids, we have an additional sales training program starting this week, and I am going to recommend a major increase in promotion. By the time we get the new sales aids and everyone has spent three more evenings in sales training, the field force should be in good shape, and with the increased promotion I think you will see the product take off.

"The only question is why no one picked this up in the test marketing, and believe me, I am asking! I don't like to see us start behind on a new product, I don't like to have to spend two weeks troubleshooting because all the bases weren't covered by my subordinates, and I am looking for some answers."

QUESTIONS

1. What functional strategies do you see in the air monitor problem? Can you judge the effectiveness of the strategy?
2. What functional strategies do you see in the Seattle plant rejection rate problem? How much attention should such a rise in rejects receive?
3. What functional strategies do you see in the water monitor problem? Can you judge the effectiveness of the strategy?
4. Do you think that the planning department is playing a constructive role? Would any other group be able to do this better?

CASE 30 VALUE-DRIVEN PLANNING AT UNIFIED INDUSTRIES

Louis Wintern, the management consultant, had been talking with the CEO for two unscheduled hours now—two very intense hours—while the staff rescheduled the president's appointments and postponed meetings. Then the president's secretary interrupted with a call from the chairman, the CEO excused himself to take the call, and Louis had a few minutes to organize his ideas. After he had washed his hands and splashed cold water on this face, he started to list his thoughts:

- panic—that is why he called me in.
- the low price of his stock was the trigger.
- shareholder value is the issue.
- this place is a sitting duck for a raider.
- if a raid has already started, it's too late for value-driven planning to help.

Just then the CEO came back in, followed by a waiter with more coffee and pastries for both of them: "Good news, Louis. This was all a false alarm. The Black Flag Partnership is filing a notification with the Securities and Exchange Commission that it now holds 5.8 percent of the stock and intends to seek control of Uniford Industries. The corporate name is so similar to Unified Industries that it confused someone who called our informant with a warning that Unified Industries was the target.

"That means we are not being threatened actively. But both the Chairman and I are very upset by this experience, what you have been saying makes a lot of sense, and I want an active program to change things before some other pirate tries to move in on us."

"Great!" Louis was smiling for the first time in several hours. "But you have to know that it will take time to build a new image for your stock in the stock market. And a new image has to be based on a new substance; that means changing some things. I think we will have to work on this together to see what changes would help and how you feel about them."

"Can you have a specific proposal by tomorrow morning?"

"Yes."

"Can you be back with it by 8 A.M.?"

"Yes."

"When will you need more information from us?"

"I need only publicly available information until we agree on a plan of action tomorrow. I have the last annual report and 10K filing, but if I could get copies of the two previous reports, any newer SEC filings, and any summary of stock price movements that is easily available, it would save time in getting my thoughts together for tomorrow." The CEO made a quick phone call to get the necessary information sent up, and Louis went off to work on his proposal.

The next morning Louis started with what he called a backwards plan of action. "The first actions to improve your stock price should be planned last, to be sure they don't put the whole organization in a turmoil." This was his list:

1. A stock buy-back—with borrowed money or hidden assets—to raise the earnings per share of the stock.
2. Restructuring—if it makes any sense—because this makes a dramatic announcement; but let's talk about what it might mean in substance first.
3. A review of investment strategy to see how the placement of the firm's capital is contributing to shareholder value.
4. A review of corporate and business planning and how the enterprise strategies are affecting shareholder value.
5. A review of your takeover potential, starting with the legal structure of your corporation, any state laws that would help you, and any obvious changes to your bylaws and pattern for electing directors.

After a week of intense joint effort Louis, the planning director, and the controller were in the corporate board room with the CEO, the Chairman of the Board, and the Management Committee, talking about planning for shareholder value. Louis was on his feet, making a presentation: "Unified Industries has three base businesses contributing 80 percent of the revenue and 95 percent of the profits. The ten businesses representing the other 20 percent of sales and 5 percent of profits vary in attractiveness, but none of them seem to represent any important corporate thrust, and most of the recent strategic and investment moves have been to expand the three base businesses."

Louis wrote on a flip chart: "Do you really want to be a conglomerate?" He turned to the audience: "Without these ten little businesses you would have a higher return on assets, a higher profitability, and a completely different image to investors—after all, two of your base businesses are in the same field, and no company with businesses in only two fields is a conglomerate."

The group talked about this suggestion for a while, and after the initial impact of the idea had passed, a consensus began to develop that such a move might be possible. But then Louis stopped the discussion: "Wait until we have talked about some of your other options, and then you can make a better choice. Next I hope you won't mind if I challenge you on the strategy for your third-largest business."

Chapter 15 Strategic Management and Value-Driven Planning

"This is a commodity business in a growing market, you have a sound position, you are growing with the market, and profits are higher every year. But this is a capital-intensive business, and you are investing heavily, year after year. This is also a low-return business, with the lowest ROI of your major activities; and because of the way construction costs have been rising, this business' return on investment goes down further with every addition to capacity. One of your stock market price problems is that your corporate return on investment is lower than most conglomerates'. Any good financial analyst can study your annual reports and see that your cost of capital is higher than the return this one business is giving, that you are investing heavily, and that each new investment makes the return on investment lower.

"I don't know whether you would consider selling that business, but I think you could get a very good price because the replacement cost of its assets is so far above what you have paid, and some of the possible buyers might not have the same pressure to expand and maintain market share—if they needed the material for captive consumption, for example."

As the discussion flowed, Louis learned that the controller had complained at length about the folly of investing money that was returning less than the cost of capital, but had been beaten back with the need to keep market share in a commodity business. And there seemed nothing sacred about that business; divestment could be discussed without raising anyone's blood pressure. Louis took the next step: "Let's talk about two visions of your future and see whether either one can start you toward something you may want to do.

"After our short acquaintance I have an impression of a good group. I haven't seen any hints of the bad things and pockets of incompetence most investors seem to expect in a large corporation these days. Your earnings record and earnings growth have both been OK; there are not many better records around—but the stock market values your earnings below almost any other conglomerate, and conglomerates are already valued below the major industrial groups. Your company's valuation by the stock market is so far below what I estimate to be the value of your businesses sold separately that you would be a sitting duck for a raider—and so many bright young financial analysts are at their computers looking for situations like this that I don't know how you have been overlooked for so long.

"But if you were to sell your commodity business and your ten little businesses, suddenly you would be an important company in one industrial area. As soon as the stock market got accustomed to that and valued you with that group, I estimate that it would increase your share price about 50 percent. Or if you were to put the assets you freed into a stock buy-back, you would have an immediate and considerably greater impact on share price. To move the stock price, you need to announce an important program and follow with action the market can see—but these things do not have to be done all at once; you can take a reasonable length of time on divestitures, for instance, as long as investors believe you are pursuing them seriously.

"Take another scenario—if you sold all of these businesses, sales revenue would fall by about 40 percent. Maybe you don't like the idea of becoming a smaller company—so acquire a business or two, but in a closely related field—so that you not only become an important company in one industrial area, but an exciting, growing leader in that area.

"I haven't run across any reason why you need to be a conglomerate, and it's easier to set growth records in a more focused sort of company. For instance, you have some very good angles for getting synergism between businesses that are almost unrelated, and instead of nickels and dimes now, those would bring a tremendous payoff in a company where the businesses are strongly related.

"I'm not done with my list—I want to try to talk you into a stock buy-back for instance, and there are some other good ways to finance it—but first I'd like to find out how you feel about some of the choices for shifting the business base of your company."

After an hour of back-and-forth discussion the group began to move more and more strongly toward the idea of concentrating their energies in one business area. The CEO finally stated this as a consensus, and the group clearly agreed. When Louis asked if this meant that they were willing to talk about divesting the 40 percent of unrelated businesses, the group said yes. The CEO restated their agreement but reserved decision on the growth question: "I think we have come a long way in one day, to a clear agreement to strip down to the business area that really interests us most anyway. I'm intrigued by the acquisitions idea, as I think some of the others are, but this needs some thought. Besides, John (the Chairman of the Board) and I need to call some of the directors that are not here, to be sure no one has objections or ideas that need to be heard before we begin to make decisions. And first, Louis, I want to hear some of those ideas of yours about financing." On this note the meeting adjourned to a friendly and informal luncheon in the nearby executive dining room.

The next morning Louis was back for an appointment with the CEO to talk about the decisions that would be needed. After half an hour the CEO called in the controller and the planning director. Louis brought them up to date: "A good way to get the attention of the stock market is to announce an exciting restructuring plan. This could probably be ready rather soon, and the sooner orderly action can start, the sooner you begin to move out of the takeover target zone. I hate the term 'restructuring,' but it is the proper jargon just now, and it often includes five bases we should touch: (1) expense reduction, (2) a review of the pension plan, (3) a statement of the divestiture plan, with at least an indication of the timetable, (4) some borrowing, and (5) a stock buy-back. The total plan and its impact have to be substantial, or else we are wasting our time, but some of the individual elements could be cosmetic, to show that the bases have all been touched, if you don't want to do anything major there.

"For instance, expense reductions are an automatic part of any restructuring announcement, and if there is a lot of money to be saved, this is a good time to do it. The problem is, you can shake the place up to the point that all of the good young people quit. In this case if you are going to concentrate on one business area, you probably can reduce the corporate-level structure a lot, and this could save a lot of money. And if there are any other areas where you should slim down, they should be included. But I hope you can handle this in a way that gives your people a chance to move to other assignments—and doesn't get the whole organization upset.

"The pension plan is the favorite 'hidden-asset' target of raiders—and if you haven't already done this, you should look around to see if there are any other hidden assets, like real estate that is worth so much now that you should sell it and move. But your pension plan seems to be a fair and honest one you have funded fully and run well for many years. In that time a lot of people have come to work for you and then left again before they gained the right to take their pension benefits with them. Between the leftover benefits and some good investment decisions the fund has a lot of extra money. A preliminary look says you can take between one and three hundred million dollars out after properly covering your obligations to all present employees and retirees. You should figure out what that surplus really is and take it out, through open and proper changes in the retirement plans. Otherwise it is an idle asset some raider may use to get back part of the cost of acquiring you.

"The divestiture plan needs a little thought, because you will need to start to put it into effect as soon as you announce it. Do you know where you would like to start, with potential buyers on the horizon, or will you need to hire a big-name investment banker to shop your companies? And with leveraged buyouts as easy to finance as they are today—are there some of the ten small companies where the present management would like to buy the business? If this makes sense, it could lead to a quick sale at a fair price, and you could help with the arrangements without taking any financing risks.

"The borrowing part of the restructuring plan can be real or cosmetic. It should be in the plan because it is fashionable to use debt to increase earnings for shareholders, because it sometimes really does increase earnings, and because you might need the money, depending on what else you do. Your corporation has a strong balance sheet, a good cash and marketable securities position, and almost no long-term debt. What we should do is to firm up the rest of the program and then project interest expense burden and earnings per share for different levels of borrowing and stock buy-back—and you probably will find that you want to carry a good deal of debt. Meanwhile some current borrowings can let other elements of the program start.

"In particular you will want to start the stock buy-back and you have to pay for the stock. You will get cash from the pension fund, if you go that way, and from the divestitures; and when you get that cash, you can repay any borrowings you don't want—but also I think it makes sense for you to look at acquisitions in your new central business area, and that might take cash.

"And some place here the review of laws and corporate bylaws should be going on, to decide if you want to create takeover defenses. I would rather see a substantial program that defends you through creating values the stock market can recognize, but this takes a little time and I know you may want to build legal barriers."

Two weeks later a major restructuring plan was announced to the public two days after a thorough briefing of employees and managers throughout the company. By then the company had quietly acquired 5 percent of its outstanding shares based on a statement of intent that had been filed earlier and not acted on, and now it announced a plan to acquire 20 percent more, automatically raising its earnings per share by 33 percent less the increased interest cost. The plans for divestiture and shrinkage of staff were announced together with a letter of intent for the acquisition of one small subsidiary by another company, and the leveraged buyout of another by its management, both at prices that brought very favorable comments from Wall Street.

The pension fund restructuring yielded about $250 million in surplus cash. A week before this was announced a favorable sale of the commodity business to a European company became public knowledge, and a week afterwards the corporation announced its acquisition of a similar-sized business in the new central business area together with a high-profile "renaming the company" competition to see which employee could suggest the new corporate name most suited to its new industry position. The stock price slowly crept up to a price earnings multiple comparable to the rest of the industry grouping, and the financial press began to talk about this new industry leader. When the president learned that his company was the subject of a very favorable feature article in the Wall Street Journal, he was very pleased and asked his secretary to find Louis. Louis happened to be with the planning director just then; the president asked both of them to come up to his office.

They shared the president's pleasure with the recognition, of course. But when the president asked him, Louis said that only 75 percent of the job was done: "You are no longer a conglomerate taking a conglomerate discount on your stock price. Your company's earnings are valued at the same level as the rest of your new industry, but that is wrong because your performance is much better, and you are undervalued by the missing premium. Also, you have done so well that you don't have as much debt as you had planned—it's time to project earnings with different levels of increased debt and stock buy-back again, to see where you want to be.

"I don't think there is a company anywhere that can match your performance in shifting market valuation from a disastrously low level to where it is now. I don't know whether you are still undervalued enough to attract a raider; but I know the value can be raised, and that's one measure of management today—its ability to build value for the shareholders.

"Another important part is what the planning director and I were working on—looking for where you could change your planning and management system and decision criteria so that your managers will be looking at every decision, and especially at every investment in assets and organization, to be sure it adds value to the firm. The stock market price is a more remote measure, but if you take and hold a leadership position in your industry and every decision adds value to the firm, earnings will grow and the stock price will grow faster. Value is the key, value-driven planning carried into action."

QUESTIONS

1. Why should the stock market value conglomerates lower? Does this make sense? Discuss.
2. Why would it be necessary to bring a consultant in, to decide to change the things that were changed here? Discuss.
3. Do you think the world is better off for this restructuring of Unified Industries? Why or why not?

PART V

PRACTICING STRATEGIC MANAGEMENT

CHAPTER 16

POLICY MAKERS— AS TOP MANAGEMENT, AND AS PEOPLE

KEY IDEAS IN THIS CHAPTER

Chapter 16 tells something about the executive environment, and the types of people who work in it.

- **the strategy and policy environment** – making decisions and living with them, use of corporate staff.
- **executive backgrounds** – no formal requirements, but most are college educated, with many advanced degrees.
- **ethical standards** – better than they used to be; need to be better yet.
- **interaction with the public** – the CEO as chief public speaker.
- **global horizons** – the need to manage all around the world.
- **the role of the master builder** – chief executives that build major complexes of businesses.

- **the management of strategy and policy** – summary and integration.

THE STRATEGY AND POLICY ENVIRONMENT

In the flow from planning to strategy and action, the action step is the one that yields the results. The final key component, therefore, of the strategic management process is the step in which the correct action is taken, based on all of the previous steps. Part Five of the book deals with this strategic management, both in general terms, and in the specifics of the management process in a variety of different sorts of organizations. As a beginning, this chapter deals with the key managers themselves.

The management in an organization must be decision makers and action takers. In taking action they exercise their authority, and with authority comes responsibility and accountability for the results. The strategy and policy environment therefore is one in which the line decision makers quickly form the habit of making decisions and taking action for which they will be held accountable.

In many organizations these decision makers use staff groups to help them in gathering information on current operations, trends for the future, and so forth. Therefore the strategy and policy environment is often also peopled with financial and corporate planning staffs; legal, technical, and personnel staffs; and others. These staffs work with and may taste of the decision-making power of the line, but do not themselves have either decision authority or responsibility for outcomes. Their recommendations may or may not be followed, or may be followed imperfectly. They may escape blame for imperfect advice in one case, only to be improperly blamed for a line manager's mistake in another.

THE PEOPLE WHO WORK IN THIS ENVIRONMENT—THEIR BACKGROUNDS

Traditionally U.S. industry has favored promotion from within, and a past pattern was that many company presidents rose from the ranks, usually from the most important parts of the company.[1] This resulted in many

---

[1] W. P. Dommersmith, "On the Odds of Becoming a Company President," *Harvard Business Review*, 44 (May–June 1966), pp. 65–72.

chief executive officers with backgrounds in production or other technical fields. Then marketing executives began to be promoted more, and then managers from other functions. In Hayes and Abernathy's classic article: "Managing Our Way to Economic Decline,"[2] they deplored the later shift to using a much higher proportion of chief executives with law and financial backgrounds. Probably there has now been a reversal, as manufacturing has somewhat regained its importance in international competitiveness. *Engineering Times*[3] recently reported that 44 percent of newly appointed CEOs had technical backgrounds, including many with degrees in engineering.

There are no specific educational requirements for a chief executive or other top management position, except those necessary for a career leading to the top level of a firm. Henry Ford had no college education, the same was true of many other early business leaders, and important CEOs without college backgrounds can still be found today. But college education is now accepted as a more rapid way to make progress, and the proportion of CEOs with college degrees and with advanced degrees has risen steadily from survey to survey. The Harvard Business Review's survey of executive mobility reports that in its sample of highly mobile chief executives none were without a college education, 25 percent had bachelor's degrees, 29 percent had MBAs, 19 percent had a master's degree other than MBA, and 25 percent had doctoral degrees.[4] These were high-profile people who changed companies to begin their current jobs in 1987; they had more education than the lower-level top management executives in the same survey, and probably much more than the average CEO, but the data served to illustrate the point that many of the high-income, high-profile CEOs are very well educated.

What kind of managers does U.S. industry want? Top managers will have trained as lower managers, often in the same company. In a major study Luthans, Hodgetts, and Rosenkranz[5] found a significant difference between how successful managers were—meaning how fast they got promoted—and how effective they were as managers—meaning how well their units performed. The successful managers emphasized networking-type contacts throughout the organization and more routine communica-

---

[2] Robert Hayes and William Abernathy, "Managing Our Way to Economic Decline," *Harvard Business Review*, July–August 1980, pp. 67–77.

[3] Alan Chapple, "Engineers as CEOs: Those on Top Show the Field Begets Managers," *Engineering Times*, Vol. 10, No. 6, June 1988, p. 1.

[4] "Worldwide Executive Mobility," *Harvard Business Review*, July–August 1988, pp. 105–123.

[5] Fred Luthans, Richard M. Hodgetts, and Stuart A. Rosenkranz, *Real Managers* (Cambridge, Mass., Ballinger, 1988).

tion with others, but gave less time to human resource activity and routine communication with their subordinates. The effective managers, based on the superior performance of their units, spent much more time on human resource activities and routine communication with their subordinates, much less time on networking outside their units, and got promoted less rapidly. From the standpoint of overall performance it would seem that the wrong managers were being promoted. If the wrong managers were being promoted as the study suggests, how does this relate to the current problems and restructuring across U.S. industry? Clearly it suggests that the effectiveness of the whole organizational system for selecting managers must be raised if the caliber of management is to be raised as a part of the effort to make U.S. firms competitive.

ETHICAL STANDARDS

An important dimension in profiling top management is some estimate of the ethical standards to which they and their organizations work. For example, the Department of Defense is a recurrent source of bidding, overcharging, and pricing scandals involving various government officials and business executives. DOD spokespeople remind us that, because of the very large scale of the procurement effort, some incidents of this sort are inevitable, as probably they are. But the issue in this discussion is the ethical standards to which business leaders work, and the problems at DOD serve to remind us that there are low as well as high standards of business ethics in everyday practice. While it is difficult to generalize to executive behavior as a whole, a few tentative conclusions are possible.

In the first place, and while there are many examples of bad ethical behavior, there is good evidence that the general tendency over time is for the ethical standards of business conduct to rise. During the so-called robber baron era of business misbehavior around the beginning of this century it was regrettably routine for large corporations to pay individual legislators to vote for bills in many state legislatures; newspaper reporters and anyone else who really cared could find out what the going price was for a vote in a particular state legislature. The public finally got upset and such flagrant misbehavior is no longer tolerated. Other abuses continue, but the general trend through better laws, better enforcement, and a more alert public is to narrow the remaining areas of abuse a little more each year.

In the second place, large business and international business have an increasing stake in high standards of ethical conduct; this is being recognized, and the business community is more and more establishing such standards for continuing business relationships. Large firms need high performance standards as well as good internal controls to prevent misuse of funds; these controls do not work as well if unethical schemes are being handled through the same payment procedures, and the simplest pattern is to do everything by the book—especially in dealings across borders and legal jurisdictions. Many dealings must depend on telephone and other verbal or electronic notification; the whole business process would be very badly hampered if good ethics and good faith were not the general rule, and the pressure for this sort of behavior grows greater every year as international trade expands. There are always individuals who take any opportunity for personal advantage, regardless of ethical issues, but the pressure from the business community against such behavior and for stricter law enforcement tends to rise steadily with time.

Finally, society is focusing increasing attention on its leaders, including all significant executives, and we expect and demand higher standards of behavior and personal ethics from our leaders than from ourselves or our neighbors. Thus, although the general social trend of focusing attention on business leaders has many anti-business aspects, it is also a force for a higher standard of ethical behavior. The conclusion is that current business ethical standards are better than ever before, that they still need to be improved in many areas, and that a number of current forces are aiding in this slow process. The best way to make profits is to run an ethical business.[6]

Some executives and some firms do not always behave ethically, and a part of wise behavior is always to use a bit of the same skepticism and caution as one would use if asked to buy large diamond rings or thousand-dollar watches from a street vendor. More difficult is the problem some firms have in dealing with cultures that have different ethical standards, as in countries where gratuities that are considered routine and proper would be classified as bribes in the United States. But having more than one ethical standard under the same management control system makes any standard difficult to enforce, and more than one company has ruled out customary payoffs and gratuities in a particular country because management did not want such things handled within its procedures at all.

A serious personal problem arises when a manager or other professional finds that he or she is being asked to behave unethically; for instance, in any one of several cases where engineers and technicians have been ordered to report incorrect test data on a drug or aircraft brake, etc. It is very difficult for any individual to deal with such a situation. "Whistleblowing," or reporting the situation outside the company, is morally attractive but often makes great difficulty for the responsible employee even where there is legal protection against corporate reprisals. The simplest advice is never to stay in a situation in which you cannot join wholeheartedly. The reluctant participant is just as guilty as any other if a legal issue arises—and by getting out one can stay clean—but getting out

---

[6] Kenneth Blanchard & Norman Vincent Peale, *The Power of Ethical Management* (New York, Morrow, 1988).

can be difficult advice for an employee with concerns about career and dependents.

INTERACTION WITH THE PUBLIC

Top management positions have become less sheltered from public view and public questions than in the past. With the rise of consumer activism, formation of environmental and other activist groups, and regulation through Occupational Safety and Health Act (OSHA) work place requirements and Equal Employment Opportunity (EEO) requirements for equal treatment of women and minorities in all positions and at all job levels, any manager at any level in the organization may find that his or her position and decisions are a part of a current public or legal issue requiring testimony or interviews that put that manager in full public view. Consequently, the training and qualification of managers for representing the enterprise to the public is getting more attention now, and most managements consider the ability of a manager as a potential public representative as at least a minor consideration in any significant executive position.

GLOBAL HORIZONS

Business is becoming more international, not only because of wider personal horizons and travel patterns, but because markets are becoming more global. Japanese companies competing for the U.S. market invite U.S. competition on their home ground also, and in every other country whose market is important to them, and more companies are analyzing their markets and planning their international business strategy to be able to compete in this way.

For the managers this means a trend toward a need for a more global point of view, and many organizations and managers have already begun to acquire it. More top managers now have had at least some experience in other countries, and more managers will be hired with the expectation that circumstances might take them to another geographic area as a part of the assignment.

THE ROLE OF THE MASTER BUILDER

Members of top management vary widely in the dimension and scope of their impact on their firms and the business world. Roger Blough, a well-qualified operating executive, was president of U.S. Steel for many years—but he is remembered principally for unintentionally provoking an ill-advised confrontation with President John Kennedy by the manner and timing of a steel price increase. Boone Pickens, a capable oil executive, is likely to be remembered primarily for his ingenuity in devising new strategies for taking control of other oil companies. More profound and long-lasting is the impact of a man such as Henry Ford, who changed the automobile market and the country in the course of learning how to build the Model T and, eventually, the Ford Motor Company.

There have been many master builders, such as the first Henry Ford, who have distinguished themselves by turning an important vision into reality. Alfred Sloan is remembered for designing an automobile strategy better than Henry Ford's and for building the General Motors organization necessary to operate that strategy. Theodore Vaill led the group that gave the United States the best telephone service in the world and built AT&T into the largest private corporation the world had ever seen. Andrew Carnegie contributed significantly to the development of the railroad system and U.S. industry by learning to produce steel at lower cost than ever before and forcing his competitors to meet the same standards.

The importance is not the list, which could be lengthened, but the concept that some top managers, including a number active in management today, have had a profound impact on the country because they were able to lead their companies into major new areas or to force the development of new systems, as General Sarnoff decided to bring color television to the United States, and used the resources of RCA to carry the color system over the difficult start-up years. The important idea is of a business leader, or a group of business leaders collectively, performing this master builder role that has contributed so much to national progress.

THE MANAGEMENT OF STRATEGY AND POLICY

Managing strategy and policy at a responsible level is a demanding assignment from which many managers draw deep personal satisfaction. It requires people able to be decisive and to live with the consequences of a decision. And today's business environment is requiring a more versatile and more international type of manager, with a more rounded training and better able to represent the company to the outside world in addition to performing his or her assigned functions.

More and more a managerial career is demanding some business education as a prerequisite, although in the recent period of recession and organizational reverses many organizations were freshly reminded that a business education is only preparation for management, and that hands-on training in the management process is still necessary in addition to lectures and coursework.

FIGURE 16–1	POLICY MAKERS AS KEY ACTORS IN THE STRATEGIC MANAGEMENT PROCESS

Living in the strategy and policy environment
What kinds of people are these?
    Attitudes
    Ethics
    Careers
Global management horizons
The role of the master builder
    Who are they?
    What is their impact?

LEADING BUSINESS AND INDUSTRY INTO THE FUTURE

Thus the nature and selection of the people that make up top management are critical components of the strategic management process, as summarized in Figure 16-1.

QUESTIONS FOR ANALYSIS AND DISCUSSION

1. From the top managers you know about, does a top management position look like an easy life or a hard one? Why?
2. List some of the currently active top managers and pick out those who have had a measurable impact on the country or the business system. Whom have you picked and why?
3. What are the standards of conduct that top managers live by? It has been said that we expect higher standards of conduct from business leaders than we set for ourselves. Do you agree?

FOR FURTHER INFORMATION

Auletta, Ken, *The Art of Corporate Success: The Story of Schlumberger* (New York: Putnam, 1948).
    A good account of the accomplishments and managerial style of Jean Riboud, who built Schlumberger to its preeminence.

Heilbroner, Richard, (Ed.), *In the Name of Profit* (Garden City, N.Y.: Doubleday, 1972).

Corporate misconduct by major U.S. firms—names and dates—whistle-blowers punished and culprits rewarded.

Luthans, Fred, Richard M. Hodgetts, and Stuart A. Rosenkranz, *Real Managers* (Cambridge, Mass., Ballinger, 1988).

Do U.S. corporations promote the best politicians instead of the best managers? Here is the data.

Pascale, Richard Tanner, & Anthony G. Athos, *The Art of Japanese Management* (New York: Warner Books, 1981).

A good contrast between the management styles and accomplishments of Harold Geneen, who built the modern ITT, and Konosuke Matsushita, who built Matsushita, both then ranked among the world's fifty largest industrial companies.

CASE 31 FIREFLY COMPUTERS

After he finished high school, Romer Gomez worked in a variety store for two years, until a distributor of business products offered him a better job and he began to learn about business and management. Then one evening he saw one of the first microcomputers and was fascinated. A few days later he bought a used computer and began to teach himself to program in BASIC. He began to take evening classes, first in FORTRAN, then in COBOL. He had joined a local computer club, and began to buy programming manuals—for Pascal, for LISP, and for a variety of more or less exotic computer languages. In each case he learned enough to understand the principles of the language, and then went on. He continued to work for the business products distributor and did well; but almost every waking hour outside of work was absorbed by his growing fascination with computers and their applications.

While negotiating for a better price on a new microcomputer, he got acquainted with the manager of the local computer store, who was so impressed by Romer's detailed knowledge of small computers, programming, and software, that he made a very good job offer. At first Romer was very happy working in the computer store. Then he realized that this was the first time that he had not been free to do whatever he wanted to with a computer; here he had to follow store rules, and to spend most of his time helping customers select equipment or solve application problems. At night, when he finally was free to do whatever he wanted, it was almost an anticlimax because he had already been working with the same machines all day.

Romer never had thought about career goals. College had not appealed to him. After high school he had taken the first decent job he could find, and followed the line of least resistance ever since. But although he still did not know what he wanted to do, he decided he did not want to spend his life as a microcomputer sales representative; with the business products distributor he had been a junior manager, and liked managing very much. Then he met his old boss on the street, discovered he was badly missed, went back to his old job at the business products distribution company with a substantial raise, and computers became just a hobby again.

As personal computers with larger memories became available, Romer helped the bookkeeping department set up inventory control and accounting records; that got him another raise, because it made his boss' firm more efficient and more competitive. This was pioneering work, but by the time Romer thought about trying to turn his work into a software product, several other people had marketed similar programs. They all did about the same thing, but Romer saw that some of the others were easier to use than the one he had written.

Romer continued to try to define his own goals. He did not feel he should spend such a large fraction of his energy on his computer hobby without relating it to something potentially useful or profitable. The more he thought about it, the more he realized how much he had enjoyed making the personal computer do something for the business products business that had not been done before. Not even the fact that other people had marketed the program before he thought of selling his took away the fact that he had done something that had not been done before— he might even have been the first. He began to dream about making computers do other things, and to collect ideas on interesting programs and applications. He spent a day at a microcomputer fair, and asked so many questions that some of the people who were trying to promote new software products lost patience with him completely.

Romer found that he did not know enough about most businesses to devise business applications for a microcomputer, more than the simple ones already accomplished, and very many people were doing that already and succeeding. An equal number were trying to make microcomputers useful and practical in the home, but they were making much less progress. There were an amazing number of products for home computers, but only the computer games and the programs a small business could use seemed ever to sell well. And he read that sales of the smallest personal computers had fallen off badly, for lack of demand by individual families. What could a home computer be made to do? The question became almost an obsession; he once told a friend that sometimes when he closed his eyes he could see microcomputers buzzing around like fireflies, looking for a home. His friend teased him afterwards about the fireflies, and when Romer started his own company, he called it FireFly Computers.

Romer had the name, and had decided he wanted to start a company, but he needed a product. This would be a true home computer. It would be called the FireFly I. He began to define what he wanted the FireFly I to be able to do, and for every capability he wanted, he began to outline the necessary programs. He knew he needed help with some of the programming, and he did not know how to start a company. But the starting point had to be something to sell, and he hoped that if he got the work of the machine well enough in mind, then he could somehow figure out what capacities it needed, so it could be designed. Romer daydreamed and also wrote programs, struggling to define what the FireFly I should be.

To be competitive the FireFly I should have capability for games, color graphics, and word processing, and be able to run the programs with the largest popular following. For utility it needed to be compatible with the widest possible range of other personal computers. But the FireFly I was really going to be designed to do new things easily. In the first place, you could talk to it—to a limited extent, but it would accept verbal commands like "yes," "no," "stop," "wait," and so forth. This allowed a variety of routine programs to be run more easily by a person also doing other

Chapter 16   Policy Makers—As Top Management, and as People   387

things around the house. The computer would come to a stopping point in the program, and sit until the operator came by, looked at the screen, and said "print" or "run." This was a convenience, and practical for the few key words he selected.

And there were a family of expert systems the FireFly I would run; actually the basic programs were essentially the same except for the memory storage, but as the expert system built experience, the results were impressive. The personal weather forecasting system, for example, always asked a standard series of questions, starting with "what was the weather like after the last forecast you requested?"; "what is the forecast now?"; "what is the temperature?"; "what is the weather like now?" and in each case the screen would segment into a large group of choices—the user would touch the appropriate choice, and the computer would go on. With the power of the expert system the memory built a pattern from past requests from the same person, and the results were uncanny; given a minimum of data and the personal biases of the user, the computer could "confirm" or "reject" the official forecast with surprising accuracy.

After six months, when Romer began to have an idea what he wanted the FireFly I to be able to do, he attempted to estimate the hardware capabilities required. He did not do well at this at all, but he met a young engineer who knew a great deal about such things, and the FireFly I began to take shape for the first time. The two of them found a sympathetic ear, and a venture capitalist who had made a great deal of money helping the start-up of other computer companies began to guide the evolution of FireFly Computers. Under his prodding the definition of the product proceeded rapidly, for in many respects it could be a clone of other widely sold personal computers. This helped with the compatibility objectives; except for one or two special chips widening the capabilities, the components could be obtained in quantity from firms already in microcomputer production, and the only question was whether FireFly should do its own assembly or subcontract the entire package.

Romer's programming had some limitations, but he had made two innovations in program structure that radically reduced the memory requirements; in fact, without these, the FireFly I would have been far too expensive for its target market. When he was pressed to do a business plan for his new company, Romer tried to visualize everything that had to be done before the FireFly I could be marketed, and he put in a good deal of money for programming, to double-check his own work.

The venture capitalist had proposed that FireFly Computers raise seed money for office and travel expenses, and to begin work on a prototype of the FireFly I. To raise this seed capital, and after necessary clearance of the prospectus, the associates of the venture capitalist went to investors they knew and suggested that these people lend FireFly Computer money for its initial operations; the understanding was that these loans would be repaid out of the proceeds from the first sale of stock to the public, and each of these early investors also obtained a share in the equity of the company at a very nominal cost.

With the seed money in hand, the company was formally organized. Romer quit his job and, as president of FireFly Computers, he began to work to get the first demonstration model of the FireFly I completed. This work went well, a preliminary demonstration for the venture capitalist and the others who now formed the Board of Directors looked hopeful, and work started on the first public offering of stock in FireFly Computers. It was anticipated that Romer would keep 25 percent of the stock, since he had started the company; 5 percent had been committed to those who had provided the seed financing; 5 percent would be divided among those who had joined the Board of Directors, plus 5 percent for the venture capitalist; and 10 percent would be reserved for stock options for the initial officers and key employees. Thus, 50 percent of the stock was allocated in one way or another. The initial public offering was planned as the sale of 20 percent of the stock, leaving another 30 percent in the corporate treasury; new companies often need additional financing, and the venture capitalist visualized a second sale of 15 percent of the stock at a much higher price (because of the progress that would have been made by then), with another 15 percent for a third offering if it should be needed.

The FireFly Computer business plan had to be converted into a formal prospectus describing the securities to be sold, and this prospectus required approval by the Securities & Exchange Commisson. The venture capitalist's office staff had prepared many similar documents, but Romer was awed by the way that the FireFly plan turned into a neatly printed 150-page prospectus full of legal language and warnings to the investors. Then there was a wait for comments and approval; more information had to be added about the risks and uncertainties for one more company entering the personal computer market at this time, and then one day Romer got a call that the prospectus was approved and the offering could be scheduled.

Romer did not know what to say, because he had just had a very bad afternoon with the FireFly I prototype. The personal weather forecasting program had been giving some trouble, which was no great concern because Romer had said from the beginning that he wanted a more experienced programmer to polish his work. But today he and the programmer had been deep inside the coding, at the interface between the expert system and the normal operating system in which the governing program was written; the expert programmer had found the basic flaw that was giving the trouble. But the expert had concluded that the problem could not be solved, and that neither the weather program nor any other of the expert system applications could ever work. He called Romer a hopeless amateur who was wasting everybody's time and left in a flurry of bad language. At that moment the venture capitalist called with his good news about the prospectus.

After Romer explained the problem, the venture capitalist called the

Chapter 16 Policy Makers—As Top Management, and as People   389

programmer, who said he had heard that Romer used to be a ribbon clerk and should go back to a job he could handle. He advised immediate abandonment of the FireFly Computer Company. The venture capitalist was upset and called an emergency directors' meeting for that evening. By then several of the other directors had also talked to the expert programmer, and the meeting was not a pleasant one. Romer told the directors that he had demonstrated several successful programming innovations in the design of the FireFly I, which they knew, that they did have a real problem, and that every one should get off of his back so that he could find out how to solve the problem. The venture capitalist proposed that the meeting be recessed for two weeks, and the board eventually approved the motion, although two directors resigned in protest.

Romer had two programmers on his small staff; the three of them started a marathon analysis of the problem. Every time one of them had an idea, it was tried immediately. Every time one of them thought of a person who might be able to help, someone picked up the phone to call that person. One lead was promising enough so that an outsider, after signing the necessary confidential disclosure forms, spent half a day with them, but was no help in the end. A week of day-and-night work went by, and then the second week. At four in the morning the day before the day the board meeting was to resume, the three of them were arguing furiously over a different approach to the interfacing of the two programs. Suddenly the solution to the flaw they were battling fell out of the discussion. It wasn't exactly what they were talking about, and none of the three of them knew afterward exactly where the idea had come from, but by noon they had a first test confirming its soundness.

Then they went back to the programs for the FireFly I prototype, but by five o'clock work came almost to a stop; they had worked straight through the night before and were too tired to go on. Romer suggested they eat, sleep, and start again at midnight, which they did. The program revisions took all night, as expected, and by eight o'clock they were running and debugging. The bugs were not serious, and by ten o'clock, the time of the meeting, the FireFly I was ready for a full-dress demonstration. Romer took his two assistants, the FireFly I performed beautifully, the board gave Romer a vote of confidence, and he went home and slept while the venture capitalist went ahead with arrangements for the public offering.

Skeptics had questioned whether anyone could get investor support for a new personal computer company at this time, but the FireFly I was different and caught people's imagination. The offering was immediately oversubscribed, which meant that most people did not get to buy as much stock as they had wanted, and continued investor interest kept FireFly Computer stock at a healthy premium over the offering price. The venture capitalist was very happy, and called for an aggressive effort to get the FireFly I into production.

The engineer who had helped work out the cost of the FireFly had been hired to oversee production, and Romer urged him on. With the help of the venture capitalist they had found another promising young person to direct the marketing; Romer started him to work on distribution and marketing plans. In addition to general oversight of what the others were doing, Romer continued to direct the programming effort, to get skilled programmers to review and polish the programs, and to make a serious effort at testing and debugging versus the widest range of operating conditions they could visualize. Romer also asked his marketing director to organize a users council of people who would be willing to work with and evaluate the FireFly I at the earliest point that machines became available. In addition Romer had another effort under way, to get the necessary adaptations negotiated or written, so that the buyer of a FireFly I computer would in fact be able to run most of the popular software programs written for other machines. The venture capitalist, who was also chairman of the board of directors, kept a general oversight of the whole effort, watching for the sorts of omissions and errors that had plagued other new companies he had worked with. Altogether the effort was an effective one, and after six months it appeared that the FireFly I would be brought to market on schedule and at a lower cost than the production budget had allowed.

Production was largely being handled by others, and while the FireFly production director was not that experienced, he had a good sense of what to do and when to ask questions, and had found two or three experienced engineers he could talk to. The only critical problem was in the synchronized delivery of components from different vendors, and since FireFly was largely using standard components and the component suppliers were just a little hungry, the delivery problems stayed under control except for the special chips, of which there were two. One was integral to the FireFly I, to give it some of its special extra capabilities, and the other was a plug-in extra accessory Romer planned to sell at cost; he would have preferred to include it in the standard package, but the list price had to be kept too low to allow this; by spending a few dollars extra the user could have the ability to run whole families of additional programs. Both special chips had been carefully negotiated custom orders, with penalty clauses and delivery protection, and the second chip came in on schedule. The first was much more critical to the program, of course.

Romer and the venture capitalist met with the production director to review the problems with this one chip, and to consider their alternatives. The vendor was badly off schedule. Worse yet, the cause of the delay seemed to be serious quality problems with the entire product line. All three of them could see FireFly losing six months or a year and then having to struggle with a marginal product, and this was not acceptable. Alternatives included starting over again with another vendor, and this had been explored, but it would not avoid a major delay. The venture capitalist asked if there were any other chips that could be substituted. The production director said that this was impossible, but Romer corrected him: "Impossible unless we can find one with the correct functions and then rewrite all of our programs to fit it." They talked a little more, and then Romer sent the production director off to survey for available chips similar in function, to see if there was anything close enough to what FireFly needed.

Surprisingly enough, a sufficiently similar chip was in production, deliveries were good enough to meet the original schedule, and costs well below the custom chip price. "But you realize," Romer said, "that we will use up the savings on a lot of units with the cost of changing all of our programs, and we will create a whole new roster of bugs we will have to find and fix before these programs go to market." They talked some more, but the governing consideration was the lack of any real choice. While it is not necessarily fatal for a new company to fall six months or a year behind its initial marketing schedule, it really hurts, and many such laggard companies find that the market has changed or the new features of their product have been bypassed, by the time that they get something to sell.

The decision was "full speed ahead" with the new chip. Romer hired more programmers, and the entire crew started a full-speed, round-the-clock effort to revise all of the FireFly I programming to accommodate the new chip, still with a separate debugging effort and the same major effort to get sound, serviceable versions of all programs before the target dates. The work pace never slackened, for Romer had broken the task into components, each with a schedule, and the group drove to keep the schedule flowing smoothly. Not all of the program revisions were routine, and several different times the group found itself in entirely new territory where one of Romer's innovations had to be readapted. Weeks went by and Romer lost weight, but the schedule held. Elsewhere the FireFly program was going well. The marketing director found it rather easy to rouse enthusiasm for the FireFly I, which was intriguingly different, priced at an appealing level, and coming from what appeared to be a well-organized effort.

The weekend before the Monday which was the official marketing date Romer collapsed. The doctor said it was exhaustion plus a mild heart attack. But Romer had the programming effort well enough organized so that it finished smoothly and the product was launched on schedule, with Romer allowed to sit in the background at the press conference in a wheel chair. The FireFly I was well received by the market; soon the financial press realized that a new success story was unfolding, and the FireFly began to appear in numerous feature articles. Not only was it unusual for a new product from a new company to appear on schedule and fulfill all of its claims, but the wide variety of available programs enhanced the appeal, and it soon became apparent that the FireFly software was unusually clean and free of troubles. As the feature writers reconstructed the FireFly story, they learned about some of the problems and tribulations. One writer called it "Determination Computers" in tribute to Romer's round-the-clock efforts.

Romer made sure that the people who had helped him were well treated, in salary, with stock options, and in position. He negotiated with the venture capitalist to trade jobs—"You be president, before I kill myself"—and began to study how FireFly could run without a great deal of his direct involvement. By the end of the second year he had withdrawn almost completely from routine operations; he said he wanted computers to be more like a hobby again, but this time he had a hand-picked development group to help him, and the hobby he was pursuing was his dream of new capabilities and accomplishments with the FireFly II.

QUESTIONS

1. To what extent does the success of a small new company depend on one or two people? Is this good or bad?
2. How can the sort of hard-driving people who start companies successfully avoid damage to their health when the pressure rises, as it did at FireFly?

CASE 32 THE MASTER BUILDER

When he sold his controlling interest in Frange International through a secondary offering to the public, the financial press estimated that Roderick Frange had received $430 million in cash after expenses, at least $330 million of which would have been profit. Reliable witnesses reported that a specialist in leveraged buyouts had offered $100 million more, to which Frange had replied: "No, I've got my capital back and a fair profit. I don't want to be greedy, and I'd rather leave it as a public company." The reporters wanted Frange to comment, but he had taken a two-week vacation "between companies" and no one knew where he was.

Monday morning of the third week Roderick Frange, his secretary, and two staff assistants assembled in a small suburban office not far from Frange's home and talked about next steps. They all had worked with him for years, and could guess the pattern of events. In the case of Frange International it had started with the acquisition of the struggling Acme Pinball Company almost four years earlier, followed by a series of acquisitions and investments, until Frange International stood on its own today as a modern, well-managed and competitive machinery manufacturer. The next step after Frange International had been discussed in a preliminary way during the weeks that the Frange International stock offering was in preparation, and Frange had begun to ask his staff for ideas about areas of opportunity for the future.

Frange also read widely, and had recently reviewed the opportunity-search recommendations from SRI International, Arthur D. Little, and one or two other major industrial consultants. He wanted to stay out of competition with Frange International, and this ruled out many types of machinery manufacture. He liked to deal with different sorts of businesses, and he liked to put together strong and competitive firms as a result of his efforts. He spent the morning of their Monday meeting in review of the data they had all gathered, contrasting the two or three areas that had come to the top during their discussion. In the afternoon, when Frange announced that they would go into the seed business next, he stated a consensus that all of them believed in. They each felt they had helped convince him of a wise choice, and yet it was very much his decision.

For the seed business they needed an action plan. From the assembled information it was clear that it should be primarily a U.S. business until it became well established, since the U.S. market for purchased (rather than saved) seeds was the largest and best organized. The questions were what the major segments of the market were, who the competitors in each might be, where the competitive advantage came from in each segment, and where Frange might have a good entry point. Parts of this information were already available, and the tasks in gathering the rest were quickly assigned. Roderick Frange started on a few days of travel, first to Washington to meet the key people in the Department of Agriculture interested in the seed business, to meet the heads of trade associations, and to stop at two or three agricultural experiment stations that were not too far off of his travel route.

Friday morning a quick review with his staff convinced him that two market areas where he wanted a position were the retail markets for packaged vegetable and flower seeds, and the major hybrid corn market. He needed much more background information on the hybrid corn market, but the universe of sound packaged seed companies large enough to provide a reasonable base was not large, and several were already divisions of major firms. He got on the phone and worked out the next week's agenda, making an appointment with the president or general manager of a significant packaged seed company every day the next week. Assuming that a tour, lunch or dinner, and a friendly discussion would take half a day, he could also visit an equal number of experiment stations or trade journals, depending on the geography, and still travel to the next appointment overnight.

At each company he used the same general approach, of an investor wishing to enter the seed business starting with the packaged seed segment they were in; then he asked the president he was visiting for an opinion as to how attractive the business area might be, and for suggestions as to how he might best gain entry. In three out of the five cases he learned that the company he was visiting probably could be acquired. In all cases he learned about the business area, saw and talked with key people, and filled his briefcase with product literature. The trade journal editors were also very helpful, because it is their business to trade information, and because they could visualize the amount of advertising Roderick Frange would buy, if he invested seriously in the seed business. And every experiment station visit was more worthwhile than the last, because Frange was learning more and more and could ask better questions.

Saturday was a full day with the staff back at the office. Further information on the packaged seed companies did not show any worthwhile companies he had not visited, with the possible exception of a division of a conglomerate Frange did not wish to deal with. "So," he said, "decision time is upon us." Two of the three companies that had indicated possible availability appealed to him, but he saw real problems that warned him away from the third. Neither of the two companies that had not indicated availability seemed worth struggling for. Frange decided to see what could be worked out with one or the other of the two promising companies. By noon his secretary had reached the presidents of both, and Frange had follow-up appointments set early the following week. He had talked with the law firm he used, which had three young attorneys who liked to travel with him when needed; he arranged for one of them to go on the follow-up visits, on the basis that it is always better to have an observer in a ne-

Chapter 16 Policy Makers—As Top Management, and as People

gotiation, and to get the legal work started immediately if things began to move toward agreement.

Saturday afternoon the staff spent reviewing the hybrid corn companies, and then talking about sorghum, hybrid wheat, and other aspects of the seed business. The hybrid corn business depended on key research and marketing elements, and Frange decided that the best approach was to get the two parts separately. He did not want to spend the large amount of capital necessary to buy the market position of one of the hybrid corn leaders—that probably were not available on a friendly basis anyway—and he did not see the real need, long-term, for such an expensive acquisition. He and the staff sorted out the smaller hybrid corn marketers who might give a credible entry, and he began to call on their presidents the following week. But he felt entitled to take Sunday off, and his first Monday appointment was close enough to be reached on an 8 A.M. Monday plane.

At the end of six weeks the staff looked tired, and Frange was enjoying himself thoroughly. He had a definitive agreement, subject to audits, to acquire a packaged seed company and a hybrid corn company. In both cases the acquisition, at a generous dollar figure, was to be for a combination of stock in a new company, Frange Seeds, and cash. In both cases the selling owners felt that they were getting stock worth about the value of the company that they were selling, plus another 50 percent in cash. The cash Frange raised by selling stock in Frange Seeds to a group of investors who had made money backing his activities in the past. One third of this pool he put up himself, so that he was a substantial investor but held far from a controlling interest.

In another six weeks Frange Seeds had agreements to acquire two more seed sales companies and a seed research firm doing basic work with corn and sorghum hybrids. As the seed world realized what was going on, proposals to sell seed businesses poured into the Frange Seeds office and were duly screened, but Roderick Frange had shifted his first priority to operations. As soon as an acquisition was definite, he visited each facility and met as many of the people as possible. After talking individually with the key managers, he asked for the opportunity to talk with the managers as a group and spoke about his dream of building a major integrated seed business with their own operation as a key component; of the opportunities that this would make for promotion beyond the boundaries of the firm, and of his own need for their ideas and suggestions as to how to proceed. Each speech ended with a brainstorming session about the best way for him to go forward from there.

Because of the nature of the seed business, the operations were too scattered for any real functional integration—in marketing or production, for example—but he started a coordinating council where the marketing people from all of the companies would meet once a quarter and talk about common problems, another for production, and another for research. As soon as he found the necessary talent, he also appointed staff assistants as coordinators for production, marketing, and research efforts in different parts of the firm; but another important part of their assignment was to help him find out how to strengthen each function. For example, he knew that seed research ties to genetic engineering research were needed in some if not all product areas, and that South American, Australian, and other off-shore production sites were needed so that more than one seed generation per year could be accomplished by growing seeds in the southern hemisphere during the northern winter. His approach was to get his managers and technical people to help define the need and the alternatives, since they were smart people already working in the field, and then to move as rapidly as possible to fill that need. In the same way he made other acquisitions, in each case buying a firm that added something tangible to the structure of the whole at a price that made the contribution attractive.

As the organization saw how rapidly Frange moved to fill their needs once they had convinced him that these needs were real, their enthusiasm grew, morale rose, and a company-wide achievement drive gained momentum. Sales grew more rapidly than they would have otherwise, and the various components of the company made full and ingenious use of the competitive advantage that the various agreements and acquisitions were intended to achieve. Frange made a public offering of a small amount of Frange Seeds stock, so that the company would have a public market and so that it could apply for a stock exchange listing, and used the money for new buildings and facilities to aid the expansion of the different parts of the company.

And as the momentum of the organization grew, Frange began to withdraw somewhat from day-to-day operations, and to spend more time on managerial selection and the way that the overall management group operated. He began to take vacations again. One of the original staff assistants stopped by Frange's office and found out from the secretary that Frange was on vacation. "That's a danger sign," he said. "When this show is running well enough for him to take vacation, he must be about ready to sell out. I wonder what kind of a company he'll have us build next."

QUESTIONS

1. Is there or is there not an economic contribution in building an organization such as Frange Seeds from its parts? How does this compare with conglomerate acquisition? Discuss.
2. What possibly could make a rich man such as Roderick Frange work so hard? Discuss.

CHAPTER 17

MANAGING IN PUBLIC AND NOT-FOR-PROFIT ORGANIZATIONS

KEY IDEAS IN THIS CHAPTER

The policy and strategy process in public and not-for-profit organizations is almost identical to that of for-profit organizations, as Chapter 17 explains:

- **living with budgets instead of profits** – public versus private sector organizations.
- **winning support for programs** – building a constituency.
- **the public face of public business** – managing for the public as a public servant.
- **designing strategy** – the same process here, except the leverages work differently.
- **public management** – chapter summary and integration.

This book has focused primarily on business organizations, yet other sorts of organizations also have missions, goals, and strategies, must establish policies by which to operate, and have the same need for value-driven planning and strategic management. As will be developed in this chapter, the management needs and the strategy and policy requirements of public and not-for-profit organizations are quite similar to those of business organizations, and most of the same tools and techniques apply. But because the purpose of such an organization is different, it has a different set of priorities and different approaches to solving its problems, and this places its management under different sorts of pressure.

BUILDING A CONSTITUENCY TO SUPPORT THE ORGANIZATION

Depending on what an organization is doing, and whether it is producing a product or delivering a service, as discussed in Chapter 11, it will face basically different approval processes for its efforts. The tools and the planning needs of management are largely the same, but the world from which a public sector organization receives approval and funding may be radically different.

If a public sector organization is permitted to do so, it often builds incrementally on its past, using its existence as a justification for continuation of its services, and attempting to negotiate for funding only on the size of the budget increases necessary to continue and expand its function. This has been a very successful tactic, and although the zero-base budgeting concept was devised specifically to cancel out this approach to obtaining funds, many politically adept managers continue to expand their budgets from year to year in this way.

More fundamentally, most not-for-profit units are service-focused, and require the good will and support of an outside constituency for their continued existence. The efforts of the organization are divided between management of an effective operation, and catering to these key constituencies. Often not-for-profit groups have several types of constituencies for which to care.

A museum, for example, has need of the good will of the general public and often derives some of its revenue from the fees and purchases as they walk through. But it is more interested in converting the interested public into museum members, who have a closer relationship and pay more. And beyond the many grades of personal and organizational members are the sponsors—those who can be persuaded to give funds. The sponsors vary from individuals and corporations who will donate, to various levels of government who can be persuaded to include the organization in current budgets, and to governmental and foundation groups who will approve grants for specific projects.

The Veterans Administration is a service-focused agency that has built a strong constituency among veterans, their relatives, and the general public, and can draw automatic support against challenges to its funding from a wide range of powerful organizations who have made themselves important in the reelection of members of Congress. In the same way, most other service-focused organizations have constituencies. The Army Engineers have long worked to develop relationships with key members of Congress, and to plan necessary harbor, dredging, and levee work so that it will benefit these supporters' districts sufficiently that they will defend the Engineers against challenges to budget or projects.

These are but a few well-known examples of a pervasive process. Any welfare department or department of public works has a constituency, as does the Tennessee Valley Authority or the Port of New York Authority. The underlying management process is the same for such an organization, but the emphasis is different due the need to cater to this constituency.

The management of any effective not-for-profit organization concentrates intensively on the strategy for building and maintaining this strong, contributing constituency. Much of the current difficulty in the not-for-profit area has come because organizations once supported by individual philanthropists find this no longer possible—a broader constituency must be found, and many of today's not-for-profit organizations have not learned how to do this. The organizational planning process and its tools are essentially identical—it is the emphasis toward which the process is directed that is different.

THE PUBLIC FACE OF PUBLIC BUSINESS

In Chapter 16 it was suggested that due to the changing demands on businesses almost any manager may be required to act as public representative of the firm from time to time. That manager may have to talk to reporters, or represent the company by testifying at a trial or before a legislative committee. Even more strongly does this requirement bear on the managers in any public organization and in a great many not-for-profit organizations.

Where the manager of a privately owned business has many sorts of obligations to customers, suppliers, employees, and the community that members of the public will invoke from time to time, the manager of a public agency or bureau is, in a literal sense, a public servant, and some members of the public will demand services on this basis that they may not be entitled to otherwise; and where the request must be refused, the public sector manager usually finds it necessary to handle the matter very carefully to avoid giving offense that could itself lead to another public issue.

In the same way, legislators and others wishing to establish themselves in the public view often find it convenient to attack public agencies—whether for inefficiency, poor performance, or bias in rendering services—and may subject a department to unfair criticism in order to make a public point.

The end product of all of this is a picture of a public sector manager and some not-for-profit organization managers as living in much more of a goldfish bowl than managers in private business organizations. In some units this relationship with the general public is a key part of the job, and its maintenance may be at least equal in importance to managerial ability.

DESIGNING PUBLIC OR NOT-FOR-PROFIT STRATEGY

The public or not-for-profit organization has the same need for product strategy or—more often—service strategy, and the process for defining it is essentially the same as for a business organization, except that the leverages that must be created in the customer's mind act toward a decision to use the agency, visit the museum, or commit funds for its support, rather than the more traditional exchange of money to purchase a product or service. In one sense this is two-sided selling—on one side to obtain the funds necessary for public or not-for-profit operation, and on the other to build a meaningful usage of services or other relationship with the necessary clientele or constituency.

PUBLIC MANAGEMENT

Managers in public and not-for-profit organizations have the same organizational needs for mission, goals, strategy, and policy formulation as their private sector counterparts, and the same need for strategic management and strategic control of the policy execution. They may be pressed less competitively, particularly if they are in service-focused organizations, but they usually will have to deal with public processes for review and approval to a much greater extent, and may manage in the public view to a greater degree.

Public and not-for-profit organization managers function in an organizational world with somewhat different parameters and challenges than

> **FIGURE 17-1** STRATEGIC MANAGEMENT AS A REQUIREMENT IN PUBLIC AND NOT-FOR-PROFIT ORGANIZATIONS
>
> **The basic challenges are the same**
> - a mission to fulfill
> - goals to achieve
> - a strategy to be designed and carried into action
> - new rules can be devised and resources created
> - organizational effectiveness can be created
>
> **Some of the ground rules are different**
> - living with budgets instead of profits
> - winning support for programs
> - building a public constituency
> - managing an organization with a very sensitive public face

APPLYING STRATEGIC MANAGEMENT

for the private sector, but with the same need for a clear linkage between planning, strategy, and action in a strategic management process, as illustrated in Figure 17-1.

QUESTIONS FOR ANALYSIS AND DISCUSSION

1. "The linkages from mission to goals to strategy are essentially the same for all types of organizations, including private business, public sector, and not-for-profit organizations." Do you agree or disagree, and why?

2. "Public and not-for-profit sector managers have the same opportunity to make up new rules and create new resources as private sector managers." Do you agree or disagree, and why?

3. Discuss some of the ways that managing against a budget in a specific agency or not-for-profit corporation may be different from working to make a profit. (You may want to look again at the discussion of productive versus service units in Chapter 11.)

4. Make a list of public sector organizations, and for each one list the constituency served by it or otherwise supporting its existence. How do the managements of these organizations act to assure themselves of this support?

5. Make a list of not-for-profit organizations, and for each one list the constituency served by it or otherwise supporting its existence. How

do the managements of these organizations act to assure themselves of this support?
6. List public and not-for-profit organizations that do a conspicuously *good* or *bad* job of managing their public face. In each case, why did you classify them that way?

FOR FURTHER INFORMATION

O'Neill, Michael O., & Dennis R. Young, *Educating Managers of Non-profit Organizations* (New York: Praeger, 1988).
  Training managers in a different sort of environment.

Wholey, Joseph S., *Organizational Excellence: Structure, Quality, and Communicating Value* (Lexington, Mass.: Lexington, 1987).
  Putting together a public-sector organization.

CASE 33 LANDS AND FORESTS DEPARTMENT

The office day at the Lands and Forests Department started with the mail. The director always came in a few minutes early, to get his papers organized, and to start on the notes and dictation. His secretary was not surprised to find several letters on the dictation machine already and the outgoing mail drawer full when she came in. She was surprised to find two legislative aides already in a meeting with her boss; but she knew that they were working on a revision of the state park regulations that had both the friends and enemies of the state park system upset. She called several staff members and delayed a scheduled 9:15 review of the newsletter program; but the unscheduled meeting ended at 9:20, and her "Good morning, Mr. Miller," greeting as the aides left was answered not only in kind, but with a request for ten minutes "for a phone call and two letters." She rescheduled the newsletter meeting at 9:30 as requested, and he was only two minutes late.

The newsletter meeting was an important one because the "Friends of Lands and Forests" newsletter had become a significant and influential bridge between the department and those of the citizenry who took an active interest in the state's park programs, management of its public lands, and assistance in forest management and fire protection. Because it was a state publication, the newsletter had to be very careful to avoid partisan editorial positions; except that the GOOD of the people and the WILL of the people statewide were always a legitimate basis for the department's arguments. The newsletter had a modest subscription fee designed to cover the extra printing and handling costs of one more copy, with editorial costs paid out of the department budget; except that in addition there were as many complimentary copies distributed as the department budget would permit, and many of the subscribers also joined the "Friends Club." Counting these contributions, the newsletter just about paid for itself, and did a tremendous amount of good in making a connection with the people who were interested in the work of the department.

The value of the newsletter was because of the way that it was written and distributed, of course, and as director of the department Michael Miller had set high editorial standards and insisted on careful, thoughtful selection of the articles and news items to be printed. As a part of his interest, he scheduled bimonthly editorial meetings at which the newsletter planning and reader reaction were discussed in detail. He had no desire to dictate the contents, and the meetings were extremely participative in their pattern, but he felt that without clear and routine evidence of his interest the staff care and enthusiasm might slacken. As was their pattern, the newsletter editorial meeting consumed the balance of the morning; in fact, he had to excuse himself a few minutes before the meeting was quite concluded because he was to host a luncheon.

The luncheon group was made up of gun club representatives who had petitioned for the right to set up target ranges on public land, and representatives of several citizens' groups, upset by the danger that firearms represented for the public, who had petitioned for more restrictions on shooting on public land. He told both groups that they should be better acquainted, as he had found good people on both sides. He also told both groups that it was his job to approve all proper use of public land, since it was the public's property, and this might include target ranges if they were safe, well located, and well supervised. On the other hand, it appeared that the present rules on the handling of firearms on public land did not always protect the other members of the public properly. So, while they were all together, why didn't the gun clubs help the citizens' groups to work out a better set of rules for handling firearms on public land so that he would be able to deal with the question of safe and proper places to set up target ranges? In effect he told them that if they could work together, they could both have what they wanted, and they began to get acquainted over lunch. Of course, there was not time to work out a specific proposal, but he did get the leaders of both groups to appoint a committee that would meet and put such a proposal together. He got one of his staff included as an observer, but really as a means of being sure that the group tried to do something, as new gun-handling rules had been needed for a long time, and he preferred to delay the request for target ranges until these rules were in place.

By 2:30 Miller was back in his office with a feeling of accomplishment, besides the fact that he had got two groups of agitators off of his back for a few weeks. But he found an urgent call from an assistant attorney general of the state. A scandal had erupted over payoffs to county officials from a lumber company that had allegedly been using county road equipment to build logging roads on state land. Lands and Forests was involved because the company was cutting state timber, and the local paper that had broken the story hinted at payoffs there, too. But an hour of phone calls and checking convinced him that the lumber company's dealings with the state were clean and in good order. They had purchased the right to cut the timber they were cutting in competitive bidding by offering far the highest price of the seven bidders; they had requested and received approval for the access roads they were constructing on state land; and Miller found a sheaf of very neat and thorough weekly inspection reports on the road-building and cutting that showed that the company was cutting according to its contract, and that Lands and Forests was supervising the job thoroughly. He called the assistant attorney general and suggested that he look through the same files, and invited him to bring a reporter or two: "You may want to make a point over the fact that the state's hands are clean this time."

Because of the lumber company problem Miller's secretary had delayed a 3:00 P.M. budget meeting to 3:30, and the weekly 4:00 P.M. operations meeting to 4:30, as she saw the way that the afternoon was going. The budget meeting, a first review of the budget the Lands and Forests Department would request for the next year, was an important one and took the full hour for which it had been scheduled. When the operations meeting started at 4:30, Miller apologized to the group: "I have been fighting fires all day, and I got a little off schedule. But somebody has to tell me what the department is doing, and I hope your spouses will understand if we don't get out of here until 5:30." They spent an intense, efficient hour, with a flow of reports, decisions, new assignments and questions for follow-up the next day, and ended promptly at 5:30, as Miller tried not to force his staff to work extra hours more than specific tasks required. He cleared his desk, put a few papers in his briefcase for after dinner, and started home just before six.

Michael Miller had headed the State Lands and Forests Department for three years now, after fifteen years of rising through the ranks. Among the ranks of state agency heads and commissioners he was always listed among the professional rather than political appointees, and he was proud of his professionalism. He was equally proud of the strong role his department played in state government affairs, and the frequency with which other agency heads or members of the legislature would ask for his suggestions on how to manage some difficult public or political issue. Miller told anyone who asked that, in order to be able to run the department at all, he had to spend half of its time, energies, and budget in maintaining relationships with key public groups, the legislature and members of the state government, and the public at large. He said that the challenge for any agency head was to accomplish the public purpose of the agency well enough with the other half of the budget to satisfy the same people with which the first half of the budget maintained relationships.

A check of the Lands and Forests Department budget by a public interest group over a three-year period showed that Miller had exaggerated the cost and extent of the public and legislative relations activity; it was probably not much more than a quarter of the total. When he was asked about this, he admitted to an overemphasis, because he said that if his staff did not manage these outside relationship activities well enough, they would not get any budget at all for the work of the department.

QUESTIONS

1. Why shouldn't Michael Miller, or the head of any other state department, just concentrate on doing the work of the department and let the public relations and communications problems be handled by someone else? Discuss.

2. Make a list of public agencies and classify them according to the degree to which the public reaction to their work is a critical part of performing it. Which departments must deal with public reactions most carefully? Which departments can pay less attention to public reactions?

CASE 34 THE DUNGY MUSEUM

Ronny Marfake, the Dungy Museum's conservator, was in a fury and his staff all were out of sight. He stormed through the office area, and secretaries trembled. He looked for Abram Weedy, the registrar, but Abram was on an errand outside of the museum. He found Wilbur Runner, the building superintendent, who was quieter but a kindred spirit: "Wilbur, how do they expect us to keep this place operating? I can't do my job without resources!" Wilbur tried to comment, but Ronny had gone on already: "Alton Dungy built this place and gave us a forty million dollar endowment to operate it. And when I discovered that the only good painting we have of Alton Dungy is falling off the canvas and asked for $25,000 extra for a good restoration, those knotheads upstairs told me there were no more funds in this year's budget. But I just learned that they approved $200,000 for expenses and a guest curator for the summer festival exhibition opening in August. And that wasn't in this year's budget until now!" Ronny stormed on, leaving Wilbur shaking his head.

Next Ronny looked for Sumner Pin, the museum director, and made the same complaint. "Ronny," the director said, "have you talked to anyone in accounting about this? They would have told you that the summer festival exhibition is happening because a certain local millionaire gave us $200,000 to put it on. We can't use the money for anything else—and, of course, we are pleased to be able to do the exhibition.

"And have you talked to Susan Williams in development? She has a really good nose for people around the community who might give us a grant for a key project. Alton Dungy still has relatives in town; maybe one of them would like to give us money enough to keep their Uncle Alton's picture from falling off of the canvas, but someone has to ask. That's Susan's job, but the rest of us have to tell her what we need and why."

Ronny was only a little deflated: "Sumner, I'm no accountant and no fund-raiser, and never pretended to be. I am here and working for museum wages because I want to keep works of art from being destroyed by carelessness and time. I have built the best conservation group in this part of the United States, and if you guys would help a little more, it would soon be the best there is. It's not my job to worry about the money. But please help me find a way to save that painting!"

Sumner called Susan and asked her to get the details from Ronny and see what she could do. As he had guessed, the Dungy family was sympathetic. Alton Dungy's surviving brother took over the fund-raising, setting up a family pool into which each branch was to contribute $5,000, and he was so persuasive he got seven contributions. The next day he called Susan back with $35,000, with the extra $10,000 for the museum conservator to use in another good cause.

Meanwhile Sumner Pin had called Abram Weedy, the registrar, whose duties started with a complete and detailed record of the works of art the museum owned. This record was supposed to include an assessment of the condition of each holding, and an estimate of the cost and urgency of any conservation work needed, so that the museum would not have these unpleasant surprises. "Abram," Sumner asked, "couldn't your people have given us a warning that the Dungy painting was in such bad shape?"

"Yes, they would have, if they had ever gotten to the fifth floor of the museum with their condition records. We have been working very hard on the fourth floor; we did the basement and the first three floors in three years, but when we hit those storage rooms full of prints, etchings, and other paper goods on the back of the fourth floor, it really slowed us down. We are almost done now, but we have been working on that floor for three years. Then we will start the fifth floor, and the Dungy painting would have been one of the first we did."

"I knew you had spent an awful lot of time on the fourth floor—but you mean that nothing at all has been done on five yet?"

"That's right, Sumner. I believe in being systematic about this, so that we not only do our job but do it right." Abram Weedy was another very good and very dedicated man; an asset to the museum because of the care he and his staff devoted to the museum records; but he wasn't trained as a manager, and Sumner Pin saw his own mistake in not paying more attention to Abram's failure to set priorities. Much of the paper collection on the fourth floor was of uncertain value, which was why it was in storage rooms rather than on display; in fact, the museum board was about to get another proposal that a great deal of it be sold or discarded to free the space. And the registrar's department, which was supposed to inspect every piece of art every five years, had already been working on the current inspection for six years because it had devoted three years to that paper collection.

Sumner Pin went back to his office to attack a museum membership problem he had been avoiding, but he found Grace Martinez, who ran the museum shop, and Farley Black, chief of the guard force, waiting to ask him to settle a dispute. The museum shop had suddenly become an important source of income, thanks to Grace Martinez' careful management and creative choice of gifts and cards. But almost from her first day, the guard force had objected because she brought so many more people in, and the more people, the more security problems. Most recently she had gotten the access doors rearranged so that people could come in from the street and shop in the museum shop without getting admitted to the exhibit area at all. This was bothering Farley Black, and not for the first time. "Chief," he said, "I don't want to be the one that keeps this little lady from selling a lot of postcards, but I don't like having people come in to the museum shop without paying admission. When they are checked past the guard at the gate and have to put down their entrance fee, you get rid of a lot of riffraff. And now we let just anybody walk into the shop and buy."

"Farley, don't you have a security guard on duty in the museum shop already?"

"Yes, we always have had a guard there."

"Grace, how do you feel about the security in the shop?"

"Sumner, we have a reasonably peaceful city. I don't mean that there aren't bad people—there are everywhere—but less than in most cities these days. The downtown area is full of retail shops about the size of the one I run here, and I don't know of one that has a full-time security guard in the store; and here Farley's whole force is on call a few feet away. I think we have the best security in the city already, without screening the people who want to come in and browse. It's partly because I respect Farley's work so much that I think it is ridiculous to make people pay and pass inspection before they can come in to shop."

The issue was fully out on the table, and Sumner Pin wondered how to settle it. He asked them to let him think about the problem, and set another appointment for the following week. Actually, he hadn't the slightest idea how to solve the problem, and just making a decision and giving an order didn't seem to work very well with the museum people. So, he carried the problem with him, until suddenly it occurred to him that Marian Martini, the museum accountant, might have an idea, and he asked her. She thought a moment and then pulled out the statement showing the museum shop sales and profits. With the change three months ago to allow the public in directly, sales had started a sharp rise. The shop was already profitable, and now it appeared that it was beginning to contribute substantially. "Chief," she said, "these numbers say that you have to back Grace and give her all of the encouragement you can. Lord knows we need the money, and she is really beginning to help with overall expenses. If Farley could understand that, he would be on her side too."

"Farley will never be much of an accountant—but didn't you tell me that the reason we could give him the extra guard he needed was because of extra income from the shop? He will understand that." Sumner then arranged for Marian to calculate every month the fraction of the salaries of the guard force that the earnings from the shop represented and show it to Farley. And before too many months had gone by, Farley was asking his guard force how they could attract more people into the museum shop.

Sumner often delayed on problems he did not know how to handle, and some of the staff had noticed this. When the problem could be resolved neatly, as the conflict between Farley Black and Grace Martinez was, Sumner could feel good about his management, but he knew he had been delaying too long on the museum membership problem, and finally he called Mark Vivian, the membership director, and Susan Williams, the development director, in to talk over the problem. It was Mark's problem, or request; he wanted to spend quite a lot of money on membership development, and the museum really did not have the money. But his reasons for going ahead were very good. Mark asked that Marian Martini be included, to help with the financial side of the issue, and the meeting was scheduled.

When the Dungy Museum had been created by the will of Alton Dungy, it started with a board of trustees and an endowment. The income from the endowment was a good base for the museum program, but did not cover all expenses, so that other donations were needed. The problem was not a severe one because the trustees were all men of means who joined the board because they wanted to help with the museum. When they found worthwhile projects that the museum could not afford, they took turns writing checks, and the programs went forward. There were other donors, of course, but the generosity of the trustees was an essential ingredient in the operating budget. With the passage of time this had changed; on the positive side the museum had received gifts which added to its endowment. On the negative side, costs had risen, and the trustees and the tax laws had changed. Few of the present trustees could afford the routine open-checkbook policy of the early years or thought it appropriate for the funding to be such a personal process. With these big personal gifts drying up, the museum had to find other sources of revenue. That is why it had a membership director at all, and the more clearly Mark Vivian understood what he had to do, the more strongly he pressed for the funds with which to do it.

Susan Williams had not heard these proposals before, and they required money the museum did not have, which suggested that as development director she would have to find it somewhere. That is why Sumner Pin had called her into the meeting, which started as a presentation by Mark Vivian of what he wanted to do and how much it would cost.

Earlier Mark had proposed a graduated series of membership levels that had been adopted and were already in effect. The public could become Members of the museum for $30 per year, with Family Membership at $50 per year, Friends of the Dungy Museum at $250 per year, and Museum Sponsors at $1,000 per year. Corporate Membership cost $2500 per year. Corresponding to each level of membership were a series of privileges to help the member justify the cost.

What Mark wanted to do now was to spend money to increase the membership at the various levels. The museum already had a Members Lounge; Mark wanted it expanded and redecorated. The museum had a one-page newsletter that went to the various levels of membership once a quarter; Mark wanted to convert it into a nice monthly newsletter on good paper and with some artwork to make it attractive. The upper levels of membership were to get privileged access to new publications; more new publications were needed to make this meaningful. The Members were to be invited to receptions, introduced to artists, given previews of exhibitions, and otherwise brought into the center of the museum world. These members were paying more, but they really had not been offered much yet, and Mark wanted these offerings expanded and made substantial. And he would also expand direct mail promotion of membership, but he wanted to experiment with other media. Museum posters on the city buses looked like an attractive way to get attention, for example. There were also some interesting ideas about radio promotion, and some museum people had claimed success with television spot advertising; Mark was not arguing for specific media so much as arguing for the need to promote aggressively in the best way that could be found.

Mark made an excellent presentation. Sumner thanked him. The room was silent. Then Marian Martini spoke up: "Before we cry out because we can't afford any of this, I think we have to look at the reasons for doing something, and then try to figure out the best thing to do. In the old days, our records show that the individual trustees donated between $25,000 and $50,000 apiece per year. Not only that, but they asked their uncles and cousins for help on specific projects and got it. The records aren't that clear on why everybody gave, but it looks to me as though the fifteen members of the board of trustees either contributed or were responsible for the contribution of over $1,000,000 per year to the museum operation, in addition to whatever was raised by specific campaigns. Allowing for inflation, that would be worth several million per year today, and today's board gives only a fraction of that. We have expanded endowments a bit, and Susan has a fertile touch in getting contributions for specific projects, but we are hurting because we don't have that wonderful flow from the trustees any more. We had federal money for a while, but that seems to be mostly dried up. Susan has had success in getting a good deal of corporate money, particularly for specific exhibitions and projects, but it doesn't close the gap entirely."

Marian continued: "What Mark was brought in for was to organize a new constituency of people interested in the museum. Nobody ever thought that we would make money from the basic museum membership; but if we make it attractive, those people will come to the museum, buy books and cards, and participate in our other activities, and we will get some return there. And, for every thousand members we can add, a fraction will get more involved. Some will become sponsors, and there is money for us there. Others will answer the phone when Susan calls, and perhaps make a gift to help with a project we are trying to finance. If we didn't have the Dungy endowment, the change in the board of trustees would have put us out of business already; but we are certainly in pain. And I don't see how things can ever get any better if we don't build a big, active membership base, along the lines of Mark's program; and that is what he was hired for. I don't think there is any choice. I think we have to decide where to get the money, what to do first, and how fast to try to build membership. But we have to go forward, or else we should all quit and go work for a museum with better financing."

"Marian, that was the longest speech I have ever heard you make!" Sumner Pin laughed.

"But she made a lot of sense, Chief," Susan added. And as the meeting went on, it turned into a development meeting. That is, Susan pressed Mark to define simple, understandable components of the program he wanted in words that a potential sponsor would understand, as she visualized the challenge of getting sponsors to pledge support for the various pieces. Sumner began to think that perhaps it could happen.

After the meeting, Sumner Pin complemented Marian on her overall grasp of the problems of the museum. "Thanks, Sumner," she answered, "but I have a big advantage over the rest of you. So far as I know, everyone on the professional staff started out either trying to be an artist, or fascinated with works of art. So here you all are, working for half of what you could get in some other organization and still each trying in their own way to be an artist or an artists' helper. I am the only one who sees the Dungy Museum Corporation as a business. And then it is very simple. We have a bottom line. Either we find enough money to pay our bills and meet our budget, or we go under. The artists don't like for me to talk about money, but that's what keeps the museum going, and we have to manage it."

QUESTIONS

1. How is running a museum different from running a for-profit corporation? Or is it different? Discuss.
2. If you had to advise the trustees of the Dungy Museum on how to plan for the future, what would you say?

CHAPTER 18

SMALL BUSINESS AND ITS SPECIAL PROBLEMS

KEY IDEAS IN THIS CHAPTER

Chapter 18 discusses the strategy and policy problems of small business, the application of the framework developed earlier, and some of the special problems and opportunities caused by being small:

- **managing without staffs and specialized resources** – small business managers as more versatile, exposed, and independent.
- **entrepreneurship** – starting new businesses; business plans; financing; assistance.
- **regulations, government, and the bias toward bigness** – small may be beautiful, but big can better afford the problems of dealing with bureaucracy.
- **assistance in finding markets and growth** – sources of information and support for small businesses.
- **small business management strategy** – chapter summary and integration.

The strategy and policy needs, challenges, and problems of large and small enterprises are very similar, but small business differs in three specific ways: (1) by being small, small business has less need for an elaborate organization structure; in this respect the management task is much simpler; (2) small business, by being smaller, has a flexibility and a speed of movement that large organizations have difficulty in matching; and (3) small business, by being small, has fewer resources, less overhead, and fewer opportunities for scale economies and learning curve advantages; in general it can afford fewer mistakes and withstand fewer adversities, and it will have higher costs for certain types of operations.

Beyond these obvious differences are several small-business strategy and policy considerations that deserve specific discussion, beginning with the need to manage with fewer specialized resources.

MANAGING WITHOUT STAFFS AND SPECIALIZED RESOURCES

As organizations grow larger, they can afford more specialization of resources. General Electric could justify a separate staff to study the environment outside of the enterprise, as could AT&T, but smaller firms with the same sort of need must solve it a different way; highly specialized staffs of this sort can be justified only by spreading the expense over many different businesses.

Where specialized elements of information are actually critical to the business performance, the larger firms will have a distinct advantage if they take full advantage of this potential. If they do not, or if imperfect internal coordination impedes the information flow, the closer contact with customers and business in a small firm may cancel out the larger part of this advantage.

Even managers of somewhat larger organizations often must do without special staff except for key areas such as accounting and personnel. Further, the managerial assignments in small businesses will be less specialized, and each manager will have to be more self-supporting than in a big organization. Services, such as an analysis of conditions in the marketplace, will be by subscription instead of custom-prepared by internal staff, and probably will not be as specifically tailored to the needs of the firm.

Smaller and smaller organizations have less and less staff. Many companies operate for years without hiring accountants and lawyers, instead using the professional services of a suitable firm on a retainer or per diem service basis. They may not be as well served as a result, because an outside firm sometimes cannot spend the time studying specific problems of one business the way that a full-time employee can.

The small-business manager works in a different sort of environment, and one that seems heavy with disadvantages as profiled, even though small-business success stories are so numerous. However, one of the key findings of *In Search of Excellence* was that the excellent organizations keep their individual business units relatively small, and achieve their excellent results by avoiding problems of bigness often so severe that they offset its advantages. But the small units discussed there may still have 600 employees, and may still look like a big business to an entrepreneur with a staff of twenty-five.

ENTREPRENEURSHIP: STARTING NEW BUSINESSES

The small-business area is the traditional seedbed for future large businesses, and much has been written about the high rate of job creation by U.S. small businesses. What this means in the practical sense is that new businesses are being created at a very high rate; many of them fail, but many others succeed. When a new industrial frontier opens—in semiconductors, personal computers, or biotechnology, for example—as potential entrepreneurs see the opportunities, many new businesses are created in that area, and the firms that will eventually dominate that area as it matures are at least as likely to come from these new start-up businesses as from major firms already established in other areas.

Start-up of a new business can be difficult but also very rewarding, and in addition to the resources available to any other small business, a large number of venture capital and other start-up financing sources look actively for promising new businesses they can assist in exchange for fees, interest payments, and equity options.

The key to start-up of any new business that needs outside financing is for the entrepreneur to assemble a basic business plan showing what the business will do, how it will do this, how much starting the business will cost, how the investment will be repaid, and how much profit there will be. This plan does not have to be massive, but it needs to be well and clearly done—to show that the entrepreneur knows what he or she is talking about, and to show that the venture is a good risk for the investors. In many cities there are venture centers, sometimes affiliated with a business school, where an entrepreneur can get advice on putting together a business plan. Or by checking with banks, venture capital groups, the nearest Small Business Administration office, or the state or city agency devoted to small business, the entrepreneur can find sources of help with a business plan, either there or by referral.

Banks are an obvious starting point for any business needing a loan, including new businesses, but banks are not supposed to risk their capital. This means that a bank's loan officer should offset the obvious risks of a business start-up by requesting security for the loan with sufficient value so that the bank will not lose even if the new business fails. An entrepreneur starting a new business can easily obtain money by taking a mortgage or second mortgage on his house, for instance, and if the business will have buildings or other property with good resale value, these can be mortgaged also. But where the cash needs exceed the amount the entrepreneur can obtain by pledging property as security, most banks would prefer not to make the loan. Small-business investment companies and the various sorts of venture capital companies are somewhat more open to risk but still want guarantees against the loss of their capital. Very many new businesses, unable to pledge property of sufficient value, go to the stock market and sell shares in the ownership of the company.

The best place to get the money depends on the specific circumstances, but with a good and clear business plan, getting adequate financing should be as easy as the business prospects warrant. That is, a great many firms make their way by helping promising small businesses get started, and if they can be convinced that a given venture is likely to be successful, they will be quite anxious to invest. None of this help is free, and the entrepreneur is caught between the requirements of good professional people for fair compensation, and the desire of less ethical financiers to get more out of the new business than their services justify.

Most start-ups have little or no money to pay for services, and the venture capital industry is normally paid in other ways. A promising venture often needs seed money, for example. Seed money can permit the founder to quit his or her job and devote full time to the new business, to begin to build prototypes, or in other ways to prepare for full-scale launch of the new enterprise. Often by getting some of these preliminaries accomplished, stock can be offered to the public from a stronger foundation, and a stock offering is more likely to be well received. Therefore the financial advisors of a new firm may organize a seed money offering, and look for investors who would like to participate. A seed money investment is often structured as a loan plus purchase of a small share in the enterprise at a low price; often the loan is 90 percent or 95 percent of the total investment and is repaid in full from the first sale of stock to the public. Thus the seed money investor takes the risk of a total loss if the new venture never gets to a public offering, but gets most of the money back quickly from that stock offering—often within three or six months—leaving that investor with a share in the enterprise acquired at a very low cost, and therefore a high profit potential if the business succeeds. This is quite fair in concept, but the fairness in actuality depends on how the terms of the offering are defined.

A new business also needs a good board of directors, to show investors the caliber of people who will be overseeing the use of their money, and to get the assistance of those people in guiding the business and in arranging its financing. Directors in large companies are paid for their time; in start-up companies where cash is scarce, the directors usually receive stock, and the stock will have little or no value unless the company begins to succeed, so the directors must be persuaded to invest their time and efforts in hopes of a substantial return several years later if they can help to make the company succeed.

When stock is sold to the public, this must be on the basis of a prospectus approved by the Securities and Exchange Commission and sometimes by a state agency. The prospectus is derived from the business plan. Its requirements may be relatively simple if the stock offering is to be made to only a few investors, and more complex if the offering is to be widely advertised and sold in more than one state. The firm handling the stock offering will charge for its services and for the expenses incurred, with these charges deducted from the proceeds of the sale, and may also ask for shares of stock or options entitling it to buy stock at a privileged price in the future.

The share of the company that should be sold to the public in a stock offering is a matter of judgment, where two factors enter. The entrepreneur will want a voice in running the company and a share of the profits, and selling stock to others reduces both. Second, business start-ups are uncertain and start-up costs are often underestimated; if a start-up is going well but the money runs out, it may be rather easy to sell more stock to the public and raise more money if some of the equity has not already been sold. Thus, it is common for an initial public offering to represent 20 or 25 percent of the equity in the company with at least an equal amount reserved for later sale, but this can vary widely.

The process of financing a new venture through sale of stock to the public can be complex, but the concept is simple and good help is available with this process. Because the process is complex, with a very large number of possible combinations of stock and options to purchase stock in the future, and because many people may have a legitimate reason to get shares in the company at a very low price, the details can be manipulated to increase the cost to the new venture and to leave very little for the people who actually start the business. An entrepreneur can gain some protection by dealing only with reputable, well-established professionals, and by comparing the terms proposed with other deals set up by other firms for other companies.

REGULATIONS, GOVERNMENT, AND THE BIAS TOWARD BIGNESS

The United States has been accused of favoring large organizations, and the entire regulatory system has an unmistakable bias in this direction. In public policy terms, this is an intense contradiction. The political tradition of the country is a small-business tradition, and many political figures have benefited themselves by becoming known as advocates of small-business causes.

In spite of this tradition the country has found need to regulate its businesses more and more closely, and most regulation by its nature has a heavy bias against the small business. For example, the desire for equal opportunity in employment resulted in a requirement that businesses make routine reports of their total employment, broken down to show distribution by sex and minority group in each different job category. Such reports do aid the enforcement effort, and they are little burden for a large personnel unit that already has people gathering and analyzing most of the same data for internal studies. But such reports are a significant additional task for a small business with a very small personnel department.

Many other examples add up to the same thing, and smaller firms across the country are struggling with the costs of fulfilling new and more elaborate regulations. In the pharmaceutical field the cost of bringing a new drug through the regulated clinical trial and approval processes is given by large companies as a minimum of several million dollars, and this cost has effectively blocked small companies from introducing new prescription products at all unless they can form a partnership with a large company. These requirements were based on public safety and appear necessary, but do have the consequence of placing small businesses at a disadvantage.

ASSISTANCE IN FINDING MARKETS AND GROWTH

Because the United States does have a small-business tradition, and because small-business issues appeal more to voters than big-business issues, many programs and agencies have a small-business-assistance focus. One federal-level example is the Small Business Administration, which runs seminars and assistance programs aimed at aiding small businesses, and has a variety of small-business-related services. In addition there are a variety of corresponding state and local agencies, including organizations making available free consulting services from retired executives, and various other assistance mechanisms for people trying to start their own businesses.

Financing help is available through the Small Business Administration, or from many local venture capital groups, some of which have formed Small Business Investment Corporations independently or in cooperation with a local bank, and which will make loans to small businesses that under some circumstances may be up to 90 percent guaranteed by the federal government. In addition several types of federal

---

FIGURE 18-1 STRATEGIC MANAGEMENT AS A SMALL-BUSINESS REQUIREMENT

The basic challenges are the same
- a mission to fulfill
- goals to achieve
- a strategy to be designed and carried into action
- the opportunity to devise new rules and create new resources
- the opportunity to create the desired degree of organizational effectiveness

Some of the problems are different
- few staffs and few specialized services
- more of working independently
- more need to master many different management tasks
- a disadvantage versus regulations and government reporting requirements
- some specialized assistance services
- much greater flexibility and freedom of action

APPLYING STRATEGIC MANAGEMENT

---

contracts give preference to small businesses, although the preferences are broader in scope where the small business is minority owned. Altogether there is a significant amount of assistance available to a deserving small business, and a start on locating this assistance is through the nearest Small Business Administration office or through any corresponding state or local agency.

SMALL-BUSINESS MANAGEMENT STRATEGY

Small-business management is like management of larger businesses in most ways, and has the same needs for strategies and policies, including strategic management and strategic control as indicated in Figure 18-1. Strategic blindness can be a much more serious problem, because, with fewer managers and multiple functions covered by each, all could suffer from the same malady and the business could come to disaster. The flexibility and ease of changing direction in a small business are tremendous offsetting advantages, and because the managers in a small business have so many functions, they are not able to get isolated from reality so easily as in a large organization. Even though the disposition and work habits of a manager may lead to strategic blindness, a customer may knock it out of him or her before too much damage is done, and the small-business sort of teamwork is proven as more effective than more clumsy big-business processes. The advantages of smallness are very great, and in many business situations these advantages can offset the superior resources and cost positions of a giant firm that give it preeminence in its central markets.

QUESTIONS FOR ANALYSIS AND DISCUSSION

1. To what extent do you agree that the basic problems of running a large or a small business are approximately the same? Discuss.
2. How much of a disadvantage do you really think the burden of regulations and paperwork is to a small company? What could be done about it?
3. Give examples of the way that small businesses sometimes move faster than large ones. Is it necessary that large organizations be so slow?
4. Small firms have a much better track record for major new innovations than large organizations. Why do you think this is so?
5. Not having a corporate staff of experts to call on in a small business would seem to be a larger disadvantage than it appears to be, from the success rate of some small companies. Why doesn't this make more difference?
6. With the assistance of the local Small Business Administration office, a state or local industrial development agency, or the office of your local representative in Congress, make a list of services available to help small businesses find markets, solve management problems, and otherwise grow and prosper.

FOR FURTHER INFORMATION

Gaedeke, Ralph M., & Dennis H. Tootelian, *Small Business Management* (2nd Ed.) (Glenview, Ill.: Scott-Foresman, 1985).
  A good general guidebook.

Silver, David A., *The Entrepreneurial Life: How to Go for It and Get It* (New York: Wiley, 1983).
  A well-presented picture of how to start a business.

CASE 35 THE GROWTH COMPANY

Ralph Frenes was raised by an uncle who owned a small company. After he finished business school, Ralph worked for a series of different firms in financial and service work, doing well, gaining excellent experience, but without really beginning to build a career. He had asked his uncle once about the family company, but the business was stable and the profits not that high. "I doubt the business could support both of us," his uncle said, and Ralph pursued the matter no further.

Then the uncle died, Ralph was his only relative, and found that he had inherited the business. He discovered that it had annual sales of $1 million. His uncle had been paying himself $30,000 per year in salary as president, and the corporation was earning 5 percent after taxes, or another $50,000 per year in net profits. Ralph could see why the uncle had not encouraged him to enter the firm. And as Ralph looked back into the financial history of the firm, he found that sales had been at about the same level for many years, growing only about as fast as the inflation rate.

A sound little business with no growth; but Ralph was puzzled about why there was no growth. He took two weeks' vacation from his current job and studied the business, visiting customers, meeting people in and out of the firm, and generally trying to find out what sort of a business world his uncle had faced. By the end of the first week he saw obvious ways to increase sales by approaching new groups of customers. By the end of the second week he had a marketing plan worked out in some detail. He called his current boss, and asked for a month's leave without pay. The boss hesitated, Ralph resigned on the spot, and from that point he was fully committed to his own company and its growth.

Three months into the effort he had proved the soundness of his insights. He now expected to double sales the first year, again the second year, and then to hold the growth to 50 percent per year "forever," because it would be disorderly and hard to manage a business growing faster than that. Marketing and administrative expenses would stay at about the same ratio to sales as the business expanded, so that the net profit after tax would grow in direct proportion to the sales volume. The company's products were manufactured in one corner of a huge company-owned brick factory built in 1923. The old machinery had long since been scrapped, and the manufacturing now consisted of a simple assembly and quality check based on components available in almost unlimited quantities from reliable suppliers. Thus, the capital cost of expansion was very small, more building space was available than could possibly be needed, and the necessary additional employees could be hired and trained as needed. The future seemed assured.

Then one night Ralph had a nightmare. He was in bankruptcy court, and his company was being liquidated. After what seemed to be hours of

EXHIBIT I — GROWTH COMPANY INCOME STATEMENT
(as of December 31)

		% of Sales
Revenues	$1,000,000.	100.0%
Cost of Sales	655,000.	65.5
Gross Profit	345,000.	34.5
Operating Expenses	250,000.	25.0
Marketing	150,000.	15.0
General & Administrative	100,000.	10.0
Income before Taxes	95,000.	9.5
Provision for Income Taxes	45,000.	
Net Income	$ 50,000.	5.0%

EXHIBIT II — GROWTH COMPANY BALANCE SHEET
(as of December 31)

Assets

Current Assets		
Cash and Marketable Securities		$ 50,000.
Accounts Receivable		100,000.
Inventories		125,000.
Total Current Assets		275,000.
Property, Plant, and Equipment		
Original Plant (1952 purchase)	$1,220,000.	
Depreciation Reserve	1,220,000.	
New Equipment	150,000.	
Depreciation Reserve	$ 100,000.	
Property, Plant, and Equipment—Net		50,000.
TOTAL ASSETS		$325,000.

Liabilities

Current Liabilities	
Accounts payable	50,000.
Stockholders' Equity	275,000.
TOTAL LIABILIITES	$325,000.

agony and attack by the lawyers for all of his creditors, a voice intruded. "I am the spirit of bankruptcies future. You deserve a lot more consideration than Scrooge. But this is what is going to happen to your company the way you are running it now." Then Ralph woke up, drenched with sweat, and called a financial consultant. Only a tape recorder answered, since it was four in the morning, but he left an urgent message and got a call back at nine.

QUESTIONS

The income statement and balance sheet for Ralph's company as he took it over are shown in Exhibits I and II.

1. Project the income statement and balance sheet and do a sources and uses of funds statement year by year for the next five years, assuming the growth rates Ralph had projected. When do you think the bankruptcy would have occurred, and why?
2. Develop two alternative financing plans that avoid bankruptcy and project them for the same period. Which do you recommend?

CASE 36 THE DRIP-DROP PAINT CO.

The Drip-Drop Paint & Varnish Company was a small regional paint company. It was long-established and quite successful in its region, but competitive pressures had become greater and greater as national paint manufacturers took market share away from local companies such as Drip-Drop. Drip-Drop had maintained its reputation for quality and its sales volume, but had obtained almost none of the growth in the total market, and profit margins had shrunk. Drip-Drop management realized that it needed a new strategy if it was to survive, and was looking for alternatives.

When the Drip-Drop sales manager met an executive of Blue Market, a major retail chain, at a conference, he suggested that Blue Market should put in a paint department. Blue Market was interested, discussions followed, and out of this meeting grew a partnership, with Drip-Drop making paint for Blue Market to sell under a Blue Market label. Blue Market opened a paint department in one store, then expanded to others, and finally to the whole eastern region of its nationwide network of home centers, so that by the end of three years the Drip-Drop plant had put on a second and a third shift and was operating at capacity. Prices on the sales to Blue Market were lower, but there was no marketing or distribution cost other than shipping to the Blue Market regional warehouse. The future of Drip-Drop began to look better, for with the plant so busy, costs improved, and retail sales under its own name began to grow again, although slowly.

Blue Market did well with its paint departments in the eastern region and continued to increase its orders. Then Blue Market management decided to open paint departments in the stores in its other three regions, and asked Drip-Drop if it would be able to supply the paint. Drip-Drop agreed, but suggested to Blue Market that if it built a plant in the midwest and another in the far west, the savings in distribution and shipping costs would soon pay for both; and then after the plant was paid for, Drip-Drop would pass the savings on to Blue Market. Everyone was pleased with this idea, suitable buildings were found in both areas, and construction went forward rapidly. Soon Blue Market had paint departments in all of its stores nationwide, the paint sales were very profitable, and both companies very pleased with the relationship that had developed.

The president of Drip-Drop was concerned about his company's increasing dependence on Blue Market purchases, however, as Blue Market was taking 85 percent of the total gallonage of paint Drip-Drop manufactured. Drip-Drop had almost no sales under its own name from either of the new plants, and continued slow growth of its own line of paints in the home region. With Drip-Drop executives spending most of their time on Blue Market business, it was surprising that there was any growth at all in the Drip-Drop sales, and the president reorganized so that a different group was responsible for development of Drip-Drop's own business.

Then Blue Market acquired another retail chain, which operated home centers also, with the intention of converting these into Blue Market centers as rapidly as might be practical. This acquisition would increase by 75 percent the number of stores in the Blue Market home center chain. But these new stores already had paint departments, and the acquired company had its own paint-making subsidiary that made the paint they sold. Blue Market management now found that it owned a paint company making paint for the new stores, and had a close relationship with Drip-Drop, which had helped it into the paint business and had supplied the Blue Market chain up to this point.

One of the key elements of Blue Market marketing philosophy was the concept of a relatively uniform national merchandise policy, so that items purchased in any store in the United States would be nearly identical in characteristics and performance. And the paint lines were nowhere near the same. Drip-Drop technical staff had an entirely different approach to paint formulation than those at the company Blue Market now owned. Both approaches worked, but painters did not like to shift from one type to the other because they had to use the paint differently to get the desired results. Blue Market management decided that this was too blatant a violation of their uniform national merchandise policy; one line of paints would have to go, and the other would have to expand to supply the full chain. Blue Market marketing argued forcefully that Drip-Drop should get the business, because of the good quality, good service, and competitive prices it had always provided to Blue Market. But the chairman of the Blue Market corporation thought about the consequences of closing two paint plants they had just acquired and putting their employees out of work, and ruled in favor of the acquired Blue Market company.

The first Drip-Drop heard of all of this was when the president got a letter telling him that the annual contract for Blue Market's paint requirements (due for renewal in three months) would not be renewed; after that, there would be no more paint sales to Blue Market.

QUESTIONS

1. What should Drip-Drop do now?
2. Drip-Drop could hardly have refused the Blue Market business. But can you think of any way it could have operated so that it would

have been less vulnerable to the sort of cutoff that occurred? List as many alternatives as you can think of; which are the best?

3. If you were the president of a company selling 85 percent of its output to one customer, how could you negotiate with that customer to maintain an adequate profit on the merchandise? Discuss.

CHAPTER 19

OTHER COUNTRIES AND OTHER CULTURES

KEY IDEAS IN THIS CHAPTER

Business policy and strategy problems in other countries and cultures are similar, because business fundamentals are the same worldwide, and different because of a multitude of important local factors:

- **universals** – the organizational hierarchy, the functions of management, the corporate form, bottom-line performance
- **local requirements and differences** – to follow the requirements of that society.
- **different legal and social systems** – where the firm must fit into them.
- **people and their culture** – they take control of the firm if they want to.
- **the multinational federation** – when each subsidiary must first meet local requirements before the needs of the parent.
- **international management strategy** – chapter summary and integration.

Many businesses operate in more than one country, so their policy and strategy considerations are multinational. Sound strategy and strategic management of an enterprise are worldwide requirements, but the details vary from country to country and culture to culture. This chapter discusses the challenge of making policy and strategy in other countries and other cultures and putting them into action. It will start by considering the ways in which the management challenge everywhere is the same, and then turn to some of the differences.

UNIVERSALS

Certain common factors run through business organizations and their management challenges worldwide. These include the organizational hierarchy, the functions of management, the corporate form, and bottom-line performance pressure.

THE ORGANIZATIONAL HIERARCHY

An organization exists for some purpose large enough so that it requires a number of people to perform it. In order that the required number of people actually perform the desired task, their efforts must be structured in some way, and the overall performance guided by someone who has been given charge over the collective effort.

While a multitude of different arrangements are in use, all significant organizations have an authority figure at the top, a pattern of delegation and subdivision of the work, and a chain of command linking higher and lower levels. Even where the workers have a share in the ownership, as in a cooperative, the basic working structure is authoritarian if not autocratic; participative management techniques are common in many organizations, but even those are not truly democratic. Because the managers at each level must bear full responsibility for the operations they control, the personal risk of permitting subordinates more than an advisory role forces the maintenance of an authoritarian structure regardless of the political or social system of the country.

THE FUNCTIONS OF MANAGEMENT

Long ago the basic functions of management were enunciated as planning, organizing, staffing, leading or directing, and controlling. While many variations of this list have been proposed, they all tend to build around a central group of functions that any and all managers must perform. And this same group of functions can be used to describe a manager's job in any country or culture in the world, even though the specifics of the jobs vary greatly.

THE CORPORATE FORM

Wherever industrial development has begun—in essentially every country of the world—the process is organized through corporations or their functional equivalents. That is, the industrial process functions by putting a pool of resources into the hands of a group of managers charged with economic performance in the fulfillment of some mission.

In the United States, this is accomplished through profit-seeking corporations with stockholders, managers, and employees. In a different political system the resources may be allocated by a state council, and the performance requirement may be fulfillment of a budget rather than achievement of a profit, but the internal dynamics of the resulting management challenge are quite similar.

BOTTOM-LINE PERFORMANCE

As indicated above, all managers in all sorts of organizations have financial targets, with quotas to fill and expense or profit budgets to meet. Even though the specific pursuit of profit is in disfavor in some countries, their business organizations are all basically economic in nature, and seek social ends by economic means, as discussed in Chapter 1.

LOCAL REQUIREMENTS AND DIFFERENCES

Even though a significant list of universal qualities can be identified in organizations producing goods and services all over the world, the actual organizations differ substantially. Primarily these differences spring from the integration of these organizations into different legal and social systems, from differences in the skill, knowledge, and desires of the people who come to work in the organization, and from differences in resource availability and cost.

DIFFERENT LEGAL AND SOCIAL SYSTEMS

Although a business does not have to be incorporated, in the United States essentially all significant businesses are—made, in the words of the supreme court opinion quoted in Chapter 1, "an artificial being created by law" and therefore governed by the specifics of that law. To do business in another country, a corporation must be established there—an artificial being must be created by that law and exists by the sufferance of that law-giving society. Laws differ greatly in some countries, and the corporation is a creature of that law, whatever it says. If the law says that no employee can be laid off without government permission, then the business must operate that way.

Social systems are also quite different. South Africa separated out the blacks as a lesser status group. Women do not have the same rights as men in countries that observe Islamic law, and the various Arab states believe that discrimination against certain races is proper. Whatever the local social system is, by engaging to do business there, under local law and as an element of the local society, a business commits itself largely to follow the requirements of that society as a condition of being permitted to operate.

There is some latitude, of course, and business self-interest is in the direction of moving toward more equitable international behavior standards. Subsidiaries of some U.S. corporations in South Africa had established constructive leadership in moving toward better pay and a closer approach to equality for the black majority. However, deviant behavior of this sort must be carefully gauged, since the operating franchise could be terminated by the host society if the offense to their social standards became sufficient in the opinion of the local authorities to warrant such action. But in this case social pressure in the United States forced most of these companies to terminate their operations and leave the South Africans to their own devices.

PEOPLE AND THEIR CULTURE

The people who come to work in an organization are a product of their background and culture, and most international companies prefer to staff almost exclusively with local people if the necessary skills and abilities can be found. In the first wave of expansion by U.S. companies into markets in less developed countries after World War II, several projects foundered because the local people "could not be trained to do the work." The problem was that they had been given U.S. training materials that assumed a grade school education and a lifelong familiarity with cars and other mechanical devices. People who had never seen machinery before required much more training because it was all so strange to them, and the training materials had to be extended and adapted to their backgrounds.

Similarly, the cultural pattern of going to a factory to work every day was not familiar to many people. The reason for having to be at work every day and at the same time had to be explained carefully again and again; where this was not done, people stopped coming regularly and the business had trouble scheduling its work.

Every culture has its own rules of conduct and behavior, and in most cases these rules take precedence over the rules of the business. To be a compatible element in a society, the managers of the business must learn what these rules are. This sounds obvious, and it is, but it is not always easy. Fairchild Camera had a very successful plant on a Navaho Indian reservation, and although this is not a foreign land, the project had a very difficult start-up due to large cultural differences poorly understood by the Fairchild managers. During the tenure of the first plant manager the plant suffered from high and unexplained absenteeism; the second plant manager began to find out more about the Navajo religion and discovered a pattern of religious holidays that explained much of the absenteeism; but the Navajo talked little about their religion to outsiders, and no one had realized these holidays even existed.

There are limits to the extent to which a business can accommodate religious preferences, and even in the United States many firms have had difficulty accepting that to some people Saturday instead of Sunday is the holy day. Where the work force of a business comes from many different races or religions, as in some African countries, there can be significant problems even in establishing a common language and a general set of work rules. The underlying theme is that organizations function productively and efficiently when they are well managed, and good management includes a sharing of goals and values, as discussed in Chapter 10, so that an effective teamwork develops among all of the members of the organization. In another country and culture, it is very challenging for managers who are not nationals to find out enough about the society they have joined to build effective team work across cultural barriers, and this is an area where good management has a clear opportunity to excel.

THE MULTINATIONAL FEDERATION

One recurrent problem of any business with international or multinational dimensions is conflict between the needs and desires of the business and the political and social policies of one or more countries. If a country has exchange controls and limits imports because of balance-of-payments problems, this may hamper the business in getting necessary imported materials or machinery, and some accommodation must be found. Perhaps the business can create an export transaction that will offset the effect of the import transaction it needs to get approved, or can otherwise find a noncontroversial means of accomplishing its purpose. Some firms have even gone to the point of investing their profits in other local businesses to generate exports, since the exports sold in the world market could give them means of generating hard-currency payment for necessary imports and for repatriation of profits that the local government could not be expected to permit directly.

When governments differ over the wisdom of a transaction, the business can be caught in the middle in a very difficult situation. Dresser Industries had established a French subsidiary to manufacture its oil and gas equipment in Europe; this subsidiary bid on the compressors needed for the Russian natural gas pipeline to Eastern Europe, with the strong encouragement of the French government. But the U.S. government took an unexpectedly strong stand against export of this U.S. technology to the Soviet Union, the French designs were based on Dresser's U.S. technology, and Dresser was caught. The French subsidiary went ahead with the sale, as required by its French citizenship, the U.S. government banned any new transfer of technology to it, and the result might have been to put the French subsidiary out of business had the United States and French governments not compromised their differences.

A corporation must behave as a citizen of the society that controls it, if it intends to continue in business. This means a multinational with subsidiaries in many countries has only a limited ability to command specific actions from its subsidiaries, because they must act in a manner compatible with the interest of the societies of which they are a part. This limitation serves the long-term self-interest of the parent corporation because it leads to the greatest long-term profits in each individual country, but it means that a multinational must operate more in the style of a federation of subsidiary companies that works out a joint operating pattern compatible both with local interests and long-term profits.

STRATEGY FOR INTERNATIONAL MANAGEMENT

The business strategy and policy problem are basically the same elsewhere as in the United States, except that complexities emerge in the international arena that may be less obvious in the United States, as Fairchild Camera did not expect to have to integrate into such a different culture here in the United States as it found on the Navajo reservation. As illustrated in Figure 19-1, the management basics are unchanged, but the checklist of options and alternatives is longer, when an operation in another country or across international borders is the basis of the planned strategic management effort.

FIGURE 19-1 INTERNATIONAL STRATEGIC MANAGEMENT

The basic challenges are the same
- a mission to fulfill
- goals to achieve
- a strategy to design and carry into action
- opportunity to devise new rules and create new resources
- opportunity to create an organization of the desired degree of effectiveness

The management universals apply
- the organizational hierarchy
- the basic functions of management
- the corporate business form
- emphasis on bottom-line performance

Local requirements must be met
- a fit into the legal and social system
- conformance with key requirements of the local culture
- membership in the local society
- minimum threat of foreign control

APPLYING INTERNATIONAL STRATEGIC MANAGEMENT

QUESTIONS FOR ANALYSIS AND DISCUSSION

1. Do you agree that the basic challenges are the same in management in the United States and in other countries? Discuss.
2. Do you agree that managers in other countries have the same opportunities to make up new rules and to create new resources? Discuss.
3. Make a list of organizations in very different sorts of countries. To the extent that the information is available, attempt to confirm that they have (a) an organizational hierarchy, (b) a requirement for the same functions of management, and (c) a corporate form or else some other structure that is functionally equivalent (professional managers responsible to a board or authority for their effectiveness in achieving economic performance from the assigned resources—whether measured by budget, profit, or quota).
4. Find examples of the ways that companies find it necessary to change their operations to fit the legal and social system requirements of the host country.
5. Find examples of the ways that companies find it necessary to change their operations to fit the local cultural requirements.

6. Find examples of businesses that have and have not managed to fit into the local society.
7. Examine the ways that different countries have used to assure themselves that foreign interests will not be able to control the operation of businesses in their countries. Does this justify business efforts to find a federated management structure or other means of allaying these fears?

FOR FURTHER INFORMATION

Dluges, Gunter, & Klaus Weiermair (eds.), *Differing Value Systems* (New York: Walter de Gruyter, 1981).
   Background on the different business environments.

Liontiades, James C., *Multinational Corporate Strategy: Planning for World Markets* (Lexington, Mass.: Lexington Books, 1985).
   Linking together the worldwide system.

CASE 37 THE PLANT IN TASPOTAMIA

The plant in Taspotamia was intended as the essence of a smooth, organized start-up by a company that knew its processes and processing better than any other in the world. In the course of its expansion it had built fifty regional plants in different parts of the United States, five plants in Canada, and five more in different parts of England. All of the plants were generally similar, so that the construction and training routines had been extended into a standard operating procedure for start-ups, and the results had been as good as might have been expected. Now this was the start of a new wave of expansion, and the present long-range plan called for 100 more plants in less developed countries in the next five years, with the Taspotamia plant as the prototype.

Start-ups had been refined to the point that the company had a start-up control center, which was now monitoring the last phases of the start-up of the last two U.S. plants and the fifth English plant. There had been some unusual communication problems to solve, but the Taspotamia plant construction and start-up were being monitored in the same way. The control center had an electronic display wall on which a complete flowchart of the construction and start-up plan could be displayed in green, together with a display in red of the progress reported to that time. Every morning the president walked into the executive dining room for coffee; he could have had it served in his office, but he preferred to create an opportunity for informal discussion. And on his way to the dining room he walked through the start-up center and pushed the display buttons for any start-ups in which he had a particular interest.

Naturally the president was interested in Taspotamia, even though it was early in the construction—and the display showed it was three days behind schedule only one week after construction had started. He asked everyone who came for coffee if they knew what was holding up progress at Taspotamia, and then when he got back to his office, he got on the phone. The manager in charge of the start-up control center had cabled for information, but had received no response. The president called directly without worrying about what time it might be in Taspotamia. There was some trouble with the phone lines in the local area there, and the call was delayed. Finally his secretary was able to tell him that she had got the Taspotamia plant for him, and the president found himself talking to a sleepy field engineer who was spending the night at the site. But not to worry; the three days lost were actually five days lost because of delays in customs clearance of the bulldozers shipped in to do the grading: "Chief, it took us four days to find out that you can't get a single thing through Taspotamian customs unless 1 percent of its value is in an envelope in cash. The government doesn't pay customs people at all—they would literally starve to death if they didn't get something from each shipment they clear. But we know that now, the bulldozers are working from dawn to dusk when we figured only eight-hour days in the schedule, and we will have the job back on schedule before you know it."

The president was somewhat disgruntled about doing business in a country that didn't pay its customs agents, and somewhat reassured by the report that they were gaining on the schedule again. Sure enough, during the next week when he punched up the Taspotamia plant display, every day the red actual line had edged closer to the green line representing the schedule.

By the time site preparation and installation of the prefabricated building framing was complete, the Taspotamia plant was two days ahead of schedule, and everyone glowed. But when the manual part of the erection process started, progress slowed down. The president didn't panic as quickly this time, but he did ask the executive in charge of the Taspotamian operation to find out what the story was and tell him immediately. But then a cable came in to the start-up center that the plant was on strike and all construction suspended. How could there be a strike when there wasn't even a union? And so many members of top management put in direct calls to Taspotamia that they could not all be accommodated; what sounded like a young male Taspotamian with an Oxford accent suggested that the managers make a priority list, so that he would know in what order to put the calls through. The executive in charge of the Taspotamian operation was allowed to make the first call, with the rest of the executive group standing in a circle around the desk.

"We have a misunderstanding with these people," the engineer in charge of the construction told his boss at headquarters; the call was on the speaker so that the others could hear the conversation. "We have been treating them just like unskilled American workers, meaning that every man is equal, the way the law says. And in Taspotamia, they don't think everyone is equal. Some of these poor fellows are born to do the dirty work, according to the local view, and aren't even allowed to touch the others. Now we don't work that way, because it is not American, and we have been having more and more static. Then this morning we decided to settle this thing once and for all, and assigned work according to the number of weeks of seniority each man has in the crew. That put some of these so-called lower types of people in the same work crews as the rest, and you should have heard the fuss. And then every man of them walked out—the high-class and low-class people both seemed just as mad at us. It isn't a strike in the picketing way—it's just that every single worker disappeared completely. It's night here now, but I have an appointment with a Taspotamian Department of Labor person first thing in the morning, and another at the U.S. embassy in the capitol. The offices start late, so by the time I leave I will know if anybody came to work here, but the way it looks, I really doubt they will be back."

Construction was shut down for three weeks. The Taspotamian government was very upset that foreign managers refuse to treat decent Taspotamians the way that they were accustomed to be treated, and it took a week to get an appointment with anyone in the government influential enough to help get work started again. Then the Taspotamians offered a one-week training course in Taspotamian culture and customs for the entire U.S. construction group, and this was an offer that could not be refused. The third week was a slow process of negotiation with local leaders, and the fourth week construction resumed. Then, under work rules approved by the Taspotamians, progress began again, although the schedules were not quite met, and there seemed to be no way to regain the lost month.

Fortunately for the construction executives and the staff manning the start-up center, start-up schedules always had a hidden cushion for the unexpected, and as bits of this cushion came into the schedule, the month behind schedule began to shrink, to the point that the plant was completed on schedule and turned over to operations for checkout, operator training, and start-up. Checkout was easy, since the equipment was in good order, but red flags started to show again in the second week of operator training. Knowing that the president was about to ask, the headquarters group involved with the start-up made an appointment and went to see him. "Chief," the spokesman began, "we have hit something we never came up against before. The Taspotamians are not learning to operate the machinery."

"What do you mean, they are not learning to operate the machinery?"

"Just that. We are using the standard training courses we have been using for new operators for years. And the Taspotamians aren't learning. A one-week basic course for the simplest machine operations—nobody seemed even to know how to take the test, so we gave the whole week again. Now we have two classes of fifty each, each with ten instructors, we have gone over the material carefully twice, and not one of the hundred trainees shows any sign of even knowing how to run the machine badly, let alone passing a test."

"Could this be a language problem?"

"It's true that none of the instructors speaks Taspotamian, and none of the Taspotamians speaks English, but we have hired a translator for each instructor, and our manuals are so thoroughly illustrated with diagrams that they should be able to learn from the diagrams. After all, we used the same technique at our plant in Quebec; the workers there learned very quickly in spite of our not being able to speak French, and that plant started up with high production and high quality from the first day."

"Those people in Quebec are a lot better educated than the Taspotamians."

"Yes, Chief, of course. None of the Taspotamians can read or write, so far as we know. But our training material works just as well with functional illiterates in the United States—we have found good workers who couldn't read or write at all."

"Then what are you doing to solve the problem?"

"We don't know what to do. To try to find out, we have six experts on Taspotamia and its culture flying in from different U.S. universities, and we have asked for embassy help to find any company from any industrial nation that has trained Taspotamian workers for machine work. We can't be the first to try, but we haven't found a good lead yet."

"Have you asked any Taspotamians?" It turned out that they had not. The president asked why they had not. And although Taspotamia was classified low on the list of less developed countries, it had a small university with a surprisingly broad curriculum, including an engineering department. The head of the engineering department welcomed a visit from the operations manager of the plant, and after apologizing for the fact that Taspotamia was not yet able to have a proper engineering school according to American standards, he asked to see their training materials, and next day visited the training sessions in the new plant.

His conclusions were pointed, and not pleasant to hear: "You can't give my people IQ tests, because the workers you are training are too poorly educated to take such a test. As far as we can learn from other approaches to the testing, however, you will find their basic intelligence the equal of workers anywhere in the world. In fact, we believe that Taspotamians also have some unusual abilities, such as ability to recognize and match patterns, somewhat like some of the U.S. Indian tribes. Anyway, the intelligence is there. But your training materials assume a basic education that these people do not have; therefore they cannot succeed unless you revise your training materials."

The training group was stunned: "We don't assume any education at all; we have many examples of illiterate workers who have trained successfully with these materials."

"You Americans! You consider reading the only measure of education. But even your illiterates are very familiar with machines and machinery, because they have been surrounded by it all of their lives. These Taspotamians do not really know what machinery is; some of them have never been close to a machine of any sort, up to the day that they came into your training class. You have three levels of training to accomplish—first, to teach these people what the machines are; second, to teach them to be comfortable working with these machines; and third, how to operate them. You have training programs only for the third part, which is the quick and easy part."

The end result of all of the discussion was a new series of training classes. The first was a class in Taspotamian for the instructors, and meanwhile some Taspotamians that the head of the university engineering department had helped them find began to teach basic machine elements. And, as was its way, the company began to try to organize and plan this training material so that it could do the same job more easily in the future. By the end of three months some of the Taspotamians had advanced to the point that they began routine production, but for only an hour or two at a time and under close supervision of the instructors. By the end of the fifth month the plant was operating at half the planned capacity, and by the end of the tenth month it reached rated capacity, although costs were still above estimate. After it had been operating for eighteen months, the Taspotamia plant began to run like any other company plant after a successful start-up. And at this point the trainers felt that they could take an unskilled Taspotamian worker and carry that worker through to successful operation of a simple machine in six weeks, as compared to one week it required elsewhere.

Back at headquarters the president was both disheartened and furious. This was the worst start-up performance for the company since the fifth plant was built many years ago. He was trying to decide whether he should fire the whole training staff when he got a direct call from the plant manager in Taspotamia. "Chief, I thought you would like to know that the training director and I just got knighted by the president of Taspotamia for making outstanding contributions to the development of the country. And we have had six requests from different multinationals for information on how we train Taspotamians. All six want to send teams to observe our operation, and we need a policy decision on whether to let them in."

After he thought about the phone call, the president felt much better. He called for his planning director and asked him to start a revision of the expansion plan. "Apparently we need to build in more time and money for training of local labor according to the country. So we had better find out a lot more about these countries before we try to operate plants there. And all of the operating staff and at least half of the construction staff we send need to be fluent in the local language; that will cost us some time and money, too. But apparently we have learned to do something right. I am going to make all of our training materials company-confidential, and ask for suggestions for R&D projects on how to make the process work better."

Things were back to normal, and the president began to look forward to the next hundred new plant start-ups.

QUESTIONS

1. Do you think that the training materials and techniques should be kept confidential? Or shared freely between companies? Discuss.
2. Based on the above, do you think the next start-up in a less-developed country will go well? Or does this company still have a lot more to learn?

CASE 38 THE CHOCOLATE MACHINE COMPANY

In the beginning it was a European company building a plant in Oklahoma to supply its U.S. markets, but its name was difficult for truck drivers to handle, and they simplified it. When the U.S. manager learned of this, he wrote to his superior at the home office: "Our name is a problem here, because almost no one is familiar with any language but English, and even for the French our corporate name is complex. I discover that our deliveries and supplies are now being directed to the "Chocolate Machine Company," a rough English phonetic equivalent. For convenience I suggest that we make this the official name of our U.S. subsidiary." While the worldwide company was a major multinational with a complex name, the U.S. subsidiary became the Chocolate Machine Company.

This multinational was often cited as an example of good management of a fast-growing and far-flung industrial empire. In many ways it was, although there are many difficulties to be overcome in managing companies in different countries with different laws and customs. The problem that caused the discharge of the manager and three analysts in the Chocolate Machine Company job evaluation unit was caused by these discrepancies between practices in different countries.

This occurred in a large research laboratory, where much glassware had to be washed, and the glassware washers had always been women. Federal law mandated the end of sex discrimination, the Chocolate Machine Company opened these jobs to men, and many of the new hires were men. Of course, the men were paid the same wages as the women, but some of the senior scientists from various European countries had a different tradition; they felt that the men should be paid more because some had families, etc. Since management had decided to adhere to federal laws very strictly, these men found another way. They created a new job classification with additional duties, which they called an assistant technician. After this was duly approved by job evaluation as a more responsible job with a higher pay rate, all of the male glassware washers were promoted to assistant technician even though they continued to wash glassware full time just as before.

Naturally someone complained of discrimination against the female glassware washers; management discovered that the complaint was valid, and fired the job evaluation people who had allowed themselves to be fooled. The women glassware washers got a retroactive pay increase to the same level as the men, and several other job classifications had to be revised as a result. But management was not quite sure what to do about the scientists who had caused all of this trouble. These were very important and prestigious members of the research staff and the scientific community nationwide, and they justified their behavior by the customs in their native countries, although they had intentionally deceived management and broken U.S. law. Finally management compromised with a stern letter warning that U.S. laws against discrimination must be upheld.

Then the U.S. subsidiary was asked to lend a technical expert to assist the parent company in start-up of a new unit. This was a frequent sort of request, and the Chocolate Machine Company staff enjoyed the chance to spend a few months as an honored guest in another country. But in this case the best qualified person for the assignment was an Israeli, and the second was a woman, and the assignment was in one of the more remote parts of a major Arab country. Another employee, a white male, could probably do the job adequately, but was clearly less qualified. The Chocolate Machine Company did not want to break federal law against discrimination, and did not want to send an employee on an impossible assignment.

Finally the manager responsible called in the Israeli and said: "We have this assignment which you are well qualified to do, and by law we can't refuse to send you. But we are afraid you will not come back alive if you have to live for several months in a rural Arab country." The same manager pointed out to the woman the cultural differences that would make it difficult or impossible for a woman working alone to accomplish the assignment. After some thought and discussion, both agreed to being bypassed for this assignment, and the man who was the third choice was sent. The job took a little longer than it might have otherwise, but was completed satisfactorily.

The corporation held one of its periodic management conferences, and the president of the U.S. company was visiting over cocktails with a group of presidents and general managers of the subsidiaries in different countries. They talked about the problems of sending their people into Arab countries, or any country with other customs. "But the worst," one of them said, "is the problem of sending people into the home office." What he meant was that no one ever got promoted from any of the subsidiaries into the corporate headquarters; only nationals of the home country worked there. And it turned out that for many of the subsidiaries this was a major problem.

"If I get a good technical director," said one, "I have no promotion to offer unless I give up my own job. And we are a small company; so an ambitious person will work for me for a few years until he gets really good. He can't go to any other part of this company, so he will quit and go to a larger company to get advancement."

"The same thing happens a lot with general managers," said another. He turned to the president of the U.S. company: "You run a big company. Maybe it doesn't mean anything to you that you can't ever be promoted into the management of our parent. But I run a little company, and most of the other men here do too. We must either be content to be minor managers for life, or change companies. I like this company and I don't want to leave it; but the largest reason we lose general managers is when they go to better jobs outside. And then we look at some of the children that have major management jobs in the home office, because the home company they are promoted out of is not very large, and everything is growing so fast that they must be moved up very rapidly to fill the jobs."

The president of the U.S. company thought about this conversation for a long time. Personally he had decided that he did not really want to move his home and family to the European headquarters city anyway, and he did have a very good job running a large company, so that he was not personally uncomfortable with this corporate policy. He was very troubled at the thought of the talent being lost worldwide because none of these people could be promoted outside of their own country. But he also knew of multinational companies that had had bad experiences with promotion of nationals from other countries into the headquarters group because they and their families found the adjustment very difficult. He decided he didn't know whether the problem was with the policies of these companies, though, or with the way they carried them out.

QUESTIONS

1. How should a multinational corporation operate in order to get the best potential from all of its employees?
2. How can a multinational move employees back and forth between countries and cultures and be fair in all of its actions, when different countries and cultures have such different rules for handling people? Discuss.
3. Should a multinational promote its top managers only from the home country? Or from the whole enterprise? How can it best manage the conflicts that come from either policy?
4. Should the scientists have been punished for maneuvering a violation of U.S. laws to pay the male glassware washers more? Or was the fact that they were behaving correctly according to the rules in their home country justification enough?

CHAPTER 20

THE POLITICAL WORLD AROUND THE ORGANIZATION

KEY IDEAS IN THIS CHAPTER

The business of business is business, but it exists in a political world; Chapter 20 discusses business relationships with political power and their implications for strategy and policy:

- **economic power versus political power** – the power of a wealthy business against the political system; the people always win if they are enough to speak out.
- **relationships with government power** – the problem is how to keep good working relationships without getting too close.
- **business policy for a political world** – chapter summary of a difficult, sensitive relationship area for strategic management.

In Chapter 6 public strategy was listed as one of the key components of the governing enterprise strategy, and the present chapter considers the consequent problem or opportunity as the business interacts with government power. When the enterprise is asked to support candidates or programs, or otherwise to make its position in the society useful to others around it, management should consider the nature of the firm's position, and the way in which its resources should or should not be used. The starting point is further exploration of the power and the limitations of a business in dealing with the political process.

ECONOMIC POWER VERSUS POLITICAL POWER[1]

Some fear corporate power, which is the power a business enterprise possesses. Corporate power is real but limited in extent. As an economic entity, a business often wields substantial economic power. Economic power can lead to political influence but not political power, and the boundary between political influence and political power is a critical one that provides an important limit to the power of any corporation.

Political power is ultimately based on the support of large numbers of people, where political influence is the ability to guide the actions of those who hold political power. Politicians or elected officials will have a base of political power so long as they have the support of the constituents from whom that power is ultimately derived. Even the political power of a dictatorship or other totalitarian form of government requires at least the passive consent of the majority of the governed, because of the ultimate power of the people as a whole. Many totalitarian states use propaganda and limit the freedom of speech of their opponents, as a means of maintaining this passive consent.

Because political power is normally delegated quietly to representatives, economic power can gain substantial control through political influence. As long as these actions do not cause enough concern to the constituency to jeopardize the political power of their representatives, these representatives can often be induced to take actions favoring a business. A large part of the art of politics is to function in such a way as to maintain a secure base of political power. As a result, the political influence of economic power will be accepted by those in political leadership only to the extent that their political power base is not jeopardized. This limita-

---

[1] George C. Sawyer, "Corporate Allegiances to the Local Society," *Columbia Journal of World Business*, Winter 1978, pp. 39–44.

tion on economic power is clear-cut, and accounts for the difference in the dynamics of the use of political and economic power.

The distinction between political influence and political power is real and critical. Business influence in political areas is based only on economic power. While the business may be a controlling force through its use of such influence, the process must be conducted subtly and must avoid any substantial confrontation with real political power based on the desires of masses of people. Through political power the rules are made; if a confrontation between economic power and political power is allowed to occur, those with the political power can change the rules, take away the economic resources, and eliminate the opposing economic power. This has happened to foreign multinationals repeatedly in African and South American countries. Business self-interest normally requires avoidance of confrontation with political power in each political jurisdiction where it operates.

This self-interest in avoiding confrontation with political power almost eliminates the potential for the great supranational corporate force that has been raised as a political spectre. For example, ITT was profiled as such a force.[2] Yet when it chose to enter the political arena in Chile to ensure the defeat of a leftist presidential candidate, ITT moved out of its position as a business entity looking to Chilean law for protection of its proper interests; it attempted to establish itself as a force in Chilean politics. Such a potential political force represented a threat to the real political power and could not be tolerated. When that candidate was elected, the ITT subsidiary was seized as an enemy of the state, while many other subsidiaries of U.S. companies were allowed to continue in operation.

A business that has economic power can exert economic influence. This economic influence can be converted to political influence but not to political power. However, if political influence is used with sufficient skill so that the holders of the political power sense no challenge, such influence can sometimes achieve political governance and effectively control public policy; this is its potential and its danger.

The control on business political influence is dual. First, the means by which political influence is maintained are subject to review. Recent progress through disclosure of improper corporate political payments forced by the SEC seems likely to lead to more cautious behavior by certain U.S. corporations and also to similar disclosure requirements elsewhere. Raising the awareness of this potential abuse of economic power increases both the risk and likelihood of discovery, thus reducing the incentive to misbehave in this way.

---

[2] Anthony Sampson, *The Sovereign State of ITT* (New York: Stein and Day Publishers, 1973).

The second and more powerful control on misuse of business economic power to influence the political process is the risk of offense to the political power latent in the people. As worldwide sensitivity to this problem grows, as from the Lockheed and Recruit scandals in Japan, it becomes more hazardous for a business to attempt to maintain improper political influence. Where many business battles in the market place can be lost in one year and won in the next, the losses in confrontation with political power tend to be more permanent. Lockheed achieved aircraft sales to Japan by improper payments that then came to light and ultimately caused a change in the Japanese government. Lockheed faces a long rebuilding task if it is ever to regain its former commercial stature in Japan.

Businesses should avoid confrontation with political power except as a last resort because the business is so likely to lose and the loss is so likely to be large. And since this political power is local to each political jurisdiction, it forms the potent, ultimate force toward requiring a business to operate as a compatible, contributing entity within the local society.

This political power did not check improper corporate use of political influence in past generations, partly because the direct, local use of their own power was not familiar to the people in many less developed countries. This situation has changed, and the awareness of actual and potential abuse of corporate power is growing daily. Consequently, local political power and the business fear of arousing it will be an increasingly effective check on corporate actions in the future.

RELATIONSHIPS WITH GOVERNMENT POWER

Political leaders almost always seek a working relationship with the leaders of the significant business firms—because these firms and their leaders are important elements of society, and because the businesses have money that would be very useful to the political process. Federal law forbids contribution of corporate funds to candidates in federal elections, and some states have similar laws.

However, the law does permit the formation of Political Action Committees among the managers of a business. Membership must be voluntary, and then the committee decides what to do with its contributions. Inevitably a committee of managers seem to decide to contribute to some of the same candidates the business would have supported, if it had been possible for it to contribute.

The same people who would offer favors and hope for donations of business funds will sometimes seek the loan of a corporate jet, the hiring

FIGURE 20–1 POLITICAL RELATIONSHIPS AS A COMPONENT OF STRATEGIC MANAGEMENT

Political realities versus the business
- business operates at the sufferance of society.
- the government exists with the sufferance of the people as a whole.
- the people of a country are the ultimate holders of the political power.
- the political power in a society cannot be ignored.

The real force is the political power
- political power derives from the desires of masses of people.
- those with the political power can make the rules— but usually delegate their power to leaders or representatives.
- business has only economic power.
- economic power can be used to gain political influence.
- political influence can sway the delegates who exercise the political power.
- the limit of political influence is the threat of a change in this delegation.
- when economic power and political power conflict, those with the political power can change the rules and take away the wealth that opposed them.

Government power and the business
- the government power is the power of the delegate establishment.
- the delegates may or may not be secure in their power.
- as society's rule-makers for now, the business needs a working relationship with these delegates in order to operate.

STRATEGIC MANAGEMENT OF THE NECESSARY LIAISON WITH POLITICAL POWER

of a relative, or another sort of favor. Because the business unit is such an influential component of society, and because its decisions have such significant impact, the desire is quietly to influence those decisions in favor of some specific person or cause.

BUSINESS POLICY FOR A POLITICAL WORLD

The political dimension of business policy and strategy is an important, sensitive dimension, but should change strategy and policy little beyond the elements already integrated as part of the enterprise strategy for public role and image, and for the management of the business' social impact. The reason for separate consideration and discussion of this political area is largely to reemphasize the nature of the relationships and their great sensitivity, although requirements for a successful policy and strategy approach were defined in earlier chapters. Figure 20-1 shows this area as another component of the necessary strategic management posture.

QUESTIONS FOR ANALYSIS AND DISCUSSION

1. Find your own illustrations of the political influence of various businesses. When is this healthy for society? When is it unhealthy? How can society ensure that such influence will be healthy?
2. Find your own examples of the interaction between political power and economic power. Is there any doubt about which is greater?
3. List a series of business relationships with government in various countries; try to get a wide variety of different types of relationships. Which are healthy and constructive? Which are not? Potentially, what could be done about this?

FOR FURTHER INFORMATION

Ball, Donald A., & Wendell C. McCulloch, Jr., *International Business*, 3rd Ed. (Plano, Texas: BPI, 1986).
   A good overview of the major considerations.

Buchholz, Rogene A., *Business Environment and Public Policy*, 2nd Ed. (Englewood Cliffs, N.J.: Prentice-Hall, 1986).
   Public policy aspects of business relationships with political power.

CASE 39 THE GREEN EMERALD MINING COMPANY

One Tuesday morning in Parliament a cabinet minister proposed the expropriation of the Green Emerald Mining Company. Green Emerald mined copper, lead, and bauxite, and its name came from a mountain lake bordering its first mining claim. In earlier years the heavy work of mining copper and lead had required legions of workers; Green Emerald had built towns and moved mountains in the course of getting the copper and lead out. Then some of its earlier properties had begun to produce less; it had found bauxite, and broadened its scope to become a significant supplier of ore to the aluminum industry. Green Emerald was profitable, of course. Its management insisted on its being classified as a socially responsible corporation, and even its critics admitted that it treated and paid its workers better and maintained better working conditions than most other foreign corporations active in the country.

But expropriation? There had been a few pickets from a group called Flaming Swords, but this didn't seem significant. Then William, the president of the local Green Emerald subsidiary, got a call from another cabinet minister, and half an hour later was in that minister's office when several other government officials came in. Expropriation? William was dumbfounded. The cabinet minister said: "This proposal will be debated for a week or two in our Parliament. It may pass, but it will be vetoed and killed for now. Our president considers it premature, although not necessarily wrong. For many years you have lived off of the wealth of our country, made large profits, and taken them out of our poor land. We are not angry at you, for you have treated our people fairly for the most part, but we are a poor country, we have only so much wealth in our mountains, and we must have that wealth used for the good of all of our people. Expropriation is not today, and I am sure that when the time comes, we will want to pay you a fair price—but it is only a matter of time. Please tell your masters in your country that this is what is going to happen."

William thought about all of this very intensely on the drive back to the mine where his headquarters were. When he got back, he called his boss in New York to report. After the two had talked for a while, William said: "Boss, this is the sort of thing we brainstormed about when we did the Green Valley proposal. I know that is still in the corporate process somewhere—and every two or three months I have tried to get you to shake it loose and get it approved. That is a very high-profit venture. I understand the only hesitation was a reluctance to increase our investment in this country, but the cash flow from the mines was going to fund the whole thing, and that cash flow is being threatened.

"I think the Green Valley plan is what we need right now. I would like to unfold that for discussion with the government—without committing us to the details—but to take their mind off of this expropriation foolishness. I know you can't make a commitment this minute, but if you could get me a green light within a day or two, I think I can convince them we have been working on this—because we have. In three or four weeks there would be no point, because they will think we dreamed it all up after we were threatened."

Two hours later the president called from New York and gave William the necessary approvals. He immediately called the same cabinet minister: "Our company has been planning major investments in new industries in your country for some of the same reasons you suggested. Our plans are at the stage that we are now developing them in full detail. We were nearing the point of discussing them with your government, then delayed a little because some of our people questioned whether we should invest so much more down here. These objections have been overcome, but I don't know how our discussion this morning will change all of this.

"I believe I should lay all of this out for you and whomever else you may wish to include, and then we can talk about how everything fits together. I could do this later today, or tomorrow." They settled on the following morning, and William's staff worked into the night making photocopies and otherwise organizing the materials to describe the Green Valley proposal.

The meeting the next day went exactly the way that William had expected—meaning that the government officials were swept off their feet by the scope and impact of the proposal. Green Emerald planned to build a series of local industries, transforming that area from mining and rural into a substantial, modern, nonpolluting industrial district. Employment needs would exceed the local labor supply, meaning that the region would draw workers out of the urban slums and poor rural districts elsewhere in the country. The mine profits and other cash flow would be diverted into the funding of Green Valley, relieving a major strain on an economy that now had difficulty earning enough foreign exchange after essential imports to offset repatriation of Green Emerald profits. Many of the new industries would be exporters, and by generating a new stream of exports, Green Emerald helped the country and gained the option of taking its profits from export sales in other currencies more easily transferable back to the United States.

Euphoria set in after William's presentation, until he asked pointedly whether the expropriation threat should cause his management to cancel the Green Valley plan. Three cabinet ministers were present; they requested time for a caucus and withdrew. They came back to say that they had called the president and the rest of the cabinet, who began to arrive within a few minutes. William made the same presentation again, received the same sort of applause, and asked the same pointed question about whether his management should go ahead. This time the whole cabinet withdrew for a caucus that took over an hour.

Chapter 20 The Political World Around the Organization

When they came back, the president of the republic spoke for the group: "Senior William, you have presented an exciting prospect for an industrial development our country needs very badly. Assuming it details out the way you have outlined it, the plan will have the full and enthusiastic support of my government. But you ask about the expropriation issue, and I must give you two answers. In the first place, you told us you had planned on the income from your mines to help finance the grand plan; my government will support you as far as it can, and that certainly means that we will not press for expropriation. But in the second place, my government represents millions of citizens, mostly poor and hungry, who have grown very angry over having our industries controlled by foreign interests who grow fat from profits earned in our poor country. And now there is this strange new political party called Flaming Sword that is rallying our poorest citizens. Their cry is not for expropriation or for any other legal remedy, but for a flaming sword to purify our soil of foreign influence.

"To come back to the question you ask—if your company and my government can agree on the details of this grand new plan, we will give it our full personal and official support. But that leaves unknown what our people will say, and whether the flaming swords can be quenched except with blood. Some of our own party proposed this expropriation of major foreign corporations as a conservative middle ground, to head off this madness. You are convincing me we should not expropriate your corporation, but this means we will have to face the anger of our people more directly."

William and his bosses talked about the situation and their options. The Green Valley plan was clearly better than expropriation. William was told to start it in motion and also—hopefully—to figure out a strategy for dealing with the power of the people. Meanwhile they learned that a parliamentary maneuver had substituted a Dutch bank and a South African bank as expropriation targets in the bill the Parliament was debating. Eventually the bill passed, it was not vetoed, and two small but universally disliked foreign corporations disappeared.

The Green Valley Plan called for a series of new industries, all logically related to each other, with a cement company as a starting point. The country now imported its cement. Having its own production would save foreign exchange and cut construction costs. The plan was for a plant with two rotary kilns, one of which had been a part of an idle Green Emerald smelter that would now house both the cement plant and a brick plant. A newer and more modern cement kiln would be added as soon as practical, but the plant could start to make cement in the old one almost immediately since the stone and other materials were readily available.

William's engineers said they would be ready to start hiring and training employees for the cement plant start-up crew in six weeks. William briefed the head of the local union and the governor of the province, telling them about the cement plant, the brick plant, the coal mines, and that this was a part of a much larger plan to be announced shortly. The Green Valley Plan was formally announced in a ceremony on the steps of the capitol by William and one of the cabinet ministers.

Many of the supervisors and skilled workers needed for the cement plant were employees promoted from the company's mines, and many new workers were hired. By the time the cement plant was in operation, a brick plant in the other part of the same old smelter was almost ready for start-up. Coal was available in the region, and a major mining development was underway very soon—plus a barge line, to provide economical water transportation for the mines, cement, brick, coal, and for the country as a whole. The company organized a construction company, and a shipping, handling, and warehousing facility in the nearest major seaport, to ensure efficient and economical linkages among the different transportation forms, and then moved into the next phase of establishing a series of industrial development areas. The country was well supplied with electricity from major hydroelectric installations, and had a basic network of railroads. The idea was, that with good services, efficient plant, and low-cost labor the country had become a very attractive industrial site for international companies planning to supply this and other surrounding countries; a Japanese manufacturer had already agreed to locate an automobile assembly plant in one industrial development area, for example.

The real target was to develop local industry, of which there was very little—except that Green Emerald had formed a venture investment company and a private development bank. These encouraged the formation of a packaged food company and a grocery chain, both of which needed extensive consultant help in the early years and then succeeded dramatically. Other local industries soon followed.

By now William had encountered the agitators for the Flaming Sword party many times and had become acquainted with one or two of their leaders. This gave him a private route for discussions of the many ways in which his program and theirs had parallel objectives—culminating eventually in the creation of a Flaming Sword venture development fund, to aid and assist poor entrepreneurs from rural areas in starting their own businesses.

Because the Green Valley Plan went forward smoothly, within two years the country could see the impact of the hiring for new industries, and the areas near the plants were feeling the benefits of the increased payrolls. In another two years the stimulus of more new industries had begun to spread across the country, and near the Green Valley plants businessmen were beginning to grumble a little because it was harder now to hire good help. The expropriation threat seemed to have vanished, and the Green Emerald's new investments were paying very well. The only problem was that William, who was president of the whole company by now, still wanted to keep reinvesting all of the rapidly increasing

Green Emerald cash flow in further growth of the country, but the profits were so attractive that the directors didn't really try to argue.

QUESTIONS

1. Why should the president of a country be so tentative in his endorsement of a plan that was so obviously beneficial? Discuss.
2. If this additional industrial development was so profitable for William's company, why do you think they waited so long to start?
3. What enterprise strategies had to be changed before Green Emerald could undertake the Green Valley Plan?

CASE 40 NERDLY ELECTRIC AND GAS COMPANY

Joe and Sam were in the bar across the street from the Nerdly Electric and Gas headquarters office building after a major sales presentation to a group of Nerdly executives. The presentation had not gone well. They were disheartened and sipped silently for some time.

"Hi, fellows, I thought you would be halfway back to the big city by now." Joe and Sam recognized a Nerdly power coordinator who had sat in on the meeting. The coordinator continued: "You guys have a very impressive line of merchandise. You must enjoy handling it."

"Ordinarily, yes," Sam answered, "but you guys seemed so darned uninterested that we are a little down right now."

"I can tell you haven't been around the utility business much. You shouldn't be discouraged, but you should learn more about what makes a company like Nerdly tick. You have great stuff, but you didn't have a chance today because you didn't give us any reason to be interested."

Joe protested: "But our machinery does a quality job for less. Why doesn't that interest you?"

"That's what I mean. You need to understand us better." He signalled for another round. "You start by thinking we want to save money, and sometimes we don't. If we can put in a machine and put it in our rate base without any fuss, we really don't care what it costs; our return is based on our investment, and the rate of return the public service commission allows is a good one; so we are on cost-plus, and you can't get us excited by cutting the equipment cost."

"But if you guys don't care that much about the costs, why do I keep reading about utilities with all sorts of cost and profit troubles?"

"Now you are getting closer to the money. You have to look at the regulatory process and the way that it works. The public service commission is getting all sorts of static about the routine twice-a-year rate increases, and since we got an automatic adjustment for changes in fuel cost, those increases are due to the rising cost of labor—our own, and the services we purchase. That is where we need to save, by cutting down on the labor and purchased services the system needs, to get better control of routine operating costs. If your machines had a higher reliability and a lower maintenance cost, that would interest us more than a savings in the purchase price."

"But our machines do have a higher reliability and a lower maintenance cost," Joe sputtered.

"Then you should have told us that, more than how much less they cost. Anyway, the areas where you get our attention are in helping with costs that we have trouble getting approval to pass on to our customers. At the moment those are the rising costs of running our network, mostly labor-related costs, and the "big surprise" kinds of costs the heavy overruns in construction expense on the big new plants have caused. Nerdly isn't much involved in the big cost overruns, fortunately."

Sam had been silent up until now: "From what you say, we missed a big opportunity, because we have a good story on lower maintenance costs and higher labor productivity, particularly at the high end of our line. But we didn't talk about that at all because our industrial customers have been so much more interested in cutting the first cost.

"We need to learn a little more about the utility business and then try again. Can we buy you dinner and talk some more?"

The result was a long evening of eating, drinking, and talking. Another Nerdly executive drifted in, and the four of them struggled with a definition of the way that a public utility operated. It operated very freely, and could do almost anything it wanted to do in planning for its future. No approval was needed to start to build a nuclear plant or any other kind of plant; except that each type of construction must be licensed for safety, environmental impact, and so forth before construction or before start-up by the agencies with that jurisdiction. But no one worried about whether the utility could afford a given new plant, or knew how to manage the construction project, or even what the project would do to the electric rates.

But the operation was tightly controlled in many ways. Whatever plan Nerdly Electric submitted for billing its customers became a rule, almost with the force of law once approved, and Nerdly could not raise or lower its charges or calculate them in a different way without going back to the public service commission and petitioning for a change. So that while Nerdly may have had a great deal to do with creating the rules at some time in the past, in the present they were cast in concrete until the commission approved a change.

Sam and Joe were fascinated. They never had encountered businesses with so much freedom in some dimensions and so many restrictions in the others. "The one thing I don't understand," Sam said, "is what difference it makes if the cost of electric power is high or low."

"You understand more than you think you do. The cost of power doesn't matter at all, unless it gets so high that it drives industry away. The rate of return is figured from what the cost is, high or low, and there is no good yardstick for what is too high. Some people think new power transmission technology will make power cheap enough to ship around so that the state public service commissions won't let a company expand if it can buy power cheaper, but everyone everywhere wants the plants to be local and no one wants to depend on long lines from somewhere else."

QUESTIONS

1. All industries are regulated, to some degree. To what extent are public utilities more regulated? Illustrate with examples from other industries. Are there areas where public utilities are less regulated? Illustrate.

2. The theory of public utility price regulation comes from microeconomics, and requires that rates be set at the lowest price that will allow the utility to recover its costs, including a fair return on the capital invested. This would work very well if the costs were always kept at the lowest possible level; but this is hard to enforce in the absence of competition. How could the comparative performance of other companies be used to make this rate-setting process work more in the public interest?

CHAPTER 21

FROM PLANNING AND STRATEGY TO ACTION

KEY IDEAS IN THIS CHAPTER

This chapter presents an integrated summary of key elements from the book as a whole:

- **creating resources** – a key strategic management talent.
- **power for the strategy** – effective strategies bring results because their leverages generate power to drive them.
- **substance governs strategy** – strategic management requires the ability to reach past the forms and procedures and work with the real substance of the strategy.
- **the entrepreneur as a rent collector** – an unfamiliar image, but a process by which some strategic managers make their companies very rich.
- **policy, strategy, and the business firm** – recapitulation of interrelationship between the different types and levels of strategy.

- **designing effective strategies** – breaking new ground, by approaching customer needs, markets, and competitors in a different way.
- **strategy and the excellence model** – often, but not always, a high-performing organization is required to make a strategy work, and the excellence model can be the basis for creating it.
- **conclusion** – good strategy design is a key component of effective strategic management.

Successful action means doing the right things at the right times. Effective strategies are those strategies that lead to successful action. What action will succeed at a given time depends on many things, including all of the circumstances and alternatives and an element of luck. Designing effective strategy is the science and art of considering and understanding enough of these circumstances and alternatives so that strategies leading to successful action are chosen.

Success means that the strategy works; that is, that it brings about the desired results. This may be easy or difficult. Most experienced managers can give examples of successful strategies that really should have failed—but some fortunate combination of circumstances carried them through. And most can name a corporate goliath with a weak strategy—a successful but vulnerable company that may continue to prosper indefinitely unless some David takes note and attacks. But most collections of strategy stories also include very good strategies that deserved to succeed but did not, for some accidental or unforeseeable reason. The conclusion is that the strategy design process can be fallible, in spite of the best efforts of the participants, because the world of real markets and organizations contains so many surprises, good and bad.

But most strategies do not encounter the sorts of radical, unpredictable good or bad fortune that overrides plans and forecasts. Most well-planned strategies can be executed largely according to these plans and do yield approximately the desired results. That is, strategy can be designed, and if the design process illustrated in Figure 21-1 and discussed in earlier chapters is well executed, the action directed by that strategy will be successful in most cases. The purpose of this chapter is to summarize that design process.

CREATING RESOURCES

One of the most important dimensions in design of a strategy is any need or plan to create resources. To cause the purchase of the specific product, perhaps a new leverage needs to be established in the customer's mind.

FIGURE 21-1 STRATEGIC MANAGEMENT: FROM PLANNING AND STRATEGY TO ACTION

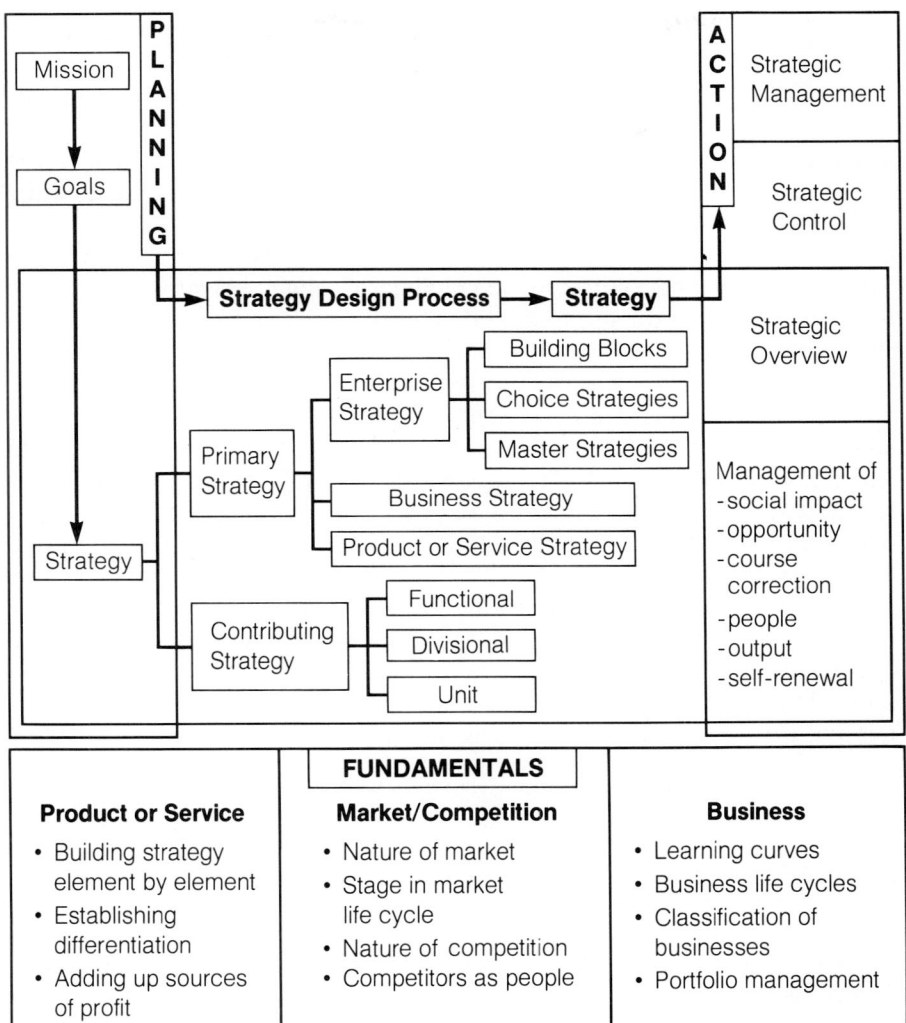

This creation has a cost, according to the effort required. If this effort builds a position, whether based on new features, lower price, brand identity, or another favorable attribute, then a resource is also created. This new position can usually be used again and should earn rent.

The process of resource creation needs specific attention because it has high potential and is so little recognized. Even though example after example of dramatic business success includes important created resources, business proposals are too often compared as if the requested amount of money defined the resource need. The resource requirement is often far larger, and if a given management can truly create the other needed resources, the investment will return handsomely; if it cannot, the business will fail even if funded with twice the requested number of dollars.

Designing strategy is something like the farm-era problem of pulling up a stump or lifting a tractor engine. Given three strong timbers to make a tripod and suitable tackle, almost any large object can be lifted. Given the problem of something heavy to lift, solution starts by finding hoisting tackle powerful enough to lift it—a chain hoist to raise an engine block, or a set of good needs-leverages linkages to raise sales in the market place. Then there must be a tripod strong enough to take the strain—three good fence posts to pull up a stump, and careful support from the characteristics of the product, the market, and the business itself, in the case of a business strategy.

Earlier chapters dealt with the product, market, and business characteristics to aid in constructing a robust basis for a given strategy in each. The needs-leverages linkages must provide the power to convince the necessary numbers of customers to buy; but their effectiveness depends on sturdy support in the fundamental characteristics of the product, competition and market, and the business. A farmer trying to pull up a stump was sometimes hurt if one leg of his tripod broke, because the power of his hoist was to no avail without strong supports. Also for strategy, good needs-leverages linkages are essential, but so are strong supports. No one wants to have a product, market, or business assumption fail and the strategy come tumbling down.

POWER FOR THE STRATEGY

The strategy tripod requires three strong supports plus needs-leverages linkages powerful enough to overcome the resistance. But the leverages do not work alone. A lever by itself does not raise a weight, but it can magnify the force available until it meets the need. The potential increase of a force by a suitable system of leverages is almost infinite if the levers are good enough; Archimedes said that with a suitable lever he himself could move the world. The working of a system of levers depends on the force applied, the nature of the leverages, and the amount of resistance to be overcome.

Needs-leverages linkages tie a product or service to a customer need in a way that is intended to cause the customer to see their value and make the purchase. The power on the lever, to make the purchase actually happen, comes from that customer's perceptions of the need and the ability of that power or service to fill it.

To get power for the levers, a marketer attempts to sharpen the customer's perception of the need, to increase urgency and reduce deferability of the purchase—and works even harder to establish the potential for a specific product or service to fill that customer's need better and more favorably than any alternative. There are two sources of power, therefore: the pressures of the customer's inherent need and the potency of the product offering, both based on the buyer's perception as reinforced by the seller.

Both sources of power are invoked first by the skill and deftness of the sales effort, and more fundamentally by the intrinsic merit of the product as filling the need in a superior way. Creation of this power is by producing an effective deliverable and presenting it well. The first Xerox copiers were so superior to their alternatives for most purposes that the issue was almost entirely one of need. If the customer could be convinced of the need for a copier, the Xerox was almost the only way to fill the need. The power to the leverages, and thus the power of the strategy, was from effective programs for spreading the use of copying.

Now many good copy machines are available. The power to the leverages for an effective copier marketing strategy is largely based on differential advantages—why one machine is better or less expensive in a certain application than the others. The customer needs are little changed, although with more flexible and less expensive machines the market has continued to expand. The purchase leverages have become comparative, and the needs-leverages linkages largely build on "a better way to satisfy your copying needs."

Some copier strategies are based on new features—advanced controls, easier care, less maintenance, and so forth. Others emphasize quality, reliability, and service relative to alternatives. Still others feature low cost—of the machine, of owning it, or of the per-copy cost of its services. The various copier manufacturers are competing to produce better copiers technically, machines and copies of higher quality, copiers easier to care for, more reliable, and requiring less service, and lower-cost machines or machines lowering the cost per copy. Each of these advances is quickly matched by the others. All of these features are demanding to obtain, and many organizations are competing for the same advances in each feature.

Various manufacturers have established positions in the copier market, with the Xerox position the most formidable, but none of these positions seems to be yielding large rents. The market has adjusted to copier availability from many vendors, and other manufacturers have had many years to match the original Xerox cost and manufacturing positions. It seems probable that the successful survivors in this market will be those able to gain competitive advantage over their competitors most rapidly and consistently.

This competition is not over the ability to do a task, but to do it better and more rapidly than competitive groups. The outcome should be determined by the relative skills of the several managements in selecting development targets and the relative effectiveness of their organizations in achieving them. This is a market in which the excellence model will make a difference. This is a market in which the power to the leverages must come primarily from performance of the organization.

With many vendors constructing needs-leverages linkages based on the same set of needs, this is a market in which one or several of the different sorts of organizational effectiveness—in developing new features; in quality, reliability, and performance; in cost; in field support of the machines—will determine who combines the most force and the best leverages; that is, who transmits the most force from its leverages to the need, and thus gains the market advantage.

Power for the strategy must be sufficient to give the best set of needs-leverages linkages if that strategy is to be effective. This means good presentation of good products, of course. As competitive pressure rises, the strategy requires better and better leverages and more and more power. Where established positions no longer yield rents to protect the leader, as they once protected Xerox, the competitive issue will be determined by quality of management, quality of organization, and some element of chance. The more difficult the competitive situation may be, the more carefully constituted the strategy must be, and the more the excellence model helps in making it effective—in making it profitable, that is.

SUBSTANCE GOVERNS STRATEGY

The need and challenge in designing strategy are to plan the right actions and execute them. This requires an ability to look at business situations and see the substance through papers, procedures, and forms, and this is not a common ability.

The manager of a Cyanamid feed blending department noticed that quantities of export orders from his plant were being returned unsold for salvage or reprocessing, sometimes a year or two later. Export shipments went to a warehouse to be held until export clearances, import licenses, and letters of credit could be obtained. This took many months, during which there were order changes and cancellations. Packages became dirty in the warehouse and bags got broken. The products, which had a limited shelf life, sometimes reached the point where not enough of their dating remained for them to be sold.

This department head asked why the products had to be produced before the clearance to ship them had been obtained. At first no one could answer the question; then someone realized that the product lot numbers were needed on the clearance papers. The department head then suggested that the lot numbers be assigned and his crew print the bags for the product; these bags would be held empty in his plant until a few days before shipping and then filled with the appropriate product.

This proposal caused confusion and met resistance because it did not follow standard operating procedures, but no one could find anything wrong with it. The department head kept insisting on an answer, his boss and his boss's boss agreed that he was entitled to an answer to his question, no one could find a defensible reason for turning him down, and finally his suggestion was tried. It worked well. A large in-process inventory disappeared, to the point that Cyanamid discovered it no longer needed a major warehouse in Fairlawn, N.J., which then was closed. The savings also included avoided loss of dated products, reduced inventory investment, and the reduced costs in handling and warehousing, but the amount was never made known to the division responsible for the cost reduction because higher-level management was embarrassed to admit how much such a simple change had saved.

After this change had been absorbed by the system and some of its managers reflected on it, embarrassment increased. They realized it was not necessary to preprint the product packages for the export shipments; lot numbers were easy to preassign and reserve; this permitted all of the paperwork to go forward, and the production could be scheduled a few days before the desired shipping date. This change was also made, and the system had finally moved to the point where it should have started, with the paper clearances managed by scheduling and sales, and production concerned only with making product when needed for actual shipments. The system would have been set up this way when the export sales strategy was defined in the first place, if any one of dozens of analysts and managers involved in its function had thought about the substance of how to fill export orders rather than building an inefficient process around existing forms and procedures.

The point is not to single out Cyanamid but to suggest that a common failing in organizations, particularly large ones, is for people to do their jobs and lay out their strategies in terms of the routine procedures and standard instructions without thinking about the substance of the task at all. Effective strategy must be based on the substance of the process, and is unlikely to be formulated by a manager who has not learned to look past the procedures and come to grips with the substance.

THE ENTREPRENEUR AS A RENT COLLECTOR

Positions are a key element of business and product strategies, as discussed before. Their value is as something to build on, a resource making possible leverages increasing the effectiveness of a strategy. As such, positions have value and earn a return in the market place. This return is a form of rent, as discussed in Chapter 4.

The rent a position earns is its contribution to the total profitability of a strategy. That total profit potentially has many sources, where effective distribution service is one and brokerage between bulk purchases and smaller sales is another. Innovation and rent can be the largest profits, but they can fade away, whereas a distribution profit or a brokerage profit tends to be more constant. Profits from innovation are the returns to the creation of a product or service with superior needs-leverages linkages—something better that people will willingly pay more for, or something equally good for less money. The impact of the innovation can be clear cut, and its profits are often generous.

Rent is less obvious, but perhaps larger over the long term. A patent, by design a monopoly, earns a rent to the extent of its profit contribution if it bars a competitor from the market. To the extent that the Hoffmann-La Roche position in the Valium market was due to a now-expired patent on this drug substance, that patent earned very handsome rents. Actually many other positions contributed also, and probably in later years the franchise of the product with the medical profession and with consumers was at least as important as the patent—but that franchise was also a position that earned rent.

Any position has the potential to help create leverages and earn rent. The manager whose zone of authority includes various positions should count them among the resources managed. That manager should be responsible for reporting on the rents each of these positions is earning, and projecting what he or she will do to increase rent collections.

This brings the discussion to the entrepreneur in the role of rent-collector, because this is a very important role. Coca-Cola long resisted any secondary use of its Coke market franchise in spite of a large rent potential, on the basis that this might dilute the position and endanger its ability to continue the long-term Coke profit flows—including a very important and substantial rent stream. Then when changes in competition and taste brought the need for variations on the traditional Coca-Cola product, the Coke brand franchise was broadened very successfully to include the diet and other new products. Some of the key management decisions at Coca-Cola in recent years, therefore, were concerned with Coca-Cola Corporation rent collections.

Whether the position is a brand name, a superior distribution access to a market, an advantageous production or raw materials position, or mastery of a difficult technology, the strategic question is how to get the most rent. Sometimes this involves broader use of the brand or other position and sometimes it does not, depending on the situation and the likely competitive consequences. But the success of major market forces—IBM comes to mind—develops in part because they know how to get maximum rents from their positions, and how to keep strengthening these positions so that these rents will continue into the future. Some of their top managers are very good rent collectors.

POLICY, STRATEGY, AND THE BUSINESS FIRM

The action directed by a strategy should be aimed at achieving one or more goals. Preceding the design of a strategy therefore should be any necessary clarification of the goal or goals at which it is aimed, and these goals exist within the framework of a mission toward which the efforts of the unit are dedicated. Basic as this seems, it is of the utmost importance because of the many cases in which failures in strategy and action trace back to uncertainties about the goal structure, or a lack of understanding of the underlying purpose or social role upon which the organization's efforts should have been focused. The mission or social role comes first; this allows definition of a series of goals for management action, and then the design of strategies to achieve those goals—the planning-and-strategy-to-action sequence stressed here.

Strategies differ greatly according to their level and relationship to the business or organizational purpose. The basis strategies governing the creation and sale of products or services are build up (1) out of a series of elements: a deliverable, resources, leverages, focus, positions, display, and cash flow; (2) through a choice of product or service differentiation as unique, strong or weak specialty, or commodity; and (3) by developing sufficient sources of profit from innovation, rent, and various sorts of distribution, brokerage, insurance, financing, storage, and other service fees. Business strategies are assembled in the same way, with the added consideration of the nature of the total product line or sales package, and the resulting financial viability of the business unit, and master strategies are built in the same pattern except that they deal with the overall shape of a complex of businesses.

Enterprise strategies are different, and deal with the nature of the organization and of the businesses in which it will engage. Leadership, opportunity, people, public, and resource strategies are the building blocks, and desirability, managing, belonging, credibility, and risk/reward choice criteria govern the flow of management decisions. Enterprise-level strategies have received relatively little conscious attention in many organizations, and in the absence of specific guidance an organization transforms the actions of its top managers into implicit policies to govern future action. Many enterprise-level strategies limit the performance of businesses and products sufficiently to establish business areas in which the enterprise cannot be profitable.

Product or service, business, and enterprise strategies are the primary strategies, so-called because they direct business actions. The functioning of an organization also requires large numbers of contributing strategies, for the various functions, divisions, or other organizational units, to aid these units in directing their action to provide appropriate support to the product or service, business, and enterprise strategies dependent upon their efforts. Few product (primary) strategies could succeed without a suitable marketing (contributing) strategy, and most primary strategies have many specific functional support requirements for their success.

DESIGNING EFFECTIVE STRATEGIES

In putting all of the enterprise, product, market, and business characteristics together with mission and goals and setting out to design a strategy, several basic characteristics of the business process need consideration also. In the first place, many of the behavior patterns of any given business area are determined by custom and habit; while there are laws and regulations, in most cases they deal with only the smaller part of the total behavior pattern, and business managers determine the rest. The managers of any business have a great freedom to change to different behavior patterns, therefore, and a large opportunity through making up new rules, if they can find rule patterns acceptable to their customers and the market and beneficial to their business. Making up new rules—for distribution patterns, for terms of trade, for the basic relationships between suppliers, manufacturers, and customers—is one of the most creative and most potent strategy options. It is usually a difficult option, because shifting market and customers to new behavior patterns is a cultural change process—not easy to accomplish but potentially very rewarding.

Another strategy design option, or even requirement, is the creation of key resources necessary to attain the desired ends. Resources are not given and constant, or obtained only from banks. What resources are really required to make a given strategy work? What resources really control the effectiveness of that strategy and the profit levels that will result? Often the requirements lists include words such as "credibility," "capability," and "efficiency," which can exist only if management somehow creates them. Many of the key resources a business needs can be created as needed; many are available only through such creation; and in many cases these created resources are much more important than the resources bought with dollars. Resource creation is not always easy—it may be very difficult and may require a high order of management ability—but it also may be the key to whether a strategy has a chance of success.

When Medi+Physics began to offer short-lived isotopes for hospital diagnostic testing, it wanted to persuade hospitals to stop making their own reagents for these purposes. To succeed, it had to make the reagents during the night, standardize, test them to the satisfaction of the Food & Drug Administration, release them, and deliver them in the morning for use later that day; because of the short half-life, those not used the same day they were manufactured had to be discarded. Medi+Physics had to create the capability of reliably manufacturing, testing, and delivering quality reagents on a rigid schedule, and create credibility with the hospitals such that they would discontinue their own less efficient reagent manufacture, and schedule procedures and patients in anticipation that Medi+Physics would in fact deliver quality materials on time day after day. The created resources represented by the manufacturing and delivery capability and the credibility with the hospitals were more critical to the success of the business than any of its other resources.

Making up rules and creating resources requires specific capabilities for successful execution from the management that devises the strategy, determines the timetable required, and directs the successful action. Often the capabilities, credibility, and efficiency requirements relate to characteristics of the organization that management chooses to build, and different levels of organizational effectiveness can be achieved. The strategy design process makes use of created resources and new rules as appropriate, but the cutting edge is in the design and choice of the leverages that become the driving force for customer action, and the needs-leverages linkages created from them.

STRATEGY AND THE EXCELLENCE MODEL

Strategy is the means of accomplishing an end. To achieve this end, management obtains and uses a wide variety of tools and resources, some purchased and some created. The most potent single management tool is an excellent organization—a tool of which the creating managers become a part, and one of the most valuable resources a management can create.

Not all strategies require excellent or even good organizations to be effective—some of the high-flying new software and computer companies did extremely well for years with organizations later shown to be weak and disorganized. A strategy needs enough power behind it to persuade the customer. If the leverages are extremely good or the competition weak, less power is required and a weak organization can succeed.

Success in strategy design is in having strategies that prove effective in use. The science is in putting them together well, with good needs-leverages linkages and sufficient power to drive them. The art is in knowing how much power is really sufficient, and the excellent organization always keeps trying to add a little more.

CONCLUSION

The message of Part Five, the concluding section of this book, is that the pattern developed in Parts One through Four should be applied, and the strategic thinking should be converted to strategic action. Strategic management, as a concept and as a practice, is and should be the embodiment of this process. Parts One and Two of the book developed the primary strategy framework and its product, market, and business foundations. Part Three presented the strategic management of the enterprise itself, first through strategic control, management of social impact, and management of opportunity, and then of the human organization—the people, the operation, and organization self-renewal. Part Four laid out a strategy design framework for product and business, its reconciliation with the governing strategies, and its fit into the strategic planning pattern a given organization uses. The resultant in Part Five is a strategy ready to be applied—to a large or medium business, as illustrated by most of the earlier examples, to a public agency or not-for-profit organization, to a small business, or in another country or culture.

This is a system for creating effective individual strategies in a very wide variety of situations. Without an effective strategy an organization cannot succeed. With the tools for designing such a strategy, as this book has attempted to provide, the road is open for success through good strategic management.

CASE 41 — GROWTH FOR THE ITHILIEN CHEMICAL COMPANY

The Ithilien Chemical Company was founded in 1936 by William Gamgee, to make chemicals from forest products. Its initial operations were based on the refining of rosin from the Ithilien pine, and it achieved modest success in the marketplace. By 1956 sales had reached $800,000 per year, and Sam Gamgee, son of the founder, persuaded his father to diversify by acquiring the Miromir Company, a small family business then in financial difficulties.

As general manager of the Miromir Division of Ithilien, Sam Gamgee found that immediate changes were necessary to save the business. A faltering cosmetic line and the fragrance products were sold, permitting Miromir to concentrate its limited resources in the flavors area, its only recent area of market success. After several difficult years Miromir developed a strong market position as a supplier of blended flavoring and microingredients to manufacturers of baked goods and bake mixes.

In 1962 Ithilien sales reached $5 million. Sam Gamgee became president, with his father continuing as chairman and owner of 100 percent of the Ithilien stock. The two men began a serious search for opportunities to broaden the base of the business. The first acquisition was Morgul Products, an industrial gas business, followed by Isengard Industries, a plastic fabricator. In 1966 combined sales reached $42 million, but the original rosin business was threatened as a fungus blight swept through the Ithilien pine, largely eliminating the source of the resin. William Gamgee was urged by friends in the industry to shift to processing of rosins from other species or to steam distillation of rosin from underwater stumps and logs. Disheartened by the passing of the Ithilien pine and reluctant to make the necessary additional investments, he hesitated, and finally sold the rosin business to a competitor on favorable terms in 1969.

With the capital thus freed Ithilien bought a 40 percent interest in Osgiliath Organics, a fine chemicals producer, and acquired the Rohan Rubber Company, a specialist in products for the tire industry, and Moria Colors, a carbon black manufacturer. The Ithilien business continued to grow in spite of the loss of the rosin sales volume, and acquisitions continued.

The next acquisition was Hornberg Products in 1974. This was a small company that had built a plant for processing gum from gianburu beans grown on contract by local farmers, and was beginning to develop industrial uses for the resulting products. Then an operating problem in an Isengard process step caused Sam Gamgee to call in Greyhame Services, a firm specializing in purifying solvents on a contract basis, and their success led to the acquisition of Greyhame by Ithilien in 1976. In the same year Ithilien bought out the other interests in Osgiliath Organics, giving it 100 percent ownership.

Difficulties at Isengard continued, and it was decided that the best way to strengthen the business was to integrate back into raw materials, thus eliminating chronic purity problems in the resin supply. A PVC monomer plant was built, although imposition of new OSHA standards delayed completion of the plant and caused a considerable cost overrun.

In 1982 Ithilien unexpectedly had to borrow $20 million, its first major debt, because of errors in financial planning and because its reserves were not liquid, and Sam Gamgee felt the need for a period of consolidation. He wanted to bring the increasingly complex company to a completely sound operating basis and to rebuild its financial resources.

Although Sam Gamgee's health had begun to fail, he had built a strong management team headed by Perry Underhill, his son-in-law. In 1984 Perry Underhill became president, although Sam Gamgee continued as Chairman and Chief Executive Officer. Through a stock offering in 1985 Sam Gamgee sold 25 percent of the Ithilien common stock to the public, and arranged for officers, employees, and others close to the company to buy an additional 20 percent either immediately or on long-term contract.

The group of Ithilien businesses was now sound and financial reserves were building. The younger managers, and Perry Underhill in particular, felt the need for new investments. Sam Gamgee, concerned about the future of the economy and perhaps affected by his own declining health, hesitated to consider acquisitions or to fund major new programs.

In November 1988 Perry Underhill was named Chief Executive Officer. Then in early February Sam Gamgee died unexpectedly. His papers showed that he had planned to announce on March 31 his retirement effective July 1, 1989. He had drafted his retirement announcement in the form of an open letter to Perry Underhill and to all Ithilien employees and stockholders. In the draft he stated his concern that he had held Ithilien back too long in making necessary new investments. He expressed his confidence in the health of the business and the competence of the management group. He charged Perry Underhill to lead Ithilien to a profitable new future by wise use of the available talents and resources.

In his will Sam Gamgee conveyed a 5 percent share of Ithilien common stock jointly to Perry Underhill and his daughter, and distributed another 5 percent among his other five children. This bequest, in addition to the stock they had purchased in 1985, made Perry and his wife together the largest individual stockholders with a 7 percent share. The balance of Sam Gamgee's stock, or 45 percent of the Ithilien common shares, was placed in a trust for the grandchildren. The trustees were instructed always to vote the stock in support of the position of the majority of the shares held by Ithilien officers and employees.

Perry Underhill, well-trained for the presidency and with a strong mandate, was now free to direct the business toward building a better and more secure future. Toward the end of February 1989 he held a three-day meeting with his management group to consider the future of the Ithilien businesses. From the meeting and from the staff work afterward a report emerged that can be briefly summarized as follows:

ITHILIEN CHEMICAL COMPANY
Status: March 1989

SALES AND EARNINGS

	Income Statement ($ millions)		
	1978	1983	1988
Net Sales	$140	$220	$260
Net Profits	$ 15	$ 22	$ 23.5
	11%	10%	9%

- current ratio 5.0
- no long-term debt
- capital reserve account (corporate balance sheet) now contains $175 million in marketable securities.
- dividends established at 25 cents/quarter on 1 million shares, or a cash requirement of $1 million per year.

INCOME BY DIVISION

Division	1988 Income by Divisions ($ millions)		
	Sales	Earnings	%
Osgiliath Organics	$ 18	$ 1.2	6.7%
Morgul Products	59	5.0	8.5
Moria Colors	71	7.0	9.9
Isengard Industries	50	3.5	7.0
Hornberg Products	17	2.0	11.8
Rohan Rubber	12	1.0	8.3
Miromir Flavors	15	1.4	9.3
Greyhame Services	18	2.4	13.3
Total	$260	$23.5	9.0%

BUSINESS OUTLOOK BY DIVISION

Osgiliath Organics

Business: Toll manufacture and custom synthesis, primarily of products requiring special expertise in sulfonation reactions. Only a small volume of regular products for its own sale.

Situation: This business has suffered low profit margins as it struggled with new OSHA and EPA regulations in a competitive marketplace. This period of adjustment appears to be over, and margins are beginning to recover. The plant is in good condition and operating at an average of 85 percent of capacity. Little gain in volume is possible without major new investment.

Outlook: Only slight growth in real production volume, with improvement in profit margins to about the 10 percent level, and full pass-through of any cost increases due to inflation.

Morgul Products

Business: Industrial gases: carbon dioxide, nitrogen, oxygen.

Situation: A good regional business with a dominant share of the local market. Market penetration has been limited by transportation costs as distance from the Morgul plants increases. Expansion could be based on water shipment to another distribution point or development of a new region. The last study showed that several attractive expansion areas had been preempted by others, but significant investment opportunities may still exist in other areas.

Outlook: Continued growth estimated at 7 percent per year based on increased local usage. Margins should continue to improve as usage grows within the same geographic areas and brings distribution economies, but pricing freedom is limited by the need not to make this region excessively attractive to competitors.

Moria Colors

Business: Carbon black producer.

Situation: This plant is running essentially at capacity. Its economics depend on favorable raw material prices, and it is very doubtful that additional supplies can be obtained at present prices. The present business is protected for ten more years until the original forty-year supply contract expires; renewal at today's market prices would raise the product cost above anticipated market prices and cause the plant to shut down; but in the near term profit margins can be widened somewhat through judicious price adjustments. Before acquisition by Ithilien, Moria Colors had once made and sold titanium dioxide and chrome yellow; these facilities still exist although they have been idle for more than 30 years; recent studies showed no potential for profit from restarting the original color processes. Expansion of the Moria Colors business requires either a new basis for carbon black production or a new approach to the other colors.

Outlook: Continued sales at the present level of real output, with full recovery of cost increases and some increase in profit margin until the raw material supply contract expires; outlook highly uncertain thereafter.

Isengard Industries

Business: Polyvinyl chloride (PVC) resins plus fabrication, although fabrication volume is now small and maintained largely as a service for certain old customers. Isengard specializes in custom resins and molding compounds for specific customer uses.

Situation: This plant is operating at 75 percent of original design capacity, but at 90 percent of the capacity that operating experience now shows to be achievable. It is a sound, efficient operation with good costs. However, Isengard has a relatively small position in a commodity industry, so that the viability of the present business could decline over the long term. Isengard management strongly favors additional investment aimed at tripling capacity and adding PVC pipe-fabricating facilities—but this is a very competitive market, and the anticipated pipe and resin market prices, and therefore the return on the additional capital, have been difficult to project accurately.

Outlook: A sound operation that can continue to do what it does now for many years, and which, if not expanded, should be able to maintain the present profit margin until there are major changes in industry market share and competitors' costs.

Hornberg Products

Business: Produces gum and related products from the gianburu bean; present markets are in the food industry with limited industrial uses. This division is nationally known for the quality of its technical service.

Situation: Gianburu gum is considered by food and industrial customers to be generally similar to guar gum in its physical properties, with small special advantages in some uses. It has found good market acceptance for those limited uses, and this has been extended by the quality of the formulation service with which Hornberg supports it. This product would displace other gums and achieve large volume if it could be offered at a lower price. The present operation is profitable and could easily be expanded. However, the markets for the present uses seem saturated, with volume growing at about 6 percent per year, and no new market in sight without a dramatic shift in price relative to other gums. Hornberg management can find no practical route to major price cuts except through genetic changes in the gianburu bean itself to produce more gum, and has been supporting a local university study of gianburu bean genetics and yield improvement for the past ten years. But while the study confirms the possibility of major improvements, actual progress to date is disappointing. Processing of similar gums has been considered, but none so far has shown good payout prospects.

Outlook: Stable, with continued slow growth and full maintenance of profit margins. The only major promise would be from a genetic breakthrough in gum yields from the beans, and the only major threat is from continuing work elsewhere with new and potentially competitive bacterial gums.

Rohan Rubber

Business: Rubber chemicals, primarily for the tire industry.

Situation: Rohan's position is good, but the tire industry has just come through a difficult period. As a supplier recognized as expert in the choice of the best chemicals for any given use, Rohan would appear secure, although it has been able to gain sales volume primarily at the expense of smaller rather than larger competitors. Considering the reduced tire industry production volume and therefore chemical requirements due to the longer life of radial tires, two years ago Rohan started an internal study of ways of establishing itself as a supplier in other rubber or related markets; an expansion proposal is now in preparation although all of the target markets are relatively mature and quite competitive; it is too soon to tell whether the return characteristics of this proposal will be favorable.

Outlook: Difficult times in the short run, with some growth of sales volume over 1988 levels in 1989, recovery in 1990, and slow growth thereafter. Margins should continue at the present (lower) level and are not likely to return to 1985 and 1986 levels over the next three to four years.

Miromir Flavors

Business: Custom flavoring and microingredient mixes for the baking industry.

Situation: Miromir is well established in its market, based on its consistent ability to develop and reproduce mixes that will produce specific flavor, texture, and moisture characteristics in the finished baked goods. While the prices of purchased flavor, spice, and other materials have risen sharply in periods of inflation, there has been no difficulty in passing on these costs. But Miromir pricing strategy requires limiting margins to about the present level unless a clear competitive advantage can be established; Miromir believes that its product superiority will guarantee the business at prices close to competition but will support little or no price premium. Thus, the business should continue as dominant in its narrow market area, with maintenance of margins and about the 8 percent per year growth projected for its customers.

Past Miromir ventures into other market segments were unsuccessful for various reasons. Microingredients for soft drinks, meat products, puddings and desserts, and other food products represent attractive growth potential, although in each case the business is in the hands of a competitor appearing to be as well established in that area as Miromir is in the bakery area. Miromir management is committed to market expansion and will soon submit a proposal for a major move into one of these adjacent areas.

Outlook: A secure business anticipating 8 percent per year growth with maintenance of profit margins. A proposal for doubling volume by moving into an adjacent market area will be submitted shortly. The question will be whether the effort necessary to dislodge or purchase a competitor is the best use of Ithilien resources in the light of other available opportunities.

Greyhame Services

Business: Solvent purification service. Reprocesses and returns solvents under contract, usually dealing in difficult mixtures or solvents with specific processing problems.

Situation: Greyhame has grown rapidly. It is a sound and profitable business with great demand for its services and a good reputation with regulators and environmentalists. However, new restrictions on handling of specific solvents and on discard of residues, and concern about unknown components in mixtures have limited expansion, and it has been necessary to refuse some of the solvents formerly processed. The building of more Greyhame solvent service plants and the extension of Greyhame solvent services to other solvent and product areas would be very profitable by past yardsticks. It would also be beneficial to customers and the public because of better handling of EPA and OSHA requirements for protecting workers and the environment. Nonetheless, the wisdom of such expansion is doubtful until operating rules and potential liabilities under federal regulations become more clear.

Outlook: Uncertain. In the short term the business can grow 10 to 15 percent per year and maintain or increase margins if compliance with regulations does not become unexpectedly expensive. In the long run the business should be expanded, initially by tripling capacity with a proposed series of new service plants. Rapid expansion is essential to prevent loss of the opportunity to others, except that present regulatory uncertainties must be better resolved before such new investment is recommended.

Outlook for Ithilien as a Whole

Situation: Ithilien is a well-managed group of separate businesses in the chemical area. While each business takes care of its own development needs, these efforts have not resulted in dramatic new products or expansion of Ithilien into new areas. Ithilien has added new types of products almost exclusively by acquisition in the past, and has no internal source of new types of products for the future.

The Ithilien divisions are regional or national businesses; the company has essentially no international interests at present.

Outlook: Sound businesses; after allowing for the uncertainty of some of the divisional projections, Ithilien management believes that the prospect is for continued sales growth exceeding the inflation rate for the next few years. Present profit margins should be at least maintained.

In the longer run the viability of the carbon black and PVC businesses must be questioned, unless major capital investments are made in both areas. Moria Colors has not proposed any expansion. Isengard is proposing major investments in the PVC area, and Miromir, Rohan, and Greyhame have investment plans also. The questions are where best to put the corporate resources and energy, and what kind of a mixture of businesses to build for the future.

Corporate Mission

Ithilien Chemical will strive to provide chemical and chemical-related products to fulfill legitimate customer needs. This is a somewhat conglomerate statement of mission; to offset any hazards due to lack of specific product or market focus, it is necessary to insist on careful mission definitions by the various component Ithilien businesses, and to strive to foster the evolution of groups of businesses sharing a common mission.

Corporate Goals

1. Ithilien must have sound projections of a 10 percent per year growth in sales and profits on a constant dollar basis (corrected for the decreasing value of the dollar) to be assured of at least maintaining its sales and profits in the face of the unforeseen.
2. Ithilien must be prepared for the loss of the carbon black business when the present raw material contracts expire. While that situation may not be hopeless, sound management requires preparation for such an eventuality.
3. Ithilien must develop further internal coherence in a product and market sense, so that there will be more reinforcement between separate successful businesses.
4. To provide real growth for Ithilien employees, managers, and stockholders, Ithilien requires further growth in sales and diversity. On the average of once every three years Ithilien should move into a new business or product area—whether from internal development or acquisition—and the overall real growth target will be set at 15 percent per year in recognition of the need for more than staying even.

Status: July 1989

1. Business outlook continues essentially unchanged.
2. Perry Underhill vetoed the proposed acquisitions of a supermarket chain and a machine tool accessories business as too foreign to Ithilien management.
3. After extensive discussions among the Ithilien officers, stockholders, and the trustees of the Gamgee estate, Ithilien has refused two surprisingly generous takeover offers, one from a large oil company, and the other from a high-technology company.
4. Having decided to remain independent and not to be conglomerate in its growth, Ithilien is searching for the best way to grow. As a part of this program Perry Underhill has retained the consulting team of which you are a part. Your team is to prepare a presentation to Ithilien management outlining your recommendations.
5. The Association of Ithilien Stockholding Employees claims to represent 10 percent of the Ithilien stock; if so, it could control the company if as many of the other employee stockholders voted with it as voted with Perry Underhill. This group has petitioned Perry Underhill for a declaration of management principles that would essentially say that, whatever the growth plans, Perry will continue to manage Ithilien in about the way that Sam Gamgee did. The key members of the group are senior divisional executives fearful that a more centralized management process would threaten their positions. Perry wishes to allay their fears, will feel obliged to fulfill any commitment he makes, has not decided whether a more centralized management is necessary, and discovers that his key advisors are sharply divided. Some feel that Ithilien's strength is its ability to run a loose federation of chemical businesses, and others see the need for a strong central management in order to survive. What would you advise (a) as a course of action, and (b) as an answer to the stockholder group?
6. The Ithilien growth goals have stirred discussion among middle management, to the point that Perry Underhill has asked your consultant team for an independent evaluation of the goals and the concepts that they represent.

QUESTIONS

Prepare answers to questions (4), (5), and (6) above.

CASE 42 THE MONTH MANUFACTURING COMPANY

"Bill, I need an in-depth confidential analysis of the Month Manufacturing Company." Bill was an experienced manager and now a Senior Management Consultant newly hired by a nationally known firm. He had become acquainted in the firm by helping with a number of projects that were in progress. His boss was giving him his first major assignment.

"Chief, I know Month Manufacturing by name only, because it's so secretive and not publicly owned. How can I get a quick briefing before I go in?"

"There isn't much, but I'll tell you what I know. Old Eben Martin named his four sons Day, Week, Month, and Year. I don't know what happened to the others, but Month showed a real aptitude for his father's business, and Eben wanted him to have his own company. He established the Month Manufacturing Company and gave it to his son on his twenty-first birthday. When his father died, Month Martin inherited the family business empire. He made Month Manufacturing the owner of most of his other businesses, and it had the reputation of being a real money machine. Shortly before Month Martin died, he shifted the operating control to a group of professional managers. That was fifteen years ago, and his estate still holds the stock. Month Manufacturing publishes no reports, owes no money, and no one outside of the company really knows much about it, which is why we were called in.

"You should read the clipping and credit files for background, but there really won't be any good source of information until you get acquainted at Month and are able to find out what is going on. We are told that the profitability of the company has fallen off somewhat over the past five years, and the trustees have talked about selling the company, either to a major buyer or through a stock offering to the public. They came to us for advice on how much the company is worth in today's market. We were still costing out an appraisal project when they learned that a leveraged buyout firm wants to buy the whole company at whatever turns out to be a fair price. The leveraged buyout firm is our client, and it's better if you don't know who they are until later. But the access to internal information is based on our promise to make our reports available to the trustees also, together with our recommendations for the management of the company. You have the initial phase of the job. Your specific assignment is to analyze the operations and recommend any action you think appropriate to strengthen the organization and improve its strategies. Then with your report in hand we will decide what to do next.

"Management has been talking to the trustees about the possible need to raise capital for some projects, and the trustees talked to Gomorrah Trust about financing in a preliminary way and were asked for basic business information they do not have. The Gomorrah people are friends of ours, and with the trustees' agreement Gomorrah will also have access to our reports. We can say that your reason for being at Month is to learn enough about operations so that Gomorrah can be convinced to raise the capital management wants. And that story is true, although it leaves a lot out.

"This is one of the largest private companies left. It has manufacturing operations and service operations, seems a little conglomerate, and something is holding profits down. Beyond that, you can get a list of the basis businesses Month is in from our credit reports, but the place has always been so secretive that they don't even put their name on their factory buildings, and the business press has never obtained enough information for a profile. The advance understanding with Month Manufacturing Company management is that you are to have full access to everything and everyone in the company, but you will have to move carefully since they have never let an outsider look around inside before."

Bill made an appointment with the president of Month Manufacturing for the following Monday, met the headquarters executive group in a friendly meeting followed by a three-hour luncheon, and then left on a two-week preliminary tour of Month Manufacturing's plants and offices. Bill was energetic and covered a lot of ground. He filled notebooks with names and titles and tried to construct organization charts. He asked for copies of all sales literature and any other papers he saw or heard of that had been released to the public, but he was deliberately slow in asking for confidential company information. He didn't know what he was really looking for yet, knew that there had to be limits to the amount of confidential information he could get, and decided to build a thorough background picture first. Most evenings he kept free, and dictated detailed notes on the happenings of the day that a stenographic service transcribed for him the next morning. On planes between cities he organized his notes and tried to define the patterns that were emerging.

Monday of the third week he met with the chief financial officer and began to study the financial performance of the company and of its individual businesses, and by then he had a sound preliminary understanding of what the Month Manufacturing organization was like. The financial overview was that corporate profits had declined only slightly over the past ten years. But as he dug deeper, he saw significant gains in sales volume, with profits as a percent of sales falling from about 5 percent after taxes to a little over 2 percent after taxes at present. Month did not calculate profits for individual profit centers, although the company was organized that way. Instead, the profit center accounting was carried only to the level of net profit contribution after divisional expenses and before corporate overhead and income taxes. Records available on this basis showed that the various Month businesses had had very different sales growth rates. None had shrunk in sales volume over ten years, and all were consistently profitable at the divisional profit contribution level, but it seemed unlikely that some of them were earning enough to carry their share of the corporate overhead.

Most of the profit in the corporation was being generated by two out of the ten businesses, both of which had had years of very rapid sales growth that now appeared to be slackening. Bill had been asked by his boss for a preliminary report as soon as he had sufficient information, and after his introduction to the Month Manufacturing financial records, Bill drafted the following summary:

PRELIMINARY REPORT—MONTH MANUFACTURING COMPANY (CONFIDENTIAL)

I have been cordially received by the Month executive group and accorded full access to any information I have requested. This is sensitive, as no one outside Month and very few inside of the company have ever had this access before, and I have been careful to ask for confidential information only when clearly required for some phase of my investigation. I am now moving into more specific issues related to the businesses and their conduct, and this question of full information access will be more fully tested than it has been up to this time.

Month Manufacturing is a diversified company with ten businesses largely organized and operated as separate entities. These are treated as profit centers, except that Month has never adopted full profit center accounting. Routine financial reports show divisional profit contribution for each of these businesses but do not allocate corporate expenses to the businesses. Subject to this limitation, sales and profits for the last ten years are summarized by business and in total in Exhibit I.

The growth in divisional profit contribution as shown in Exhibit II matched against the almost flat net profit figure invites audit of the corporate level of expense. The ten businesses seem to operate very independently with almost no shared or central services except for a somewhat variable part of the accounting, data processing, and personnel work that is done at the corporate level. While pensions and fringe benefits are centrally administered, the benefit costs are paid by the divisions and only the administrative cost is unallocated. I will gather more information on the nature of the services that this corporate expense represents.

The picture that emerges from the total sales and profits table is of a company losing profitability in spite of some continued growth. The picture of the individual businesses on a profit contribution basis gives further detail.

Return on assets data show the same down trend as in

EXHIBIT I	DIVISIONAL SALES AND TOTAL PROFITS Month Manufacturing Company ($ millions)									
	1979	1980	1981	1982	1983	1984	1985	1986	1987	1988
Total Sales	450	510	570	630	700	780	870	960	1070	$1185
Instant Package	$ 10	30	50	75	100	125	150	170	190	210
Integrated Axles	90	94	99	104	105	102	110	120	134	150
Shoebox Constr.	109	119	128	132	135	122	133	147	165	185
Beaver Chips	5	10	20	35	70	140	170	195	210	220
Instant Chimneys	73	77	80	82	83	84	90	97	107	120
Streaky Frames	60	64	67	69	69	70	74	80	89	100
Shadows on Demand	26	29	32	32	33	34	36	39	44	50
Everloving Tugs	46	50	53	56	57	56	60	65	75	85
Historic Sites	7	8	9	10	11	12	12	13	17	20
Puffin Hoists	24	29	32	35	37	35	35	34	39	45
Divisional Expense	$350	400	450	500	560	630	710	790	890	995
% of Sales	78	78	79	79	80	81	82	82	83	84
Profit Contribution	100	110	120	130	140	150	160	170	180	190
Corporate Expense	$ 59	69	79	89	98	108	118	128	137	$ 147
% of Sales	13	14	14	14	14	14	14	13	13	12
Profits before Tax	41	41	41	41	42	42	42	42	43	43
Taxes	18	18	19	19	19	19	19	19	19	19
Net Profits	$ 23	23	22	22	23	23	23	23	24	$ 24
% of Sales	5	4	4	3	3	3	3	2	2	2

profitability and another dimension of the differences among the ten businesses. Return on gross fixed assets in 1988 was 8.01 percent, and gross fixed asset allocation by business is available. Net fixed asset data are not available in the same summary form, nor are the figures for current assets actually used by each business. For the corporation, overall return on current plus net fixed assets for 1988 was only about 2.7 percent, but while this indicates the importance of including the current assets, it exaggerates the problem since Month Manufacturing carries an unusually large amount of cash and marketable securities, as shown on the balance sheet that follows Exhibit IV. Management does have plans to request a loan from Gomorrah Trust, and I am promised details I do not yet have. When this was discussed, I was not yet aware of the unusually large current asset position, which must relate to a very conservative management philosophy, but I will question this

EXHIBIT II — DIVISIONAL PROFIT CONTRIBUTION
Month Manufacturing Company

	1979	1980	1981	1982	1983	1984	1985	1986	1987	1988
$—millions										
TOTAL	$100	110	120	130	140	150	160	170	180	$190
Instant Package	1	5	11	20	28	37	45	50	52	53
Integrated Axles	17	15	13	11	12	7	6	6	6	8
Shoebox Construction	24	32	32	31	27	25	22	20	24	28
Beaver Chips	+	1	2	5	13	35	47	57	56	55
Instant Chimneys	16	15	15	15	15	12	8	8	10	11
Streaky Frames	13	12	12	11	11	9	9	9	10	11
Shadows on Demand	7	7	7	7	8	6	6	5	6	6
Everloving Tugs	13	14	15	15	13	9	9	7	8	9
Historic Sites	2	2	3	3	4	4	3	4	4	5
Puffin Hoists	7	7	10	12	9	6	5	4	4	4
% of Sales										
TOTAL	22%	22	21	21	20	19	18	18	17	16%
Instant Package	10	17	22	27	28	30	30	29	27	25
Integrated Axles	19	16	13	11	11	7	5	5	4	5
Shoebox Construction	22	27	25	23	20	20	17	14	15	15
Beaver Chips	2	10	10	14	19	25	28	29	27	25
Instant Chimneys	22	19	19	18	18	14	9	8	9	9
Streaky Frames	22	19	18	16	16	13	12	11	11	11
Shadows on Demand	27	24	22	22	24	18	17	13	14	12
Everloving Tugs	28	28	28	27	23	16	15	11	11	11
Historic Sites	29	25	33	30	36	33	25	31	24	25
Puffin Hoists	22	22	21	21	20	19	18	18	17	16

specifically. In the absence of divisional profit data the best available return on assets comparison is between the levels of divisional contribution calculated as a return on gross fixed assets in Exhibit III.

BRIEF REVIEW, BUSINESS BY BUSINESS

Instant Package Delivery. Instant Package Delivery is one of the newer Month businesses and a strong contributor to its growth in sales and profits. Its business is package pickup and delivery, primarily as a local ser-

EXHIBIT III	GROSS FIXED ASSETS AND RETURN ON FIXED ASSETS Month Manufacturing Company									
	1979	1980	1981	1982	1983	1984	1985	1986	1987	1988
Assets ($ millions)	$148	166	189	212	231	249	260	271	280	$296
Instant Package	5	10	15	20	25	30	35	40	45	50
Integrated Axles	45	47	49	51	52	53	54	55	57	62
Shoebox Construction	13	15	20	23	24	25	25	25	25	26
Beaver Chips	7	10	15	18	28	40	47	52	56	60
Instant Chimneys	16	16	16	23	23	22	21	21	18	18
Streaky Frames	12	12	12	15	17	17	15	15	16	17
Shadows on Demand	4	8	8	8	8	8	8	8	8	8
Everloving Tugs	35	35	40	40	40	40	40	40	40	40
Historic Sites	1	2	2	2	2	2	3	3	3	3
Puffin Hoists	10	11	12	12	12	12	12	12	12	12
% Return on Assets	15%	14	12	11	10	9	9	9	8	8%
Div. Contr. as % return	68	66	63	61	61	60	62	63	64	64
Instant Package	20	50	73	100	112	123	129	125	116	106
Integrated Axles	38	32	27	22	23	13	11	11	11	13
Shoebox Constr.	185	213	160	135	112	100	88	80	96	108
Beaver Chips	1	10	13	28	46	88	100	110	100	92
Instant Chimneys	100	94	94	65	65	55	38	38	56	61
Streaky Frames	108	100	100	73	65	53	60	60	62	65
Shadows on Demand	175	88	88	88	100	75	75	62	75	75
Everloving Tugs	37	40	38	38	32	22	22	18	20	22
Historic Sites	200	100	150	150	200	200	100	133	133	167
Puffin Hoists	70	64	83	100	75	50	42	33	33	33

vice operated in a number of different cities and with intercity ties among the areas where it is active. It advertises little except to local businesses in its areas of activity, and competes on the basis of a price advantage over its national competitors. It enjoyed rapid growth, which has slowed, although division management feels that a new era of growth is just ahead.

Integrated Axles. An old business based originally on axles and now including a number of other mechanical components. It sells primarily to

| EXHIBIT IV | BALANCE SHEET AS OF 12/31/88 |
Month Manufacturing Company ($ millions)

Assets

Current		$633
Cash and Marketable Securities	288	
Accounts Receivable	152	
Inventories	193	
Fixed		$243
Property, Plant, & Equipment	296	
less reserve for depreciation	53	
Net Fixed Assets	243	
Total Assets		$876

Liabilities

Current Liabilities		$ 87
Accounts Payable	66	
Accrued Taxes & Misc.	21	
Long-Term Debt	-none-	
Stockholders' Equity		$799
Total Liabilities		$876

auto, truck, and farm equipment manufacturers, as well as to suppliers of the secondary market for repair parts. Growth has been slow and returns below the corporate average. Division management is very proud of their plant modernization program as well as indications of new markets in other machinery areas. They look forward to a resurgence of growth and profits.

Shoebox Construction. This is another of the older Month businesses. Originally it was founded for factory construction of prefabricated homes, and continues in this line. However, it branched into commercial construction when the prefabricated home sales proved disappointing, and current volume is divided about equally between the two. Shoebox earns profits above the corporate average, but the variation from year to year is significant. Management feels that a two-year-old program for prefabricated home sales through a national chain of retail home centers is beginning to show great promise, and has great hopes for rapid future growth.

Beaver Chips. The other "new" Month business, Beaver Chips, began operation just over ten years ago. It is a specialized silicon chip manufacturer and has benefited from the strong growth of demand from electronic and computer companies. This industry has been in some difficulties due to slackening demand and import competition over the past several years. Beaver Chips growth in sales has slackened, and profitability is down somewhat even though it is still one of the more profitable Month businesses. Division management sees Beaver as uniquely positioned because of the mix of specialized chips it makes, so that it will not be hurt by the commodity-level Japanese competition; resumption of rapid sales and profit growth is predicted.

Instant Chimneys. Instant Chimneys is another housing industry venture. It specializes in prefabricated components, and its business is built around a line of prefabricated fireplaces and chimneys plus related components and accessories. Growth has been relatively slow, and margins have fallen over recent years although there have been some signs of improvement. In this business, too, division management points to plant modernization, hard work, and improvements in the market situation as a basis for optimism about the future.

Streaky Frames. Streaky Frames was a struggling aluminum window company before Month Martin acquired it. Twenty or more years ago it introduced a line of higher-quality windows, in an effort to tap a part of the market that Andersen and others have developed. It has marketed primarily through the major home center chains, with slow growth in sales and some loss of margins. Over the last two years it has begun to see success with a new premium window that also yields a higher profit margin, and the prediction is that Streaky Frames business will grow and regain its former margins over the next few years.

Shadows on Demand. At about the same time that Month Martin acquired Streaky Frames, he bought Shadows on Demand, an awning company, on the basis that there should be great synergism between windows and awnings. The synergism never developed and the two businesses operate very independently. The awning business has grown over the last ten years but profits have not, although divisional contribution has not fallen below the corporate average. A new line of custom slatted blinds has been developed over the past several years and tested in local areas over the past two years. The belief is that local hardware and home center dealers can take orders on a basis that will be very profitable for them and for Shadows on Demand, and the test data look good, so this division projects a bright future.

Everloving Tugs. A shipbuilding business specializing in tugboats and related craft. It was one of the first Martin family businesses, but its growth has hardly exceeded inflation, and margins have shrunk. A new general manager has spent the depreciation reserves from the old yard on a five-year modernization program and reports success in bidding competitively for tug contracts again. In addition, the yard has begun to build a few pleasure craft and sees the opportunity to expand this business.

Historic Sites. Historic Sites is both a management company that operates historic mansions and other historic sites on contract for the foundation or other owner, and a tour operator, where it specializes in organizing tours of the type of historic areas where it also manages. It is the smallest Month Manufacturing business in spite of good growth and good profits. Management sees further growth, but could use outside help to get a clearer idea whether this business may have the potential for major expansion.

Puffin Hoists. Originally this was a steam winch company founded with the help of Month Martin's grandfather. Currently it makes a sound, well-respected line of winches and hoists which are sold primarily to shipbuilders. Growth has been steady but not exciting, and profit margins have fallen. A new general manager took charge three years ago, leading to the recent gains in sales volume. These have not been translated into profit contribution because of development costs for two new lines. For the first time in the forty or so years that the Martin family has owned both companies, Puffin is building a winch suitable for use on a tugboat, guided by Everloving Tugs specifications. Both see an unfilled need that will bring new sales and profits to both divisions. Also, Puffin has begun to work for the first time on designs that meet U.S. Navy specifications. With the present shipbuilding program and what Puffin feels are highly competitive costs, significant gains in sales and profits are predicted.

Month Manufacturing Overall. From a distance, the company looks better, as both sales and profits have grown steadily over the last ten years. Closer, the fall in return on sales and return on fixed assets is very disturbing. Business by business, all seem to have problems, with the possible exception of the smallest, Historic Sites. The two growth divisions, Instant Package and Beaver Chips, both show signs of topping out. Shoebox Construction is erratic. Instant Chimneys, Streaky Frames, and Shadows on Demand, the three building component businesses, have only average margins and uncertain prospects. Integrated Axles, Everloving Tugs, and Puffin Hoists are three old industrial businesses with poor margins. While all of the Month Manufacturing businesses project a bright future, the resulting picture is too good to be believable. Overall, it is not certain what is going to happen to the company in the next few years.

Inside the company are a lot of nice people who seem intelligent and well motivated. Morale is good, and people seem to know what they are doing and how to do it. Operations in most divisions make a favorable impression on a visitor. On the other hand the company has been very insulated from the outside and some of the management systems and procedures are not very modern. The best example is the accounting system, which, while appearing to be very comprehensive and adequate in many dimensions, does not produce much of the data needed for a more complete analysis of the company and its problems. As mentioned earlier, there is no attempt at profit center accounting beyond the routine reporting of divisional profit contribution, even though the businesses are organized and run as profit centers. Fixed assets are classified by business, perhaps in part because the different businesses tend to be at different geographic sites; but inventory, receivables, and payables data by business are not available. I have no reason to question the quality or adequacy of the accounting work, but it is worth noting that there never seems to have been any kind of outside audit of the Month family enterprises, and Month Manufacturing seems to have only a minimal internal audit effort.

QUESTIONS

As Bill went off to learn more about the individual Month Manufacturing businesses and their business strategies, the details of the accounting systems, and how Month management intended to use the money they might borrow, his boss pondered the preliminary report. It was good work but showed a truly massive task ahead, if they were to do a thorough job. He considered the objectives and wrote down questions:

1. What do we need to know to put a fair valuation on the Month Manufacturing Company in comparison to other companies in today's market?
2. What do we need to know in order to tell the Month trustees what sort of a program should be instituted to bring profitability up?
3. What do we need to know in order to tell the Gomorrah Trust people how to appraise the risks in lending capital to Month Manufacturing?

    Prepare your own answers to these three questions.

SUPPLEMENTAL CASES

CASE 43 MODERN MEDICINES, INC.

Modern Medicines was a medium-sized pharmaceutical company selling a line of ethical (prescription) and over-the-counter (nonprescription) drug products. It had enjoyed a number of years of growth that its managers were looking for ways of continuing and extending. However, additional competition was expected in several product lines, so that new products or other new sources of sales would be needed to continue the growth. And while the Modern Medicines' Research Department had several promising drugs under development, none was ready yet for submission to the Food and Drug Administration for approval, and therefore they all were several years away from approval and sale.

In order to consider ways to improve near-term results during the years before new drug approvals could be expected, a major study of alternative programs had been carried out. The president and the management committee reviewed these proposals with some care, dropping out many of the less attractive, in preparation for another more careful review intended to lead to approval of the best program or programs. Some of the contenders are discussed below:

VITAMINS

Modern Medicines had a complete line of vitamin and related nutritional products that represented $20.1 million of 1988 sales and $0.98 million net profit after taxes, on a fully allocated basis. The vitamin product manager had proposed a large "buy now, pay later" promotion to encourage broader distribution and more complete shelf stocks of Modern Medicines' vitamin line, coupled with an aggressive promotion by local advertising and direct mail. The product manager projected that he could increase sales to $50 million per year within a year; but after explaining his projections and getting top management to agree to their logic, he asked the financial group to base the projections on a $25 million gain, "to leave room for the unexpected." This manager had a very good track record, having doubled vitamin sales in the three years he had been product manager, and having exceeded every sales or revenue projection for the line that he had submitted.

In this case the projection was that after allowing for the extra promotion expense, the $25 million in increased sales would yield $2.5 million in extra income after taxes. However, since an extended payment plan was a part of the proposal, the accounts receivable for the vitamin line, now at about the same average age as for the rest of the line, would shift to an average age of 180 days, thus calling for an increased investment in working capital. Otherwise, the increased volume could easily be manufactured in existing capacity and would cause no significant change in other cost factors. Assuming that sales would increase as projected, how interested should Modern Medicines' management be in this method of increasing sales and profits, and why?

BIOLOGICALS

The marketing manager once worked for another company that had a good line of biological products, and had long wanted to broaden the Modern Medicines product line to include them. Spurred by the desire for more sales, he and the chief purchasing agent had been canvassing the remaining biological products producers to see whether Modern Medicines could buy reputable products for resale. Modern Medicines already sold several products actually made for it by other companies, and there was no policy barrier to such a proposal if its economics were attractive. In this case a Canadian producer was actively interested in increasing its volume through Modern Medicines' sales in the U.S. market. Its products were licensed for sale in the United States; at least initially those additional products would not cause extra product liability expenses, and the marketing manager had proposed that Modern Medicines sign a contract with the Canadian producer. He projected first-year sales of $15 million and second-year sales of $30 million with 10 percent net profit after taxes on sales. But because of the long production and inventory cycle the Canadian producer would require advance payment for the purchases; after cutting through the complexity of the agreement, this meant that on the average Modern Medicines' purchase price of 60 percent of sales price would be paid an extra year before the products would be sold, with this extra cost carried as an inventory expense. How interested in this sales increase should Modern Medicines be, and why?

BIOTECHNOLOGY

Modern Medicines had a small equity investment in a genetic engineering firm and a place on its board of directors. This firm was now waiting for approval of a new line of monoclonal antibodies able to target and destroy specific tumor and other cells. Modern Medicines could have marketing rights if it would help to finance the necessary production facilities. The proposed contract would give Modern Medicines exclusive U.S. rights for an investment of $25 million. The products would be ready for market in less than two years, first-year sales were projected at $53 million and second-year sales at $150 million, with net profit after taxes of $12 million and $42 million, respectively. Assuming that Modern Medicines wants to recover its investment in six years, and that sales and profits continue at the $150 million per year rate, how interested should Modern Medicines be in this sales increase, and why?

MORE BIOTECHNOLOGY

The president of Modern Medicines was concerned about risks in the biotechnology area, and requested a consultant study. The consultant projected probabilities as follows: (a) of reaching market and reaching sales targets on schedule = .25; (b) of reaching market and sales targets within a year of schedule = .4; (c) of never reaching market = .2; (d) of recovering the capital within 10 years from sale of this or some other product, .8. How do these probabilities affect the calculations you did in the preceding section? Based on these probabilities, how interested should Modern Medicines' management be in this sales increase, and why?

MODERN MEDICINES, INC.
Income statement for the year ended December 31
($ millions)

	1988	1987
Net sales	254.5	241.2
Cost of sales	105.6	99.0
	148.9	**142.2**
Research	28.0	25.5
Marketing	62.2	55.5
General & administrative	29.7	28.2
Total operating expense	119.9	109.2
Operating profit	**29.0**	**33.0**
Other expenses		
Interest and financing	6.8	6.5
Misc. expenses	2.3	3.8
Other income	4.7	1.9
Total other expenses	4.4	8.4
Net income	**24.6**	**24.6**
Taxes	7.3	8.4
Net income after taxes	17.3	16.2

MODERN MEDICINES, INC.
Consolidated Balance Sheet as of 12/31
($ millions)

	1988	1987
ASSETS		
Current Assets:		
Cash	$12.2	$13.0
Accounts receivable	50.5	46.9
Inventories	55.3	54.1
Prepaid expenses	18.0	15.5
Total current assets	**136.0**	**129.5**
Long-term Assets:		
Investments	.6	.6
Property, plant & equipment	215.4	190.2
Depreciation reserves	90.8	73.4
Net PP&E	**124.6**	**116.8**
Intangibles, after amortization	4.2	5.1
Total long-term assets	**129.4**	**122.5**
Total Assets	**265.4**	**252.0**
LIABILITIES		
Current Liabilities		
Short-term debt	8.8	16.5
Current portion of long-term debt	5.2	5.2
Accounts payable	38.8	63.7
Accrued taxes and liabilities	11.4	11.8
Total current liabilities	**64.2**	**97.2**
Long-term Liabilities:		
Long-term debt	50.8	47.4
Reserve for indemnities	16.1	13.8
Advances from licensees	6.6	5.9
Deferred income taxes	15.7	11.6
Total long-term liabilities	**89.2**	**78.7**
Stockholders' Investment	**112.0**	**76.1**
Total Liabilities	265.4	252.0

CASE 44: THE BYTE-SO SOFTWARE COMPANY

The Byte-So Software Company is a computer software company that has been in business for several years. Earlier its investors believed that several of its forthcoming products had major sales potential, and one industry analyst wrote a widely quoted feature: "Lotus and Microsoft Move Over—Here Comes Byte-So." Sensing the potential for hundreds of millions in very profitable sales, the investment community became very enthusiastic, and Byte-So was able to obtain generous financing.

The actual development of the business has followed a much less glamorous course. The company has a proven ability to generate large numbers of useful new programs, and it has released a large number of individually successful products for small business applications, but it seems to be geared to developing many products for small markets. Also, Byte-So has undertaken custom programming at relatively low profit margins in order to extend its applications experience in certain fields. Byte-So management has invested very heavily in development, with the result that the company has lost money on operations, although the income from its investments more than balanced this loss in 1988.

You are a member of the venture capital group of a large industrial company. Your company is in discussion with Byte-So about possible acquisition, since it would fit logically into a group of computer-related activities in one division. If acquired, Byte-So would operate as an independent profit center. The amount of synergism between Byte-So and your company's other operations is still uncertain, and you have been told to disregard it in the initial appraisal. That is, Byte-So is to be considered on its merits as a free-standing business.

You have available the income statement and balance sheet for the past two years. In addition you have the Byte-So management projections for total revenue and total costs and expenses plus certain other costs and credits for the next three years:

BYTE-SO SOFTWARE COMPANY, INC.
($ millions)

	1987	1988	1989	1990	1991
Total revenue	$ 7.3	14.6	21.5	28.5	$35.5
Total costs and expenses	10.4	15.1	19.6	24.0	27.8
Income from operations	$ (3.1)	(.5)	1.9	4.5	$ 7.7
Tax-loss carryforward available	—	.3	.7	1.2	1.5
Capital investment	2.0	1.6	5.9	18.2	7.3

You have been asked for two calculations:

1. Assuming the growth in revenue and costs as projected by Byte-So management, what will happen to earnings per share in the next three years? (Assume 5.0 million shares outstanding.)
2. Up to this point the price/earnings multiple at which the stock has traded has not been meaningful, because of losses now turning into small profits. Assuming (a) stock outstanding stays constant at 5 million shares, (b) the price/earnings multiple fluctuates around a mean of 15, and (c) a 66⅔ percent premium over market price is necessary in order to acquire the company, how attractive an acquisition would Byte-So be (i) at the beginning of 1990, and (ii) at the beginning of 1991?

BYTE-SO SOFTWARE COMPANY, INC.
Income statement for the year ended 12/31
($ millions)

	1987	1988
Total revenue	$ 7.3	$14.6
Costs and expenses:		
Cost of goods/services	3.4	5.2
Research & development	2.9	3.0
Marketing, G & A	4.1	6.9
Total costs and expenses	10.4	15.1
Income from operations	$ (3.1)	$ (.5)
Interest income	.2	1.3
Interest expense	(.2)	(.1)
Income before taxes and extraordinary credit	$ (3.1)	$ .7
Taxes	—	.3
Extraordinary credit tax loss carryforward	—	.3
Net income	$ (3.1)	$ .7
Shares outstanding, millions	2.0	5.0

BYTE-SO SOFTWARE COMPANY, INC.
Balance sheet, as of 12/31
($ millions)

	1987	1988
ASSETS		
Current assets:		
Cash	$ .7	$ .2
Marketable securities	2.9	37.8
Accounts receivable	2.7	5.4
Prepaid expenses	.2	.8
Total current assets	$ 6.5	$44.2
Plant, property & equipment	5.4	7.0
Reserve for depreciation	1.1	1.6
Net PP&E	4.3	5.4
Other assets	.2	.5
TOTAL ASSETS	$11.0	$50.1
LIABILITIES AND STOCKHOLDERS' EQUITY		
Current liabilities:		
Accounts payable	$ .5	$ 1.4
Accrued payroll & employee benefits	.6	.9
Current portion of long-term debt	.3	.1
Other liabilities	—	.1
Total current liabilities	$ 1.4	$ 2.5
Long-term debt	.7	—
Other liabilities	—	.1
Total liabilities	$ 2.1	$ 2.6
Stockholders' equity	8.9	47.5
TOTAL LIABILITIES AND STOCKHOLDERS' EQUITY	$11.0	$50.1

CASE 45 SWINGING GENES

Swinging Genes first came to public attention when Wilder Brooks, the president, held a press conference that got national television news coverage. Two of Swinging Genes' founders were prominent in genetic research, and on a television interview show they and a famous clinician discussed the genetic engineering breakthroughs that had led them to found a new company. The whole incident caused a lot of excitement, in part because Swinging Genes appeared to be on the track of several dramatic medical discoveries, and in part because the Securities and Exchange Commission lawyers thought the publicity was too much like a promotion for a stock issue they were preparing. But after a good deal of discussion the SEC withdrew its objections, the offering went ahead, and Swinging Genes went into business with $30 million in the bank and an ambitious research program to spend it on.

Swinging Genes needed laboratories for this research, and an attractive plant was available. The Woodwind Pharmaceutical Company had gotten into quality problems. Then it went out of business after the Food & Drug Administration banned its major product, and Wilder Brooks was able to obtain its facilities on very favorable terms. Woodwind had built a small, new pharmaceutical research laboratory, plant, and warehouse complex in Peanut Blossom, an affluent suburban community with some light industry. The Woodwind laboratories could easily be adapted for the Swinging Genes program, and there was plenty of space for future expansion. Swinging Genes was ready to begin operations in a remarkably short time.

The community of Peanut Blossom had become very worried about the Woodwind plant as its quality troubles made headlines, and was glad to see it go. Then no one really knew what Swinging Genes planned to do, genetic research has uncertain connotations, and a certain flamboyance of the management served to increase the nervousness of the community. The same day that a timid-looking delegation from one local group called on Wilder Brooks to ask if he was really planning to do genetic research, the lawyer for another group went to court to request an injunction to prevent any experiments that would change living things as found in nature.

Swinging Genes found itself embroiled in a strange and confusing local controversy. It had not actually done anything yet or announced any specific program, but it also found itself the target of a proposed zoning ordinance that could have prevented its operation altogether. Wilder Brooks had a long talk with the mayor of Peanut Blossom, and discovered that the mayor understood his community very well. That afternoon Wilder sent everyone at the plant on a two-week paid vacation and stopped all construction without explanation to anyone. The plant was locked, lights out, and abandoned so far as anyone could see.

A week later there was a "letter to the editor" published in the local paper protesting the rough treatment of Swinging Genes by the community; it was cosigned by the head of the local building trades council and the former head of the Woodwind Pharmaceutical union local, now unemployed. The paper also carried a short editorial suggesting that Swinging Genes had never had a chance to tell its side of the story. Wilder Brooks knew that in a town like Peanut Blossom the union endorsements and the loss of the former pharmaceutical plant jobs meant little, but at least this was a start.

The Town Board invited Wilder Brooks to a meeting, and quizzed him about Swinging Genes' plans, which sounded very bland and beneficial as they were reported in the local paper. Then the mayor asked for a public hearing, on a "voluntary" basis, since no specific complaint was pending against the company. A wide variety of citizen and activist groups testified at the hearing, which was also widely reported in the media. The question-and-answer portion of the meeting became quite rough at some points in the meeting, but the net public impression was rather favorable.

Following the hearing Swinging Genes released a carefully prepared public statement. For this it bought a full page in the local paper, distributed the statement as a mailing to all postal patrons, and otherwise broadcast it around the community. In this the company restated its program, outlining its anticancer program and its plan for attempting control of diabetes and arthritis, and reemphasizing its adherence to the prescribed genetic research guidelines as well as agreeing to additional stipulations developed from the confrontations with citizens' groups around other genetic research facilities. It invited the creation of a citizens' advisory council that would meet with the research director from time to time, to learn more about what was actually in progress and to express any community concerns.

After another week Wilder Brooks quietly began to restart operations, and no one said anything. The citizens' advisory council was formed, and had a rather bland first meeting, since no operations had yet started. But the way finally seemed clear for Wilder Brooks and Swinging Genes to do what the company had been founded for. "I think we will accelerate our attack on the cancer problem," he told the mayor over a quiet lunch after he had thanked him for helping so much. "I never thought that the hardest part of starting a new company would be in getting acceptance from the neighborhood, but now that we have it, I'd like to show them some worthwhile results."

QUESTIONS

1. Why would a business such as Swinging Genes have so much trouble getting community acceptance when the products could be so life-saving?
2. Should the company have looked for a rural area away from people?
3. Would you want Swinging Genes (or any similar company) in your town?

CASE 46 THE LOOSE-LEAF TOBACCO COMPANY

One day the chief executive officer of the Loose-Leaf Tobacco Company gave up smoking. He was on vacation at the time; he had gone off for two weeks to get away from the company and think about its future. Giving up smoking was a personal thing, but it partly grew out of disquiet about the future of the business. The chief came back from vacation with a new attitude toward the business and its problems. He had been too long an industry spokesman to say anything about smoking, except that he had switched to smoking a pipe. He had gathered a collection of foul old pipes from his uncles and started carrying three or four of them around with him; there were complaints about the way the pipes smelled, but no one noticed that he never actually smoked.

More important, the chief began to look at Loose-Leaf and its opportunities in a different way. He was chairman and CEO. His president and chief operating officer had been running the tobacco business for the past two years; he was a very good executive, dedicated to the tobacco business and its people, and smoked enough cigarettes, the CEO thought, to count for both of them. Loose-Leaf's nontobacco businesses were small and unimportant, and the CEO began to question whether that was the way it should be.

Loose-Leaf was one of the major tobacco companies in the United States and in the world. Consequently it had a very large number of employees in many communities, and a much larger number of tobacco farmers and other suppliers were dependent on the prosperity of the company. An internal study had suggested that if for any reason Loose-Leaf ceased to operate, a dozen small cities and many rural counties would be very hard hit. Yet it was hard for even the most optimistic tobacco industry enthusiast to find a basis for predicting future growth; the consensus forecasts had shifted toward the tobacco industry either maintaining its present volume, or beginning to shrink at a significant rate, depending on how rapidly society insisted on restricting smoking further.

Loose-Leaf needed to find areas for growth. The chief got a fresh review of the options and of the experience of the other tobacco companies. The summary was as follows:

1. Some tobacco companies had diversified by acquiring companies in other industries. This had not always worked; some of these companies had been sold again, perhaps because of the difficulties of managing strange businesses. Even if it did work for us, it could only maintain the business base in the interests of the investors, and would do nothing for the present employees, dependent communities, and tobacco producers.

2. No tobacco company had diversified in any way that seemed to benefit its present organization.

The chief felt that the situation demanded a better response from Loose-Leaf. The business was very profitable, a good corporate citizen, and well-liked except by those opposed to legal sale of tobacco. Loose-Leaf would be a leading tobacco company as long as society allowed sale of tobacco—but he felt that tobacco sales and profits would begin to shrink at a significant rate within a few years. While the president did his best to maximize the profits from the tobacco company, the chief would put his energies into an effort to find other ways to use Loose-Leaf resources so that the company, the Loose-Leaf people, and those outside of Loose-Leaf and dependent on it could begin to build another business base—a nontobacco alternative for corporate growth and employment of its people and resources.

QUESTIONS

1. Is this a realistic objective?
2. List some of the specific diversification options for Loose-Leaf.
3. Construct a preliminary outline of a diversification program for Loose-Leaf.

CASE 47 THE UPSCALE SUITS COMPANY

"An Upscale Suit is the mark of an educated man." This was one of the key advertising slogans during the rise of the Upscale Suit Company. Ronald Scale, the founder and president, had learned the garment business working for his father and his uncles. He returned from the South Pacific after World War II a year short of his college degree, finished under the GI Bill, and then stayed on for a masters from the business school. He had some savings from the war years, and when he graduated, he went back to the same Mississippi River city where he had gone to high school to organize the Upscale Suit Company.

The business did well. He had learned a good deal about selling suits from his father and uncles, and got good advice from them in any unexpected situations. He had learned as an officer that he had managerial ability, the business school training served him well, and he had made a good choice in the initial positioning of the product line.

"An Upscale Suit, the mark of an educated man." Ronald Scale sought means of reinforcing this image, which seemed so well to capture the attention of the aspiring managers of the early and later 1950s. The advertising copy often drew from the English and on the aspirations of the ambitious young man outdoing those who had come before him. Not every year's sales gain was as good as the year before, because fewer people buy clothes in recessions, but the uptrend of the business was pronounced, and not until after 1970 was there a year when sales fell below the year before—and that was in a recession year.

Over the next eight years sales were up in six years and down in two. Ronald Scale was not that concerned—the long up-trend was still running—but he was a little puzzled. He had not changed anything. The products were good, cost-competitive, well tailored, and the advertising copy just as bright and upscale as ever. Then, starting in 1985, there were four years when sales fell a little each year. The business was still profitable and supported Ronald Scale and his family well—but for sales to fall for four years? And the fifth year started badly. Ronald knew he should do something, and decided on a large advertising campaign.

The advertising increased sales, although barely enough to pay for the cost, and then someone started defacing the Upscale Suits billboards. When Ronald Scale saw one where the Upscale educated young executive had been given an Afro haircut, he managed to laugh it off. But when the graffitti spread, this began to bother Ronald Scale, and he went to see the police chief, an acquaintance from high school. "I realize you really can't do anything about the billboards—but what is happening in this town?"

The Chief looked at him. He was in civilian clothes that day. "Ron, this is an Upscale Suit, and I have worn them for a long time. My son buys from you too. But I wonder how many of the newer people do. This city has changed a lot since the days when we came back from the war and you started a clothing business. Have you really looked around? I think you are selling to the people who were here back then, and some of us are still left. But there are a lot of others now who have never tried your clothes and maybe don't think that much of your advertising."

Ronald Scale was slow to yield the point: "But the people who come in the store seem about the same now as they did then. I haven't seen that much change."

"Ron, that's the point. The rest never come in. Besides driving from your parking space behind the store to that nice house of yours in the suburbs, have you ever studied the city? Look around this town, see what kind of people are on the streets, and try to figure out which ones ever go inside your store."

Ronald Scale parked his car and walked across the business section. He took a bus for a few blocks, cut through the main floor of a department store, and out into another street. He went back to his car and began to drive a pattern just outside of the business district, looking at the residential areas and the neighborhood shopping areas. He had known all of these streets as a high school boy, but the neighborhoods looked so different he had to stop and buy a map. Three hours later he was in the office of the local chamber of commerce talking to his friends there. "Where can I get some survey data on what kind of people live in this city? By races, and colors, and income levels? I've lived here all of my life and built a business on selling to one kind of man, but I can hardly find any of them on the street. I never tried to sell to blacks or Hispanics, or anyone else but young white middle Americans. How could I get so out of touch with the city?"

QUESTIONS

1. How do you think that Ronald Scale got so out of touch with the city?
2. How could he have avoided this?
3. What can he do about it?

CASE 48 WATCH DISPLAY CHEMICALS

Amazon Industries was a major multinational corporation. An unexpected offshoot of its fundamental research processes was a better way to make the chemicals required for watch displays. Amazon obtained patents protecting its rights to make the chemicals or use them for watch, calculator, and other types of displays. This was a fast-growing new area, and Amazon Industries decided to enter this market to sell these chemicals in the United States (and elsewhere).

For this business the mission was that of supplying the display chemical needs of the electronic industry, and among the goals Amazon Industries set was the achievement of a preeminent and profitable market position. The business strategy included (1) an ongoing R&D effort to maintain leadership in a rapidly evolving market, (2) initial emphasis on chemicals needed for watch and calculator displays, with products for calculators, instruments, signs, and even flat TV screens to follow, (3) patent protection of the business, insofar as possible, (4) marketing to display manufacturers based on developing an exclusive supply position since Amazon planned to sell superior chemical mixtures of a proprietary nature, and (5) an attempt to bring the business to a positive cash flow as soon as possible.

These watch and calculator displays consisted of a very thin sandwich of specially coated glass. Sealed between these thin sheets of glass were display chemicals that changed from clear to opaque under the influence of a very small electric current. These were the chemicals Amazon Industries decided to make and sell. They would replace LED (light emitting diode) displays, which were bulkier and required a great deal more electric power to operate. Many other laboratories had made chemicals for liquid crystal watch displays, but the family of products covered by the Amazon Industries patents were better.

Different chemicals gave different display characteristics, and to get the type of display a watch or calculator manufacturer wanted required blending several different chemicals. Amazon planned to sell proprietary mixtures of these blends—that is, they would make a blend and guarantee it to have certain performance characteristics, but they would not tell the customer exactly what the ingredients were. This would help Amazon to develop a position difficult for competitors to match exactly, and also give flexibility to change the mixture slightly from time to time if necessary to meet the performance specifications. While a number of electronic industry, governmental, and other research groups in various countries were actively searching for further improvements in the chemical display technology, no competitor had yet tried to establish a position as the leading chemical supplier to the industry.

The existence of this business resulted from Amazon Industries' decision to develop the opportunity the research discovery presented. Management had reviewed alternatives ranging from abandonment of the patents to direct entry into display, semiconductor, and watch manufacture. To go into the electronics and semiconductor business would have meant direct competition with various semiconductor companies, and Amazon decided this was not justified. But it wanted a return from the patents, so it decided to sell the watch display chemicals.

No social impact problems were forseen, in part because the chosen business role affected society only indirectly, through supply of products to consumer products industries. Operations requirements were judged to be well within the established competence of the firm, although this effort was not without its start-up problems.

In constructing a strategic model of such a business, the technique is to examine the selected strategy as it must be developed in the light of the technical characteristics and business realities of the effort, to see what the consequences of the strategy must be. These consequences are then examined, to see whether any of them may be undesirable, or suggestive of unsuspected vulnerabilities of the business.

In this case, the analysis began with a more detailed consideration of the technology and the product line that it could generate. These were by nature small-volume products since a gram of chemical could be made into a very large number of watch displays. Because of the complex chemistry, these were high-cost products. They also required pricing to give a high gross margin, in order to recover the R&D investment and to have hope of a profit from sales of relatively small amounts of material. The initial expectation was of a market that could be developed at a price of $4 per gram (or $4,000 per kilo) with individual sales in multikilo quantities. In deciding to sell proprietary mixtures based on their superior performance, the firm had chosen a packaged performance approach to the market, based on the unique or strong specialty products it hoped to offer.

Chemicals for these displays had extremely high purity requirements but of an unfamiliar type, because they related to electronic industry needs for control of conductivity and electrical characteristics as well as conventional chemical quality and purity standards. The product line for this business was conceived as intrinsically small, with a handful of chemical components formulated into proprietary blends tailored to specific application needs.

Product life was expected to be short due to the dynamic nature of the field, with obsolescence after about two years. This defined the challenge to R&D, which had the burden of providing the successor products more effectively than competing electronic and chemical laboratories.

The market characteristics suggested that the chemical needs for watches and calculators would support a successful small business. But the growth potential justifying the development was largely in other display applications likely to develop in future years. Because of the rapid technology shifts in the electronic industry, Amazon Industries' entire approach to the display market was vulnerable to potential replacement of this liquid crystal display technology by a newer one, in the same way that this liquid crystal system had replaced an earlier liquid crystal display, which itself had replaced light emitting diode watch displays, all within a few years.

Given the decision to enter the marketplace, the strategic model shows that there were remarkably few managerial choices as to how to proceed. The dynamics of the market and the technology mandated an R&D effort sufficient to renew the line in the face of short product life, and the R&D investment was essential to the long-term position regardless of near-term sales success. Only those few firms able and willing to compete in manufacture of watch and other display markets could be customers, so the market would remain relatively small until other display applications developed. An approach to the market with superior proprietary mixtures gave the only near-term hope of obtaining a large enough share of this small market to make the effort profitable.

The value of developing a strategic model was to discover the tightness by which the course of action was constrained even before entry efforts started, with a large market share essential for profitability until the market grew much larger. This also allowed analysis of the vulnerability of the strategy to disturbances in the chosen environment. In this case the strategy was very vulnerable, because management had so little freedom of action if conditions changed.

Application of this specific strategy started in a promising manner but then encountered two problems. The most critical was the buying posture of the major electronic companies. They resisted the idea of buying anything from only one supplier, because this made them too dependent on that supplier's performance. They even refused to test product mixtures with superior properties where the composition of the mixture was not fully disclosed, since this implied dependence on one vendor.

This difficulty was based on bitter experience with chemical and pharmaceutical companies as suppliers, which had led the electronic companies to the generalization that any chemical bought from outside the electronic industry would have to be purified anyway, before it would be suitable for their use. This caused a number of electronic companies to manufacture their own specialty chemicals in spite of the obvious inefficiencies.

Over the long run such an attitude could be overcome by demonstrating reliable performance and service as a supplier, but at a small initial sales volume based on only a portion of each company's requirements. The purchasing policy of most companies required a second supplier, and many companies continued to make a part of the material for their own use. This purchasing policy also barred all proprietary products and led to a situation favoring development of price competition.

A second major difficulty in implementing the chosen strategy was the failure of the prospective customer group to obtain their anticipated share of the U.S. consumer market. Unexpectedly the Japanese and others led in successful innovation, at the expense of established U.S. and European companies. Poor sales of the finished products meant less need for display chemicals in the United States, especially as a number of display manufacturers withdrew from the market.

In evaluating the performance of this strategy after about four years, it appeared basically sound and likely to work out in the long run, although greatly delayed by the painful process of developing a reputation for reliability with the electronic companies. Because the strategy had been so tightly constrained from the first, management had had no choice but to accept the delay, short of total abandonment of the venture. Up to that point the customers had accepted the products only on a commodity basis, even though the goal still was to move back to selling packaged performance of strong specialty products.

Sales and market growth were proceeding, but far behind original projections. And the U.S. electronic companies, while not competing effectively for watch displays for conventionally priced watches, had increased their sales volume by enlargement of the market for low-priced watches. Amazon Industries made no public statements, but industry analysts suggested that the display chemicals business had not begun to make a profit. No new display technology had yet threatened, and the investment still had long-term prospects for return of the investment and eventual profits.

This example illustrates some of the key elements of a conceptual model of the business strategy being employed. A numerical model could also be constructed, but this effort is usually not justified unless at a later stage. Initially the emphasis is on defining a strategy, developing the framework for putting it into action, and then looking at the consequences, the physical limits, the vulnerabilities, and the robustness of the strategy to random events. The normal purpose is to develop an understanding sufficient so that design of the strategy can be further improved beforehand to reduce the chance of misadventure. Quantification can then represent a further refinement of the design, if time permits and the potential increase in precision seems to justify the effort.

Such a conceptual strategic model can be built from the mission and goals that provide the strategy its initial validity, and modified by the requirements of the strategic overview components. Then the strategy should be analyzed (1) to confirm the definition of its seven elements, especially focus, (2) for degree of differentiation and sources of profit from the strategy, (3) as to stage of growth of the business, (4) for protection from competitive forces, (5) as to the nature of competitive advantage, (6) regarding the profile of the customer group, and (7) regarding the technology horizon—when will today's technology be obsoleted, and by what? From this information, the size of the product line and the likely distribution of product sizes, product life, and profitability can be estimated, so that both the likely shape of the business and the nature of the constraints around it begin to emerge more clearly.

QUESTIONS

1. Discuss this Amazon Industries venture; up to the end of the case, to what extent was it a failure or success, and what were the key factors determining this?

CASE 49 MODELING A SPECIALTY CHEMICAL BUSINESS

Ambitions, Inc. was a successful specialty chemical business founded by a group of very good chemists. The company had taken as its mission the supplying of customer needs for high-performance specialty chemicals from two strong technology positions—both of which required successful operation of difficult synthetic organic reactions that most companies did not attempt. The management had set goals almost entirely in terms of sales and profit growth, and aspired to very high growth rates. Ambitions planned to do the difficult, and its strategy called for aggressive development of pharmaceutical intermediate plus chemical and electronic industry applications of products from these two technologies. This strategy development required a strong research and development group, and the company had also successfully pursued some R&D contracts, to increase the span of its more fundamental research.

Ambitions, Inc. became a conspicuously successful small chemical company within a few years, as it succeeded in making its strategy work. Especially, marketing opportunities for its products had been pursued into international markets to an extent unusual for a relatively small firm, and this had helped the growth in sales.

A strategic overview analysis had called for further strengthening of corporate operations, and the gathering of additional resources to hasten the already favorable rate of development of corporate opportunity. No social impact problems had come to light, and potential need for corporate course correction had been minimized.

The competitive advantage of the firm was based on good chemistry and two difficult technologies applied to small markets. The business was young, fast-growing, profitable, and the technology position sound for the foreseeable future. Most of Ambitions' products were not patentable, but the processes were, and Ambitions had obtained as many process patents as possible. The customer group was defined by the specific applications, with many small single-use products.

The nature of the synthetic chemical made these products expensive, and therefore they were used only for superior performance when an application justified this. The products were priced to be profitable, with long product life in many of the smaller applications. While margins were high, the relatively small sales volume of most products required this high margin in order to pay R&D and other overheads and produce some net profit. In such a line of small, high-margin products, those few products that grew to a larger volume provided the major source of profit. But any product that became large enough to interest a commodity chemical supplier could be preempted and produced by such a company at equal or lower cost, since Ambitions did not have a basic patent position that would prevent such an entry. The competitor would have to work out a process that did not violate Ambitions' process patents, but with the advantages of larger volume their costs were likely to be lower. Thus, success of a specific Ambitions product could lead to the loss of the product, at least as a major source of profit.

This vulnerability to loss of large, successful products is common among small specialty chemical companies, and, so long as it is recognized, is not a barrier to significant levels of success. In this specific case, however, the vulnerability had received little attention, even though most of the firm's profits were derived from two excellent products both large enough to be lost in this way. Worse still, the product line contained no intermediate-sized products, where the model of the strategy would require that the product line always contain intermediate-sized products as potential replacements for products that might be lost. Thus, the development of a strategic model based on the performance of a very attractive and fast-growing business showed that a fundamental vulnerability had been neglected. Action aimed at building intermediate-sized products was strongly recommended, in hope of maintaining the growth momentum of the firm in the face of predictable product losses.

QUESTIONS

1. Explain in your own words why Ambitions was vulnerable to losing only its large products.
2. How should this change the product and business strategy, and the way that the top management ran the company?

CASE 50 PROMISES FOR THE FUTURE, INCORPORATED

John Edwards, the controller, was trying very hard to see the president. Jack James, the president, had disappeared again. His secretary apologized: "He's so wound up in this big proposal, I think he forgot he asked you to come up here."

"Well," John Edwards grunted, "Tell him I've got the cost estimates he needs for 'this big proposal,' and call me again when he will be here long enough to catch him." He picked up his bundles of paper and trudged back toward the accounting section.

The president came back, picked up a paper from his desk, and left again immediately by the other door of his office, to the frustration of the secretary. Five minutes later he was back with the vice-president of marketing, and they spent a heated twenty minutes in debate, broke abruptly and both reached for telephones. Before the secretary could say anything, the president had his party and was selling hard to win his participation.

When he hung up, the secretary said, "John Edwards was up to see you. He said you sent for him. Shall I call him?"

"No, I don't have time 'till later. I'm going over to marketing." And the afternoon went on and on this way. About two hours later John Edwards trudged back up with his papers, still uncalled, and asked the secretary what was going on.

"Still the same pace on the same proposal. And I really don't know what's going on, so I can't tell you. But if you stand right where you are and he doesn't pop either in or out of his office within ten minutes, it will be the first time this afternoon."

John Edwards stood. Time passed. Ten minutes later the president charged in, perspiring a little. "John, how did you know I was about to call you?"

"I didn't—but I have to leave at five for a doctor's appointment, and I knew you were working on this proposal, and I figured I had better get the cost data to you somehow before I had to leave." He laid out his papers, and briefly presented the cost estimates.

"Good. Add an extra 30 percent and put it in that way."

John Edwards was thunderstruck. "Chief, that's the first time you ever accepted a cost estimate from anyone without a 25-minute grilling on the details—let alone adding a fudge factor."

"John, this job is different. We are proposing to do something very important that has never been done before. From the proposal they have to *know* we can do it; that's why we have two former cabinet officers and a senator signed on as consultants. If the proposal convinces them we can do the job, we will get the job, regardless of the cost; otherwise not. We never wrote a proposal before where we had to prove our qualifications to do something that had never been done; but I think we have done it this time."

John Edwards shook his head, as he walked back to his office to get his coat.

QUESTIONS

1. To what extent do companies—or job candidates—have to prove they can do things they never have had a chance to do? Discuss.
2. Why do businesses make the unreasonable sort of request that question 1 represents?
3. How does a company try to overcome this sort of barrier?

CASE 51 THE MEDICAL METER COMPANY

At Western University Professor Jones had discovered and patented a new approach to measuring the light spectrum transmitted through an organic substance. Both the Colder Controls Company and the Medical Meter Company wanted the exclusive right to manufacture and market the professor's invention. The royalty was set by the university, and both companies had agreed to pay it. Now they were trying to persuade the professor and the university representative that each could do a better job than the other. Traditionally Western University let the faculty member have a large voice in the decision, so both companies concentrated their presentations on Professor Jones.

Colder Controls spoke first, and the representative built up the importance of Professor Jones to their effort; they would name the instrument after him, put his picture on the nameplate if he wished, and the presentation went on in this vein.

When the representative from Medical Meter got up, he dealt with Professor Jones only very briefly: "We agree that this invention should be sold as the Jones Meter, and plan to use Professor Jones as a consultant to be sure that we make the best use of his prestige. But the reason that the Medical Meter Company ought to be your licensee is that we can design an attractive, reliable meter quickly, build it at a reasonable cost, and get it to market in minimum time. Our design group is staffed to handle six instrument concepts a year, with an average of twelve months from start to a working production prototype, and twenty-four months to production models on the distributor's shelves. We sometimes can go a little faster, but we can speak confidently of having the new Jones spectrum meter available for sale two years from today.

"More than that, we have built up an excellent instrument service facility available through all of our distributors, to the point that Medical Meter is known for having the best supporting service in the industry. And, having got the service base, we have told our design groups to make it obsolete, by building machines that don't need service, or can be serviced by replacing modules right in the user's laboratory. Medical Meter is now the best for operating reliability, and the service is still there if you need it. And with reliability and service like that, and reasonable prices, our meters are easy to sell. But we don't depend on that; we have a topnotch sales force geared to handling six new products a year; but they don't often get the chance to sell a real winner like the new Jones meter we hope to build, and they will really set the market on fire with it when it gets there.

"We are the best at designing, building, selling, and servicing instruments for this market. We would be most proud to add the Jones Meter to our line, and to bring its benefits rapidly to the waiting world."

Colder Controls had a good design and service group, too, but Professor Jones didn't really know much about them. He had heard good things from his friends about Medical Meter, and they sounded so competent. He told the university he thought that Medical Meter should get the license, they did, and they introduced an attractive, well-designed Jones Meter to the marketplace two years later.

QUESTIONS

1. How important is the capability to develop good products on schedule?
2. How does a company establish this capability?

GLOSSARY

Differentiation (of products or services)   The degree to which one firm's product or service is different from that of its competitors. Any degree is possible, with the following four categories defining the major possibilities:

  Unique product   A product for which there is no substitute at any price in the opinion of the buyer.

  Strong specialty   A product whose substitutes are sufficiently inferior so that the buyer will willingly pay a premium price.

  Weak specialty   A product sufficiently better than its substitutes that the buyer will always select it, if price and other considerations are equal.

  Commodity   A product normally bought from the seller with the best price or delivery among those able to meet the product specifications.

Elements of product and business strategy   *See* Strategy.

Enterprise strategy   *See* Strategy.

Excellence model   A pattern for management of a group or of an organization in a manner that can lead to maximum individual contribution, maximum organization competence, and maximum effectiveness in executing strategies. This pattern sets requirements for purpose, leadership, commitment, relevance, learning, and excellence.

Fees   Payments for services rendered corollary to a sale—see Profit sources.

Goals   Specific targets for achievement within the area defined by its mission. Goals and objectives are treated as roughly equivalent here, although goals are more likely to be larger or longer-term, and the very specific and short-term are more likely to be called objectives, in the management-by-objectives sense.

Innovation profits   From creating something new and useful—see Profit sources.

Management of social impact   Anticipating the impact of organization actions on society, modifying these actions to reduce unfavorable impacts, or balancing these actions in such a way as to make them more acceptable to society.

Management operating system   That network of linkages by which a management group communicates among its members and with the organization, gathers information from organization and environment, and directs the performance of its operation. Its nature is defined by the accumulated impact of all of the policies, rules, and procedures laid down by management plus the habit patterns the organization has developed during past operations.

Mission   The social role a business will fulfill by satisfying certain needs of customers or society well enough so that these customers will pay more for the necessary goods or services than it costs the business to deliver them.

Policies Guidelines or rules management sets for itself and for the organization in the operation of the business. These rules can arise by specific decisions, as when management chooses a new direction for the business, or can grow out of habitual operating patterns.

Profit The net return from a particular business activity after direct and allocated costs and taxes; that is, revenue less costs and taxes.

Profit sources

True profit the *returns to innovation;* usually fading away after a few years.

Fees

for **distribution services:** making merchandise conveniently available for purchase; retailing of all sorts, mail order outlets, industrial distributors and supply houses.

for **production services:** the assembly and testing of the final product.

for **trading services:** bringing together interests of buyer and seller; securities and real estate brokers, trading between countries.

for **breaking bulk:** reselling lesser quantities not otherwise available; odd lots of common stock, small packages of coal, or potting soil for plants.

for **use of capital:** a return on the investment required for the business pattern; financing of retailer via trade credit from wholesaler, hospital supply inventory necessary to guarantee same-day delivery.

for **insurance:** protection against inventory and other business risks carried in the customer's interest; spoilage and obsolescence of inventories, hedging of commodity and currency risks.

for **specialized services:** customs processing, personal shopping, custom design.

Rents

earned by **differential productivity of resources,** such as a superior cost position.

based on **brand names,** reputation, customer habits, or other market franchise.

due to **patents,** trade secrets, control of natural resources, or any other sort of monopoly position.

due to **economies of scale** in purchasing, production, distribution, or marketing.

Rent A payment for the use of intangible or tangible property. *See* Profit sources.

Social impact The impact on society of an organizational action—in terms of changes in life style, schedules, health, or welfare for individual members of society, the community, or society as a whole.

Strategic blindness An inability to see the strategic dimension in everyday issues; an occupational consequence of the concentration necessary for successful operating management. It arises because most operating executives condition themselves to function from a limited viewpoint, considering only events and data with a proven relevance to daily decisions. From such a viewpoint a new transistor or a potential new invention to make photocopies is invisible; it can have no proven relevance because it never existed before.

Strategic control The process of ensuring that the policies put into action and the results generated represent real progress toward the selected goals. The control component of the normal management process focuses on how competently a plan is being translated into action, but strategic control looks also at how appropriate these actions are for getting the desired results in the environment as it now exists and as it will become tomorrow. In particular, strategic control is necessary to ensure that strategic decisions are made from the necessary overview perspective, and to exercise control over the enterprise strategies that themselves govern the evolution of the enterprise.

Strategic management The effective integration of a well-conceived strategy with management of the on-going business process.

Strategy A basic approach for designing the action that will solve a problem or accomplish a goal; any strategy should answer a "how" question—that is, how progress is to be made toward achieving a goal.

  Contributing strategy A how-to-accomplish-our-goals statement dealing with the pattern of action by which a specific function, department, or other unit will contribute to the accomplishment of one or more primary strategies.

  Primary strategy A how-to-accomplish-our-goals statement dealing with the whole of a given accomplishment; strategy for a product, a service, a program, a business, an enterprise.

  Building block strategy *See* Strategy components.

  Business strategy A how-to-accomplish-our-goals statement laying out the way in which a business will be managed.

  Choice strategy *See* Strategy components.

  Enterprise strategy A how-to-accomplish-our-goals statement laying out the way in which a firm will be guided, and the way in which it will apportion its assets and capabilities—see Strategy components.

  Functional strategy A contributing strategy for a specific function. *See* Contributing strategy.

  Master strategy *See* Strategy components.

  Product strategy A how-to-accomplish-our-goals statement laying out the way in which a product will be managed.

  Program strategy A how-to-accomplish-our-goals statement laying out the way in which a program of related products or services will be managed.

  Service strategy A how-to-accomplish-our-goals statement laying out the way in which a service will be managed.

Strategy, product and business; **ELEMENTS**

  Deliverable(s) The product or service (or the catalog of related products or services) for which the strategy is designed, and which, in a cost-effective manner, must meet and satisfy customer needs in the opinion of that customer; the deliverable must be an effective satisfier of those needs.

  Resources The necessary combination of technology, equipment, time, talent, money, and position required to implement a strategy successfully.

  Focus The defined relationship with the customers and the market place upon which a strategy is based.

Leverages The specific incentives to buy a given product or service, *as perceived by the buyer;* the reasons why the customer sees the deliverable product or service as a satisfier of his or her specific needs.

Position Any consequences of past operations that can become a resource providing leverages for strategies. Valuable positions include those based on brand names and other market success; unusually effective production, service, distribution, or selling organizations; low raw material costs or control of raw material supply; superior or protected processes and technology; cost advantages; unusual management or organizational competence; and strong ties to customer need and habit patterns.

Display requirement The arrangements necessary so that potential customers can become sufficiently familiar with a product or service and how and where to buy it. Because it brings additional interaction with the customer, display is often coordinated with focus, and with advertising of the leverages.

Cash flow A progress measure and control element, to predict and track the action pattern of a strategy and to gauge its vulnerability to sudden failure or success.

Product line (business strategy only) Choice of the assortment of products or services to be offered by the business in order best to achieve its potential.

Strategy, enterprise; COMPONENTS

Building block strategies Basic organization characteristics, largely set as a result of management preferences, that determine the nature of the enterprise and the sorts of businesses in which it can succeed.

Leadership strategy The strength, style, and intensity of management direction of the organization's activities, and the manner and formality or informality with which the management group chooses to work among itself and with the organization as a whole.

Opportunity strategy The aggressiveness or passiveness of the opportunity search and the way in which detected opportunities are evaluated and developed, or not.

People strategy The kind of employee community and the nature of the teamwork and of the long- or short-term relationships the organization builds and maintains.

Public strategy How the organization relates itself to the public; the degree to which the impact of enterprise actions on the public is emphasized or minimized, the extent to which organization actions are open and visible, and the way in which the contacts of the organization with the public and the media are managed.

Resource-getting strategy The money-spending and money-obtaining policy, the adequacy of the resource supply it can tap, and the way in which it interrelates with the other strategies.

Choice strategies Decision criteria used by management in allocating resources as it receives resource requests and makes choices among them.

Desirability The degree to which a specific project is a good undertaking, according to the standards set by the organization's mission and goals.

Managing How diverse or how homogeneous the enterprise should be, how many types of management challenge should be compounded, and how complex the overall management task should be permitted to become.

Belonging   The degree to which a given product, business, or project will mesh into the fabric of the enterprise.

Credibility   For each request for resources, the specific requirements management sets for the quality of the underlying plan and the ability of the proposing managers to make it work.

Risk/reward   The acceptability of the projected payoffs and the likelihood that they will be achieved; the risk/return criteria, and the way these criteria change with specific circumstances.

Master strategies   A pattern or patterns defining how to build a business or complex of businesses; this may include integration or coordination of different components of the enterprise or changes in these components, including creation of new units, restructuring of old ones, and acquisitions or divestitures; actions planned with a perspective longer in range or broader in scope than the self-interest of the managers of the various components would dictate.

Third-wave management   A management system based on an intensely participative network in which subordinates at all levels take major responsibility for managing their own jobs; John Sculley uses this term to describe the management system at Apple, using Alvin Toffler's third-wave nomenclature.

Value-driven planning   A planning process under strategic management that requires that every action planned and put into action adds value to the firm or enterprise over the long run.

INDEX

Achievement, 243, 250, 280–283
Ackoff, Russell, et al., 3
Action
  bias for, 245
  development of, 25–34
  as objective, 35
  planning toward, 457–488
  policies and, 26, 28–29
  strategy toward, 34, 457–488
Adaptability, in five-fold way, 248
Adkins-Phelps, 105, 147
ADL. See Arthur D. Little
Air Products and Chemical, 105, 147
Alcon, leverage and needs, 318
Allegiance guideline, 208
Allen-Bradley, 355
Allen, Robert J., 247–248
American Cyanamid, 323, 463
American Express, 105
American Home Products, 220, 334
American Hospital Supply, 62
American spirit, principles of, 296–297
Andrews, Kenneth R., 238
Ansoff, H. I., 137
Ansoff, H. Igor, et al., 29
Army Engineers, 399
Arthur D. Little matrix, 111–112
AT&T, 382, 414
  as a basic business, 219
  changes and, 297–298, 301
Atlanta Federal Reserve Bank, 247
Atrophy, organization risk, 292
Automobile industry, 80–81
Autonomy, fostering, 246
Avon Products, 144

Bache, 176
Bank of America, 176
Banks, for small businesses, 415, 418
Barnard, Chester, 243
Base business, planning for, 219
BCG portfolio planning matrix, 110–111
Beatrice Foods, 334
Bell System, breakup of, 298
Belonging strategy, 144–147, 152, 153

Belonging strategy (continued)
  choice strategy, definition, 519
  for excellence model, 253
  relations of, 333–334
  strategic control over, 177–178
Berg, Norman A., 137
Bigness
  bias toward, 417–418
  as problem, 276–279, 284
Black & Decker, 175
Blanchard, Kenneth, and N. V. Peale, 380
Blough, Roger, 381–382
Bobst, Elmer, 79
Boot's, British firm, 220
Bork, Robert H., Jr., 9
Boston Consulting Group (BCG), 107, 110–111
Boundaries, in strategy matching, 336
Brand names, 59, 60, 516
Bristol-Myers, 150, 220
Building blocks, 137–143
Building-block strategies, 138, 151–153, 517, 518
  components of, 334
  relations of, 333
Business/Businesses, 5
  adding, 223–224
  appraisal of, in strategic plan, 357–358
  classification of, 108–114
  growth stages, 113–115
  life cycles and, 107–108
  natures of, 105, 119–121
  society and, 201–203
  strategic units of, 115–116
Business policy, 1 et passim
  nature and role of, 2–24
Business strategies, 465–466
  definitions, 31–34, 517
  elements of, 45–51
  examples of, 11
  foundations for, 73–170
  master. See Master business strategy
  matching, 332–338
  relations of, 334, 335
  types of, 314–316
  universals of, 428–429

Index   521

Capital, use of, 59, 516
Capital goods, short product life cycle, 55–57
Capital guidelines, 209
Cash cows, 110–111
Cash flow, 46, 49, 50, 518
Caterpillar, 336
Chandler, Alfred D., 245, 301
Change, organizational, 297–301
Changeovers, product, 277
Chaos, 278
Chapple, Alan, 378
Chief executive officers, 378
Choice criteria, 138
  boundaries of, 188
  component strategies in, 334
  for enterprise, 143–148
  strategy relations, 333
Choice strategies, 148, 151, 152, 153, 174–179
  definitions, 517, 518, 519
Chrysler, strategic blindness, 181
Coate, Michael B., 110, 112, 113
Coca-Cola, 48, 464
  bottle design, 317, 318
Comfort, 177
Comfort strategy, 145, 146
Commercial Solvents, 324
Commitment, 283
  excellence model and, 250, 252, 255, 256, 283
  organizational, 248
  worker and employer, 242
Commodity, 53–57, 515
Commodity market, competition in, 85–86
Commodity strategy, 316
Community, 204, 206–207
Compaq Computer, 178–179
Compensation, 256
  leadership and, 240–241
  of managers, 293–294, 301
Competence, 10–11, 243–252
Competition, 81–87, 90–91
  strategic control and, 179
Competitive action potential (CAP), 87–91
Competitive advantage, 314–315, 325
Competitive intelligence, 84, 89
Competitive process, 85–87
Competitors, kinds of, 82–84
Conal, 319
Concentration, perceptual barrier and, 183–184
Conglomerates, 226, 276–277, 333–335
Congruent managerial systems, in five-fold way, 248
Consensus principle, 296

Conservation guideline, 207
Constituencies, for organizations, 398–399
Consulting services, for small business, 418
Consumer goods, life cycle of, 55–57
Continuity, social, 206, 207
Contributing strategy, 31–32, 275–276
  definition, 517
  examples of, 36–37
Contribution guideline, 208
Contributor model, 281–284
Control/Controls, 173, 205
Controllability strategy, 146, 147
Corporate organization, 5
  universality, 428–429
Cost/Costs, social, 206, 210
Cost-plus-profit equation, 281
Course correction, management of, 185, 186, 228–238
Credibility, definition, 519
  for excellence model, 253
Credibility strategies, 147, 148, 152, 153
  relations of, 334, 335
  strategic control over, 178
Cultures
  business practices and, 430–431
  foreign, 427–442
  organization, 295–299, 301
Currency risks, 59
Customers
  learning from, 246
  quality and, 353–354

Dartmouth College decision, 5
Davis, Stanley M., 297
Debt/equity ratio, 118
de Geus, Arie, 352
De Kalb, 151
Deliverables, 45, 46, 50, 517
Dependence guideline, 208
Desirability, 334, 518–519
Desirability strategy, 143–145, 152–153, 175
Differential productivity, rents and, 516
Differentiation, 515
  elements of strategy and, 54–55
  in strategy design, 316, 318, 325
Directors, for new businesses, 418–419
Dis-integration, 221–222
Display requirement, 46, 48, 50, 518
Distribution function, 272–273
Distribution service fees, 58–60, 516
Distribution strategy, 276
Diversity, opportunity management and, 225–226
Dogs, 110–111
Dominant theme, in five-fold way, 248

Dommersmith, W. P., 377
Drucker, Peter, 282
Dumps guideline, 208
Du Pont
  market structure analysis, 80
  strategy, 301, 334
Durability, for excellence model, 253

Economic means
  social ends and, 6–7
  in strategy design, 12
Economic power, 444–446, 447
Economies of scale, 277–278
  rents due to, 517
Efficiency, people and, 280–283
Emerging issues, social, 26–28, 34
Empiricism principle, 296
Employee affiliation, excellence and, 247
Enterprise
  building of an, 142
  organizing, 268–271, 284
Enterprise strategy/strategies, 136–169, 465–466
  achievement strategies and, 151–153
  components of, 334
  definitions, 31–33, 515, 517, 518, 519
  how they govern, 333–335
  matching, 332–338
  problems of, 181
Entrepreneur, as rent collector, 463–465
Entrepreneurial management, 247
Entrepreneurship
  fostering, 246
  small and new businesses, 415–417
Environment, 357, 377–381, 383
Equity/debt ratio, 118
Ethical standards, of top managers, 379–381, 383
Ethics, 205, 207
Evolution of markets, 78–79
Excellence, 245–246
Excellence model
  alternatives to, 254–256, 271
  commitment and, 250, 252, 255, 256, 283
  credibility and, 253
  definition, 515
  enterprise strategy requirements, 252, 253
  leadership in, 249–256
  learning in, 251–252
  loyalties in, 254–256
  for management, 249–252, 253
  strategy and, 253, 467
Excellence principle, 296
Executive mobility, 378
Experience curves, 106–107

Fairchild Camera, 411, 412
Fayol, Henri, 29
Federal management guideline, 208–209

Fees, 515, 516
  as profit source, 59, 60
Financial analysis, in strategic plan, 357, 359–360
Financing, of new and small businesses, 415–417
Firms, 5, 6, 11–12. *See also* Businesses
Fit strategy, 146, 178
Five-Fold Way, 247–249, 256
Flexibility of structure, 275
Focus, 46, 47, 50, 84, 517
Ford, Henry, 378, 384
Ford Motor Company, 81, 82, 181, 221, 242, 382
Forecast, in strategic plan, 357, 359
Foreign countries, 427–442, 445
Foreign cultures, 427–442
Foresight, management function, 188
Formality, in leadership, 238–239, 256
Frito-Lay, 9, 10
Functional competence, 248
Functional plans
  in the strategic plan, 357, 359
Functional strategies, 275–276, 517
Future, creating, 227

General Electric, 175, 414
  classification schemes, 108–110, 111, 113, 114
  SBU organization, 155, 268, 270–271
  sector management, 184
General Foods, 61
General Mills, 228
General Motors, 225–226, 242, 382
  acquisitions, 276
  Ford competition, 81–82
  market structure analysis, 80
  organizational problems, 300, 301
  strategic blindness, 181
Generalized distribution rule, 89
Generic products, as profit source, 61–62
Ghemawat, Pankay, 50
Global horizons, for top managers, 381, 383
Goals
  definition, 5, 515
  development of, 30–31
  shared, in leadership, 240, 245, 256
  in strategic plan, 357, 358
  in strategy/action, 465
  in strategy design, 12
Governments
  in international business, 432
  power of, 446–447
Grace, Peter, 336
Grace, W. R., 144, 323, 336
Growth, small business assistance, 418

Habits, 34
  policies and, 26

Hamel, Gary, and C. V. Pralahad, 137
Harrigan, Kathryn Rudie, 222
Hasbro, 56
Haspeslagh, Philippe, 111
Hauser, John R., and Don Clausing, 353, 354
Hayes, Robert, and W. Abernathy, 378
Hedging, 59
Heller, Robert, 246
Henderson, Bruce D., 107, 110
Hewlett, William, 246
Hewlett-Packard, 246
Hierarchy, as organization universal, 428
Higgins, James M., 151
Hiring
　in excellence model, 256
　leadership and, 240–241
Hofer, Charles W., 112–113
Hoffmann-La Roche, 54, 84, 464
　compensation policy, 241
　master business strategy, 150
　resource-getting strategy, 141–143
Homogeneity of market, 76
House of Quality theme, 353, 355
Human resources, use of, 204, 205

IBM, 7–9, 48, 464
　job security, 242
　people strategy, 141
Individual, respect for, 239–240
Informality, in leadership, 238–239, 256
Information, market, 75–76
Innovation
　design boundaries and, 326
　excellence and, 247
　opportunity management and, 226–227
　as profit source, 59, 60
Innovation profits, definition, 515
Innovation strategy, for excellence model, 253
Insurance, fees for, 59, 516
Integration, 221–222
Integrity principle, 297
International Business Machines. *See* IBM
International Harvester, 181
International management, strategy for, 432
Intimacy principle, 297
Inventories, insurance of, 59
ITT, 445

Job security, 242
Johnson & Johnson, 225, 271, 334
Just-in-time production, 355

Katz, Daniel, and R. L. Kahn, 293
Kendall, M. G., 80
Kennedy, John F., 382
Koch, Donald L., *et al.*, 247

Kodak, 181
Kroc, Ray, 246

Laborer model, 281–284
Law, in business principle, 206
Leadership, in excellence model, 249–250, 252, 253
Leadership strategy, 138, 139, 152, 153, 238–240
　definition, 518
　in excellence model, 254–256
　relations of, 334
Learning
　in the excellence model, 251, 252
　organizational, 352–353
Learning curves, 106–107
Legal systems, foreign, 429–430
Leontiades, Milton, 298, 299
Leverage/Leverages, 458–462, 464, 467
　creating, 318, 325
　example of, 50
　needs linkages, 325, 335, 458–462, 467
　in strategies, definition, 46–47, 518
Leveraged buyouts, 223
Levitt, Theodore, 63
Lire cycles
　businesses and, 107–108
　of markets, 77–79, 108
　of products, 55–57, 79
Lincoln Electric, 282
Lockheed, 446
Loctite, 52–53
Logical incrementalism, in organizational structure, 298, 301
Loyalty/Loyalties
　business impact on, 205
　in excellence model, 254–256
Loyalty guidelines, 209
Luthans, Fred, *et al.*, 378

McDonald's, 246, 255
McGregor, Douglas, 239
McKesson, 317–318
McKinsey & Company, 108, 244–245
Maintenance function, 273
Management
　course correction planning, 228–230
　definition distinction, 172
　entrepreneurial, 247
　foresight function, 188
　functions of, 428–429
　information requirements, 186–188
　nonspecialized, 414–415
　of operations, 267–290
　organization models and, 283
　processes of, 188
　in public and not-for-profit organizations, 397–412
　redirection of, 253
　of small business, 414–415

524 Index

Management (*continued*)
  of social impact, 206–210, 515
  strategic, 28–29, 34, 517
  strategic control and, 187–188
  third-wave, 279–280, 519
  universals of, 428–429
Management operating system, 253–254, 256, 515
Manager/Managers
  competence of, 293–294, 301
  top level, 376–396
Manager model, 281–284
Managerial systems, 248
Managing strategy/strategies, 144, 145, 152, 153, 518–519
  for excellence model, 253
  international, 432
  relations of, 333
  strategic control over, 175–177
Manufacturing service fees, as profit source, 60
Manville, public strategy, 334
Market/markets
  as basis for strategy, 74–103
  boundaries, 77
  competition-strategy link to, 90, 91
  entry into, 80
  evolution of, 78–79
  finding, for small businesses, 418–419
  geographic size, 76–77
  homogeneity of, 76–79
  life cycles of, 77–79, 108
  nature of, 75–77
  organization of, 75
  product differentiation in, 85–86
  product life cycle and, 56–57
  value appraisal in, 117–118
Market competition, 81–82
Market information, availability of, 75–76
Market leadership, excellence and, 246
Market structure, 79–81, 180
Marketing strategy, 275–276, 334
  excellence and, 247
  relations of, 334
Marshall, John, 5
Maslow, Abraham H., 282
Master builder, role of, 381–383
Master business strategy, 138, 149–157
Master strategies, 151, 152
  definition, 517, 519
  design and redesign of, 335–336
  diagram for, 338
  for opportunity, 224–225
  relations of, 333–335
Matrix organization, 246
Medi + Physics, 466–467
Merrill Lynch, 176
Miller Brewing Co., 224
Miller, Lawrence M., 296, 297

Mission, 3–4
  definition, 3, 315
  development of, 29–31
  in strategic plan, 357, 358
  in strategy/action, 465–466
  in strategy design, 12
Mission statements, 4, 6
Mitsubishi, 353–354
Mobil, public strategy, 141, 334
Mobility, executive, 378
Monopoly positions, 59
Multinational federation, 431–432
Musashi, Miyamoto, 82–83

Naisbitt, John, 27
Navajo tribe, 411, 412
Naylor, Thomas H., 116–117, 137, 269
Needs-leverage linkages, 325, 335, 458–462, 467
Neighborhood guideline, 208
New products guideline, 209, 219
New services, 219
New York Stock Exchange, 75, 76
Newman, William H., and J. P. Logan, 3, 137
Niche strategies, 316
Norton, public strategy, 14
Not-for-profit organizations, 397–412

Objective, action as, 35
Ohmae, Kenichi, 83, 354
OPEC, 229
Operations
  day by day, 284
  management of, 185, 186, 267–290
Operations strategy, 272–276, 283–284
Opportunity
  innovation and, 226, 227
  management of, 185–186, 217–236
  master strategy for, 224–225
  planning for, 218–222
Opportunity costs, 208
Opportunity guideline, 208
Opportunity strategy, 138–139, 140, 152, 153
  definition, 518
  master, 224–225
  relations of, 324
Organization/Organizations
  aging of, 292
  atrophy of, 292
  of the enterprise, 268–271
  for excellence, 246–247
  hierarchy in, 428
  local differences and requirements, 429
  management for change, 291–310
  political world around, 443–456
  varieties of, 11–13, 279–280
Organization competence, 10–11
Organization culture, 295–299, 301

Organization model, management and, 283
Organization requirements, for strategies, 256
Organization vitality, 180
Organizational commitment, in five-fold way, 248
Organizational learning, planning in, 352
Osborne, 179
Ouchi, William C., 295
Overhead costs, 282
Overview
  opportunity management and, 230
  strategies, 183–187

Participation, leadership and, 249–250
Pascale, Richard T., and A. G. Athos, 244, 245, 295, 297
Pascarella, Perry, 297
Patents
  as profit source, 60
  rents from, 59, 516
People
  management of, 237–266
  in the policy environment, 377–381
  roles of, 280–283
People competition, 82–85
People component in excellence model, 256–257
People strategy, 139–141, 152, 153
  definition, 518
  in excellence model, 253–256
  IBM, 141
  in leadership, 240–242
  relations in, 234
Perceptual barriers, 183–184
Performance, management of, 237–266
Performance principle, 296
Peters, Thomas J., 63, 278, 279, 280, 282, 354
Peters, Thomas J., and R. H. Waterman, Jr., 9, 176, 239–240, 243–247, 255, 295–297, 415
Pharmaceuticals, as profit source, 62
Phillip Morris, 224
Physical resources, use of, 204, 205
Pickens, Boone, 382
Pillsbury, product linkage, 337
PIMS, 114
Planning,
  action from, 457–488
  as a learning process, 352–353
  long-range, 350
  value-driven, 349, 373, 519
Policy/Policies
  action and, 26, 28–29
  definition, 8, 516
  development of, 25–34
  habits and, 26

Policy/Policies (continued)
  management of, 382
  strategy and, 465–466
Policy environment, people in, 377–381
Policy makers, 376–396
Political influence, 445
Political power, 444–447
Political world, organization in, 443–456
Pollution guideline, 208
Port of New York Authority, 399
Porter, Michael, 83–86
Portfolio management, 115–117
Portfolio matrices, 111–112
Positions, 518
  example of, 50
  in strategies, 46–48
Power, economic vs. political, 444–447
Power guideline, 209
Price, maintenance and cutting, 86–89
Primary strategy/strategies, 31–34
  definition, 517
  examples of, 36–37
Procter & Gamble, 105
Product/Products
  as basis for strategy, 44–71
  differentiation of, 52–53, 85–86
  life cycles of, 55–57, 79
  as profit sources, 58–63
  strategy link to, 63–65
Product line strategy, 49, 518
Product program, in strategic plan, 357, 358
Product strategy/strategies, 31–34, 465–466
  definition, 517, 518
  elements of, 45–51
  examples of, 50
  foundations for, 73–170
  matching, 332–338
  product life cycle and, 56–57
  relations of, 334, 335
Production function, 272–273
Production services, fees for, 59, 516
Production strategy, 276
Productive units, 272–274
Productivity, through people, 246
Profit/Profits
  definition, 516
  as guidelines, 209
  maximization, social costs of, 210
  organization and, 269
  product life cycles and, 56–57
  sources of, 58–63, 516
  true, 59
Profit Impact of Marketing Strategy (PIMS), 114
Profitability, 111, 117
Program strategy, 31, 517
Promotion, leadership and, 241–243
Promotion policies, in excellence model, 256

Prudential, 176
Public, management and, 381
Public businesses, 399–400
Public issues, business impact on, 205
Public organizations, managing, 397–412
Public role of business, 207
Public service, 399–400
Public strategy/strategies, 141, 142, 152, 153, 284
　definition, 518
　relations of, 334
　role of, 271–272
Purpose, in excellence model, 249, 252
Purpose principle, 296

Q.S.C.&V., 246
Quality
　customers and, 353–354
　in planning and strategy, 353–354
　strategy and, 353–354
Quality function deployment (QFD) system, 353
Quality guideline, 207
Question marks, 110–111
Quinn, James Brian, 298

RCA, 227, 382
Realism, in strategic plan, 337, 360
Recruit scandal, 446
Regulation, 205, 417, 418
Regulation guideline, 209
Reimann, Bernard C., 224
Reith, John E., 80, 81
Relevance, in the excellence model, 250–252
Religious preferences, 431
Rents, 516
　entrepreneurship and, 463–465
　as profit sources, 58, 60
Research-development strategy, 276
Research function, 273
Resource/Resources
　creating, 8–10, 458
　examples of, 50
　human and physical, 204, 205
　in strategies, 45–46, 517
　use of, 204–206
Resource-getting strategy, 141–143, 152, 153, 518
Resource productivity, rents from, 51, 59
Resource requirements, 357, 359
Resource strategy
　for excellence model, 253
　relations of, 334
Responsibility, social, 206, 207
Restructuring, opportunity and, 223–224
Retailing, as profit source, 58, 59
Return on investment, 59
Ricardo, David, 58

Risk/reward strategy, 147–149, 152–153, 178–179, 519
　for excellence model, 253
　relations of, 334, 335
Rothschild, William E., 109
Rules of business, 7–8, 12

Safety guideline, 207
Sales, social impact of, 204
Sales function, 272–273
Sammon, William, 84
Sampson, Anthony, 445
Sarnoff, David, 382
Sawyer, George C., cited, 44, 45, 185, 204, 329, 356
SBUs, 115–116
Scale economies, 54–60, 66
Schendel, Dan E., and C. W. Hofer, 29
Schoeffler, Sidney, 114
Schumpeter, Joseph, 58
Sculley, John, 519
Sculley, John, with J. A. Byrne, 279, 280
Sears, Roebuck, 78, 317
Securities and Exchange Commission, 417
Seed money, for new business, 418
Self-direction, 279–280
Self-interest guideline, 208
Self-renewal
　change and, 300
　management for, 185–187, 291–310
　society's need for, 300, 301
　strategic blindness and, 294–295
　supervision of, 294–295, 301
Selznick, Philip, 238
Service/Services
　differentiating, 53
　fees for, 59
　not-for-profit focus on, 398
Service guideline, 207
Service-line strategy, 51
Service program, 357–358
Service strategy, 465–466, 517
　examples of, 50
Service units, 272–274
7S framework, 244–245, 256
Severance guideline, 209–210
Shared goals, in leadership, 240, 245, 256
Shareholder value, 117–118
　management for, 351
Shell, planning, 352–353
Silver, Morris, 221
Simon, Herbert, 243
Skills, in 7S framework, 244
Sloan, Alfred, 382
Small business, 413–426
Small Business Administration, 415, 418, 419
Small Business Investment Corporations, 418
"Small is beautiful," 278

Smallness, advantages of, 419
Sobel, Robert, 8
Social balance, 205–206, 211
Social change, 26–28
Social-change guideline, 208
Social-control guideline, 209
Social costs, 205–206, 210
Social ends, means and, 6–7
Social impact, 516
  adverse, 210
  anticipating and understanding, 204
  areas of, 204–205
  direct, 204, 211
  guidelines for managing, 207–210
  management of, 185, 200–216, 515
  systemwide, 205
Social responsibility, 206, 207
Social role of a business, 3–4
Social systems, foreign, 429–430
Society, business impact on, 201–203
South Africa, 430
Specialized services, 516
Specialty, definition of, 515
Speculation, profit source, 58
Staff, 244, 246, 414–415
Staffing costs, for efficiency, 282
Stalk, George, Jr., 355
Standard business units (SBUs), 268–269
Standard Oil, strategy change, 301
Standards guideline, 208
Stars, 110
Start-ups, 415–417
Steiner, George A., 137
"Stick to the knitting," 246
Stock offerings, 417
Strategic action, strategic control and, 171–310, 312
Strategic blindness, 181–184, 516
  self-renewal and, 294–295
Strategic business units, 115–116
Strategic control, 517
  in management, 187–188
  as ongoing process, 179–180
  process of, 188
  strategic action and, 172–199, 302
Strategic management, 28–29, 34, 349–373, 517
  overview, 184–188
  political relations in, 447
  practicing, 375–488
  in public and not-for-profit organizations, 401
  relation to strategic planning, 350–372
Strategic plan, 356–361
  executive summary in, 356, 357
  recommendations in, 357, 360
Strategic planning, strategic management and, 350–372
Strategy/Strategies. *See also* entries for specific kinds of strategy

Strategy/Strategies (continued)
  action and, 34, 457–488
  classes of, 31–34, 517–519
  competition and, 83–85, 90, 91
  components of, 518–519
  defining, 34
  definitions of, 517–519
  development of, 25–34
  differentiation and, 54–55
  effectiveness of, 321–323
  elements of, 51–52, 54–55, 61–63, 517–518
  excellence model and, 467
  functional, definition, 517
  governing, 136–137, 333–335
  how to design, 311–373. *See also* Strategy design
  integrating, 337–338
  levels of, 31–34, 334
  link to business nature, 105, 118
  management of, 382
  matching of, 332–348
  mission in, 465–466
  models for, 319–321, 325
  organization requirements for, 256
  policy and, 1–71, 465–466
  product link to, 44–71
  profit sources and, 60–63
  quality and, 353–354
  relations among, 333–338
  requirements of, 323–324
  in 7S framework, 244
  in strategic plan, 357, 378
  structure and, 269–271
  substance as governor of, 462–463
  summary of, 33–34
Strategy design, 12, 154, 311–373, 466–467
  competitive advantage in, 314–315, 325
  mission in, 12
  motivation and, 256
  process and fundamentals of, 313–314, 325
  for public and not-for-profit organizations, 400
  review of, 361–365
  rules in, 12
  steps in the process of, 313–314, 315–316, 325
Strategy environment, people in, 377–381, 383
Strategy matrix, 116–117
Strategy requirements, for excellence model, 248–253
Strong specialty, 53, 515
Structure, 244, 246, 269–275
Style, in 7S framework, 244
Substance, strategy governed by, 462–463
Sun Tzu, 82, 83, 354

Superordinate goals, in 7S framework, 244
Systems, 244, 292–303

Takeda company, 84
Takeovers, 118, 223–224
Targets, 429
Taylor, Frederick W., 282
TEAM, 247, 256
Technology, 180, 219–220, 247
Technology guideline, 209
Tender offers, 220
Tennessee Valley Authority, 399
Texas Instruments, 179, 182
Theme, dominant, 248
Third wave management, 279–280, 519
Third wave organization, 284
3M, 225, 255
Time, as strategic variable, 355–356
Time Energy Systems, 9–10
Toffler, Alvin, 28, 279, 519
Top managers, 377–396
Trading services, fees for, 58, 59, 516
True profit, definition, 516
Typewriters, market, 76–77

Union Carbide, 207
Unique product, 52–53, 515
United Auto Workers, 242
  unity principle, 296
Universals, 428–429
Upjohn, 220

Use of capital, fees for, 59, 516
U.S. Steel, 187, 381–382

Vail, Theodore, 382
Value
  market appraisal of, 117–118
  measure of, 111
  shareholder, 117–118
Value added, 88
Value-driven planning, 349–373, 519
Value guideline, 207
Veterans Administration, 399
Vitality, organizational, 292–293
Volkswagen, 9–10
Vulnerabilities, course correction for, 229

Warehousing, reduction of, 462–463
Warner-Lambert, 79
Wastes, 204
Wastes guideline, 208
Watson, Thomas, Jr., 246
Watson, Thomas, Sr., 7–9
Weak specialty, 53–54, 515
Wealth-production guideline, 209
Whistle blowing, 380
Whitehall Laboratories, 220
Work planning, structure and, 274–275
W. R. Grace, 144, 323, 336
Wrigley, managing strategy, 144

Xerox, 62, 182, 461